ISRAEL
AND THE
AMERICAN
NATIONAL
INTEREST

ISRAEL

AND THE

AMERICAN NATIONAL INTEREST

A Critical Examination

CHERYL A. RUBENBERG

University of Illinois Press
Urbana and Chicago

This book is printed on acid-free paper.

LIBRARY OF CONGRESS CATALOGING-IN-PUBLICATION DATA

Rubenberg, Cheryl.
  Israel and the American national interest.

  Bibliography: p.
  Includes index.
  1. United States—Foreign relations—Israel.
2. Israel—Foreign relations—United States.
3. Israel—Strategic aspects.   4. United States—
Foreign relations—1945-   . I. Title.
E183.8.I7R83 1986   327.7305694   86-4352
ISBN 0-252-01330-1 (alk. paper)

TO
Marty
WITH LOVE AND APPRECIATION

CONTENTS

ACKNOWLEDGMENTS

I have many debts of gratitude to people who have helped me in a variety of ways: they all have my sincerest thanks and my deepest appreciation. The two individuals who contributed most to helping me improve this book are Ibrahim Abu-Lughod and Sheila Ryan. Each in very different, but critical, ways opened countless avenues of thought for me. I am enormously indebted to both (though I recognize that neither may like the results). Special thanks go to John Stack, Martin Slann, and Thomas Breslin for their careful reading of and helpful comments on an early draft. In addition, John's persistent support and belief in me when I doubted myself will not be forgotten. Thanks also are due to Khalil Nakhleh for his reading and comments. Elmer Berger gave generously of his insights and information on many issues. Albert Aghazarian taught me things about the Middle East on a walk through Jerusalem that left an indelible impression—as did Albert. Assam Salameh introduced me to Palestinian life in West Beirut before the 1982 war and asked me a question that profoundly altered the way I viewed all the issues that I was considering. Thanks go to Hatem Husseini for insisting that I go to Beirut. I appreciate, too, the opportunities to see parts of the Middle East and to meet people there, opportunities that were facilitated by Don Wagner. I have learned from and been inspired by Francis Boyle and Naseer Aruri. Bernard Schechterman, who directed my doctoral research, must bear the responsibility for having introduced me to the Middle East and starting me on the long road that culminated with this book. (He, too, will not be pleased with the results.) Bernard Reich helped me in countless ways in the early years. Robert W. Tucker and George Liska introduced me to the concept of the "national interest." I am grateful to my department for its consistent support and to my friends and colleagues at Bay Vista who shared the ups and downs—especially on Thursdays. Richard L. Wentworth and the University of Illinois Press deserve thanks for their willingness to publish a "different perspective." Susan L. Patterson's careful editing and critical questions immeasurably improved the final work.

To my son, Scott, I want to offer a special thanks for his patience and understanding—not many children have to put up with a mother who is so totally absorbed in "politics" and research. And to my husband, Marty, there are not words adequate enough to express the appreciation I feel for the endless reservoir of patience, support, encouragement, and understanding he has given. He has been father and mother to Scott, husband and friend to me; and in addition he has done all my editing, spending countless hours at the word processor after his own long and draining work days ended.

PREFACE

This book is the product of ten years of research, writing, and reflection. When I first began the work, my perceptions of Israel, of U.S. foreign policy, and of the international system in general conformed to the dominant views and conventional wisdom in American political culture. Like most Americans, I was the product of a typical socialization process and an undergraduate and graduate education that reinforced the accepted norms as both self-evident and empirically correct. Not until after I left graduate school and began to travel widely and observe the world firsthand—especially the Middle East—and subsequently, motivated by my experiences, to read materials that as a student I was never exposed to, did I begin to question the conventional wisdom. I spent time in Lebanon, Jordan, Egypt, Israel, and the occupied West Bank and Gaza as well as North Africa, Turkey, and Europe. I saw the Palestinian refugee camps throughout the Middle East. I talked with Palestinians—subjects of the Israeli occupation authority, successful diaspora academicians and professionals, and PLO leaders; with Israelis—Orientals, Ashkenazim, religious and non-religious, right wing and left wing; and with Arabs from all walks of life and of all persuasions. Eventually I absorbed a literature that included the works of Ibrahim Abu-Lughod, Samir Amin, George Antonius, Martin Buber, Noam Chomsky, Johan Galtung, Antonio Gramsci, Ahad Ha'Am, Judah Magnes, Edward Said, and many others.

I gradually arrived at a world view quite unlike what I possessed on completing my formal education. It is a weltanschauung that differs considerably from that of the individuals who have acquired the power and influence to determine what ideas constitute conventional wisdom in American society. The process of arriving at where I am today has been long and sometimes painful, though always rewarding. This book has been part of the process, undergoing countless revisions, each reflecting the (then) current state of my understanding. In some ways this is a weakness. If I were to begin writing today, I would utilize a different framework—questioning the fundamental assumptions that underlie the definition of American national interest and the general purposes of American foreign policy. That, however, will have to wait for another book. I have kept the framework I began with—assessing the U.S.-Israeli relationship in terms of American national interests as those interests have been traditionally defined. I have attempted, however, within the limitations and context of that structure, to convey some of my major concerns about U.S. foreign policy in the Middle East and to illustrate some of the distortions that are prevalent in the standard literature about Israel, the Palestinians, the Arab-Israeli conflict, and the U.S.-Israeli relationship. This book represents a different perspective for viewing some of these issues.

A word about different perspectives. The ideas I express in this book are neither new nor original. Numerous other scholars have written about one or more of them in various contexts. They are not, however, part of the standard literature on the Middle East. Indeed, notwithstanding an important tenant of conventional wisdom in American society about the "free market place of ideas," what we have in regard to many issues—the Middle East being a particularly pointed example—is not "the cacophony of many varied and challenging voices, but the monotony of the chorus, the straining toward conformity."[1] Indeed, on the politically crucial issues involving Israel, what often passes for an untrammelled interplay of ideas frequently involves only differences of opinion expressed within the bounds of well-defined "respectable discourse." Moreover, the boundaries of what is considered scholarly, acceptable, and respectable have been firmly set and are continually reinforced through both positive and negative inducements. Individuals who deviate from the political orthodoxy are accused of "partisanship," "lack of objectivity," and often either "anti-Semitism" or "pro-PLOism." Indeed, the Anti-Defamation League of the B'nai B'rith and the American-Israel Public Affairs Committee have both published "enemies' lists" in which a number of such scholars are targeted, "labeled," and slandered. Others who voice different perspectives are merely ignored.[2]

On the other hand, those who advance the dominant perceptions—confining their expressions of differing opinions within acceptable limits—are considered "realistic," "moderate," "unbiased," "balanced," and "objective." In large measure this situation results from the fact that certain ideas, quite apart from their truth, accuracy, or merit, have gained such legitimacy and long-standing support as to become a force of their own, internalized in the minds of millions, and as such considered objectively existing reality. It is in this manner that certain ideas become political orthodoxy. Opposing ideas, then, are delegitimized by being labeled "not objective"; or worse, they are subjected to a critique of disinformation from the conventional wisdom that questions the integrity of the scholarship.

It must be stated at the outset that this book does not purport to be objective in the sense of being value-free and scientifically neutral. It has a thesis, openly stated in Chapter 1. Historical evidence, deductive reasoning, and insights gained from experience and reflection are brought to bear on the argument. I believe the argument to be convincing, logical, and well substantiated. However, I reject the possibility of objectively existing reality or of objective scholarship, despite the claims of the purveyors of conventional wisdom that their books are objective. All human beings are possessed of certain values—either those by which they are socialized or those that they have chosen to accept. Values are by definition subjective. Most scholars assert that their work is value-free, and many do not recognize their intrinsic values, i.e., the subjective nature of their world view. However, whether we recognize or deny that we possess a value framework that informs our scholarship, I submit that as human beings we are all value-laden, and our values are reflected, for example, in how we select certain facts from an infinite array of facts and through the meaning that we give to those facts.

I fully recognize the necessarily subjective nature of my own values, which essentially center around justice and justification. I reject the narrow world views of religion, ethnicity, and nationalism. I believe we live on a very small planet and that regardless of the color of our skin, our place of birth, or our language, we are all of equal worth and equal dignity, entitled to live with the full measure of that dignity, dominated, repressed, and exploited by no one. I recognize that these values inform my view of the world and color my scholarship. Thus, for example, I cannot look at the Palestine-Israel conflict and not see the Palestinians, both Muslims and Christians, as fully human and with the same inherent dignity as Jews. I cannot condone the domination, displacement, dispossession, and subordination of one people by another. I cannot accept the notion of racial, ethnic, or religious superiority—whether God-given or militarily taken. I cannot look at Palestine without the concept of injustice informing my understanding. I would hope that the critics of my work first examine their own values and make them equally as explicit in their critical evaluation of this book.

Because of my concern with questions of justice, I have, in addition to analyzing U.S.–Israeli relations in the framework of traditionally defined national interest, made an attempt to focus on some of the nuances and complexities of the question of Palestine. I have also made an effort to point to some of the little-known facts about Israeli history that cumulatively present a rather different picture of the Jewish state than the idealized version that much of American scholarship paints. In that sense, too, the book may appear "unbalanced." But in an area that is so massively unbalanced to favor interpretations based on Israel's perceptions and interests, it is my hope that this volume will represent a modest contribution to improving the balance in the literature in general. Moreover, it is my hope that the addition of a different perspective will constitute a positive contribution to the general understanding of the Middle East and to the policy debate (or lack thereof) on appropriate American policies with respect to the region.

The imbalance in the general literature on Israel, the Arab-Palestinian-Israeli conflict, and U.S.–Israeli relations is quite striking. The field is dominated by books reflecting the basic tenets of the conventional wisdom—e.g., that Israel is a strategic asset to U.S. interests; that Israel has constantly been embattled as a result of the efforts of its aggressive neighbors to "drive it into the sea"; and of the humane and enlightened nature of the Israeli state. The most important and influential work of this genre is Nadav Safran's *Israel: The Embattled Ally*,[3] although there is a plethora of others too numerous to mention. It is significant, I think, that out of approximately 390 references cited in a comprehensive bibliography at the end of Safran's book, not more than twenty-five could be considered to represent a "different" viewpoint. Moreover, I know from my experience as both an undergraduate and a graduate student that the textbooks, reading assignments, and accompanying bibliographies contained no more than a token (if any) reference to different points of view—usually by an Arab writer, which in the context of American political culture automatically delegitimized the work, rendering reading of the obscure citation hardly worth the effort. I also know the pressures I am subject to as a professor for exposing my students to as many diverse points of view as possible.

Because of the inevitable questions that will be raised, I should like to be very explicit about my own politics relative to the Arab-Palestinian-Israeli conflict. Israel is a fait accompli, and despite my general preoccupation with issues of justice, I believe that discussions about the justice or injustice of its establishment are counterproductive at this point. Approximately 4 million Israelis have known the state as home since 1948, and it would be an incomprehensible travesty to dismantle the state and create a whole new generation of refugees. Therefore, let me state categorically that I recognize the existence of Israel and its right to continued existence in peace within secure and recognized boundaries. However, *what* boundaries constitute the state of Israel is one of two crucial questions. The second is what to do to rectify the massive injustice that was inflicted on the Palestinian people, who today, thirty-five years later, remain state-less and homeless refugees.

While my preference for reality would be an ideal democratic, secular state in all of Palestine where Muslims, Christians, and Jews could live together in equality, neither Israelis nor Palestinians are capable of making such a state work at this stage of their history. Moreover, this seems to be an age of ever more discrete and intense national, ethnic, and religious identities. It is assuredly not an era in which ideas of universalism, humanism, or equality based on the intrinsic worth of the individual find any receptivity. Therefore, consistent with what is realistically attainable, I support a two-state solution, including Israeli withdrawal to the pre-1967 boundaries in the Golan, East Jerusalem, the West Bank, and Gaza. I support an independent Palestinian state established in the West Bank and Gaza, with Jerusalem either partitioned into an Eastern and Western sector along the pre-1967 lines with the respective parts of the city serving as the capital of the two states or entirely internationalized as was mandated by the 1947 partition resolution. Based on U.N. Resolutions 181 and 194, and modeled on Israel's "Law of Return," Palestinians living in the diaspora should have the right to immigrate to the new Palestinian state, to return to their original homes in what is now Israel, or to be compensated for their properties expropriated by Israel. I recognize the PLO as the legitimate representative of the Palestinians, and I believe it is incumbent upon Israel, as conqueror and occupier, to recognize unilaterally the PLO and initiate negotiations.

I would also like to add that while I have been harshly critical of Israel and the United States in this book—it is a book *about* Israel and the United States—in other contexts I have been equally critical of the Arab governments.[4] My deep sense of concern for the Palestinian people—my personal outrage at the grave injustice that was, and continues to be, perpetrated against them—as well as my affection for the warmth, generosity, and hospitality of the Arab peoples does not translate into an apology for the Arab governments. Indeed the Arab regimes have done as great a disservice to the Palestinians as anyone; nor have they represented their own people in an enlightened, democratic, and egalitarian manner. I would be the first to speak against human rights violations in the Arab world, the lack of regime legitimacy, the unrepresentative nature of governments as well as Arab state persecution of the Palestinians. That, however, does not diminish a legitimate critique of the nature of Israeli "democracy," the repression of Palestinians under occupation, and the aggressive, expansionist policies pursued by Israel throughout the region. All too often the evils of one system are used to justify, legitimize, or comparably favor another. One must be principled: terrorism is terrorism whether it is Palestinian terrorists planting a bomb on a crowded bus or Israeli terrorists dropping bombs from F-16's on a refugee camp. Democracy means a system based on equality for all peoples, not merely those of one particular religion. Occupation is occupation: the phrase "benign occupation" is a contradiction in terms. The book does not dwell on these issues, but I believe the reader has a right to know my personal political positions. Again, I would ask my critics to be equally open about their personal politics.

CHAPTER ONE

ISRAEL AS A STRATEGIC ASSET
The Elite Consensus and Its Fallacies

The American involvement in Vietnam, which began in earnest in 1954 after the defeat of the French at Dien Bien Phu and lasted until the signing of the Paris Peace Accords in 1973, is widely regarded as an example of a major foreign policy that despite the best of intentions and efforts contravened American interests rather than serving them. As David Halberstam eloquently illustrated in *The Best and the Brightest,*[1] the majority of the finest minds in the policymaking elite genuinely believed that the policies and objectives the United States was pursuing in Vietnam were assuredly serving its national interest. Eventually all of the perceptions about Vietnam and the policies that flowed from them were demonstrated to be utterly fallacious, and the United States was forced to painfully extricate itself from the quagmire into which it had fallen. Providentially there was no powerful pro-Saigon lobby in Washington that prevented the policy change when officials finally comprehended the magnitude of their errors. However, the Vietnam involvement, with all its complexity and destruction, is not the first, nor the last, situation in which Washington has pursued a course of action, believing that its policies were enhancing the vital interests of the United States when in fact they were not.

The entanglement of Israel with the definition of American national interests in the Middle East, together with the belief that by arming and supporting Israel to the fullest extent (validating the Jewish state's objectives of achieving a "Greater Israel") U.S. vital interests will be enhanced, has resulted in a policy as misdirected as was that involving Vietnam, and one that has potentially far more disastrous consequences than the Southeast Asian debacle. There are a number of contemporary conflicts in various areas of the world, but none presents such dangers of superpower confrontation as those in the Middle East. And of the several flash points in that region,

1

none approaches the Arab-Israeli conflict—at heart the Israeli-Palestinian conflict—in the threat it holds of global nuclear war.

The United States has traditionally defined its national interest in the Middle East in terms of the containment of Soviet expansion. The containment doctrine has been pursued as a means of (1) preventing a shift in the global balance of power, (2) ensuring the security and Western freedom of access to the region's oil supplies, (3) assuring access to the region's markets for American manufactured goods, and (4) securing the environment for American investment opportunities.[2] To realize the objectives of containment the United States had to develop strong, positive relationships with the Arab states of the Middle East and had to promote the stability of the region, for war and instability invited Soviet exploitation, threatened the security of the oil link, and endangered American commercial concerns.

It is commonly argued that Israel promotes American interests in the Middle East by acting as a barrier against Soviet penetration, by maintaining regional stability through its absolute military superiority, and by ensuring the survival of pro-American Arab regimes. The result is the thesis that Israel is a "strategic asset" to the United States.[3] There is, however, a contrary view: the existence of Israel and the policies it has pursued have made the Arabs susceptible to Soviet influence and have enabled Moscow to extend its penetration of the region.[4] Indeed, it was in direct response to Israeli aggression that several Arab states turned to the Soviet Union for arms and forged alliances with Moscow to maximize their own security. Likewise, it is the Israeli refusal to recognize Palestinian nationalist aspirations or to deal with the Palestine Liberation Organization (PLO) as the institutional expression of those aspirations (and its success in preventing the United States from so doing) that perpetuated the Palestinians' resort to force as a means for securing their ends and impelled them to turn to Moscow. Moreover, as a result of the protracted Arab-Palestinian-Israeli conflict—and in spite of Israel's absolute military superiority—the region has been in a constant state of instability, including seven major wars—1948, 1956, 1967, 1969-70 (the War of Attrition), 1973, 1978 (the first Israeli invasion of Lebanon), and 1982—and almost continuous raids and reprisals. America's vital interests thus have been in serious and perpetual jeopardy. Further, the U.S.–Israeli relationship in and of itself has impeded the efforts of the United States to further the stability of pro-American governments throughout the Middle East and has led to less than optimal conditions concerning American access to markets, raw materials, and investment opportunities.[5]

Israel and its supporters have been consistent in placing the onus for the ongoing conflict with the Arabs, and indeed most Americans have come to accept the thesis of the aggressive, warlike Arabs, ever-ready to bring about the destruction of Israel. But Israel has initiated four of the wars (1956, 1967, 1978, 1982) and has contributed significantly to the onset and/or intensification of the other three. For example, in 1973 Syria and Egypt launched a limited war against Israel in an effort to regain some of their national territory that Israel had seized in 1967 and as a means of making a strong statement regarding the unacceptability of the post-1967 status quo. In addition, while Gamal Abdul Nasser, president of Egypt, escalated hostilities along the Suez Canal in what came to be known as the War of Attrition, it was Israel's deep penetration raids, i.e., Israeli bombing and strafing of Egyptian military and civilian targets, including the suburbs of Cairo, that intensified the war and brought large quantities of Soviet equipment and personnel to Egypt.

Moreover, while Americans look with sympathy on Jewish efforts to construct a national home in Palestine after 2,000 years of dispersal and in the wake of European institutional genocide, they are oblivious to Arab interests, desires, and perceptions in general and have failed to comprehend why the Arabs view the Zionist movement quite differently. The massive injustice that was sustained by the indigenous Arab population of Palestine would be self-evident in any other context. Reality, however, has been distorted by the emotions generated in the West as a result of the Holocaust and by the enormous disparities between the ability of Jews and Arabs to influence Western, particularly American, perceptions. This distortion, which has been reinforced by the legacy of the Judeo-Christian tradition and Western misunderstanding of and hostility toward the Arab world, Islam, and the Orient in general, has in turn given rise to a powerful mythological orthodoxy. Thus, for instance, the PLO is understood to be simply a "terrorist organization" because of its operations against Israeli civilian targets, but Israeli state terrorism directed at Arab civilian targets is portrayed as "self-defense" and "retaliation."[6] The magnitude of American misunderstanding of the Arab-Palestinian-Israeli conflict is suggested, in one example, by the little-known statistic that the total number of Israeli civilians killed in all acts of terrorism from 1967 to 1982 was 282,[7] less than the number of Arab civilians killed in *one* Israeli bombing raid of Beirut on July 17-18, 1981.

After thirty-five years of this protracted and destructive conflict, rationality demands that Americans deal with the realities of the Middle East and attempt to comprehend the weltanschauung and sensibilities of the Arabs who did not eagerly welcome the usurpation of their land, the dispossession and displacement of their people, and the creation of an exclusive Jewish state in their midst. Moreover, as Nahum Goldmann, former president of the World Jewish Congress noted, the Zionist demand for a Jewish state "was in full contradiction with all principles of modern history and international law." Goldmann further observed, "If this demand were to serve as a precedent, the Indians of North America could claim for themselves the United States, and the descendants of other American natives in Mexico, Peru, and so on."[8]

It is also important for Americans to understand that in the post-1967 period the Arab states have moved one by one to accede to Israel's presence in the region and to seek accommodation with it. By 1982 all of the Arab governments had accepted Israel in the context of the original U.N. formula, i.e., Arab state acceptance of the Jewish state has been predicated on an Israel limited to the pre-1967 boundaries and, in most instances (Egypt being a notable exception), on the creation of the Palestinian Arab state called for in the 1947 U.N. resolution that recommended the partition of Palestine and legitimized Israel. Israel, however, has considered these terms unsatisfactory and has rejected every Arab state attempt to reach accommodation except that pursued by Egypt. Some examples (though not inclusive) of Arab efforts to reach a settlement with Israel include these instances. In February 1970 President Nasser declared that "it will be possible to institute a durable peace between Israel and the Arab states, not excluding economic and diplomatic relations, if Israel evacuates the occupied territories and accepts a settlement of the problem of the Palestinian refugees."[9] Israel neither withdrew from the occupied territories nor even considered a satisfactory solution for the Palestinians. (The Israeli position regarding the Palestinians was made explicitly clear by Labor Prime Minister Golda Meir in 1969: "It was not as though there was a Palestinian people in Palestine considering itself as a Palestinian people and we came and threw them out and took their country away from them. They did not exist."[10])

After Nasser's death, the new Egyptian president, Anwar Sadat, in February 1971 offered Israel a full peace treaty, with security guarantees, based on Israel's return to the pre-June 1967 borders.[11] Israel did not respond. The same year Jordanian Foreign Minister Abdullah Salah announced that Jordan, too, was ready to recognize Israel if it returned to the pre-1967 boundaries.[12] Again Israel did not respond. In 1972 the Israeli government strongly rejected a proposal offered by King Hussein to establish a confederation of Jordan and the West Bank.[13] After the failure of these diplomatic efforts Egypt, together with Syria, decided to undertake the limited (October 1973) war. The diplomatic process initiated by Henry Kissinger after this war resulted in disengagement agreements between Egypt and Israel and Syria and Israel and demonstrated both Arab states' willingness to exchange territory for peace. Moreover, Jordan offered extensive concessions and a full peace to Israel in the aftermath of the 1973 war, which Israel flatly rejected.

In January 1976 a resolution, backed by Egypt, Syria, Jordan, the PLO, and the Soviet Union, was introduced in the U.N. Security Council. It called for a Middle East settlement based on the 1967 borders, with "appropriate arrangements ... to guarantee ... the sovereignty, territorial integrity, and political independence of all states in the area [including Israel and a new Palestinian state] and their right to live in peace within secure and recognized boundaries." Israel insisted that the United States use its veto to kill the resolution.[14] In 1977 Egypt, Syria, and Jordan "informed the United States that they would sign peace treaties with Israel as part of an overall Middle East settlement."[15] On March 20, 1977, the Palestine National Council, the PLO's legislative body, issued a declaration calling for "an independent national state" in Palestine (a significant departure from their previous call for a democratic secular state *of* Palestine). Labor Prime Minister Yitzhak Rabin of Israel responded that "the only place the Israelis could meet the Palestinian guerrillas was on the field of battle."[16] The PLO endorsed the Soviet-American joint statement of October 1977 on a comprehensive peace in the Middle East; Israel rejected it.[17] Egypt's Sadat went to Israel in November 1977, but not until September 1978 (and then only under duress) did Israel agree to a settlement with Egypt. It required another six months of American intervention to persuade Israel to sign a formal peace treaty with Egypt. Two other efforts by the Arabs to reach accommodation, both rejected by Israel, were the Fahd (1981) and Fez (1982) peace plans. (The unanimous adoption by the Arab states of the Fez Plan signified the formal acceptance of Israel in the entire Arab world.) In addition, Israel categorically rejected the 1982 Reagan Plan for a Middle East settlement within hours of its enunciation, even before the Arab states had an opportunity to comment on it, as it had the Rogers Plan thirteen years earlier.

Indeed, not the Arabs, but Israel, through increasingly expansionist policies—in the Golan, East Jerusalem, the West Bank, and southern Lebanon—has impeded all efforts to reach accommodation. Israel—including both Labor and Likud governments—has been adamant since 1967 that Jewish sovereignty over Jerusalem is absolute and indivisible; that the Golan Heights will never be returned to Syria; that a Palestinian state on the West Bank is not even a topic for possible negotiation; that under no circumstances will Israel talk to the PLO; and that the West Bank will not be returned to Arab sovereignty. Given the intensity of feeling in the Arab world—particularly at the mass level—over the issues of Jerusalem and the Palestinians (and in Syria, additionally, over the Golan Heights), in the context of problems of regime legitimacy within the Arab states it is not difficult to understand why Arab elites often express hostile statements regarding Israel. As the foregoing suggests (and as this book will illustrate in detail), they have also offered opportunities for accommodation. Israel ignored or rejected Arab statements seeking accord and rapprochement, fixing instead on the hostile statements as "proof" that no peace was possible. But since Israel never responded to Arab overtures and made no proposals itself (save ones circumscribed by its negative absolutes on Jerusalem, the PLO, a Palestinian state, and the Golan), I am forced to conclude that the onus of responsibility for the ongoing conflict resides with Israel. The absence of a Middle East settlement and the regional instability such a condition engenders work to the detriment of American interests with respect to the containment of Communism and freedom of access to commercial markets, in addition to increasing the potential for great power conflagration.

Moreover, the constraints imposed on American diplomacy in the Middle East by virtue of the U.S.–Israeli relationship have impeded Washington's ability to achieve stable and constructive working relationships with the Arab states, a necessary prerequisite for the realization of all American regional interests. Unquestionably, alliances with the instinctively anti-Communist Arab governments (South Yemen being a notable exception) would have been significantly enhanced in the absence of the U.S.–Israeli partnership. Even those regimes that pursued close associations with Washington in spite of the American-Israeli union were constrained from publicly normalizing the ties for fear of the domestic opposition an overt affiliation with the United States would bring. For example, as unequivocally pro-American and anti-Communist a government as the Saudi monarchy, and one so crucial in the oil and geostrategic equation, has refrained from an open alliance with the United States. The pro-American Jordanian regime likewise has remained aloof from a formal association with the United States. Only the iconoclastic Egyptian leader Anwar Sadat ignored the domestic risks in such collaboration and forged a total alignment with Washington: for his disregard of his country's sensibilities Sadat was assassinated. The contradictions in this situation were particularly apparent in the summer of 1984, in one instance, when the traditionally pro-American Kuwaiti government purchased arms from the Soviet Union because of Israel's ability to prevent the United States from responding to its request for defensive weapons in the context of increasing threats to Kuwait's security from the Iran-Iraq hostilities.

American corporate and commercial interests in the Middle East have been constrained in other ways as a result of the U.S.–Israeli relationship. To cite but one example: as a result of pressure that pro-Israeli groups were able to exert on Congress, a set of antiboycott laws was passed that severely limit business in the Arab world. As a consequence, American companies and the United States economy suffer an estimated $1 billion loss per year.[18]

Of greatest significance, however, is that as a result of the U.S.–Israeli partnership, the Soviet Union has been afforded numerous opportunities to extend its power and prestige in the Middle East, in direct contravention to America's most important objective. Indeed, each increment of growth in Soviet influence in the region has been directly related to Israeli policies, beginning with Israel's large-scale, unprovoked attack on Gaza in February 1955, after which Nasser turned to the Soviet Union for arms (marking the Soviet entrée into the Middle East), through the 1982 war in Lebanon during which Israel dealt Syria a humiliating blow, knocking out all its missile batteries in the Bekaa and destroying nearly one-third of its air force. Subsequently the Soviet Union provided Syria with more highly sophisticated weapons than previously, including SAM 5's, which were accompanied by a coterie of Soviet advisors. Indeed, the final outcome of Israel's war in Lebanon was characterized by (1) a marked decline in U.S. influence throughout the region and the virtual exclusion of Washington from Lebanon; (2) an upsurge of Soviet power and the power of Soviet-supported states such as Syria; (3) a renewed situation of regional instability as Syrian and Israeli troops confronted each other in Lebanon; and (4) new groups of Arab resistance fighters struggling against the Israeli occupation of Lebanon, causing Israel daily attrition and provoking the traditional "retaliation" bombardments with all the attendant potential of precipitating a new Syrian-Israeli war in which the likelihood of Soviet and American involvement was greater than ever before. In addition, in the wake of the U.S.–backed Israeli war in Lebanon, Egypt withdrew its ambassador from Israel, "cooled" the peace process, and began to reevaluate its alignment with Washington. Jordan refused to take the risks that President Ronald Reagan expected after his September 1, 1982, peace initiative. America found itself with extremely limited leverage to deal with the escalating Iran-Iraq war, which threatened the Arabian Gulf oil lifeline and the stability of a number of Arab regimes supportive of U.S. interests. Terrorist attacks on American lives and property escalated to unprecedented levels. And the Palestinian issue remained unresolved.[19]

The post-1982 period was a replay, albeit with more potential danger for the United States, of a scenario that had occurred many times in the previous thirty-five years. Still ignoring all the obvious lessons, American policy remained wedded to Israel. In fact, the partnership grew stronger when Congress in November 1982, in spite of Israel's categorical rejection of the Reagan peace initiative, appropriated more funds for Israel than the administration had requested, appearing to reward the Jewish state for its adventurism in Lebanon and its defiance of the administration. A year later, in November 1983, the administration itself forged a formal military and strategic alliance with Israel (actually a reinstatement of a 1981 accord that had been suspended when Israel annexed the Golan Heights). To most Arab regimes, this was the final indication that Washington had lost all credibility as a mediator or impartial negotiator in the Middle East conflict.

The most obvious and yet perplexing question, given that the policy of tying U.S. Middle East interests to Israel and providing absolute (de facto, if not in principle) support for the foreign policy objectives of the Jewish state has not served American interests, is why has Washington pursued such a policy for thirty-five years?

There are various answers to this question, including: the historical and cultural affinities that are believed by many to exist between Israel and the United States;[20] the inability of U.S. diplomacy to devise a bold and effective Middle East policy and implement it; the irreconcilability of competing Palestinian and Jewish claims to the same territory and the resulting depth of Arab-Israeli animosity impervious to third-party influence; the inability of the Arab states to organize effectively and press their interests on the American government; the Holocaust syndrome in Israel of fear and "preemptive" aggression; the power of the pro-Israeli lobby in American domestic politics; the pressure of Congress on the Executive branch; the failure of State Department professionals to prevail over White House advisors, who have been more attuned to domestic political concerns than national security matters; and the impossibility of any president conducting a strong and positive Middle East policy designed to maximize U.S. interests, given the imperatives of presidential election politics.[21] Seth P. Tillman, a scholar who grounds the contradictions of America's Middle East policy squarely in the domestic political process, puts the matter thus:

American presidents have sought to avoid a direct confrontation with Israel and its strong supporters in the United States because of the terrific domestic controversy sure to be engendered by such a face-off; because of the powerful and apparently undiminished hold Israel and its supporters have upon the Congress; because of the exorbitant amount of political capital that would have to be expended in such a battle, placing at risk an administration's other objectives, foreign and domestic; and because of the uncertainty that even with the use of the full political and educational powers of his office, a president would prevail in a domestic showdown designed to put the weight of American power in back of even so imprecise a program as the Reagan Plan. . . . It has been, I think, conclusively demonstrated over the years that the legislature on its own is incapable of throwing off the shackles of special interest and ethnic politics. Except in the special cases of the Saudi arms sales—F-15's in 1978 and AWAC's in 1981—Congress has seldom withstood pressures of the pro-Israel lobby, and it has *never* withstood these pressures in the area that matters most—the amounts and conditions of American military and economic aid to Israel. It is this and this alone that gives Israel the means to withstand all verbal pressures and reproaches and to continue to impose solutions contrary to the desires and interests of the United States.[22]

All of these factors provide pieces of the puzzle, but to understand such a complex situation requires an evolutionary look at the U.S.-Israeli relationship. In the final analysis the explanation for the extraordinary and contradictory union rests on two factors: (1) a perception, based on erroneous assumptions and a total misunderstanding of the complexities of the Arab world but that nevertheless acquired the legitimacy of absolute truth in dominant sectors of the American foreign policymaking elite, that saw Israel serving as an extension of American power in the Middle East and a strategic asset to U.S. interests; and (2) the power of the pro-Israeli lobby in American domestic politics. It must be noted at the outset, however, that the extraordinary success of the domestic pro-Israeli effort is, to a considerable extent, related to the fact that the interests of the lobby have *coincided* with the official government position toward Israel, which has been one of support since 1948. A detailed discussion of the second factor is presented in Chapter 8. The remainder of this chapter examines the first.

No one, not even the Israelis themselves, argues that the United States supported the creation of the Jewish state for reasons of security or national interest. Some argue that support was based on humanitarian concerns; others suggest complex historical, religious, and moral factors; still others point to psychological reasons of guilt and obligation associated with the Holocaust. There is no doubt some truth in all of these assertions; however, as the material in Chapter 2 demonstrates, support for the creation of Israel was primarily a matter of domestic political considerations. Virtually every professional in the foreign affairs bureaucracy, including the secretaries of state and war (later, defense) and the joint chiefs of staff, opposed the creation of Israel from the standpoint of U.S. national interests. However, politically, Zionism was organized on a worldwide scale by 1942 and was able to secure direct access to the highest echelons of the American government. For example, as a result of the intervention of Eddie Jacobson, President Harry Truman's close friend and business partner, Chaim Weizmann, a prominent world Zionist leader, was able to meet with the president and argue the Zionist case. More important, the issue of support for a Jewish state became enmeshed in domestic politics, and Truman's chief political advisors, David Niles and Clark Clifford, were able to convince the president that supporting the Zionist program would assure success in his uphill battle for the presidency in 1948. Indeed, the issue became so entangled in party politics that the Democratic party platform of 1948 contained planks specifying policies identical to the interests of the Zionists.

After the creation of Israel, in the face of the opposition and resistance of Palestinian Arabs, including support for the resistance from the armies of neighboring Arab states, the United States assumed what was termed a "moral commitment" to assure the security and survival of the Jewish state. It is worth noting, however, that contrary to the popular wisdom perpetuated in most academic literature, of Israel as an embattled underdog in the 1948 war struggling against vastly superior odds, recent research has demonstrated a quite different reality. One well-documented study concludes: "In addition to being generally better equipped than, and numerically superior to, the Arab forces, the Jewish army was more mechanized and mobile. The result was that in the vast majority of individual engagements, Jewish soldiers simply outnumbered Arab soldiers. In most instances . . . it was superior Jewish numbers and firepower that carried the day."[23]

Yet based on the myth of the imminent destruction of Israel, the definition of U.S. national interest in the Middle East was expanded to include "the security and survival of Israel." Such a moral commitment to another state, especially one founded on psychological imperatives, is unique in the annals of international relations and foreign policy. Morality, as Realpolitik writers from Niccolo Machiavelli to Henry Kissinger have argued, should not constitute the rational for state behavior in the international system. Rather, the basis for foreign policy should be the "national interest," which is derived from core values peculiar to each state, including the "good" of the nation, of the territorial state, of the particular way of life of the society, and of the society's elite. Nothing in the core values (as this concept is understood in international relations theory) of American political culture accounts for a definition of the national interest that includes a commitment to the security and survival of Israel. Even the destruction of Israel, a possibility that was never an aspect of the objective reality of the Middle East, would in no way threaten the territorial integrity of the United States, the way of life of the American system, the preservation of the American nation, or the interests of the elite.[24]

Significantly, the myth of the mortally threatened Israel was sustained despite the spectacular Israeli invasion of Egypt in 1956 (in concert with France and Great Britain, two of the world's foremost imperial powers) and its occupation of Gaza and Sharm el-Sheikh. In addition, Washington's inability to deal with Egypt made Israel seem a more desirable ally.

President Dwight Eisenhower and his secretary of state, John Foster Dulles, were particularly outraged by the independence of Egyptian President Nasser. Nasser's purchase of weapons from the Soviet Union—the so-called Czech Arms Deal—deeply angered the American leaders. Nasser bought those weapons, however, in direct response to Israel's massive raid on Gaza and *after* his request for American arms was turned down. The Egyptian leader's subsequent nationalization of the Suez Canal was even more galling to Eisenhower and Dulles. Yet Nasser undertook the nationalization specifically in retaliation for Dulles's withdrawal of an American offer to finance the Aswan High Dam project. Washington was also unhappy because Nasser refused to join the Baghdad Pact, because he was the unchallenged leader of the Arab world and an effective and articulate spokesman for pan-Arab nationalism, and because he was a leader (together with Josip Tito and Jawaharlal Nehru) of the nonaligned movement.

From the Eisenhower administration until Nasser's death in 1970, Washington was intent on unseating this "radical" Arab leader, who refused to align himself with the United States on its precise terms. It seemed in government circles that "Nasserism" represented as much a threat to American interests in the Middle East, as did Communism in Southeast Asia. The two were not comparable, however; indeed Nasser was a staunch anti-Communist.

For a while it appeared as if John F. Kennedy might come to terms with Nasser and accept Egyptian nonalignment, but for Lyndon Johnson and his advisors Nasser represented an intolerable challenge to American hegemony. The Johnson administration became bogged down in Vietnam, and Washington saw few options for dealing with Nasser; thus by 1967 Israel's ability to defeat Egypt seemed an important asset to America. During this time Kennedy had inaugurated the thesis of a "special relationship" between the United States and Israel and had also begun the policy of massively arming the Jewish state. In general, relations between Johnson and Israel grew even warmer.

Of greatest significance, and closely related to Washington's frustrations with Nasser, by the early 1960s some individuals in Washington began to conceive of an Israeli "Sparta" that could dominate the Middle East in the interests of American power.[25] Specifically, it was believed that Israel could assist in bringing about an end to Nasser's reign, an idea that Johnson apparently came to accept. Mired in Vietnam, angered by Nasser's policy of nonalignment and his advocacy of pan-Arabism regionally and Arab socialism internally, and encouraged by advisors such as Walter and Eugene Rostow who were sympathetic to Israel's interests, Johnson seemed to conclude that a swift, decisive defeat of Egypt by Israel (which American intelligence was fully aware Israel could deliver) would bring about the demise of the Egyptian leader and open new possibilities for the United States in the region. Johnson understood, however, the negative implications of being perceived as supporting Israeli aggression against Egypt and Syria, and the administration presented itself as working for a diplomatic solution to prevent war. Indeed, many officials at the State Department did sincerely attempt to avert war; still, in the end, there appears to be little doubt that Johnson gave Israel the "green light" to initiate hostilities. In addition, in the aftermath of the conflict the United States pointedly did not call for Israeli withdrawal to the prewar lines as it had in 1956. This represents a striking example of a common characteristic of U.S. Middle East diplomacy—the dichotomy between principle and practice. In public and in principle, the United States maintained its opposition to Israel's initiation of hostilities, but in practice Washington probably encouraged and may have facilitated it.

The June 1967 War marked a turning point in the U.S.-Israeli relationship. Israel's stunning military performance, defeating three major Arab states in six days, led many policymakers to adopt the premise that Israel could serve as an instrument of American power, a strategic asset to U.S. regional interests. Then, in 1970, Israel's mobilization in support of the Jordanian regime during the "Black September" crisis added a crucial and unique reinforcement to its image as an American surrogate. Although Israel performed no military functions during that battle other than the mobilization and Jordan on its own crushed the Palestinians, in the aftermath of "Black September" many argued that Israel was the bulwark protecting pro-

American regimes from Jordan to Saudi Arabia and beyond from domestic insurrection.

This new perception concerning Israel was not universally shared (though no one questioned the underlying assumption), and several important individuals, such as Undersecretary of State George W. Ball and Senator J. William Fulbright, chairman of the Foreign Relations Committee, dissented heartily. Most sectors of the policy-making elite, however, adopted the idea. Israel and its American supporters understood the advantages that would flow to the Jewish state from such a perception and propagated the idea throughout the corridors of Washington, academia, and the media. The perception took hold in significant areas of American society and soon became political orthodoxy. Indeed, any questioning of it brought intense denunciation, including, not infrequently, labels of "anti-Semitism." Nevertheless, the fallacies in the idea were clear, and Ball aptly summarized several of them: "What can Israel protect and against whom? . . . the threat of hostile forces primarily means the menace of Soviet attack against the oil production of the Gulf. But in spite of the formidable arsenal we have provided, and the high quality of Israel's fighting forces, what could a nation of only a little more than three million people do by itself to halt a serious Soviet attack? Moreover, not only is Israel a substantial distance from the Gulf, but any attempt by the United States to use it as a forward base would automatically alienate the Arab oil-exporting states we would be seeking to protect." More important, as Ball also noted, the Soviets are highly unlikely to initiate a direct attack on any of the states in the Gulf region, since they would be acutely aware that such an action would threaten an American interest so vital as to result in almost certain confrontation.[26]

In spite of these and other flaws, the perception of Israel's strategic utility gained widespread legitimacy and soon acquired the force of absolute truth. This occurred in no small measure because of the credibility it was given by Henry Kissinger, President Richard Nixon's national security advisor and later secretary of state, who was the dominant foreign policy decision-maker during the Nixon and Ford presidencies. Kissinger was particularly wedded to the notion of Israel as an extension of American power and was highly instrumental in institutionalizing the thesis both in ideology and practice. Kissinger oversaw massive transfers of armaments and economic aid to Israel and provided the Jewish state with absolute diplomatic and political support, even undermining the efforts of Nixon's first secretary of state, William P. Rogers, to develop a comprehensive peace settlement for the Middle East (the Rogers Plan).

The Nixon Doctrine, enunciated in 1969 with respect to the Far East, formalized and legitimized the idea of regional surrogates and placed America's view of Israel's role in a larger global and strategic context. The promulgation of this doctrine contributed to the institutionalization of the idea of Israel as a strategic asset.

Simultaneous with the promotion and institutionalization of the perception of Israel as an extension of American power occurred the intensified propagation and further inurement of another, though contradictory, perception concerning Israel: that of a beleaguered underdog, surrounded by hostile neighbors poised to drive it into the sea. Given the magnitude of the military victory Israel enjoyed in the June War, in addition to its regional military superiority from 1948 on, this second perception would seem to have no basis in reality. Yet it became virtually universally accepted in American political culture and elicited great sympathy in U.S. public opinion. No one ever questioned the contradiction of how a country could be *both* a besieged, vulnerable prey *and* the guarantor of American interests in a critical region vital to U.S. interests. But such was the mythology surrounding Israel in the post-1967 period. And significantly, whichever image one adopted—and some people even internalized both—the end result was to favor more arms, more aid, and more political support for Israel, either so it could protect itself or so that it could protect the United States. Such a situation suited Israel's purposes and allowed it to pursue its regional objectives with tremendous latitude.

Indeed, Israel proceeded to fulfill its interests with significant disregard for America's. Israel's security in its position as America's partner was enhanced by the knowledge that if the policymakers in Washington had a change of heart, the organizational and financial strength of Israel's American supporters, the "pro-Israeli lobby," exercising their influence through the domestic political process, would assure the dominance of the perception and the continuation of the policies that were derived from it. The praetorian achievements of Israel in the June War engaged the imagination of American Jews, strengthening their pride in and support for Israel. Thereafter, they organized themselves with renewed fervor on the domestic scene. Outstanding organizational skills backed by huge financial resources and combined with a passionate emotional commitment catapulted the pro-Israeli lobby to a force of almost unparalleled power in Washington.[27] Tillman comments on the nature of the lobby: "This is not a lobby in the conventional sense in which farmers, organized labor, the oil companies, [etc.] are a lobby, with commitments to specific economic or social objectives. It is rather a commitment rooted in powerful bonds of kinship, in memory of a common history and the conviction of a common destiny. The root strength of this most formidable of domestic political lobbies . . . lies not in its skills in public relations, access to the media, or ample financing, although all of these are impressive, but in the solid, consistent, and usually unified support of the Jewish communities of the United States."[28]

The unique success of the pro-Israeli lobby on the American political landscape was also related to other factors:

(1) The *congruence* of the lobby's objectives with elite perceptions;

(2) The ability of the lobby to tie Israel into the cold war anti-Communist consensus—a careful strategy that includes the issue of Soviet Jewry;

(3) The evolving role of Congress on Middle East issues and the ability of the lobby to influence Congress;

(4) The strength of pro-Israeli sentiment in public opinion, in part a reflection of the Judeo-Christian tradition, sympathy for the Jewish people as a result of the Holocaust, and a general distrust, fear and prejudice toward the Arab world, and in part a reflection of the ability of pro-Israeli individuals and organizations to shape public opinion consonant with their perceptions, interests, desires, and world view (a phenomenon especially notable in the media, including movies, television, radio, popular literature as well as journalism[29]);

(5) The growth of "Christian Zionism" as part of the increasing Christian fundamentalist movement in the United States;[30] and

(6) The success of Jewish groups and individuals in the social process known as interfacing, which led to coalition-building with non-Jewish groups. (Seymour Martin Lipset, a sociologist at Harvard University, has called this the "dynamic core of Jewish political effectiveness."[31])

The objective power of the pro-Israeli groups grew tremendously in the years after 1967 and assured Israel that its interests became American policy, even as U.S. interests were compromised along the way.

Indeed, in the period following the June War the pro-Israeli groups in Washington garnered power equivalent to that which Israel amassed in the Middle East. The promotion and institutionalization of the perception of Israel as a strategic asset were major objectives of the Israeli lobby (as was obtaining unlimited quantities of economic and military aid). Perhaps the singularly greatest achievement of these groups was that at the same time they successfully promoted the perception of Israel as a tiny, threatened David facing imminent destruction from the Arab Goliath. Both images were incorporated into American political orthodoxy, and both assured Israel a limitless flow of weapons and aid as well as the persistence of the Israeli prism as the correct way of perceiving the Middle East.

There were, as noted, numerous fallacies in the idea of Israel as an extension of American power. One particularly questionable argument was the thesis (which grew out of the Jordanian crisis in 1970) that Israel was protecting conservative Arab regimes from domestic insurrection. The weakness of this argument was demonstrated by the fall of the shah of Iran in 1979, when both the United States and Israel could only watch helplessly as indigenous forces overthrew the most staunchly pro-American (non-Arab) government in the region. Indeed, the idea of Israel shoring up any Arab regime against domestic subversion and political instability would appear to have no basis in reality. On the contrary, as Ball argues, "The United States [has been] hurt rather than helped by its uncritical support for Israel, since the anxieties and resentments we engender in the Arab world by our obvious deference to the will of Israel do us irreparable harm [among the Arab peoples] and clearly weaken the moderate Arab regimes on which our influence depends."[32] Yet from 1970, this argument was cited repeatedly as an alleged illustration of Israel's strategic value.

This was in part an extension of the larger American misperception that if enough force was applied and sufficient quantities of arms and money made available, any pro-American regime, regardless of how unpopular domestically or how despotic and repressive, could be kept in power. And indeed, American policymakers supported leaders in the Middle East and elsewhere (the monarchy and Nuri Said in Iraq, the shah of Iran, Anastasio Somoza in Nicaragua, Ferdinand Marcos in the Philippines, among others), no matter how reactionary, corrupt, and tyrannical, so long as they were pro-American and anti-Communist. In the process Washington ended up supporting the status quo, even when the great majority of people living under these regimes longed for economic, social, and political changes and ultimately held America responsible for the perpetuation of their plight.[33] As Fred Khouri, a Middle Eastern scholar, observes, American policymakers have consistently failed to understand that "while leaders come and go, the people stay forever; and that [while] repressive regimes (especially with United States aid) can for a time maintain their rule, sooner or later the situation will explode. . . . American security can be based only on the support of the peoples themselves, and not merely on some transitory and unpopular regime. . . . No one world power could hope to dominate indefinitely any state or region against its will."[34] To which it might be added that no one world power, even with the assistance of a militarily superior proxy, can keep an unpopular regime in power; the fall of both the shah and Somoza clearly illustrate the point. Yet the dominant perception remained unchallenged. In this context it is also worth noting that each time Jordan or Saudi Arabia (the two regimes Israel was supposedly protecting for the United States) requested arms from Washington, Israel, utilizing its domestic lobby, mobilized all its resources and power in the Congress to defeat the arms sales and was usually successful. Thus, even given the widely held belief that the United States could maintain any government in power if it applied the correct combination of force, economic incentives, and military equipment, it is difficult to comprehend how Israel fit into this equation in the Middle East.

Another aspect to the perception of Israel's strategic value to the United States is its alleged protection of the region from Soviet penetration. One commonly cited example involves the situation along the Suez Canal from 1967 to 1970. In the aftermath of Egypt and Syria's defeat in 1967, both states turned to the Soviet Union for arms and aid. Soviet weapons and advisors poured into Egypt, and as the War of Attrition along the Suez Canal intensified, many U.S. officials became concerned that this new extension of Soviet influence posed a serious security threat to American interests. This situation, in turn, contributed to the argument that Israel should get all of the advanced weapons it requested, so that it could contain the growing Soviet threat. (Israel also contended that it needed more weapons to strengthen its bargaining position with the Arabs.[35])

The Soviets, however, would not have had an opportunity to expand in Egypt if Israel had not invaded that country in 1967 and occupied a large portion of Egyptian territory. Moreover, the intensification of Soviet involvement in Egypt was directly related to Israel's escalation of postwar hostilities along the Suez Canal in the form of deep penetration raids inside Egypt. Reflecting on this situation a Central Intelligence Agency official who held a key post in the Middle East at the time commented: "When they began [the deep penetration raids] we tut-tutted and asked the Israelis, 'Are you sure you know what you are doing?'. . . They assured us the Soviets would do nothing, but they were wrong, dead wrong. It was predictable that the Soviets would have to do something and that they would come in with massive equipment and personnel. That may really have been precisely what the Israelis wanted—because it was the Israelis that benefited the most when the Soviets were in there."[36] In addition, Washington's unwillingness to induce Israeli withdrawal from the occupied Arab territories, based on Resolution 242, further impelled the Arab states to turn to the Soviet Union. The end result was that the more arms Israel received from the United States, the more dependent the Arab states became on Soviet weapons and the less willing Israel was to engage in meaningful negotiations that would lead to a settlement acceptable to all the parties.[37]

During the Camp David process Israel's image as an asset to the United States received another boost, since it was believed by many that Israel could "deliver" Egypt to the United States through a peace treaty and thus significantly extend American influence in the Arab world, first over Egypt, then over the remaining states, which were expected to "fall into line," one by one. In fact, Egypt delivered itself to the United States as early as 1972 when President Sadat expelled his Soviet advisors without asking for any quid pro quo from Washington; in 1973, immediately upon initiation of the October War, Sadat contacted Washington and indicated his willingness to cooperate with the United States in a postwar settlement after his limited military action. Sadat's desire for an American-Egyptian alliance was evident during the postwar negotiating process directed by Kissinger. The 1979 Egyptian-Israeli treaty did firmly ensconce Egypt within the American sphere of influence, although the achievement of the treaty came about in spite of, rather than because of, Israel, since the positions taken by the Jewish state during the negotiations were so extreme that only Sadat's ardent and unflagging wish to be a part of the American fold (and President Jimmy Carter's painstaking intercession) prevented the collapse of the process that the Egyptian leader had initiated. Moreover, the terms of the treaty (regarded by some as permanently extending Israeli sovereignty over the West Bank) were such that instead of increasing America's influence in the rest of the Arab world, U.S. credibility was again diminished as America was seen to be totally in the service of Israel.

In addition, Camp David afforded the Soviet Union another opportunity to extend its influence, as disillusioned Arab regimes and the Palestinians searched for political support and armaments. On the one hand, the fear engendered in the Arab world by the military potential of an Israeli-Egyptian axis backed by the United States was palpable. On the other, since the accords foreclosed the possibility of Palestinian self-determination, Moscow appeared as the only possible party that could perhaps alter the political status quo. (The emasculation of the European states on the Middle East question— begun in the post–World War II period and accelerated after the Sinai/Suez crisis—was, by the 1970s, nearly complete, although there was a consensus throughout Western European countries on the necessity of a Palestinian state alongside Israel as the essential prerequisite for regional peace.[38]) Middle Eastern instability also increased significantly after Camp David as Israel pursued aggressive policies against Iraq, Syria, Lebanon, and the Palestinians and then used the treaty (the military neutralization of Egypt and the "legitimization" of Israel's sovereignty over the West Bank) to launch a major war against the Palestinians in Lebanon in 1982.

At the time of the invasion of Lebanon, important sectors of the policymaking elite still adhered to the perception of Israel as a strategic asset. Kissinger's expansive arguments about the benefits that would accrue to the United States as a result of the Israeli initiative were particularly notable.[39] But the aftermath demonstrated conclusively that America's interests were in no measure served by Israel. Nevertheless, key members of the policymaking elite (President Reagan among them) still clung to the illusion, although it was difficult to ascertain who believed in the orthodoxy and who were responding to domestic political considerations. The success of Israel and its American friends in tying the Jewish state into the cold war anti-Communist ideological framework was an important factor in the Reagan administration's pro-Israeli orientation. But at the same time pro-Israeli groups had such a grip on the domestic political process that congressmen and presidents alike feared for their political lives should they dare to deviate from the demands of Israel. By 1982 the lobby targeted and worked for the defeat of congressmen based on its determination of their support for Israel, and presidential candidates competed ardently for the votes and money that the lobby could deliver. During the 1984 primary season, the spectacle of Democratic presidential contenders Walter Mondale and Gary Hart irresponsibly compromising the interests of the United States in their zeal to demonstrate which one more fervently supported moving the American Embassy in Israel from Tel Aviv to Jerusalem was an indication of how seriously candidates took the power of the lobby. The tarring of Democratic contender the Reverend Jesse Jackson with the label "anti-Semite" because of his advocacy of a Palestinian homeland demonstrated the lengths to which the pro-Israeli groups were willing to go to ensure that Israel's interests and the prevailing dogma remained intact.[40]

The primary purpose of this book is to demonstrate the extraordinary magnitude of U.S. support for Israel in the context of the thesis that Israel has not served the national interests of the United States in the Middle East as those interests have been traditionally defined. To the contrary, America's objectives in the region—containing the expansion of Soviet influence and ensuring freedom of access to the oil reserves, to markets, and to investment opportunities—all require regional stability and the formation of secure alliances between the United States and the Arab states, and these objectives have been seriously jeopardized, even thwarted, as a result of the U.S.-Israeli partnership. This book illuminates the breadth and depth of American support for Israel, which, indeed, has amounted to a virtual marriage between the two states in the post-1967 period, when the definition of American national interest became so intimately bound up with Israel that the objectives and purposes of American foreign policy became indistinguishable from those of Israel, despite the obvious contradictions in the goals of the two states. Indeed, while both countries wished to extend their domination over the Middle East, insofar as Israel was successful in furthering its hegemony, America's ability to strengthen its influence was impeded.

A further objective is to view the U.S.-Israeli relationship from several levels of analysis. Thus in each historic period the book considers the international situation, the inter-Arab situation, and America's relations with both the Soviet Union and the Arab world. These dimensions afford new insights into the understanding of the contradictions in U.S.-Israeli relations.

Another objective is to demonstrate the dichotomy between principle and practice in U.S. Middle Eastern policy. From the outset, the United States, in public and in principle, has been committed to certain policies, but in practice, it pursues very different and contradictory policies. The numerous instances of this situation will become apparent as the text progresses.

It is a final aim, albeit one that is not fully developed, to shed some new light on Arab-Palestinian-Israeli relations. For too long discussions of this conflict have been viewed solely through the prism of Israel's perceptions and interests. Scant consideration or attention has been given to Arab perceptions, particularly Palestinian ones. Few American scholars have taken the trouble to examine the Middle Eastern conflict from the perception of the three million homeless and stateless Palestinians who were forced to leave their homes and lands—their country—so that European Zionists could realize their dream of a Jewish state in Palestine. Few American scholars have seriously considered the Arab perception of Zionism as that of an extension of European colonialism and imperialism, which mitigated all the aspirations of the Arab nationalist movement by the implantation in the heart of the Arab world of a foreign nation, colonized and settled by European Jews, who have demonstrated that the indigenous Arabs cannot be equal citizens in this "enlightened and humanistic" Jewish state.[41] Moreover, few Americans have considered the very real security threat that Israel has presented to the Arab states since 1948.

Indeed, despite the persistence of the mythology to the contrary, in reality Israel has always been stronger than the Arab states. While it is true that until 1967 (some also continued after 1967) Arab leaders frequently made highly inflammatory and hostile statements regarding Israel, were not prepared to engage in normal interstate relations with it, and undoubtedly wished that such a state had not been interposed in the Arab heartland, at no time was Israel's survival in jeopardy and at no time was the state in danger of extinction. On the contrary, it was Israel that threatened the security of the Arab states while repressing and even denying the existence of the Palestinians. In 1948, within six months of its founding, Israel defeated the armies of every Arab state in the Middle East, including the Palestinian irregulars, and engaged in a major successful offensive against Egypt. In 1956 Israel invaded Egypt and in less than ten days had occupied the Gaza Strip as well as the entire Sinai down to Sharm el-Sheikh. In six days in 1967 Israel crushed the armies of Egypt, Syria, and Jordan in a war it initiated and occupied vast amounts of Arab territory after the war was over. In 1973 Israel quickly reversed a Syrian-Egyptian initiative and occupied even more Arab land. In 1978, and again in 1982, Israel invaded Lebanon. In the spring of 1985 Israel still occupied one-third of Lebanon as well as Syria's Golan Heights and the totality of historic Palestine, including Jerusalem. Nevertheless, the objective fact of Israel's superior military strength has somehow been shrouded in unreality and myths about its imminent destruction. At least until the 1982 war in Lebanon, Israel was typically perceived as being the underdog, on the defensive and constantly threatened by hostile Arabs. This myth was used in turn to induce the United States to provide Israel with all of the sophisticated weapons it demanded, while the consequences for U.S. interests of America's sponsorship of Israel's militarism and expansionism were never even openly debated in this country.

I do not purport to do justice in this book to the complexity of Arab-Palestinian-Israeli relations. The narrative and analysis do attempt, however, to raise certain issues that have been particularly distorted in American scholarship and journalism. It is my hope that the reader might be inspired to delve further into the reality of the Middle East and might be less willing to accept the traditional assumptions associated with that region.

The various objectives of this book are grounded in analyses of six major historic events that have profoundly affected Israel and have likewise inexorably involved the United States. The book spans the period from 1947-48 to 1984 but focuses on these events:

(1) The partition of Palestine, the creation of the state of Israel, and the first Arab-Israeli war;

(2) The Sinai-Suez crisis of 1956;

(3) The June 1967 "Six-Day War";

(4) The 1973 October War;

(5) The Camp David accords; and

(6) The Israeli invasion and occupation of Lebanon in 1982.

I hope that the analysis contained herein will offer a new prism through which Americans may view the U.S.–Israeli relationship and the Middle East in general.

CHAPTER TWO

PARTITION AND WAR, 1947-49

Introduction

The United States emerged from World War II as the most powerful nation in the international system. Prior to the war it had limited its involvement outside the Western Hemisphere (with the exception of World War I) to commercial concerns; in the aftermath the United States became politically and militarily active in every region of the globe. In the context of America's new global perspective, policymakers considered the Middle East an area of vital importance because of its oil reserves, its geostrategic location, and its potential commercial advantages. However, by 1947 the Middle East was rent with conflict as the movement of political Zionism intensified its drive to establish a Jewish state in Palestine, and the Arab states, together with the indigenous Palestinians, increased their resistance to the Zionist goal. Britain, since 1921 the mandatory power for Palestine, was no longer capable of managing the conflict and turned the problem over to the United Nations. The United States then became directly enmeshed in the issue, ultimately lending its influence to the idea of partitioning Palestine into a Jewish state and a Palestinian Arab state. The American decision to support partition, and thereafter to support Israel, profoundly affected the future of U.S. Middle East diplomacy.

Historical Antecedents to the 1947-48 Conflict

Jews date their association with Palestine to about 1800 B.C., when the Jewish patriarch, Abraham, migrated there from Mesopotamia. When Abraham and his tribe arrived, Palestine was inhabited by the Canaanites and the Philistines. Eventually Abraham's descendants left Palestine and migrated to Egypt, where they lived for several centuries before Moses led them back to Palestine sometime in the 12th century B.C. During the first years after their return to Palestine, the Jews were weak and fragmented; later, after defeating the Ca-

23

naanites, they were united into a kingdom under Saul and reached their zenith under his successor, David, in the 10th century B.C. David's son Solomon built the First Temple in the city of Jerusalem during this period. It is this first united kingdom, which lasted about 100 years before dissolving into the kingdoms of Judah and Israel, that provides most of the historical basis for political Zionism's claims to the area.[1]

In 721 B.C. the Assyrians invaded the northern kingdom of Israel and destroyed part of it. The small southern kingdom of Judah continued to exist until the Babylonians attacked Jerusalem in 586 B.C., destroyed the First Temple, and scattered the people. Fifty years later Persia captured Babylonia and permitted some Jews to return to Palestine. A Second Temple was built in the early part of the 6th century B.C. Subsequently, Alexander the Great, the Ptolemies of Egypt, and the Syrian-Greek state to the north ruled all or part of the area. The Jews enjoyed a century of dominance again in Palestine from about 168 B.C. (after the Maccabean revolt) until the Roman conquest in 63 B.C. In the wake of a revolt against Roman authority by Jewish Zealots, the Second Temple was destroyed in 70 A.D., and thereafter the majority of Jews were scattered to other parts of the world, with only a small remnant remaining in Palestine.[2]

Palestine is also the birthplace of Christianity. It was under Christian dominance from the time of the conversion of the Roman emperor Constantine (except for a brief Persian conquest) until 634 A.D., when it was conquered by the Muslims.

During the early part of the 7th century the prophet of Islam, Muhammad, united the various Arab tribes on the Arabian peninsula. After his death in 632 A.D., his followers acquired a vast empire, extending at its peak from Pakistan to Spain and including all of what is considered the Middle East today. In 691 A.D. Caliph Abd al-Malik built the Dome of the Rock in Jerusalem, near the site where Muhammad was believed to have ascended to heaven. His son, Caliph al-Walid, built the Mosque of al-Aqsa near the Dome of the Rock in 715 A.D. Thus the area, known as the Haram al-Sharif, is holy to Muslims, and Jerusalem is the third most sacred city in Islam, after Mecca and Medina. For 300 years Arabic culture and civilization flourished in the Middle East under united and independent Arab governance, and it is from this period that modern Arab nationalism takes its inspiration. Many of the Palestinian people claim descent from the Canaanites and the Philistines. Indeed, they did not arrive with the Muslim Arab conquest in 634; in fact, the indigenous people absorbed the bearers of Islam, mingling cultures but adopting the language and religion of the Arabian invaders.[3]

Rule by the Abbysid Caliphate in Palestine ended in 1071, when the Seljuk Turks invaded. They were, in turn, defeated by the Crusaders, who ruled during the 12th and 13th centuries. Then came the Tartars and the Mongols (1244-60), the Mamlukes of Egypt (1260-1517), and the Ottoman Turks (1517 to World War I). After World War I Palestine was given to Great Britain as a "mandated territory," meaning that Britain was charged with establishing a "responsible government" in the area. Throughout this tortuous and convoluted history in the centuries following 1071 A.D. the majority of people living in Palestine remained Arab and Muslim, with Christian Arab and Jewish minorities scattered among them.

Modern Arab nationalism began its development in the second half of the 19th century.[4] It encompassed both Christian and Muslim Arabs and included a number of diverse ideas and organizations, which ultimately coalesced in the goal of independence for the Arab world from Ottoman rule. During World War I the British induced the Arabs to revolt against the Ottoman Turks and thus join the Allied war effort. In return, the British pledged to facilitate the independence of the Arab East after the war. The British commitments to the Arabs were contained in the Hussein-McMahon Correspondence, which included specifications concerning the boundaries of the area designated as the independent Arab state and explicitly encompassed Palestine.[5] The Arabs kept their part of the bargain, significantly aiding the Allied cause. But the British subsequently promised Jewish Zionists to help them establish a homeland in Palestine and, moreover, agreed with France to carve up the Arab East into "protectorates" under French and British rule. The promise to the Zionists was contained in the Balfour Declaration,[6] while the accord with France was known as the Sykes-Picot Agreement.[7] These agreements contradicted each other and the original British promise to the Arabs.

Political Zionism was born in 1897, when the first Zionist Congress met in Basel, Switzerland, under the leadership of Theodor Herzl.[8] In large part it arose in response to widespread anti-Semitism throughout Eastern (and to a lesser extent Western) Europe. Like the Arab nationalist movement, Zionism originally subsumed several distinct concepts and ideas (including the idea of a binational Jewish and Arab state), but was solidified in 1942 with the adoption of the Biltmore Program, a formal declaration of Zionist aims with regard to the establishment of a Jewish state in Palestine. The most important policy statement of the Biltmore program declared: "The new world order that will follow victory cannot be established on foundations of peace, justice, and equality, unless the problem of Jewish homelessness is finally solved. The conference urges that the gates of Palestine be opened; that the Jewish Agency be vested with control of immigration into Palestine and with the necessary authority for upbuilding the country, including the development of its unoccupied and uncultivated lands; and that Palestine be established as a Jewish Commonwealth integrated in the structure of the new democratic world."[9] After the adoption of the Biltmore Program, the Jewish Agency[10] acted diplomatically on behalf of the World Zionist Movement and the Jewish population of Palestine. Political Zionism reached its apogee in the years between 1942 and 1947 as it worked toward the establishment of the Jewish state and unlimited Jewish immigration into Palestine.

In terms of the debate over the disposition of Palestine, several statistics concerning demographic trends and land transformation are relevant. Turkish sources reveal that in the mid-nineteenth century slightly more than 600,000 people lived in the Ottoman provinces that were later designated as the entity of Palestine. Of those, 80 percent were Muslim, 10 percent were Christian Arab, and 5-7 percent were Jewish.[11] In 1822, according to Jewish sources, there were 24,000 Jews in the general area of Palestine.[12] In 1922 (twenty-five years after the Basil Congress and intense efforts to induce Jewish immigration), a British census found 83,794 Jews in Palestine out of a population of 757,182; the Jews thus constituted approximately 11 percent of the population.[13] In December 1931 the British conducted a second census (the last official one before Israel was created) and found 1,035,821 individuals living in Palestine, of which 174,006, or approximately 16 percent, were Jewish.[14] The growth of the Arab population in Palestine (both Muslim and Christian) resulted primarily from natural causes, while the growth of the Jewish population was mainly due to emigration from Europe. Between 1932 and 1936 approximately 174,000 more Jews arrived in Palestine.[15] In March 1947, according to the last officially released figures, the total population of Palestine was estimated at 1,908,775, of which 589,341 (approximately 31 percent) were Jewish.[16]

Statistics on land ownership are equally relevant. Prior to 1880 Jewish holdings were infinitesimal, as the vast majority of Jewish people were urban dwellers.[17] A major part of the Zionist program outlined at the Basil Congress was the purchase of land in Palestine by Jews to "upbuild" the national home. By 1947, after fifty years of Zionist land purchase efforts, Jews owned approximately 180,000 hectares of land, representing 7 percent of the total land area.[18] In the 1947 partition resolution the Jewish state was allotted approximately 5,500 square miles and was to have included upward of 500,000 Jews and 400,000 Arabs. The area allotted to the Arab state was 4,500 square miles and was to contain approximately 800,000 "non-Jews" (Arabs and "others") and 10,000 Jews.[19] In the aftermath of the 1948 war, Israel emerged with one-quarter more land than it was originally given in the partition resolution, and the land was virtually emptied of its Arab inhabitants.

The Emerging Crisis in Palestine: British Decline and American Ascendancy

By 1947 Palestine had become an area of raging conflict. Relations on all sides—Arab-Jewish, Anglo-Jewish, and Anglo-Arab—had deteriorated significantly. Britain, as noted, was in the untenable position of having made contradictory promises to the Arabs and the Jews about the disposition of Palestine, and with its power to influence events circumscribed by wartime losses, London became increasingly reluctant to deal with the Jewish demand for statehood in the face of vehement Arab opposition.[20]

In light of Britain's dilemma and diminished power, the United States rapidly assumed the role of the dominant foreign power in the evolving Palestine crisis. Prior to this period the United States had been viewed very favorably in the Arab world. As a result of extensive private American educational, philanthropic, and missionary activities and the absence of American imperial involvement, most Arabs perceived the United States to be a champion of self-determination, human rights, and democratic freedoms. The United States had not, however, been entirely aloof from the Palestine question.[21] For example, on September 21, 1922, the American Congress had passed a joint resolution stating its support for a homeland in Palestine for the Jewish people.[22] And in May 1943 President Franklin D. Roosevelt gave his personal assurances to King Ibn Saud of Saudi Arabia that both Arabs and Jews would be given ample opportunity to express their views before any long-range decisions were taken about the settlement of the Palestine issue.[23]

In January 1944 identical resolutions were introduced in the House of Representatives and the Senate declaring that the U.S. government supported the establishment of a Jewish state in Palestine.[24] However, because of wartime considerations and Arab opposition to the creation of a Jewish state in the Arab heartland, the War Department persuaded Congress in March to shelve the resolutions temporarily. In October Secretary of War Henry L. Stimson withdrew his department's objection to the resolutions, declaring that since political considerations now outweighed military ones, the issues should be determined on a political rather than a military basis. The resolutions were reported back to both houses in December, but action was again postponed, this time resulting from intervention by the Department of State. That department, concerned about the diplomatic and political repercussions for the United States from an overtly pro-Zionist position, argued that "the passage of the resolutions at the present time would be unwise from the standpoint of the general international situation."[25] Consequently, the resolutions were dropped permanently.

At the executive level President Harry Truman explicitly contradicted Roosevelt's promise to King Ibn Saud in a letter to the king made public by the White House on October 28, 1946. Truman was responding to the Saudi monarch's expressed displeasure over Truman's support of massive Jewish immigration into Palestine: "The American people have supported the concept of a Jewish home in Palestine since the first World War. It is only natural, therefore, that this government should favor at this time the entry into Palestine of considerable numbers of displaced Jews in Europe, not only that they may find shelter there, but also that they may contribute their talents and energies to the upbuilding of the Jewish National Home."[26] How "natural" Truman's position was is subject to considerable dispute. In fact, an official American investigation concluded just the opposite. The King-Crane Commission (Dr. Henry C. King, president of Oberlin College, and Charles Crane, a businessman), appointed by President Woodrow Wilson in 1919 with the approval of the Supreme Council at the Paris Peace Conference, had warned against "the extreme Zionist programme for Palestine of unlimited immigration of Jews, looking finally to make Palestine a Jewish state." The American commissioners felt that some of the aspirations and plans of the Zionists were praiseworthy but concluded that the Zionist proposals as a whole would be unfair to the Arab majority. They recommended that Palestine be kept as part of Syria and only a limited part of the Zionist program be carried out.[27] By the late 1940s, however, the United States under the Truman administration committed itself to the Zionists in the conflict over Palestine and soon dissipated the good will Americans had enjoyed in the Arab world.

In 1947 Britain turned the Palestine issue over to the United Nations, and there, with the influence of the United States, the political drama evolved while the military conflict in Palestine intensified.

The United Nations and Palestine

The United Nations appointed an eleven-member Special Committee to investigate the conflicting Palestinian and Jewish claims.

Composed of representatives from Australia, Canada, Czechoslovakia, Guatemala, India, Iran, Netherlands, Peru, Sweden, Uruguay,
and Yugoslavia, the committee was charged with recommending to
the General Assembly an appropriate solution to the situation.

Although it did agree on certain general principles, the committee
was unable to produce a unanimous report and thus submitted two
proposals. The minority report called for extension of the British
mandate for three years, followed by the creation of an independent
federation of Arab and Jewish states with Jerusalem as the capital.
The majority report recommended the partition of Palestine into an
Arab state and a Jewish state, each politically independent but with
an economic union (including a common currency and a customs
union), and an internationalized zone under permanent U.N. trusteeship for Jerusalem.[28] The Arabs rejected both plans; most Zionists
accepted the majority report, albeit with reservations, and then made
the partition of Palestine the focus of their subsequent diplomacy.
Responding to those who felt the partition resolution provided insufficient land for the Jewish state, Zionist Labor leader and Israel's
first prime minister, David Ben-Gurion, argued forcefully for the
acceptance of the partition plan, noting that since the Arabs refused
the U.N. proposals, there was no danger that the borders of the
partition plan would actually become the borders of Israel. Ben-
Gurion commented: "There will be war and in the course of the war,
the borders will be changed."[29]

When the two reports were presented to the General Assembly in
the fall of 1947, there was serious division within the American
government over which position to support. The issue was whether
the establishment of a Jewish state in Palestine was really in the
national interest of the United States, given the intense opposition
of the Arabs to such a state and the very real and vital interests
America had within the Arab world. For many Americans, however,
the question was colored by the fact that six million Jewish lives
were lost in the Nazi Holocaust.

U.S. Global Concerns, Middle East Regional
Linkages, and American National Interests

The development of U.S. involvement in the Middle East during
1947-48 must be considered in the context of the larger international
scene. For the majority of American government officials, Washington's policy in the region was intimately bound up with the global
great power situation. For other individuals involved in the policymaking process, the immediacy of domestic political concerns out-

weighed calculations of long-term consequences of national interest. In the end, the arguments of the latter prevailed, but the positions of the former cannot lightly be dismissed.

In the postwar world only the United States and the Soviet Union possessed significant great power status. Moreover, the wartime alliance between the two countries shifted quickly to a cold war with global ramifications. Both the Soviet Union and the United States had interests in the Middle East, and the potential clash of those interests in the context of the emerging global conflict was thought by most American officials to portend serious problems. The major foreign policy objectives of the United States in the post–World War II period, devolving from the definition of the national interest, were: (1) containment of Communism, and (2) expansion of banks and corporations. Both had direct applicability to the Middle East. Moreover, in the postwar years the dominant perception of the Soviet Union in foreign policy circles was of a world revolutionary state bent on overturning the international system and dominating the entire globe. This view, with the concomitant conception of any Russian activity outside the borders of the Soviet Union as a threat to America's interests, inspired the United States to become actively involved in regional discords everywhere on the globe and to intervene overtly in many of these conflicts. Indeed, no area of turbulence was exempted from U.S. intervention—political or military.

As a civil war in Greece dragged on, Washington charged that the Soviet Union was directly responsible for aiding and encouraging the Greek left; in response the United States developed the containment policy, formally enunciated in the Truman Doctrine on March 12, 1947. The essence of the containment policy was the American pledge to: "help free peoples to maintain their institutions and their national integrity against aggressive movements that seek to impose upon them totalitarian regimes. This is no more than a frank recognition that totalitarian regimes imposed on free peoples, by direct or indirect aggression, undermine the foundations of international peace and hence the security of the United States."[30] The speech was followed by a $400 million grant to Greece and Turkey, which marked the first step in the new policy of containing Soviet expansion. On June 5, 1947, Secretary of State George Marshall called for massive economic aid to rebuild Europe to prevent its succumbing to Communism. Congress enacted the Marshall Plan in April 1948, granting over 12 billion dollars during the next four years for European reconstruction.

As the cold war intensified, U.S. policymakers, including Secretary Marshall, Navy Secretary (later the first secretary of the newly created

Defense Department) James Forrestal, Undersecretary of State Robert Lovett, John Foster Dulles, and Robert McClintock, grew increasingly suspicious of Soviet intentions, and their anxiety was superimposed onto an analysis of every regional situation, including the question of Palestine.[31] At the same time, domestic politics and personal relationships appear to have exercised the primary influence over President Truman's decisions regarding the establishment of Israel during this period.

Indeed, it is questionable whether Truman thought through the long-term international consequences for American interests of his position on Palestine or if he simply responded to the pressures of the moment. Truman was not ideologically committed to the cause of political Zionism, although he was sympathetic to the idea of a Jewish homeland in Palestine. He was, however, clearly aware of the positive domestic political implications of a pro-Zionist stance. Ultimately he became a forceful advocate for Zionism, but that appears to be related more to domestic politics than deep personal conviction. Truman once bluntly told a group of State Department representatives concerned about the direction and implications of the policies he was pursuing: "I am sorry, gentlemen, but I have to answer to hundreds of thousands who are anxious for the success of Zionism: I do not have hundreds of thousands of Arabs among my constituents."[32] Truman seems also to have been genuinely concerned about the humanitarian issues involved with the remnant of world Jewry in the postwar period.[33] However, the president did not demonstrate any awareness of the humanitarian problems his policies were creating for the indigenous Arab inhabitants of Palestine. Moreover, in light of Truman's humanitarian concerns, one could legitimately ask why he did not open the United States to the refugees of the Holocaust.

The Debate over the Partition of Palestine: National Interest versus Domestic Politics

As the debate over Palestine intensified and the British role waned, President Truman became increasingly enmeshed in the issue. Of his position Truman wrote: "My purpose was then and later, to bring about the redemption of the Balfour Declaration and the rescue of at least some of the victims of Nazism. I was not committed to any particular time schedule for its accomplishment. The American policy was designed to bring about, by peaceful means, the establishment of the promised Jewish homeland and ease access to it for the displaced Jews of Europe."[34]

Truman's involvement with the cause of political Zionism appears to have originated in the fall of 1946. With the November congressional elections approaching and Democratic fortunes, especially in New York, looking bleak, David K. Niles, a member of the presidential staff, convinced Truman of the political advantage of an "immediate commitment" to the Zionist program.[35] Thus the president issued a statement on Palestine on the most sacred day in the Jewish religious calender, Yom Kippur. In his speech Truman reiterated a previous call for "substantial immigration into Palestine . . . at once"; but, more significantly, he endorsed the establishment of "a viable Jewish *state*" in Palestine,[36] a more explicit ratification of Zionist goals than his previous support of a Jewish *homeland.* (Shortly thereafter he communicated the new American policy to King Ibn Saud.) John Snetsinger, a prominent scholar of that period, records that a week after the 1946 elections Forrestal visited Truman and recommended that from then on Palestine be handled in a nonpartisan manner. According to Forrestal, however, Truman "seemed to feel that not much will come of such an attempt, that political maneuvering is inevitable, politics and our government being what they are."[37]

In addition to the practical political considerations Truman's domestic advisors pressed on him, the president was also subjected to pressure from his old friend and business partner, Eddie Jacobson. Indeed as Peter Grose illustrates, American Zionist leaders used Jacobson (who Grose argues was not a particularly ardent Zionist himself) as a valuable channel to Truman.[38] Many scholars credit Jacobson with deepening Truman's sympathies for the cause of political Zionism.

However, while the president, his best friend, and some of his closest political aides were inclined to support the Zionist position, most of the major actors in the foreign policymaking process were not. Almost without exception, career officers in the State Department, in particular the staff of the Near Eastern Affairs Section and the Policy Planning Section as well as Secretary Marshall, opposed the idea of a Jewish state. They argued that Great Britain had maintained its position in the area by establishing good relations with the Arabs; now that Britain was no longer able to hold this position and the United States was assuming the dominant role in the region, Washington, too, should forge strong ties with the Arabs.[39] The major issues of concern for individuals at State were centered on the concerns that American support for the Zionist program would create an opportunity for Soviet penetration of the Middle East, including the real possibility of a permanent alignment between the Soviets and the Arabs; create a barrier to continued American access to the oil and markets of the region; violate the principle of self-determination in Palestine for the Palestinian Arabs; engender an unworkable policy that would require force for its implementation; and result in destabilization of the entire Middle East.[40]

The State Department was joined in its opposition to the partition plan by the Department of the Navy, the War Department, and the Joint Chiefs of Staff. The Joint Chiefs were unanimous and unequivocal that the United States should commit no armed forces either to carry out the recommendation of the Anglo-American Committee of Inquiry (established in November 1945 to evaluate the problems of European Jewry and Palestine) for immediate admission of 100,000 European Jews into Palestine or to support implementation of the U.N. resolution on partition.[41] They argued that no action should be taken that would cause more trouble in Palestine than what British troops could control. Much as the State Department did, the Joint Chiefs warned that if antagonized by Western policy in Palestine, the Arabs might make common cause with Moscow and the Soviet Union could replace the United States as a power in the region, with serious consequences for Western access to the area's oil. The Joint Chiefs concluded that since the United States had vital security interests in the area, no action should be taken that would reorient the Middle East away from the West.[42] Navy was particularly concerned about the issue of oil. It believed that continued access to Arab oil for U.S. military forces and for European reconstruction required Arab good will, which would be jeopardized by U.S. support for the creation of a Jewish state in the Arab heartland.[43]

Thus the issues of "Communist penetration," "freedom of access," and "regional instability" were cited vigorously and frequently by those who opposed U.S. support for Zionist aims. Each concern involved vital interests of the United States and proved to be well founded, despite the fact that they were not the primary determining factors in the formation of policy—a situation that seems anomalous, given the intense fear of Soviet expansionism prevalent during this period.

The Zionist movement was organized on a global scale by the time the United Nations took up its debate on partition, and Zionist diplomacy, exercised vis-à-vis President Truman, became extremely important. Truman's own comments on his experiences with the Zionists are instructive: "The White House was subjected to a constant barrage. . . . I do not think I ever had as much pressure and propaganda aimed at the White House as I had in this instance. The persistence of a few extreme Zionist leaders activated by political motives and engaging in political threats disturbed and annoyed me. Some were even suggesting that we pressure sovereign nations into favorable votes in the General Assembly. I have never approved of the practice of the strong imposing their will on the weak, whether among men or among nations."[44]

The question of whether the United States exerted pressure on other states in the United Nations to vote for partition (and, if so, how much pressure) is an issue worthy of some note, especially given Truman's stated disapproval of such measures. In the early weeks of the debate the United States did not take a particularly strong position in favor of partition, and Washington did not announce its support of the partition plan until October 11, over a month after it had been introduced. Yet in the last week of the debate it is certain that the United States exerted considerable pressure on several uncommitted countries.[45] Moreover, the evidence strongly suggests that the activities of the American delegation in the final days before the vote in soliciting the ballots of other countries were the result of a direct order by President Truman. While Truman does not admit this in his memoirs, David Horowitz of the Jewish Agency recounts the following: "America's line of action had swung in a new direction. As a result of instructions from the president, the State Department now embarked on a helpful course of great importance to our own interests."[46]

In the final analysis, however, the amount and extent of pressure on other countries were probably less important than the effect of America's very strong and overt support for the partition plan just before the vote was taken. Again, Horowitz: "The improved atmosphere [created by America's active support] swayed a number of wavering countries. The United States exerted the weight of its influence almost at the last hour, and the way the final vote turned out must be ascribed to this fact. Its [American] intervention sidetracked the manipulation of the fringe votes against us."[47] Thomas Hamilton, a *New York Times* correspondent, wrote in a similar vein. "It is clear that the attitude of the United States was primarily responsible for the Assembly's decision. . . . Questions of pressure apart, it is obvious that American support was a *sine qua non* of the partition decision. Therefore, the fate of partition will be of special importance to the United States."[48]

Following the passage of the partition resolution (Resolution 181) on November 29, 1947, by a vote of 33-13, the level of violence and armed conflict between Arabs and Jews escalated sharply in Palestine. Many of Washington's subsequent policy shifts must be viewed through the prism of concern over embroiling the United States in armed conflict in the Middle East; at the same time the administration was concerned about the impact of its policies in the domestic political arena.

Issues and Concerns Created by the Partition Decision

Arms for the Jewish Movement?

During the period immediately following the passage of the partition resolution, the main goal of the Zionists was to gain effective control over the territory allotted to them by the U.N. partition plan. This was their objective in both the civil war and in the war with the Arabs that followed the Declaration of Independence in May 1948. To be successful, of course, they needed to secure arms and weapons, which the Jews assumed they would be able to purchase from the United States. But such was not to be the case, at least not officially. Even before the U.N. vote on partition, the State Department had recommended an embargo of arms to the Middle East.[49] A formal embargo was instituted on December 5, 1947, to the dismay of Jewish nationalists, who viewed it as an indication that the Truman administration would not work to implement the partition plan.[50] The State Department argued that the embargo was consistent with long-established policies and that it was undertaken to prevent conflict or, in the event of conflict, to reduce its nature and scope.[51] The effort to prevent a regional arms race was consistent with the American view that security and stability were essential for Washington to pursue its other interests in the area. In the end, however, despite the official embargo, Jews were able to secure some military supplies illegally in the United States and, more important, to raise huge sums of money in America with which to purchase arms elsewhere. The Zionist movement obtained most of its heavy arms from the Soviet Union (via Czechoslovakia) and France. But significantly, as David Ben-Gurion later acknowledged, when Israel purchased arms from Paris and Prague, it was with American support and blessing: "They both wanted dollars from us—and dollars are only to be had in one certain country. We got many millions of dollars from the United States."[52]

As for the illegal flow of arms from the United States to Israel, a number of writers have described the activities of the Sonneborn Institute (later called Materials for Israel) and other dummy companies through which war materials were purchased from U.S. government surplus stores and other sources and sent to Palestine. For example, a Land and Labor organization was created in Palestine—on paper—so that tanks with gun turrets removed could be sent to it disguised as tractors; military uniforms, minus the brass buttons, were dispatched as work clothes, and so on. One author relates: "As the result of secret 'Thursday Night Meetings' held all over the country [United States], Jewish-owned firms contributed everything from sandbags—for protecting orphanages and old people's homes . . . to classical records for the lifting of Haganah morale; and American-Jewish war veterans left souvenir firearms at gun-drops, usually Jewish owned stores. . . . Nor were professional gunmen ignored as a possible source of weapons."[53] Nevertheless the embargo on arms remained the official American policy throughout 1947-48.

Troops to Implement Partition?

The United States was also unwilling to commit military troops to enforce the partition resolution, despite the fact that the Zionists wanted outside help, as Moshe Shertok of the Jewish Agency indicated: "The Jews regard an international force in aid of their defense of the Jewish State territory as most desirable."[54] However, the view that prevailed in Washington—even with the president—was that political support was fundamentally different than military assistance. A report prepared by the Policy Planning Staff at the State Department outlined explicitly the reasons for not sending troops to Palestine:

Any assistance the United States might give to the enforcement of partition would result in deep-seated antagonism for the United States in many sections of the Muslim world over a period of many years and would lay us open to one or more of the following consequences:

(a) Suspension or cancellation of valuable United States air base rights and commercial concessions, cessation of United States oil pipeline construction, and drastic curtailment of United States trade with that area.

(b) Loss of our present access to the air, military, and naval facilities enjoyed by the British in that area, with attendant repercussions on our overall strategic position in the Middle East and Mediterranean.

(c) Closing or boycotting of the United States educational, religious, and philanthropic institutions in the Near East, such as the American University at Beirut established in 1866 and the American University at Cairo.

(d) Possible deaths, injuries and damages arising from acts of violence against individual United States citizens and interests established in the area. Official assurances of the Arab governments to afford protection to the United States interests could not be relied upon because of the intensity of popular feelings.

(e) A serious threat to the success of the Marshall Plan. The present oil production of the Middle East fields is approximately 800,000 barrels a day. To meet Marshall Plan requirements, production must be raised to about 2,000,000 barrels a day, since no oil for Europe for this purpose could be provided from the United States, from Venezuela, or from the Far East. Before the current disturbances, United States oil companies had made plans for the required development in the Middle East, without which it will be impossible to proceed if the present situation continues.[55]

These were all realistic and critical concerns for America's vital interests in the Middle East and the world. The prophetic accuracy of each of the predictions is indeed striking from the vantage point of 1985.

Truman, too, was worried about these possibilities, and despite intense pressure from American Zionists and the arguments of some of his political advisors, the president remained committed to the position that no American troops would be sent to Palestine.[56] However, Truman recorded in his memoirs the pressures to which he was subjected: "The Jewish pressure on the White House did not diminish in the days following the partition vote in the United Nations. Individuals and groups asked me, usually in rather quarrelsome and emotional ways, to stop the Arabs, to keep the British from supporting the Arabs, to furnish American soldiers, to do this, that, and the other. I think I can say that I kept my faith in the rightness of my policy in spite of some of the Jews. When I say 'the Jews,' I mean, of course, the extreme Zionists."[57]

Fighting between Jews and Arabs in Palestine intensified during the last weeks of 1947 and the early weeks of 1948. Moreover, as the British prepared to depart, Washington feared that partition could only be implemented by American troops, and high administration officials warned repeatedly of irreparable damage to American interests if an all-out war erupted, particularly if the United States was fighting on the side of the Jews.[58] At the same time, the international situation was becoming increasingly tense between the United States and the Soviet Union. Washington was concerned that the coming elections in Italy might produce a Communist government and the crisis in Czechoslovakia was growing as were the problems over Berlin. Because Truman feared a possible conflagration in Europe, he was anxious to avoid a war in the Middle East: if American troops were tied down in Palestine, the United States would have less military leverage in Europe.[59] Thus the president did not reject the advice of State and the Joint Chiefs on the issue of troops to implement partition.

The Trusteeship Proposal

In the context of the deteriorating situation in Palestine and the increasing international tensions, on March 19, 1948, the U.S. ambassador to the United Nations, Warren Austin, formally proposed to the Security Council the establishment of a U.N. trusteeship for Palestine in place of the partition plan. If the trusteeship proposal had been adopted by the Security Council, it would have meant that the partition resolution was no longer valid. Austin's speech was made shortly after a secret meeting in the White House between Truman and Chaim Weizmann (a Russian-born British chemist and one of the most prominent Zionist leaders), in which both men apparently felt that the other understood and accepted each other's position. The meeting had been arranged by Eddie Jacobson, at the request of his Zionist friends, and had required some fairly firm "friendly persuasion" on Jacobson's part.[60] The near coincidence of Austin's speech with the Truman-Weizmann meeting caused Truman considerable chagrin.

A great deal of controversy surrounds Truman's role in the trusteeship proposal. Most analysts insist that the president knew nothing about the plan. Truman is evasive about the issue in his memoirs, but a close examination of the historical record demonstrates that he did indeed know and approve of the State Department plan for trusteeship. He apparently did not know precisely when Ambassador Austin was going to introduce the plan at the United Nations and was embarrassed by the timing of the presentation.[61] Subsequently he made every effort to distance himself from the proposal.

Zionist reaction, both at home and abroad, to the trusteeship idea was swift and extremely negative. Shertok wrote of the plan and the truce that the United States intended to arrange with it: "The proposed plan entails the deferment of statehood and renders its attainment in the future most uncertain, thereby gravely prejudicing our rights and position."[62] Speaking on behalf of the Jewish Agency, he stated: "It is the feeling of the Jewish world that it [the time for a Jewish state] . . . is now or never."[63] The secretary general of the United Nations, Trygve Lie, likewise castigated the United States for the trusteeship plan.[64] Yet, regardless of the reactions of the Zionists or the U.N. secretary general, national interest was taking precedence over domestic political concerns at this point, and the trusteeship proposal could have assisted the United States in achieving a number of its regional objectives. The Security Council voted to convene a special session of the General Assembly to consider the trusteeship plan, but after a month's debate the council had not reached a decision on the proposal, and events overtook the discussion.

Because of the negative domestic political fallout from the plan — which could have been potentially disastrous, since 1948 was a presidential election year — Truman's chief political advisors, David Niles and Clark Clifford, urged him to pursue a more pro-Zionist policy. They argued that it was essential for the president to repair the damage caused by the trusteeship proposal to secure the support of Jewish voters, particularly in New York.[65] Their successful efforts were reflected in Truman's recognition of the state of Israel immediately following its proclamation of independence.

Recognition of the State of Israel

The declaration of U.S. recognition of the state of Israel on May 14, 1948, was issued while the General Assembly was debating the trusteeship plan. Minutes after the announcement of independence by the Israeli authorities, the president gave official recognition to the "the Provisional Government as the *de facto* authority of the new State of Israel." This diplomatic act of immediate recognition had momentous importance. Israeli diplomat and historian Walter Eytan commented: "Without recognition a new state must stifle. It cannot exist if other states will not recognize its existence. Thus it was of prime importance for Israel to secure recognition as quickly as possible by the greatest number of states. . . . To be recognized by the United States was a near-miracle, certainly the greatest thing that could have happened at that moment to the infant state."[66] Indeed, with that one political gesture Truman placated his domestic Jewish critics and set the United States on a long-term course of support for the new state. Yet the juxtaposition of the statement of recognition with the discussion of the trusteeship plan occurring in the General Assembly demonstrated the lack of a thoughtful, long-term American policy for the Middle East.

Truman had been given contradictory advice regarding the advisability of early recognition. Secretary Marshall, Undersecretary Lovett, Fraser Wilkins, Robert McClintock, and Austin all strongly counseled the president against immediate recognition. Austin decried it as a "vulgar attempt to win votes. . . . The transparent dodge to win a few votes would not in fact achieve this purpose. The great dignity of the office of the president would be seriously diminished. The counsel offered by Mr. Clifford was based on domestic political considerations while the problem which confronted us was international. I said bluntly that if the president were to follow Mr. Clifford's advice and if in the elections I were to vote, I would vote against the president."[67] The major objection to immediate recognition was that such a precipitous step would unnecessarily alienate the Arabs and, combined with the developing cold war, would work against the most vital interests of the United States. State Department documents indicate that its officials believed that the president understood their position and would take their advice.

At the same time, Niles and Clifford were concerned about Truman's uphill campaign to win the presidency in 1948, and they believed that the Jewish vote in New York would be crucial.[68] Clifford felt strongly that the president could and should use the issue to his political advantage. On May 12 he remarked that "prompt recognition of the Jewish state after the termination of the Mandate . . . would have distinct value in restoring the presidential position for support of partition of Palestine."[69] Prominent Democratic politicians also urged Truman to recognize Israel immediately. Jacob M. Arvey, Chicago's leading Democrat, wrote Truman to discuss the "political repercussions implicit" in the establishment of a Jewish state. "I fear very much that the Republicans are planning to exploit the present situation to their further advantage. This ought not to be permitted." (A nationwide series of pro-Zionist rallies had been planned for Sunday evening, May 16, 1948, to hail what would then be the day-old state of Israel.) Arvey went on: "Only a declaration [of American recognition of the new state] before Sunday evening can transform the sentiments of the multitudes who are certain to attend these meetings from bitter criticism to unparalleled laudation."[70]

Indeed, there is little disagreement, from either those who supported immediate U.S. recognition or those who opposed it, that Truman's decision was a matter of practical domestic political consideration, although in his memoirs Truman takes issue with those officials who opposed his action. "I was told that to some in the State Department this announcement came as a surprise. It should not have been if these men had faithfully supported my policy. The difficulty with many career officials in the government is that they regard themselves as the men who really make policy and run the government. They look upon the elected officials as just temporary occupants. Every president in our history has been faced with this problem: how to prevent career men from circumventing presidential policy. Too often career men seek to impose their own views instead of carrying out the established policy of the administration."[71]

Perhaps, however, career officials, who are not dependent on the vagaries of domestic politics and reelection campaigns, are in a better position to view the national interests of the country in a dispassionate and rational manner. In fairness, it must be said that Truman was not oblivious to America's vital interests. Undoubtedly he believed that the decision to recognize Israel on May 14 did not involve immediate national security concerns and would not imperil world peace: the president no doubt felt he could take such an action, which would help him at home politically, without harming the United States internationally. Yet on the broader issue of the creation of a Jewish state in Palestine, it is clear that domestic political considerations outweighed calculations of long-range national interest.

Moreover, in terms of future consequences, as significant as Truman's support for the establishment of the state of Israel was his lack of effort to facilitate the emergence of the Palestinian Arab state that was also recommended in the 1947 partition resolution. Truman's inaction on this matter set the precedent of dualism in U.S. Middle East diplomacy—the contradiction between principle and practice. In principle Truman maintained the American commitment to Resolution 181, but in practice he ignored the provisions relating to a Palestinian state. For this monumental oversight Truman alone must bear responsibility.

American Support for Israel: American versus Israeli Interests

Following the recognition of Israel, President Truman made a series of decisions favorable to the new state. The first, a symbolic gesture, was to invite Israel's new president, Chaim Weizmann, to be his guest in Washington. Upon arriving in Washington, the Israeli statesman found Pennsylvania Avenue decked with flags of the United States and Israel. During a White House conference on May 25, Weizmann discussed the problems that beset the new state and raised the issue of a substantial loan. Truman told him confidently, "There is no trouble about that because the Jews pay their debts."[72] As time went on, greater urgency was attached to the request for a loan, which grew to $100 million. Truman's public endorsement of the loan came shortly before the election in November, although the president had given private assurances earlier that the loan would be made.[73] Soon after the election Truman honored his commitment: on January 19, 1949, the White House announced the authorization of an Export-Import Bank loan of $100 million to Israel.[74] This marked the beginning of America's public financial commitment to Israel, which subsequently came directly from the U.S. treasury and grew continuously in succeeding years.

A second decision by Truman also pleased the Israelis and their American supporters. The State Department had recommended that a career foreign service officer head the American diplomatic mission in Tel Aviv.[75] Truman, however, rejected the department's candidates and chose instead James G. McDonald, who had sympathized with the Zionist position while serving on the Anglo-American Committee of Inquiry.[76] McDonald's work in assisting the Jewish refugees who had immigrated to Israel also commended him to the Zionists. An official announcement of McDonald's appointment as the special representative of the United States to Israel was issued less than three hours after Clifford asked McDonald to accept the position.[77] The speed and manner of handling McDonald's appointment indicated that the entire matter was arranged by Clifford in the White House, and not through the standard procedures followed in the State Department.[78] The State Department made little effort to conceal its displeasure over McDonald's selection, but reaction in Israel and among American Zionists was enthusiastic: Weizmann, for example, cabled his "heart-felt thanks" to Truman for an appointment that brought "deep satisfaction to the community of Israel and to Jewry generally."[79] Zionists had no cause for disappointment in McDonald's performance: he worked tirelessly to impress the American government with the desirability of acceding to Israel's requests.

In mid-July the Democratic National Convention adopted several platform planks concerning Israel. One claimed for Truman a significant share of the credit for establishing the Jewish state and pledged that a Democratic administration would extend a program of diplomatic support and economic assistance to Israel. A Democratic administration would not, according to another plank, agree to modifications of Israel's boundaries (as a number of government officials were suggesting as a means of bringing peace to the Middle East), unless such changes were "fully acceptable" to the Jewish state. A promise to sponsor Israel's bid for membership in the United Nations was also made. Moreover, according to the platform, the arms embargo should be lifted so that Israel could defend itself against "aggression."[80]

Israelis and American Zionists were pleased by the Democratic platform in 1948 and saw in it the basis of strong American support for the new state. Indeed, the 1948 election marked the marriage between the American Jewish community and the Democratic party, a union that proved mutually beneficial to the interests of both and endured until the late 1970s (when significant rifts appeared during President Jimmy Carter's reelection campaign).[81]

On the question of U.S. support for Israel's admission to the United Nations, the Democrats kept their platform's promise on both Israel's first application, made November 29, 1948, which was rejected, and on the second, made February 24, 1949, which was accepted. The request to end the arms embargo was another matter, however. Even though Truman was plagued with requests to lift the embargo, he was persuaded by the State Department that any unilateral revocation would be exhibiting "a virtual American alliance with the Jewish war effort and an American declaration of war against the Arab states."[82] A compelling reason for presidential inaction on this matter also derived from the public response to the embargo. Although the

Zionist program generally met with either mild public approval or indifference, one nationwide poll indicated that 82 percent of the electorate opposed any change in the status of the embargo.[83]

There were several other important issues on which Israel's interests conflicted with American interests and resulted in some discord between Truman and his Jewish supporters. One of these was the so-called Bernadotte Plan. Count Folk Bernadotte was the U.N. mediator for Palestine, and he used his good offices to attempt to negotiate a cease-fire in the 1948 Arab-Israeli war and to facilitate a resolution of the Palestine conflict. A truce, one of several he arranged, took effect on June 11, 1948, and lasted almost a month, until July 9. In the interval Bernadotte proposed a plan that included a readjustment of Israel's boundaries in an effort to reduce friction points; a formal recognition of the Jewish state by the Arab states; and a guarantee of return for Palestinian Arab refugees to their homes. Particularly controversial was the proposal that the Galilee become part of the Jewish state and that the Negev become part of the Arab state.[84] The Israeli government strongly objected to the entire plan but viewed the loss of the Negev as intolerable.[85]

The British government formally endorsed the Bernadotte Plan, and it appeared for a time that Anglo-American cooperation might oversee a peaceful resolution of the Palestine conflict when in September Secretary Marshall announced that the United States "considers that the conclusions contained in the final report of Count Bernadotte offer a generally fair basis for settlement of the Palestine question."[86] The reaction among Israel's American supporters to Marshall's endorsement of Bernadotte's proposals was strongly negative, and they vigorously lobbied President Truman to repudiate the secretary's statement. Truman notes in his memoirs that he "did not like" the aspect of the Bernadotte Plan related to the Galilee and the Negev: "It looked to me like a fast reshuffle."[87] Yet a State Department memorandum relates that "the plan itself was in essence almost identical with the Department's suggestions for territorial changes in Palestine which had been explicitly approved by President Truman in his own handwriting."[88]

Whether or not he originally approved the plan, it is clear that after the negative domestic political reaction to Marshall's statement, Truman wanted to disassociate himself from it. State Department officials advised him, however, that if he were to repudiate his own secretary of state he would "impugn the integrity of the United States which would have far reaching repercussions on our foreign policy not only with respect to the Palestine problem, but in every other matter where the pledged word of the United States might henceforth be regarded as valueless."[89] Even his political advisors suggested that such a repudiation would be unwise, given accepted campaign norms in foreign policy matters. Nevertheless, late in October, Truman made a forceful statement of his position on Israel's boundaries that converged with Israel's interests; he minimized the Bernadotte Plan, noting only that it offered a possible basis for negotiation.[90] Thus domestic political pressures resulted in U.S. abandonment of a plan that sought to resolve the Palestine crisis, a precedent for every subsequent effort—through President Reagan's 1982 initiative—that attempted to bring about a settlement of the Arab-Palestinian-Israeli conflict.

Bernadotte and his assistant, Colonel Andre-Pierre Sarrault, were assassinated in Jerusalem on September 17 by a Jewish terrorist group known as the Fatherland Front, an off-shoot of the terrorist Stern Gang of which Yitzhak Shamir, later prime minister of Israel, was the leader. Ralph Bunche was appointed Bernadotte's successor as U.N. mediator for Palestine.

The First Arab-Israeli War

The civil war raging in Palestine was transformed into a formal war after the Israeli proclamation of independence, when Arab regular armies from Syria, Egypt, Iraq, Lebanon, and Transjordan, together with token troops from Saudi Arabia, joined the resistance efforts of the local Palestinian Arabs. The war began on May 14, 1948, and lasted until January 7, 1949, when Egypt notified Bunche that it was ready to negotiate a cease-fire under U.N. sponsorship. It should be noted, though, that with the sole exception of the Egyptian army of 10,000 men that crossed the Negev Desert (the status of which had not yet been decided), the Arab armies engaged the Israelis in the area of Palestine designated as the Arab state, not the territory of the Jewish state.[91]

On May 22 the Security Council adopted a resolution demanding a comprehensive cease-fire within thirty-six hours. Israel accepted the resolution, but the Arab states initially rejected participation in the proposed truce. Eventually, however, the Arabs bowed to diplomatic and political pressure and accepted a cease-fire. The truce went into effect June 11. Israel used the break in fighting to augment its forces, raising the number of Jewish men under arms to 100,000 (compared to a maximum of 35,000-40,000 Arab troops), and airlifting in huge quantities of heavy arms from Czechoslovakia and France as well as substantial amounts smuggled from the United States and Britain.[92]

By July 8, in spite of Bernadotte's efforts, war broke out again.

On July 13 Philip C. Jessup, a member of the American U.N. delegation, made a speech in the Security Council in which he implicitly threatened sanctions against the Arabs if they did not cease fighting.[93] Trygve Lie records that this implied American threat induced the Arabs to yield, and a second armistice went into effect on July 18.[94]

During the period of the second truce, serious strains developed between Israel and the United States over a number of issues, including a negotiated peace versus the maintenance of the truce, the status of Jerusalem, and the Palestinian Arab refugees.[95]

The Palestinian Arabs

Approximately 770,000 Palestinian Arabs (Muslims and Christians), over half of the total number in Palestine, were made homeless as a result of the creation of Israel.[96] Most of these people fled to escape the hostilities of the war, expecting to return when the fighting ended. Israel's refusal to permit the return of these wartime refugees created the permanent Palestinian refugee problem. The majority of the refugees were forced to reside in squalid camps in Lebanon, Syria, Jordan, Gaza, and the West Bank. The camps were eventually administered by a special agency of the United Nations—the U.N. Relief and Works Agency for Palestine Refugees (UNRWA)—created to provide the Palestinians humanitarian services (e.g., food, clothing, medical care, education, and temporary shelter) until they could return home. Unlike the U.N. High Commission on Refugees, UNRWA was not mandated to seek the resettlement of the Palestinians in the various countries to which they had fled. (Additional Palestinians were made homeless by the June 1967 War, and today there are over three million stateless Palestinians dispersed throughout the Middle East and elsewhere.)

Removing the indigenous Arab population from the area of Palestine allotted to the Jews had been an issue for Zionist leaders, who were concerned about the ethnic purity of the Jewish state. The portion of Palestine given to the Jews would have contained, as noted, approximately 400,000 Arabs as well as 500,000 Jews.[97] Traditional Israeli historiography has argued that the Palestinians fled their country because they were told to leave by their own leaders and by the leaders of other Arab countries. Recent research by an Israeli investigator has demonstrated that of the 400,000 Palestinians that fled Palestine between November 29, 1947, and June 1, 1948, 70 percent fled because of Jewish military action. According to Dr. Benny Morris, a report prepared by the Israeli Defense Forces (IDF) Intelligence Branch in 1948 states that 55 percent of the Palestinians fled because of direct, hostile Haganah operations against Arab settlements and because of the effect of Haganah hostile operations on nearby Arab settlements, especially the fall of neighboring centers, while 15 percent fled because of the operations of the "dissident Irgun Z'va'i Leumi and Lohamei Herut Yisrael."[98] While considerable information has been available about the terrorist underground, this is the first evidence from official Israeli sources of organized attacks by regular IDF units against Arab civilians.

The most extreme act of the "dissident" terrorist campaign was the deliberate massacre of 250 people in the Arab village of Deir Yassin in April 1948 by the Irgun, in which old men, women, and children were mutilated, raped, and disemboweled. This single operation spread terror throughout Palestine and gave great momentum to the flight of the population.[99] In his memoirs Menachem Begin, the leader of the Irgun and later prime minister of Israel, described the "usefulness" of the panic and terror associated with Deir Yassin. In a footnote to the revised edition of *The Revolt,* published in 1977, Begin writes: "Out of evil, however, good came. This Arab propaganda spread a legend of terror amongst Arabs and Arab troops, who were seized with panic at the mention of Irgun soldiers. The legend was worth half a dozen battalions to the forces of Israel."[100] In the original American edition of *The Revolt,* published in 1951, Begin had written that in the wake of Deir Yassin, Arabs throughout Palestine "were seized with limitless panic and started to flee for their lives. This mass flight soon turned into a mad, uncontrollable stampede. Of the about 800,000 Arabs who lived on the present territory of the State of Israel, only some 165,000 are still living there. The political and economic significance of this development can hardly be overestimated."[101] Begin thus claimed, as Seth P. Tillman, a Middle East scholar, notes, that in effect "the terror associated with Deir Yassin precipitated events that enabled the new State of Israel to rid itself of the bulk of its Arab population and thus to acquire its demographic character as a Jewish state."[102] The report prepared by the IDF Intelligence Branch demonstrates the even greater role of the Haganah in initiating the mass exodus of Palestinians.

Israel's subsequent official position on the refugee question was that the return of the refugees was contingent upon the establishment of peace treaties with all the Arab countries. It is clear, however, that Israel never intended to permit the return of the Palestinian Arabs to their homeland. To do so would have meant compromising the "Jewish" character of the state.

In 1949 the United Nations passed Resolution 194, which called for the repatriation of the Palestinians to their homes or for compensation to be paid to those who chose not to return. Israel ignored the resolution, and Truman did nothing to foster Israeli compliance, although the United States voted for it—again, a dichotomy between principle and practice. Resolution 194 (and Resolution 181) remain as valid as when they were originally passed, though U.S. officials today do not even refer to them. In actuality Washington has appeared to encourage resettlement of the Palestinians in Arab countries, despite several additional U.N. resolutions to the contrary, and in spite of opposition by both the Arab states and the Palestinians themselves. It is also important to note that PLO Chairman Yasir Arafat's repeated statements that he recognizes all U.N. resolutions on Palestine are meant to include these as well as later ones in spite of Israeli and American preference to ignore them.

Jerusalem

Israel, viewing Jerusalem as an integral part of the Jewish state, its "eternal" capital, also rejected the concept of internationalization of Jerusalem as defined by the partition resolution. Israel occupied West Jerusalem in the 1948 war and, as early as March 1949, began moving governmental agencies there. (In July 1967, one month after its occupation of East Jerusalem in the June War, Israel declared that Jerusalem was one indivisible city, the capital of Israel. In 1980 Israel formally annexed East Jerusalem.) Significantly, again, the United States—in violation of its stated principles—took no action with regard to Jerusalem in 1948-49 to ensure Israeli compliance with the U.N. resolution that legitimized its existence.

There was a brief period in the fall of 1948 when it appeared as if Washington might be prepared to press for a solution to both the Palestinian refugee problem and the internationalization of Jerusalem; but, due to the influence of Ambassador McDonald, who retained direct access to President Truman, and as a result of preelection political pressures and the advice of Niles and Clifford,[103] the administration did nothing.[104] A report written by McDonald describing the depth of Israeli determination to resist American pressure on these issues was a major factor in convincing the president to back down: "I am convinced that neither Ben-Gurion nor Shertok, in their talks with me exaggerated when they said in substance: 'On no matter adversely affecting our independence or our security will we yield to the threat of United Nations sanctions, even if these are backed by your government, which we know to be our friend. What we have won in the battlefield, we will not sacrifice at the council table!' "[105] U.S. capitulation on these crucial issues resulted in long-term negative consequences for American interests in the Middle East. A firm stand, ensuring the internationalization of Jerusalem, the return of the Palestinians to their homes and land, and the creation of the Palestinian Arab state as recommended in Resolution 181, would have assuredly reduced the conflict and instability that have plagued the region for the past thirty-five years and would have markedly enhanced America's vital interests.

The End of Hostilities

The second truce held until October 1948, when fighting resumed with major Israeli offensives against Egypt in the south and in the Galilee in the north. The administration issued pointed and public objections to the Israeli invasion of Egyptian territory and even threatened—but did not implement—sanctions against Israel.[106]

On November 4, immediately after Truman's stunning reelection, the Security Council passed a resolution calling on both sides of the conflict to withdraw to the boundaries that they had held before the Israeli-Negev offensive began.[107] The Israelis strongly opposed the resolution, arguing that possession of the Negev was crucial to Israel's viability[108] and pleaded for U.S. help.[109] As a result of American efforts, the U.N. resolution was never implemented, and the Israelis concluded their military campaign successfully. Israel entered the armistice discussions in January with more territory than it had been allotted in the partition plan and with the armies of the Arab states shattered and in disarray.

Under the auspices of the United Nations, Israel concluded armistice agreements with Egypt, Lebanon, Jordan, and Syria between February 24 and July 20, 1949.[110] As noted above, since armistice demarcation lines were determined approximately in accordance with the territory under the military control of each country, the 1949 settlements left Israel one-quarter larger than it would have been under the original partition resolution. Jordan illegally occupied the West Bank (subsequently—and just as illegally—annexed it), and Egypt illegally occupied the Gaza Strip: the Palestinian Arab state mandated in the partition resolution did not come into existence.[111] With the armistice negotiations completed, an uneasy truce settled over historic Palestine, whose name disappeared from the world's new maps.

Conclusion

This chapter has clearly illustrated that American support for the creation of the state of Israel was based primarily on domestic political considerations, not on calculations of U.S. national interest. Indeed, the vast majority of individuals in high policymaking circles considered American support for the creation of a Jewish state in Arab Palestine to run counter to all vital American interests.

The key to comprehending how and why the crucial decisions on the Palestine question were made in 1947-48 is understanding the role of the president as the ultimate arbitrator of the decision-making process. It is significant that Truman's decisions on Palestine were taken without the "advice" or "consent" of Congress and were in direct contradiction to the recommendations of virtually every senior career official in the State Department and the military. This represents a striking example of what is usually considered a transcendent reality in analyzing U.S. foreign policy—that the locus of decision making resides in the Executive Branch, ultimately with the president.

Indeed, there is a long tradition of presidential prerogative and preeminence in the making of foreign policy in U.S. diplomatic history—a tradition that has only been strengthened in the second half of the twentieth century. Congress typically plays a subsidiary role, a reactive rather than a policy-initiating role. But Congress does have one important Constitutional power relative to foreign policy— its power to allocate financial aid. Significantly, partly because of this power and partly for other reasons (primarily related to the nature and influence of the pro-Israeli lobby), over time, on Middle East policy issues, Congress has come to assume a dominant role in the formation of policy, virtually usurping traditional presidential prerogative and fundamentally altering the historical relationship between the Executive and the Legislature. This trend has been particularly pronounced in the post-1967 period, but no subsequent president ever enjoyed such unfettered independence in deciding Middle East policy as did Harry Truman (though Henry Kissinger, President Richard Nixon's national security advisor and subsequent secretary of state, came close during 1969-74).

Thus, while debates continue over the nature of the U.S.–Israeli relationship, it cannot be denied that the relationship had its genesis in American domestic politics. Certainly no one in the U.S. government, least of all President Truman, envisioned Israel as a strategic asset to the United States, dominating the Middle East in the interests of American power. Truman's motivations were clearly and overwhelmingly related to domestic political calculations. It was at least ten years before the idea that Israel could serve as an extension of American power began to be considered and another ten years before it became political orthodoxy. Nevertheless, the ramifications of Truman's domestically motivated decisions profoundly affected America's position in the Middle East, impinging on U.S. relations with all the states in the area as well as altering the course of the region's history and reverberating on the international scene. The creation of Israel led to the protracted Arab-Palestinian-Israeli conflict, involving thirty-five years of turmoil, instability, and war in the Middle East, and resulted in the region becoming a major arena of great power contention as the Arab states sought ties with Russia to offset the security threat posed by Israel. Moreover, America's role in the creation of Israel and its subsequent support of the new state led to the dissipation of long-standing Arab good will and affinity for the United States and to continuous problems for American interests in the Arab world. The heart of the Arab-Palestinian-Israeli hostility resides in the conflicting Palestinian nationalist (which until approximately 1967 found expression in pan-Arab nationalistic sentiments) and Jewish nationalist claims to Palestine. That the United States so wholeheartedly supported the claim of one group while undertaking no effort on behalf of the other is further testament to the political expediency that characterized the American position.

It is understandable why Palestinians, who lost their homes and lands and were transformed from a secure, stable existence on a land to which they had profound cultural and historic attachment into destitute refugees cramped into squalid camps, were unaccepting of the "legitimacy" of the Jewish state and the "right" of Jews from all over the world to immigrate there. It is also not surprising that the Arab states did not welcome the imposition of this foreign state in their heartland. However, the Arab states gradually came to accept the reality of Israel as a fait accompli and by 1982 all had signaled their willingness to reach peaceful accommodation with it (most had done so long before 1982). But the Palestinians remained dispersed, dispossessed, repressed, brutalized, and discriminated against in every country in which they were forced to reside after 1948. By the end of the 1960s their amorphous conviction of having suffered a grave injustice had crystallized into a coherent sense of national identity: a genuine Palestinian nationalism, expressed in an ideology of armed resistance and national liberation. But even they, too, came to accept the reality of Israel, finally insisting only that the Palestinian state called for in the original partition resolution be implemented and that they had the right to select leaders of their own choosing. The refusal of Israel to recognize the legitimacy of Palestinian self-determination and Israel's ability to force the United States to deny the validity of Palestinian nationalism — or even to talk with Palestinian leaders — are two of the greatest tragedies of American foreign policy. From the vantage point of 1985 there can be no doubt that the unresolved question of Palestine is the crux of the continuous Arab-Palestinian-Israeli conflict.

Finally, based on a false orthodoxy that grew out of the 1948 war concerning the imminent destruction of Israel at the hands of superior and determined Arab armies, the United States assumed what was termed a "moral commitment" to the security and survival of the Jewish state, which became incorporated in the definition of American national interests. In practice this moral commitment amounted to the assurance of Israel's absolute military superiority vis-à-vis the entire Arab world. During the 1950s the United States facilitated that superiority by encouraging France, Canada, and other Western countries to provide Israel weapons, while Washington supplied the dollars that allowed for their payment. The result, however, of fostering the absolute military superiority of Israel was to encourage the growth of Israeli militarism, to provide the means for Israel to realize expansionistic objectives, and to create a powerful disincentive for Israel to negotiate a just Middle East settlement. Despite arguments to the contrary, none of these consequences has served American interests.

CHAPTER THREE

THE 1956 SINAI-SUEZ CRISIS

Introduction

Almost immediately after the armistice agreements were concluded, disagreements surfaced between Arab and Israeli officials over the meaning of various provisions in the agreements. At the same time a series of "incidents" occurred along the demarcation lines as Palestinians attempted to return to their homes. Problems also developed over Arab efforts to establish an economic boycott against Israel, over the Israeli plan to divert the waters of the Jordan River, over Israel's encroachments into the demilitarized zone with Syria, and over Arab interdiction of Israel's use of international waterways. The conflicts escalated, and a series of raids and retaliatory assaults intensified the tension, which eventually culminated in the invasion and occupation of the Gaza Strip and the entire Sinai peninsula in November 1956. The Eisenhower administration, aware that U.S. acquiescence in the Israeli occupation would have very adverse consequences for Washington's relations with Arab states and could serve as an opportunity for Soviet penetration of the region, acted firmly, even threatening sanctions in order to secure Israeli withdrawal. At the same time, however, skillful Israeli diplomacy and the willingness of the United States to accommodate Israel's interests allowed Israel to emerge from the episode with significant gains.

The International Context, Regional Linkages, and American National Interests

President Dwight D. Eisenhower came into office in 1953; he appointed as his secretary of state John Foster Dulles, whose foreign policy orientation was based on containment and deterrence. Dulles attempted to prevent Communist expansion by drawing an imaginary line around the Sino-Soviet periphery and threatening a nuclear response to Communist penetration beyond that frontier. Dulles was cognizant of the substantial public dissatisfaction with the Korean

War, which explains, in part, his idea that the United States could avoid fighting future foreign ground wars with the threat of massive retaliation for actions that Washington would define as "Soviet aggression." Yet even as the Korean War concluded, American involvement in Indochina began.

Dulles also adhered to the concept of regional security alliances and sought to create others patterned on the North Atlantic Treaty Organization (NATO). The Southeast Asia Treaty Organization (SEATO) was the first to take shape; it was followed by the Baghdad Pact (later renamed the Central Treaty Organization or CENTO), which linked Europe through the Middle East to South Asia. The strategic position of the Middle East as the crossroads between Europe, Africa, and Asia gave special significance to the formation of a security alliance in that region. Moreover, Europe's increasing dependence on Middle Eastern oil led American strategists to fear that Soviet penetration of the region would allow the Communists to dictate the future of Europe by controlling its crucial energy resources. Indeed, from the perspective of Washington it seemed that for Moscow the Middle East could be the means to outflank and disintegrate NATO.[1]

Thus, in October 1955 Dulles forged an alliance between Britain and the Northern Tier countries of Turkey, Iraq, Iran, and Pakistan, known as the Baghdad Pact. The United States did not join this organization, despite its singularly significant creative role, primarily out of concern over angering those countries not included in the association.[2] Indeed, Egyptian President Gamal Abdul Nasser was outraged over the alliance, condemning it as contrary to the "positive neutralism" he advocated for the Arab states vis-à-vis the global great power conflict. Nasser also resented the pact as an Anglo-American effort to strengthen Iraq and other Arab elements opposed to the Arab nationalist movement that he inspired and desired to lead.[3]

Israel likewise was incensed over the Baghdad Pact, though for different reasons. That country viewed the pact's provision of arms supplies to Iraq as a threat to its national security and immediately demanded membership in NATO and a bilateral defensive arrangement with the United States.[4] The refusal of both requests led Israel to claim justification for its policy of massive military preemptive and reprisal raids into neighboring Arab countries.[5]

Actually, the Baghdad Pact was a major blunder for the United States. It contributed to a convergence of interests between Russia and Egypt and gave Israel additional impetus for its preference for military solutions to political problems. In turn, the security threat Israel posed to the Arab states as a result of this policy led them to seek assistance from the Soviets. Thus, instead of creating a barrier against Soviet influence, the pact virtually cultivated it; instead of contributing to Middle Eastern stability, it led to greater instability.

Indeed, instability was a major characteristic of the Middle East in the post–World War II period, and the Baghdad Pact was certainly not the only contributing factor. Essentially the instability resulted from the nature of the decolonization process itself, as well as from the divide-and-rule policies instituted by the colonial governors and from the unpopular regimes the Western powers attempted to institutionalize in the new states as Arab nationalist sentiment grew rapidly throughout the region. By 1950 the European powers, which had exercised control over much of the area between World Wars I and II, had been forced to withdraw. The former French mandates of Syria and Lebanon and the British protectorates of Iraq and Jordan had all achieved independence by 1946. Egypt had won its independence from Britain in 1922 (though British influence was still considerable), and the British withdrew from Palestine in 1948.

But independence did not translate into stability. For example, in Syria an army coup in 1949 led to a military dictatorship that ruled until 1954 when the Ba'ath party emerged. Washington's relations with the nationalist Ba'athist leadership were antagonistic from the outset. A British-imposed monarch (Faisal, son of the Sharif Hussein of Mecca) sat on the throne of Iraq, while a discredited general, Nuri al-Said, exercised effective control. That country was ripe for revolution, which came in 1958. Prior to the revolution, the United States had worked closely with Nuri Said, drawing Iraq into CENTO; thus the nationalist leaders who overthrew the monarchy and Nuri Said viewed the United States with considerable suspicion. King Abdullah of Jordan (another son of Sharif Hussein also sitting on a British-created throne) was assassinated in 1951. Abdullah's grandson, Hussein, eventually established control with the assistance of the United States, marking the beginning of a close and enduring relationship between Jordan and Washington. In fact, for a number of years Hussein received regular payments from the Central Intelligence Agency.[6]

A revolution in Egypt in 1952 replaced the British-backed monarchy of King Farouk with a government of nationalist officers, ultimately led by Nasser. Washington initially wooed Nasser and attempted to bring him into the American fold, but when the Egyptian leader insisted on a policy of nonalignment and refused to follow Washington's directives, the administration became almost obsessive in its desire to see Nasser replaced. Eventually, the strength of Nasser's influence in the Arab world combined with the intensity of Washington's desire to bring an end to his rule was one of the most important elements in catalyzing the U.S.–Israeli relationship.

In 1953 the nationalist prime minister of Iran, Muhammad Mosaddeq, attempted to unseat the British-imposed shah, who was promptly resettled on his throne in a coup assisted by the Central Intelligence Agency. Thereafter, non-Arab Iran was a solid friend of the United States until the 1979 revolution. Finally, Palestine remained in ferment as its indigenous people, more than half of whom were refugees in neighboring countries, attempted to return to their homes despite Israel's adamant refusal. The practical effect of U.S. policies in this dispute was to uphold the interests of Israel and ignore the plight of the Palestinians.

Thus, the end result of these circumstances was that the Soviets were afforded numerous opportunities to extend their influence in the Middle East. Indeed, America's most vital interest as then defined—containing Soviet expansionism—was thwarted by Washington's support for the wrong parties throughout the region during the Eisenhower-Dulles tenure.

Simultaneous with its efforts to fill the power vacuum in the Middle East in the wake of the decline of British and French influence, Washington also initiated a vast program of economic penetration. For example, in the aftermath of World War II, U.S. corporations came to dominate exploitation of Middle Eastern oil, and the profits realized on oil production as well as concern for the supply of oil to Europe were important issues for U.S. policymakers.[7] For this reason, the United States sought to establish a close relationship with the monarchy in Saudi Arabia, which like the Jordanian kingdom became a loyal U.S. ally.

In addition, as part of its effort to replace British influence, the United States actively encouraged Great Britain to withdraw from the Suez Canal. Then, after the conclusion of the Anglo-Egyptian treaty in 1954, Dulles offered to finance construction of the Aswan High Dam in Egypt. Subsequently, however, in a fit of pique at Nasser's persistent policy of nonalignment, Dulles abruptly withdrew the offer. Nasser retaliated by nationalizing the Suez Canal, which led to the tripartite British, French, and Israeli invasion of Egypt and the Sinai/Suez crisis of 1956.

Britain's stated reason for the invasion—its concern with the maintenance of freedom of transit through the canal, especially for vital oil shipments—explains only part of the British reaction to the nationalization. In the face of the loss of India and the crumbling of its imperial positions in the East over the span of a decade (and in spite of its withdrawal from Suez itself), the canal had remained a symbol of empire for the British. With the Egyptian nationalization, Britain's entire position as a world power seemed to be at the mercy of a nation that many Britons had no respect for. France joined England in the Egyptian invasion primarily as a way of retaliating against Nasser for his aid to the rebel leadership in Algeria. Indeed, the French seemed to feel that if Nasser could be eliminated, their problems in North Africa would be solved. Britain and France then extended to Israel the opportunity to participate in the war against Nasser.[8]

Israel's motivations for undertaking the Sinai campaign involved the desire to eliminate fedayeen guerrilla bases in Gaza (established after a massive Israeli raid on Gaza) and to open the Straits of Tiran to Israeli shipping.[9]

The Arab-Israeli Context

Beginning in 1949, acts of infiltration along Israel's borders became frequent as displaced Palestinian refugees tried to resettle their properties, return to their villages, contact their relatives, and reclaim their possessions that the Israelis had expropriated. Some incursions undoubtedly had the objective of injuring and/or killing Israelis and there were also occasional stealing and smuggling. But these early infiltrations were not part of a coordinated campaign, nor were they organized and directed by any united Arab front in which Arab governments took part. The vast majority of these acts in the early years were simply the reactions of frustrated individuals and families attempting to reclaim what was rightly theirs. Nevertheless, once such incursions became a regular occurrence, Israel developed an official policy of massive retaliation against the towns and villages of neighboring countries from which the infiltrators were suspected to have come. Subsequently, the pattern of Palestinian incursion and Israeli reprisal became the fulcrum around which Israeli strategy and policies and those of neighboring Arab countries revolved.

From 1951 on, some of the larger Israeli raids were made by military units, and it may be assumed that the Israeli government ordered these attacks, although for a few years it denied responsibility for them.[10] For example, on the night of October 14, 1953, a 600-man battalion of the regular Israeli army attacked the village of Qibya (population 2,000), one and a half miles inside the West Bank (then under Jordanian rule). Sixty-six men, women, and children were killed. U.N. military observers, who reached the scene two hours afterward, described it thus: "Bullet-riddled bodies near the doorways and multiple bullet hits on the doors of the demolished houses indicated that the inhabitants had been forced to remain inside until their homes were blown up over them."[11] The Israeli government denied responsibility for the raid, and Prime Minister David Ben-Gurion said, in a special broadcast, that the massacre might have been the work of impulsive border settlers, who were "mostly Jewish refugees from Arab countries or survivors of Nazi concentration camps." In fact, Qibya was the first operation of a special force, Unit 101, created by the Israeli army for the specific purpose of such attacks. For the next decade Unit 101 terrorized Palestinian towns in the West Bank and Gaza (its commander, Ariel Sharon, later became minister of defense).[12] By 1955 Israeli authorities began to acknowledge publicly responsibility for the assaults made from Israeli territory.[13] In the October 10, 1956, Israeli raid on the Palestinian village of Qalqilya (under Jordanian control on the West Bank), in which eighty-three were killed and fifteen wounded, an Israeli para-troop brigade was used as well as armor and artillery. The official nature of the operation was without question.

The stated objective of the Israeli raids was to stop the Palestinian incursions. More broadly, however, the raids were the result of the belief of Ben-Gurion and General Moshe Dayan (who became chief of staff in 1953) that by applying massive military force against neighboring Arab states, Israel could compel the Arab governments to stop the Palestinian incursions, to recognize Israel's right to exist, and to agree to formal peace treaties with the Jewish state. Since Dayan and Ben-Gurion saw Egypt as the key to peace with the Arab world, it became the primary object of Israel's military lessons.

A number of raids were carried out against Egypt; the one with the most serious repercussions was the raid on Gaza on February 28, 1955. After months of calm along the Egyptian-Israeli border, two platoons of Israel's army attacked the town of Gaza with machine guns and bazooka rockets, burning tents and trucks, shooting animals, and demolishing stone and sheet-iron buildings with TNT charges. The pump house that supplied one-third of the water used by Gaza's 100,000 inhabitants was dynamited, and the guard killed. Hand grenades were tossed into the railroad stationmaster's bedroom, wounding his nine-year-old son. A seven-year-old boy was killed and his father wounded in a grenade-and-demolition attack on another home. An Egyptian truck carrying thirty-five soldiers was blown off the road. Twenty-two of the men were burned or shot to death and twelve were wounded. A year later Nasser reflected on the Gaza raid, saying: "Peace could have been achieved with the passage of time. In fact, peace reigned on the borders, except for a few minor incidents which took place. . . . But on February 28, 1955 we were not merely threatened but nightmared."[14]

On August 31, 1955, Israel carried out another major raid against Egypt. In a two-pronged attack on the village of Khan Yunis in the Gaza Strip, Israel killed thirty-nine Egyptians, including four soldiers, several policemen and Palestinian guards, and civilian villagers.[15]

A seemingly senseless attack occurred at Kafr Qasem on October 29, 1956. At about 5 o'clock that evening, only hours before the invasion of the Sinai, a group of farmers were returning to their small village, unaware that the Israeli Frontier Guard had declared a curfew half an hour earlier, though even if they had known, they would have been unable to reach their homes before the curfew took effect. Just outside of Kafr Qasem, Israeli soldiers saw the returning villagers and, without warning, opened fire, killing forty-seven persons, among them fourteen women and several children.[16]

In addition to the raids and reprisals, other factors contributed to the Arab-Israeli conflict and the crisis of 1956. One was the continuing problem of Israel's attitude toward the Palestinians. Despite U.N. Resolution 194 calling on Israel to allow the Palestinian refugees to return to their homes or to be compensated for their lost property if they chose not to return,[17] the Israeli government consistently refused either repatriation or compensation. Furthermore, Israel's treatment of the Palestinian minority that remained within its borders inflamed the feelings of Arabs in neighboring countries.[18]

The Arab boycott of Israel also contributed to the heightening of tensions between Israel and the Arab states. Initially the boycott was directed at Israeli trade with Arab countries. Eventually the Arabs attempted to extend it to cover all Israeli commercial activities, though they were far less successful with the secondary measures. The boycott was intended to delay Israel's economic development and was justified on the grounds that a state of war continued to exist between Israel and the Arab countries. Although the boycott was somewhat detrimental to Israel, particularly in the earlier years when the state had a large influx of immigrants and limited material resources for their settlement, its potentially more serious effects were offset by the massive infusions of private aid from Jews living abroad, from public aid given by the American government, and from reparation payments from Germany.[19]

Another factor was internal political developments in Israel. Ben-Gurion had retired as prime minister and defense minister in January 1954, and Moshe Sharett took his place. Sharett adopted a more conciliatory posture toward Egypt and attempted to involve Israel in several peace initiatives. These initiatives, however, were consistently undermined by supporters of Ben-Gurion (such as Dayan) who remained in the government. Ben-Gurion returned to the ministry of defense in February 1955 and reassumed the position of prime minister in November, and he wanted to demonstrate that his return signaled a new policy, or at least a new national mood, of militancy toward the Arabs. The Gaza raid of February 28 was a major tactic in the implementation of this policy. Ben-Gurion attempted to justify the Gaza raid, in view of the dearth of incursions along the Egyptian-Israeli border, by arguing that it was undertaken in response to two specific issues: the Lavon Affair and the *Bat Gallim* incident.

Pinchas Lavon was the Israeli minister responsible for intelligence when, in late 1954, Egyptian authorities uncovered an Israeli-led ring of spies and saboteurs who had been involved in incidents of bombing and arson of American facilities in Cairo. Lavon denied the Egyptian charges, although it later became public knowledge that the bombings had been carried out by Israeli intelligence. The operation grew out of the Israeli government's concern over any improvement in relations between the United States and Egypt, believing such a relationship would threaten its special ties with Washington. By 1954 there were several cultural and economic agreements under discussion between Washington and Cairo, and the Egyptians were hoping that Washington would aid in the construction of the Aswan Dam. In addition, an American aid program of $50 million had been established, and the American ambassador to Egypt, Henry Byroade, had developed a personal friendship with Nasser. Most threatening, from Israel's perspective, were American efforts to induce Egyptian participation in the emerging Baghdad Pact. Thus the espionage ring in Cairo was designed to sabotage the prospect of Egypt's joining a U.S.-sponsored Middle Eastern alliance organization and to disrupt the development of Egyptian-American friendship.[20] Egypt hanged two of the thirteen persons accused of participating in the sabotage, and Israel used the hangings as a pretext for the Gaza raid.[21]

The second incident that Ben-Gurion presented as justification for the Gaza raid was the seizure of the Israeli ship *Bat Gallim* in the Suez Canal in September 1954. However, the Israeli decision to send the *Bat Gallim* through the canal had been undertaken with the knowledge that Egypt would most likely seize the vessel. Egypt had confiscated Israeli ships on previous occasions when they had entered its territorial waters, and Israel had seized several Arab ships in Israeli waters.[22] The *Bat Gallim* was, in fact, the first Israeli ship to seek passage through the Suez Canal after 1949, since previously there had been no desire to provoke confiscation. When the *Bat Gallim* set off on its voyage, Britain was negotiating the Suez Canal Treaty with Egypt. The Israeli government hoped that an incident in the canal would pressure Britain to force Egypt to end the blockade against Israeli shipping in the canal as part of the final agreement. The ship was impounded, as expected, and the crew was imprisoned for a short time, but Britain did not force an end to the blockade on the Egyptian government.[23] Ben-Gurion used the seizure of the ship and the temporary detention of the crew as reasons for attacking Gaza.

Despite the many sources of tension between Israel and the Arab states in this period (the problems between Israel and Syria were the most intense), Egypt professed an interest in a political settlement with Israel. In the early weeks of 1955 President Nasser asked Elmore Jackson, a prominent American Quaker, to undertake a secret diplomatic assignment to attempt to facilitate such a settlement. Jackson also had the backing of the U.S. government and made three round trips between Egypt and Israel. In a summary of his mission Jackson wrote: "Nasser had a unique position in the Arab world. He was the symbol of Arab nationalism, and the Egyptian revolution had stirred deep emotions throughout the Arab world. The fact that Nasser explored seriously the possibilities of a peace settlement with Israel— before he turned to Eastern Europe for arms supply—should be of major interest to all those who seek an end to the cycles of violence which periodically convulse the Middle East."[24] Nasser's peace initiative was received with interest by Prime Minister Sharett, but Ben-Gurion aborted it with the Gaza raid.

The Gaza raid had profound consequences on subsequent events in the Arab-Israeli conflict. It resulted in the formation of the first government-sponsored Arab guerrilla organization, the fedayeen, and it set in motion a chain of reactions between Egypt and Israel— raids, reprisals, an arms race, new alignments with the great powers, and the Israeli invasion of Egypt in November 1956. The most important and far-reaching of these consequences was the spiraling arms race in the Middle East, which led directly to the formal entreé of the Soviet Union into the region. Immediately after the Israeli attack on Gaza, Nasser became intent on securing arms, so that "for peace or war, Egypt would not deal from weakness." Nasser stated in an interview with the *New York Times* that the Gaza raid caused him to open negotiations for Soviet arms and the Khan Yunis raid made him decide to accept the Soviet offer.[25] Mahmoud Riad, a prominent Egyptian diplomat, wrote that "Nasser had always referred to this attack [Gaza], which was completely unprovoked, as the turning point. He was taken unaware and began to give serious consideration to the dangers posed to Egyptian security by the Israeli compulsion for expansion and aggression: henceforth, Nasser gave an equal priority to arming and consolidating Egyptian armed forces."[26]

While the Gaza raid was surely precipitating in Nasser's decision to acquire Soviet weapons, the Egyptians later developed an official position that it was not the only reason. Cumulative developments, including the Baghdad Pact, the increasing French supply of arms to Israel, and the failure of U.S.-Egyptian arms negotiations, in addition to the raid, were said to be responsible. Indeed, Nasser had attempted to buy arms from the United States. Since Washington was anxious to bring Nasser into a Western defense alliance and to strengthen American influence with him, the sale of arms was considered to be an excellent means of accomplishing these ends. Administration officials thus discussed with the Egyptians various proposals for the sale of American equipment running from $40 million to $100 million.[27] Some scholars have argued that Nasser did not get American arms because he refused to agree to U.S. stipulations that the arms be used solely for defensive purposes[28]—a sensitive point for the Egyptians, who would have been reluctant publicly to foreswear war against Israel. (Israel agreed to such stipulations—a provision of the Arms Export Control Act—then persistently disregarded them.) Others have argued that the United States was not forthcoming because Egypt refused to join the Baghdad Pact.[29] Whatever the explanation, Washington ultimately rejected the Egyptian request.

Subsequent to the breakdown in arms negotiations with the United States, and in the context of Egypt's security concerns after the Israeli attacks on Gaza and Khan Yunis, Nasser concluded an agreement with the Soviet Union in September 1955, commonly referred to as the "Czech Arms Deal." This transaction marked the beginning of the extension of Soviet influence in the Middle East. It put an end to American hopes that Nasser could be persuaded to join a Western alliance, and it broke Western control over the flow of arms to the area. Quite simply, it created a whole new power situation: the Arab-Israeli dispute was now squarely enmeshed in the global great power competition, and this could not but bode ill for U.S. national interests in the Middle East.

The Israelis viewed the Soviet deal with Egypt in the gravest light. They considered it a serious threat to their security and asked the United States for arms to match those that Egypt had acquired.[30] The request was formally rejected, as had been similar requests on previous occasions, with the answer that it was not the policy of the United States to contribute to an arms race.[31] In actuality, however, the United States had sold Israel weapons even before the Czech

Arms Deal, despite its official policy.[32] But more important than direct arm sales were the U.S.–facilitated Israeli arms purchases from third countries, primarily France. From 1949 the United States supplied Israel with substantial financial aid, knowingly making possible its purchase of weapons from Canada, France, and Britain.[33] At the same time Washington turned a blind eye (or perhaps actually encouraged) its allies to sell Israel weapons. Such sales constituted a direct violation of the 1951 Tripartite Declaration in which London, Paris, and Washington agreed to prevent an arms race in the Middle East by not supplying arms to any of the region's nations. By the early part of 1955 the French began to increase significantly their arms sales to Israel, a process that did not pass unnoticed in Egypt. In addition, once Dulles decided, sometime in April 1956, that Israel needed planes and heavy weapons from the West to counter Soviet arms, he exerted considerable pressure on other countries, especially Canada, to provide those weapons. In fact, in May 1956—in a pointed and public gesture—the United States agreed to relinquish NATO priority over some French military equipment and permit their sale to Israel. Nasser responded by offering diplomatic recognition to the People's Republic of China, an action that provoked Dulles into withdrawing the American offer to finance the Aswan Dam project. Nasser then nationalized the Suez Canal, and Britain, France, and Israel began laying plans for war.

Parallel to these issues of raids and reprisals and arms escalation was the issue of Egyptian interdiction of Israel's use of international waterways. Egypt, as noted, prohibited Israeli shipping in the Suez Canal, although a more significant restriction for Israel was the problem of passage through the Straits of Tiran, a vital Israeli link to the rest of the world, as ships leaving Eilat, Israel's southernmost port, had to pass through the Straits to enter the Red Sea. In 1953 Egypt introduced blockade regulations against Israeli shipping in the Straits and established a coast guard unit at Ras Nasrani, at the southern tip of the Sinai where the Straits join the Red Sea. This unit stopped all vessels entering the Straits and subjected them to search to ensure that they were not Israeli ships (though cargo reached and left Israel on ships bearing other flags). At the beginning of September 1955, in the context of the heightening tensions after the Gaza and Khan Yunis raids, Egypt strengthened this blockade, stating that neither Israeli ships nor planes would be allowed through or over the Straits of Tiran.[34] Opening the Straits to Israeli shipping was one of the objectives of Israel's Sinai campaign in 1956.

The American-Israeli Context

The advent of the Eisenhower administration brought a subtle but perceptible shift in American-Israeli relations. In the spring of 1953 Secretary of State John Foster Dulles, the preeminent foreign policy decision-maker during the Eisenhower period, went on a fact-finding expedition to all the principal countries in the Middle East. When he returned, he delivered a major foreign policy speech stressing the importance of Arab good will and American impartiality in the Arab-Israeli dispute.[35] He emphasized the need for strengthening the interrelated defenses of the Arab countries so as to forge a regional security system, and stated: "The United States should seek to allay the deep resentment against it that has resulted from the creation of Israel. In the past we had good relations with the Arab peoples. . . . Today the Arab peoples are afraid that the United States will back the new state of Israel in aggressive expansionism. We cannot afford to be distrusted by millions who could be sturdy friends of freedom."[36] Dulles continued: "Israel should become part of the Near East community and cease to look upon itself, or be looked upon by others, as alien to this community." Dulles also asserted that at least some of the Palestinian refugees "could be settled in the area presently controlled by Israel." Furthermore he suggested that America should increase its economic aid and technical assistance to the Arab states.[37]

The speech reflected in part the cold war mentality that dominated U.S. foreign policy—the fear that if the Americans did not win the support of the Arabs, the Soviets would. But it also reflected the thinking of a new administration that genuinely believed there were two sides to the Palestine issue. In addition, Dulles thought that if the Arab states were in the Western fold, they could best be prevented from taking any warlike action against Israel and that an Arab-Israeli peace was more assured if only one great power dominated the region. The Israeli government, however, was extremely resentful of this speech and the new attitude in Washington. Israel believed that American impartiality in the Middle East would "unjustly and dangerously blur . . . the distinction," as Israel perceived it, between "the potential aggressor and his potential victim."[38] The Israeli government also viewed Dulles's statement regarding the return of some of the refugees as a "thinly veiled" attack on Israel's vital national interests and its "very survival."[39] None of Dulles's recommendations was ever implemented.

Subsequent American statements and actions indicated other underlying differences between the United States and Israel. For example, on July 25, 1953, the United States rejected, "for the time being," Israel's request for a $75 million loan.[40] In part, Washington intended this announcement to signal its disapproval of Israel's creeping annexation of Jerusalem. Indeed, on July 28 Dulles publicly voiced American displeasure over the transfer of the Israeli Foreign Ministry to Jerusalem, suggesting that it was likely to increase tension in the area, and added that the American Embassy would not follow.[41] The move of the Foreign Ministry specifically contradicted existing U.N. resolutions on Jerusalem, including the 1947 partition resolution, which considered Jerusalem an international city, not part of the Jewish state.[42] The aid request was subsequently fulfilled, however, and the Israelis continued to construct government offices in Jerusalem. Thus, the dichotomy between principle and practice was evident even in the early part of the Eisenhower administration.

Nevertheless, there were a number of issues of discord between the United States and Israel. For example, on September 18, 1953, Washington announced the temporary suspension of aid to Israel for its violation of the U.N. Truce Supervision Organization's request to suspend work on its hydroelectric project on the Jordan River in the Israeli-Syrian demilitarized zone. With this project Israel intended to divert the Jordan's waters to the Negev. The plan included the construction of a hydroelectric installation to exploit the drop in the river's flow between Lake Huleh and Lake Tiberias (the Sea of Galilee). The site of the project, near the bridge of B'nat Ya qov, was in the demilitarized zone in close proximity to the Syrian border. The Syrians objected to the Israeli plan on the grounds that it was taking from Syria (and Jordan) water that was rightfully theirs and much needed and that in the long run it would give Israel a significant military advantage. General Vagn Bennike, the UNTSO chief of staff, sustained Syria's objections and ordered Israel to stop its activities until Syria gave its consent. The Israelis refused to comply and continued digging the channel. Syria lodged a complaint with the Security Council, and the United States temporarily supported Syria's position.[43] Subsequently, Israel announced suspension of work on the project whereupon Dulles recommended the resumption of aid to Israel, although Israel eventually completed the project on its terms. The incident is significant, however, in that for the first and only time in U.S.–Israeli relations the American government took a principled position in a dispute between Israel and the Arabs and suspended aid to Israel until it complied.[44]

Another source of discord involved the verbal condemnation by the United States of Israel for its October 1953 raid on Qibya.[45] From the outset, at least in principle, America opposed Israel's policy of massive retaliation, rightly fearing the potential repercussions of the policy both in terms of regional instability and American interests. Again, however, the United States never undertook any measures to see that Israel desisted from this dangerous policy. Nevertheless, Israel deeply resented Washington's public position.

There were yet other issues that caused friction between Israel and the United States. On April 14, 1954, Washington announced that its grant-in-aid to Israel for fiscal year 1955 would be pared to $52.2 million because Israel was "nearer self-support and no longer required the large sums that had been made available in the three previous years."[46] On April 10 Assistant Secretary of State Henry Byroade delivered a speech (with a sequel on May 1) in which he attempted to outline the U.S. assessment of the main issues in the Arab-Israeli dispute and to put forward some ideas for improving the situation. He stressed the need for Israel to abandon the "attitude of the conqueror and the conviction that force and a policy of retaliatory killings is the only policy your neighbors will understand." He advised Israel to cease thinking of itself as the center of world Jewry and suggested that a limit on immigration would be likely to have a beneficial effect on Arab attitudes toward Israel, which could be the beginning of a rapprochement. Byroade also accused the Arabs of attempting to maintain a state of affairs suspended between peace and war while desiring neither—a policy he considered dangerous—and argued that world public opinion would increasingly condemn the Arab position. He admonished the Arabs to accept the existence of the state of Israel and move toward a *modus vivendi* with it.[47] Despite Byroade's evenhanded approach, Israel was outraged by the speech, arguing that the assistant secretary's suggestions struck at the very concept of Israeli statehood.[48] No American policy was developed reflecting Byroade's analysis and recommendations.

Israel was also extremely unhappy about U.S. efforts to forge the Baghdad Pact in 1954. Israel viewed American military and economic assistance to Iraq as especially unacceptable, arguing that arms to Iraq were a direct threat to Israel's security, since Iraq had participated in the war of 1948 but had not later signed an armistice agreement with Israel.[49] The administration did not believe that arms to Iraq were a threat to the Jewish state, and, moreover, was interested in regional security and the prevention of Soviet expansion. The conflict of interest between the two countries was readily apparent, and in this case Washington continued its relationship with Iraq. (It was in 1954, however, that Israel initiated the sabotage operation against American facilities in Egypt which contributed to the rupture in U.S.-Egyptian relations.)

In August 1955 Dulles again turned his attention to the Arab-Israeli problem. In an address before the Council of Foreign Relations in New York City, he outlined the main problems of the region, which included the "tragic plight of the 900,000 Palestinian refugees who formerly lived in the territory that is now occupied by Israel" and the "lack of fixed permanent boundaries between Israel and its Arab neighbors."[50] He suggested a number of possible approaches for dealing with the problem, including a resettlement and repatriation of the refugees. He proposed that resettlement could be facilitated by the creation of more arable land through water development projects that the United States could fund, and he stated that America would participate in an international loan to Israel that could be used to pay the refugees for their homes and land that Israel had expropriated. He suggested more formal treaty arrangements in order to provide both the Arabs and Israelis a greater sense of security. Moreover, he offered the good offices of the United States to aid in negotiations for final boundary settlements.[51]

Israel reacted vehemently to Dulles's speech. The Israeli government feared that the speech suggested that the United States saw Israel's boundaries as a subject for negotiation and might support a reduction of Israel's territory to satisfy Arab wishes.[52] Again the conflict of interest and the divergent perspectives were very real, yet Dulles's clarity of perception concerning America's vital interests in the Middle East was not translated into a concrete policy that the administration was willing to implement. Nothing was done for the Palestinians, and Washington did not use its good offices to fix Israel's boundaries.

Moreover, despite the many areas of tension and conflict between the United States and Israel, Washington continued throughout this period to give Israel very substantial economic and financial assistance (see Table 1). With regard to this government aid, Nadav Safran, a prominent scholar of Israeli affairs, has commented: "On a per capita basis of the recipient country, this is probably the highest rate of American aid given to any country."[53] Moreover, the American government never seriously attempted to question the classification of the nearly $1 billion of donations given annually by American Jews as tax-exempt charity, even though this money went into the general development budget of Israel. David Ben-Gurion himself has publicly acknowledged that without this public and private aid, given or sanctioned by the American government, Israel would have been unable to develop its economy on the scale that it did, institutionalize and develop its state structures, absorb the vast number of immigrants that were encouraged to come, and pursue its military objectives.

TABLE 1. U.S. Assistance to Israel, 1948-59

Year	Total Aid	Economic Loans	Economic Grants	Military Loans
1948				
1949				
1950				
1951	0.1		0.1	
1952	86.4		86.4	
1953	73.6		73.6	
1954	74.7		74.7	
1955	52.7	30.8	21.9	
1956	50.8	35.2	15.6	
1957	40.9	21.8	19.1	
1958	61.2	49.9	11.3	
1959	50.3	39.0	10.9	0.4
TOTAL	490.7	176.7	313.6	0.4

SOURCE: *The Link*, Dec. 1982, 3.
NOTE: Data are in millions of dollars and do not include loans through the Export-Import bank.

The accommodation of U.S. policy to Israel's interests during this period, in spite of the many areas of conflict and divergence, resulted from a number of factors, including: (1) the "Western orientation" of Israeli leaders, which enabled them to understand the workings of the American government and to interact positively with governmental personnel and processes; (2) the ability of Israeli leaders to secure access to high government officials—elected and nonelected—to explain their views; (3) the ability of Israeli leaders and pro-Israeli Americans to reach and influence the American public, successfully shaping "informed" public opinion by creating perceptions about the Arab-Israeli dispute consonant with Israel's interests; (4) the existence of important advocates among the American Jewish community working on Israel's behalf with the government, the media, and crucial sectors in American society (such as labor); and (5) general cultural and historical considerations that seemed to give Israelis and Americans a natural affinity for each other. By contrast, Americans tended to view Arabs with suspicion and hostility—as part of the inferior races and civilizations which could not be admitted with equality to the councils of the Western world's order. In addition, Arab leaders were not as successful at comprehending the nature of the American system and had little direct access to high echelons in Washington. They understood little, if anything, about the necessity or the means of influencing American public opinion (indeed, the Arabs tended to believe that because their position was "just," it would prevail naturally). And, save for a few "Arabists" (so labeled derisively by Israel's domestic supporters) in the diplomatic corps and the State Department, Arab countries had no domestic constituency advocating their position. The Palestinians had no representatives at all.

The Sinai-Suez War

The Hostilities

On October 29, 1956, Israel invaded the Sinai. On the following day, by prior arrangement, Britain and France issued an ultimatum to Egypt and Israel, to withdraw to ten miles on either side of the Suez Canal and to allow the British and French to establish themselves along the canal or they would "intervene in such strength as was necessary."[54] The ultimatum provided Britain and France with an excuse to intervene militarily when Egypt rejected the demand. Nasser refused the ultimatum, as expected, while Israel accepted it, since it enabled the Jewish state to advance on all fronts.

British and French troops landed along the canal, and by November 7 the military campaign was completed. At the termination of hostilities Israel was in command of the Gaza Strip, giving it control over the bases used by the fedayeen, as well as the entire Sinai up to ten miles from the Suez Canal, including Sharm el-Sheikh, thus affording Israel control over entry to the Straits of Tiran.[55]

The U.S. Response

Toward the end of October the United States had learned of the heavy mobilization of Israeli armed forces, and Eisenhower had cabled Ben-Gurion twice, as Moshe Dayan's comments below indicate, urging him not to resort to the use of force.[56] Israel's total disregard of America's pleas, as well as U.S. regional concerns, was said to have enraged Eisenhower and Dulles.[57] It is instructive to see how the Israelis viewed the matter. Dayan recorded the following analysis in his *Diary* on October 29 concerning the effect (or lack thereof) relations with the United States had had on Israeli decision-makers on the eve of war:

The situation with the United States is complicated and not at all agreeable. Israel, wishing and needing to maintain close ties of friendship with the United States, finds herself in the difficult position of having to keep from her—and even be evasive about—her real intentions. The alternative, however, is to forgo military action and just put up with the Arab acts of enmity—blockade of the Gulf of Aqaba, fedayeen terrorism.... The United States is adamantly opposed to any military action on the part of Israel.... I was struck by the hollowness of the president's words in both cables [October 27 and October 29] that "only a peaceful and moderate approach will genuinely improve the situation"; and also his notification, which is presumably expected to allay anxiety in Israel, "that I have also directed that my concern be communicated to other Middle Eastern countries, urgently requesting that they refrain from any action which would lead to hostilities."[58]

This important statement demonstrates many fundamental Israeli policies and attitudes toward the United States. Dayan admitted that there was no prior consultation with Washington; he even acknowledged that there was deception. He noted American opposition to Israeli military activity but asserted that Israel rejected U.S. efforts to find a peaceful resolution. Dayan also clearly intimated the Israeli preference for military solutions. These attitudes have endured in Israel's postures and policies in subsequent years.

In response to the Israeli invasion, the administration immediately brought the matter before the Security Council. On October 30 the American ambassador to the United Nations, Henry Cabot Lodge, asked the council to find a breach of the peace, to order a cease-fire, and to instruct the Israeli forces to withdraw behind the frontiers as established in the armistice agreements.[59] Lodge also strongly warned other members of the United Nations to refrain from giving assistance which might continue or prolong the hostilities.[60]

The Security Council produced a resolution on October 30 that: (1) called on Israel to "immediately withdraw its armed forces behind established armistice lines"; (2) called on all members to refrain from the use of force or threat of force in the area in any manner inconsistent with the purposes of the United Nations, to assist the United Nations in assuring the integrity of the armistice agreements, and to refrain from giving any military, economic, or financial assistance to Israel so long as it has not complied with this resolution; and (3) requested the secretary-general to "keep the Security Council informed on compliance with the resolution and to make whatever recommendations he deems appropriate for the maintenance of international peace and security in the area by the implementation of this and prior resolutions."[61]

Britain and France ignored the U.N. resolution and Washington's requests. They issued their ultimatum, and then invaded Egypt. The U.S. response was firm and unequivocal: it strongly condemned the resort to war by Britain, France, and Israel and worked through the United Nations to end the hostilities and secure the withdrawal of all foreign forces.

The American decision to condemn the tripartite aggression was officially depicted as the result of Eisenhower's and Dulles's concern for a viable world order for which the United States stood.[62] No doubt this is an accurate analysis, but American motivation was not entirely based on principles of international law.[63] The U.S. position during the Sinai-Suez crisis must also be understood as having three objectives: (1) the final eclipse of British and French influence in the Middle East; (2) minimizing Soviet opportunities for expansion; and (3) preventing further alienation of the Arab regimes from the United States.[64]

On October 31 President Eisenhower delivered a major radio and television address, outlining United States policy in the crisis. Eisenhower reiterated American support for Israel and friendship with the Arab countries but stated that "the action taken [by Israel] can scarcely be reconciled with the principles and purposes of the United Nations to which we have all subscribed." He also declared that "it is and will remain the dedicated purpose of your government to do all in its power to localize the fighting and to end the conflict."[65] The speech signaled a shift in the locus of U.S. diplomatic strategy from the Security Council to the General Assembly, and the following day Dulles made a strong speech to that body. The secretary's November 1 remarks to the General Assembly condemned the Israeli resort to force, arguing that there was a "better prospect" for the resolution of conflicts than "armed aggression." Dulles also noted that there had been armistice violations both by Israel and against Israel, but stated that "the violent armed attack by three of our members upon a fourth, cannot be treated as other than a grave error, inconsistent with the principles and purposes of the Charter."[66] Following Dulles's speech the General Assembly passed a resolution on November 2 calling for an "immediate cease-fire . . . the halt of military forces and arms into the area . . . the withdrawal of all forces to the armistice lines . . . the scrupulous observance of the armistice agreements," and "the withholding of military goods to the area by all members of the United Nations." At the termination of hostilities, the resolution declared, efforts should be made to "reopen the Suez Canal and restore secure freedom of navigation."[67]

Israel's response to the General Assembly resolution, transmitted in an *aide memoir* on November 3, indicated a willingness to cease-fire, provided Egypt agreed; but Israel refused to withdraw to the armistice lines, arguing that Egypt's "all out attempt to eliminate Israel by force . . . has undermined the peace agreement and deprived the armistice agreement of all its functions." Israel asserted that "a return to the armistice agreement would be a return to a system which has served as a cover for the victimization, the boycott, and the blockade of Israel, and for a policy aimed at Israel's ultimate annihilation."[68] Egypt accepted the November 2 resolution contingent on the cessation of attack by Israel.[69]

On November 3 the Canadian foreign secretary, Lester B. Pearson, proposed a measure in the General Assembly to facilitate the implementation of the cease-fire. He suggested the creation of a U.N. Emergency Force (UNEF) to be positioned between Israel and Egypt, in place of Britain and France, to supervise the cessation of hostilities and to assure freedom of transit through the Straits.[70] The Canadian resolution supported Britain and France morally, yet enabled them to halt their military operations without losing face. Major General C. L. M. Burns, chief of the UNTSO, initiated formation of the UNEF immediately after the cease-fire went into effect on November 7; it was in place by November 15. It is worth noting, in terms of future events, that Israel always adamantly refused to have any U.N. peacekeeping forces stationed on its soil. British and French troops withdrew immediately after the stationing of the UNEF.

The Soviet Union complicated the situation by not only supporting the resolutions introduced by the United States condemning Britain, France, and Israel but also by sending ominous notes to each country. The Soviet Union demanded the "cessation of aggression against the Egyptian people"; described the actions of the three states as "aggression affecting the interests not only of Egypt, but of other states also"; and stated emphatically that "the Soviet Government is fully determined to apply force in order to crush the aggressors and to restore peace in the East."[71] Such a threat had implications for a great power confrontation; however, given the problems the Soviets were having in Hungary at that time (the Soviet suppression of the Hungarian revolution occurred simultaneous with the Sinai-Suez affair), Washington viewed the Soviet notes as being fundamentally rhetorical, and Moscow did not follow through on its hostile words. A more serious concern, however, was the American fear that in view of the collusion between Israel and the Western powers in the invasion of Egypt, Cairo might subsequently form an alliance with Moscow to provide for its future security.

Israel's postwar statements and policies contributed significantly to Washington's apprehension. Israel's Sinai campaign had realized important strategic gains for the Jewish state, and it was not anxious to relinquish the "fruits of victory."[72] Thus Israel developed a postwar political strategy with the primary objective of turning the military victory into a political success. Ben-Gurion set the tone for Israel's postwar efforts in a "victory speech" he delivered to the Knesset on the evening of November 7. The prime minister described the Sinai campaign as "the greatest and most glorious military operation in the annals of our people and one of the most remarkable operations in world history."[73] Ben-Gurion also noted that:

(1) The armistice agreement with Egypt is dead and buried and cannot be restored to life. . . .
(2) In consequence, the armistice lines between Israel and Egypt have no validity. . . .
(3) We are ready to enter into negotiations for a stable peace, cooperation and good neighborly relations with Egypt, on condition that there are direct negotiations, without prior conditions, on either side and not under duress from any quarter whatsoever. . . .
(4) On no account will Israel agree to the stationing of a foreign force, no matter how it is called, in her territory *or in any of the area occupied by her.* . . (emphasis added).[74]

The fallout from this speech was immediate and negative. Pearson is said to have remarked to Abba Eban that Ben-Gurion's speech must have been equally offensive to the British, the French, the Americans, and the Arabs. "If you people persist with this," he allegedly went on, "you run the risk of losing all your friends."[75] According to Eban, "The general reaction was confusion and consternation. . . . and the demand for greater pressure to withdraw increased." Moreover, Eban noted, "Much of the sympathy that we had acquired after October 29 was dissipated."[76] One indicator of Israel's dismal position was its total isolation in the General Assembly on the night of November 7: the vote for the resolution calling for an immediate cease-fire and withdrawal was 65 to 1 (Israel), with 10 abstentions. Nevertheless, Israel remained determined to turn its military victory into a political success.

Indeed, Ben-Gurion's speech was merely the prelude to Israel's postwar diplomatic strategy, which essentially centered around the policy of no withdrawal from the territories occupied in the war until *after* certain specific Israeli conditions were obtained. This policy led to serious strains in the U.S.–Israeli relationship, since Washington's policy called for unconditional Israeli withdrawal, coupled with the threat of economic sanctions as a means of facilitating that withdrawal, as a *prerequisite* to fulfilling Israel's conditions. In addition, the issue of sanctions became a matter of significant discord between Israel and the United States. Eisenhower relates in his memoirs that he instructed Dulles to draft a statement announcing the suspension of all U.S. military and governmental aid to Israel until it complied with the U.N. resolutions.[77] One account reports that sanctions were threatened as early as October 31, when Dulles told Israel's Abba Eban: "You know, it [continuing operations in the Sinai] will be bound to affect our relations. We could hardly continue economic aid and all the other kinds of assistance you get from us."[78] By

November 4 the threats were extended to private aid. Ben-Gurion wrote of a White House meeting between American and Israeli officials in which the Israelis were told: "Israel's attitude will inevitably lead to grave consequences, such as the stoppage of all governmental and private aid to Israel, sanctions by the United Nations, and perhaps even expulsion from the United Nations Organization."[79]

It is significant, however, that while the threat of sanctions was bandied about quite extensively during this crisis (from October 1956 through April 1957), there is almost no evidence to suggest that sanctions were ever actually imposed.[80] Perhaps Washington's reluctance to follow through on its threats, in comparison to its direct and immediate action in suspending aid in 1953, accounts for the difficulties it encountered in obtaining Israeli withdrawal from Egyptian territory. Had all governmental and private aid actually been suspended, it seems certain that Israel would have promptly withdrawn its forces from Egypt. In lieu of imposing sanctions, the major problem for American policymakers in the aftermath of the war was how to secure Israeli withdrawal in light of Israel's stated intention to remain until its demands were fulfilled.

The Political Struggle over Israeli Withdrawal

On November 7 Eisenhower sent a sternly worded letter to Ben-Gurion, warning that any delay in Israel's immediate withdrawal would have the gravest consequences: "Any such decision by the Government of Israel . . . could not but bring about the condemnation of Israel as a violator of the principles as well as the directives of the United Nations. . . . It would be a matter of the greatest regret to all my countrymen, if Israeli policy on a matter of such grave concern to the world should in any way impair the friendly cooperation between our two countries."[81]

Ben-Gurion was aware that at least partial withdrawal was unavoidable, not only because of the difficulty of a permanent military occupation of so large an area at that stage in Israel's economic development, but also because of the constellation of forces strenuously opposed to Israel's retention of the captured lands. Nevertheless, he was determined not to withdraw until Israel's conditions were satisfied. Thus Ben-Gurion wrote to Eisenhower on November 8: "We will, upon conclusion of satisfactory arrangements with the United Nations in connection with this international force entering the Suez Canal area, willingly withdraw our forces."[82] No mention was made of Gaza. The prime minister cabled a similar message to the U.N. secretary-general and urged the United Nations to pressure

Egypt to renounce its state of war with Israel, to end the boycott and blockade, and to cease sending into Israel "gangs of murderers."[83] Ben-Gurion thus tied Israeli withdrawal to the prior success of the UNEF and in so doing gave the offer of withdrawal a conditional nature. The Israeli strategy then was predicated on a phased withdrawal, related to the achievement of specific concessions and guarantees from the United States and the United Nations. Abba Eban wrote of the strategy: "It was obviously not possible . . . to remain in most of Sinai. The decision was to delay and stagger the withdrawal while mustering support for international control both in Sharm el-Sheikh and in the Gaza Strip."[84] The Israelis felt that if freedom of navigation in the Straits could be guaranteed and return of the Gaza Strip to Egyptian control (and thus, presumably, to the fedayeen) prevented, the war effort would not have been in vain.[85] The problem for the United States was Israel's demand for the guarantees *prior* to its withdrawal: Washington felt that providing such guarantees before Israel withdrew would be viewed as American ratification of Israeli aggression. On November 8 Ben-Gurion delivered a radio broadcast to his nation informing the Israeli people of the various pressures on the government and the government's decision for a conditional withdrawal, contingent on guarantees for freedom of navigation. He was firm in response to the pressure being applied by the United Nations and the United States: "Our foreign policy is dictated by our essential needs. . . . It is not and will not be decided by any foreign factor."[86]

The Israeli policy on withdrawal was opposed by U.N. Secretary-General Dag Hammarskjöld as well as the United States. Both felt that Israel should withdraw unconditionally and then seek a solution for Gaza and the Straits. That fundamental conflict set in motion an intense diplomatic struggle in New York and Washington. The Eban-Hammarskjöld dialogue at the United Nations went on for almost three months (November 21, 1956–February 11, 1957), while the Eban-Dulles dialogue was all-consuming from February 11 through February 28. Israel proceeded with craft and calculation—exerting pressure on the United States and the United Nations by the resoluteness with which it held to its strategy of phased, conditional withdrawal. Thus, in response to a November 24 General Assembly resolution demanding immediate and complete Israeli withdrawal,[87] Ben-Gurion announced that by December 1 Israeli troops would withdraw to a position thirty miles east of the canal. However, on December 9, Ben-Gurion instructed Eban to "do everything possible to gain time, to avoid a clash with the secretary-general, and to demand free passage through the Canal." Ben-Gurion insisted that if pressure for further withdrawal continued, Israel would halt at El Arish in the first week of January 1957 and wait for "real" assurances. It was not at all clear, however, that the Israelis would even pull back as far as El Arish. An agreement on December 16 between General Burns and General Dayan provided for two steps in the phased withdrawal—thirty miles that week and fifteen miles the week after—but Hammarskjöld strenuously objected to the slow pace. Eban finally persuaded Ben-Gurion to agree to expedite the withdrawal to the El Arish line by the end of December.[88]

On December 25 Ben-Gurion cabled Eban with a new policy directive—the focus of Israel's political strategy was to be shifted from U.N. "assurances" to U.S. "guarantees" with a clear scale of objectives: (1) demilitarization of eastern Sinai; (2) retention of Israeli troops at Sharm el-Sheikh until concrete guarantees were achieved; and (3) the non-return of Egyptian administrative control to Gaza (potentially implying permanent Israeli occupation).[89] On December 29 Foreign Minister Golda Meir met with Dulles and asked for an outright U.S. guarantee of Israel's freedom of passage in the Straits of Tiran and the non-return of Gaza to Egypt.[90] Dulles reproached Israel for not consulting the United States prior to the invasion and asserted that Israeli aggression had reduced its chances of rectifying what injustices it had suffered. Dulles agreed that the Gulf of Aqaba was an international waterway and that the Gaza Strip had not traditionally been part of Egyptian territory, but he eschewed the idea of any kind of U.S. guarantees.[91]

By January 13 the Israeli government had withdrawn from the territories it had occupied during the invasion, except for Gaza and a strip from Eilat to Sharm el-Sheikh from which Israel could assure its access to the Straits of Tiran. The United States remained firm, however, that Israel evacuate these areas as well. Eisenhower wrote of the American position after January 13: "If Israel did not desire to defy the United Nations it was first necessary that her forces withdraw unconditionally behind the borders fixed by the truce of 1948. Only then could the nation expect the support of the rest of the free world in securing by peaceful means her legal rights."[92]

Throughout January 1957 tension mounted between Israel and the United States, and the problems of securing Israeli withdrawal from Sharm el-Sheikh and Gaza became entangled in the larger geopolitical view of Dulles and Eisenhower toward Middle East problems in general. As Eisenhower described it: "In this confusion one danger loomed above all others: the leaders of the Soviet Union had their eyes on the Middle East. The Soviet goal was by no means merely the right to move ships through the Suez Canal. . . . neither was the goal Middle Eastern oil. . . . The Soviet objective was, in plain fact, power politics; to seize the oil, to cut the Canal and pipelines of the Middle East, and thus seriously to weaken Western civilization."[93]

Washington's continuing worries about potential Soviet inroads in the Middle East and Western freedom of access to the region's raw materials and markets were reflected in its attitudes and policies toward Egypt and Saudi Arabia. On the one hand, the administration feared that Nasser might form an alignment with the Soviet Union in the aftermath of the 1956 war. And such concern was well founded. It was Israel's earlier aggression—the Gaza raid—that had originally impelled Nasser to seek arms from Moscow. Egypt's concern for its national security would surely be heightened after the 1956 invasion and occupation. Moreover, since Britain and France had joined in the attack on Egypt, and given continuing American hostility, Nasser had few options in seeking to provide for his country's security and territorial integrity. Even so, Nasser attempted to maintain his policy of nonalignment and his desire to keep Egypt free of dependence on any one great power. Washington, however, seemed incapable of developing constructive policies for dealing with Egypt; rather, the United States persistently antagonized the Egyptian president. For example, the desire to ensure Western access to Arabian oil led to an American effort to strengthen relations with Saudi Arabia. However, instead of focusing on improving bilateral ties between Washington and Riyadh, Dulles attempted to build King Ibn Saud up as a counterweight to Nasser in inter-Arab politics, which merely served to alienate further the Egyptian leader.[94]

The intersection of the Arab-Israeli conflict with American-Soviet global competition led to a major new foreign policy initiative in early January. The Eisenhower Doctrine was proclaimed by the president before a joint session of Congress on January 5, 1957. Its stated purpose was "supporting the sovereignty of each and every nation of the Middle East against the predatory desires of international Communism." The doctrine was primarily aimed at Nasser (which did not escape him) and its essence was contained in three points. (1) Congress was asked to authorize the president to employ as he deemed necessary the armed forces of the United States to secure and protect the integrity of any nation or group of nations in the general area of the Middle East requesting aid against overt armed aggression from any nation controlled by international Communism. (2) Congress was to authorize the president to undertake programs of military aid to any nation or group of nations desiring it. (3) Congress was to authorize American cooperation with such states in the development of economic strength for the maintenance of their national independence.[95]

Nasser was incensed by the Eisenhower Doctrine and feared that it signaled a direct U.S. attempt to unseat him and to reverse the course of Egyptian development. The doctrine was welcomed by some conservative elements in the region, such as King Hussein of Jordan and President Camille Chamoun of Lebanon (though not because they feared the spread of international Communism), but it was rejected by Arab nationalist leaders and by nationalist movements that were influential factors in many Arab countries, including Jordan and Lebanon. Indeed, President Chamoun's formal acceptance of the doctrine contributed to the fissure in the "National Pact" between Lebanese Christians and Muslims and proved to be one of the major factors precipitating the 1958 civil war, during which American marines landed in Lebanon. Moreover, as the United States became increasingly identified with Israel, the suggestion of military bases on Arab territories or military pacts with America was viewed by even conservative Arab leaders as a grand design by Washington to impose U.S.–Israeli domination over the region.[96] In addition, the Eisenhower Doctrine was faulty conceptually: the Arab regimes did not perceive the Soviet Union or Communism as their greatest security concern; rather, they viewed Israel, with its increasingly militaristic and expansionist tendencies, as the major threat to their security. (Some conservative leaders also viewed Arab nationalism as a serious threat: for them "international Communism" became a convenient inducement to secure U.S. backing to maintain their unpopular power positions.) But in the final analysis, much like the Baghdad Pact, the Eisenhower Doctrine proved to be a major blunder of American diplomacy, ultimately alienating the Arabs, fostering regional instability, and providing new opportunities for the expansion of Soviet influence.

In keeping with the concerns that gave rise to the Eisenhower Doctrine, however, the United States remained firm in its position that Israel had to withdraw unconditionally. On January 17 Ambassador Lodge spoke in favor of a resolution pending before the General Assembly: "The United States has spoken clearly and unequivocally in favor of prompt [Israeli] withdrawal of all forces behind the armistice lines. . . . We have supported each of the resolutions . . . giving effect to this general principle. We continue to hold this view and will vote for the resolution before the Assembly now."[97] The resolution, which reiterated the U.N. demand for complete Israeli withdrawal, passed.

U.S.–Israeli tensions escalated on February 2, when Ambassador

Lodge made two separate statements in support of two resolutions that were pending a vote.[98] The first resolution deplored Israeli noncompliance with previous U.N. resolutions and called on Israel to withdraw without further delay behind the 1949 armistice lines.[99] The second resolution recognized that Israeli withdrawal must be followed by action that would assure progress toward the creation of peaceful conditions; it therefore called on Egypt and Israel to observe the provisions of the 1949 armistice and directed the secretary-general to place the UNEF on the 1949 demarcation line to keep peace in the area.[100] The resolutions were passed on February 4. Israel was unhappy about both resolutions but was even more concerned with the implied threats of sanctions in Lodge's speeches, particularly the second. A more overt threat was contained in a personal message from Eisenhower to Ben-Gurion on February 4. Eisenhower wrote: "I feel it necessary to make the strongest possible pleas to Israel that she cease ignoring the United Nations resolutions which, taken as a whole, can help, I believe, to bring tranquility and justice to your country and her neighbors. Continued disregard for international opinion, as expressed in the United Nations resolutions, will almost certainly lead to further United Nations action which will seriously damage relations between Israel and United Nations members, including the United States."[101]

Notwithstanding the various threats, the Israeli government rejected the U.N. resolutions in a strongly worded letter to the secretary-general on February 5.[102] Moreover, on February 8 Ben-Gurion bluntly rejected pressure from all sources: "It is unthinkable," he wrote to Eisenhower, "that now that we have recovered our independence in our ancient homeland, we should submit to discrimination: our people will never accept this no matter what sacrifice it might entail."[103]

By this time countervailing pressures from the American domestic scene had coalesced and undoubtedly affected the resolution of discord between Israel and the United States. Forty-one Republican congressmen signed a statement that they presented to the president, calling on the United States to oppose Israeli withdrawal until Egypt began to negotiate. Seventy-five Democratic congressmen demanded in a letter to the president that the United States insist on free passage through the Suez Canal and the Straits of Tiran before Israel's evacuation. Moreover, there was considerable vocal pressure against any form of sanctions from influential individuals including William Knowland, the Republican Senate leader, and Democratic Senator Paul Douglas. The AFL-CIO issued a statement urging the demilitarization of Sinai as well as continued Israeli civil administration of Gaza. In addition, a large portion of the American media supported

Israel's demand for guarantees regarding free passage through the Straits and for security against future Egyptian hostility. The *Washington Post* was the first to call for a guarantee through the United Nations and, if necessary, a separate U.S. guarantee of free passage and secure borders. These expressions of support for Israel's position demonstrated the successful efforts of Israel's American supporters in convincing crucial sectors of American society of the correctness of Israel's positions and perceptions, as well as illustrating the extent of perceived cultural affinity between Americans and Israelis. In the face of such domestic opposition, the administration's threats of sanctions were seriously undermined, and the Israelis were aware that subsequent threats were little more than empty words.

February 11 marked the beginning of American acquiescence to Israel's position. On that day Secretary Dulles addressed an *aide memoir* to the Israeli ambassador promising that if Israel withdrew to the prewar lines, the United States would support the stationing of the UNEF at Sharm el-Sheikh to ensure nonbelligerency and freedom of passage in the Straits and in the Gaza to prevent fedayeen raids. Most important, the United States put in writing its support for the principle that the "Gulf [of Aqaba] comprehends international waters and that no nation has the right to prevent free and innocent passage in the Gulf and through the Straits." Dulles continued, "The United States . . . is prepared to exercise the right of free and innocent passage and to join with others to secure general recognition of this right." The memorandum added, however: "It is of course clear that the enjoyment of free and innocent passage by Israel would depend upon its prior withdrawal in accordance with the United Nations resolutions." With regard to Gaza the United States maintained its original position that according to the armistice agreement Egypt had the right and responsibility of occupation.[104]

The proclamation declaring the Gulf of Aqaba an international waterway open to free and innocent passage went a considerable measure toward meeting Israel's basic objective. Abba Eban confirmed this and added that "the practical solution of stationing United Nations forces was enriched and deepened by Mr. Dulles' memorandum of February 11."[105] Still, the U.S. position was not conciliatory enough for the Israeli government. According to Ben-Gurion, it was unsatisfactory "in that it stipulated prior withdrawal to the armistice demarcation lines in the Gaza Strip and evacuation of the coast of the Straits of Eilat [Tiran]."[106] Ben-Gurion also continued to oppose the idea of Gaza being returned to Egyptian administrative control.

On February 12 Dulles reiterated the assertions in the *aide memoir* and again urged immediate Israeli withdrawal.[107] Israel remained unmoved. In frustration, Eisenhower raised the issue of sanctions anew on February 16. At a meeting that day with Dulles, Lodge, and Treasury Secretary George M. Humphrey, Eisenhower stated: "I rejected . . . any more United Nations resolutions designed merely to condemn Israel's conduct. I preferred a resolution which would call on all United Nations members to suspend not just government, but private assistance to Israel. Such a move would be no hollow gesture."[108] It seems apparent, however, that by this time domestic political pressure was a serious impediment to the president's undertaking such measures.

On February 17 President Eisenhower issued a major news statement from Thomasville, Georgia.[109] In this address he made public the February 11 *aide memoir*, reviewed some of the events that had occurred to that date, and stated that the United States was aware that Israel had legitimate grievances and should be able to find a remedy to them, but concluded with the statement: "Accordingly, the United States had renewed its plea to Israel to withdraw in accordance with the repeated demands of the United Nations and to rely upon the resoluteness of all friends of justice to bring about a state of affairs which will conform to the principles of justice and of international law, and serve impartiality and proper interests of all in the area. This, the United States believes, should provide a greater source of security for Israel than an occupation continued contrary to the overwhelming judgment of the world community."[110]

The Israelis felt that the tone of the president's statement was at odds with the spirit of the *aide memoir* (that they had found insufficient in any event), and they correctly perceived it as being condemnatory—putting Israel in the wrong for using force to seize Arab lands as bargaining power. The response came in two forms. Ben-Gurion immediately cabled instructions to Eban, reconfirming the non-negotiability of Israel's position on the Straits and Gaza. The cable specified: (1) no evacuation until *after effective* guarantees of free passage through the Straits, and (2) the non-return of Egypt to Gaza.[111] Second, Ben-Gurion wrote to Dulles, rejecting the U.S. position and requesting that he arrange a postponement of a scheduled U.N. General Assembly debate on the possibility of implementing sanctions against Israel as a means of enforcing its compliance with United Nations resolutions.[112] Dulles did, in fact, secure a delay of the debate.

On February 20 President Eisenhower was subjected to pressure from a group of twenty-six congressmen petitioning the president on behalf of Israel's interests. In a meeting held just prior to a scheduled radio address, Senators Lyndon Johnson and William Knowland strongly pressed Eisenhower to explain why he was insisting on unconditional withdrawal and why he continued to threaten Israel with sanctions.[113] According to an official present at the meeting: "The president told the legislators that he was well aware of their opposition to sanctions against Israel and that he could understand their attitude. . . . Then Eisenhower stated flatly that he did not know how to protect American interests in the Middle East except through the United Nations. . . . If the United States failed to support the United Nations on the Israel issue he declared, it would be a lethal blow to the principles of the world organization. . . . Nobody likes to impose sanctions, but how else can we induce Israel to withdraw to the line agreed on in the 1949 Armistice?"[114]

Eisenhower believed that Israel's best chance for security and peace with its neighbors resided in its behaving according to accepted principles of international law and the U.N. Charter. If Israel was going to violate those norms flagrantly, then it was the responsibility of the United States to ensure that it abided by them. Moreover, to protect wider U.S. interests in the Middle East, Eisenhower argued that Israel had to be induced to act within the context of the U.N. Charter and to abide by international law. The congressional leaders declined to support Eisenhower's position, but the president made the broadcast as planned. The tone of the president's message was strict, the content was essentially the same—Israel had to withdraw unconditionally, relying on the United Nations and the United States to ensure that it would obtain the two conditions it sought after its withdrawal.[115]

The following day, February 21, Ben-Gurion reiterated his opposition to the U.S. position in a speech before the Knesset. He argued again that "the people of Israel cannot submit to discrimination in international relations."[116] Ben-Gurion sent Eban back to the United States, after a brief respite in Israel, with a new strategy. The problem of freedom of navigation was to be *separated* from the problem of Gaza; however, freedom of navigation was to be insured *before* there would be a retreat from Gaza.[117] Moreover, Eban was armed with five points that Israel considered "essential" in this regard. They included:

(1) That its ships be permitted to sail in the Gulf of Aqaba and carry on trade to Eilat, including the transport of oil to Eilat;

(2) That the U.S. government publicly acknowledge that if Egypt interfered with Israeli shipping in the Gulf and in the Straits after the evacuation, Israel would have the right of self-defense to adopt all forceful means necessary to secure freedom of passage;

(3) That the definition of "free and innocent" should include

warships, and that Israel's warships should have complete freedom to sail in the Straits and the Gulf;

(4) That in the event the U.N. General Assembly passed no resolution calling for the stationing of an international force on the western shores of the Straits until peace is achieved, there should be a resolution calling for a U.N. naval force to patrol the Straits and the Gulf until peace is achieved; and

(5) That the U.S. government should obtain declarations from as large a number of states as possible, recognizing the Gulf as an international waterway and the terms of (2) above.[118]

Dulles allegedly gave Eban an "encouraging" response to the five points and inferred to the Israeli ambassador that the United States would work to fulfill these conditions.[119] However, as the Israeli proposals involved U.N. cooperation and Hammarskjöld refused to go along with them,[120] the situation remained at an impasse.

At this point, the French made a proposal that led to the final settlement.[121] The crucial point in the French formula was that if Israel were *attacked* in the Gulf of Aqaba—nothing was said about its right to use force in the event of closure of the Straits—it could act in self-defense under Article 51 of the U.N. Charter. This proposal became the basis of an agreement between Israel and the United States and Israel and the United Nations. Ben-Gurion pressed Eban to insist on the necessity for at least an "assumption" in any form, even if the assurance was secret, from the United States and the United Nations that Egypt would not return to Gaza. The prime minister wanted the United Nations to authorize Israel to remain in the strip until a formal peace agreement was arrived at, and he insisted that no reference be made to the 1949 armistice agreement.[122] Neither Hammarskjöld nor Dulles agreed to this demand.

The implementing session took place at the State Department on February 28. "We went over the document sentence by sentence," commented Eban, "and agreement was unqualified." When the discussion ended, Dulles said that Ambassador Lodge would receive instructions to note favorably the forthcoming Israeli announcement on the various issues.[123]

The Israeli government approved both the Dulles-Eban document and the text of a statement that Meir was to give at a special session of the General Assembly on March 1. Meir's statement began: "The Government of Israel is now in a position to announce its plans for a full and prompt withdrawal from the Sharm el-Sheikh area and the Gaza Strip, in compliance with Resolution 1 of 2 February, 1957."[124] However, the foreign minister then listed a number of "qualifications" concerning Israel's perception of its "rights" both with regard to the Straits of Tiran and the Gaza Strip, under which it was making this withdrawal, including the "freedom to act" militarily in situations that Israel would define as "deteriorat[ing]."[125]

Following Meir's declaration, Lodge presented a statement on behalf of the American government, reflecting the totality of U.S. interests in the Middle East. He said that Israel's assumptions about the Straits were "not unreasonable"; but on the issue of Gaza, Lodge emphasized the validity of the armistice agreement and the secretary-general's primary role therein. He also reiterated the position that no member of the United Nations had the right "to seek political gains through the use of force or to use as a bargaining point a gain achieved by means of force." He reaffirmed the U.S. commitment to support "the right of free and innocent passage and to join with others to secure general recognition of this right." Lodge further emphasized that in the overall context of peace in the Middle East, the United States "would like to see as rapidly as is practical a definitive settlement of the Palestine problem" and he condemned "acts of aggression or other breaches of the peace" by members of the world organization. He also stipulated that the UNEF's function in the Straits "would, of course, be without prejudice to any ultimate determination which may be made of any legal questions concerning the Gulf of Aqaba," emphasizing the administration's often-repeated suggestion that the status of rival claims in the Gulf of Aqaba should be determined by the World Court.[126]

Israel was extremely angered by this speech, particularly so because of Lodge's statement on Gaza, but also because of the ambassador's reference to the Palestinian issue.[127] In an effort to mollify the Israelis, Dulles met again with Eban and subsequently announced that President Eisenhower would send the Israeli prime minister a letter indicating that the "assumptions and hopes" expressed in the General Assembly by Meir were acceptable and that the United States would work for their implementation.[128] On March 2 Eisenhower cabled a letter containing such reassurances to Ben-Gurion.[129]

On receiving the letter, Ben-Gurion called a special cabinet meeting and proposed the evacuation of the Gaza Strip. The resolution was passed by the Knesset, but many Israelis, who believed that what had been gained militarily had now been lost politically, were disappointed.[130] Ben-Gurion expressed some reservation, commenting that "there is no certainty and no clear and authoritative undertaking that the Egyptians will not return or be restored to Gaza"; but nevertheless he indicated general satisfaction with the outcome: "The main objective has been reached: freedom of navigation in the Straits of Eilat, through the Red Sea, and into the Indian Ocean; and the introduction of a United Nations force outside our territory to safe-guard this freedom of navigation and quiet in the Gaza Strip."[131] Thus on March 4 Ben-Gurion issued orders for full and prompt withdrawal of all Israeli forces from Sharm el-Sheikh and the Gaza Strip. By March 7 the evacuation was complete, and the Sinai-Suez crisis was ended.

On March 8 Ben-Gurion wrote to President Eisenhower: "Now that we have withdrawn from the Sinai Desert, as I promised in my letter of November 8, and have also withdrawn from the Gaza Strip, which I profoundly believe we should not have done, for both political and security reasons, please permit me to point out that we did so in large measure because of your letter of March 2 in which you expressed your conviction that 'Israel would have no reason to regret' such an action and that 'the hopes and expectations' expressed by her Foreign Minister 'would not prove groundless.' "[132]

On March 13 the Egyptians returned to Gaza and assumed ad-ministrative control. The Israelis were greatly distressed at the time; however, in retrospect, Abba Eban wrote of the extremely positive outcome of the Sinai-Suez affair for Israel: "For the next ten years there was not a single violent collision between Israelis and Egyptians from the Gaza Strip; and during that period, Israel translated its navigation rights in the Straits of Tiran from an abstract principle to a living reality expressed in hundreds of sailings under dozens of flags, and in the swift development of Eilat as Israel's outlet to the Southern and Eastern worlds. To these gains in Tiran and Gaza was added the psychological boost which Israel derived from its successful military operations. So in the end, the balance sheet in March 1957 was in decisive credit."[133]

Conclusion

Of greatest significance with regard to this period (1949–1956/57) is that as a direct result of Israel's aggression against Egypt, the Soviet Union was afforded an opportunity to extend its influence in the Middle East, specifically contravening America's most vital interest in the region. The Israeli raid on Gaza in February 1955 impelled the Egyptians to turn to the Soviets for armaments, and the Israeli invasion of the Sinai in 1956 led Nasser to seek increased support from Moscow. Moreover, Israel's persistent refusal to deal with the Palestinian issue on the basis of U.N. resolutions, including the orig-inal partition resolution (Resolution 181), which called for an in-dependent Palestinian Arab state alongside the Jewish state, or Res-olution 194, which stipulated repatriation and/or compensation for the Palestinians; its defiance of the provisions in Resolution 181 defining the international character of Jerusalem; its attempt to divert water from Arab sources illegally; its encroachments on the demilitarized zone with Syria, coupled with its efforts to assert sovereignty over Lake Tiberias; and its growing militarism, manifested in the policy of "massive retaliation" and in the invasion of Egypt all served to antagonize the Arabs, perpetuate and heighten regional instability, and fuel the overall Arab-Israeli conflict. Moreover, insofar as the United States was associated with these Israeli policies, or was unable to prevent Israel from pursuing them, the Arabs perceived America to be aligned with Israel, making it difficult for Washington to establish beneficial relationships in the Arab world, particularly with the emerging nationalistic elements throughout the region. Arab verbal hostility toward the Jewish state was certainly a prominent feature of this period. The Arab states also undertook an economic boycott of Israel, Egypt restricted its use of the Suez Canal and the Gulf of Aqaba, and Palestinians continually attempted to infiltrate Israel in order to return to their homes. Nevertheless, it was Israel that physically violated the territorial integrity of the Arab states and threatened their national security through its large-scale and persistent military attacks.

It must be noted, though, that the U.S. choice of Arab partners among the various factions in the area was far from astute, e.g., the monarchy and Nuri Said in Iraq. Moreover, it is clear that Dulles's actions vis-à-vis Nasser were totally counterproductive and contributed significantly to America's difficulties in the Arab world. Indeed, the Eisenhower administration's inability to deal with Nasser—its unwillingness to accept the Egyptian policy of nonalignment; its pointed opposition to Nasser's advocacy of pan-Arabism regionally and Arab socialism domestically; its attempt to build up other Arab states (e.g., Iraq and Saudi Arabia) as "counters" to Egypt's influential position in the Arab world; its contradictory policies toward Nasser (intensely pressuring him to join the Baghdad Pact, offering to sell him American arms then not following through, offering to finance the Aswan Dam then withdrawing the offer)—can hardly be analyzed as rational or constructive diplomacy. In the end, Eisenhower's and Dulles's frustrations with Nasser and their desire to bring an end to his tenure became an integral aspect of American Middle East policy and contributed considerably to the decision to build up Israel—on the one hand, as a means of unseating Nasser, and on the other, as an outpost of American power that would protect all the American interests in the Arab world that Washington had been unable to protect through direct relationships with the Arab states themselves.

Washington's refusal to support Nasser was one of the greatest failures of American policy during this time and had profound consequences for all subsequent U.S.–Middle East relations. (Israel's attempts to disrupt U.S.–Egyptian relations should not pass unnoticed.) In addition, both the ill-conceived and ultimately unsuccessful Baghdad Pact and Eisenhower Doctrine must be counted as major policy blunders of this period and also contributed to later American failures in the region.

While the Executive branch was still the locus of decision-making on Middle East issues during the Eisenhower-Dulles tenure, this period also marks the beginning of congressional action on behalf of Israel. In addition, the emergence of important sectors of American society, particularly organized labor, as strong and vocal supporters of Israel's interests was an important factor at this time. The role of the media and of informed public opinion was also of growing significance.

While it is interesting to speculate about, it is impossible to know with certainty to what extent Israeli policies during the Sinai-Suez crisis were affected by the American threat of sanctions. My best judgment is that probably they were affected less than would seem from a reading of the text. Israel did indeed withdraw from the territory it occupied during the war; however, it never intended to remain on that territory, as it did not have the capabilities to do so at the time. Both Ben-Gurion and Dayan make explicitly clear that prolonged occupation was not an Israeli objective in 1956-57. Withdrawal, thus, did not signify a capitulation to American wishes: at issue was the timing of the withdrawal in relation to the obtaining of American guarantees. Israeli strategy called for the use of phased withdrawal as a mechanism for obtaining international, and particularly American, ratification of its policy objectives (including the destruction of the fedayeen bases in Gaza and the opening of the Straits of Tiran to Israeli shipping). The United States did not disagree with these objectives but believed that Israel should not have undertaken a war of aggression to achieve them and should not have them ratified until after it withdrew from the territory it occupied as a result of its aggression. The war proved highly successful for Israel. The fedayeen bases (created in the aftermath of Israel's 1955 attack on Gaza) were destroyed, and, despite Egypt's administrative return to Gaza, there was not, as Abba Eban points out, one incident of guerrilla activity from Gaza for the next ten years. Moreover, the Straits of Tiran were opened to Israeli shipping, and much of Israel's subsequent economic development can be attributed to its freedom of access in these Straits. Thus Israel achieved its objectives, American pressure notwithstanding, and saw its military success translated into political victory. The threat of American sanctions in the whole crisis seems in some ways moot, although it is clear that the Eisenhower administration genuinely believed that to maximize American interests in the Middle East, the United States had to pursue a policy reflecting some balance between Israeli and Arab interests and not align itself wholeheartedly with Israel.

Still, despite the tensions between Israel and the United States during the Sinai-Suez crisis and despite the obvious conflicts of interest between them, including Israeli policies that directly contravened American interests, the United States remained the strongest supporter of Israel in the world community. In large measure this situation resulted from the following factors: (1) extremely effective Israeli diplomacy contrasted with largely inept Arab diplomacy; (2) the growing antagonisms between Washington and Egypt; (3) the support that Israel was able to garner in important sectors of American public opinion; (4) the sympathies and obligations for Israel that were still strongly felt in the United States associated with the Holocaust and America's deeply rooted bias against the Muslim world and the Orient in general; (5) the perceived cultural and historical affinities that Americans and Israelis enjoyed which Americans and Arabs did not; and (6) the fortuitous situation of having a vocal and dedicated group of domestic pro-Israeli Jews who were willing to advocate Israel's objectives with the American government and its public.

Still, the Eisenhower administration has been the only administration to condemn Israeli aggression, to act in a principled manner vis-à-vis Israel in the United Nations, and to threaten the withholding of American aid as a means of influencing Israeli policy. (In the 1953 dispute over Israel's plan to divert the Jordan River waters for exclusive Israeli use, Eisenhower actually did suspend aid until Israel complied with the U.N. requests.) Whether or not the threat of sanctions was the actual reason for Israeli withdrawal from Sinai is probably less important in the final analysis than Washington's willingness to use it. Later, when Israel's dependence on American economic and military aid increased enormously, and when Israeli policies seriously threatened vital American interests, it is certain that various administrations could have exercised considerably greater influence over Israel if they had threatened *and used* sanctions as a means of pressuring their tiny, belligerent client.

CHAPTER FOUR

THE JUNE 1967 WAR

Introduction

The June 1967 War shattered the prevailing stasis of the Arab-Israeli conflict so profoundly that the Middle East has never been the same. The third Arab-Israeli war began with an Israeli air attack on Egyptian air fields on the morning of June 5, 1967, and ended on June 10, when a cease-fire on the Syrian front went into effect. In those six days the map of the Middle East was redrawn as the Israeli military overran territory more than three times the size of prewar Israel. The geostrategic situation created by Israel's victory transformed all previous Israeli political and military calculations. All of Israel's centers of population and industry were, after the war, securely behind Israeli lines, while the capitals of Israel's main adversaries were within easy striking distance of Israeli air and ground forces. Israel occupied the Gaza Strip, the entire Sinai down to Sharm el-Sheikh, the West Bank of the Jordan River, East Jerusalem, and Syria's Golan Heights.

Israel's stunning performance was rewarded by America's refusal to insist on Israeli withdrawal from the territories it seized during the hostilities. In the aftermath of the war the U.S.–Israeli relationship assumed a profound new orientation and dimension. Most important, the idea of Israel as a strategic asset to American interests was rapidly enshrined as an absolute tenet of political orthodoxy.

The United States in the International System, 1956-67

The continuity of the fundamental U.S. foreign policy of containment was expressed in America's increasing intervention in Indochina during this period. From Dwight Eisenhower to John Kennedy through Lyndon Johnson, each administration escalated American involvement in Southeast Asia, and the Vietnam quagmire provides an important backdrop to events in the Middle East in 1967. At the same time, the aftermath of the nearly disastrous Soviet-American confrontation during the Cuban missile crisis in 1962 saw the beginning of a thaw in U.S.–Soviet relations.

The first indication of a potential relaxation of tensions between the great powers was the signing of the Nuclear Test Ban Treaty in 1963, followed by some resolution of the Berlin problem. Moreover, by the early 1960s the Sino-Soviet split indicated to U.S. policymakers that Communism was no longer quite the massive, monolithic threat it once seemed. China was becoming an additional factor in the global equation. Thus, the international setting in 1967 was not the same as in 1956, but the Soviet Union had both allies and interests in the Middle East, and the United States was acutely aware of the competitive and inherently conflictual nature of the pursuits of both powers in that region. American policymakers attempting to deal with the Middle East and the vicissitudes of international politics were faced with vexing dilemmas resulting from the ongoing, if somewhat modified, cold war; the quantitative and qualitative changes in the arms race between the Soviet Union and the United States; the deepening American involvement in Vietnam; the persistence and intensity of the Arab-Palestinian-Israeli conflict; a growing inter-Arab "cold war"; Washington's continuing frustrations with Gamal Abdul Nasser; the real interests that America had in the Arab world; and the increasingly intimate association of the United States with Israel's interests and policies.

The United States and the Middle East between 1956 and 1967: Policies and Interests

The Eisenhower Doctrine was applied in Jordan in 1957 to shore up the monarchy of King Hussein, which was faced with severe domestic opposition. Under the aegis of the doctrine the United States extended $10 million in military and economic aid to the ailing Jordanian regime and dispatched the Sixth Fleet to the eastern Mediterranean as a demonstration of support. Again under the rubric of the doctrine, the United States sent 14,000 troops to Lebanon to restore order and the status quo after the eruption of a civil war in 1958 threatened the prevailing power structure and the pro-Western orientation of that country. Neither state, it should be noted, was threatened by Communist aggression, the problem with which the doctrine purported to deal.

The Baghdad Pact suffered a serious blow in the summer of 1958, when a group of nationalist Iraqi army officials led by General Abdul Karim Kassem overthrew the pro-Western monarchy of King Faisal

II and promptly signed an alliance with the United Arab Republic (UAR), a union forged between Egypt and Syria in February 1958. U.S. policymakers viewed the alliance between Iraq and the UAR as signaling the disintegration of Western influence in the region: it seemed to Washington that only Lebanon, Jordan, and Saudi Arabia were outside the Nasser camp. However, the alliance was short-lived, as the new regime in Baghdad began to challenge Nasser's claim to leadership of pan-Arabism. In the early 1960s Kassem was over-thrown and the Ba'ath party came to power in Iraq; the Iraqi Ba'ath-ists were soon engaged in serious discord with the Syrian Ba'athists as well as with Egypt. This and the severance by Syria in 1961 of its four-year-old alliance with Egypt marked the beginning of the period known as the "Arab cold war."[1] For a short time thereafter both Jordan and Saudi Arabia improved their relations with Egypt, but the *modus vivendi* deteriorated quickly over a conflict in the Yemen, in which Cairo and Riyadh supported opposing parties. Pan-Arabism was given fresh impetus, however, in the first Arab summit conference, which met in Cairo in January 1964, but by mid-1966 the Arab world was rent with internal conflict again.

In the wake of Iraq's "defection," the U.S. became a de facto member of the Baghdad Pact (renamed the Central Treaty Organi-zation and relocated in Turkey) by joining the economic, military, and countersubversion committees. Washington also forged bilateral defense agreements with the remaining Muslim members of the pact, Turkey, Iran, and Pakistan. In the end, however, the failure of CENTO to fulfill its expectations, the bankruptcy of the Eisenhower Doctrine, the inter-Arab rivalries, and the persistent virulence of the Arab-Palestinian-Israeli conflict led American decision makers to abandon attempts to organize the Middle East in a military alliance linked to the West. Instead, when Kennedy became president, the U.S. gov-ernment attempted to both strengthen the U.S.-Israeli relationship and to woo Nasser, by then the undisputed leader of the Arab world.

During this period certain policymaking circles began to discuss the potential advantages to the United States of a militarily superior Israel that could dominate the Middle East in the interest of American power. This idea grew out of several circumstances, including: (1) the intense competitions and hostilities within the Arab world—its seeming instability; (2) Washington's difficulties in establishing sat-isfactory relationships with the increasingly nationalistic Arab re-gimes; (3) the ongoing hostility toward Nasser; (4) the overriding and persistent concern with Soviet expansion in the Middle East; and (5) Israel's stability, firm pro-American orientation, exceptional military capability, and eagerness for a formal tie with the United States. The idea of even an informal alignment with Israel as a means of furthering American hegemony was a sharp reversal of the attitude that had been dominant throughout the 1950s, i.e., that American preeminence in the Middle East would be best served by maintaining a balance between Israeli and Arab interests — extending and fulfilling American commitments to all the major regional actors and restraining Israeli militarism and expansionism. Indeed, despite the many apparent "good" reasons for the policy shift, it was an ill-conceived and misdirected idea. Nevertheless, by the end of the decade it became institutionalized in American Middle East policy.

When Kennedy assumed office in 1961, he initially took the position that peace in the Middle East was dependent on a balance of military power between Israel and the Arabs; however, he shortly began to perceive certain advantages in the idea of an Israeli Sparta acting as a U.S. surrogate. Kennedy thus initiated the concept of the "special relationship" with Israel and began the policy of providing the Jewish state with sophisticated American weapons. France had been supplying Israel with arms since the early 1950s under the terms of a secret Franco-Israeli arms arrangement (in violation of the Tripartite Agreement, but with American support and encouragement). However, after Charles de Gaulle's ascension to power in 1958, the French reoriented their policy toward the Middle East and by the early 1960s the supply of French arms to Israel began to diminish. This decline, combined with the Soviet Union's provision to Egypt of MIG-21's and TU-16's (in the aftermath of Israel's 1956 invasion) and in the context of the emerging perception regarding Israel's potential usefulness to the United States, induced Kennedy to respond favorably to Israel's insistent demand for American arms. In September 1962 Washington agreed to sell Israel short range Hawk missiles. That sale was followed by tanks in 1964 (under the Johnson administration) and Skyhawk planes in 1966. These sales marked the beginning of Washington's commitment to assure the absolute regional military superiority of Israel, which has continued to be a cornerstone of U.S.–Israeli relations and of American policy in the Middle East.

Kennedy's introduction of sophisticated American weapons into Israel was predicated on the belief that by fostering Israeli military superiority vis-à-vis the Arabs, peace would more likely obtain in the region. The president and his advisors assumed that the Arabs would never challenge such an obvious superiority of force and therefore regional stability would be assured. Israel, however, wanted the more advanced arms to pursue its own political and military aims, which included expanding its territory and dominating its Arab neighbors.[2] Thus the policy of assuring the absolute military superiority of Israel ultimately resulted in precisely the conditions Washington hoped to avoid—instability, war, and increased Soviet involvement.

Kennedy's inauguration of the special relationship occurred in 1962 when the president privately assured Israeli Foreign Minister Golda Meir that the United States and Israel were de facto allies.[3] In the autumn of 1963 Kennedy wrote a letter to Prime Minister Levi Eshkol that allegedly contained a virtual guarantee of Israel's territorial integrity[4]—a rather problematic guarantee since Israel continued to refuse to define its borders or specify the parameters of what constituted its territory. In addition, Kennedy accepted Israel's map of its share of the Jordan River's water. Formal sanction was given to the Israeli plan for diversion of the waters in a note Kennedy sent to Prime Minister David Ben-Gurion in 1962,[5] despite the fact that the Israeli plan seriously compromised the vital national interests of both Syria and Jordan. (During 1963 Ben-Gurion again resigned as prime minister and Levi Eshkol assumed the office again.)

Kennedy made a major statement on the Arab-Israeli conflict at a press conference in May 1963. In a sense it was a unilateral replay of the Tripartite Declaration, but more important, the speech obscured the burgeoning U.S. involvement in providing arms to Israel. Kennedy did, however, avoid a formal commitment to Israel (which the Jewish state wanted) and reaffirmed—in principle—U.S. opposition to the threat or use of force in the Middle East.[6]

The American president also attempted to demonstrate U.S. understanding of the problems facing the Arab states in the Middle East by selecting ambassadors who were sensitive to and informed about Arab interests; for example, John S. Badeau, former president of both the American University in Cairo and the Near East Foundation, became Kennedy's ambassador to Egypt.[7] In addition, Kennedy accorded Nasser recognition as a leader of the nonaligned movement and of the Arab world and attempted to establish a more positive bilateral U.S.–Egyptian relationship.[8] Minimal as these efforts were, however, they ceased after Kennedy's death.

Johnson, who assumed the presidency after Kennedy's assassination in 1963, treated Middle East issues in general as being of only secondary importance. Vietnam received most of his attention, and problems in the Middle East were left largely to the State Department. American diplomacy in the Middle East during the Johnson administration—at least until May-June 1967—was directed mainly at the use of Washington's good offices to minimize local conflicts (mostly between "moderate" Arab states) and toward extending and solidifying American influence. Unlike the early years of the Eisenhower administration, during this period the United States did not even address in principle the core of the regional problems and made no attempt to resolve the Arab-Israeli conflict or to find a solution to the Palestinian question.

Johnson had little sympathy for the Arab nationalism and Arab socialism advocated by Nasser, although for a time he seemed to waiver between a desire to try to come to terms with Nasser and a belief that Nasser's prestige and regional ambitions had to be trimmed. The latter approach came to dominate fairly quickly, and U.S.–Egyptian relations deteriorated steadily between 1964 and early 1967. In part this was because of the conflict in Yemen, a civil war with regional and extra-regional implications. Egypt sent troops to the Yemen on the side of the Republican regime, which represented modernization and progress. But Washington believed that Egyptian participation in Yemen constituted a threat to the security of Saudi Arabia and to the oil fields in the Arabian peninsula. Thus Johnson sent aid to the Yemeni Royalist forces, siding with Saudi Arabia and the Royalists and further eroding Washington's relations with Egypt. Thereafter U.S.–Egyptian relations disintegrated rapidly over Washington's sale of arms to Israel, Egypt's arms build-up, friction over various crises in Africa, and quarrels about aid. Indeed, in 1965 Johnson withdrew all American aid to Egypt, though it amounted to less than $100 million and went mainly to pay for surplus American wheat on easy repayment terms. Shortly after this act, Johnson concluded an arms deal with the Israelis that included more Hawk missiles. Johnson sent Nasser a message informing him of the arms sale, justifying it on the grounds that Egypt was in possession of Soviet bombers and warning Nasser that any attempt to "make capital" out of this issue would bring about a polarization in the Middle East situation. However, in the words of Egyptian diplomat Mahmoud Riad:

It was this flagrant American position—previous arms supplies to Israel were channeled through Britain, France and Germany—that was to accelerate the process of polarization in the region. . . . and so the year 1966 began with all the lines of communication established by Presidents Dwight Eisenhower and John Kennedy between the United States and Egypt crumbling one by one. Nasser had given up all hope of improving relations with Johnson. He also felt that the timing of the deal reflected a new dimension in United States–Israeli relations, coming as it did at a time marked by the singular absence of tensions along the Arab-Israeli borders. In his determination not to be drawn into an armed conflict with Israel and with the pressing demands of Egyptian development, Nasser had brought pressure to bear on the Palestinians to refrain from commando raids, whether from across the Egyptian borders or the armistice lines in the Gaza sector.[9]

In contrast to his relations with Egypt, Johnson's sentiments toward Israel were friendly, supportive, and admiring. Abba Eban wrote of Johnson that "within a few months he had established with Prime Minister Levi Eshkol the kind of intimate confidence that had never existed between heads of American and Israeli governments. . . . I found that his intuition about Israel had filled out and deepened."[10] Johnson advanced the special relationship concept and went further than Kennedy in commitments to Israel during his discussions with Eshkol in June 1964. Johnson still did not provide Israel the absolute guarantees regarding American commitments in specific situations that the Israelis wanted, but new and promising machinery was created for joint consultations on political and military levels, and implicit assumptions were definitely conveyed. Shimon Peres, then deputy defense minister, wrote that Eshkol reported that Johnson had said to him: "The United States stands four square behind Israel," that America would "not be idle if Israel is attacked," and that this pledge, given by both his predecessor and himself, was a "solemn and serious commitment."[11]

Indeed, the commitment to Israel's security was, by the Johnson tenure, accepted as a basic tenet of American foreign policy. In reality, however, Israel's objective military superiority was a fact (though one that generally went unacknowledged), and the tremendous emphasis that was placed on American "guarantees" of Israel's "survival" and "security" seems anomalous. Moreover, the unanimity concerning America's commitment to Israel's security tended to conceal important areas of ambiguity and disagreement: the question of what actually constituted a threat to Israel's security; how to reconcile the American involvement with Israel with U.S. interests in the Arab world; the question of the Palestinians; the point at which and the manner in which America would intervene should the Soviet Union increase its support for the Arabs against Israel; and other equally difficult questions.[12]

Several individuals close to Johnson were proponents of a strongly pro-Israeli foreign policy and appear to have played significant roles in transforming Johnson's personal sentiments toward Israel into official actions. Among these were Eugene V. Rostow, undersecretary of state for political affairs; his brother Walter, the national security advisor; and Arthur Goldberg, ambassador to the United Nations. Other persons close to the president with particularly intense pro-Israeli inclinations included Abe Fortas, later appointed by Johnson to the Supreme Court; Clark Clifford, a Washington attorney and former political advisor to President Harry Truman; Abe Feinberg and Arthur Krim, wealthy Jewish contributors to the Democratic party; and John P. Roche, Johnson's "intellectual-in-residence."[13] In addition (perhaps in part because of their sentiments concerning Israel), these men were also advocates of the thesis that Israel could serve as a strategic asset to the United States.

In a number of specific areas the United States moved perceptibly closer to Israel's views during the Johnson administration. For example, on the Palestinian issue, Washington shelved the Joseph Johnson Plan after Israel expressed its opposition to the proposals. Dr. Johnson, president of the Carnegie Endowment for International Peace, had been appointed by the U.N. Conciliation Commission in August 1961 to explore practical means for dealing with the Palestinian refugees. After months of study Johnson made five proposals: (1) each Palestinian would be given an opportunity, free from all external pressures, to express whether he preferred repatriation or resettlement; (2) Israel's legitimate security interest would be safeguarded by allowing it, subject to U.N. review, to reject individual Palestinians as security risks; (3) both repatriation and resettlement would be handled on a gradual, step-by-step process and would be undertaken simultaneously; (4) a special fund, to which Israel would be expected to make a substantial contribution, would be set up to pay compensation for Palestinian properties expropriated by Israel as well as to provide financial help to assist the resettled Palestinians to become self-supporting; and (5) the United States would play a vital role in supervising all aspects and stages of the program.[14]

Israel and its American supporters were quick to condemn the plan, and President Johnson agreed in an "informal" understanding with Israel that the great majority of the Palestinians would have to be settled in Arab states, that an unspecified minority "could" be repatriated, and that the United States would negotiate directly with the Arab governments (not the Palestinians themselves) over the resettlement of the Palestinians. It is doubtful that Israel would have agreed to the resettlement of any significant number of Palestinian Arabs, given its commitment to an exclusive Jewish state; however, since the United States and the Arab governments failed to reach an agreement, the pressure on Israel to deal with the Palestinian issue faded, and Israel conveniently ignored it from then on. The United States formally continued to adhere to Resolution 194, but Washington took no action to foster the repatriation of the Palestinians or to provide for their compensation. The continuing contradiction between the principle and practice of U.S. Middle East diplomacy is again apparent.

Another issue on which Washington moved closer to Israel's views was that of Jerusalem. The United States continued to withhold recognition of Jerusalem as Israel's capital, but it ceased applying pressure on other states that wished to establish their diplomatic missions there.

In addition, U.S. aid to Israel grew significantly in this interwar period, as reflected in Table 2.

TABLE 2. U.S. Assistance to Israel, 1957-68

Year	Total Aid	Economic Loans	Economic Grants	Military Loans
1957	40.9	21.8	19.1	
1958	61.2	49.9	11.3	
1959	50.3	39.0	10.9	0.4
1960	55.7	41.8	13.4	0.5
1961	48.1	29.8	18.3	
1962	83.9	63.5	7.2	13.2
1963	76.7	57.4	6.0	13.3
1964	37.0	32.3	4.8	
1965	61.7	43.9	4.9	12.9
1966	126.8	35.9	0.9	90.0
1967	13.1	5.5	0.6	7.0
1968	76.8	51.3	0.5	25.0
TOTAL	732.2	472.0	97.9	162.3

SOURCE: *The Link,* Dec. 1982, 3.
NOTE: Data are in millions of dollars and do not include loans through the Export-Import bank.

American National Interests: International and Regional Linkages

As in earlier periods, American interests in the Middle East during the decade that culminated with the June 1967 War still remained: (1) limiting Soviet influence and maintaining the balance of power in the area; (2) assuring access to the supply of oil for the United States and its Western European and Japanese allies; (3) ensuring American freedom of access to the region's markets and investment opportunities; and (4) guaranteeing Israel's "security and survival." And as earlier, realization of the first three was significantly complicated by the manner in which the fourth was undertaken. Additional complications resulted when American policymakers decided to use Israel as an instrument of American power.

By the mid-1960s the Soviet Union was deeply involved in the Middle East on the side of several Arab states. This situation posed a new and potentially critical problem—creation of yet another arena in which "confrontation" between the two nuclear superpowers was possible. Many individuals in government believed that the nature and configuration of U.S. and Soviet interests in the Middle East were such that the two powers might inadvertently be drawn into a local war. The military intervention of one superpower on behalf of its client would almost certainly be met with counterintervention by the other. Consequently, the risk of great power nuclear confrontation seemed especially acute in the event of an outbreak of hostilities between Arabs and Israelis. This situation would seem to have further intensified the need for peace and stability in the region, suggesting the necessity of fostering an equitable settlement of the Arab-Palestinian-Israeli conflict, rather than attempting to impose American domination on the Arab world through Israeli military superiority. Regardless of the short-term technological advantages that the United States could provide Israel, logic dictated that the vast demographic and territorial quantitative advantages of the Arabs (coupled with their assured nonacceptance of such an arrangement) would render U.S.-Israeli hegemony unworkable in the long run and could, moreover, result in precisely the great power confrontation everyone feared.

Johnson's awareness of the potential for superpower conflict is reflected in his memoirs: "The danger implicit in every border incident was not merely war between Israelis and Arabs, but an ultimate confrontation between the Soviet Union and the United States and its NATO Allies."[15] Eugene Rostow wrote in the same vein: "The Middle Eastern crisis is not a regional quarrel about Israel's right to exist. It is, on the contrary, a fissure in the foundation of world politics—a Soviet challenge to the relationship of Western Europe and the United States, and therefore to the balance of power on which the possibility of general peace depends."[16] Thus Rostow too understood that an Arab-Israeli war might not be merely a local conflict, but could be a stage in a process which would threaten the security of Europe and the United States. Yet, while avoiding a confrontation with the Soviet Union was seen as a paramount concern of American foreign policymakers, and the linkage between regional conflicts and potential international crises was clearly understood, the United States nevertheless proceeded to create conditions that increased rather than decreased the likelihood of such a disaster.

The U.S. interest in Middle Eastern oil involved certain ambiguities during this period. Following World War II, most experts believed that the United States would soon exhaust its reserves of petroleum. Many drew the conclusion (as discussed in Chapters 2 and 3) that since Middle Eastern oil would be vital to American and NATO security, the United States should do nothing to jeopardize friendly relations with the Arab states. Above all, these individuals argued, America should try to keep its distance from Israel. However, during the 1950s and the 1960s the predicted oil shortage did not occur. Instead, oil was abundantly available in the world market and at comparatively low prices. American production covered most domestic needs and Arab embargoes in 1956 and 1967 proved ineffective and short-lived. On the other hand, American allies in Europe and Japan were heavily dependent on Middle Eastern oil and thus vulnerable to potential embargoes. Nevertheless, the American mood of the mid-1960s was one of comparative optimism regarding oil. What is more, U.S. oil companies were realizing at least $2 billion in profits annually from their Middle Eastern operations, and the United States was selling about $1 billion worth of goods annually to Arab countries.[17]

The Arab-Israeli Context

From the end of the Sinai-Suez conflict until the beginning of the 1967 crisis, the Israeli-Egyptian border was peaceful. This was almost exclusively the result of Egyptian preference rather than a consequence of the presence of the U.N. Emergency Force (UNEF), although the UNEF did supply Nasser with something of a rationale for refraining from sponsoring guerrilla activities against Israel. However, as tensions escalated in the spring of 1967 and in the context of public Israeli threats against Syria, inter-Arab pressures forced Nasser to ask for the partial withdrawal of the UNEF and the positioning of Egyptian troops in the Sinai. This then allowed Israel to portray Egypt as the aggressor in the June War.

On the other hand, in the post–1956-57 period the Syrian-Israeli border was not as tranquil for several reasons. First and foremost was the basic Arab-Israeli conflict, which always seemed at its most intractable between Syria and Israel. But specific issues also contributed to the tense atmosphere, including conflicts over fishing rights in Lake Tiberias (the Sea of Galilee); guerrilla incursions into Israel from Syrian territory; Israeli encroachments on the demilitarized zone along the border; and the Israeli development of the Jordan River Project, called the "National Water Carrier." This last issue, though part of the overall Arab-Israeli conflict, had a specifically Syrian aspect because it was centered along the Syrian border, and it eventually became one of the main problems in Israeli-Syrian relations. The escalation of these various Syrian-Israeli conflicts triggered the June 1967 crisis.

Other regional developments that provide a backdrop to the 1967 war include the first Arab summit conference, which met in Cairo in January 1964. At the conference Nasser took the position that the Arab states needed to coordinate their military apparatus to provide for their common defense against another Israeli invasion. To this end they organized a United Arab Command, although it never materialized in serious form. The conference also established an authority for the implementation of an Arab project for the utilization of the Jordan waters, but it never functioned successfully. An agreement was also reached that the Palestinians should have an organization of their own through which to pursue their rights. On this issue, the Egyptians were motivated in large measure by a desire to be relieved of the burden of responsibility for the Palestinians; but, in addition, they hoped to use (and in practice did until 1969) such a Palestinian organization as an instrument of Egyptian policy in inter-Arab politics.

Ahmad Shuqairy was appointed by the summit conference to organize the Palestine Liberation Organization (PLO), and he spent five months touring Palestinian communities in the various Arab countries to promote support for such a body. Palestinians seized the opportunity to have Palestinian political interests represented independently of the Arab governments, and in May 1964, 422 Palestinians from a wide variety of backgrounds, mostly professional, met in Jerusalem in the first Palestine National Congress and proclaimed the PLO. The PLO was not originally a guerrilla organization, although it did include the rudiments of a conventional army, the Palestine Liberation Army (PLA). (In practice, however, the Arab states fully controlled the contingents of the PLA stationed in their respective countries.) Not until 1969, catalyzed by Israel's victory over the Arab states and its occupation of the West Bank and Gaza, did the PLO become dominated by guerrilla groups and assume an important military function.[18] Unfortunately, despite genuine efforts by the leadership of the PLO after Yasir Arafat assumed the chairmanship to steer an independent course for the Palestine national movement, the Palestine issue was cynically and ruthlessly manipulated by the Arab regimes to the perpetual detriment of the Palestinians and their quest for self-determination.[19]

Prior to the formation of the PLO, a number of small, independent guerrilla groups had appeared, and the activities of these groups, particularly insofar as they were sponsored or condoned by Syria, contributed to the 1967 war. In 1957-58 al-Fatah (the Palestinian National Liberation Movement) emerged under the leadership of Yasir Arafat and several close associates.[20] In addition, the Popular Front for the Liberation of Palestine (PFLP), headed by Dr. George

Habash, emerged from the Arab Nationalist Movement. The PFLP later splintered, with Nayif Hawatmeh forming the Democratic Front for the Liberation of Palestine (DFLP). (These three groups, from a total of eight, were the most powerful organizations—and in the post-1967 period the most independent of Arab governments—within the PLO.)

By 1965 Fatah began to carry out guerrilla operations against Israel. It was based primarily in Syria, but sometimes initiated operations from Jordanian territory, though King Hussein made every effort to prevent such incursions.[21] The Ba'athist leaders in Damascus sponsored Fatah in part as a means of countering Egyptian influence in inter-Arab politics on the Palestinian issue and also to embarrass Nasser by creating conflict along the border with Israel. Israel responded to the Palestinian commando incursions with massive retaliatory raids, usually against Syria, although occasionally against Jordan. Thus the cycle of guerrilla raids and Israeli reprisals began again, but with greater ferocity. Israel believed that massive military action against Syria was necessary both to force it to rein in the Fatah guerrilla campaign and to deter Egypt from coming to Syria's help. In practice, the Israeli attacks had the effect of increasing Syrian hostility toward Israel and driving Damascus closer to the Soviet Union.

Thus, by 1965 the outlines of the third Arab-Israeli war were beginning to take shape around two sets of issues. The first set was made up of inter-Arab competition and conflict, including Nasser's desire to maintain his leadership of pan-Arabism in the context of the rivalries among Egypt, Syria, Jordan, Saudi Arabia, and Iraq. The second set lay within the broad context of animosity between Israelis and Arabs, but centered on the continuous conflict between Israel and Syria over the demilitarized zone and the National Water Carrier Project, as well as the Fatah guerrilla campaign and the Israeli strategy of massive retaliation.[22]

The intensity of inter-Arab competition—the Arab cold war—significantly complicated the regional scene. Syria's domestic instability, its support of the Fatah guerrillas, and its special relationship with Moscow contributed to serious conflict between Damascus and Cairo during 1966-67. Syria condemned Egypt for its prohibition of Palestinian guerrilla activity from Egyptian soil (and from Gaza) and for its reluctance to either provoke Israel or come to the aid of Damascus when Israel attacked Syria. Indeed, all Nasser's rivals taunted him for "hiding behind the UNEF skirt," charging him with cowardice, dishonor, and "fear unworthy of an Arab leader." Jordan was even more aggressive than Syria in articulating these accusations, while Saudi Arabia, Iraq, and the Palestinians also harassed the Egyptian leader. In addition, relations between Syria and Jordan were intensely hostile, at times almost overshadowing the Syrian-Israeli conflict; and the PLO's Shuqairy (who sounded the most strident verbal attacks on Israel) also accused King Hussein of disloyalty to the Arab cause and castigated Nasser. In short, the inter-Arab feuding induced uncertainty of tenure and rash behavior among the Arab leaders. In particular, Nasser came to feel increasingly isolated, and his most serious miscalculations in the spring of 1967 may be seen in terms of attempting to preserve his status in the inter-Arab context.[23]

The Arab-Palestinian-Israeli conflict was further complicated by the Jewish state's continuing attempts to divert water from disputed sources and its encroachments on the demilitarized zone. Israel initiated numerous provocations, the most serious of which was described by General Karl von Horn (a Swede who served as a member of UNTSO) as "a premeditated Israeli policy to edge east through the demilitarized zone towards the old Palestine border (as shown on their maps) and to get all of the Arabs out of the way by fair means or foul."[24] Moreover, because of these on-going conflicts (in addition to motivations growing out of its competition with Cairo), Damascus encouraged Fatah guerrilla raids across the Israeli border. Through the latter part of 1966 there were increasing numbers of these incursions. In October 1966 two incidents, in which several Israelis were killed, caused Israel to appeal to the U.N. Security Council. The Soviet Union vetoed a resolution that was critical of the guerrilla raids. After the U.N. vote, the Syrian prime minister declared: "We are not sentinels over Israel's security and are not the leash that restrains the revolution of the displaced and persecuted Palestinian people."[25] Israel's response to the Syrian statement came in the form of massive military action on November 13 against the West Bank Palestinian towns of Es Samou, Jimba, and Khirbet Karkay. Why Israel chose Jordan rather than Syria is not clear, although the following reasons have been suggested: (1) the rugged, uphill terrain along the Syrian border made land assaults against Syria difficult and costly for Israel; (2) Syria's relationship with the Soviet Union might induce a response from Russia against Israel; and (3) the degree of American influence with Amman would serve as a deterrent against a Jordanian retaliatory strike.[26] In any case the attack, generally referred to as the Es Samou raid, was without provocation. The Israeli force of 4,000 men was transported in armored cars and tanks and supported by several air squadrons. According to U.N. observers, eighteen Jordanians were killed and fifty-four wounded (including civilians) while 140 houses and other buildings, including the school, clinic, and mosque, were demolished.[27] The long-term political consequences of this action were considerable: it may be compared to the Gaza raid in terms of repercussions.

The U.N. Security Council by a vote of 14 to 0 censured Israel "for this large scale military action in violation of the United Nations Charter and of the General Armistice Agreement between Israel and Jordan," emphasizing to Israel that "actions of military reprisal cannot be tolerated and that if they are repeated, the Security Council [would] have to consider further and more effective steps as envisaged in the Charter to ensure against the repetition of such acts."[28] While this resolution had the effect of encouraging the Syrians not to interfere with Fatah incursions, it enraged Israel and contributed to its belief that more and greater military pressure was the only means to deal with the area's problems. Israel was to a considerable extent a prisoner of its own conviction that the only option for dealing with the Palestinian issue was massive military action against the Arab states. But such assaults, which always resulted in high civilian casualties, served merely to threaten the governments of the attacked countries and to strengthen their animosity toward Israel while also strengthening the resolve of the Palestinian guerrillas to continue their campaign. Nor did the enormous military destruction in any way deal with the crux of what was a political problem: the Palestinians. In the aftermath of the Es Samou attack the Arab governments began to talk openly about the necessity of acting against Israel. In addition, King Hussein charged Egypt and Syria (both of whom had been denouncing his regime) with failing to bear their share of the burden of confrontation with Israel. Hussein specifically accused Egypt of failing to supply promised air cover and urged that Egyptian troops be withdrawn from the Yemen and sent to the Sinai on Israel's southern flank as a deterrent to further Israeli attacks on Jordan or Syria.

From January to April 1967 the Syrian-Israeli border saw an escalating series of clashes. Then on April 3, 1967, the Israeli government announced that it had decided to cultivate all areas of the demilitarized zone, specifically lots 51 and 52, which the Syrians insisted belonged to Arab farmers.[29] At 8:00 o'clock on the morning of April 7, a tractor began work on a strip of Arab land south of Tiberias. The Syrians fired mortars at the tractor, and the Israelis struck back with artillery, tanks, and aircraft. Seventy Israeli planes penetrated Syrian airspace and shot down six Syrian planes, one over the outskirts of Damascus. One of the most serious aspects of the affair, which in retrospect marks the prelude to the June War, was that for the second time in six months Arab forces suffered severe humiliation at the hands of Israel without the Unified Arab Command in Cairo lifting a finger, as both Syria and Jordan were quick to remind Nasser. Then followed five weeks of both Arab and Israeli inflammatory rhetoric, including specific Israeli threats against Syria, and finally a partial Egyptian mobilization on May 14, an Israeli mobilization on May 15 and 16, and the expulsion of the UNEF on May 16.

Israeli Perceptions

Several factors were of particular significance to Israeli decision-makers as the April-June events built to a crisis. The most prominent scholar of the foreign policymaking process in Israel, Michael Brecher, has identified three: (1) the historical legacy of 1957, (2) the "Ben-Gurion complex," and (3) the "Holocaust syndrome."[30]

The primary lesson for Israeli leaders from the Sinai-Suez experience was their acute sensitivity to the pressure the United States had placed on Israel to withdraw from the Sinai, Sharm el-Sheikh, and the Gaza Strip after the war. Thus in the spring of 1967 Israeli officials were anxious to secure American compliance with what Israel perceived to be previous U.S. commitments relevant to the current situation, and, more important, with long-range Israeli policy objectives related to the impending hostilities: as Israel prepared to initiate war it wanted to ensure that in the aftermath of the fighting the United States would not pressure it to withdraw from the newly occupied territories.

The "Ben-Gurion complex" was essentially the perception of Ben-Gurion (and most of his closest associates) that military force was the preferred means for dealing with all regional problems—"the only language the Arabs understand." Ben-Gurion also believed that Israeli military action without U.S. support was risky, though he would never have forsaken Israel's military option simply because Washington opposed it. But there was extensive Israeli consultation with American leaders throughout the pre-1967 war period, unlike 1956, to ensure American political support for the fruits of the expected Israeli military victory.

Finally, the "Holocaust syndrome" reflects a widely shared perception in Israel, adroitly manipulated by its leaders, that Israel's very survival is at stake in every situation. Thus, every event assumes proportions far exceeding its actual magnitude or significance and begets and "justifies" a reaction totally disproportionate to its importance. An example is Yitzhak Rabin's statement in 1972 about the 1967 crisis: "The problem [was] not freedom of navigation: the challenge [was] to the existence of the State of Israel."[31] Indeed, by construing every militant Arab statement or action in the months and weeks preceding the June War as a threat to Israel's survival, Israeli leaders committed themselves, a priori, to a military solution. It seems apparent, however, that Israel's decision makers saw in the situation in the spring of 1967 an opportunity to launch a war, for which they were well prepared, to expand their territory and subdue "once and for all" the Arab states. The Holocaust syndrome was a useful pathology in rallying mass support. General Mattityahu Peled, one of the architects of the Israeli victory in 1967, compares the reality with the whipped-up survival rhetoric:

'There is no reason,' he said, 'to hide the fact that since 1949 no one dared, or more precisely, no one was able, to threaten the very existence of Israel. In spite of that, we have continued to foster a sense of our own inferiority, as if we were a weak and insignificant people, which, in the midst of an anguished struggle for its existence, could be exterminated at any moment.' 'True,' General Peled went on, Arab leaders may have sounded menacing, 'but it is notorious that the Arab leaders themselves, thoroughly aware of their own impotence, did not believe in their own threats. . . . I am sure that our General Staff never told the government that the Egyptian military threat represented any danger to Israel or that we were unable to crush Nasser's army, which, with unheard-of foolishness, had exposed itself to the devastating might of our army. . . . To claim that the Egyptian forces concentrated on our borders were capable of threatening Israel's existence not only insults the intelligence of anyone capable of analyzing this kind of situation, but is an insult to Zahal [the Israeli army].'[32]

Moreover, General Rabin himself, a few months after the war, offered the following commentary concerning Nasser's intentions and means in 1967: "I do not believe that Nasser wanted war. The two divisions he sent into the Sinai on May 14 would not have been enough to unleash an offensive against Israel. He knew it and we knew it."[33] Nevertheless, Israel declared that the Egyptian forces move to the Sinai, the expulsion of the UNEF, and the closure of the Straits of Tiran were clear and present threats to its existence.

Yet while some Israeli leaders chose to define these events as constituting a life-threatening situation, the United States had no legitimate reason to sustain the Israeli position. Another Arab-Israeli war was certainly not in the interest of the United States, despite the illusions of a few in Washington who were obsessed with ending Nasser's tenure. Nevertheless, in the final analysis Johnson was apparently persuaded to give Israel an American "green light" for its war and then oversaw the political ratification of Israel's territorial expansion.

The Crisis in Spring 1967

Prelude: Israeli Policies

Israeli policies in April and May 1967 took four main tacks:[34]

(1) Israel attempted to persuade the Soviet Union to pressure Syria to restrain Palestinian guerrilla activity.

(2) Israel threatened Syria with military action. For example, on May 11, General Rabin said on Israeli radio: "The moment is coming when we will march on Damascus to overthrow the Syrian Government, because it seems that only military operations can discourage the plans for a people's war with which they threaten us."[35] The day after this verbal provocation by the chief of staff, General Aharon Yariv, director of military intelligence, gave a background briefing for forty correspondents in which he repeated Rabin's threats to Syria and taunted Nasser by claiming that Egypt was weak and that Nasser, "the all-Arab leader," would never intervene. "I would say that as long as there is not an Israeli invasion into Syria extended in area and time, I think the Egyptians will not come in seriously.... they will do so only if there is no other alternative. And to my eyes no alternative means that we are creating such a situation that it is impossible for the Egyptians not to act because the strain on their prestige will be unbearable."[36] Thus the Israelis were both provoking the Arabs—directly threatening to overthrow the Syrian government and shaming Egypt into some kind of action—while acknowledging that Israel faced no serious threat from them.

(3) Israel attempted to stop the Fatah infiltrations through massive reprisals. In a discussion of Israel's plans for a reprisal raid against Syria for Fatah incursions, Nadav Safran notes: "I have already intimated that the Israelis definitely contemplated some kind of action against Syria in the course of the month of May."[37] In fact, on May 13, the *New York Times* reported that Israeli leaders had "decided that the use of force against Syria" might be "the only way to curtail increasing terrorism."[38]

(4) Israel promoted the perception in the United States that Israel was mortally threatened by its aggressive neighbors.

Israel's attempts to put pressure on the Soviet Union and threaten Syria had no practical success; if anything, they had the opposite result. Moscow took a series of steps to stimulate Egyptian militancy and to create an Egyptian military presence on Israel's southern border to ease the pressure on Syria. Moreover, the Fatah guerrillas continued their border incursions—they suffered not at all from Israel's military policy. In addition, Israel's threats to Syria and taunts to Nasser contributed to the escalation of the crisis by: (1) inducing fear on the Arab side regarding Israeli intentions (which the Arabs always viewed as aggressive and expansionistic); (2) putting pressure on Nasser to behave with "pride" in the inter-Arab context; and (3) engendering counterstatements, each more strident than the other. The traditional maxim that action begets reaction in international politics is certainly accurate, and no less so for verbal pronouncements. On the other hand, Israel was extremely successful in depicting itself in the United States as a beleaguered David, about to be driven into the sea by the Arab Goliath.

Some analysts have argued that Johnson's sympathy for Israel, coupled with his forceful personality, should have led him to take a strong and unambiguous stand during the crisis, firmly conveying to Israel that the United States would not tolerate military action by its client and pressing it to de-escalate the rhetoric and the tensions, especially as such a stand might have helped to calm Arab rhetoric and ease tensions in the Arab world. Serious pressure from the American president could surely have prevented Israeli military action. In addition, a strong stand vis-à-vis Israel might well have induced the Soviet Union to behave more responsibly with its clients.[39] Instead, as the Middle East crisis unfolded in May and early June 1967, American behavior was at best ambiguous and at worst insensitive to the danger that war was inevitable at Israel's instigation; undoubtedly that attitude encouraged the Israeli initiative. Moreover, America's strong and overt support for Israel and the sorry state of U.S. relations with the Arabs left Washington unable to influence the Arab states or to play any role even approaching that of an honest broker in the conflict.

The Conflict Escalates: Israel and Washington—Action, Reaction, Inaction, Duet

The initial American reaction to Nasser's dispatching troops into the Sinai on May 14 was calm. His move was interpreted as a means of appeasing the Syrians and Jordanians (in the wake of Israel's attack on Es Samou and the dogfight over Damascus) and of applying minimal pressure on Israel, not as a preparation for an attack on Israel (indeed, the deployment of forces was defensive in formation). Thus U.S. policymakers did not believe any reaction was called for. High government officials assured the Israelis that the Egyptian troop movements were demonstrative and without military intent.[40] Israeli intelligence and government officials concurred in this analysis.[41]

Nevertheless, even though its own assessment of Egypt's troop movements was initially identical to Washington's, i.e., that it involved "no immediate military threat,"[42] Israel took what it termed "precautionary" measures. On May 15 Israel's chief of staff, General Yitzhak Rabin, reinforced the Negev positions with a full armored brigade. The Israelis informed the Arab regimes, through the U.N. secretary-general, that Israel had no aggressive intentions against any Arab state.[43] This was not, however, the way that the Arabs perceived the situation: the public threats against Syria and the buildup in the Negev were seen as highly menacing. Indeed, fifteen years later Israeli Prime Minister Menachem Begin admitted that the June War was *not* a defensive operation: "In June 1967, we again [referring to the 1956 Sinai Campaign] had a choice. The Egyptian Army concentrations in the Sinai approaches did not prove that Nasser was about to attack us. We must be honest with ourselves. We decided to attack him."[44]

On May 16 Israel began to mobilize its forces rapidly, although ranking decision-makers in the United States, as well as most in Israel, still concluded that Nasser's moves were not a military threat. That Israeli mobilization, however, prior to any serious provocative Egyptian actions made war inevitable. Late that evening, after the Israeli mobilization, Egyptian General Mohammed Fawzi requested that the UNEF troops leave the Sinai, although the request specifically did not mention Sharm el-Sheikh or the Gaza. The U.N. secretary-general, U Thant, responded almost immediately—to the general surprise and consternation of all the parties—that the presence of the U.N. forces in the area was inseparably linked to its freedom of action and movement and Egypt would have to choose between two alternatives: either to maintain the status quo in the Sinai or have *all* the U.N. forces in the area withdrawn. Egypt was thus left with no alternative but to ask for the removal of all the UNEF troops.

It must be assumed that the dangers inherent in Nasser's request for partial withdrawal of the UNEF were apparent to Johnson and his policy advisors. Moreover, the possibility that once the UNEF was withdrawn, Egypt would be under great pressure to close the Straits of Tiran and return the situation to its pre-1956 status seems evident also. In addition, Israel made it clear that such action would be regarded as a *casus belli*.[45] Thus, as former American government official and Middle Eastern scholar William Quandt perceptively argues: "In light of these dangers, one might have expected some action by the United States after May 16 aimed at preventing the complete removal of the UNEF. After all, Nasser had not asked for withdrawal of the force from either of the two most sensitive zones, Gaza or Sharm al-Shaykh. But the record shows no sign of an urgent approach to U Thant on this matter, and by the evening of May 18 it was too late. The U.N. Secretary General had forced Nasser to choose between no withdrawal of UNEF or full withdrawal. Not surprisingly, Nasser opted for the latter."[46]

In fact, no direct American approach was made to Nasser until May 22, the day he announced closure of the Straits. The generally negative condition of U.S.–Egyptian relations under Johnson undoubtedly contributed to the delay in raising the matter with Egypt; a bureaucratic problem may have also added obstacles. Ambassador Lucius Battle, a veteran of four years of service in Egypt, had returned to the United States to become undersecretary of state for Near Eastern Affairs in early March. The new ambassador, Richard Nolte, an academician rather than a career diplomat, was not sent until May 21. A high-ranking member of the Johnson administration related in an interview that Nolte's lack of diplomatic experience left him unable even to use the machinery of sending cables; this, exacerbated by Nasser's refusal to allow him to present his credentials immediately, was a great impediment to American policymakers. The United States had no one in Egypt who could talk to Nasser; moreover, the Egyptian ambassador in Washington, the aging Mustafa Kemel, described by this official as "a relic of the 'ancient regime,'" had no influence. Eventually, senior diplomat Charles Yost was sent to Egypt by the State Department to try to talk to Nasser, and Robert B. Anderson was sent as President Johnson's special envoy to attempt to arrange for an exchange of vice-presidential visits between the two countries in an effort to establish dialogue. However, both initiatives were undertaken far too late to have any effect on the outcome of the crisis. Indeed, they merely served to heighten Egypt's sense of Washington's duplicity, given the contradiction between the administration's stated positions and the policies it pursued in practice.

In the wake of U Thant's precipitous decision and the withdrawal of the UNEF from Egypt, Undersecretary of State Eugene Rostow told the Israeli ambassador to the United States, Avraham Harman, and his minister, Ephraim Evron, that it would be desirable for the U.N. troops to reassemble on the Israeli side of the border. Secretary-General U Thant made a similar request of the Israeli government. The Israelis refused.[47] President Johnson, in his own words, then "threw the full weight of United States diplomacy into an effort to forestall war. The first necessity being to persuade the Israelis not to act hastily."[48] It is significant that Johnson understood that it would be Israel that would initiate a war. The president sent Prime Minister Eshkol the first of several letters exchanged during the crisis, dated May 17, in which he urged "restraint" and specifically asked to be informed before Israel took any action. In this regard he wrote: "I am sure you will understand that I cannot accept any responsibilities on behalf of the United States for situations which arise as the result of actions on which we are not consulted."[49] Thus, in essence, all that the president requested of Israel was that it forewarn Washington of any action it was planning. Johnson did not demand that Israel not initiate a war.

Johnson communicated with the Soviet Union, calling Soviet Premier Aleksei Kosygin with a request that the Soviets coordinate diplomatic activity with the United States before the situation got out of control.[50] Simultaneously, Secretary of State Dean Rusk contacted the British and French to rally support for any diplomatic policy that might be developed to deal with the crisis. The British response suggested that they would be co-operative, the French response suggested otherwise.[51] Johnson also indicated that the United Nations was to be the focal point of U.S. diplomatic efforts, although American policy at the United Nations in 1967 was quite different than during the 1956 Suez conflict.

In summary, the initial response of Washington to the 1967 crisis involved an expression of "hope" that a Middle Eastern war could be avoided; a request to Israel for consultation before it initiated any military action; the establishment of a communications link with the Soviets; and the attempt to find a multilateral framework for possible diplomatic action. The Israeli reaction differed from the American position on two important points: (1) from the outset of the crisis, war was the preferred Israeli option, and (2) Israel demanded unilateral guarantees from the United States, rejecting both multilateral diplomacy or the use of the United Nations as a means for resolving the conflict.

Concerning Israel's preference for war, note that on May 19 the Israelis undertook a full-scale mobilization, including reserve troops. This action, coming after the May 16 mobilization, set in progress a chain of events both within Israel and the region that made war inevitable. Israel also sent a series of messages to France, Great Britain, and the United States, informing them that if Nasser closed the Straits of Tiran, Israel would regard such action as a *casus belli*.[52] According to Abba Eban, Egypt's imposition of a blockade would challenge Israel to defend or abandon a vital national interest and would indicate Nasser's willingness to resort to war. Nasser, however, made a clear statement to the contrary: "I am not in a position to go to war; I tell you this frankly, and it is not shameful to say it publicly. To go to war without having the sufficient means would be to lead the country and the people to disaster."[53] Moreover, Egypt viewed the navigation issue as amenable to peaceful settlement. As former Egyptian Foreign Minister Mahmoud Riad wrote: "Navigation in the Gulf of Aqaba was a matter to which a final solution could be secured, either through the International Court of Justice as was proposed at the time by Senator Fulbright [chairman of the Senate's Foreign Affairs Committee], or through the redeployment of United Nations forces at Sharm el-Sheikh, once Israeli threats were eliminated."[54] In addition, President Nasser promptly accepted a set of proposals concerning the Straits of Tiran and the Gulf of Aqaba brought to him by U Thant on May 25, proposals that the Egyptian president believed had been underwritten by the United States. Nasser answered U Thant's question regarding Egypt's military intentions by declaring: "We have never at any time intimated that we will attack Israel. It was Israel who has formally threatened to invade Syria. What we are attempting now is a defensive measure to prevent such a threat from materializing. You may have my word therefore that we will never begin an attack."[55] Nevertheless, Israel's preparations for war continued, and it is thus not improper to question Israel's motivations in undertaking this war.

Concerning Israel's rejection of the United Nations and its demand for U.S. guarantees, note that Israel allegedly objected to using the United Nations as a forum for resolving the crisis because the Soviet veto in the Security Council was available upon Arab request. Of course, the U.S. veto was available in a similar way to the Israelis. The Israelis also believed that if they lost a political battle at the United Nations, it would give further encouragement to Nasser. Of greatest concern to Israel, however, was that if the issue was brought before the Security Council, this would place a constraint on its ability to undertake military action before the debate came to an end. Israel's demands vis-à-vis the United States were expressed in a letter from Eshkol to Johnson on May 18. Eshkol presented five main points:

(1) The serious crisis presently threatening the Middle East originated in the attitude of Syria. Until now Israel has shown great patience by not taking reprisals for the fourteen acts of Syrian sabotage during the past month.

(2) Egypt has spread out over the Sinai peninsula an offensive force of at least 500 tanks. It is advisable to insist that country return its forces immediately to the other side of the canal.

(3) The United Nations force should not abandon its positions. The Secretary General of the United Nations ought to inform Egypt that only the General Assembly can order the evacuation of the UNEF.

(4) Cairo and Damascus seem to believe that the Soviet Union is

on their side in the present crisis. The United States should publicly reaffirm the guarantees it has given Israel in the past.

(5) On the occasion of Eshkol's visit to the United States in 1965, President Johnson promised that his country would act either with the United Nations or independently to preserve Israel's integrity and independence. The United States should honor that pledge.[56]

On both May 20 and 21 the Israelis tried to persuade the United States to announce publicly that it would honor its pledges to protect Israel's "independence." There was little discussion in Washington about the question of whether or not Israel's independence was being threatened, since American policymakers did not think it was. Israel, however, continued to pressure the government, demanding that both the State Department and the White House renew the declaration of March 1, 1957, concerning U.S. recognition of the international character of the Straits of Tiran and the right of "free and innocent passage" to all ships regardless of the flags they flew. The administration initially demurred on the demand for a public statement; but Israel was given conflicting signals that could have been interpreted as possibly indicating that the United States might not totally disapprove its resort to force. Israeli journalist Michael Bar Zohar reports that Rostow told Harman and Evron: "We advise you not to use force against Egypt. . . . we prefer to act within the frame of the United Nations. In order not to be overtaken by events, we should not undertake any unilateral action. . . . If you want us to be with you at the crash landing, then you had better consult us at the takeoff."[57] Rostow's admonition not to use force must be interpreted as very weak; it certainly did not constitute a demand that Israel not resort to war.

On May 22 Johnson wrote to Nasser, assuring him of America's friendship for Egypt and his understanding of the "pride and aspirations of your people." Johnson further urged him to avoid war as his first duty and promised that "if we come through these days without hostilities," he would send Vice-President Hubert Humphrey to talk to him and other Middle Eastern leaders in a new attempt to find a solution to the old problems there. The note concluded: "We believe the general armistice agreements remain the best basis for maintenance of peaceful conditions along the borders. . . . The government of the United States maintains firm opposition to aggression in the area in any form, overt or clandestine, carried out by regular military forces or irregular troops. . . . [this] has been the policy of this government under four successive administrations, a record of our actions over the past two decades within and outside the United Nations is clear on this point."[58] It is not difficult to understand why the Egyptians viewed the U.S. as duplicitous in light of Washington's behavior during and after the June hostilities.

On the same day, May 22, Johnson sent a carefully worded letter to Eshkol, again eschewing the public statement on the Straits that Israel continued to demand. He wrote that he supported "suitable measures in and outside of the United Nations" to deal with the crisis, and he advised Israel to make contact with Britain and France.[59] Johnson also sent a second message to Kosygin that day, suggesting again a joint effort to calm the situation.[60] Subsequent to the sending of these letters, the president received word that Nasser had closed the Gulf of Aqaba to Israeli shipping. After the departure of the UNEF and the full Israeli mobilization on May 19, Nasser had been under intense pressure from the Arab regimes to reinstate the pre-1956 restrictions on Israeli shipping in the Straits. Nasser was aware that Israel had stated such an action would constitute a cause for war; but, on the one hand, he did not wish to appear in the inter-Arab context to be afraid of Israel, and, on the other, as indicated above, the Egyptian president believed that the issue could be resolved through international arbitration, especially since he had no intention of initiating a war and made that clear in every possible context. Nevertheless, the action played into Israel's hands, giving the Jewish state another "reason" to portray Egypt as the "aggressor" in 1967. President Johnson understood the inevitability of the Israeli response, and thus on receipt of the information concerning Nasser's move he immediately ordered the fifty-six ship Sixth Fleet with its two aircraft carriers, the *Saratoga* and the *America,* to begin moving toward the eastern Mediterranean, along with a third carrier, the *Intrepid,* an action that implied support for Israel and a "warning" to the Soviets.[61]

Still, despite this activity, U.S. policy vis-à-vis the emerging conflict was ambiguous and ineffective insofar as preventing the escalation of the crisis. In considerable measure American ineffectiveness resulted from Israel's disregard of Washington's admonitions to calm the situation and cease preparations for war, though, as suggested, Washington's warnings were mild, to be sure. Whether the administration understood Israeli intentions at this point is not clear: it is likely that some officials in the United States were operating with the knowledge that war at Israel's instigation was inevitable, while others may genuinely have believed they could "restrain" the Israelis. There were also important voices in the administration who favored the idea of an Israeli assault against the Arabs. The argument for "unleashing" the Israelis included the likelihood that it would serve to discredit Nasser and possibly bring about his downfall; it would end Egyptian participation in the civil war in Yemen, facilitating a

Royalist victory; it would embarrass the Soviets by crushing the armies of states that they had been heavily arming; it would weaken and destabilize the Ba'ath regime in Syria; it would provide the United States with information about Soviet weapons systems; and it would leave Israel in such a powerful position that it could act as an instrument for the extension of American dominance in the region.[62] Most scholars maintain that President Johnson was steadfast in his opposition to an Israeli resort to force throughout the crisis;[63] the evidence, however, seems to suggest otherwise. Indeed, the oft-repeated phrase made by American officials in this crisis—"Israel will only be alone if it decides to go alone"—was understood in Israel as obviously *not* a prohibition on initiating the war, and indeed even as a "green light."[64]

May 23 was a particularly eventful, indeed in some ways a critical, day. In the early morning hours Johnson sent a formal message to the Israelis, requesting them to delay any action for forty-eight hours and, during that respite, to take counsel with the United States. Again the president warned them that he would take no responsibility for actions on which he was not consulted.[65] In addition the State Department summoned Evron and told him that President Johnson was sending an urgent message to Moscow, requesting its influence for de-escalation of troop movements and respect for free navigation in the Gulf of Aqaba.[66] Johnson also sent a message to the Egyptians, through Ambassador Nolte, reminding them that the United States was firmly opposed to any act of "terrorism" on the territory of neighboring states, demanding unconditional observation of the armistice agreement, and urging a gradual reduction of the troop concentrations. No similar demands were made of Israel. Nasser replied by reiterating that the measures adopted by Egypt were an attempt to offset Israeli military escalation against Syria and were a reaction to the threats to invade Syria leveled in public pronouncements by the Israeli leaders. The Egyptian president further asserted that not only was Egypt committed to the cause of peace but also that Egypt would never initiate an act of aggression.[67]

On another level, President Johnson undertook a most decisive step; on May 23 he secretly authorized an emergency air shipment of armored personnel carriers, spare parts for tanks and the Hawk missile air defense system, bomb fuses, artillery ammunition, and gas masks, among many other items (parts of the list have been excised).[68] The items were packed and sent just prior to the June 5th invasion at a time when the president had publicly declared an arms embargo on all items going to the Middle East.[69] In addition, on the evening of May 23 the president publicly supported the Israeli demand for an American affirmation concerning the Straits of Tiran. In a nationally televised statement Johnson declared that "the United States considers the Gulf [of Aqaba] to be an international waterway and feels that a blockade of Israeli shipping is illegal and potentially disastrous to the cause of peace. The right of free and innocent passage of the international waterway is of vital interest to the international community."

Earlier in the day Secretary of State Rusk had briefed the Senate Foreign Relations Committee and had advised President Johnson that there was general agreement in Congress that "the Arabs should not be permitted to drive the Israelis into the sea."[70] Significantly, Congress, the media, and "informed" public opinion were very supportive of Israel's arguments and actions throughout this crisis. For example, prior to the president's televised declaration backing Israel's interests, George Meany, a labor leader of great influence, informed the White House that he was preparing to make a public statement similar to a statement issued by twenty-four members of the House of Representatives that day containing the following passage: "We pledge the fullest support to measures which must be taken by the Administration to make our position unmistakably clear to those who are now bent on the destruction of Israel, that we are now prepared to take whatever action may be necessary to resist aggression against Israel and to preserve the peace."[71]

The British proposed two steps on May 23 that became the crux of American diplomatic efforts in the May-June crisis. First, the British suggested that as many nations as possible should sign a public declaration reasserting the right of freedom of passage through the Gulf of Aqaba. Second, they called for the maritime powers to set up a naval task force to break Nasser's blockade and open the Straits of Tiran if the Egyptians failed to respond to the public declaration.

In Israel on May 23 the Cabinet Defense Committee began finalizing the strategy for the coming military confrontation, although Eban continued to argue for the necessity of effective diplomatic measures prior to the military initiative so as to maximize American support. Eban's effort had four aims, as he described them: (1) to ensure U.S. arms and aid when the war began, (2) to retain the "fruits of victory," (3) to compel fulfillment of pledges by "friendly states," and (4) to mobilize international opposition to Nasser.[72] All the cabinet members were aware, however, that this political effort was only a prelude to military action. Arrangements were made on May 23 for Eban to visit Washington for talks prior to unilateral Israeli action. Eban's main purpose, initially, was to find out what Washington was prepared to do about the closure of the Straits of Tiran.

However, while Eban was en route to the United States the Israeli military establishment declared that it perceived a change in the strategic situation vis-à-vis Egypt, supposedly portending a surprise attack. Two urgent cables, the first signed by Eshkol, the second by the head of military intelligence, Chaim Herzog, were forwarded to Eban; they substantially changed the direction and thrust of his mission in Washington.

When Eban met with Rusk on May 25, he conveyed the Israeli assessment (contained in the cables) that an Arab attack was imminent and requested that the United States issue a statement "at once" to the effect that any attack on Israel would be regarded as an attack on the United States.[73] Rusk replied that such a request raised constitutional issues and that while the trend of discussion in the Senate Foreign Relations Committee was in favor of supporting Israel's cause, the United States would be unlikely to take unilateral action against Egypt.[74] Rusk did, however, take the cables and Eban's request to Johnson. Later, after conferring at length with the president, Rusk told Eban that, first, the United States did not share the Israeli appraisal that Egypt (or any other Arab state) was planning an attack on Israel; and, second, Washington did not regard the Egyptian order of battle in the Sinai as offensive. Furthermore, Rusk relayed that the president had said he could not even consider making such a statement as Israel requested without full congressional approval. A declaration to the effect that an attack on another country would be considered an attack on the United States had been introduced only in the NATO alliance, and even there it had been accepted only after a long, heated debate.[75]

Eban responded that his government would not have forwarded such urgent messages if its information regarding an imminent Egyptian attack was not reliable; he requested that the Americans check further into the matter. American intelligence experts spent the night of May 25-26 analyzing the Israeli claims. Several specific items had been presented by the Israelis in making their case, and by the morning of May 26 the intelligence community had analyzed each of these charges as well as a wealth of its own information and concluded definitively that an attack was *not* imminent.[76] Thus Israeli credibility came into serious question, and Johnson is reported to have become suspicious that Israel was providing unreliable reports to pressure him to make commitments that lay beyond his constitutional powers or that were premature from his perspective.[77] Johnson met with Eban on May 26 and told him frankly: "Three separate intelligence groups had looked carefully into the matter, and it was our best judgement that a United Arab Republic attack was not imminent. 'All of our intelligence people are unanimous.' I added that if the U.A.R. attacks, you will whip hell out of them.'"[78]

It is clear that Washington knew precisely that Egyptian intentions were not offensive and that it knew that when war came, Israel would win easily. It is difficult to imagine that Israeli intelligence, considered among the world's best, did not concur. Moreover, the statements of various Israelis presented above demonstrate that Israel *was* aware that Egypt had neither the means nor intention of going to war. The cables may thus be understood as Israeli pressure on the United States to hasten and strengthen American support for Israel's military plans.

The following day, May 27, the Israeli cabinet came close to a decision to go to war. Pressures were building within the country to such an extent that many Israeli decision makers saw no reason to delay further the initiation of hostilities. By this time Israel had been fully mobilized for more than a week, the country's economy had slowed considerably, and the civilian population, as well as those called for military duty, were anxiously awaiting a decision. Michael Brecher writes that the spiraling economic cost of the mass mobilization from May 16 onward made the economic factor especially relevant: "The withdrawal of a quarter of a million men from the labor force brought Israel's economy to a near standstill in production. To 'wait indefinitely' for a peaceful resolution was imposing an increasingly intolerable burden."[79]

Of course, it could be argued that if Israel had intended to pursue a peaceful solution, there would have been no need to undertake a major mobilization on May 16 followed by a full-scale mobilization on May 19 (prior even to the closure of the Straits), when everyone, including the Israelis, assessed the Egyptian movements as without offensive intent. The evidence continues to suggest that Israel wanted this war. It is then only necessary to ask why. The answer, which becomes clearly apparent in the war's immediate aftermath, involves both Israel's desire to deal the Arabs a decisive military defeat and to expand the territory of the Jewish state. The tensions of April-May 1967 provided an excellent opportunity for a full-scale military campaign, while the Holocaust syndrome facilitated the support of the entire population. Clearly, once the May 19 mobilization was undertaken, Israel committed itself to an irrevocable course of action: the subsequent discord within the cabinet was between those ministers who wanted to get the war underway as soon as possible (for economic and other reasons) and those, like Eban, who wanted to delay action until unequivocal American support was assured. Even Eban complained, however, that "the public temper was deeply affected" by the single week of mobilization. "Israel had been used to short, sharp campaigns: the agony of waiting has never been part of our military experience. The pressure of this impatience was being brought to bear by reservists at the front and on their families at home."[80]

On May 27 Washington finally attempted direct contact with Nasser when Yost and Anderson were sent to Egypt. Mahmoud Riad, the Egyptian foreign minister, received Ambassador Yost on June 1 and told him: "For our part we shall never begin an armed attack. We have, at your request, confirmed this. Should Israel, on the other hand, initiate aggression, then I would caution you, as a friend of long standing, that both the prestige and the interests of the United States in the area will be seriously damaged and Soviet gains will be further consolidated."[81] After his meeting with Riad, Yost cabled Johnson, suggesting that it would be advisable to give Nasser a way out. Indeed, James Reston, in two dispatches to the *New York Times* from Cairo on June 4 and 5, stated that Egypt did "not want war, . . . [was] certainly not ready for war," and had been making little preparation for war.[82]

On May 31 Anderson met secretly with Nasser and they agreed that Vice-President Zakariyya Mohieddin would come to Washington on June 7.[83]

In a further effort to delay Israeli action, Johnson sent a cable to Eshkol on May 27 containing a communication from the Soviet Union. Moscow had informed Washington that the Soviets possessed information about Israeli preparedness for military action and that a conflict with grave consequences could ensue. The Soviet Union had asked the United States to take all measures to ensure that there would be no military conflict. Johnson told Israel yet again that it should not take preemptive military action and thereby make itself responsible for the initiation of hostilities, and he requested once more that the Israelis give American diplomatic efforts a chance before undertaking unilateral action. Johnson's requests were clearly inconsistent. In an addendum to the president's message, Secretary of State Rusk wrote that Britain and the United States were proceeding urgently to prepare the military aspects of the international naval escort plan and that other nations were responding positively.

Rusk's addendum was not an accurate reflection of reality, however. The declaration as it was being redrafted at that time by the maritime powers contained no threat of the use of force. Moreover, three maritime states—Canada, Denmark, and Norway—had quietly indicated they would not participate in either the threat or use of force against Egypt. Indeed, a former high State Department official intimately involved in the crisis related that "this multilateral fleet became almost a joke with some of us because it was perfectly obvious that time didn't permit us to do it. And it was perfectly obvious that nobody was going to join with us. In the closing days of the issue, there were no ships anywhere near it [the Gulf of Aqaba] that could possibly have joined. The Dutch might conceivably have gone along with us and even they pulled back—eventually everybody pulled back. By the end of the period the British were terrified we were going to start in. . . . It was obvious days before the government gave it up, that nobody was going to go through with it. You could see them falling away—the British were the first."[84] In the end, only four nations agreed to sign the maritime declaration—Great Britain, the Netherlands, Australia, and New Zealand; the United States was conspicuously absent from the list of signatories. The declaration was never issued, and a naval task force was never formed.

American efforts at the United Nations were equally unavailing. The Security Council convened on May 23, at the initiative of Canada and Denmark, but adjourned on May 24 without having produced a resolution; it did not meet again until May 29. At that time Ambassador Goldberg introduced a draft resolution that stated in part:

The United States believes that the Council . . . should endorse the Secretary General's appeal and call upon all parties concerned, in his words, to exercise special restraint, to forego belligerence and avoid all other actions which could increase tension, to allow the Council to deal with the underlying causes of the present crisis and to seek solutions. . . . We believe from the context of the situation that with respect to the particularly sensitive area of Aqaba, foregoing belligerence must mean foregoing any blockade of the Gulf of Aqaba during the breathing spell requested by the Secretary General, and permitting free and innocent passage of all nations and all flags through the Straits of Tiran to continue as it has during the past ten years.[85]

The American ambassador thus called on Egypt to lift its blockade in the Straits without asking for any quid pro quo from Israel, least of all an end to the mobilization that had prompted the imposition of the blockade and that the Arabs viewed as a grave threat to their security. However, because France abstained, the United States was unable to muster nine votes in the Security Council to force the issue. The council met again on May 30 and 31 and on June 3, just prior to the outbreak of war, but accomplished nothing at any of these meetings.

In the meantime, in Israel a political crisis was growing over a lack of confidence in Eshkol's leadership. On June 1 a National Unity government was formed in which Eshkol retained the prime ministership, but Moshe Dayan, Ben-Gurion's protege, was made defense minister. The momentum for war gathered speed rapidly; the only restraining factor was the desire to maintain favor in world (especially American) public opinion, so that the "fruits of victory" would not be lost after the war was ended. The pressures within Israel to begin the war were reflected in a cable Eshkol sent to Johnson on May 31, which stated inter alia: "I welcome the assurances that the United States will take any and all measures to open the Straits of Tiran to international shipping."[86] Johnson is reported to have reacted angrily to that cable, raging to Walter Rostow: "I have no right to make such promises without the consent of Congress. This is not what I told Eban. Tell the Israelis so!"[87] The cable may be interpreted as further Israeli pressure on the United States. Moreover, it cleverly gave the Israelis an excuse to act on their own when the United States did not take "any and all measures" to open the Straits.

On June 2 Evron met Walter Rostow at the White House, primarily to seek reassurance that the United States would not object if Israel now proceeded with its plans for war. Evron stressed that time was working against Israel and that the economic cost of Israel's mobilization was rising every day. In an effort to provoke an "excuse" for the initiation of hostilities, Evron reportedly asked what the American response would be if an Israeli ship trying to break the blockade drew Egyptian fire, and Israel then responded with an attack on Sharm el-Sheikh. Rostow told Evron he would discuss this possibility with Johnson. In reply to a question by Rostow regarding how much time the United States had, Evron acknowledged June 11 as a possible deadline, but indicated there was nothing ironclad about it so far as the Israelis were concerned.[88] The Israeli proposal to initiate a provocation and attempt to force Egypt to take military action was also a clever tactic. On the one hand, it could have provided the Israelis the pretext they wanted to initiate the war (assuming Nasser responded); on the other, it was a face-saving device for the United States—letting it off the hook with regard to exercising force to open the Straits. Also at this meeting Evron apparently mentioned the 1957 commitment, stressing that it had two parts: an American pledge to assert the right of free passage in the Straits (which the president had fulfilled in his May 23 television address); and an "acknowledgment" of Israel's right to act with force if the Straits were closed. The second part also represented a new Israeli tactic, and not an accurate interpretation of the 1957 U.S. commitment. But in this vein Evron pointed out that it would be better for U.S.–Arab and U.S.–Soviet relations if Israel acted alone, rather than relying on Washington to force open the Straits.[89]

Johnson's reaction to Evron's ideas is not recorded, though it would clearly be in Washington's interest to have Israel undertake such an action unilaterally and thus lessen the strains between the United States and both Moscow and the Arab states. There was also the consideration, again discussed at this juncture, of the potential advantages that could accrue to American interests in the aftermath of the expected resounding Israeli victory, when Israel would enjoy a position of unchallenged dominance in the Middle East. On another level, some officials were eager for the technical information that a battlefield testing of American against Soviet weapons would provide. Indeed, at this point it seems that Johnson and his closest advisors lost sight of all the inescapably negative consequences from Israel's military aggression and deluded themselves that this swift, decisive Middle Eastern war would be a healthy counterpoint to the quagmire of Vietnam and would extend American power in the Middle East. Thus with the inevitability of Israel's initiating war becoming more pronounced by the hour, the administration made no further attempts to restrain the Jewish state.

It is also worth noting that the perception in Israel was that it had a "green light" from the United States. Brecher writes: "At the same time the perceived impression was that if Israel took the initiative . . . the United States would not take an unfriendly view."[90] Abba Eban writes in a similar vein: "My own reading of the Washington position told me that . . . the United States would feel relieved at being liberated from its dilemma."[91] And, more explicitly: "There were some in our military establishment who . . . believed that it might be American policy to 'unleash Israel.' "[92]

Israel Initiates War

On June 4 Israel decided that there was no further reason to delay and on June 5 launched an attack on Egypt that was euphemistically labeled a "preemptive" strike. Defense Minister Dayan had stated the minimal military objectives of the war to be the destruction of the Egyptian army, the capture of the entire Sinai peninsula, and reopening the Straits of Tiran.[93] Israel's military objectives, however, were considerably broader than Dayan indicated. Moreover, from the outset, Israeli policymakers were acutely mindful of the urgency of certain political objectives. One was to ensure that Soviet intervention be prevented.[94] Nevertheless, Israel's awareness of the potential of Soviet involvement, the threat of great power confrontation, and the danger to U.S. interests did not deter it from proceeding with its plans, especially with regard to Syria. Indeed, Israel conveyed to Washington its belief that the United States was responsible for protecting it from the Soviet Union, even if it was Israeli actions that provoked a Soviet response. The second aim was to ensure that once the war began and Egypt and Syria were engaged, Jordan could be induced to avoid involvement; a simultaneous three-front war was of great concern to Israel. The third objective was that Israel not be forced to return to the prewar boundaries; there was a clear recognition at the beginning of this war that the expansion of Israel's territory was desirable and necessary.

In order to implement these political goals, Eban and Eshkol drafted a letter to President Johnson early in the morning of June 5. It began with a description of the alleged dangers Israel claimed that it had been facing since mid-May through that morning: "All of this amounts to an extraordinary catalogue of aggression abhorred and condemned by world opinion, in your great country, and amongst all peace-loving nations." The letter expressed the Israeli concern that the United States prevent the Soviet Union from coming to the aid of its allies and attempted, in what was to become a standard Israeli argument when it undertook military operations, to suggest that there would be advantages to the United States from its actions. "The hour of danger can also be an hour of opportunity. It is possible to create conditions favorable to the promotion of peace and the strengthening of freedom in the area."[95] In transmitting the letter to the president, the Israelis indicated that the sentence about the Soviet Union was the most crucial point. Israel's actions did provoke a Soviet response: on June 10 as Israel prepared to march on Damascus, the Soviets sent a message to Johnson on the "hot line" threatening military action if Israel did not desist. Johnson responded by turning the entire Sixth Fleet toward the Syrian coast, signaling that the United States was prepared to meet any Soviet military challenge with a military response. Thus Washington risked a conflagration with the Soviet Union, including the potential of escalation to nuclear confrontation by its support for the Jewish state. Israel was undoubtedly most satisfied by Washington's stance on its behalf vis-à-vis Moscow; the rest of the world must have shuddered at American "policy."

The Israelis used open diplomatic channels to assure King Hussein that they would abstain from an attack on Jordan if he stayed out of the war.[96] Realistically, however, there was little likelihood that Jordan could have avoided entering the war once Israel attacked Egypt. King Hussein and Nasser had signed a mutual defense pact on May 30, making them formal military allies. Then, too, emotions in the Arab world in general, and among the Palestinian population of Jordan in particular, were running extremely high. The king would have been considered a traitor if he had not stood with the Egyptians once they came under assault from Israel. Moreover, it seems apparent that Israel would have attacked Jordan even if Hussein had refrained from joining the fighting, after the Egyptians and Syrians were crushed: the temptation to seize the remainder of Jerusalem and the rest of historic Palestine would have been overwhelming.[97] Indeed, a series of events following the war clearly suggests such premeditation: the immediate (June 28, 1967) move to "reunify" Jerusalem; the rapid destruction of Palestinian villages in the West Bank (begun even before hostilities ceased), including Beit Nuba, Imwas, Yalu, Beit Mersin, Beit Awa, and others; the program to colonize and settle the West Bank (begun within four months after the termination of hostilities); Israel's subsequent position on the absolute strategic necessity of the territorial depth provided by the West Bank; and the intense ideological attachment of important and powerful sectors within Israel to "Judea and Samaria." All of these factors, in addition to Israel's desire for the war and its clear intention to initiate it regardless of the Arab disinclination to fight, certainly call into question Israel's stated intentions with respect to Jordan in 1967.[98]

In addition to its bilateral diplomacy vis-à-vis the United States, Israel also sought to fulfill its political objectives, particularly concerning no return to the prewar boundaries, through a careful strategy at the United Nations. Israeli decision makers were very concerned that the United Nations would become the medium through which Israel would "lose at the conference table what was being gained on the battlefield."[99] Indeed, while Israel recognized that a call for a cease-fire was inevitable, it was greatly concerned that the cease-fire might be coupled with a unanimous international demand for a return to the status quo ante bellum. Such a position, the Israelis feared, would deprive Israel of its battlefield gains or, at best, leave it with its new boundaries intact, but in a situation of international isolation, boycott, and political blockade. Eban writes: "It was a normal United Nations practice to accompany a cease-fire resolution with a call for restoration of previous lines. A special effort of imagination and intellectual resourcefulness would be needed if these two concepts were to be separated. My own tactic was to ensure that a cease-fire resolution was not accompanied by any automatic restoration of the territorial status quo."[100]

Israel initiated its diplomatic strategy on June 5, when its ambassador, Gideon Rafael, requested an urgent meeting of the Security Council and presented to the members a recapitulation of alleged Egyptian aggression and a report on supposed Israeli attempts to seek a peaceful solution to the conflict. The following day, June 6, Abba Eban arrived in New York and worked with Rafael on securing a resolution for an "unconditional" cease-fire. In accordance with Israel's wishes, and due in considerable measure to the efforts of U.S. Ambassador Goldberg, a simple cease-fire resolution was passed on June 6, with no call for a return to the prewar lines. In his speech following the vote, Eban praised the resolution and declared that Israel would comply on condition that the other side also complied. Jordan immediately accepted the cease-fire, but Israel continued to press its attack on Jerusalem and the West Bank. On June 7 a resolution was presented to the Security Council calling for Israeli withdrawal to the prewar lines, but it was vetoed by the United States. A second simple cease-fire resolution was passed instead. Israel completed the capture of Jerusalem on June 7. On June 8 Egypt accepted the cease-fire, though Israel continued with "mopping up" operations along the Suez Canal and in the West Bank. Moreover, on June 8 Israeli troops and planes massed for an attack on Syria. Undoubtedly aware of the impending attack, Syria accepted the cease-fire, which went into effect at 5:20 A.M. local time on June 9. However, at 11:30 A.M. on June 9, Israel invaded Syria.

In four days Israel had destroyed the entire Egyptian air force on the ground (actually this was accomplished on the first day) and routed the Egyptian army, capturing Sharm el-Sheikh and occupying all of the Sinai from Gaza south. The Jordanian air force was likewise destroyed and its army defeated, facilitating the seizure of East Jerusalem and the West Bank of the Jordan River. By June 10 Israel was in possession of Syria's Golan Heights, including the city of Quneitra, and the road to Damascus was open. At that point apparently even Johnson began to blanch, and in his own words the American government "used every diplomatic resource to convince Israel to work out an effective cease-fire with Syria."[101] Washington was concerned that an Israeli drive on Damascus might bring the Soviets into the war. Indeed, it was on June 10 that Soviet Premier Kosygin warned of possible Soviet intervention if Israel did not stop its attack on Syria. The United States military response was coupled with pressure on Israel to halt the march to Damascus, and the great power tensions were defused when Israel agreed to a cease-fire with Syria late on June 10, marking the end of the war.[102]

American Policy during the War

American policymakers were confronted by a completely new diplomatic situation once Israel initiated the war. After three weeks of declaring its opposition to an Israeli resort to force, publicly warning

Israel that "you will only be alone if you go it alone," and in the face of Israel's clear-cut initiative, Dean Rusk commented on June 6 that the United States would not make a judgment about who was the aggressor. Moreover, although in his memoirs Johnson attempted to disassociate the United States from Israel's actions, writing "I have never concealed my regret that Israel decided to move when it did,"[103] at the time he, too, declined to criticize Israel's aggression.

The dichotomy between principle and practice was never starker. It is clear that in the end the administration not only did not oppose Israel's actions but also gave the Jewish state a nod of approval, at least for the war against Egypt. There is also the possibility that the United States lent physical support to the war effort. Stephen Green, author of *Taking Sides: America's Secret Relations with a Militant Israel*, alleges that the U.S. air force flew aerial reconnaissance for the Israelis throughout the war. According to Green, American RF-4C's had white Stars of David on a blue background painted on the planes fuselages and new tail numbers affixed, corresponding to inventory numbers in the Israeli air force. Green states that American pilots from the 38th Squadron (Ramstein) and technicians from the 17th Squadron (Upper Heyford) were dressed in civilian clothes, stripped of their military IDs, and carried out the reconnaissance assistance.[104] He notes that such reconnaissance was not a factor in the Israeli victory, but argues that "the aerial reconnaissance assistance that the United States provided to Israel during the Six Day War . . . help[ed] the Israelis to achieve certain territorial objectives within a very finite, limited time. United States and Israeli strategists knew well before the commencement of the fighting that diplomatic pressures for a cease-fire would be enormous. It was important for the IDF to capture certain strategic ground in a very short time, before the cease-fire lines were frozen. In this respect, the United States tactical reconnaissance assistance was not only important, it was critical."[105]

If Green's allegations are correct, the reconnaissance would likely have come as a result of a direct order from the president of the United States. At the time Nasser accused the United States of providing Israel with tactical air support, and Johnson publicly denied that the United States was providing any assistance of any kind to Israel. However, citing both the allegations of American assistance, as well as the totality of Washington's duplicity in dealing with him throughout this crisis, Nasser broke diplomatic relations with the United States. I could not ascertain whether the United States provided Israel physical support in the form of aerial reconnaissance in June 1967; however, the diplomatic support America gave Israel at the United Nations is beyond question, as is Washington's deceitfulness in dealing with Egypt. The Arab world believed that the United States acted in collusion with Israel in the May-June crisis—a perception that is reflected in the words of Egyptian Foreign Minister Riad, "The crux of the problem was that we had received in an official communication, assurances from President Johnson that Israel would not initiate hostilities if we refrained, which we had. He had pledged that the United States would maintain firm opposition to aggression in the area. Now that Israel had started the war, by attacking us, the least we could expect, in light of these assurances, was that President Johnson would demand the immediate withdrawal of Israeli forces to their original positions; then perhaps we could move to a debate of the Palestine question . . . and of the basic causes of strife in the area."[106] Johnson did not call for an Israeli withdrawal, and no discussion commenced at the war's end on any of the basic problems in the area, least of all the Palestinian issue. Nasser's response to the war is likewise important: "The problem now is that while the United States objective is to pressure us to minimize our dealings with the Soviet Union, it will drive us in the opposite direction altogether. The United States leaves us no choice."[107]

This was precisely the outcome of the war. While it was the primary strategic objective of the United States in the Middle East to decrease Soviet influence, Israel's second offensive war against the Arabs brought about greater Soviet penetration of Egypt and Syria than at any previous time. In the aftermath of the third major Israeli invasion of Egyptian territory, Egypt concluded that only the Soviets could offer them some protection against Israeli aggression. Soviet weapons and advisors poured into Egypt in the wake of the June War and seriously increased Soviet-American rivalry and competition in the area.

The strangest incident of the war and an aspect of U.S. policy that remains difficult to analyze is the Israeli attack on the American ship *Liberty.* On the morning of June 8, the fourth day of the war, a U.S. navy communications ship, the *Liberty,* was torpedoed in international waters off the Sinai coast. Johnson writes: "For seventy tense minutes we had no idea who was responsible but at 11:00 we learned that the ship had been attacked in error by Israeli gunboats and planes."[108] James Bamford, an American investigative reporter who wrote a seminal work on the National Security Agency, commented on the *Liberty* affair: "Nearly as bizarre as the attack itself was the reaction of the American government to the incident. A foreign nation [Israel] had butchered American servicemen, sending thirty-four to their graves and more than a hundred others into hospitals, and a virtually unarmed American naval ship in international waters was torpedoed, set on fire with napalm, then left to sink as crazed [Israeli] gunners shot up the life rafts. The foreign nation then says, sorry about that, and offers an explanation so outrageous that it is insulting, and the American government accepts it, sweeps the whole affair under a rug, then classifies as top secret nearly all details concerning it."[109] While the careful research of Bamford, James Ennes (the officer of the deck at the time of the attack), Stephen Green, and Donald Neff provide convincing arguments that the Israelis knew the ship was an American intelligence ship and intentionally attacked it, both U.S. and Israeli governments officially deny it. I could not determine with absolute certainty the truth of the matter. However, if the Israelis did knowingly and intentionally hit the ship, as seems likely, the most plausible explanation resides in the fact that Israel did not want the United States to know of its plans for an invasion of Syria after the cease-fire, fearing that Washington's concern over the likely Soviet response would bring serious pressure on the Israelis to cancel their battle order—something they were not about to do, regardless of the risks of Soviet involvement.

Conclusion

The most important outcome of the June War was that for the majority in the policymaking elite, Israel's spectacular military performance validated the thesis that Israel could function as a strategic asset to the United States in the Middle East. Thereafter, within a remarkably short period of time, that idea became enshrined as an absolute tenet of orthodoxy in American politics. The belief about Israel's strategic utility was expressed in U.S. policy through the provision of virtually unlimited quantities of economic assistance and military equipment, a de facto alliance between Washington and Israel, and in American support for virtually every Israeli foreign policy objective. In general, the period from 1956-57 through 1967 was a time of increasing American support for the Jewish state, and while U.S. backing for Israel's war effort in 1967 was not public and forthright, it was nevertheless very strong.

A second major outcome of the war was the rapidly increasing activism of American Jews on behalf of Israel. The praetorian achievements of the Jewish state during the fighting galvanized the sentiments of thousands, and for many transformed the traditional reverence for the Torah into worship of the Israeli state and the political ideology of Zionism.[110] Subsequently, pro-Israeli forces rapidly acquired power and influence within the American political system—a phenomenon that derived from the *convergence* between elite perceptions concerning Israel's ability to serve U.S. interests, the general public's fascination with Israel in the wake of the June triumph, and the tremendous activism of the pro-Israeli effort. Together these factors catapulted the movement into a position of unrivaled influence on the domestic scene. The pro-Israeli effort was directed at promoting and reinforcing the strategic asset thesis, generating economic and military assistance for Israel, and creating and maintaining an image of Israel as a struggling, democratic little country—America's "only friend" in the Middle East—facing nearly insurmountable odds against aggressive, warlike Arabs, ever poised to bring about its destruction. This highly successful public relations effort characterized the new occupation over East Jerusalem, the West Bank, Gaza, the Golan, and the Sinai as the "most benign and humane in history" while effusively portraying the state as a "light unto the nations."

The question of why the United States gave such strong support to Israel in May-June 1967 is perhaps the most interesting question with regard to this period. Several factors are involved. Certainly Johnson's general foreign policy dilemma created the context in which the administration's regrettable decisions were made. Johnson had failed to come to terms with Nasser and Egyptian nonalignment, and he apparently became convinced that Egypt's defeat would strengthen Washington's position in the Middle East. Moreover, since the United States was mired in Vietnam, and Washington intelligence was certain that Israel could deliver a swift and decisive defeat to the Arabs, administration officials apparently persuaded themselves that Israel's achievement of its objectives would be a much-needed psychological victory for the West. There were, in addition, the very real benefits in which various officials saw merit, such as the battlefield testing of American weapons and the intelligence to be obtained from captured Soviet equipment.

Outspokenly pro-Israeli officials in high positions in the administration, as well as private individuals with personal access to the president who also had strong pro-Israeli affinities, seem to have had considerable influence on Johnson's decision to support Israel in its military objectives and later to provide the wherewithal for Israel to retain the fruits of its aggression. Johnson's own affection for Israel, together with his other international difficulties, would have predisposed him to listen carefully to the list of seeming benefits accruing from support for Israel's war that these individuals offered. In the final analysis, however, Johnson's own shortsightedness was probably the primary factor in determining U.S. support for Israeli objectives. Bedeviled by an elusive enemy in Indochina and mounting opposition at home and certain of Israel's military capability vis-à-vis the Arabs, the president undoubtedly persuaded himself that a rapid route to American hegemony in the Middle East was to be found in following Israel.

American policy in May-June 1967 validates the thesis of presidential prerogative in foreign policymaking. While it is clear that the Congress, as well as the media and "informed" public opinion wholeheartedly supported Israel in this crisis, viewing the Jewish state as being victimized by aggressive, warmongering Arabs, President Johnson did not seek the "advice and consent" of Congress before making the crucial decisions that further entangled the United States with Israel's regional objectives and compromised American interests. While the president expressed concern throughout the crisis about having congressional support for any U.S. action in the Middle East (clearly mindful of the growing negative sentiment in Congress over the Gulf of Tonkin Resolution he had pushed through the Senate and the escalating American involvement in Vietnam derived from it), once he was assured that Israel could manage its military campaign without any U.S. military assistance, Johnson never discussed with Congress the ramifications for American interests such an Israeli action would engender.

Yet Johnson, like the presidents who followed him, failed to comprehend that insofar as the United States extended support for Israel's policies of regional domination, America's ability to further its influence was compromised, as were all of America's interests in the region. President Johnson failed to evaluate properly and prudently the long-range problems that would inevitably arise from the course of action he chose in 1967; he failed, it seems, to foresee anything like the 1973 oil embargo by Arab oil producers, whose patience with the United States became strained to the breaking point, or the developing militancy of the Palestinians, who could not tolerate the new occupation and the new mass of displaced refugees. Johnson also failed to perceive the advantages that would fall to the Soviet Union as a result of his flawed policies.

Indeed, while officials were reveling in Israel's "victory for the West," the fallacies in the strategic asset thesis became apparent almost immediately. Soviet influence in the Middle East increased vastly as Moscow moved to rebuild the militaries of Syria and Egypt (including the dispatch of advisors to Cairo in the context of the War of Attrition), to support the PLO, and to befriend the Arabs in the wake of their defeat. American influence with even "moderate" Arabs declined, and six Arab states severed diplomatic relations with the United States. Moreover, the region became significantly less stable as a result of conditions created by the war: approximately 200,000 more Palestinians became refugees; the occupation of the West Bank and Gaza led to a spiraling cycle of resistance and repression; and the PLO arose like a phoenix out of the ashes of the devastation wrought by Israel. In addition, the War of Attrition along the Suez Canal began within months. Those hostilities lasted three years and involved Israeli bombardment of the Egyptian cities in the Canal zone, creating hundreds of thousands of internal refugees. Moreover, within a year after the June conflict Israel launched the first of many massive ground and air attacks against Lebanon. Subsequent Israeli bombardment of Lebanon, in addition to territorial incursions, was a precipitating factor in that nation's plunge into civil war in 1975. Finally, contrary to the predictions of those officials who had favored an Israeli assault on the Arabs, Nasser survived and continued as president of Egypt while retaining his position of leadership in the Arab world; the Ba'ath party remained in power in Syria; and South Yemen eventually became the first—and only—Marxist state in the region. Contrary to Israel's premise and America's wishful thinking, the 1967 war brought neither peace nor stability to the Middle East. American policymakers, however, appeared oblivious to these results.

CHAPTER FIVE

THE OCTOBER 1973 WAR

Introduction

The fourth Arab-Israeli war, often called the October War, erupted on October 6, 1973, when the armies of Egypt and Syria launched an attack on Israeli positions along the Suez Canal and in the Golan Heights. The campaign was a limited war in that Egyptian and Syrian goals extended only to regaining parts of their territory occupied by Israel in 1967 and to serving forceful notice on Israel and the United States that the post-1967 status quo was untenable. The war lasted eighteen days, until a third cease-fire resolution, passed by the United Nations on October 25, was observed by the Israelis. It was technically (i.e., militarily) a defeat for the Arabs, but because of the ability of Egypt and Syria to launch a surprise attack successfully, and because the Egyptian and Syrian militaries fought credibly, the war became a symbol of progress to the Arabs. A sense of self-esteem replaced the humiliation that followed 1967, and it therefore became possible, in ways it had not been previously, for certain Arab states to seek peace with Israel. The October War was significant in another respect. The use of an oil embargo as a political weapon by the Arab states— the first such concerted Arab action—transformed the regional conflict into a global one involving all of Western Europe and Japan as well as the United States. Moreover, a second near-confrontation between the Soviet Union and the United States during the hostilities further emphasized the global ramifications of the Arab-Palestinian-Israeli conflict.

Immediately after the war a period of intense American diplomatic activity ensued, designed first to disengage the Israeli and Egyptian forces in the Sinai, and then to disengage the Israeli and Syrian forces in the Golan Heights. On January 18, 1974, an agreement was signed by Israel and Egypt, and on May 31, 1974, by Israel and Syria. These agreements were considered significant in American foreign policy-making circles since it was believed that they would diminish the likelihood of renewed conflict and, more important, improve the prospects for a broader settlement on the Egyptian-Israeli front. However, the preeminent foreign policy decision maker, Henry Kissinger, mistakenly assumed that a bilateral Israeli-Egyptian peace (rather than a comprehensive settlement) would best serve the American interests of regional stability, containment of Soviet influence, and extension of U.S. hegemony.

The Middle East in the Aftermath of the June War

The June War produced a significant change in Israel's general attitude about the Middle East. Most important, Israel became more confident of its own strength and its strategic position, which the war had totally transformed in its favor. The first question facing Israel was how much of the captured land should be held. There were differences of opinion within Israel over this question, but virtually all major sectors of the Israeli establishment agreed that *some* of the captured territory should be held permanently. Thus, Israel needed to determine means for retaining what land it would keep, for peopling and developing it, and for expelling or otherwise controlling the Arabs who would oppose the extension of Israeli rule. In addition, Israel needed to develop a policy that would legitimize the retention of territory. Various groups in Israel articulated a number of differing justifications. The ruling Labor party tended to favor justifications based on arguments of "security" and "strategic necessity," while other sectors preferred justifications based on biblical claims of God-given "rights" and/or nationalist ideologies of a "Greater Israel."[1]

In general, the post-1967 Israeli world view broke down into a number of axioms that, by virtue of continuous repetition, soon acquired the force of objectively existing reality. Amnon Kapeliouk, an Israeli journalist and political commentator, describes them as follows: "We shall maintain the status quo in the region for as long as we like; security frontiers deter the Arabs from attacking; the Bar Lev Line (along the East bank of the Suez Canal) is impregnable; our intelligence services are infallible; the Arabs only understand the language of force; war is not for the Arabs; the Arab world is divided and without military options; the oil weapon is a mere propaganda tool; the Palestinians of the occupied territories will resign themselves to their fate; time is on our side; it does not matter what the Gentiles say, but what the Jews do."[2] Given these attitudes, it is understandable why Israel's intelligence services as well as its political leaders misread the signs of impending attack in October 1973. It is also understandable why the June victory did not translate into peace or security.

Concomitant with its newly emerging world view, the ruling Labor party drew its "red lines" quickly and clearly in the aftermath of the war: no return to the 1967 borders, no "redivision" of Jerusalem, and a "security border" along the Jordan River.[3] What was left beyond these nonnegotiable conditions—which were soon expanded to include no return of the Golan, no negotiations with the PLO, and no consideration of a Palestinian state, and which were regularly characterized as equivalent to an Israeli national consensus—was described as open to compromise.

A series of Israeli actions paralleled its diplomatic stances, confirming Arab fears of Israeli expansionism and creating fertile ground for the growth of the Palestinian resistance movement. Within weeks after the end of the June War the Knesset legislated the "reunification" of Jerusalem, effecting the de facto annexation of the Arab sector of the city. In addition, the Israeli authorities destroyed the Palestinian villages of Imwas, Beit Nuba, and Yalu in the Latrun area and expelled their inhabitants and also partially destroyed other Palestinian villages. Moreover, while U.N. resolutions urged the return of the wave of refugees that had fled the fighting in June, and the Red Cross had received applications for repatriation from 150,000 people exiled during the war or in the immediate postwar period, Israel readmitted 14,000 of the applicants and then summarily refused to allow the return of the others. In yet another ominous step the Israeli government began in September 1967 the construction of Jewish settlements in the occupied areas.

In contrast to the Jewish state's bold self-confidence, the Arab military defeat and Israel's occupation of more Arab territory resulted in great turmoil in the Arab world and a number of significant transformations.[4] Relations among the Arab states shifted and reshifted in the postwar period and the overall picture was one of a group of states lacking cohesion, leadership, and orientation. In general, 1968 and 1969 marked a low period in pan-Arabism; indeed, some analysts argue that the 1967 war signaled its end.[5] At the very least, the formation of a Cairo-Amman axis in the postwar period in an attempt to secure the return of the occupied territories was a major blow to the pan-Arab and particularly to the Palestinian cause.

The war led Gamal Abdul Nasser to undertake a considerable modification of a number of his previous policies; for example, Egyptian involvement in the civil war in the Yemen was terminated since Egypt needed the moral and financial support of its former rivals, particularly Saudi Arabia. In response, Saudi Arabia, Kuwait, and Libya agreed to pay Egypt and Jordan 135 million pounds sterling per year as compensation for loss of territory in the war and for losses from the closure of the Suez Canal (blockaded by Nasser during the 1967 hostilities). This was a significant step toward détente between some previously hostile parties, although the rapprochement between Egypt and Saudi Arabia was short-lived. Indeed, after the Arab summit conference at Khartoum in August 1967, the Saudis avoided further contact with Egypt because they suspected the Egyptians of encouraging the Soviets to enter the conflict in the Yemen. Moreover, the Saudis failed to follow through with financial assistance to Egypt and Jordan to the extent promised. In addition, there was a major rift in Egyptian-Syrian relations in the immediate postwar period because the Egyptians came to feel that the Syrians had misled them in the May-June crisis through false allegations of Israeli troop concentrations on Syria's border. The Ba'ath regime survived in Syria, but leadership passed to General Hafez Assad in 1971; and not until after Assad's takeover did Syria and Egypt begin to mend fences.[6] King Hussein remained on the throne in Jordan, though he fought a bloody civil war with Palestinian nationalists in 1970.[7] There was a military coup in the Sudan in May 1969 by Colonel Ja'far al-Numairi, and in Libya in September 1969 by Lieutenant Mu'ammar Qaddafi; the young officers in both countries claimed that the traditional monarchies had surrendered to Israeli domination.[8]

Nevertheless, the states involved in the June War—Egypt, Jordan, and Syria—survived, reaffirmed their domestic political authority, and then proceeded, primarily with the help of the Soviets, to replace the military equipment that had been lost in the war.[9] Moreover, while they were unwilling to engage in direct negotiations with Israel from a position of weakness, they were willing to seek a political solution through the United Nations or its leading members. The statement at Khartoum of "no recognition, no negotiation, no peace" with Israel was issued largely as a concession to popular Arab feeling and to the most radical Arab regimes. The more significant call of the summit conference was for "unified efforts at international and diplomatic levels to . . . assure the withdrawal of the aggressive forces . . . from Arab lands."[10] This resolution sought a political solution and contained no reference to military action. Nasser and King Hussein were more disposed to a political solution than the leaders of Syria, Iraq, and Algeria, but even the latter regimes did not categorically rule out the possibility of such a settlement.[11] In November 1967, during his first postwar visit to Washington, King Hussein made a peace offer that included recognizing Israel's right to exist in peace and security and ending the state of war on condition that Israel evacuate the newly captured territories.[12] In February 1970 Nasser declared that "it will be possible to institute a durable peace between Israel and the Arab states, not excluding economic and diplomatic relations, if Israel evacuates the occupied territories and accepts a settlement of the problem of the Palestinian refugees."[13] After Nasser's death, the new Egyptian president, Anwar Sadat, offered Israel a full peace treaty in February 1971 based on the pre-June 1967 borders and including security guarantees.[14] The same year Jordanian Foreign Minister Abdullah Salah stated that Jordan was ready to recognize Israel if it returned to the internationally recognized boundaries.[15] In 1972 King Hussein proposed to establish a confederation of Jordan and the West Bank.[16] Israel ignored every Arab overture, and Washington made no effort to pursue the Arab openings. In the end, the failure of both Israel and Washington to respond to any of the proposed initiatives prompted Sadat to undertake the 1973 war.

Additional testimony of the willingness of certain Arab countries to end the state of belligerency and recognize the existence of Israel was the acceptance by Egypt and Jordan of U.N. Resolution 242 (see below for a discussion of this major postwar diplomatic initiative by the international community on behalf of Middle East peace). In addition, both states cooperated with U.N. representative Gunnar Jarring in his search for peace as mandated by the resolution, and both accepted the Rogers Plan—a U.S. State Department initiative that sought the exchange of territory for peace.[17] On the other hand, Israel equivocated on Resolution 242, did not cooperate with Jarring, and rejected the Rogers Plan.

While the various concessions Jordan and Egypt were prepared to offer in the post-1967 period were entirely insufficient to satisfy Israeli demands, they were more than enough to shock the Palestinians into a realization of their isolation and of the readiness of Arab governments to sell out their cause. That realization, combined with the new Israeli occupation and the displacement and dispossession of more Palestinians, contributed to the evolution of the Palestine national movement into a new and more radical phase. The PLO itself came to be dominated by the Palestinian guerrilla groups, led by Fatah, and the commitment to resist Israel's occupation was intensified.

In July 1968 Nasser spoke to Yasir Arafat about Resolution 242 and about what the Palestinians could expect in the way of future assistance from the Arab regimes: "You have every right not to accept it. There is no reason why you should not publicly oppose the resolution because it is not designed for you. But, why not be our Stern? Why not be our Begin? You must be our irresponsible arm. On this basis we will give you all the help we can."[18] Thus Nasser signaled the PLO that the Arab governments would pursue their own state interests vis-à-vis Israel, implicitly acknowledging that they would not be pursuing Palestinian interests. Nasser suggested that the regimes would tolerate PLO guerrilla activity as an irritant to Israel, so long as it did not interfere with the course set by the Arab governments. Indeed, Nasser continued to prohibit—as he had since 1956—Palestinian guerrilla activity from Egyptian territory.

Moreover, it was Nasser's willingness to ignore Palestinian interests in the service of Egyptian "national security" that contributed to the first major blow that the Palestine national movement suffered from its Arab brothers. Renewed Egyptian-Israeli conflict began within months of the end of the June 1967 hostilities and continued until 1970, when it was terminated through an American-sponsored cease-fire. The hostilities between Egypt and Israel were played out along the Suez Canal and ultimately involved a proxy war between the Soviet Union and the United States. Concerning that conflict the renowned Egyptian journalist Mohammed Heikal writes that although Israeli snipers were continuously active and Israeli planes bombed military and civilian targets near the Canal zone beginning in July 1967, Nasser initially issued an order forbidding the return of fire to avoid furnishing Israel with a pretext to resume full-scale war. Instead, Heikal writes, "In October 1967 Nasser decided to evacuate the three canal cities, Port Said, Ismailia, and Suez. As a result, more than 400,000 refugees from the Canal zone flooded into Cairo and the rest of Egypt."[19] Eventually the conflict escalated—one cease-fire was arranged and broken—and then in April 1969 Nasser proclaimed the "War of Attrition" along the Canal. Israel responded by initiating a series of deep penetration raids into Egyptian territory, profoundly disrupting civilian life in that country. By the time the war ended in August 1970—the result of the American-sponsored truce—the number of internal Egyptian refugees had reached some 750,000 persons.[20] The Palestine national movement viewed the American-arranged cease-fire, which ended the hostilities, with serious concern, particularly because of the diplomatic context then developing, including Nasser's acceptance of the Rogers Plan. The Palestinians saw in these events the portent that the Arab states were preparing to conclude peace over the heads of those most affected by the conflict, e.g., the Palestinians themselves, and a serious breach erupted between the PLO and Nasser.

King Hussein took advantage of this fissure to curtail the growing power of the PLO in Jordan. Previously, Palestinian social and political activity had been flourishing under the organization of Palestinian commandos and militia; the Jordanian police had even had to forego enforcement of the myriad regulations that restricted labor, political organization, and the press in Jordan in the areas that were under PLO control. The Jordanian army had gradually moved out of Amman and the population centers in the northern region, where Palestinian refugees were concentrated and where political and armed mobilization was at a high level. The PLO had become a semisovereign authority in Jordan, sharing power with the king, indeed, challenging the king's position.

Complicating the situation in the fall of 1970 were the activities of George Habash's group, the Popular Front for the Liberation of Palestine (PFLP), which hijacked several international flights to Dawson Field in the Jordanian desert. In addition to endangering the lives of the civilian passengers, the hijackings provided a dramatic manifestation of the king's limited control over his own territory. Hussein thus decided to move against the PLO, abruptly turning power over to the military, forming a military government, and calling the army into Amman and the cities and refugee camps of the north to suppress it. The ensuing battle pitted Hussein's modern and relatively well-equipped army against a small force of trained commandos and a larger group of hastily and lightly equipped militia— part-time fighters with generally almost no training.[21] Heavy fighting wracked Jordan on September 16 and 17, but by September 26 the battle was over. Syrian tanks, which entered Jordanian territory supposedly to assist the Palestinians, were repulsed, and the PLO was defeated by Jordanian air strikes and ground attacks. The support Syria provided was limited to troop and tank ground assaults; Damascus never supplied the air cover that it had promised, rendering the tanks and troops ineffective. Iraqi support was purely rhetorical; Baghdad partially mobilized its forces but did not intervene. Indeed no Arab state came to the aid of the Palestinians. "Black September" was thus a victory for Jordan, indeed for the Arab state system as such, but a disaster for the Palestinians, as estimates of Palestinian deaths range from 5,000 to 20,000 and the PLO lost the ability to have any independent military, political, or social organization in Jordan.

In the aftermath of the September fighting Nasser attempted to arrange a *modus vivendi* between Jordan and the PLO. While unprepared to compromise Egyptian interests for the sake of the Palestinians and having tacitly acquiesced in Hussein's assault, Nasser was nevertheless unwilling to see the PLO completely destroyed. Thus, he invited Hussein, Arafat, and other Arab leaders to Cairo to work out an agreement to prevent further clashes, and he presided over the signing of an accord on September 27, 1970. The following day Nasser died; in July 1971 Hussein carried out several massacres of Palestinians, the major ones in Jerash and Ajlun, and then totally expelled the PLO from Jordan. The PLO regrouped in Lebanon, where it had secured an arrangement with the Lebanese government in November 1969, known as the "Cairo Agreement," a formal recognition of the PLO's right to an autonomous presence in Lebanon.[22] Subsequently the PLO established a "state within a state" in Lebanon and carried out its guerrilla operations from there—primarily because the Lebanese government was too weak to restrain it. No other Arab state permitted any independent Palestinian military activity from its soil and each took every opportunity to constrain the Palestine national movement when such constraint served its ends.

The years between 1967 and 1973 in the Middle East were characterized by considerable violence and instability that foreshadowed even greater violence in later periods. Israel turned its policy of "massive retaliation" toward Lebanon, leading to the deaths of approximately 880 Lebanese and Palestinian civilians and the wounding of thousands more between mid-1968 and mid-1974.[23] Two major Israeli raids included a February 1972 incursion into Lebanon, which had the stated aim of eliminating the guerrilla bases near Israel's northern border, and a June 1972 operation in which more than seventy civilians were killed or wounded. In July and August 1972 a number of Palestinian leaders in Beirut were killed or seriously injured by letter bombs sent to them by the Israeli intelligence agency, the Mossad. In September during the Olympic games in Munich, Palestinian commandos captured several Israeli athletes and held them hostage in an effort to obtain the release of Palestinians held captive in Israel. The hostage exchange attempt became a nightmare when West German police, after promising the Palestinians safe conduct out of Germany, opened fire at Munich airport; the Palestinians killed the hostages and were themselves either killed or captured. The Munich attack was followed by heavy Israeli ground and air raids into Lebanon, whose government the Israelis held responsible for the Munich affair.

Letter bombs posted to Israeli representatives in various countries were the next round in the cycle of violence; then representatives of the PLO were assassinated by the Mossad in Rome, Stockholm, Paris, and Nicosia. In February 1973 Israel attacked a Palestinian refugee camp in northern Lebanon and shot down a Libyan civilian airliner whose French captain had accidentally strayed over the occupied Sinai during a sandstorm. These two incidents, within twenty-four hours, caused the deaths of 150 people, almost all of them civilians. In mid-April 1973 Israeli commandos raided West Beirut, killing three top PLO leaders and nine Lebanese civilians. The on-going

Israeli violations of Lebanese territory and sovereignty were a major drain on Lebanon's thin governmental legitimacy, though Washington appeared to take no notice of their implications.[24] It is clear, however, that Israel's smashing victory in 1967 and its absolute military superiority thereafter did not usher in an era of peace or stability in the Middle East.

In the aftermath of Nasser's death, Sadat consolidated his power in Egyptian domestic politics, then boldly proclaimed 1971 a "year of decision," though nothing, in fact, was decided. Sometime in mid-1972, however, Syria and Egypt began planning for the October War. In July 1972 Sadat abruptly expelled the Soviet advisors from Egypt. Mahmoud Riad's assessment of the expulsion is telling:

The factors that contributed to this decision were Soviet procrastination on one side and United States extravagance in promises made to Sadat. The Soviets were apprehensive of our resorting to military action, although they were quite convinced that the United States would never move towards complete implementation of Resolution 242. Yet they were anxious to avoid any possibility of a confrontation with the United States in this area. Talks with Nixon in May drove the Soviet Union into the field of international bargaining where issues other than the Middle East were of a more pressing nature to the Soviets. Though there was unanimity over the impossibility of Moscow forging its support to the Arab countries' right to restore their occupied territories, yet delay in helping them accomplish this end, after five years of occupation, represented to Cairo a kind of backing down on the undertaking.[25]

The Soviet expulsion served two major purposes for the Egyptians. It removed an impediment to an Egyptian attack on Israel, since Sadat believed that his Soviet advisors would not permit Egypt to initiate military operations; at the same time, Sadat was hoping to induce a more active role for the United States in the search for a Middle East settlement and to move Egypt into the American sphere of influence.

The United States in the International System: Middle East Regional Linkages and American National Interests

The years from June 1967 to October 1973 saw several significant changes in the international system. Most important were the move away from a tight, bipolar structural arrangement and the shift in American foreign policy from "Idealpolitik" to "Realpolitik." U.S. foreign policy under President Richard Nixon (elected in 1968) and his national security advisor (and also later secretary of state), Henry Kissinger, accepted the legitimacy of national interest and reason of state for all major powers, Communist as well as non-Communist. The Soviet Union was now perceived as a traditional great power, pursuing its interests within the framework of the existing international system. Soviet-American competition was not expected to cease, but the essential mode of foreign policy shifted from "containment" to "détente" and was predicated on the concepts of interdependence and linkage.

For Kissinger interdependence suggested the possibility of mutually beneficial agreements in areas ranging from trade to arms control. The Strategic Arms Limitation Talks (SALT) were one fruitful aspect of this concept, and the SALT I Treaty in 1972 was tangible confirmation of the validity of the administration's assumption concerning the mutuality of certain interests. The linkage concept derived from the belief that various global issues could be linked together in such a manner that progress on one front would be tied to progress on another: it was expected that the interdependence that would result from increasing economic linkages would serve as a constraint on Soviet political and military adventurism around the globe. In effect, for Kissinger, détente was another means to "contain" the Soviet Union. The Soviet concept of détente, however, was more limited to the bilateral U.S.–Soviet relationship: Moscow saw no reason why a relaxation of political tensions and an increase in trade with the United States should eliminate the natural competition between the powers in other areas of the world. Nevertheless, détente did serve to limit to some degree Soviet influence in the Middle East, though other forces contributed to its expansion.

Kissinger's ideas about global linkages were clearly evident in U.S. Middle East policy. For instance, the national security advisor continually urged Nixon to discourage the State Department from going ahead with joint Soviet-American initiatives that called for Israel to give up some of its occupied lands in return for a peace guaranteed by the powers. Kissinger believed that if Israel agreed either to participate in such talks or to exchange land for peace under those auspices, it would appear to be a triumph for Arab radicals and, more important, for the Soviet Union.[26] Thus the overall effect of détente on the Middle East was to freeze the post–June War territorial status quo. On one hand, the Soviets, who were eager for American technology, investment, and trade, were disinclined to press Washington on matters of concern to the Arabs. On the other, under Kissinger's influence, Washington discouraged potential Israeli compromise, considering it a victory for Moscow. In addition, Kissinger was wholly wedded to the idea of Israel as a strategic asset to American interests and sought to reinforce Israel's regional power so that it could better fulfill its functions in the American grand design. The most important aspect of Kissinger's commitment to strengthening Israel's power was massively arming it with the most sophisticated weapons in the American arsenal. However, the Soviet Union responded by arming its clients—principally Syria and Egypt—with the most advanced Soviet weapons. Moreover, as the Arabs saw that Washington had no intention of responding to Arab interests, they looked increasingly to Moscow for assistance. Thus, despite the defeat of Soviet-equipped and -trained Arab troops in 1967, and notwithstanding the inability of the Soviets to influence Israel (and their unwillingness to pressure Washington to do so), the Soviet political, economic, and military presence in the region expanded significantly in the post-1967 period.

In reality U.S. Middle East policy was rent with contradictions during the interwar years. To a considerable extent this reflected the varying sets of perceptions that different American officials had about the Middle East and the internal power rivalries among these individuals within the government. Secretary of State William P. Rogers was officially in charge of Middle East policy; however, Kissinger, who vehemently disagreed with Rogers's approach to the Middle East, managed to undercut the various initiatives undertaken by Rogers and his staff.

Kissinger, as suggested, was primarily concerned about the global implications of the Arab-Israeli conflict. This preoccupation resulted in his viewing Middle Eastern events almost solely through the prism of Soviet-American competition and in minimizing the internal dynamic of the regional conflict. At the same time, cognizant of public dissatisfaction with American involvement in the Vietnam War, Nixon and Kissinger developed the idea that regional surrogates should be built up that could act to further American interests in the absence of a direct U.S. presence. This policy was specifically formulated with respect to Southeast Asia and became known as the Nixon Doctrine; but it had special ramifications in the Middle East, where Iran and Israel were to be the major surrogate powers (to a lesser extent, Saudi Arabia, although Israeli opposition precluded the military development of Riyadh). For a time (until the fall of the shah in 1979) Iran functioned effectively as an American proxy; Washington provided it with enormous quantities of American weapons and Teheran acted to further American interests. Israel was another matter. While it received unlimited military supplies and massive economic support (Iran paid for its weapons with its oil revenues, while the American government either gave, or loaned at extremely favorable repayment terms, Israel the money it needed to acquire weapons), Israel persistently pursued policies that undermined rather than served American interests. Eventually (in 1974-75) Kissinger became aware of this anomaly, but by then the power of the pro-Israeli constituencies in the domestic political process undercut whatever efforts the administration undertook to modify Israel's behavior.

On the other hand, Rogers and most of the officials in the State Department were more sensitive to the indigenous nature of the Arab-Palestinian-Israeli conflict. They worried about the erosion of American influence and about the deterioration of the American position in the Arab world; they were also concerned that trends toward radicalization and polarization among the Arab states, intensified by Israel's new occupation, would damage U.S. interests. Many of these officials believed that this situation, fueled by the continuing Arab-Israeli conflict, would ultimately work to the advantage of the Soviet Union, resulting in the isolation of Israel in a sea of angry, anti-American Arabs supported by Moscow, as well as possibly excluding American influence from the region. Rogers and his colleagues were also anxious about the development of the Palestine national movement. The PLO, as noted, became an increasingly militant and significant regional force in the aftermath of the 1967 war; not even the crushing blow dealt by King Hussein in September 1970 eliminated the insurgent Palestinian organizations. When the PLO regrouped in Lebanon after its expulsion from Jordan, State Department strategists grew even more concerned that the movement would pose a direct threat to American interests in the region, be a force for destabilization, and possibly spark a new Arab-Israeli war. No initiatives were undertaken, however, to deal with the Palestinian issue.

Oil, as always, was a matter of concern. The Organization of Petroleum Exporting Countries (OPEC) was evolving into a force to be reckoned with, although Europe, Japan, and the United States continued to increase their dependence on Middle Eastern oil, oblivious to the implications of the emergence of this new international actor. American dependence on Middle East oil was less than that of its allies, prices remained low, and alternate sources were available; thus Washington's attention focused primarily on continued freedom of access for Japan and Western Europe and on the repatriation of profits by American multinational oil companies with their favorable impact on the U.S. balance of payments.[27] Again, however, officials at State were far more concerned about the implications of OPEC than was Kissinger, who tended not to comprehend the nature of the international petroleum market or the potential power of the cartel.

During the years between 1967 and 1973 the American interest in assuring Israel's security and survival was transformed into a de facto alliance between the two states, predicated on the perception that Israel was a valuable strategic asset to the realization of American interests. The perception was allegedly validated by Israel's powerful military performance in the 1967 war and later its willingness to mobilize in support of the Jordanian regime in 1970. It was also fed by skillful and intensive propaganda disseminated by the Israeli lobby. The result was the institutionalization in conventional wisdom and political orthodoxy of the ideas that Israel could contain Soviet expansionism in the Middle East, protect "moderate" Arab regimes from threats by "radical" forces, and maintain regional stability through its military superiority. These mistaken assessments led the Nixon administration to supply Israel with all the sophisticated weapons it desired and to provide full support for Israel's regional political objectives, without any evaluation regarding the compatibility of Israeli and American interests. These misperceptions also resulted in the United States misreading the signs of impending war in 1973.

With remarkable rapidity Israel's vast military superiority (backed by the powerful new activism of the Israeli lobby on the domestic political scene, especially in Congress) induced Israel to behave with increasing disregard for American views or interests. Indeed as one Middle Eastern scholar observed: "The United States created such a strong military force in Israel that there was little incentive to make those major concessions considered in Washington to be necessary for peace with the Arabs. In addition, the more Israel was armed by the United States, the more dependent the Arab states became on Soviet military and economic aid. In short, Israel's superior military power, and its resulting unwillingness to make the concessions needed for peace, made Israel more of a liability than an asset in preventing the spread of Soviet power and influence in the Middle East."[28]

Israel received not only military but also economic assistance from the United States, and in the years between 1967-73 the actual amounts of both grew enormously. Table 3 is illustrative.

In addition to these official amounts, the General Accounting Office, in a study entitled *United States Economic Assistance for Israel,* listed the following aid:

(1) A $55 million Ashdod-based water desalination project.

(2) $125 million in loan guarantees from 1974 to 1975 for private U.S. financing of mortgages for low-cost housing in Israel.

(3) Export-Import Bank Loans & Overseas Private Investment Corporation investment guarantees.

(4) More than $10 million in grants to the Intergovernmental

TABLE 3. U.S. Assistance to Israel, 1967-75

Year	Total Aid	Economic Loans	Economic Grants	Military Loans	Military Grants	Soviet Jews' Resettlement Funds[a]
1967	13.1	5.5	0.6	7.0		
1968	76.8	51.3	0.5	25.0		
1969	121.7	36.1	0.6	85.0		
1970	71.1	40.1	0.4	30.0		
1971	600.8	55.5	0.3	545.0		
1972	404.2	53.8	50.4	300.0		
1973	467.3	59.4	50.4	307.5		50.0
1974	2,570.7		51.5	982.7	1,500.0	36.5
1975	693.1	8.6	344.5	200.0	100.0	40.0
TOTAL	5,018.8	310.9	499.2	2,482.2	1,600.0	126.5

SOURCE: *The Link,* Dec. 1982, 3.
NOTE: Data are in millions of dollars and do not include loans through the Export-Import bank.
[a] The resettlement funds were a special new grant given to the Israeli government to help in the absorption and settlement of Soviet Jews in Israel. During this period of détente, large numbers of Soviet Jews were permitted to immigrate to Israel.

Committee for European Migration, to help transport refugees to Israel.

(5) U.S. contributions of about $100 million to set up three U.S.–Israeli binational research foundations for industry, science, and agriculture.

(6) $40 million in grants from the American Schools and Hospitals Abroad program to Israeli institutions.

(7) $29 million in debt cancellation, to Israeli institutions.

(8) $4.2 million in excess U.S. government property provided to the United Israel Appeal.

(9) Import privileges to export 2,700 products to the U.S. duty-free if they are of Israeli origin.[29]

American Policies in the Middle East, June 1967 to October 1973

The first important statement of the American post–June War attitude toward the Middle East was made by President Lyndon B. Johnson on June 19, 1967, in a speech at a Department of State foreign policy conference. Johnson committed the United States to an Arab-Israeli peace based on five principles: "(1) Every nation in the area has a fundamental right to live in peace and to have this right respected by its neighbors; (2) justice for the refugees; (3) the right of innocent maritime passage must be preserved for all nations; (4) limits on the wasteful and destructive arms race; and (5) respect for the political independence and territorial integrity of all states in the area."[30] Johnson pointedly avoided a call for return to the status quo ante, as Dwight D. Eisenhower had done in 1956, declaring instead: "A return to the fragile and perilous armistice is not a prescription for peace but for renewed hostilities." This avoidance lent tacit support to the Israeli government's determination to retain the conquered territories. Johnson also called for direct negotiations, implicitly ruling out the possibility of American involvement, as in the post-1956 war period, to secure Israel's withdrawal.[31] Israel was extremely pleased by the president's statement. Israeli scholar Shlomo Slonim commented, "Those points which the president chose to stress, whether of substance such as the need for a real peace or of procedure such as the necessity for direct negotiations fully accorded with Israel's position."[32]

When the U.N. General Assembly convened in the fall of 1967, the United States used the occasion to find ways to develop some momentum toward the achievement of peace based on Johnson's five principles. After much debate about procedure and the offering of several alternative resolutions, a compromise resolution was presented by Great Britain's Lord Caradon. On November 22, 1967, the Security Council adopted Resolution 242, which the framers believed contained the elements for a just and lasting peace for the Middle East. Resolution 242 states:

The Security Council,
Expressing its continuing concern with the grave situation in the Middle East,
Emphasizing the inadmissibility of the acquisition of territory by war and the need to work for a just and lasting peace in which every State in the area can live in security,
Emphasizing further that all Member States in their acceptance of the Charter of the United Nations have undertaken a commitment to act in accordance with Article 2 of the Charter,
   1. Affirms that the fulfillment of Charter principles requires the establishment of a just and lasting peace in the Middle East which should include the application of both the following principles: (i) withdrawal of Israel's armed forces from territories occupied in the recent conflict; (ii) termination of all claims or states of belligerency and respect for, and acknowledgement of, the sovereignty, territorial integrity and political independence of every State in the area and their right to live in peace within secure and recognizable boundaries free from threats or acts of force;
   2. Affirms further the necessity: (a) for guaranteeing freedom of navigation through international waterways in the area; (b) for achieving a just settlement of the refugee problem, (c) for guaranteeing the territorial inviolability and political independence for every State in the area, through measures including the establishment of demilitarized zones;
   3. Requests the Secretary General to designate a Special Representative

to proceed to the Middle East to establish and maintain contacts with the States concerned in order to promote agreement and assist efforts to achieve a peaceful and accepted settlement in accordance with the provisions and principles in this resolution;

4. Requests the Secretary General to report to the Security Council on the progress of the efforts of the Special Representative as soon as possible.[33]

The governments of Egypt and Jordan accepted Resolution 242, Syria rejected it, and Israel neither rejected it outright nor accepted it. Indeed, while the Israeli representative at the United Nations endorsed the resolution, the Israeli government did not formally agree to it and carefully avoided any reference to the resolution until May 1970, when, in the context of the second Rogers Plan (B), Prime Minister Golda Meir finally announced Israel's "acceptance" of Resolution 242.[34]

The interpretation of Resolution 242 and of its role in the effort to achieve a Middle East settlement has been controversial from the outset. Much of the debate on the resolution has centered on the difference between the English and the French texts. The English version refers to "territories" while the French talks of "*the* territories" ("des territoires"). The two versions are equally valid legally, but each side in the dispute has used one or the other to suit its purposes. Israel took the position, supported by the United States, that the English version implied that Israel was not required to withdraw from all of the occupied territory.[35] (By extension, however, Israel committed itself to withdraw from some part of all the occupied areas.)

In the view of its primary architect, Lord Caradon, the resolution meant total withdrawal by Israel from all the occupied territories.[36] In response to a question as to whether the resolution required Israeli withdrawal from "some, but not all the territories," Caradon replied: "Of course not. The text means all and not some of the territories. Proof of this is that the resolution in the preamble emphasizes the inadmissibility of the acquisition of territory by war. This is my language. Mr. Minister, I assure you the text conveys the meaning you want. This English text is taken from the United States draft. . . . Furthermore, the term 'the territories' is in the text of the draft in the four other official languages (French, Russian, Spanish and Chinese)."[37] The Arabs, the French, and most of the rest of the world understood it to mean what Lord Caradon intended.[38] However, it seems fair to say that a certain amount of ambiguity was built into the resolution to assure the support of all the parties—the Palestinians not being considered a "party."

The PLO has consistently rejected Resolution 242 on the basis that it refers merely to the "refugees" and makes no statement about the legitimate right to self-determination of the Palestinian people. Why, the PLO has asked, should it be required to accept a resolution recognizing Israel's right to exist without any comparable quid pro quo? Indeed, by so doing it would virtually relinquish any claim to a state in its native homeland. (The PLO has said, however, that it would accept Resolution 242 in the context of all U.N. resolutions pertaining to the Palestine/Israel question—having in mind particularly Resolutions 181 and 194. The United States has rejected this compromise.) The U.S. demand that the PLO accept Resolution 242 as a precondition for any recognition by or discussions with Washington was a concession Kissinger made to Israel in seeking to persuade it to sign the Sinai II Accord with Egypt in 1975. The American stance, indefensible at the outset, became increasingly anomalous as time went on and Israel negated the resolution in various ways. In 1978 Israeli Prime Minister Menachem Begin explicitly declared that Resolution 242 had no applicability to the West Bank, clearly undermining the American position. In 1981, when Israel annexed the Golan Heights after having legislated the reunification of Jerusalem in 1980, the resolution became completely moot. Nevertheless, the United States has consistently maintained in principle its adherence to Resolution 242 as the basis for a Middle East settlement and as a prerequisite for its talking to the PLO. There is thus not only a verbal dichotomy between the principle and practice of American diplomacy with regard to Resolution 242, but in addition Washington has provided Israel with the financial wherewithal to invalidate the resolution, further undermining its credibility.

During the presidential campaign of 1968 both major candidates, Richard Nixon and Hubert Humphrey, made support for Israel a cornerstone of their strategies, and both went further than President Johnson had in their statements regarding U.S. commitments to Israel's security. Both also competed ardently for the Jewish vote. In a speech to the B'nai B'rith Convention in Washington, D.C., on September 8, 1968, Nixon advocated the sale of supersonic Phantom F-4 jets to provide Israel with technological military superiority.[39] Earlier, in July 1968 Congress had approved an amended version to the Foreign Assistance Act of 1961, which noted the "sense of Congress" that the president should sell supersonic planes to Israel. Thus in October President Johnson, in an effort to garner Jewish support for Humphrey, announced that he had authorized negotiations leading to the sale of the Phantoms, and on December 27, he announced the completion of an agreement to sell Israel fifty Phantom jets. The

Jewish vote, as well as Jewish financial contributions, went over-whelmingly to Humphrey in the election.[40]

Once elected, President Nixon initially signaled the possibility of change in American policy: significantly, this was prior to the advent of Kissinger. Shortly before his inauguration, Nixon sent former Pennsylvania Governor William Scranton on a fact-finding tour of the Middle East. When he returned, Scranton specifically called for the United States to be more "even-handed" in its approach to the Middle East. However, as policy actually evolved, it became apparent that the Department of State was more interested in even-handedness than the administration, which under Kissinger's influence adopted consistently pro-Israeli positions.

By the time of the transition from the Johnson to the Nixon administration, the Middle East was demanding attention. On December 28, 1968, one day after the announcement of the sale of the fifty Phantoms to Israel, Israeli commandos destroyed thirteen civilian airplanes of Lebanon's Middle East Airlines on the ground at Beirut International Airport. According to Israel, the raid was in retaliation for a Palestinian guerrilla attack on one Israeli airliner at Athens a few days earlier. President Nixon addressed the urgency of the situation in his first press conference on January 27, 1969: "I believe we need new initiatives and new leadership on the part of the United States in order to cool off the situation in the Mideast. I consider it a powder keg, very explosive. It needs to be defused. I am open to any suggestions that may cool it off and reduce the possibility of another explosion, because the next explosion in the Mideast, I think could involve very well a confrontation between the nuclear powers, which we want to avoid."[41]

Thus Nixon authorized two sets of parallel talks in the first year of his administration—"Two Power" talks between the United States and the Soviet Union (negotiated by Undersecretary of State for Near Eastern Affairs Joseph Sisco and Soviet ambassador to the United States, Anatoly Dobrynin), and "Four Power" talks among the United States, the Soviet Union, France, and Britain. The primary proposal in both sets of talks centered around Israeli withdrawal from the entire Sinai Peninsula and the Gaza Strip, from most of the Golan Heights, and from the major part of the West Bank.[42] Kissinger, as suggested, did everything possible to discourage the emergence of any concrete initiative from these talks, fearing that any Israeli participation or concession would appear as "appeasement" to the Soviets.[43]

Quite apart from Kissinger's involvement, however, Israel strongly objected to both sets of talks, allegedly because they undercut the principle of direct negotiation and portended an imposed settlement. Israel also objected to the principle on which the talks were based (i.e., land in exchange for peace) despite (or perhaps because of) its direct derivation from Resolution 242. Israel and its American supporters mobilized in opposition to the procedures and proposals put forward by the State Department while Nixon and Kissinger disassociated themselves from the initiatives and even spoke out against them when addressing Jewish audiences.[44] Thus all the efforts undertaken by the State Department to find a solution to the Middle East conflict amounted to naught, though for a time it seemed as if the Two Power talks might prove fruitful.

Sisco and Dobrynin put forward a plan in October 1969 that was in essence a separate Egyptian-Israeli peace. It called for Israeli withdrawal to boundaries agreed on by Egypt and Israel and the partial demilitarization of the Sinai with an Israeli military presence at Sharm el-Sheikh.[45] Israel and Egypt both rejected it, Egypt because it would have left Israel in parts of Egyptian territory, Israel because it had no interest in any withdrawal.[46] Moreover, when Secretary of State Rogers formally transmitted the Sisco-Dobrynin agreement to Moscow, the Russians, too, rejected it, partly because of Egypt's reaction but also because of the rapidly deteriorating military situation along the Suez Canal.

By the summer of 1969 Israel had significantly escalated the War of Attrition. In the words of author Seymour Hersh: "Its air force began flying across the Sinai to bomb and strafe Egyptian forts and artillery emplacements. Air-to-air battles were fought with the Egyptian Air Force, and a dozen Soviet-supplied Egyptian planes were shot down. . . . Israel's Ministerial Defense Committee authorized a series of 'deep penetration' air raids, far inside Egypt; some missions involved the bombing of civilians in the suburbs of Cairo, including the destruction of at least one school. Neither Kissinger nor Nixon made any attempt in late 1969 or early 1970 to halt the Israeli attacks."[47] Thus, instead of pushing Egypt to accept the Sisco-Dobrynin plan, Moscow concluded an arms deal with the Egyptians that exceeded the total amount of arms the Egyptians had procured in the previous twelve years. The arms supplies and the escalating war both contributed to growing Soviet influence in the area, although Israel's responsibility for the increased Soviet presence went unremarked in the United States. On the contrary, the argument was advanced that Israel should receive more American weapons so that it could better contain Soviet expansionism. In any case, as a result of the increasingly dangerous regional situation, and in the face of continuing complaints about his diplomacy from the Israeli Embassy and the American Jewish community, Rogers decided to make his ideas on a Middle East settlement official.[48] On December 9, 1969, he outlined an initiative, subsequently known as the Rogers Plan for the Middle East.[49]

This was actually Rogers Plan A, since a second plan, outlined in the spring of 1970 by the secretary, came to be known as Rogers Plan B. The first is the more well known and controversial. Rogers listed four principles that he considered essential for securing peace in the Middle East: (1) that an agreement among outside powers not be a substitute for agreement among the parties themselves, (2) that a durable peace meet the legitimate concerns of both sides, (3) that the framework for a negotiated settlement be in accordance with the entire text of Resolution 242, and (4) that there not be a protracted period of no-war/no-peace, since recurrent violence and spreading chaos would serve the interests of no nation in or out of the Middle East.[50] After recounting the various obstacles to the achievement of such a peace, Rogers noted that the United States would attempt to overcome these roadblocks through continued pursuit of a "balanced" policy: "Our policy is and will continue to be a balanced one. We have friendly ties with both Arabs and Israelis. To call for Israeli withdrawal as envisaged in the United Nations Resolution without achieving agreement on peace would be partisan toward the Arabs. To call on the Arabs to accept peace without Israeli withdrawal would be partisan toward Israel. Therefore, our policy is to encourage the Arabs to accept a permanent peace based on a binding agreement and to urge the Israelis to withdraw from occupied territory when their territorial integrity is assured as envisaged by the Security Council Resolution."[51]

In addition, Rogers believed that a sense of security on both sides was needed for a lasting peace. To achieve this end, Rogers endorsed the concept of demilitarized zones and related security arrangements to be formulated by the parties themselves. With respect to changes in preexisting boundaries, Rogers said that "such change should not reflect the weight of conquest and should be confined to insubstantial alterations required for mutual security." On the future status of Jerusalem, Rogers emphasized that the United States opposed "unilateral actions by any party to decide the final status of the city" and stated that "Jerusalem should be a unified city within which there would no longer be restrictions on the movement of persons and goods. There should be open access to the unified city for all persons of all faiths and nationalities. Arrangements for the administration of the unified city should take into account the interests of all its inhabitants and of the Jewish, Islamic and Christian communities.

And there should be roles for both Israel and Jordan in the civic, economic and religious life of the city." Rogers avoided mentioning any specifics regarding a resolution of the Palestinian issue, but commented that the United States believed that a "just settlement must take into account the desires and aspirations of the refugees and the legitimate concerns of the governments in the area."[52]

Jordan forthrightly accepted Rogers's proposals, and Egypt indicated a willingness to accept them on the basis of certain clarifications. Nasser was pleased that they called for total Israeli withdrawal from occupied Egyptian territory and constituted a plan for a comprehensive settlement dealing with the concerns of all the states in the region, but he asked for a statement on how the United States proposed to facilitate implementation. The Egyptian president stated that on receiving such clarification, especially with regard to the Syrian and Jordanian fronts, he was prepared to accept the plan.[53] Syria rejected Rogers's proposals as did the Soviet Union. Russia's objection no doubt stemmed from the fact that the plan represented a unilateral American initiative in the Middle East and excluded it. Israel declined to accept the peace proposals, arguing that they took no account of Israel's need for secure boundaries and that advocating a withdrawal to the pre-1967 lines with only minor changes prejudiced Israel's bargaining position. Israel felt that the proposals regarding Jerusalem portended a redivision of sovereignty over the city, which it was determined to resist at all costs, and alleged that the provisions concerning the refugees were a threat to the continuation of Israel's character as a Jewish state.[54]

As ensuing events suggested, Rogers and his advisors at the State Department had seriously underestimated Israel's will and ability to resist an American plan that did not dovetail with its own policy. Rogers also apparently misread the attitude of the White House: Nixon and Kissinger appeared to work in tandem to undercut the secretary of state and distance themselves from any association with the Rogers Plan. For example, on December 17, Nixon asked White House aide Leonard Garment, who served as an occasional intermediary with the Israelis, to give private assurances to Prime Minister Golda Meir that the State Department initiative did not have the president's backing and that he would not seek to implement it.[55] Thus, the convergence of Kissinger's misperceptions with the interests of Israel resulted in the demise of a major peace initiative that sought a resolution to the protracted Middle East conflict—a settlement that would have better served U.S. interests in the region than the status quo.

In early April 1970 Sisco traveled to Cairo and met Egyptian

Foreign Minister Mahmoud Riad. Sisco requested a resumption of U.S.–Egyptian diplomatic relations and asked that Egypt place its confidence in the United States. Riad was not receptive. When Sisco met with Nasser, he asked him: "Why don't you initiate a political and diplomatic dialogue with us, why do you let the Soviet Union speak on your behalf?" Nasser answered him bluntly: "Because we do not trust you, because of your alignment with Israel. Every time you present us with a new project you ask for new concessions."[56]

As noted, by the early summer of 1970 Israel's deep penetration bombing raids over Egypt had resulted in considerably increased Soviet military presence and activity in Egypt. At the same time the isolation of the United States in the Arab world was growing, and anti-American sentiments were mounting throughout the region. These unfavorable regional developments were complicated by intense domestic pro-Israeli pressure on the administration. For example, on June 4, eighty-five Senators, responding to pro-Israeli pressure, delivered a petition to Secretary of State Rogers, demanding that Washington supply Israel with 125 additional fighter aircraft (e.g., Skyhawks and Phantoms). These factors prompted a new diplomatic initiative in June, the Rogers Plan B, in which Rogers proposed that Israel, Egypt, and Jordan restore the cease-fire for at least ninety days, affirm their commitment to Resolution 242 in all its parts, and agree to discussions under the auspices of Ambassador Jarring with the aim of seeking a lasting peace. On July 23, 1970, Nasser announced his country's acceptance of the proposed cease-fire (which led to the breach with the PLO), Jordan concurred on July 26, and on August 4 Prime Minister Golda Meir announced Israel's affirmative decision.

However, Meir hedged in a speech before the Knesset in which she repeatedly stressed that it was only on the basis of "clarifications" received from the United States regarding American "guarantees to maintain the military balance" that Israel agreed to the initiative. She also indicated that she had received two important pledges from Washington: first, the assurance that the United States had obtained an agreement from Egypt and the Soviet Union to refrain "from changing the military *status quo* by emplacing SAMs or other installations in an agreed zone west of the Suez Canal cease-fire line." Second, America agreed to supply Israel with military aid "in all that concerns the maintenance of her security and balance of forces in the region."[57] In other words, Israel's price for agreeing to a cease-fire was an unlimited supply of American weapons.

The terms of the cease-fire (which were only between Egypt and Israel, since Jordan had never formally renounced the 1967 cease-fire) did not bar either country from massing troops or weapons behind their standstill zones. Nor did the agreement include a limit on U.S. arms shipments to Israel or Soviet shipments to Egypt. The assumption was, therefore, that Egypt would continue to receive SAM 2's and SAM 3's from the Soviet Union and that Israel would continue to receive sophisticated electronic equipment, antiaircraft missiles, and Phantoms and Skyhawks from the United States. Neither side, however, was to construct any new military installations in the standstill zones after the cease-fire went into effect. Activities within the zones were to be limited to the maintenance of existing installations at their present sites and positions and to the rotation and supply of forces presently within the zones.[58]

The Egyptians believed that these terms could have several interpretations and, at the same time, were very concerned that a neutral body or party would not supervise their implementation.[59] For these reasons, according to Riad, during the few hours before the cease-fire became effective Egypt completed the preparation of missile bases in the standstill zones to strengthen its missile-defense system. Because it occurred before the hour the agreement went into effect, Riad argues that it did not constitute a violation of the agreement.[60] Israel discovered the reinforced Egyptian missile bases on August 8, two days subsequent to the implementation of the cease-fire, and claimed that Egypt had violated the agreement by undertaking the changes after the truce went into effect.

However, because there had been no American U-2 reconnaissance or photographs at the time the cease-fire commenced, it was not possible to determine if a violation had occurred. Many officials in the State Department suspected that Israel wanted to stall the negotiations with Jarring and thus doubted the veracity of the Israeli reports. On August 19 the administration issued a statement declaring that American intelligence had confirmed that Egypt had violated the cease-fire by making the alterations after the truce had become effective. No explanation was given of how such a determination was possible two weeks after the fact. In any case, prior to this "confirmation"—indeed immediately upon receiving the Israeli charges—President Nixon authorized a $7 million package of arms for Israel to use against the missile sites along the Canal if the cease-fire broke down. This equipment, including anti-SAM electronic devices, strike missiles, and cluster bomb units, was highly sophisticated and had not previously been provided to any foreign country, including the NATO allies.[61] The United States further "compensated" Israel for the alleged Egyptian violation by relieving it of the requirement to participate in the Jarring talks. Since the only interest Israel had in

Rogers's initiative was the cease-fire, the outcome was consonant with its objectives. Israel was able to avoid the Jarring talks, to which it had objected from the outset, and to receive all the new weapons it desired. On September 1 President Nixon agreed to sell Israel at least eighteen additional F-4 Phantom jets, just one day after the Senate approved a military authorization bill that gave the president virtually unlimited authority to provide arms to Israel with U.S. financing. Thus not only would Israel get all of the most sophisticated arms it wanted, but in addition the United States would now provide a significant portion of the new weapons as outright gifts.

September 1970 brought civil war to Jordan, and even though the conflict was essentially an issue between the Palestinians and King Hussein, the administration chose to view the affair in the context of Soviet-American rivalry. Nixon's initial reaction was to "face down" what he described as a Soviet challenge by destroying the fedayeen. On September 8 the president ordered American navy planes from the Sixth Fleet in the Mediterranean to bomb the guerrillas' hideaways.[62] Defense Secretary Melvin Laird delayed, claiming that the weather was too severe for such a strike.[63] Nixon then took other steps to show that the United States was prepared to take military measures, if necessary, to rescue the hostages (in the hijacked planes at Dawson Field) and to bolster Hussein's rule. The president ordered a carrier task force in the Mediterranean to deploy off the coast of Lebanon and placed several army units in Europe on "semi-alert." The Pentagon drew up plans for the deployment of American paratroop units in the Middle East within a short flight of Jordan and leaked the plans to the press. The PFLP responded to the reports of American troop movements by destroying the three remaining aircraft on the ground on September 11 and shifting the hostages to a new hiding place.[64]

In his memoirs Nixon relates that when King Hussein decided on September 15 to attack the PLO, Kissinger said: "It looks like the Soviets are pushing the Syrians and the Syrians are pushing the Palestinians." Nixon, too, apparently believed that the Soviets were the villains, and wrote: "One thing was clear. We could not allow Hussein to be overthrown by a Soviet inspired insurrection."[65] The president's perceptions may well have been influenced by his national security advisor. The distorting lens of Kissinger's reductionist world view could not have been more apparent.

The Israeli government saw in this situation an opportunity to demonstrate its mettle as a geopolitical "strategic asset" to the United States and at the same time to crush the Palestinian movement. Thus Israel readily agreed with the Nixon-Kissinger assessment; indeed,

Israel provided Nixon and Kissinger with the data to make their assessment. It is significant that throughout the Jordanian crisis the president and the national security advisor relied almost exclusively on Israeli intelligence (and reports from King Hussein), despite Israel's special interest in the outcome of the conflict. There was no American satellite coverage and no reports from undercover CIA agents in Syria.[66] The most important misconception entertained by Nixon and Kissinger in this affair concerned the Soviet attitude and behavior toward the major actors, especially Syria and the Palestinians. Evidence that came to light after the crisis from United States and pro-Western Arab intelligence sources demonstrates that contrary to Kissinger's view, the Soviets were urging restraint on all parties in the crisis.[67]

Nixon and Kissinger made a particularly significant decision during the Jordanian affair that had a profound impact on the subsequent development of U.S.–Israeli relations: they urged the Israelis to mobilize and intervene on the side of Jordan if it "became necessary." (For all their posturing, the president and Kissinger were not anxious for an American ground engagement in Jordan.) Israel, however, extracted a high price for its willingness to act as Washington's surrogate: a guarantee of American military intervention in case the Soviet Union or Egypt came to the aid of Syria or the Palestinians, and an explicit promise of support if Israel attacked northern Jordan.[68] Both pledges were clearly dangerous commitments, the latter especially so, given what many in the State Department considered Israeli "designs" on certain portions of northern Jordan. Some officials in Washington believed that the Israeli government coveted the Irbid Heights; if so, Israel could have foreseen in this situation not only an opportunity to seize Irbid but also the possibility of moving on to Damascus.[69] Such an action would have assuredly provoked a Soviet response, to which the United States was then committed to respond.

In the end the Jordanians themselves crushed the Palestinians and repulsed the Syrian tank force. The Israelis performed no function other than the mobilization. The Soviets played no role (save their efforts to urge restraint) and therefore were essentially unaffected by the outcome. The major winner in the situation was Israel, which, having joined in a partnership with the United States in supporting Hussein's regime, further enhanced its image as a strategic asset. Indeed, in the aftermath of Black September, Israel was said not only to be containing the spread of Soviet influence in the Middle East, but also to be providing the critical support that kept conservative, pro-American governments in power. Israel benefited materially as well: on September 17, shortly before the Syrians sent their tanks into Jordan, Nixon authorized $500 million in military aid for Israel and agreed to accelerate the delivery of previously promised F-4 Phantom aircraft. In addition, according to Seymour Hersh, Yitzhak Rabin (in his memoirs) told of a telephone call from Kissinger on September 25, conveying a message of victory and thanks from Nixon to Prime Minister Meir. Kissinger also discussed new and far reaching commitments to Israel and allegedly told Rabin: " 'The president will never forget Israel's role in preventing the deterioration in Jordan and in blocking the attempt to overturn the regime there.' He said 'that the United States is fortunate in having an ally like Israel in the Middle East. These events will be taken into account in all future developments.' Rabin understood the significance of the Kissinger message, as he wrote: 'This was probably the most far reaching statement ever made by a president of the United States on the mutuality of the alliance between the two countries.' "[70]

The major legacy of the Jordanian crisis for U.S. Middle East diplomacy was the elimination of any consideration in the White House of even-handedness as a policy option, despite continuing pronouncements from Secretary of State Rogers. Moreover, since it was believed that the absolute military superiority Washington was providing Israel would serve as a deterrent to any potential Arab consideration of war against Israel, counteract internal instability in the Arab states, and contain Soviet expansionism, the president and his national security advisor essentially forgot the Middle East. The preoccupation with Vietnam undoubtedly contributed to the com-placency with which the administration viewed the region, but, more important, Nixon and Kissinger seem to have adopted the same mistaken perceptions about the Arab world that characterized Israeli attitudes (expressed above by Amnon Kapeliouk).

The period of time between the Jordanian crisis in 1970 and the October 1973 war was unremarkable from a diplomatic standpoint. Jarring was unsuccessful despite his persistent efforts, and Washington saw no reason for diplomatic activity, since it believed the region was stable as a result of Israel's unchallengeable military might. U.S.–Israeli relations grew closer during this period. In the latter part of October 1970 Prime Minister Meir came to the United States in search of more aircraft and arms. The White House gave her assur-ances of assistance of $500 million and a favorable response to her arms request for 1971. In April 1971 the administration announced that the United States was supplying Israel with additional Phantoms and considering a new request for more.[71]

Sadat's expulsion of Soviet advisors in July 1972 should have had a resounding effect in Washington, but Nixon virtually ignored the Egyptian president's momentous decision. He did send Sadat several secret messages through intelligence channels acknowledging the expulsion as "important" and pledging that his administration would concentrate on the Middle East as soon as the Vietnam negotiations and the presidential elections were concluded.[72] While the administration's concern with Vietnam and its potential for damage in the up-coming elections made an opening to Egypt politically untimely, it is also undoubtedly true that Nixon did not want to antagonize pro-Israeli groups close to an election, as any overt communication with Egypt would surely have done. Nevertheless to publicly disregard such a dramatic move seems a striking diplomatic blunder.

Kissinger established several parallel diplomatic tracks or channels of diplomacy with Egypt, although his motivations in undertaking these initiatives were not primarily directed toward finding a just resolution of the Arab-Israeli conflict. One channel involved a formal State Department track allegedly aiming at an interim disengagement along the Suez Canal; a second centered on a secret relationship between Kissinger and Egypt's national security advisor, Hafez Ismail, in which Kissinger agreed to consider Egyptian proposals for a solution to the Arab-Israeli problem; and a third channel was established between Kissinger and Dobrynin to discuss the possibility of joint Soviet-American approaches in the Middle East.[73] The latter tract seems particularly disingenuous, given Kissinger's determination to exclude the Soviets from participation in any Middle East settlement. Indeed, Kissinger writes of his own chicanery: "To provide a semblance of coherence, I sought to delay any new State Department initiatives in the second term and stall Soviet overtures until I could determine in the meeting with Hafez Ismail what the Egyptians had in mind. This was no easy matter since I was the only person aware of all three tracks, and the State Department was being stonewalled."[74]

In the end the machinations of Kissinger resulted in further antagonizing Egypt. In February 1973 Ismail met secretly with Kissinger on three occasions. According to journalist Edward Sheehan, Ismail was distressed that Kissinger perceived the parameters of the problem to be limited to sovereignty and security (i.e., a separate, bilateral Israeli-Egyptian peace) and that Kissinger insisted on delaying discussions until after the Israeli elections in October. Nevertheless, Ismail advised Sadat that at least the United States "now seemed serious" about promoting negotiations.[75] However, Riad relates that Kissinger's specific proposal to Ismail—in essence that a final agreement between Egypt and Israel would include the recognition of Egyptian sovereignty over Sinai on condition that Israel maintained surveillance posts in Sinai for long periods—was categorically rejected by both Ismail and Sadat.[76]

In Paris, en route home from one of his secret meetings with Kissinger, Ismail read a *New York Times* report stating that Nixon had decided to furnish Israel with thirty-six new Skyhawks and forty-eight Phantoms. Kissinger assured Sadat, through the secret channel, that the report was false and that the Israeli request was still "under study." The report, however, was only premature: shortly thereafter Nixon affirmed his intention to send Israel the planes. Ismail and Sadat felt deceived and in early April Sadat told Arnaud de Borchgrave of *Newsweek:* "If we don't take things into our own hands, there will be no movement. . . . Every door I have opened has been slammed in my face by Israel—with American blessings. . . . The situation is hopeless. . . . The time has come for a shock. . . . The Americans have left us no other way out. . . . Everything is now being mobilized for resumption of the battle—which is now inevitable."[77] The road toward war was clearly widening.

In February 1973 Kissinger had an important meeting with King Hussein of Jordan. Kissinger wrote: "Hussein, alone among the Arab leaders, at that time was prepared to be specific about peace terms. . . . Israel's fundamental demand for direct negotiations was, in fact, granted by Hussein."[78] This, of course, was not the first time Hussein had made such an offer, but Kissinger's comments are significant:

He gave me a paper that spelled out the elements he had described to Nixon and me a few weeks earlier. Jordan would negotiate directly with Israel about the West Bank. There would be some border changes provided the Gaza Strip was given in return. If Jordanian sovereignty was restored, there could be Israeli military outposts along the Jordan River or even Israeli settlements provided they were isolated enclaves on Jordanian territory: he could not agree to the annexation of the Jordan valley by Israel. Wryly the King said that all these proposals had already been made directly to Israel and had been rejected. . . . On March 1 she [Golda Meir] proclaimed that "we never had it so good" and insisted that a stalemate was safe because the Arabs had no military option.[79]

Thus the real intentions of Israel with regard to the West Bank were again made abundantly clear: even in the face of a Jordanian proposal for direct negotiations, a full peace, recognition, and territorial changes to meet Israeli security requirements, Israel refused negotiations with Jordan.

Why the administration went along with Israeli rejection to such an extent is indeed puzzling. Kissinger's concern with international linkages and Soviet opportunities does not explain this: indeed, a Washington-brokered Jordanian-Israeli peace could have given the

United States an advantage in the regional/global chess game. Such a settlement would have also served a number of U.S. Middle Eastern interests. Moreover, Jordan was a loyal American client, and Washington should certainly have given some consideration to the interests of its Arab ally (although perhaps Jordan's extreme loyalty led Kissinger to believe he could cavalierly disregard Amman's interests without negative effect). It is also clear that a Jordanian-Israeli settlement would have served Israel's long-term interests better than the status quo; thus, even if the Israelis were incapable of making rational decisions to maximize their future security, it might have been expected that Washington would have provided some guidance. Is it possible that Kissinger considered Israel so valuable to American interests that he was willing to permit it to dictate *any* regional condition regardless of how unreasonable? Or were Nixon and Kissinger so concerned about offending the sensibilities of the domestic pro-Israeli establishment that they dared not disagree with any Israeli government position? The only valid reason for Kissinger to have ignored the Jordanian initiative would have been if he was seriously considering the Palestinian issue and planning to seek a comprehensive solution that included legitimate Palestinian interests, e.g., self-determination in an independent state of their own. Of course, Kissinger *should* have been thinking along these lines, for only with such a settlement will the Arab-Palestinian-Israeli conflict finally be resolved, American interests maximized, and Israel's security protected. But there is nothing in either Kissinger's subsequent behavior or his own writings to suggest that he gave any thought to a genuine resolution of the Palestinian question. The answer to why Kissinger did not press Israel to respond to King Hussein's repeated initiatives remains illusive; the consequences, however, are apparent for all to see.

By 1973 some officials in the United States were beginning to become aware of the possibility of an energy crisis, although Kissinger was not among them, and no new policies reflected the potential problems such a crisis would bring. Nevertheless, signs of impending difficulties could be observed: the price of oil had been rising rapidly since 1971, American production was stagnating, the capacity of American refineries was insufficient to meet domestic demand, and many experts considered shortages of gasoline and fuel possible by the end of 1973.[80] Moreover, in mid-April 1973 Saudi oil minister Sheikh Ahmad Zaki Yamani meeting with Secretary of State Rogers and other U.S. officials, specifically linked the output of Saudi oil for the United States with the question of a satisfactory settlement of the Arab-Palestinian-Israeli conflict.[81]

By the autumn of 1973 the Watergate scandal was seriously threatening the Nixon presidency. Kissinger became secretary of state on September 25 while retaining the post of national security advisor. Less than two weeks later the October War erupted.

From War to Cease-Fire

Both the American and Israeli governments were taken by complete surprise at the outbreak of hostilities on October 6, 1973. Both countries possessed information on Egyptian and Syrian military buildups but had failed to evaluate and interpret that intelligence adequately. The failure of the Israelis can be attributed in large measure to their overall attitude of extreme self-confidence in the post-1967 years. Yitzhak Rabin, chief of staff in 1967, a reserve general at the time of the October War, and subsequently prime minister, reflected this attitude in a statement made on July 13, 1973:

Our present defense lines give us a decisive advantage in the Arab-Israeli balance of strength. There is no need to mobilize our forces whenever we hear Arab threats, or when the enemy concentrates his forces along the cease-fire lines. Before the Six Day War, any movement of Egyptian forces into Sinai would compel Israel to mobilize on a large scale. Today there is no need for such mobilization, so long as Israel's defense line extends along the Suez Canal. We are still living within a widening gap of military power in Israel's favor. The Arabs have little capacity for coordinating their military and political action. To this day, they have not been able to make oil an effective political factor in their struggle against Israel. Renewal of hostilities is always a possibility, but Israel's military strength is sufficient to prevent the other side from gaining any military objective.[82]

Chaim Herzog, former head of Israeli military intelligence, provided further insight into Israel's failure to evaluate the significance of developments on the Syrian and Egyptian fronts: "The dogmatic manner in which a concept [that the Arab armies could not and would not go to war] was adhered to, influenced all concerned."[83]

America's inclination to rely on Israeli intelligence and analysis partially accounts for its failure. In addition, Kissinger and other officials shared Israel's attitudes concerning the ineffectiveness of the Arabs and their unwillingness to challenge the obvious military superiority of Israel.

After Israeli officials determined conclusively, about six hours prior to the outbreak of the war, that the Egyptians and Syrians were going to attack, they decided against a preemptive strike. Prime Minister Golda Meir and Defense Minister Moshe Dayan advocated this course of action for two reasons: (1) they felt that preemptive action might hurt Israel's support in Washington; and (2) more significant, they did not consider the Arab threat serious enough to warrant a preemptive strike.[84] It is important to stress that the initial Israeli assessments—which persisted for four to five days into the fighting—were that Israel would achieve another swift, decisive defeat over the Arabs. Israeli officials expected this war to be as easy as the June 1967 one had been; they were supremely confident of their military capability vis-à-vis the Arabs. Moreover, they communicated their strategic calculations and their confidence to Washington. Since Kissinger's entire Middle East policy was based on his faith in the invincibility and military superiority of Israel, he had no reason to doubt the Israeli assessments. If independent American intelligence sources presented any other evaluations, they are not part of the official record of the war; and moreover, if they were available, Kissinger and his principal advisors—particularly General Alexander Haig—ignored them.

It is also important to note at the outset that it was Kissinger, virtually by himself, who made policy throughout the October crisis. He did so not only as a result of his institutional positions but also because President Nixon was deeply preoccupied with the Watergate scandal.[85] (During the October War the following Watergate-related events occurred: Spiro Agnew resigned as vice-president, Gerald Ford was chosen to succeed him, the U.S. Court of Appeals upheld Judge John Sirica's order that the White House tapes had to be surrendered, the "Saturday Night Massacre" [Nixon's firing of the first Watergate special prosecutor and the resignation of Attorney General Elliot Richardson and his assistant] took place, and forty-four Watergate-related bills were introduced in the Congress, including twenty-two that called for an impeachment investigation.[86])

Kissinger outlined America's contradictory concerns at the outset of the war: (1) assuring the survival and security of Israel; (2) maintaining relations with moderate Arab countries, such as Jordan and Saudi Arabia; (3) preventing Europe and Japan from pursuing a different course than that of the United States; and (4) preserving U.S.–Soviet détente and avoiding a confrontation with the Soviets.[87] While Kissinger does not say explicitly, the oil-energy problem must have been of some concern (at least it should have been) as well as the credibility of the American presidency in the wake of Watergate. Nevertheless, despite all of the obvious potential problems, Kissinger was firmly convinced that "we were in a good position to dominate events,"[88] though he discovered that his control was not as absolute as he had imagined. The most striking aspect of American policy during the October War is the extraordinary degree of support Washington provided Israel, including diplomatic and economic measures and military resupply. Indeed, the United States jeopardized—in fact, damaged—its relations with its NATO allies, Japan, the Soviet Union, OPEC, and the Arab world to stand "four square" behind the Jewish state, in a situation that resulted from Israel's policies of territorial expansion, militarism, and refusal to participate in a regional diplomatic settlement.

Kissinger's initial decision was to direct the commander of the Sixth Fleet to move four ships—the aircraft carrier *Independence* and three destroyers—from Athens to Crete, 500 miles from the coast of Israel, as a signal to the Soviets not to intervene and of U.S. resolve to support Israel. Kissinger then ordered the U.S. delegation at the United Nations to pursue a "diplomatic maneuver" with the Soviets in the Security Council, involving "joint action" between Moscow and Washington. The secretary of state considered such a maneuver important for several reasons: (1) to keep the Soviets from introducing independent proposals that would be harmful to Israel; (2) to drive a wedge between Moscow and the Arabs; and (3) to delay a call for a cease-fire.[89] Because of the initial Israeli and American view—that Israel would quickly regain the initiative and win a swift and decisive military victory—Kissinger wanted to evade any appeal for an early cease-fire in order to give the Israelis time to reverse the Arab thrust. In Kissinger's words: "We wanted to avoid this [a cease-fire call] while the attacking side was gaining territory, because it would reinforce the tendency to use the United Nations to ratify the gains of surprise attack."[90] The Soviets procrastinated in answering the request for joint action and thus played into the "buying-time" scheme perfectly. Simultaneously, Kissinger instructed the American delegation to oppose a General Assembly debate because of the allegedly pro-Arab sentiment among the majority of the world's nations.

Significantly, on the second day of the war, Egypt communicated with Washington and indicated that its military purpose was limited: the objective of the war was to demonstrate to Israel that a defense line along the Suez Canal did not represent security; Israel's security could be based only on mutual respect with its Arab neighbors and withdrawal from Arab territory.[91] Egypt's message reinforced American and Israeli calculations of the limited threat to Israel that the hostilities posed. (The message was a further indication, in addition to the expulsion of the Soviet advisors, of Egypt's strong desire to move firmly and fully into the American sphere.)

On the second day of the war, October 7, the Israelis informed the Americans that they were confident of an early and definitive success.[92] This evaluation, which was shared independently by Kissinger and his staff and by every other major political and military analyst in the government, leads to the issue of military resupply. (By the end of the first day the Israelis had made two separate requests—one for hardware and one for specialized equipment.) Since it was expected that this war would last no longer than the June War, no senior American official believed that a significant arms resupply could reach Israel before the war would end. Moreover, there were two important political calculations from the American perspective. (1) A U.S. resupply might spur the Soviets to similar action, thereby escalating and prolonging the hostilities and risking a potential U.S.–Soviet confrontation. (2) A major resupply in the existing situation (in which the Israelis had all the equipment they needed and expected an early victory) would negate any attempt by the United States to portray itself as impartial. Kissinger expected from the outset (particularly given Sadat's obvious interest in an American-brokered peace with Israel) to use the conditions created by this new war as an opportunity to initiate a peace process between Israel and the Arab states, or at least with Egypt. Thus he was concerned about not unnecessarily antagonizing the Arabs with a resupply to Israel when Israel did not need it.

At the same time, however, Kissinger was concerned, as he discusses in his memoirs, about assuaging the sensitive Israeli psyche, and he believed that it was important for "psychological" reasons to meet Israel's demands for weapons so that the Israelis would not feel they were "standing alone" in their hour of crisis. Kissinger also believed that by meeting the Israeli demands for resupply it would then "affect and perhaps moderate her territorial claims in the negotiations" expected at the conclusion of the war.[93] This seems a highly questionable assumption, considering that the absolute military superiority the United States had provided Israel from 1967 through 1973 had not moderated its negotiating position in the interwar period but rather had hardened it. In fact, Israel's post-1973 negotiating stance was not at all affected by the massive aid the United States gave. Nevertheless, Kissinger continued to subscribe to this thesis and proceeded to oversee a secret resupply of weapons to Israel.

On October 7 Kissinger instructed Secretary of Defense James Schlesinger to make arrangements for ammunition and other high-technology equipment, especially Sidewinder missiles, to be picked up at a naval base in Virginia by Israeli El Al commercial planes that had had their markings painted out. On October 8 the first El Al planes arrived at the Oceana Naval Air Station and took eighty Sidewinder missiles.[94] This secret resupply remained in continuous operation throughout the war. On October 9 President Nixon publicly committed the American government to providing all the armaments the Israelis requested (which in the end included aircraft, tanks, antitank munitions, antitank weapons, laser guided bombs, and "smart" bombs). Nixon also promised that "if it should go very badly and there is an emergency, we will get the tanks in even if we have to do it with American planes."[95]

In addition, when it became apparent that the seven jets of the El Al fleet were insufficient to pick up all the equipment the Israelis wanted, the administration granted Israel permission to employ private American air charter companies to ferry equipment to Israel. The use of air charters was devised as part of the effort to maintain the secrecy of the resupply, but it turned out to be unworkable, as no charter company was eager either to court an Arab boycott or to risk its planes in a war zone. The Defense Department could have brought pressure on the charter companies (which rely on Pentagon business) but felt no urgency, as its calculations indicated that Israel had ample stocks for two weeks, far longer than any projection of military operations. The Department of Transportation apparently wanted to stay out of the military confrontation. Thus there were some bureaucratic delays in meeting the Israeli demands, but, as Kissinger notes, the two-day delay (between the efforts to arrange for private air charters and the commencement of the official airlift) did not make any substantial difference in the military calculation: "Even had the military airlift started immediately, it could not have influenced Israeli military operations prior to the launching of the first cease-fire initiative of October 12-13 which aborted."[96]

By October 13 (seven days after the outbreak of hostilities) a massive military airlift of equipment to Israel was underway. From October 14 to 25, the resupply effort delivered approximately 11,000 tons of equipment: forty F-4 Phantoms, thirty-six A-4 Skyhawks, twelve C-130 transports, and twenty tanks. From October 26 until the airlift ended on November 15, another 11,000 tons of equipment were delivered. In all, 147 sorties were flown by C-5's with 10,800 tons of equipment aboard, and 431 sorties were flown by C-141's with 11,500 tons. During the same period El Al aircraft carried about 11,000 tons of military supplies to Israel, in over 200 sorties. By November 15 American transport ships were beginning to reach Israel with more supplies.[97] Moreover, according to James H. Noyes, the deputy assistant secretary of defense for international security affairs, the United States "had to disarm some of our active units and ships in order to respond to the continuous Israeli requests for more arms and spare parts."[98]

On October 19 the American Congress passed emergency legislation providing Israel $2.2 billion to pay for the new weapons. This financial aid was indeed a watershed in U.S. support for Israel, both quantitatively and qualitatively. Moreover, the dollar amount appears to be unrelated to calculations of weapons cost. The Pentagon had considered $850 million adequate to cover the cost of resupplying Israel. Spokesmen for the administration were unable to tell Congress exactly how $1 billion of the total $2.2 billion would be used, though Congress, in its zeal to demonstrate support for Israel, was apparently not disturbed by this lack of information.[99] Moreover $1.5 billion of the total $2.2 billion was to be an outright grant, entailing no repayment. Kissinger is said to have argued for even more—at least $3 billion and all in outright grants.[100]

The important question is "why" the shift from a secret resupply to a massive public airlift.

Almost all military analysts agree that the American airlift had little effect on Israeli military strategy and tactics or on the outcome of the war. One Defense Department official involved in all phases of the 1973 war told me: "The Israelis didn't need the airlift of arms—it was a psychological and morale booster. In reality they could have mopped up the operation without any of our weapons." Another official in the State Department's Bureau of Intelligence and Research commented: "The Israelis themselves said that they didn't really need the American arms to win the war against the Egyptians and Syrians—in December, at U.C.L.A.—all three top generals agreed."[101] William Quandt, a Middle East scholar and former State Department official, also arrives at the same assessment: "From interviews with top Israeli officials I have concluded that the impact of the airlift on strategic decisions was minimal."[102] The point remains a matter of some dispute, however. The official Israeli position is that Israel was in dire need of a resupply. Others maintain that it was this highly sophisticated equipment from the American airlift that allowed the Israelis to mount their massive counteroffensive.[103] The absolute degree of Israeli need is probably not objectively determinable, at least not by me. However, assuming that Israel could have achieved a military victory without the airlift, the question again becomes why?

There are several possible explanations. By October 12 it was apparent that the war would not be as much of a pushover for the Israelis as the 1967 one had been. Israel had sustained heavy losses in men, and several of its battlefield tactics had not proven successful. Israel's survival certainly was not in jeopardy, but the overweening self-confidence of the prewar period and the early days of the war had given way to what might fairly be described as hysteria. Undoubtedly, the Holocaust syndrome was a factor: if Israel could not totally defeat the Arabs in a short, sharp, and decisive victory "the end" was near. That sense of panic was then communicated, literally hourly, to Washington. Meir cabled Nixon personally on October 12 and, according to Nadav Safran, may have implicitly threatened to resort to the use of Israel's nuclear option in the face of the "threat to Israel's existence."[104] The administration would certainly have taken such a threat seriously and would have understood the dire consequences for the Middle East and for international peace in general. The airlift may thus have been a way of calming the Israelis and restraining their most dangerous potential.

Kissinger was also concerned about domestic politics. With Nixon mired in Watergate, it would not help the president's situation for the pro-Israeli lobby to accuse Nixon of abandoning Israel. But Israeli Ambassador Simcha Dinitz was threatening to do just that; he repeatedly told Kissinger he would "go public" and "unleash his shock troops"[105] if the administration did not respond immediately to Israel's demands. Kissinger did not require prompting to know that the lobby would not hesitate to pressure Congress and take its case to the American people through the media. The spearhead of the lobby was the American Israel Public Affairs Committee (AIPAC), and by 1973 it was indeed a force to be reckoned with.[106]

Kissinger also apparently believed that such an overwhelming demonstration of American support would make Israel more forthcoming in the postwar diplomatic process. Indeed Kissinger states that this was one reason for the airlift.[107] But this reasoning would not seem to be predicated on any rational assessment. In fact, Kissinger later admitted its futility: "When I ask [Prime Minister] Rabin to make concessions, he says he can't because Israel is too weak. So I give him arms, and he says he doesn't need to make concessions because Israel is strong."[108]

Finally, the Soviets had initiated an airlift to Syria on October 9, though Kissinger himself characterized it as "moderate" and of no serious threat to Israel.[109] Nevertheless, Kissinger's ever-present world view of Soviet-American competition may have impelled him to "show the Soviets" that the United States would provide greater quantitative and qualitative support to its client than the Soviets to theirs. Indeed, despite the limited nature of the Soviet resupply to Syria (Moscow provided none to Egypt), Edward Sheehan argues that "the Soviet airlift provoked Kissinger to . . . release immense quantities of arms to Israel. He was resolved . . . to teach the Russians a hard lesson. For now . . . this was a test of wills between Washington and the Kremlin."[110]

Whatever the motivation, the resupply had profound consequences, reverberating far beyond the Middle East. Washington's
Western European allies were extremely distressed. No European
government was prepared to ignore the fact that on October 9 the
Kuwaiti Council of Ministers had announced that it was organizing
a meeting of Arab oil producers to discuss the role of oil in the
conflict. By the next day Egyptian and Saudi Arabian officials were
publicly discussing ways in which the "oil weapon" might be used.
At that time Western Europe obtained over 70 percent of its oil from
the Arab states. These factors led to prohibition of U.S. overflights
of Europe or landing rights for its airlift to Israel and to serious strains
between America and its NATO allies. Thus, the United States had
to channel its airlift through the base it leased from Portugal at Lajes
in the Azores, not the optimum route. (For permission to use its
facilities, Portugal demanded Washington's help in staving off U.N.
pressure to force changes in Portugal's colonialist African policies.[111])
Within a week after the start of the resupply, the Saudis denounced
the airlift and the $2.2 billion in aid granted by Congress. Led by
Riyadh, OPEC imposed an oil embargo on the West, coupled with
a price hike for what oil was sold, that threw the Western world into
economic turmoil.

Paradoxically the official Israeli view (and that of Israel's American
supporters) of the issue of resupply is quite negative. The quantities
of weapons that were shipped were considered insufficient, their
arrival was deemed "tardy," and the administration was accused of
manipulating the provision of weapons to serve American interests
in the Arab world while Israel faced imminent destruction. Even in
the United States, common wisdom holds that Kissinger "brought
Israel to the brink of annihilation." However, contradicting this popular view, Israeli General Herzog writes: "In many ways the Israeli
officers and troops were fighting for more than the existence and
freedom of Israel alone" (i.e., Israel was defending the free world
from the Soviet menace). Herzog notes that "only the United States
appreciated the significance of Israel's struggle," and he acknowledges
"the courageous and unequivocal American stand in favor of Israel."[112] One does not have to accept Herzog's argument about Israel's
role in the global crusade against Soviet expansionism to appreciate
his recognition of America's absolute support for the Jewish state in
1973.

The issue of a cease-fire is second only to that of military aid in
an analysis of American support for Israel during this war. The Israelis
themselves were not always clear about whether they wanted a cease-
fire or not. However, until after the joint U.S.–Soviet call for a simple

cease-fire in place (with Israel positioned deep inside Egyptian territory on the west bank of the Suez Canal) on October 22, the United States maneuvered in every possible way to accommodate Israel's position on a cease-fire. The initial American view with regard to a cease-fire was to delay it until Israel could reverse the early Egyptian gains. In the end, when Israel held a decisive upper hand militarily, Kissinger insisted on a cease-fire rather than allowing Israel to totally destroy the Egyptian Third Army, as it wanted. For this action, many Israelis and their American friends have never forgiven him. Nevertheless, Kissinger permitted Israel extraordinary latitude in pursuing the Egyptians after a formal cease-fire was to have been implemented.

Israel's policy on the issue of a cease-fire underwent several changes from the beginning of the war. At the outset Israel demanded that there be no cease-fire until there was a return to the status quo ante bellum.[113] Kissinger was in complete agreement and maneuvered the Soviets and the United Nations to delay any vote on a cease-fire. As he explained, "We had to delay the diplomacy until there was a change on the war front."[114] Quandt and others argue that on October 11 and 12 the United States began to discuss with Israel the idea of a cease-fire in place. According to Quandt, Kissinger asked the British to introduce a cease-fire resolution in the hope that Egypt would accept, since it would not involve great power "imposition." Egypt (and the Soviet Union) rejected the idea. But according to this version, while the Israelis still opposed a cease-fire in place, they agreed "in principle" to the idea. However, since Egypt objected, the British refused to introduce the resolution and Israel asked the United States *not* to introduce it.[115] Kissinger's version is somewhat at variance with this account. Kissinger states that the Israelis approached him on October 12 asking that the United Nations pass a standstill cease-fire resolution, and he then requested the British to introduce such a resolution. When the British declined because of the Egyptian refusal to go along, Kissinger claims that Meir asked him to have the United States introduce the resolution, but that he refused.[116] According to Kissinger, he was certain that the Israelis could turn the situation around on the Egyptian front (they already had on the Syrian), and he did not want the Soviets to have even the slightest intimation of American/Israeli "capitulation." Indeed, Kissinger states that "Israel was, if anything, too eager to proceed [with a cease-fire]."[117] In any case, the first cease-fire effort aborted. Kissinger's various machinations are best expressed in his own words:

That morning [October 11] Israel's strategy also became clear. Israel was sweeping across the prewar lines on the Syrian front and carrying the air war deep into Syria. Defense Minister Moshe Dayan was quoted . . . as saying that the Israeli army was heading for Damascus. By the end of the day, Israel occupied a salient on the Golan Heights eleven kilometers deep and twelve kilometers wide, beyond the prewar lines. Forward Israeli positions were only thirty-five kilometers (or twenty-five miles) from Damascus. The Israeli gain accorded with our preferred strategy if only the Israelis had kept quiet about it. After all we had been stalling the Soviets for over 24 hours on a cease-fire in place—a position we could hardly maintain if Israel announced that it was advancing on the capital of a Soviet ally. . . . But, I continued to stall with Dobrynin, this time using the excuse that we needed to consult with Israel and other parties before a meaningful cease-fire proposal could be put forward.[118]

If, however, the Israelis were prepared to accept a cease-fire on October 12, by October 17 they definitely were not (although Prime Minister Meir agreed in principle to the idea), for the tide of battle on the Egyptian front had now also turned decisively in their favor. Indeed, early on October 16 the first paratroopers landed on the west bank of the Suez Canal. Moreover, Meir objected to the suggestion that the cease-fire be linked to Resolution 242; instead, she insisted that a cease-fire be tied to direct negotiations.[119]

On October 20 Kissinger departed secretly to Moscow at the invitation of the Soviet Union to work out cease-fire arrangements. On Kissinger's arrival, the Soviets immediately dropped all their previous demands regarding a cease-fire (undoubtedly because of the severe setbacks sustained by Syria and Egypt) and agreed to go along with the American-Israeli position, including: (1) a cease-fire in place, (2) no Israeli withdrawal to any previous lines, including no call for an implementation of Resolution 242, and (3) immediate negotiations between the parties concerned under appropriate auspices, i.e., the cease-fire would lead to direct negotiations. In addition, both sides agreed that they would serve as co-chairmen of an eventual peace conference and that prisoners should be immediately exchanged by the parties after the cease-fire. (The haste with which the Soviets agreed to the American-Israeli stance made it very difficult for Kissinger to stall for time in order to give the Israelis additional time to push the Egyptians harder.) The text of this American-Soviet agreement became United Nations Resolution 338, which was introduced in the Security Council on October 22. The resolution was adopted unanimously and was to go into effect within twelve hours.

While Kissinger was in Moscow, he received a special message from President Nixon stating that the United States and the Soviet Union should use the end of the war to facilitate a comprehensive peace in the Middle East. "The current Israeli successes at Suez must not deflect us from going all out to achieve a just settlement now," Nixon declared. "We would serve even Israel's best interests if we now used 'whatever pressures may be required in order to gain acceptance of a settlement which is reasonable and which we can ask the Soviets to press on the Arabs.' " Nixon concluded by saying: "United States political considerations [i.e., domestic pro-Israeli pressure] will have absolutely no, repeat no, influence on our decisions in this regard. I want you to know that I am prepared to pressure the Israelis to the extent required, regardless of the domestic political consequences."[120] Thus there existed an extraordinary situation: an American president looking beyond domestic politics, considering the spectrum of American national interests, possessing a clarity of vision with regard to Israel's long-term security interests, and prepared to act on these perceptions; yet Nixon was so crippled by Watergate that his secretary of state was able to treat the message as if he had never seen it and proceed with his own plan. The last thing Kissinger ever envisaged was a comprehensive settlement imposed by the great powers. His desire to check Soviet influence in the Middle East precluded his working with the Soviets in any meaningful sense to obtain an overall agreement. Moreover, his desire to maintain Israel as the dominant regional power, as well as his sensitivity to Israel's interests, precluded even the slightest consideration of "pressuring" Israel into a just settlement. Kissinger simply ignored the president's message.

Despite the fact that the cease-fire agreement favored Israel in every respect, the Israelis were shocked and furious at the joint accord arranged by Kissinger in Moscow. They were particularly outraged that Kissinger had not consulted with them before going to Moscow and claimed that this joint cease-fire call portended future great power solutions that would be imposed on them.[121] They were also unhappy about the timing of the agreement; Meir wrote: "We would have liked the call for a cease-fire to have been postponed for a few more days so that the defeat of the Egyptian and Syrian armies would be even more conclusive."[122]

Kissinger had wired Israel from Moscow, informing government officials of the impending cease-fire call. President Nixon sent Prime Minister Meir a note from Washington urging that the Israeli government make an immediate announcement consenting to the joint agreement.[123] Meir, however, was so enraged over the Moscow "thing" that she demanded that Kissinger come to Israel before returning to Washington; and to assure his appearance, the prime minister indicated that Israel's acceptance of Resolution 338 would be dependent on Kissinger's appearance in Israel.[124] The visit apparently was not easy, and in his great desire to placate the Israelis, Kissinger, by his own admission, indicated that it would be acceptable for Israel to proceed with operations *after* the cease-fire: "I also had a sinking feeling" [after the massive Israeli violations of the cease-fire became known] "that I might have emboldened them. In Israel, to gain their support, I had indicated that I would understand if there was a few hours 'slippage' in the cease-fire deadline."[125]

The "few hours slippage" that Kissinger encouraged amounted to a major Israeli offensive, undertaken after the cease-fire went into effect and lasting some six days. During that time thousands of Israeli troops and hundreds of tanks (emblazoned with the label "Cairo Express") poured across the Suez Canal, cut the main roads from Cairo to Suez, and tightened a huge ring around the Egyptian Third Army, which was trapped on the east side of the Canal.[126] By the end of the operation an Israeli division was on the outskirts of Ismailia threatening its links to Cairo; two divisions had sealed off the Third Army; Israeli forces held a corridor on the west bank of the Canal, with three bridges across it; and Israel occupied an area of 1,600 square kilometers inside Egypt, down to the Port of Adabiyah on the Gulf of Suez.[127] During this massive, illegal offensive the Israelis deliberately lied to Washington, telling Kissinger that the Egyptians had mounted a major attack and that Israel was merely defending itself.[128] Kissinger voiced no public criticism of Israel, despite the fact that in violating a cease-fire arranged by the United States, Israel undermined American credibility with the Arab world (especially Egypt) and precipitated a crisis between Washington and the Soviet Union. Indeed, as Kissinger correctly observed later: "Israel wanted . . . a veto over all our decisions regardless of the merits of the issue and a free hand to destroy the Egyptian Third Army."[129] He further commented: "We had no interest in seeing Sadat destroyed—even less so via the collapse of a cease-fire we had co-sponsored."[130] Nevertheless, Kissinger permitted Israel to engage in a prolonged breach of the cease-fire that amounted to a major military offensive.

A second cease-fire call, Resolution 339, was passed in the Security Council on October 24. It reaffirmed the October 22 cease-fire and "urged" but did not "demand" the parties to return to the original cease-fire lines (this muting reflected U.S. pressure in the Security Council on Israel's behalf). Sadat accepted Resolution 339 although it still left his Third Army surrounded. Nevertheless, within hours after the new cease-fire was to have gone into effect, the Israelis again resumed their assault on the Third Army. Significantly, even though Kissinger knew in each instance that Israel had initiated the hostilities and while Sadat was pleading for American help to enforce the cease-fire, he refrained from any condemnation of Israel and instead warned the Egyptians not to undertake "offensive" operations. As a result of this obvious American duplicity and because no American pressure was being applied on the Israelis to desist from their strangulation of the Third Army, Sadat turned to the Security Council. He asked that American and Soviet forces be sent to the Middle East to bring about an end to the fighting and to supervise a cease-fire, a request that triggered a near-confrontation between the United States and the Soviet Union.

Kissinger's response was unequivocal: "We were not prepared to send American troops to Egypt, nor would we accept the dispatch of Soviet forces. We had not worked for years to reduce the Soviet military presence in Egypt only to cooperate in reintroducing it as a result of a United Nations Resolution. Nor would we participate in a joint force with the Soviets, which would legitimize their role in the area and strengthen radical elements."[131] The Soviets, however, saw merit in the idea and informed Washington that they would support such a resolution if it was formally introduced. Washington responded that it would veto any resolution calling for the introduction of Soviet and American forces. The stage was set for a crisis.

Late in the evening of October 24, Soviet Ambassador Dobrynin phoned Kissinger with a "very urgent" message from Premier Leonid Brezhnev. First, he condemned Israel for drastically violating the cease-fire and suggested that Soviet and American contingents go to Egypt to enforce the truce. Then followed a serious threat: "I will say it straight," Brezhnev cabled, "that if you find it impossible to act together with us in this matter, we should be faced with the necessity urgently to consider the question of taking appropriate steps unilaterally. We cannot allow arbitrariness on the part of Israel."[132] The United States responded with a military alert of ground, sea, and air forces, including both conventional and nuclear units (a DEF CON 3), and a diplomatic note from Nixon asking the Soviets to cooperate in a U.N. peacekeeping initiative. In the midst of this great power crisis, the Israelis demanded that Washington not ask them to pull back to the line they had occupied when the original cease-fire went into effect on October 22, and Kissinger assured them that no such request would be made.[133] Moreover, the American airlift continued.

Egypt provided the way out of the crisis by changing its request in the Security Council from a Soviet-American contingent to an international force. The Soviets agreed to accept such a force, to be composed of non-permanent members of the Security Council, and the crisis was defused. On that same day, October 25, the Security Council passed Resolution 340, establishing a U.N. peacekeeping force, excluding the great powers, and "requested" that the parties return to the lines they had occupied at the October 22 cease-fire. That the resolution did not "demand" that the parties return to the lines of October 22 again reflected American intervention on Israel's behalf. Nevertheless, the Israelis strongly objected to the resolution.

Israel was actively pursuing the humiliation of Egypt by starving the Third Army into surrender—refusing to let food, water, or medical supplies pass to the trapped army. Finally even Kissinger reacted: "We had supported Israel throughout the war. . . . We had just run the risk of war with the Soviet Union. . . . But our shared interests did not embrace the elimination of the Third Army. The issue of the Third Army was quite simply that Israel had completed its entrapment well *after* a cease-fire (that we had negotiated) had gone into effect."[134] He did not, however, stop the airlift to Israel, nor did he publicly criticize its actions. There was some discussion within the administration of mounting a U.S. resupply to the trapped Egyptian Third Army. That idea was discarded at Kissinger's insistence, however, for fear of angering the Israelis, even though as late as October 26 Israel was still attacking Egyptian troops. Kissinger again asked Israel to cease attacking and to allow food, water, and medical supplies through; Israel ignored the American request. The situation of the Third Army was becoming increasingly desperate. Still, Kissinger, in his own words, "procrastinated" in response to Sadat's frantic pleas for help, replying: "You must recognize that it is impossible for us to make proper judgements on who is keeping and who is violating the cease-fire."[135] Kissinger reassured the Israelis once more on October 26, "You won't be pressured one second before it becomes inevitable."[136]

Again it was Egypt that finally managed to break the stalemate. On October 27 Sadat signaled that he was prepared for *direct* talks between Egyptian and Israeli officers at the rank of major general, "to discuss the military aspects of the implementation of Security Council Resolution 338 and Resolution 339 of October 22 and 23, 1973." Sadat suggested the talks take place under U.N. supervision at the route marker denoting Kilometer 101 on the Cairo-Suez road. The only conditions he required were a "complete" cease-fire, to go into effect two hours before the meeting, and the passage of one convoy carrying nonmilitary supplies (food, water, and medicine) to the Third Army under U.N. and Red Cross supervision.[137]

The situation could not have been more favorable for Israel. It was about to enter the first direct talks between Israeli and Arab representatives since the independence of the state, and it retained control over the access route to the Third Army even while the

United Nations, almost unanimously, was pressing for Israeli withdrawal back from that line to the October 22 line: all this in return
for permitting one convoy of nonmilitary supplies to pass. Yet Israel
was bitter and angry. Moshe Dayan made the following statement
later in an interview with Terrance Smith in the *New York Times:*

> The Americans, in order to smooth the way with the Arabs, confronted
> us with an ultimatum to the effect that if we would not enable the Third
> Army to receive food and water, we would find ourselves in a political
> conflict with them [the Americans]. . . . The United States moved in and
> denied us the fruits of victory. It was an ultimatum—nothing short of it.
> Had the United States not pressed us, the Third Army and Suez City would
> have had to surrender. We would have captured 30,000 to 40,000 soldiers,
> and Sadat would have had to admit it to his people. We might only have
> held them for a day and let them walk out without their arms, but it would
> have changed the whole Egyptian attitude about whether they had won or
> lost the war. It would have given us more cards in the practical negotia-
> tions.[138]

Despite Israel's bitterness at being denied total victory over Egypt,
the secretary of state finally insisted that Israel accept the Egyptian
proposal. On October 28 Israeli and Egyptian military representatives
met for direct talks under the auspices of U.N. observers, although
not until late on October 29 did the convoy reach its destination.[139]
The meeting at Kilometer 101 marked the end of the October War.

This third major Arab-Israeli war had profound repercussions for
American national interests. Détente with the Soviet Union was
severely jeopardized, indeed a near-confrontation between the two
great powers occurred. Relations with the European and Japanese
allies were severely strained. And the supply of oil, vital to all the
Western industrial economies, was interrupted. Even Kissinger acknowledged that the war "had the most drastic consequences" for
the United States; he calculated that it "cost us about $3 billion
directly, about $10-15 billion indirectly. It increased our unemploy-
ment and contributed to the deepest recession we have had in the
postwar [World War II] period."[140]

Moreover, the October War challenged virtually every prewar assumption of U.S. Middle East policy. Before the October fighting
Nixon and Kissinger had believed that stability in the Middle East
could be best ensured by Israeli military predominance; however, the
vastly superior Israeli military power did not ensure stability or prevent war. The administration had doubted that Arab oil could be
effectively used to pressure the West; the embargo shattered that
assumption. It had become almost conventional wisdom that
U.S.–Soviet détente would serve to minimize the danger of regional
conflicts; the near-confrontation of the superpowers was indeed a

sobering lesson. And, finally, the traditional perception of the Arabs as inept both at war-making and cooperating among themselves was severely eroded by their performance in the war. However, of greatest significance in analyzing the October hostilities is that in spite of all the objective contradictions this crisis illustrated with regard to the American perception of Israel as a strategic asset to U.S. interests in the Middle East, the idea was not subject to reevaluation—its merits and drawbacks were not even debated in decision-making circles, while the policies derived from the perception were continued and even intensified.

Indeed, despite the numerous and serious challenges to the conventional wisdom, U.S. policy underwent no fundamental transformation. The only change from the interwar years was a commitment on the part of Kissinger to devote more attention to the Middle East—in fact, the region became a top concern, and Washington made a conscious effort to improve its relations with the major Arab countries, especially Egypt. It is significant, however, that Kissinger expected Washington to be able to better its ties with the Arabs without altering its wholehearted support for Israel or its policy of maintaining Israel as an extension of American power in the region. Kissinger apparently believed that the strength of the U.S.-Israeli tie, with the perceived influence in the Arab world this gave Washington over Israeli policy, would impress the Arabs and convince them that the United States held most of the diplomatic cards. The Soviets could provide them with weapons, but only the United States could get their territory back.[141] Yet, except for Egypt, which simply "fell into the arms" of the United States in spite of its policies, Washington was unable to improve its relations with the Arab regimes—in large measure because Washington did not use its potential leverage with Israel to make progress on issues of concern to the Arabs, and because Kissinger completely acceded to Israel on the Palestinian question.

Washington's unwillingness and/or inability to influence Israel's behavior in the post-1973 period was related both to the absence of any serious reevaluation of the faulty assumptions on which America's Middle East policy was predicated and to the power of the pro-Israeli lobby, acting on behalf of the Israeli government's interests through the domestic political process. Even Kissinger remarked on the constrictions imposed by the lobby: "It's easy to say what we've done is not enough, but . . . they were the *attainable*—given our prevailing domestic situation."[142] In addition, an aide to Kissinger commented that pro-Israeli sentiment in Congress was "the greatest constraint" on Kissinger's efforts to pursue some measure of a Middle

East settlement, and "the constraint became the determinant."[143] Indeed, the pro-Israeli groups successfully pressured Congress to resist the administration's efforts to strengthen American ties with Arab states, principally by denying the administration a critical tool— reduced aid—that could have been used to persuade Israel to adopt diplomatic positions more congenial to U.S. interests, and by blocking administration-proposed arms sales to the Arab states.

The Postwar Diplomatic Process

U.S. Postwar Objectives

The eight months that followed the October War saw unprecedented American involvement in the search for a settlement of the Arab-Israeli conflict, although the parameters of that effort were very narrowly defined, conforming to the limitations imposed by Israel. Indeed, no attempt was ever made to raise the core of the Middle East conflict, the Palestinian issue. U.S. policy focused on (1) facilitating a disengagement between Israel and Egypt and between Israel and Syria; (2) laying the groundwork for a separate, bilateral Egyptian-Israeli peace; (3) persuading King Faisal and his OPEC colleagues to lift the oil embargo; and (4) preparing a peace conference. Even the mode of diplomatic activity—a step-by-step approach that avoided linking initial accords to the nature of a final peace agreement—a method that obfuscated the most critical issues, circumventing even a discussion of a comprehensive settlement—was defined by the constraints imposed by Israel.

In fact, step-by-step diplomacy was essentially designed to avoid having to exert pressure on Israel to be forthcoming in a genuine peace settlement, though it also served to divide the Arab world. As John F. Roehm, Jr., aptly described it: "Kissinger's selection of the step-by-step approach to negotiations was partially motivated by his concern that attempts to move Israel too far, too fast, as would be likely in a comprehensive peace plan, would cause the Israeli lobby to activate its 'legions' of supporters in Congress and thereby threaten Kissinger's efforts to transform relations with the Arabs."[144] Regardless of the reasons behind it, the strategy was a failure in terms of American interests in the Middle East.

The problem with Kissinger's belief that America's special relationship with Israel would force the Arabs to deal with the United States in the diplomatic arena was that diplomacy had to hold more promise than war, for in the event of war the Soviet Union could provide more than the United States (though Soviet weapons were repeatedly shown to be inferior to American arms). However, progress toward a settlement, which was essential for maintaining the confidence of the Arab governments, meant at a minimum the return of some territory and eventually at least the appearance of movement toward resolution of the Palestinian issue. For such a policy to be successful Israel would have to make some concessions. The United States might try to extract comparable Arab concessions, but, given the nature of the issues, this would clearly be difficult. Because of this, U.S. diplomacy would have to "compensate" Israel with aid and implicitly threaten Israel with the withholding of such aid if circumstances dictated.[145] In practice, the compensation became endless, and the threat of withholding aid was never entertained.

In addition, there would also have to be promises of assistance to Egypt, Syria, and Jordan to strengthen bilateral U.S. relations with each of these countries.[146] Thus, in the absence of Israeli concessions, which it quickly became apparent would not be obtained, Kissinger attempted to use the sale of limited arms to Arab states as a means of improving relations with them. These efforts, however, were vigorously opposed by the Israeli lobby in Congress, which compelled Kissinger to reduce substantially or withdraw the proposals he initially made for sales to Jordan, Egypt, and Saudi Arabia.[147] Moreover, in responding to the lobby's intense pressure, Congress's public and harsh treatment of the Arab nations seeking U.S. arms and aid tended to cancel out whatever goodwill the transactions were intended to achieve. In the final analysis American interests were very poorly served by Washington's postwar diplomacy.

Israeli Postwar Objectives

Israel's post-1973 position was even more inflexible than its post-1967 stance. Its determination to retain all of the territories it occupied hardened; its desire for absolute military superiority also increased and produced endless requests for the most modern and sophisticated U.S. equipment. Israeli officials believed even more strongly that military solutions were the best overall means for dealing with the complex political problems of the region. As in the past, there was some recognition of the desirability of separating Egypt from the Arab side of the Arab-Israeli conflict, but there were no innovative ideas about how this might be accomplished. In addition, Israel's refusal to consider the issue of Palestinian self-determination became more rigid, as did its refusal to deal with the PLO. Its basic postwar objectives were simply to retain as much of the "fruits of victory" as were possible and to increase the margin of its military superiority. Israel was far more successful in maximizing its interests in the postwar period than was the United States.

Arab Postwar Objectives

The major objective of Egypt and Syria, as well as Jordan (though Jordan had not participated in the 1973 war), was to regain their national territory (in the case of Jordan to regain Palestinian territory); in exchange, they were prepared to recognize Israel. Israel's commitment to retain the Golan Heights thwarted the possibility of such an agreement with Syria. Jordan's hopes were dashed by Israel's determination to hold onto the West Bank and East Jerusalem, and its refusal to engage in a negotiating process with Amman. Jordan's hopes were also dampened by the regional and international legitimacy won by the PLO in the postwar period and by the PLO's refusal to permit Jordan to reassert its illegitimate authority over any part of historic Palestine. Egypt did regain some of its territory in the aftermath of the war, but Cairo's success may be ascribed to Sadat's unflagging commitment to locate Egypt fully in the American fold and its willingness to compromise on virtually every issue to achieve agreements with Israel.

Arafat sent a message to Washington on October 10 indicating the PLO's willingness to participate in a postwar negotiating process;[148] however, Kissinger denied the Palestinians any opportunity to participate in the postwar diplomacy.

Postwar Accords and Conferences

The Six Points at Kilometer 101

The first postwar accord was an Egyptian-Israeli agreement signed on November 11, 1973, by Israeli Major General Aharon Yariv and Egyptian Major General Ghany el Gamasy at Kilometer 101 on the Cairo-Suez road.[149] This Six Point Agreement laid the foundation for the Sinai I Accord (of January 1974) by relieving the acute military tensions, stabilizing the cease-fire, and providing some time for the preparation of the groundwork for broader Israeli-Egyptian negotiations. After November 11 discussions continued between Israeli and Egyptian military representatives on ways of implementing the six points; however, the talks were broken off on November 29, primarily because of Israel's unwillingness to make any commitments prior to its national elections, which were scheduled for December 31.

In considerable measure the agreement reached at Kilometer 101 was the work of Kissinger's personal diplomacy: his first Egyptian-Israeli shuttle between November 5 and 11 led directly to the signing of the agreement. Of greater significance, however, to the achievement of the agreement was that Sadat dropped the demand (being made in the United Nations and elsewhere, by virtually the entire international community) for Israel to return to the October 22 cease-fire lines. After the suspension of the talks on November 29, Kissinger focused on organizing a Middle East peace conference at Geneva in accordance with Resolution 338.

The Algiers Summit

At a summit conference in Algiers in November 1973, the Arab leaders affirmed the necessity of: (1) liberating all occupied territories, including Jerusalem, and (2) restoring the national rights of the Palestinian people according to the decisions of the PLO. In addition, the PLO was designated as the sole, legitimate representative of the Palestinian people, and Jordan was effectively stripped of the right to speak for the Palestinians. (King Hussein refused to accept the Algiers draft resolution on the PLO but had little choice, a year later at the Rabat Summit in 1974, except to defer to the Arab consensus.) It was also decided that the oil embargo should be lifted, giving the Saudis a face-saving device in the context of intense American pressure on Riyadh to end the embargo. The decision concerning the embargo involved the establishment of a link between its termination and a disengagement on the Syrian front. (In the end the Saudis agreed to terminate the embargo before any progress was accomplished on such a disengagement.) Finally, a resolution was adopted stating that the U.S. policy of complete alignment with Israel would adversely affect American interests in the region. At the close of the meeting the ministers issued a statement declaring their willingness to participate in a peace process based on Israeli withdrawal and the achievement of the legitimate rights of the Palestinians.[150] Thus the Arab regimes clearly demonstrated their willingness to recognize and accept Israel as a state in the Middle East; however, Israel and the United States interpreted the Algiers resolutions in a completely negative light.

The Geneva Conference

The Geneva Conference was to be convened on December 18, with the participation of Egypt, Syria, Jordan, and Israel; the United States and the Soviet Union were co-sponsors, and the United Nations was the official host. Kissinger was undoubtedly aware that the conference could not resolve the basic issues in dispute; more important, he personally opposed both a comprehensive settlement and Soviet participation in the Middle East peace process. But he believed that the convening of such a conference would give him time for behind-the-scenes personal diplomacy and that the psychological factor of bringing Arabs and Israelis together in a singular setting for diplomatic intercourse could set an important precedent. Egypt, however, was the only willing participant among the Middle East actors. Jordan's enthusiasm for a Geneva Conference was significantly dampened as a result of the Algiers Summit (because of the transference of responsibility for the Palestinians to the PLO), although Jordan's wavering was overcome with relative ease. Israel was strongly opposed to participation in a Geneva Conference, and its disinclination to attend was less easily resolved than Jordan's.

Israel put forward a number of demands, the satisfaction of which it announced was a prerequisite for its attendance at Geneva. Israel demanded an explicit provision in the conference invitations stating that the original composition of the conference could be expanded only unanimously. This demand, to which Kissinger agreed, was intended to make sure that the PLO would be formally barred from Geneva and that its later participation at any reconvened conference would be subject to an Israeli veto. Israel was also given a private, written assurance that the United States would oppose, to the point of veto, any invitation to the PLO without Israel's consent. This was a substantial concession on the part of the United States, considering the intense feelings in the Arab world on this issue and the centrality of the Palestinian question to any final resolution of the Arab-Israeli conflict. Israel also demanded that there be no more than a ceremonial role for the United Nations, arguing that granting the auspices for a peace conference between Israel and the Arab states to an organization in which the Arabs had an automatic majority was unacceptable. Kissinger acquiesced, essentially by arranging the meeting so that the participants would split up as rapidly as possible into subgroups, minimizing the role of the United Nations and assuring that diplomacy would proceed in a bilateral fashion, and by manipulating the program to assure that the United Nations would only "convene" the conference, and not "supervise" it.[151] Finally, Israel also refused to sit in the same room with the Syrians unless they complied with Israel's demands for a list of prisoners of war and Red Cross visits before the conference. Syria refused to come to Geneva, thus letting Kissinger "off the hook" regarding Israel's demands vis-à-vis Damascus.

When Syria's President Hafez Assad declined the invitation to Geneva, he stated that he was interested in a peace process, but would not attend a formal peace conference until after he had an initial disengagement agreement with Israel. He was extremely disturbed by the fact that there was to be an agreement concerning the Egyptian front before there was one on the Syrian front. This was, for him, a serious threat to the Egyptian-Syrian alliance and to Syria's vital interests. Moreover, Assad correctly suspected that Sadat had not informed him of all the arrangements he had concluded with Kissinger. In Riad's words, Kissinger "had played his role craftily in provoking ill-feeling between Syria and Egypt in this critical period by his double-dealing and innuendoes."[152]

In any case, with all its prerequisites met, Israel no longer had an excuse for not attending the Geneva Conference, though the Israelis continued to tell Kissinger that they might not appear. In the end, a letter from President Nixon to Prime Minister Meir and personal encouragement from Kissinger (in addition to the substantive concessions to Israel's demands) induced Israel's attendance. Kissinger writes of his attempts in Israel to persuade the Israelis to attend Geneva: "All our sympathy for Israel's historic plight and affection for Golda were soon needed to endure the teeth-grinding, exhausting ordeal by exegesis that confronted us when we met with the Israeli negotiating team. . . . Just before leaving Jerusalem I visited Yad Vashem, the memorial to the six million Jews who had died at the hand of the Nazis. . . . It was intended as a reassurance to the people of Israel that I understood and would respect their fears in a process of peacemaking."[153]

The Geneva Conference was convened on December 21, under the formal auspices of the U.N. secretary-general, with representatives of the United States and the Soviet Union as co-chairmen, and with the foreign ministers of Egypt, Jordan, and Israel in attendance. Each participant presented opening remarks, and the conference was then recessed indefinitely. Kissinger's evaluation of the success of the conference is very positive: "The Geneva Conference, whatever its bizarre aspects, was not an inconsiderable achievement in itself. For the first time two Arab states — Egypt and Jordan — sent high level representatives to sit around the same table as the Israelis."[154] Others are less generous in their assessments; some, including members of the American government, have called the whole thing a farce.

Egyptian-Israeli Disengagement: The Sinai I Accord

In the wake of the Geneva Conference, Kissinger was anxious to proceed with an Egyptian-Israeli disengagement agreement. Thus early in January 1974, after the Israeli elections returned Golda Meir as prime minister, Moshe Dayan came to Washington with a plan for an Israeli-Egyptian accord. It essentially involved an Israeli pullback from the west bank of the Suez Canal and allowed Egypt to keep territory Israel had won on the east bank, roughly six to ten kilometers forward from the Canal. More important, however, were the political demands Dayan attached to the proposal, which were presented as non-negotiable: (1) an end to the state of belligerency between Egypt and Israel, (2) lifting the blockade of Bab el-Mandeb (a strait forming the southern gate of the Red Sea), and (3) a pledge to reopen the Suez Canal and permit transit of Israeli ships and cargoes. Israel also demanded that the United States underwrite any Egyptian-Israeli agreement with an assurance of long-term arms supply.[155]

On January 11 Kissinger set out for the Middle East to present Dayan's proposals, in the guise of an American plan, to the Egyptians. Sadat greeted Kissinger with enthusiasm and a commitment to complete the agreement by January 18 (thereby undermining his negotiating position). He also told Kissinger that once the agreement was finalized, he would make the rounds of the various Arab capitals and urge an end to the oil embargo, even offering, as Kissinger relates it, "to promote the lifting of the embargo in any manner that would publicly give Nixon the credit—showing that our domestic difficulties [Watergate] had not gone unnoticed in Egypt."[156] Sadat's position before Kissinger's arrival had been that Israel should withdraw beyond and vacate the strategic Mitla and Gidi passes in the Sinai. He had wanted one and one-half divisions on the east bank and had been unwilling to accept stringent restrictions on types of weapons. Israel's plan stipulated no more than two or three battalions (1,000 men) on the east bank and no heavy weapons; on the west bank, Israel insisted on a maximum of 300 tanks in the thirty-kilometer zone from the Canal. When Kissinger put forward the proposals he was carrying, Sadat immediately consented to ending the blockade of the straits when a disengagement agreement was concluded and agreed that cargoes bound to and from Israel would be able to use the Suez Canal. The Egyptian president also promised not to raise the Palestinian or Syrian issues during the disengagement phase and did not raise any objections to the exclusion of the Soviets from this process.

On January 12 Kissinger went to Israel and for the remainder of the week shuttled back and forth between the two parties. The complexities of this effort have been amply recorded elsewhere.[157] The resulting agreement, the Sinai I Accord, was reached on January 17 and was signed the following day. In it Israel achieved all of its most important aims, while Egypt compromised on each of its original points. Israel did drop the demand for a formal end to belligerency and agreed to some minor changes in force levels and the line of disengagement. However, Israel retained control of the Gidi and Mitla passes, and Sadat agreed to a reduction in forces from 70,000 to

7,000 men and tank reductions from 700 to 30. Egypt also agreed not to deploy SAM antiaircraft missiles in an area reaching back thirty kilometers west of the Suez Canal. Egypt agreed to reopen the Suez Canal and to permit the transit of Israeli ships through it. Israel consolidated its defense line, was separated from the Egyptian army in a way that reduced the possibilities of either a war of attrition or a surprise attack, and was able to release reservists to help in the normalization of the home front.[158] In addition, it was generally agreed in Israel that the Egyptian pledge to reopen the Canal, together with the expected rehabilitation and repopulation of Canal zone cities, would reduce the prospects for conflict and improve the momentum for peace.

Moreover, Israel demanded and received a separate, bilateral agreement with the United States. This detailed ten-point "Memorandum of Understanding" contained several important American commitments to Israel, in addition to conveying several Egyptian "statements of intention" concerning the Suez Canal and the demobilization of its armed forces, which Washington essentially guaranteed. Further, the United States promised that the completion of the disengagement agreement would take precedence over new steps at Geneva; that U.N. troops would not be withdrawn without the consent of both sides; that the United States considered the Straits of Tiran an international waterway; and that Washington would be responsive to Israel's defense needs on a continuing and long-term basis. In substance, the administration underwrote—politically, economically, and militarily the Israeli-Egyptian agreement.[159]

The Sinai I Accord is a high point of convergence of Israeli and American interests. It was essentially an Israeli plan, sponsored by the United States and accepted by Egypt. Some in the Arab world, largely as a result of Sadat's promotion of the Sinai agreement, saw the accord as a possible turning point in U.S. Middle East policy in the direction of more even-handedness. Sadat was the most enthusiastic, commenting publicly: "Previously it [United States policy] was completely favorable to Israel. Today without having changed radically, it is new. Now that the Americans have made a gesture, the Arabs should make one too."[160] Rather quickly, however, it became apparent to the Arabs that there was little new in American policy.

The Palestinians were caught in a number of contradictions. First, it was clear that the Arab states were prepared to make peace with Israel in exchange for return of their territory (as noted, in the case of Jordan, in exchange for Palestinian territory) without pressing for Palestinian interests. Second, the PLO itself was split over what course—both ends and means—to pursue. The Fatah leadership wanted to participate in the peace process then evolving, and even individuals regarded as uncompromising as Abu Iyad began talking about a Palestinian state "on twenty-three percent of Palestine" (i.e., the West Bank and Gaza).[161] However, since Israel and the United States refused to permit their participation, the willingness and/or ability of the Fatah leaders to deliver such a compromise was never tested. On the other hand, "rejectionist" groups led by George Habash's PFLP denounced the Fatah "capitulations" and any PLO program short of the liberation of all of Palestine. Yet in spite of the radicals, within a few years formal PLO ends were altered from the ideal of a democratic secular state to the "two-state" solution. This process was begun at the twelfth Palestine National Council (PNC) meeting (Cairo, June 1-9, 1974) and was institutionalized at the thirteenth PNC meeting (Cairo, March 12-20, 1977). The PNC functions as a parliament-in-exile for Palestinians and is the supreme legislative body within the PLO.

Of greater consequence to Middle East peace, American interests, and Israeli security was that since the Palestinians were denied participation in the peace process, armed struggle appeared (to many in the PLO) to be the only alternative means available to them. Thus, in the aftermath of the October War, while Fatah succeeded in curtailing the international terrorism of the interwar period, guerrilla operations remained a continuing—though by no means the sole—tactic for a number of years. Two of the most serious guerrilla attacks on Israeli soil—Kiryat Shmoneh and Ma'alot—occurred in April and May 1974. The first was carried out by the Popular Front for the Liberation of Palestine–General Command (PFLP-GC), a group strongly influenced by Syria, founded by Ahmad Jibril, and having virtually no grass-roots support, but a leader among the radicals; the second, by the DFLP (Hawatmeh's group). The PFLP-GC undertook the suicide mission at Kiryat Shmoneh on April 11 to derail the discussions then underway among Fatah, the DFLP, and Sa'iqa (a group set up by the Ba'athist leaders in Damascus after the June War that has functioned in Palestinian politics to serve the interests of Syria) concerning the acceptance of a Palestinian state in the West Bank and Gaza and participation in the Middle East diplomatic process (specifically the Geneva Conference). Hawatmeh apparently decided to undertake the Ma'alot operation because of the lack of response in Israel to an interview he gave to Yedioth Aharonot (a leading Israeli newspaper) in which he set out his views on a two-state solution, because of the negative response with which his ideas were received in the Palestinian context, and because of the favorable popular reaction among the Palestinian masses to the Kiryat Shmoneh attack. The Fatah leadership was not pleased by these operations, but ultimately took responsibility for them—in part because of the enthusiasm they engendered among the Palestinian masses and in part because Kissinger successfully closed all the diplomatic doors while Israel increased its intransigence on the question of Palestine.[162]

Israel's response to the two attacks was to resume the bombing of Lebanese towns and cities and Palestinian refugee camps in Lebanon, and the violent cycle of raids and reprisals began again.

Jordan's Fruitless Search for a Peace Settlement

Kissinger relates that following the conclusion of the Sinai I Accord between Egypt and Israel, King Hussein invited him to Jordan and indicated that although he realized that the Syrian problem was next on the agenda, he hoped that an Israeli-Jordanian peace process with regard to the West Bank could begin soon thereafter. He was thus signaling his willingness to undercut the PLO, which only months previously (at Algiers) had been declared by the Arab states the sole, legitimate representative of the Palestinians, and the only party entitled to negotiate the status of the West Bank. Hussein told Kissinger that his double nightmare about the West Bank involved either indefinite Israeli occupation or a PLO state, whose first target he believed would be the Hashimite kingdom.

Kissinger apparently assured Hussein that given the logic of his position, Israel would surely be willing to engage in negotiations. Indeed the Jordanians put forward a very modest disengagement proposal for the Jordan Valley, involving principally Israel's withdrawal from Jericho on the Jordan River, allowing Israel significant modifications in the border, and special security arrangements in the area itself. However, this proposal was rejected outright by the Israeli government, which claimed it needed the Jordan Valley as a security line.[163] It was again clear that Israel had no intention of relinquishing the West Bank. It might have been expected that American officials would understand the negative long-term consequences from such a situation and thus exert some influence on Israel to reach a compromise concerning the West Bank; however, no pressure was exerted on Israel either to respond to Jordan or to the PLO.

The Syrian-Israeli Disengagement Agreement

The effort to arrange a Syrian-Israeli disengagement began on January 20 when Kissinger flew to Damascus. Assad indicated that he was ready to proceed with negotiations, but, on returning to Israel the same day, Kissinger discovered that the Israelis were not. The

Israelis were interested only in a list of prisoners of war and Red Cross visits to verify the proper treatment of Israeli prisoners. Moreover, on February 9 Prime Minister Meir implicitly negated Resolution 242 when she declared Israel's position regarding negotiations on Syria's Golan Heights. Meir told Israeli settlers on the Golan that she regarded the Golan and its settlements as inseparable from Israel and could not conceive of any withdrawal from the post-1967 cease-fire lines.[164]

In the ensuing weeks the Arab oil-producing states made a feeble attempt to implement the linkage agreed upon at Algiers between an Israeli-Syrian disengagement and an end to the oil embargo. On February 3 King Faisal informed President Nixon that the oil embargo could not be lifted until an agreement was reached on the Syrian front. The Americans took just the opposite tack. When Egyptian Foreign Minister Ismail Fahmy and Saudi Foreign Minister Omar Saqqaf came to Washington on February 16, Kissinger told them that if they wanted to see President Nixon while they were in Washington, they would first have to agree to lift the oil embargo regardless of how the Israelis responded to the initiative on the Golan.[165] On February 18 the two ministers informed the secretary of state that their governments had agreed to an unlinking of the embargo from the Syrian disengagement process. In fact, the lifting of the oil embargo, which was formally taken at a meeting of the Arab oil ministers in Vienna on March 18, was completely unconditional.[166] Thus the Arabs gave up what leverage they possessed vis-à-vis the United States without receiving any quid pro quo in return.

On February 20 Syria sent Kissinger a list of Israeli prisoners, which the secretary transmitted to Israel on February 27. Kissinger returned to the Middle East on February 24, for the beginning of the Syrian-Israeli disengagement process. His first visit was with Assad, of whom he writes, "[His] actions bespoke a desire for accommodation. . . . the leader of the most militant of Israel's neighbors was putting all his chips on the United States. In the Syrian context this was an act of daring comparable to Sadat's change of course some weeks earlier."[167] Again, it might have been expected that the administration would consider America's long-term interests (as well as Israel's) and act accordingly. It did not, as usual unwilling to pursue a policy with which Israel disagreed.

Assad wanted not only a disengagement of forces on the Golan but also an Israeli pullback beyond the pre-1973 war lines, for which he was willing to negotiate an end to belligerency and a normalization of relations. Meir had already made it clear that such a withdrawal was out of the question. Indeed, the Israelis saw no reason for negotiations at all because they believed Israel had nothing to gain from them, especially as the Syrians had already met their demands on the prisoners of war and Israel was in occupation of more Syrian territory, without the unstable troop configuration situation that had existed with Egypt. Thus the initial Israeli plan left Israel occupying a salient forward of the old post-1967 war line, allowed for a narrow U.N. zone, and proposed the return to Syria of only the easternmost section of Israeli-occupied Syrian territory. Even Kissinger considered the Israeli proposition worthless as a basis of negotiation, and when he returned to Damascus on March 1, he suggested that some further groundwork would have to be done in Washington and so presented nothing. Kissinger then flew to Saudi Arabia, where he was reassured that the oil embargo would be lifted, then on to Amman where he held several friendly meetings with King Hussein.

During March and April American and Israeli and American and Syrian diplomats held discussions in Washington in an attempt to find a resolution. Dayan presented an Israeli plan that not only involved disengagement purely within the line captured in the 1973 fighting but also demanded that there be no negotiations until all prisoners of war were released. Further, the defense minister demanded that an article banning terrorism be included in the agreement, as well as an article allowing the emigration of Syrian Jews. In addition, Dayan argued that even if there were a disengagement agreement with Syria, it would not mean peace, and therefore Israel needed the most up-to-date aircraft and other types of sophisticated weapons. He specifically asked for 1,000 tanks, 4,000 armored personnel carriers, and other equipment.[168]

Kissinger attempted to persuade the Israelis to soften their position on the Golan. One of the carrots he used was a waiver on repayment of the $1 billion of the $2.2 billion in aid that Congress had allocated in October. The Israelis, however, barely acknowledged the gesture; they were extremely angry over a U.S. vote in the Security Council condemning Israel for a massive raid into Lebanon in mid-April in which twenty-one civilians were killed and 134 wounded.[169] The administration hastened to make amends to Israel for its U.N. vote. In a written statement Washington promised to support all future Israeli "retaliatory" activities against "terrorist" raids. Meir made the pledge public before the Israeli Knesset. It said in part: "Raids by armed groups or individuals across the demarcation line are contrary to the cease-fire. Israel, in the exercise of its right of self-defense, may act to prevent such actions by all available means. The United States will not consider such actions by Israel as violations of the cease-fire and will support them politically."[170] The granting of such a license for military aggression against Arab states would seem to be an extraordinary and highly dangerous act on the part of the United States; it was further evidence of the extremes to which Washington would go in its support for Israel.

Nevertheless, the Israelis remained suspicious of Kissinger's motivations regarding the Syrian-Israeli negotiations and unremittingly intransigent in the negotiating process. The final shuttle was long and difficult, beginning on April 28 and not concluding until May 31, when Syria and Israel signed a disengagement accord in Geneva. According to the agreement, Israel was to withdraw from the salient captured in the October War, the city of Quneitra, and a narrow strip of territory conquered in 1967; Israel thus retained the Golan Heights. U.N. troops were to be stationed in a buffer zone, and on either side of that zone two areas of thinned out and limited forces were permitted. Specific disengagement procedures were to be ironed out by a joint military working group. Technical agreements resulting from this accord were signed on June 5 and provided for the exchange of prisoners and other details of the implementation of the agreement.[171]

In the view of many of Israel's generals and strategic planners, the new Israeli lines and positions in Syria were as good, if not better, than the ones that existed prior to the 1973 war.[172] Additionally, it was understood that the U.N. force between the Israelis and the Syrians and the thinning of forces in the forward zones would act as inhibiting factors to a Syrian attack. On another level, the accord also strengthened the Egyptian agreement by lessening the prospects for a war in which Egypt might be forced to join. Thus, in spite of Israel's opposition to the disengagement process, it maintained its occupation of the Golan and strengthened its regional position.

Conclusion

The end of the 1967 war through the post–October War diplomatic activity in 1973-74 saw extraordinarily strong American support for Israeli interests and policies, in the context of the perception that Israel served as a "strategic asset" to U.S. interests and an extension of American power in the Middle East. The institutionalization of the idea of Israel as a surrogate power and the concomitant growth in U.S. support for Israel resulted both from the faulty assumptions of certain powerful policymakers, especially Henry Kissinger, and from the extensive and effective propaganda disseminated by pro-Israeli groups whose influence with numerous sectors on the American domestic scene expanded greatly in the interwar years. The perception of Israel's surrogate utility was allegedly validated by the Jewish state's stunning military performance in the June War and enhanced by its mobilization in support of Jordan in 1970. According to proponents of the surrogate thesis, by providing Israel absolute military superiority the American interests of containing Soviet expansionism, promoting regional stability and preventing war, and assuring Western freedom of access to the area's raw materials, markets, and investment opportunities would be maximized. (In addition, advocates claimed that providing Israel unlimited arms supplies would make it secure, and therefore increasingly flexible with regard to a comprehensive settlement of the Arab-Palestinian-Israeli conflict.) The strategic asset thesis came to be accepted during these years as absolute dogma in the conventional wisdom of American political culture. The most tangible expression of this perception was the provision to Israel by Washington of unlimited quantities of the most sophisticated weapons available as well as increasing economic assistance. Further evidence of Washington's willingness to accommodate Israel in the context of the belief about its surrogate power were Kissinger's relentless and successful efforts to exclude the Palestinian issue from all diplomatic forums and to bar the PLO from participation in the diplomatic process. Indeed, no single American has done more to negate Palestinian interests than Henry Kissinger.

This chapter has also clearly illustrated the fallaciousness of the strategic asset thesis and the fact that the policies that grew out of it were completely counter to American interests. These policies undermined the entire framework of détente with the Soviet Union; increased Soviet influence and presence in the Middle East; provoked a second U.S.-Soviet confrontation; increased Arab hostility to the United States; produced an Arab oil embargo and a phenomenal spiraling of oil prices; estranged the United States from its Western European and Japanese allies; and led to almost continuous instability in the Middle East. Despite the manifold contradictions between theory and reality, neither the perception nor the policies derived from it were altered to conform to reality. This was due to the convergence between the strength of the thesis in certain powerful elite circles and the power and influence of pro-Israeli constituencies.

The tradition of executive prerogative in foreign policymaking was again evident during this period, though when Kissinger attempted to pursue certain policies that did not accord precisely with Israel's, the erosion of that norm was apparent, with the Congress able to block administrative initiatives that Israel's American friends mobilized to oppose. The beginning of the following period more clearly illustrates this transformation.

CHAPTER SIX

THE CAMP DAVID PROCESS

Introduction

The time between the signing of the Israeli-Egyptian and the Israeli-Syrian disengagement agreements in 1974 and the conclusion of the formal Israeli-Egyptian peace treaty in 1979 saw crucial and inter-related developments on the international scene, in the Middle East, and in American domestic politics. The mistaken assumptions and premises on which U.S. Middle East policy was predicated between 1967 and 1973 were reinforced, further institutionalized both in practice and in conventional wisdom, and culminated in the con-clusion of a separate, bilateral treaty between Israel and Egypt.

The "Camp David process," an expression of the totality of efforts aimed at the realization of an Egyptian-Israeli treaty between 1974/75-79, was qualitatively different from the previous events here ana-lyzed. They were wars, and this was peace, but a peace that may have been as cataclysmic as any of the wars. The process received a dramatic boost when the Egyptian president, Anwar el-Sadat, made a pilgrimage to Israel in November 1977. Sadat expected that by giving the Jewish state recognition and offering it full peace and a normalization of relations, Israel would return all the occupied Egyp-tian territory. Israel did not, however; and it began to seem as if Sadat's bold move would go nowhere. Then the American president, Jimmy Carter, committed himself to bringing the process to fruition. He invited Israeli Prime Minister Menachem Begin and President Sadat to Camp David, the presidential retreat in the mountains of Maryland, to work out the details of a peace treaty.

The three leaders and their aides met for thirteen days, from September 5 through 17, 1978, when a "framework" for peace was signed. The Camp David negotiations produced two documents: the first constituted the basis of a peace treaty between Israel and Egypt; the second, a framework for a larger peace in the Middle East that purportedly would resolve the Palestinian issue.

On March 26, 1979, a formal Egyptian-Israeli peace treaty was signed. Thereafter the Egyptians and the Israelis proceeded to implement the provisions of their agreement: ambassadors were exchanged on February 26, 1980, the final tract of land in the Sinai was returned to Egypt on April 25, 1982, and a process of full normalization of relations was underway. No progress was accomplished on the Palestinian issue; on the contrary, Israel expanded its settlements and intensified its hold over the West Bank, then undertook a war against the Palestinians in Lebanon in 1982.

The Inter-Arab Context and the Israeli Context

The Arab World

The Arab world after 1973 was a compendium of contradictions. Despite the desperate situation of the Egyptian Third Army at the end of the October fighting and Israel's obvious military advantage, the war became enshrined in Arab public opinion as a historic victory.[1] Subsequently, all other events in inter-Arab politics were overshadowed by Sadat's diplomacy vis-à-vis Israel, made possible in considerable measure by his ability to cite the 1973 campaign as a victory. In addition, the weakness of pan-Arabism (which had become increasingly apparent after the Arab defeat in 1967) considerably facilitated the Egyptian president's pursuit of peace with the Jewish state.[2] Sadat was also motivated by a desire to situate Egypt firmly in the American sphere and by the belief that it was the United States that could obtain for the Arabs the concessions they sought from Israel. Unfortunately, this perception of Washington as being able to "deliver Israel" (shared by several other Arab regimes) was not predicated on reality. Nevertheless, when Sadat claimed that the United States held "99 percent of the cards" in any Middle East settlement, initially there was a pervasive feeling that if any movement could occur in the intractable Arab-Palestinian-Israeli dilemma, it would be generated by Washington.

The desire of many of the Arab regimes for a solution fashioned and guaranteed by the West, specifically the United States, after the October War was to a great extent related to the economic interests of the Arab elites. Fouad Ajami, a prominent analyst of the Arab world, has observed that the enormous wealth amassed by the oil-producing countries after 1973 led to an infatuation with the consumer goods that the United States produced, although the attraction to American materialism did not lead to an acceptance of any of its positive values, e.g., personal and cultural freedom, democracy, and accountability of leaders.[3] Thus, in the years following 1973, the Arab regimes became progressively more repressive and decadent, the gap between elites and masses widened, and the internal contradictions of Arab polity and society became more clearly pronounced than at any previous time. By 1975-76 the Arab world was in disarray, interstate discord was increasing, domestic upheavals were occurring within most countries, and the collapse of Lebanon into a devastating civil war marked the end of the period of euphoria that had characterized the Arab region in the immediate aftermath of the October War.[4] By 1979 reverberations from the Iranian revolution were being felt throughout the region and regime elites in every Arab state had reason to question their longevity.

Sadat pursued his diplomacy with a combination of contempt for other Arab leaders and a naive belief about the inevitable success of his efforts, which he then thought would ineluctably carry Jordan, Syria, Iraq, Saudi Arabia, and other Arab states along with him. Such, however, was not to be the case. Sadat ruled a relatively stable and homogeneous political system with a complex identity related in part to the ancient Egyptian civilization of the pharaohs and transcending to some extent Arabism; thus he could potentially take risks in the context of Egyptian domestic politics that other Arab leaders could not contemplate. Yet Sadat even misjudged his own society, overstepping the normative parameters of Arabism and Islam that provide the major constraints on foreign policy formation in all Arab states. Moreover, the nature of the final agreement Sadat accepted, in the context of the internal weaknesses of the Arab states, precluded the possibility of other regimes joining in. The blatant disregard of Palestinian interests would have been far riskier for elites in other countries, where mass sentiment concerning the question of Palestine was still strong and where regime legitimacy was extremely precarious—often resting on little more than the ideological rhetoric of pan-Arabism (a cornerstone of which was the issue of Palestine), in addition to the personalism and paternalism of leaders and evermore sophisticated security systems.[5]

Hafez Assad, for instance, as a member of the Alawites, an unpopular minority group in predominantly Sunni Syria, had to be infinitely more cautious than Sadat in seeking accommodation with Israel.[6] The Damascus government rested on Assad's personal rule, a ruthless internal police system, and the ideology of pan-Arab nationalism, any element of which was subject to erosion. In addition, Damascus was continually concerned about the possibility of an Israeli invasion, and this preoccupation colored all Syria's regional policies—both with respect to Israel and to the Arabs—in the post-1973-74 period. Damascus's concern with an Israeli military threat explains the Syrian intervention in the Lebanese civil war against its former allies, the Lebanese National Movement (LNM) and the Palestinians.[7] But the meaning of that bloody suppression against the only organized progressive force in the region was lost on no one: Arab state interests would not tolerate any situation that carried the potential of an Israeli provocation. Undoubtedly the Palestinians were shattered—even more by that realization than the repetition (i.e., Jordan 1970) of Arab physical repression. Indeed, for all of its radical rhetoric and pan-Arab ideology, Syria, too, was a status quo state, mainly interested in the return of the Golan Heights, for which it was prepared to negotiate with Israel. The 1974 Syrian-Israeli disengagement agreement demonstrated Syria's willingness to seek such a settlement, and in his memoirs Henry Kissinger gives additional evidence of Assad's intentions. Nevertheless, the wartime alliance between Egypt and Syria disintegrated after 1973 in the wake of Egypt's diplomatic embrace of Washington, Syria's internal problems, and the civil strife in Lebanon.[8]

Sadat's diplomacy contributed indirectly to increasing tension between Syria and Iraq during this period. Such tension, with its long historic antecedents, stems in part from the traditional competition between the two states for leadership of the Fertile Crescent and exists despite the fact that both countries are ruled by Ba'athist parties directly descended from the Ba'ath socialist movement of the 1940s. Nevertheless, this tension was given fresh impetus in the aftermath of the October War.[9] Iraqi President Saddam Hussein saw an Egypt aligned with the United States and Israel as providing a unique opportunity to realize his personal ambitions for regional hegemony; as he moved to assume that role, the animosity between Baghdad and Damascus escalated. The extent of the hostility between the two regimes became apparent in 1980, when Iraq initiated a war with Iran[10] and Damascus sided with Teheran.

Sadat's diplomacy also resulted in a breach with Saudi Arabia, which was considerably more problematic for Cairo than that between Egypt and Syria, since Riyadh provided the Egyptian economy with regular and substantial monetary infusions. It is significant, though, that despite the evolving rapprochement with Israel from 1974, Saudi financial sustenance for Egypt remained constant until 1978. Support was not withdrawn until after the first Baghdad Summit in November of that year, following the signing of the Camp David accords. Egyptian-Saudi relations worsened considerably after the second conference in Baghdad in March 1979. At that meeting the members called upon all the participants to sever diplomatic relations with Cairo and impose a total economic embargo on Egypt, including termination of economic aid. Saudi Arabia, which as much as or more than the other Arab states faced internal contradictions and domestic discontent (dramatically illustrated in an attack on the Grand Mosque in Mecca in November 1979), acquiesced in the program of the so-called hard-liners.[11]

Jordan's ability to participate in a peace process during this period was complicated by the growing regional and international legitimacy of the PLO, which ultimately constrained Hussein from following Sadat's lead. The Arab summit conference held in Rabat in October 1974 produced a unanimous resolution (based on the Algiers decision a year earlier) designating the PLO as the sole, legitimate representative of the Palestinian people both in the diaspora and in the occupied West Bank and Gaza. That decision represented a major victory for the PLO and its chairman, Yasir Arafat, but it was a defeat for King Hussein, since it nullified his aspirations for Jordanian control over the West Bank through an Israeli-Jordanian accord. As discussed in Chapter 5, Jordan had specifically offered Israel direct negotiations in pursuit of such an agreement in the immediate post–October War period (as well as numerous times before the war), although Israel had rejected the offers. The Rabat decision officially took the matter out of Hussein's hands; in addition, widespread support for the PLO among both East Bank and West Bank Palestinians after 1974, the explicit opposition of West Bank Palestinians to the Camp David formula, and Jordan's Palestinian majority made it impossible for the Jordanian monarch to support Sadat publicly. However, Jordan never abandoned its illegitimate objective of control over the West Bank, despite subsequent diplomatic maneuvers appearing to support Palestinian interests.[12]

One particularly important reaction to Sadat's diplomacy was the rise of Islamic fundamentalism that swept Egypt and the Middle East in general (though Egyptian diplomacy was by no means the sole reason for the upsurge in Islamism).[13] No country in the Middle East was immune—the attack in Mecca in 1979 was perhaps the most unexpected manifestation of the trend, the revolution in Iran was the most significant, and Sadat's assassination in 1981 the most extreme expression within Egypt.

At the same time, while Egypt pursued its separate peace with Israel (implicitly sacrificing Palestinian interests in the service of the Egyptian state), the Palestine national movement matured and consolidated, altering both its fundamental objective and its primary means, solidifying its support with the Palestinian people, and garnering widespread international legitimacy and recognition.

During 1974-79 the PLO underwent significant transformations, formally pursuing a two-state solution (relinquishing its goal of liberating all of Palestine, abandoning its subsequent proposal for a democratic secular state of Palestine, and finally agreeing to accept a mini-state alongside Israel), and focusing increasingly on diplomacy and politics (rather than primarily on armed struggle) to achieve an independent Palestinian state. The March 1977 PNC meeting endorsed the idea of a Palestinian state in the West Bank and Gaza, and agreed to participate in the Geneva Conference and other diplomatic forums. The outcome of this parliamentary session represented a victory for the "moderates" over the "radicals" within the PLO.[14] However, the fact that all of the concessions made by the PLO were met with complete rejection by Israel (and the United States) eventually weakened the position of the moderates within the organization. The radicals were able to point out that the moderates had gained nothing in return either for their pursuit of diplomacy or for their substantive compromises, a charge that acquired increased meaning after the Israeli war against the Palestinians in Lebanon in 1982 and contributed to a civil war within the PLO in 1983. Yet it requires little imagination to understand that had the moderates been able to "deliver" any slight victory—recognition of the Palestinian right to self-determination by Israel or the United States, recognition of the PLO as the legitimate representative of the Palestinians by Israel or the United States, formal dialogue with the United States— it would have created a momentum within the organization around which the radicals would have ultimately coalesced. (Of note, too, is that the open dissension within the PLO between 1974 and 1979— the closest approximation to real democracy in the region—was used by Israel, in one of its more disingenuous arguments for not dealing with the representatives of the Palestinians, as "proof" that it would be useless to negotiate with the PLO since the organization would not be able to deliver the dissidents to any agreement that might be reached.)

As important as the changes in objective and strategy of the PLO in the post-1973 period is the widespread legitimacy—among Palestinians and non-Palestinians—won by the PLO. Indeed, by 1973 the PLO was accepted by virtually all Palestinians, both those living under occupation and those scattered throughout the world, as being the legitimate spokesman for their nationalist aspirations.[15] This was evidenced in one instance by the fact that nearly all the municipal leaders elected in 1976 in the West Bank (in the last elections Israel permitted in the occupied territories) campaigned as "pro-PLO" candidates. It was also demonstrated in a poll conducted for *Time* magazine by an Israeli firm, with the help of Israeli sociologists, showing that 86 percent of all respondents, randomly selected in the

West Bank, wanted an independent Palestinian state, headed solely by the PLO.[16]

The PLO also emerged as a formidable actor on the international scene during this period and was accepted by a majority of the world's governments as the official representative of all Palestinians. Immediately following the Rabat decision, on November 13, 1974, Arafat addressed the U.N. General Assembly, the first head of a nongovernmental organization to do so. His invitation to speak before the General Assembly had been approved by a vote of 105 to 4. (Only Israel, the United States, Bolivia, and the Dominican Republic voted against it.) The subsequent invitation to the PLO to take part, with the status of special observer in the General Assembly debates, further reflected the PLO's acceptance in the international community. In addition, shortly after being recognized as a special observer at the United Nations, the PLO was invited to participate in the Euro-Arab dialogue, which was initiated in 1974 but entered a more significant phase in May 1976 at a General Committee Meeting in Luxembourg.[17] As a result of these openings, the PLO was invited to establish quasi-embassies, i.e., "information offices," in Italy, France, Holland, Belgium, Britain, and Germany. France and Italy were the most cordial to PLO officials, Germany and Britain the most reserved; but the dialogues begun through these contacts laid the foundation for an important new approach to the PLO (independent from the United States) on the part of many European countries. By 1978-79 a consensus existed among the European governments on the necessity of an independent Palestinian state as a sine qua non for Middle East peace. Indeed, in June 1980 the members of the European Common Market issued the "Venice Declaration," which endorsed the principle of Palestinian self-determination, and called for the PLO to participate in the peace process.[18] Unfortunately, the European states were effectively powerless in the realpolitik of the Middle East. But this international recognition, the widespread legitimacy the PLO enjoyed among Palestinians, the existence of expatriate Palestinian communities in most Arab countries, and the continuing potency of the issue of Palestine among Arab masses all added to the unwillingness of other Arab regimes to follow Sadat's lead.

A number of factors contributed to the transformation of the PLO. One of the most important was its situation in inter-Arab politics. Ultimately the PLO reflected the post-1973 change in the Arab state system concerning the acceptance of Israel as a fait accompli and the necessity of seeking accommodation with the Jewish state on the basis of the pre-1967 borders. The PLO was confronted with the dilemma of maintaining a balance between the pursuit of Palestinian interests while not offending Arab state interests.[19] At the same time, it faced relentless Israeli and American refusal to acknowledge its existence as a legitimate actor in Middle East politics, let alone negotiate with it over issues of substance. Additionally, the United States was the dominant external power in the region and was fully committed to Israel while simultaneously enjoying close relations with a number of key Arab regimes. PLO leaders thus concluded that the organization would not survive if it were to operate outside the parameters of the Arab state system. Moreover, the results of its commando warfare were uncertain, even portrayed in the most favorable light. After the 1970 disaster in Jordan and the loss of access to their bases in the East Bank with its lengthy boundary along the occupied areas, the Palestinians were relegated to bases in Syria and Lebanon. Damascus kept a tight rein on the guerrillas, rarely allowing them to operate from its territory. The Lebanese border with Israel is short and was relatively easy for the Israelis to defend, particularly considering Israel's willingness to use massive fire power and aerial bombardment of Lebanese towns and villages and Palestinian refugee camps. In addition, the Israeli strategy added to the politically difficult circumstances of the PLO in Lebanon, generating animosity toward the Palestinians on the part of the Lebanese who were subjected to Israel's massive bombing raids and land incursions.[20] The Lebanese civil war worsened the Palestinian position in Lebanon. Finally, the PLO devoted enormous energy and resources to the development of a wide variety of civilian social institutions in the refugee camps in Lebanon—educational, medical, economic, welfare, cultural, etc.— that served both to meet the needs of the Palestinians and to provide prototypes for a future independent state. The involvement in institution-building was also a moderating and organizationally transforming force. Thus for all these reasons, PLO guerrilla activity declined markedly in the post–1975-76 period and was replaced with an emphasis on diplomacy and an effort to find a political solution to the Palestinian situation. However, the rapidly evolving moderation of the PLO (evidenced in the acceptance of the two-state solution and in a variety of other indicators such as the endorsement of a joint U.S.–Soviet peace proposal put forward in October 1977[21]) was met with continuous Israeli intransigence. The Palestinian dilemma became increasingly difficult as a result of Sadat's particularistic political initiative, which negated the most basic concern of the Palestinians, i.e., self-determination.

The shattering impact of Sadat's diplomacy in the Arab world was paralleled by the devastation of the civil war in Lebanon—a war that involved class, religious, tribal, ethnic and social conflict, and was in a sense a microcosm of the entire Arab world.[22] The war was not entirely an internal affair, however; external forces contributed significantly to the intensity, duration, and outcome of the conflict. Indeed, once hostilities erupted, Israel directly supported the rightist, Christian-dominated coalition, perpetuating the fighting and ultimately pressuring Syria into siding with the rightist factions against the leftist Lebanese coalition (the LNM and the Palestinians).[23] The war ended as a result of the entry of the Syrians on the side of the rightist forces (to forestall Israeli action on their behalf) in the latter part of October 1976, but its termination merely set the stage for events to come.

In March 1978 Israel launched a full-scale invasion into Lebanon, allegedly in retaliation for a Palestinian guerrilla raid carried out across Israel's northern border. A more important motivation for the invasion was the desire to establish a "security belt" in southern Lebanon. Israel occupied that area until June 13, when the security zone—an area some seven miles wide—was firmly established. The area was placed under the nominal control of a renegade Lebanese major, Saad Haddad, whose militia subsequently was fully integrated into the Israeli Defense Forces.

The Iranian revolution and the overthrow of the shah in 1979, while not in and of itself part of the inter-Arab context, had profound consequences for the stability of the region. In general the revolution affected the Arab world through its moral impact on the Arab people, in the context of the decadent and illegitimate nature of political authority in the Arab states. Iraq, Saudi Arabia, and the other countries of the Arabian Gulf were acutely aware of the potential domestic crises they could face if the ideas and activism of the revolution spread to their countries. Iraq's concern, heightened by Iran's incitement of the Shi'ite majority in Iraq to overthrow the government of Saddam Hussein (a Sunni), led Baghdad to initiate a war with Iran in 1980 to put an end to Khomeini and his Islamic revolution.[24]

Israel's Internal Politics

In June 1977 Menachem Begin, leader of the Herut party, came to power in a coalition government, the Likud, that brought a new emphasis and a new style to Israeli foreign policy. The Labor party, which had been in power without interruption since the establishment of the state in 1948, found itself defeated and disorganized. The Herut party had been formed by Begin in 1948 from the terrorist organization the Irgun Zvai Leumi. (The Irgun was famous—or infamous—for blowing up British military installations in Palestine, dynamiting the King David Hotel, and executing British soldiers as well as massacring 250 men, women, and children at Deir Yassin.)

In addition, the Herut party was part of the revisionist strain of Zionism, fathered by Vladimir Jabotinsky, which opposed the partition of Palestine and called for the creation of a Jewish state in all of historic Palestine (defined to include Jordan). And indeed, the bond that held the Likud coalition together in 1977 and through subsequent years was the commitment to the concept of "Eretz Israel" (Greater Israel): the belief that the territories acquired in the 1967 war were "rightly" Israel's and should be incorporated into the Jewish state. However, while Begin was committed to Jewish sovereignty in all of what he considered ancient Palestine, he was not committed on ideological grounds to retaining the Sinai. In part it was this lack of emotional/ideological attachment to Sinai that made it possible, in the end, for the prime minister to accept an accord with Egypt, although many members of his coalition opposed the peace treaty intensely. Begin was also motivated to conclude the Egyptian-Israeli treaty because of the second document he secured at Camp David, which, in effect, ceded the West Bank to Israel after a five-year transitional period—an important step toward the realization of Eretz Israel.

Under the Begin government Jewish settlement in the occupied West Bank was greatly accelerated as the Likud proceeded with plans for annexation of the territory. At the same time repression and terrorism against the Palestinians living in the West Bank and Gaza assumed new and more ominous dimensions, ultimately designed to foster the emigration of the indigenous population. Though Washington denounced the settlements as "illegal" and an "obstacle to peace,"[25] the dichotomy between principle and practice in American Middle East policy was particularly apparent on this issue. Statements calling the settlements "illegal" had no practical meaning when the United States continuously provided the financial assistance that permitted their construction, and American economic aid to Israel grew enormously throughout this period.

The Likud's position on the Palestinians, while seemingly harsher than previous Israeli governments, was in fact quite consistent. The leaders of both the Labor alignment and the Likud coalition were steadfast in denying the existence of the Palestinians as a people, in refusing to consider the Palestinian right to self-determination, in refusing to engage in any negotiations with the PLO, and in defining the PLO as a "terrorist" organization. Prime Minister Golda Meir had stated in 1969: "It is not as though there was a Palestinian people in Palestine considering itself as a Palestinian people and we came and threw them out and took their country away from them. They did not exist."[26] When Yitzhak Rabin became prime minister, he explained why Israel would refuse to negotiate "with any Palestinian element." This would provide "a basis for the possibility of creating a third state between Israel and Jordan," which Israel would never accept. "I repeat firmly, clearly, categorically: it will not be created."[27] Some years later, speaking in support of Prime Minister Begin, Rabin reiterated Israel's long-standing opposition to negotiating with the PLO. The PLO, he said, could not be a partner to any negotiations, "even if it accepts all of the conditions of negotiations on the basis of the Camp David agreements [in addition to Resolutions 242 and 338], because the essence of the willingness to speak with the PLO is the willingness to speak about the establishment of a Palestinian state, which must be opposed."[28] (Meir and Rabin, of course, were spokespersons for the Labor party).

The International Context, Regional Linkages, and American Interests

Great Power Relations and the Continuing U.S. Interest in Limiting Soviet Expansion

In the international system in the period after the October War and the two disengagement agreements, détente remained the cornerstone of American policy vis-à-vis the Soviet Union (despite the serious challenge to the concept that had arisen during the war). However, the U.S. failure in Vietnam, marking the final collapse of the containment policy as enunciated by Harry Truman and pursued by subsequent administrations, gave the policy of détente even greater significance.

Washington had not, as discussed in Chapter 5, abandoned its effort to limit the expansion of Soviet influence; rather the perceptions dominant in elite circles about the nature of the Soviet state had changed and, more important, the means used to contain Moscow had been altered. Washington continued to believe in "interdependence" and "linkage" as the basis of its policy; thus trade with the Soviet Union was considered a major instrument to achieve the objectives of détente. In addition to its profitability for American industrialists and farmers, U.S. officials felt that trade would provide a powerful material incentive for a Soviet foreign policy of "restraint and accommodation" around the globe. But as questionable as were the linkage assumptions in the international context, when they were extended to the Soviet domestic sphere, "linkage" contributed to the unraveling of détente. That extension came about as a result of efforts by pro-Israeli groups to connect U.S. trade with the Soviet Union to the issue of Soviet Jewry. This was part of a complex strategy to tie Israel—with a professed commitment to the well-being of every Jew everywhere in the world—into the fundamental American policy of limiting Soviet expansionism (sometimes referred to as the "cold war anti-Communist consensus" in the United States). By focusing U.S. public attention on Soviet mistreatment of Jews and Israeli efforts to rescue them, pro-Israeli elements expected that the image of Israel as a strategic asset to America's objective of containing Soviet influence in the Middle East would be enhanced. (Israel was also motivated on this issue by its interest in fostering the immigration of Soviet Jews, whose skills, education, and Ashkenazi ethos, it was hoped, would offset the growing demographic domination of the Oriental-Sephardim in Israeli society.) Just how politically motivated the campaign on behalf of Soviet Jewry was became apparent in the controversy over the persecution of Jews in Argentina during the mid-1970s by a Fascist, anti-Semitic regime. During that ugly affair Israel attempted to stifle criticism of the Argentine government— most notably the criticism of Jacobo Timmerman, an Argentinean Jew who had been imprisoned, tortured, and subjected to official anti-Semitism—to preserve Israel's burgeoning trade relationship with Argentina.[29]

On the one hand, the lobby's linkage campaign was highly successful from the perspective of Israel's interest in appearing as a valuable asset to the United States. On the other hand, the pro-Israeli effort contributed in considerable measure to the deterioration of détente. A major "victory" in the lobby's efforts was the Jackson-Vanik amendment of 1974, which formally tied Soviet-American trade to the emigration of Soviet Jews. But in early 1975 Moscow rejected the trade agreement that had been concluded with Washington, considering that this amendment was a serious intervention in Soviet domestic affairs. Moreover, at home Moscow temporarily suspended Jewish emigration entirely after this amendment was passed, and when emigration resumed, the number of Jews permitted to leave the Soviet Union dropped from approximately 35,000 in 1973 to less than 15,000 in 1975 and 1976.[30] Obviously no state, let alone a great power, would publicly admit that it mistreated part of its population and allow itself to be placed on probation by a foreign nation in return for trade. Moreover, since to a great extent Soviet motives for pursuing détente were economic, this lack of payoff reduced its reasons for maintaining détente.

The Carter administration, which took office in 1977, initially adopted the world view that there were limits to American power; that America should act in a more restrained manner than it had in the past in terms of intervention in foreign countries; and that human rights for all peoples were an important American value that should be pursued at the international level. However, Jimmy Carter's selective pursuit of human rights did not impress the Soviets, causing additional strain in the détente framework. Nevertheless, U.S.–Soviet relations were reasonably good, but ambiguous, in the years 1974-79, although toward the end they deteriorated seriously as a result of Soviet involvement in Afghanistan. Note also that in spite of the ups and downs in relations between Washington and Moscow and despite Soviet involvement with a number of Arab regimes, the Soviet Union has been consistent since 1948 in supporting Israel's right to exist (it voted for the 1947 resolution to partition Palestine and supplied the Zionists with arms in the first Arab-Israeli war). Moscow has also been consistent since 1967 in supporting Israel's right to secure national boundaries within the pre-1967 lines; it has steadfastly backed Resolution 242 even in the absence of diplomatic relations with the Jewish state (broken after the June War).

Relations between the United States and the Soviet Union evidenced notable cooperation on the Middle East during the first year of President Carter's tenure. In the context of the president's efforts to facilitate a comprehensive solution in the Middle East and to reconvene the Geneva Conference as a way of breathing life into the stalled peace process, the United States participated with the Soviet Union in issuing a joint statement on October 1, 1977, outlining a comprehensive settlement for the region. The communiqué called for: (1) Israeli withdrawal from occupied Arab lands; (2) resolution of the Palestinian question, including insuring the legitimate rights of the Palestinian people; (3) termination of the state of war between Israel and the Arabs with the establishment of normal, peaceful relations among the countries on the basis of mutual recognition, sovereignty, territorial integrity and political independence; and (4) international guarantees (in which both the United States and the Soviet Union would participate) to ensure compliance with the terms of settlement.[31] The statement was also significant for what it did not say: it did not call for direct PLO participation in the talks at Geneva, it did not mention a Palestinian state, and Israel was not asked to return to the 1967 borders or to abandon East Jerusalem. Moreover, the Soviets had sent a message to Prime Minister Begin on September 23 stating that Moscow would restore diplomatic relations with Israel on the day the Geneva Conference was reconvened.[32]

Nevertheless, the Arab governments and the PLO welcomed the Soviet-American statement.[33] In fact, William Quandt (a member of the National Security Council staff from January 1977 to July 1979 who reported directly to National Security Advisor Zbigniew Brzezinski and whose primary area of responsibility was the Arab-Israeli conflict[34]) relates that Egypt, in particular, was extremely enthusiastic about the communiqué.[35] Moreover, it was Egyptian President Sadat who transmitted to Carter the PLO's decision to accept representation at Geneva within a unified Arab delegation. (The Palestinian contingent was to be headed by Edward Said, a professor of English literature at Columbia University and a member of the PNC.)[36] Relinquishing the demand for independent representation constituted a significant compromise for the PLO. Moreover, by agreeing to participate in the Geneva Conference the PLO was very clearly signaling its acceptance of Israel's right to security and peaceful existence within internationally recognized boundaries and its acceptance of diplomacy as the fundamental means to achieve political objectives. Israel, however, immediately rejected any PLO participation in negotiations at Geneva while reiterating its opposition to the reconvening of the conference. (Israel had objected to Carter's proposal for a resumption of Geneva—and its underlying principle of a comprehensive settlement—from the outset, but had reluctantly participated in preparatory plans and discussions for the conference.) In addition, Moshe Dayan forcefully restated Israel's policy that it would never negotiate with the PLO under any circumstances.[37] Given Israel's opposition to the Geneva Conference and to a comprehensive settlement, its refusal to deal with the PLO, and the intense pressures pro-Israeli constituencies exerted on Carter after the October 1 communiqué (discussed below), it seems highly unlikely that the U.S.–Soviet initiative could have been implemented. However, Anwar Sadat's journey to Israel and the dynamics he created as a result of that trip preempted the initiative, and it was never resurrected.

America was preoccupied throughout most of 1978 with the Egyptian-Israeli peace process and with the deteriorating situation in Iran. Washington was also concerned about a Soviet-inspired coup in Afghanistan. When the Soviets invaded that country in 1979, the Carter administration reversed its earlier premise regarding the limits of American power and projected the urgency of a direct U.S. military presence in the area. Contingency plans were drawn up for U.S. troop movements to the Gulf, a Rapid Deployment Force was established, and the rhetoric of a new aggressive Carter Doctrine was in vogue. Indeed, the cold war was once again joined.

Access to Oil: An Ongoing American Interest

OPEC was an important actor on the international scene after the October War. The enormous price increases OPEC instituted had a profound impact on both developed and underdeveloped countries. Moreover, it seemed, at least for a time, that Saudi Arabia and the other Arab oil-producing states would continue to cut production and raise prices if a satisfactory solution was not found to the Palestinian issue and other Arab concerns. Thus, the United States attempted to co-opt Saudi Arabia. The sale of sixty F-15 fighters in 1978 and five sophisticated electronic surveillance planes (AWACs) in 1981 (both sales intensely opposed by Israel and its American friends) were important parts of this effort, as was tying Saudi economic interests to the American-dominated, Western capitalist system. Significantly, however, after its spectacular entry on the world scene in 1973 with the embargo and the rapid series of price increases, OPEC never again used its potentially powerful tool to affect American policy. This was mainly the result of the successful integration of the interests of the oil-producing states with the Western economic order, resulting both from adroit American diplomacy and, probably more important, from the desire of the elites of the oil-producing states to have it that way.[38] Indeed, by the advent of the Carter administration, the governing elites of Saudi Arabia as well as of most other Arab countries saw their own interests—personal and state—as best served by some sort of alignment with the United States, however ambiguous and rhetorically denied. Nevertheless, the alleged threat of OPEC action remained a part of the American political scene.

The U.S. Interest in Regional Stability

Both Lebanon and Iran were major areas of instability in the Middle East with potentially serious consequences for American interests. Washington accorded less attention to Lebanon than Iran, though Lebanon's civil strife and its continuous penetration by Israel made it a certain source of problems for the United States. Moreover, Washington appeared not to notice that Israel was a major cause of the instability in Lebanon at the same time that it was unable to quell the turbulence in Iran.

Indeed, the United States never appeared to comprehend how seriously and negatively Israel's military policies—massive raids into neighboring countries, bombing forays, and invasions—affected regional stability; at least it never took measures to prevent them. The Carter administration demonstrated more concern than previous governments, and President Carter responded with some firmness to the Israeli invasion of Lebanon in 1978. Two days after the invasion began, on March 16, Washington formally asked the Israelis to withdraw. The administration also introduced a resolution in the U.N. Security Council (Resolution 425) that called for total Israeli withdrawal from Lebanon and the establishment of a U.N. observer force. A United Nations contingent (UNIFIL) entered Lebanon on March 23, although Israel did not withdraw until June 13. Israeli involvement in Lebanon continued until July 1981 when the United States arranged a cease-fire between Israel and the PLO. That truce maintained quiet on the Israeli side of the border (though Israel repeatedly violated Lebanese sovereignty) until Israel invaded Lebanon again in June 1982.

At the beginning of 1979 the Pahlavi dynasty in Iran collapsed. After almost thirty years of extensive American support to this despotic but pro-American government, and after massive transfers of sophisticated weapons to the Iranian military, the shah was toppled by mass insurgency. It was unremarked in Washington that America's strategic asset, Israel, was helpless to assist the Pahlavi regime or to prevent insurrection in Iran. Yet if Israel could not assist a non-Arab regional government (with whom it had excellent, if covert, relations) to maintain itself in power, how could it be argued that Israel was protecting conservative Arab governments from radical uprisings on behalf of the United States? This question was not even debated, and conventional orthodoxy was maintained.

The Iranian revolution had serious implications for Middle East stability and was deeply unsettling to Washington strategists; it not only demolished the shah's government but also ushered in a government that clearly was not going to function in the service of American interests. The revolution dealt a severe blow to the prevailing wisdom of the Nixon Doctrine concerning the utility of regional surrogates. In addition, the United States perceived a threat to its interests throughout the Middle East in the rise of militant Islamic fundamentalism. The Iranian revolution touched a positive nerve in the Arab peoples in the region, and this in turn raised serious questions about the stability of the Gulf states, including Saudi Arabia. Concern was then generated about future Western freedom of access to Gulf oil supplies and other Western commercial and strategic interests. Indeed, Islamism proved to be a genuine threat to American interests, but the United States never grasped how to deal with this phenomenon. Nor did Washington ever comprehend how much its own policies in the region—support for the shah, disregard of the Palestinians, alignment with Israel—contributed to the intense anti-American element in the growing fundamentalist movement.[39]

The American Commitment to Israel's "Security"

In the period immediately following the conclusion of the Israeli-Egyptian and Israeli-Syrian disengagement agreements in 1974, there was considerable optimism in the United States about the prospects for an ongoing peace process. A trip by President Richard Nixon to Egypt, Saudi Arabia, Syria, Israel, and Jordan in June 1974 was intended to emphasize America's commitment to facilitating a resolution of the Arab-Israeli conflict, to improve relations with the Arab states, and to strengthen its traditional ties to Israel.

In their strategy for continuance of the peace process, most officials in the United States believed that Israeli-Jordanian negotiations were essential to secure Israel's withdrawal from the West Bank. King Hussein informed Washington of the substantial concessions he was prepared to make, and at the end of a visit to Washington by the king on August 18, 1974, a joint American-Jordanian statement indicated the willingness of the United States to support a Jordanian-Israeli disengagement process.[40] Israel, however, was not interested in negotiating with Jordan over the West Bank, and the initiative was scuttled. Since Israel was even more emphatic that it would never negotiate with the PLO, there were few options for a resolution of the West Bank occupation. Indeed, Israel attempted to foreclose possibilities regarding the West Bank both by rejecting negotiating opportunities and by continuously constructing illegal settlements—creating "facts on the ground"—leading to a gradual de facto annexation of the area. The Labor party took the lead in this strategy, though it was significantly accelerated by the Likud in 1977 and thereafter. Washington appeared to take little notice.

Henry Kissinger went to the Middle East in November 1974 in an attempt to avert a collapse of his step-by-step diplomacy, but the regional scene was complicated from the Israeli–U.S. perspective as a result of the Rabat conference and the Soviet Union's call for a return to Geneva. The secretary of state returned home without achieving any progress. Significantly, however, in the communiqué issued at the end of the Vladivostok Summit (also in November), it appeared that the Soviet Union would accept Kissinger's step-by-step approach.[41] The PLO was not mentioned in that communiqué.

After considerable preparatory groundwork both in Washington and the Middle East, Kissinger returned to the region and undertook an intensive shuttle from March 8 through March 23, 1975, in an attempt to attain a second agreement between Israel and Egypt. But even after five months of preliminary efforts, the positions of the two countries were still far apart. Israel wanted to minimize its territorial withdrawals, while obtaining broad political concessions; Egypt was primarily interested in the return of its territory, particularly the Mitla and Gidi passes and the Abu Rudeis oil fields. Prior to Kissinger's departure Israeli officials had been explicit in expressing their demands concerning what was expected of Egypt. For example, Yigal Allon stated in a lecture at Tel Aviv University on December 26, 1974, that an interim agreement would see partial Israeli withdrawal only in exchange for "significant strategic and political commitments by Egypt."[42] The Israeli ambassador to the United States, Simcha Dinitz, in a televised interview on the "Today" show in February 1975, presented a list of Egyptian actions that Israel considered essential concessions:

They can shift the emphasis of their national effort from the accumulation of weapons of war to the reconstruction of their towns and the development of their economies; the Egyptians can reopen the Suez Canal and allow Israeli ships to pass through without let or hindrance; the Arab governments can call off their economic boycott of Israel (instead of intensifying it); they can desist from their diplomatic ostracism of Israel at the United Nations and other international forums; they can curtail their incendiary anti-Israeli broadcasts and the dissemination of hate by other means (schools, mosques, newspapers, books, and so on); they can open their borders with Israel to the movement of people and goods in both directions.[43]

It is not surprising that the shuttle ended in failure. Indeed, Israel had demanded a written agreement from Egypt ending the state of belligerency between the two countries and had insisted on a normalization of relations (in the form of a political agreement that would allow for free movement of tourists, an end to the economic boycott, and much more) while agreeing to retreat only 30 to 50 kilometers, still leaving the Abu Rudeis oil fields and the Mitla and Gidi passes in its control.[44] In response to Israel's demands Sadat asked: "What am I supposed to give them? I can't give them land. I can't give them anything against my sovereignty. . . . Isn't it sufficient that I have already started reconstruction in the Suez Canal zone and more than half a million refugees are returning to the three cities and up to this moment they are under the range of the Israeli artillery?"[45]

In fact, the administration believed that it was incumbent on Israel, under Resolutions 242 and 338, to make a gesture that would demonstrate that it did not intend to occupy Egyptian territory permanently and was committed to the principle of territory in exchange for peace. Thus on March 23, President Gerald Ford, backed by Kissinger, issued a statement announcing his intention to "reassess" U.S. policy in the Middle East. The announcement was designed to signal Israel of the administration's displeasure with the Jewish state's intransigence. Washington never publicly criticized Israel, but the Israelis deeply resented even this subtle pressure and successfully undermined the administration through a dramatic coup staged by their American supporters, who mobilized all their resources in an extraordinary effort that evidenced the decline of presidential prerogative with respect to Middle East policymaking and highlighted the growing congressional influence on these issues.

In late May seventy-six Senators were induced to sign a letter to President Ford (drafted in part by the American-Israel Public Affairs Committee), pledging their support for Israel. The letter stated that American policy should seek a settlement "on the basis of secure and recognized boundaries that are defensible," demanded that the military balance not be allowed to shift against Israel, and demanded that the United States be responsive to Israel's economic and military needs. The letter called on the president to make it clear that "the United States acting in its own national interests stands firmly with Israel in the search for peace in future negotiations, and that this premise is the basis of the current reassessment of United States policy in the Middle East."[46]

The letter was published just prior to a meeting between President Ford and President Sadat in Salzburg, Austria, at a time when the two nations were engaged in delicate negotiations aimed at resuming the Israeli-Egyptian talks.[47] The Egyptian People's Assembly bitterly denounced the letter as "a flagrant bias in favor of Israel" and characterized the signers as "hostile to peace."[48] The *New York Times* carried a story from Israel, which quoted a senior Israeli official as stating: "Buoyed by recent demonstrations of congressional support, Israel has decided to ignore repeated United States requests that it produce new negotiating proposals before the American-Egyptian meeting in Salzburg."[49] One White House official commented that the Senators' letter cost the United States an extra $500 million in aid tied to the second Sinai agreement.[50] Former Undersecretary of State George Ball argues in a similar vein that the pro-Israeli strength demonstrated by the letter weakened Kissinger's ability to secure concessions from Israel and increased the amount of the "subsidy" the United States had to pay Israel in order to achieve Sinai II.[51] Whatever else it may have done, the letter clearly betrayed Kissinger's claim that Washington was an honest broker in Arab-Israeli negotiations.

Kissinger and Ford pressed ahead in the attempt to secure a second agreement between the Israelis and the Egyptians, even though their ability to exert any real pressure on Israel was effectively undercut by the pro-Israeli strength evidenced in Congress. In August 1975 Kissinger undertook another shuttle, which lasted fourteen days, in a further effort to produce the desired accord. This time he was successful, but only after providing Israel with extensive and far-reaching secret commitments that placed serious constraints on the conduct of American foreign policy in the Middle East. The complex of agreements known as Sinai II were formally initialed on September 1 in Jerusalem and Alexandria and were signed in Geneva on September 4 by representatives of Egypt and Israel.[52]

Under the terms of Sinai II the lines in the Sinai were redrawn in an ambiguous way: Israel evacuated the Gidi and Mitla passes (essentially a route through the peaks of a chain of hills) but was allowed to put its forward defense line at the bottom of the eastern slopes of the hills. Egypt was allowed to bring troops to the western slopes of the hills, and a U.N. buffer zone was established at the peak of the hills proper. Thus Egypt could say it had "gotten back" the passes, and Israel could say it had not given them up. The use of American personnel in an "early warning system" in the hills near the passes was a face-saver for Israel, although it established a dangerous precedent for the United States by introducing American troops into an area of potential Arab-Israeli conflict. Egypt renounced belligerency and committed itself to move toward a formal peace. As in the past, the UNEF remained on Egyptian soil.

The compensations provided by the United States to Israel for its signature on the accord, contained in four secret Memoranda of Agreement, were extraordinary. Washington pledged (1) to provide Israel immediately with approximately $2 billion in military and economic aid and new military hardware; (2) to drop the push for a Jordanian-Israeli withdrawal agreement; (3) that in case of involvement of a great power in a war with Israel there would be active counterinvolvement by the United States; (4) to be "fully responsive" on an "ongoing and long term basis to Israel's military and defense requirements, to its energy requirements and to its economic needs." (Indeed, Kissinger committed the United States, in the midst of an acute American oil shortage and crisis, to providing Israel with all its oil needs if it could not meet its requirements by itself, even to the extent of transporting the oil to Israel.)[53]

In addition, Washington pledged (5) to "take into account in calculating" the figure for annual aid "Israel's additional expenditures for the import of oil to replace that which would ordinarily come from Abu Rudeis and Ras Sudar (4.5 million tons in 1975)"; (6) that Israel would not have to implement its part of the Sinai II agreement until Egypt permitted passage of all Israeli cargoes from Israeli ports through the Suez Canal; (7) to support the Israeli position "that the next agreement with Egypt should be a final peace agreement"; (8) to vote against any Security Council resolution unfavorable to Israel, including a pledge "not to join in and to seek to prevent efforts by others to bring about consideration of proposals which it and Israel agree are detrimental to the interests of Israel"; (9) to conclude with Israel "as soon as possible" the "contingency plan for a military supply operation to Israel in an emergency situation"; (10) to never recognize or negotiate with the PLO so long as the PLO did not formally recognize Israel's right to exist and did not accept Security Council Resolutions 242 and 338; (11) to "consult fully and seek to concert its position and strategy at the Geneva Peace Conference . . . with the government of Israel." Finally, on military matters: "The United States is resolved to continue to maintain Israel's defensive strength through the supply of advanced types of equipment such as F-16 aircraft. The United States agrees to an early meeting to undertake a joint study of high technology and sophisticated items, including the Pershing ground-to-ground missiles with conventional warheads."[54]

This "marriage contract" was unique in the annals of American foreign policy, the more so in that it was secret in form, an "executive agreement" that was never submitted to Congress for ratification under the constitutional provision requiring the advice and consent of the Senate on treaties with foreign nations. (There is no reason to assume that the Senate would have objected to the agreements if they had been submitted, however, given the pro-Israeli orientation of Congress by this time.) And it was all for a limited and partial Israeli pullback of its occupation forces in the Sinai desert.

The remainder of 1975 and 1976 were devoted primarily to the upcoming presidential elections. The Republican candidate (incumbent Gerald Ford) and the Democratic candidate (Jimmy Carter) outdid themselves in pledging support for Israel and fidelity to its interests.

The Carter Administration: A New Approach to American Interests in the Middle East

Once in office the Carter administration initially seemed prepared to take a fresh approach to the Middle East, although there was no debate and apparently no questions raised about the concept of Israel as a strategic asset and a guarantor of American interests in the region. Nevertheless, in mid-February 1977, Carter sent Secretary of State Cyrus Vance to Israel, Egypt, Lebanon, Jordan, Syria, and Saudi Arabia to prepare an administration initiative. That spring Carter met with Prime Minister Yitzhak Rabin of Israel, President Sadat of Egypt, King Hussein of Jordan, and President Assad of Syria. Carter forthrightly addressed the need for a comprehensive settlement in the Middle East (reversing his predecessor's step-by-step approach) and undertook specific steps to reconvene the Geneva Conference. In addition, the new president seemed to show some understanding of the centrality of the Palestinian issue.[55] William Quandt outlines Carter's approach to the Middle East on both process and substance: "The president was openly committed to an active American role in trying to break the deadlock in Arab-Israeli negotiations. He saw the Middle East dispute as closely related to both the energy crisis and the danger of superpower confrontation. He was also convinced that progress must be made in 1977.... On substantive issues ... he ... spoke publicly of three basic requirements for Middle East peace. First, peace should entail normal relations, such as exchange of ambassadors, trade, open borders, tourism, and regional economic cooperation. . . . He was sensitive to the Israeli argument that there was an asymmetry in asking the Arabs to make peace and the Israelis to give up territory. . . . Second, . . . was the need for borders that would be recognized and arrangements for security that might go beyond the borders. . . . He thus tried to meet Israel's concern for security by placing heavy emphasis on these technical arrangements. . . . Carter was also prepared [to] bolster Israeli security, up to and including a U.S.–Israeli defense pact as part of an overall settlement. . . . [Third] Carter took the lead in articulating a new position for the United States on the Palestine question, calling for the creation of a 'homeland' for the refugees."[56]

Carter encountered opposition from Israel and its domestic supporters on both his substantive concept of a comprehensive settlement and his procedural approach of attempting to reconvene the Geneva Conference. But it was over his statements about the Palestinians that the president was subjected to the most extreme abuse and intense opposition from pro-Israeli quarters. No matter how strongly and concretely Carter demonstrated his support for Israel, the Jewish state and its American friends were relentless in their condemnation of any expressions of concern about the Palestinians.

The president first publicly articulated some thoughts on the Palestinian issue in a speech on March 15, 1977, in Clinton, Massachusetts, where he spoke of the need for a Palestinian homeland[57] (to be distinguished, it is to be noted, from a Palestinian state). But it was the first time that such a concept had been part of any official American statement since 1947, when the United States supported the U.N. partition resolution dividing Palestine into a Jewish and an Arab state. However, immediately following the Clinton speech Israel and its American supporters heaped disapprobation on the president. Carter then significantly qualified his original comments: "The exact definition of what that homeland might be, the degree of independence of the Palestinian entity, its relations with Jordan, or perhaps Syria and others, the geographical boundaries of it, all have to be worked out by the parties involved."[58] In practice, as did all previous presidents, Carter opposed Palestinian self-determination, subscribing rather to some form of "autonomy" for the Palestinians under one or another foreign domination.[59] Still, Israel and its domestic friends remained outraged and deluged the White House with protests. Subsequently, a more detailed statement on the "homeland" issue came from Vice-President Walter Mondale, speaking for the Carter administration before the World Affairs Council in San Francisco on June 17, 1977.[60] Mondale's statement embodied all of Carter's qualifications plus new ones and was intended to satisfy the Israelis and their domestic supporters, who were not, however, placated.

Then, when on October 1, 1977, President Carter participated in issuing the joint Soviet-American statement on the Middle East, Israel and its American backers reacted vehemently. The Israeli government rejected the joint statement, in the words of Finance Minister Simcha Ehrlich (speaking for Prime Minister Begin, who was in a hospital), "with both hands" because it was "the first step toward an imposed solution" and because "it indicated American willingness to have the PLO participate in a Geneva Peace Conference." Ehrlich suggested that the Carter administration's action represented an effort to relieve its frustration from policy failures in other areas by forging ahead at all costs to convene a Middle East peace conference. The Labor party supported the Likud government, likewise strongly denouncing the Soviet-American statement. A former foreign minister, Yigal Allon, pronounced it "unnecessary, ill-timed, and ill-phrased."[61] Israeli officials charged that the phrase "legitimate rights" was a code word for their greatest fear, a Palestinian state on the West Bank and Gaza. They were especially outraged at the absence of any specific reference in the joint statement to U.N. Resolutions 242 and 338: "We hang onto those with all our strength because they say nothing about the Palestinians."[62] (It is not difficult then to understand why the PLO has been unwilling to accept these resolutions by themselves.)

The opposition to the Soviet-American initiative from domestic pro-Israeli sources was equally severe. Rabbi Alexander M. Schindler, chairman of the Conference of Presidents of Major American Jewish Organizations, said that the joint statement, "on its face, represents an abandonment of America's historic commitment to the security and survival of Israel." Senator Henry Jackson, one of Israel's most vigorous supporters in the Senate, and George Meany, president of the AFL-CIO, warned that any attempts by the Carter administration to "undercut" Israel would backfire politically on the president.[63] In addition, wealthy Jewish Democrats refused to purchase tickets for a fund-raising dinner that the president was scheduled to attend.[64]

To emphasize its disapproval of the Soviet-American declaration, the Israeli government dispatched Foreign Minister Moshe Dayan to the United States to "consult" with President Carter. On October 4 the two men met at a hotel in New York, and after a lengthy session the president agreed to a series of proposals presented by Dayan, including a specific promise never to use military or economic sanctions to pressure Israel to make concessions on any issue in future negotiations. Carter also promised Dayan that Israel would be informed in advance who the Palestinians would be at Geneva and could "screen" them to ensure that no PLO members were seated. The president then added that Israel could always refuse to participate if it did not approve of the Palestinians. Quandt makes the important observation that because Carter approached Dayan from the perspective of seeking help from the Israeli foreign minister on his domestic problems with American Jews, Dayan thus had great leverage in their negotiations. The result was that while the evening began with Israel and the United States on the verge of a major confrontation, it ended with the United States fully siding with Israel. The Israeli–U.S. joint statement issued that night was a triumph for Israel on both form and substance. It included U.S. commitments that Resolutions 242 and 338 would remain the basis for the resumption of the Geneva Conference and in effect absolved Israel of the need to accept the U.S.–Soviet joint statement.[65] Moreover, in a speech to the U.N. General Assembly earlier on October 4, the president had spoken of the need for a "true peace" based on Resolutions 242 and 338, stated that Israel must have "borders that are recognized and secure," and reiterated America's absolute commitment to Israel's "security."[66] Subsequently, it was reported that Carter and his aides were so relieved to have the rift with Israel smoothed over, and the prominent members and leading contributors of the American Jewish community once again (seemingly) friendly to Carter, that the president did not mind that he was perceived as having capitulated to Israel.[67] The *modus vivendi,* however, was short-lived, as Carter attempted to provide President Sadat some support for his peace initiative.

(Arab leaders meanwhile were stunned at Carter's acquiescence. Egyptian diplomat Mahmoud Riad records his perception: "While Israel succeeded in invalidating a document which had been agreed upon by the two superpowers, the Arab capitals were astounded at the amount of American subservience to Israeli pressure. Further evidence of this was soon to emerge when, on 28 October, the United States refrained from voting on a General Assembly resolution denouncing the establishment of Israeli settlements, while 131 countries voted in its favor."[68])

The most concrete manifestation of the solidification of the U.S.–Israeli partnership from 1974 through 1979—in addition to the commitments surrounding the Sinai II accord—may be seen in the ever-increasing amounts of financial aid given by the American government. Table 4 is illustrative.

The figures in this table do not include the private, tax-exempt transfers of money made by American citizens to Israel, estimated to be approximately $1.4 billion annually. In addition, there are non-aid accounts, including Export-Import bank loans, grants and contracts from the Department of Energy and the National Institutes of Health, and military contracts; economic infrastructure expenditures (not official foreign economic aid as listed in the chart), including trade support, foregone exports, and technology transfers; contingent aid, including the oil supply agreements of 1975 (and later 1979); and consequential aid, including the U.S. contribution to UNRWA, aid to Lebanon, including multinational forces and observers, and funds for reconstruction. In addition, Egypt later received aid as compensation for Camp David.[69]

TABLE 4. Assistance to Israel, 1974-79

Year	Total Aid	Economic Loans	Economic Grants	Military Loans	Military Grants	Soviet Jews' Resettlement Funds
1974	2,570.7		51.5	982.7	1,500.0	36.5
1975	693.1	8.6	344.5	200.0	100.0	40.0
1976	2,299.4	239.4	475.0	750.0	750.0	15.0
1977	1,757.0	252.0	490.0	500.0	500.0	15.0
1978	1,811.8	266.8	525.0	500.0	500.0	20.0
1979	4,815.1	265.1	525.0	2,700.0	1,300.0	25.0
TOTAL	13,877.1	1,031.9	2,411.0	5,632.7	4,650.0	151.5

SOURCE: *The Link,* Dec. 1982, 3.
NOTE: Data are in millions of dollars and do not include loans through the Export-Import bank.

Toward an Egyptian-Israeli Peace

September 1977 to September 1978:
Sadat's Visit to Israel: U.S., Israeli, and Egyptian Interests

There was at least one substantive, secret, preparatory meeting between the Israelis and the Egyptians prior to Sadat's visit to Israel in which both sides made their positions on negotiations clear. Moshe Dayan, Israeli minister of defense, met with Dr. Hassan Tuhamy, special envoy to President Sadat, on September 16, 1977, in Rabat, Morocco, under the auspices of the Moroccan monarch, King Hassan.[70] Dayan's account of the meeting demonstrates that the Israelis were aware of the Egyptian position and agenda for peace, and he conveys his impression that the Egyptians were "definitely interested in securing peace" and were prepared to compromise significantly on the Palestinian issue.[71] The Egyptian position as presented at the Rabat meeting was essentially full peace and a formal normalization of relations in exchange for Israeli withdrawal from territories occupied in the June War, Arab sovereignty in those territories, and Palestinian "nationhood" under the "control" of the various Arab countries. Tuhamy also conveyed Sadat's conviction that once Egypt formally initiated this process and received tangible results, Syria and Jordan would follow, and Saudi Arabia would give the process support.[72] It is significant that Sadat's opening bargaining position negated the concept of Palestinian self-determination, proposing instead an Arab-Israeli peace that excluded Palestinian national rights and ceded the West Bank to Jordan.

Dayan was explicit about Israel's position. Israel would not withdraw from all the territories occupied after June 1967, particularly not the West Bank; East Jerusalem would not come under Arab sovereignty; and the Palestinians were an Arab problem—the Arab states should absorb, control, and resettle them. Israel was not going to permit their return to Palestine, nor was it going to permit any Palestinian state or entity on the West Bank. The only possible concession Israel might consider was to eschew formal sovereignty over the West Bank and Gaza in favor of de facto annexation and continued military rule.[73] Significantly, King Hassan supported the Israeli position on the Palestinians at the meeting: "He said he accepted my [Dayan's] argument that the Palestinians were likely to prove a danger to Israel's future, just as they endangered the position of the King of Jordan. This problem had accordingly to be dealt with and settled in a reasonable manner: the Arab states should assume collective responsibility for the Palestinians, maintain supervision over them, and devise security measures which would satisfy Israel. The Palestinian problem after all, was basically an Arab problem: it should therefore be considered and solved by the Arab countries, and not by Israel or the United States."[74]

Thus not only did Sadat begin the "peace" process with the limited concept of "nationhood" under Arab "control" for the Palestinians, but he was also clearly aware of Israel's position concerning the Palestinians and the West Bank and proceeded knowing that this issue would have to be circumvented if Egypt was to regain its territory. The Egyptian president's frequent and seemingly forceful comments about "Palestinian self-determination" and "legitimate rights" in the months following his visit to Israel are explained by his need to placate his domestic opposition and his regional adversaries. It is clear that Sadat never had any interest in the establishment of an independent Palestinian state.

Dayan followed his meeting with Tuhamy by a meeting with President Carter and his advisors on September 19 (two weeks before the decisive October 4 session). Dayan informed Secretary of State Cyrus Vance about his meeting in Rabat. Later, with the president, Dayan urged the Americans to deal exclusively with Sadat and to ignore his advisors, especially Ismail Fahmy, the Egyptian foreign minister.[75] Indeed, Israel, and ultimately the United States, sought to isolate Sadat from Egyptian officials who disagreed with the president's bilateral approach.[76] Dayan also restated Israel's negative views concerning the Geneva Conference and the concept of a comprehensive settlement. The foreign minister informed Carter categorically during this meeting that the West Bank would never be returned to Jordan nor would it become a homeland for the Palestinians: "If the West Bank were annexed to Jordan, it would lead to the destruction of the State of Israel. It would mean our return to the pre-1967 borders; the dismantling of our military installations on the mountain ridges; and the pullback of our armed forces from the Jordan Valley. The territory would be ruled by the PLO and would serve as a base for a devastating attack on Israel."[77] However, Dayan did promise Carter that for one year there would be no new civilian settlements in the occupied areas.[78]

The president recorded his thoughts at the time: "When Israeli Foreign Minister Dayan came to Washington . . . I was then convinced that some of Israel's recent actions were the main obstacles to progress on the peace talks. I told him I thought the gratuitous endorsement of a new group of settlements, the recent Israeli invasion of Lebanon [one of the frequent reprisal incursions], and the failure to make any reasonable proposals or counterproposals on the question of Palestinian representation [at Geneva] were almost insuperable obstacles."[79] Dayan, too, wrote about the September 19 meeting. He labeled the president "hostile" and described the atmosphere in Washington as "ugly."[80]

The matter of settlements became an increasingly contentious issue between the United States and Israel in the aftermath of Dayan's departure, and remained so for the duration of the Camp David process. On October 10, the Israeli cabinet authorized six new settlements inside military camps on the West Bank (technically not violating Dayan's pledge to Carter concerning civilian settlements, but hardly in keeping with the spirit of the Dayan-Carter understanding). Moreover, a few days later work was begun on a civilian settlement near Jerusalem, at a site called Maale Adumim. In addition, shortly after Begin and Sadat met in Ismailia on December 25, 1977 (subsequent to Sadat's visit to Israel), Israel began construction on four new civilian settlements in the Sinai—an action that Carter considered a direct affront to Sadat's peace overture. And on January 23, 1978, work commenced on another civilian settlement in the West Bank, at Shiloh.[81] It is little wonder that Begin and Dayan were not considered trustworthy negotiators. On the other hand, the president never seriously attempted to prevent the construction of new settlements either through withholding aid or through any other measure.

The next Dayan-Carter meeting, on October 4, brought not only an end to Carter's advocacy of a resumption of the Geneva Conference, but also the abandonment of the Soviet-American initiative on the Middle East and a further reassessment by the president of his concerns about the Palestinian question. In ten months Israel and its American friends had engineered a major change in the direction of U.S. policy. Concerning the role of the domestic pro-Israeli effort President Carter made a revealing admission to a delegation of Egyptian officials in a White House meeting on September 21: "It is important that you do not forget that my influence on Israel is proportionally related to the scope of support which I get from American public opinion, Congress and the Jewish circles in this country. I want to be abundantly clear that in the absence of such a triangular support my ability to influence Israel is minimal."[82] Quandt adds that Carter told Fahmy he could never pressure Israel because to do so would be "political suicide."[83]

On November 9 Sadat announced to the Egyptian parliament that he would be willing to go to Israel. On November 15 Prime Minister Begin sent the Egyptian president a written invitation to address the Israeli Knesset, and on November 19 Sadat arrived in the Jewish state. Sadat's speech before the Knesset called for peace and mutual recognition. The Egyptian president offered Israel "security and le-gitimacy" and declared, "We really and truly welcome you to live among us in peace and security." Sadat also called for Israeli with-drawal from the territories occupied in 1967, "including Arab Je-rusalem," and for recognition of the rights of the Palestinian people to self-determination, "including their right to establish their own state."[84] Sadat maintained then, and thereafter, that he was interested in a comprehensive peace, not a separate, bilateral agreement on the Sinai, and that he would never "sell out" the Palestinians.[85] But the outcome of the process Sadat initiated, as well as what transpired prior to the initiative and during its unfolding, belie the Egyptian president's claim.

Sadat's motivations for bypassing the Geneva Conference and deal-ing directly with Israel are somewhat complex. Many analysts argue that he did so in direct response to the U.S.–Soviet communiqué, though this seems unlikely for a variety of reasons.[86] It appears rather that Carter's capitulation to Israeli pressure after the dispute over the U.S.–Soviet joint statement shook the Egyptian president's con-fidence in Carter's willingness and ability to facilitate a meaningful Geneva Conference.[87] In any case, Carter's plans for a resumption of Geneva were ended with Sadat's initiative. The United States could do little else but support the initiative, though significantly Wash-ington was no longer in control of the process. Administration officials expressed hope that Egypt and Israel would not settle on an exclusive bilateral agreement, but in the end the particularistic interests of both parties overwhelmed those hopes. Quandt writes that in the imme-diate aftermath of Sadat's visit to Israel, Carter was still committed to a comprehensive settlement in the Middle East and was not willing "to throw his weight fully behind a separate Egyptian-Israeli deal. . . . The American strategy would be to support talks between Egypt and Israel but to try to use the opening provided by Sadat to move forward on the Palestinian issue as well."[88] That strategy was abandoned in less than four months.

According to an account by Moshe Dayan, in early December the Egyptian president informed an American delegation (composed of Secretary Vance and his top aides, Philip Habib, Harold Saunders, and Alfred Atherton) that he was prepared to conclude a bilateral peace with Israel. Sadat added that it would be necessary to set the agreement in the context of a wider framework in order to avoid domestic problems and alienation from the Arab world. But in this regard he stated that he only wanted a "declaration of principles" on the Palestinian issue—something formulated in general terms, committing Israel to no territorial concessions, just giving him the necessary defense against his Arab critics.[89] There is no reason to doubt this aspect of Dayan's report since Sadat repeatedly stated that such was his interest. However, according to Dayan, the American officials were quite willing to accept this approach: "[They] gave us happy impressions of their Cairo visit and were optimistic about the prospects of the negotiations."[90] Here one must question Dayan's interpretation and ask if Vance and his associates were as willing as Dayan indicates to go along with Sadat's strategy, especially given its serious deviation from the concept of a comprehensive settlement and its negative implications for American interests. True, in the end, this is precisely what the United States settled for. Yet surely the Americans must have had some reservations.

Prime Minister Begin came to Washington on December 16 to present to President Carter Israel's plans for a peace agreement. Begin's proposal contained two parts: one, an Israeli withdrawal in the Sinai with the caveat that Israeli settlements be permitted to remain under the protection of U.N. forces and that Israel retain control over the Sinai air bases; the other, an "autonomy plan," called "Home Rule for Palestinian Arabs, Residents of Judea, Samaria, and the Gaza District."[91]

In its essence the autonomy plan proposed to withhold Israeli claims of sovereignty over the West Bank for a "limited period" and to grant the residents of the occupied territories authority over their domestic affairs, but not over the land on which they lived. The autonomy plan contained several specific points: Israelis would have the unrestricted right to acquire land and to establish settlements in the West Bank. Palestinian Arabs would be allowed to acquire land in Israel on the same basis that Israelis could acquire land in the territories (a curious point since Israel's Arab citizens cannot acquire land on the same basis that its Jewish citizens can;[92] but in any case the point was later modified to say that Arabs who became Israeli citizens could acquire land in Israel). The return of Arab refugees "in reasonable numbers" would be regulated by a joint committee in which Israel would retain the right of veto. Israel would stand by "its right and its claim to sovereignty" over the territories, although the issue would be left in abeyance for "the present." The entire plan would be subject to review within five years, with Israel retaining a veto over all final outcomes. The plan also proposed an elective administrative council to sit in Bethlehem, with jurisdiction in fields such as health, housing, education, and agriculture; security and public order would remain under Israeli authority.[93]

In his memoirs Carter says he found the Israeli proposals "not acceptable." Still, he wrote: "Begin sounded much more flexible regarding the West Bank than I had expected, but I was to discover later that his good words had multiple meanings, which my advisors and I did not understand at the time."[94] Quandt writes that Carter and his advisors were "disappointed" with Begin's "home rule" proposals, but that Carter told Begin in a second meeting on December 17 that the plan was "constructive." Begin pressed the president for a stronger endorsement "by reciting a long list of prominent Americans who reportedly favored his proposals. He quoted Senator Henry Jackson to the effect that the American people would support them." This comment, Quandt writes, "came very close to Israeli meddling in United States domestic politics and was not much appreciated by the White House. But since such behavior had long been part of the U.S.–Israeli relationship, no one objected."[95]

Whatever Carter's reservations concerning the autonomy proposal, immediately after the Israeli prime minister formally presented the plan to the Knesset on December 27, Carter called it a "long step forward."[96] Carter further stated that while President Sadat "so far is insisting that the so-called Palestinian entity be an independent nation, my own preference is that they not be an independent nation, but tied in some way with the surrounding countries, making a choice, for instance, between Israel and Jordan."[97] It is possible that the president saw more flexibility in the autonomy plan than there actually was, but it is clear that Palestinian self-determination was not even to be considered. As such the failure of the peace process in any wider sense was foreordained. (Even from the limited perspective of Jordanian interests—to say nothing of Syrian concerns—the course Washington appeared willing to follow contained the seeds of inevitable Arab rejection.)

Eventually an American position on the West Bank was developed by Brzezinski, Vance, and other administration officials including Saunders, Atherton, Peter Day, and Quandt. The features of what came to be known as the "nine point" West Bank–Gaza approach provided: (1) the inhabitants of the West Bank and Gaza would have self-rule during a five-year transition period; (2) authority for the self-rule would derive from Israel, Jordan, and Egypt, the arrangements to be negotiated by these three states and the Palestinians (from the West Bank and Gaza); (3) self-rule would be by an authority freely elected by the inhabitants of the West Bank and Gaza; (4) Israel and Jordan would refrain from asserting sovereignty over the area during the five-year transition period; (5) Israeli forces would withdraw to limited and specified encampments; (6) during the transition period, in order to implement Resolution 242, the self-governing authority, Israel, Jordan, and Egypt would negotiate about the issues of an Israeli withdrawal from the territories occupied in 1967, secure and recognized final borders (including possible minor modifications), the security arrangements to accompany Israeli withdrawal, and the terms and conditions of the long-term relationships between the West Bank and Gaza to Israel and Jordan; (7) the agreement negotiated by the parties would come into effect by the expressed consent of the governed to the substance of the agreement; (8) the parties also would negotiate about issues such as the introduction of a U.N. or Jordanian military presence, resettlement of Palestinian refugees from outside the territories in the West Bank and Gaza, and arrangements for reciprocal rights for Israelis and the inhabitants of the area; and (9) a regional economic development plan would be established including Jordan, the West Bank–Gaza authority, Israel, and Egypt.[98] It is significant that the United States was unable to facilitate the implementation of any of these points.

The Nitty-Gritty of the Follow-up to Sadat's Initiative

In the weeks following Sadat's dramatic visit to Israel, it became apparent that the Israelis and the Egyptians viewed the Egyptian initiative from substantially different perspectives. Sadat believed that he had given "everything" in going to Israel and offering it recognition, security, and legitimacy. He thus expected Israel to be forthcoming on the issue of territory.[99] The Israelis, on the other hand, viewed Sadat's visit as merely ceremonial and expected detailed, protracted negotiations to follow. Sadat and Begin met a second time, at Ismailia on December 25, 1977, but they failed to reach agreement even on the framework for a peace process or on the language of a joint "statement of principles." They did agree to set up two negotiating committees to work out details of a settlement: a political committee to meet in Israel and a military committee to sit in Cairo. Sadat's agreement to establishing the two committees reflected a retreat from his original expectation of a substantive response from Israel and a recognition that protracted negotiations were going to be necessary. However, after the Ismailia encounter, six months passed before the two leaders met again.

On January 4, 1978, President Carter visited Aswan, Egypt, and made a speech that included the statements that a Middle East settlement must resolve "the Palestinian problem in all its aspects" and that the Palestinians must be permitted to "participate in the determination of their own future."[100] These ambiguous remarks— a significant retreat from earlier statements—suggested only that Palestinians might "participate" in deciding their eventual fate, while implying that Israel, and no doubt others, would participate in negotiations about, if not determine, that future. Sadat indicated that Carter's statement was "identical" with his own thinking.[101] The Israelis expressed some satisfaction that Carter had said nothing about either a Palestinian state or self-determination, though they were very displeased by several of his comments.[102]

On January 15 the Egyptian foreign minister, Mohammed Ibrahim Kamel (who succeeded Ismail Fahmy after his resignation protesting Sadat's unilateral initiative), arrived in Israel to begin participation in the political committee. In his first public statement Kamel called on Israel to cease its occupation of Arab lands and recognize the "national rights" of the Palestinians. Two days later at a state dinner, Prime Minister Begin castigated Kamel for these remarks, suggesting that he was a young man, inexperienced, and unaware of history, and asserted that Israel would never return to the "fragile, breakable, aggression-provoking and bloodshed-causing lines" of pre-1967 Israel. He also vehemently reiterated Israeli rejection of the concept of Palestinian "self-determination."[103] President Sadat, reacting to the affront to his foreign minister, called the Egyptian delegation home, thus halting the political committee.[104] The Israeli cabinet then issued a statement declaring that this "extreme" action "proved" that the Egyptian government "deceived itself that Israel will submit to demands it has never considered feasible."[105]

In addition to this unpleasant diplomatic incident, there remained considerable divergence over the "form" of any joint statement of principles (though in reality there was little, if any, difference on substance). Israel was adamant that there be no reference to the "legitimate rights" of the Palestinians in such a statement and insisted that President Carter's reference in the Aswan speech to the "need to solve the Palestinian problem in all its aspects" be altered. The administration agreed to Israel's demands and thereafter eliminated this phrase from its comments on the issue. Egypt continued to insist on a statement of principles that would be acceptable domestically and elsewhere in the Arab world.

In the wake of Carter's capitulation regarding the phrase about solving the Palestinian problem in all its aspects, Egyptian officials began to question whether Washington would support them at all. Sadat believed that Carter had deserted him in so far as legitimizing his initiative in the Arab world (by retreating in his public pronouncements on support for the Palestinian issue), and felt in general that Carter was not adequately backing him.[106] Hermann Eilts, the American ambassador in Egypt, sent a cable to Carter entitled, "Sadat and the USG: An Incipient Crisis of Confidence," that strongly conveyed Sadat's growing doubt about the strength of the American commitment. Eilts pointed out that Sadat believed Carter was not supporting him sufficiently on the question of Israeli settlements in the Sinai and that he was concerned about the likelihood of the United States selling more advanced aircraft to Israel.[107] The Egyptian president came to Washington in early February and pleaded for American backing. While in the capital he told a reporter that he was "discouraged and disappointed" by the slow progress toward peace and said he wanted the United States to play a more forceful role as an "arbiter"—and as a source of pressure on Israel.[108] Sadat specifically asked the president to spell out an American position on the peace process. Carter agreed that an American position was important but said that the United States could not put forward a proposal immediately after Sadat's visit: "That would look like collusion. American Jews, public opinion, and Israelis would reject it."[109] The president added that he would first have to consult with the Israelis before an American position could be advanced. As Quandt aptly comments, "Domestic political realities . . . were much more on Carter's mind in 1978 than they had been in 1977."[110] Carter also told Sadat that he would not lean on the Israelis and insisted that he did not have much influence with Prime Minister Begin.[111]

Quandt relates a rather Byzantine aspect of the Egyptian-American talks, which he suggests gave them an appearance of wide agreement when there were actually a number of divergencies. One involved which party—the United States or Egypt—should exert pressure on Israel for compromise on the statement of principles concerning the Palestinians. Sadat felt that it was Carter's responsibility to pressure Israel on Resolution 242 and was reluctant to get into details about the West Bank and Gaza.[112] On the other hand, Carter and his advisors hoped that Sadat would take a firmer line on the Palestinian issue so that the Egyptian president could later be seen as making concessions and abandoning hard-line Arab demands under U.S. pressure. This was apparently part of a convoluted American scheme to "confront" Israel in order to elicit concessions.[113] Sadat, however, was interested in concluding a bilateral accord even without an agreement on general principles concerning the West Bank and Gaza (though his main advisors strongly opposed that approach). In any case, not until after the Camp David summit in September 1978 did Sadat take a genuinely strong stand on the Palestinian issue (by which time the United States had reversed itself and was backing the Israeli position). There was also disagreement between the United States and Egypt over a request by Sadat for 120 F-5E jet fighter aircraft and "some" F-15's and F-16's. Carter did not think that Congress would support the sale of planes to Egypt; thus he was reluctant to make a specific commitment to Sadat. On the other hand, he was sympathetic to Sadat's need for some form of American support and felt he had to provide the Egyptian president with some planes to maintain his trust.

The most important outcome of the Carter-Sadat meeting—an outcome that Quandt notes is difficult to prove, but that he clearly accepts—was an understanding on the necessity of moving quickly toward a separate Egyptian-Israeli agreement.[114] Quandt relates an interview he had with Carter on May 22, 1985, in which the former president said he could not recall if there were specific discussions about such an accord during his meetings with Sadat, and was not sure when his own thinking shifted from the idea of a comprehensive settlement through negotiations at Geneva toward the idea of bilateral Egyptian-Israeli talks.[115] But regardless of when, it is of considerable significance that the president acknowledges this change in his approach to the Middle East, and Quandt provides substantial evidence to suggest that the February meeting with Sadat was an important factor in Carter's shift to the bilateral concept.[116] What is more, according to Quandt, Carter eventually came to feel that almost any agreement was better than none at all, and that whatever Egypt and Israel could agree on would be fine with him: "As time went by he seemed to think the primary strategic objective for the United States was to conclude a peace treaty between Egypt and Israel, not resolve the Palestinian question."[117]

One must ask how and why President Carter altered his position so significantly. Part of the answer undoubtedly lies in the momentum generated by Sadat's initiative as well as in the fact that neither Sadat nor Begin was interested in a comprehensive peace.[118] Indeed, Quandt notes that Carter "probably understood better than the rest of us that Sadat was prepared to yield on the West Bank"[119] and Israel's objections have been amply recorded herein. Still, it might have been expected that the president of the United States would have understood that American interests in the Middle East are greater than the sum of individual Israeli and Egyptian interests. Certainly a major aspect of the explanation must reside in the fact that Carter was never committed to a solution to the Palestinian question that would have been acceptable to the Palestinians themselves. It is thus reasonable to conclude that since the president lacked any commitment to the principle of Palestinian self-determination or to an independent Palestinian state, he was unwilling to expend "political capital," i.e., to antagonize his pro-Israeli constituencies, over a solution that the Palestinians would have rejected. And indeed, the reaction of domestic elements was a significant determinant in policy formation by this time.[120] Nevertheless, before all these things became crystal clear both the president and Sadat made a number of statements that appeared to demonstrate a concern for the Palestinians.

On February 8, the day Sadat left Washington, the White House issued a statement affirming the American commitment to Resolution 242 and its applicability to all fronts, and repeating the American position that Israeli settlements in the occupied territories were contrary to international law.

Israel's reaction to the White House statement is recorded by Moshe Dayan: "The Israeli government felt gravely injured by the unjust accusations [that the settlements were illegal and that Resolution 242 included the West Bank] by one who maintained that he was an honest broker and even claimed a special friendship with Israel." Dayan further commented: "Whatever the position taken by Washington, however, she had to recognize that without Israel's agreement, the conflict would not be resolved. Throughout the thirty-year existence of Israel, tough words from Washington had not brought Israel to her knees and had not achieved their purpose."[121] Dayan's defiant remarks indeed reflected the reality of U.S.–Israeli relations: America's interests did not prevail over Israel's—primarily because Washington never used more than "tough words" to induce Israeli compliance with its interests.

During Sadat's visit to Washington, Israeli leaders had become concerned about the possibility that the administration might deviate from the path of their objectives. An official in Israel commented at the time: "We're not too worried about Congress, where we have many good friends, and we're convinced Sadat will fall on his face if he tries to weaken our ties with American Jewry. But we are apprehensive about what will come out of Sadat's meetings with Carter, who likes to please his guests by saying something they want to hear."[122] Israel was also not happy that Carter had declared, concerning the January 23 ground-breaking for the new settlement at Shiloh, "I am confident that Prime Minister Begin will honor the commitment personally made to me and thus will not permit this settlement to go forward."[123] Begin did not honor his commitment to the American president; indeed, he denied having made it and construction at Shiloh was completed. Moreover, Begin took a new, more aggressive tack by declaring *publicly* that Resolution 242 did not apply to the West Bank, which he claimed was Jewish by ancient right and therefore liberated, not occupied, land. Concerned with the dilemma this pronouncement created for Sadat, Carter replied that this "reinterpretation" of the U.N. resolution could be a blow to the prospects for peace in the Middle East. But the president's reaction to the Israeli negation of Resolution 242 was mild, to say the least, and Begin continued his public declarations about Israel's intention to expand its settlement program and to retain permanent control over the area. Washington continued to provide the funds that made the settlements possible. Once again the dichotomy between principle and practice in American Middle East policy is starkly outlined.

Dayan was dispatched to Washington, arriving just after Sadat departed. His visit was billed explicitly as a "public relations counterattack against Sadat."[124] Dayan belittled Sadat's historic visit to Israel: "It didn't risk a single inch of the security of Egypt." Dayan also expressed his approval of the settlement at Shiloh: "I admire them [the settlers] rather more than I admire Israelis who go to live in Canada and Zionists who do not come to live in Israel."[125] In a meeting with Carter, Dayan restated the Israeli position that Resolution 242 had no applicability to the West Bank.[126] "Israel, he said, wanted a peace agreement with Jordan without withdrawal. Israel intended to keep its military positions, its settlements, and its right to settle."[127] Quandt relates that Dayan showed the president and his advisors a document that supposedly represented what Carter had told a group of American Jewish leaders a few days earlier. "In it Carter allegedly said that Israel might be able to keep one airfield in Sinai; that Israel could retain a military presence in the West Bank beyond five years; and that the West Bank Palestinians would be allowed to participate in a referendum after a five-year transitional period and would have the choice of affiliation with Jordan or Israel or continuation of the status quo, but not the choice of an independent state. Carter reportedly had told the Jewish leaders that even the Saudis did not favor an independent Palestinian state."[128] Quandt notes that while most of the points accurately reflected the president's thinking, the point concerning the retention of an Israeli airfield in Sinai was a misunderstanding.[129] But Dayan's possession of a document containing such U.S. "commitments" to American Jewish leaders obviously strengthened the Israeli position: the interface between domestic politics and Middle East policymaking could not have been clearer. Dayan also "warned" President Carter against any sale of sophisticated weapons to Egypt, saying it would have "a very negative effect on the peace process." In Israel, Deputy Defense Minister Mordechai Zippori told the Knesset that in order to block any weapons sales to Egypt, Israel intended to "mobilize all our friends" in America.[130]

In response to Israel's opposition to the sale of arms to Egypt, the White House released a statement that reaffirmed America's "historic commitments" to Israel's security, but nevertheless submitted a proposal to Congress on an arms package that offered Egypt fifty F-5E's (considerably fewer than the 120 it had requested and no F-15's or F-16's); Israel, fifteen F-15 interceptors and seventy-five F-16 fighter bombers; and Saudi Arabia, sixty F-15's.[131] The idea of the "package" was an attempt to circumvent Congress's likely disapproval of the requests for Egypt and Saudi Arabia while approving the request for Israel. Presented with the package arrangement, Congress would have to either decline to disapprove the sales to all three countries or to none.

Despite the fact that the arms proposal maintained Israel's absolute military superiority—indeed, it reinforced Israel's qualitative advantage—and represented no more than a token to the Arabs, the Israelis were outraged. (In reality the proposed sale of planes to the Arabs was a political move; the F-5E's were intended to bolster Sadat's confidence in the United States, since he was receiving no substantive help from Washington in his peace initiative. The F-15's for Saudi Arabia were intended to reward the Saudi monarchy's moderation both on Middle East issues in general and on oil prices in particular. The plan was also designed to garner Saudi support for the Egyptian-Israeli peace process and to tie Riyadh even more closely to the United States. Indeed, it was acknowledged in Washington that if approved, the F-15 sale would virtually guarantee an oil-price freeze through 1978 and would ensure that Saudi Arabia would remain on the dollar basis indefinitely, rather than switching its huge holdings out of the hard-pressed American currency.) However, disregarding the important advantages from the arms package for the United States, Israel and its American supporters fought the proposed sale at every level. After a bitter battle, the Senate, on May 15, declined to disapprove the package, giving the Israeli lobby one of only two losses it experienced in its efforts to block the sale of American arms to Arab states. It was not, however, a victory that emboldened Carter. On the contrary, he appeared to think that he could not afford any more such confrontations with Israel and its friends in Congress.[132] According to Quandt: "His [Carter's] decision to sell F-15's to Saudi Arabia brought him into sharp conflict with the Jewish community. He won the battle but seemed to conclude that it was a costly victory. . . . As a result, Carter decided to work through Begin, not against him [in the negotiations with Egypt]. Whatever Begin could be brought to accept without a confrontation would [now] define the outer limits of the agreement."[133]

As events unfolded in the emerging peace process, the PLO leadership grew increasingly dismayed. In February 1978 Yasir Arafat wrote a private letter to President Carter in which he suggested that the continual exclusion of the PLO from the diplomatic and political context left it little alternative means save the *ultima ratio* of force.[134] The United States ignored Arafat's plea for inclusion in the peace process, thus assuring the PLO's resort to violence.

That violence came in a Fatah-sponsored guerrilla raid. Thirteen commandos seized a civilian bus, north of Tel Aviv, on March 11, 1978. Majed Abu Sharar, a PLO spokesman, stated after the raid: "This was our answer to Sadat's peace initiative." Thirty-seven Israelis were killed as the Israeli Defense Forces attempted to stop the hijacking by force, causing a fierce firefight with the guerrillas. The Israeli retaliation was swift and massive: on March 14 Israel launched Operation Litani, in which 20,000 Israeli troops invaded Lebanon in a combined air, sea, and ground assault. (There is substantial evidence, as indicated above, to suggest that this operation may have been at least two years in the planning and was waiting for an excuse to happen.)[135] During the first stage of the operation the security belt was created in southern Lebanon, and Saad Haddad was placed in charge of the area. A second stage of the operation involved moving toward the Litani River and the outskirts of Tyre. During the full operation approximately 2,000 civilians died, many thousands more were wounded, 200,000 fled their homes, and 300 PLO troops were killed.[136]

The administration's essential position on the invasion was reflected in a statement read by Hodding Carter, a White House spokesman, who commented on the "painful and serious dilemma" that the Palestinian raid had created for Israel and noted that the "legitimate security interest" of Israel was involved.[137] Nevertheless, on March 15, after Israel had successfully completed the first stage of its operation (indeed on that night Prime Minister Begin publicly declared that the Israeli forces had accomplished their mission in Lebanon), Carter sent Begin a message asking that Israel discontinue its advance and pull its army behind the frontier. Carter also asked that Israel permit a U.N. force to be posted in southern Lebanon.[138] Additionally the United States convened the Security Council and introduced Resolution 425, which was adopted on March 19, calling for a cease-fire, withdrawal of forces, and the establishment of a U.N. Interim Force for Southern Lebanon (UNIFIL).[139] Begin responded by ordering the campaign expanded, despite his statement that Israel had accomplished its objectives. Israel eventually accepted Resolution 425, and UNIFIL troops entered Lebanon on March 23, though the cease-fire was not yet in effect. Moreover, Israel did not withdraw its forces until June 13, when it determined that the security zone was reasonably stable under the control of Saad Haddad. Handing over control of the the frontier area to Haddad meant that Israel pointedly ignored the mandate of UNIFIL.

The Lebanese government credited American pressure with securing the Israeli withdrawal.[140] Carter also asserts that it was his move in the Security Council, combined with a threat to notify Congress that Israel was using American weapons illegally by invading Lebanon, that was responsible for Israel's departure.[141] More to the point, Israel had achieved its goal (the establishment of the security zone under the control of an Israeli surrogate) and had no reason to remain. Its withdrawal did not signify capitulation to U.S. pressure.

(Concerning the issue of Israel's illegal use of American weapons: on April 5, 1978, Secretary of State Vance sent a letter to Congress, in response to queries from Congressmen Paul Findley and Charles Whalen, in which he pointed out that under the 1952 Arms Control Export Act certain weapons were to be provided to Israel only on condition that they be used for self-defense, and reported that "a violation of the 1952 agreement may have occurred by reason of the Israeli operations in Lebanon."[142] If the letter had stated that a violation *had* occurred, the president or Congress would have been required to suspend all military assistance to Israel. According to Vance: "The fact was that we had little doubt Israel's use of United States–origin military equipment had gone beyond the requirements of self-defense. However, since our principal interest was in Israel's compliance with the United Nations withdrawal order . . . we did not want to trigger a counterproductive crisis. At the same time, we protested Israel's use of cluster bombs in Lebanon in violation of its agreement with the United States that it would use this antipersonnel weapon only when attacked and only against military targets. On April 20, Defense Minister Ezer Weizman conceded using the cluster bombs had been a mistake."[143] It is instructive to note that no interruption in the transfer of aid or military equipment, including cluster bombs, occurred, despite the secretary's admission that Israel violated both American law and a specific bilateral agreement. Indeed the flow of arms and aid increased. Moreover, as a result of raising such sensitive questions on more than one occasion, Representative Findley became a target of pro-Israeli groups at reelection and ultimately lost his seat due in considerable measure to their intensive efforts.[144])

While Israeli troops still occupied Lebanon, Prime Minister Begin was welcomed in Washington on March 21 by President Carter. The main focus of discussion between the two leaders was the statement of principles or declaration of intentions that Sadat wanted in order to proceed with the negotiations. The Israelis remained adamant in insisting that any such declaration exclude references to Palestinian rights or the future of the West Bank.[145] Carter records that when he pressed Begin on what points he would be willing to show some flexibility, Begin replied that there was nothing beyond what he had already proposed.[146]

Carter then arranged for another meeting with Begin during which the president outlined the American position and what he understood to be the Israeli position. The American position (with which Sadat concurred) as described by Carter was:

No complete withdrawal by Israel from the West Bank; no independent Palestinian nation; self-rule in the West Bank–Gaza strip; withdrawal of Israeli forces to negotiated security outposts; some modification of the western boundaries of the West Bank; devolution of power to the local authorities from both Israel and Jordan; no claim of sovereignty [by either nation] for a five-year period; at the end of the five-year period the Palestinian Arabs who live in the occupied territory will have the right to vote either on affiliation with Israel or Jordan or continuation of the so-called "interim government," if they find it to be attractive; the ceasing of new or expanded settlements during time of negotiation.

Then Carter read what he understood the Israeli position to be:

Not willing to withdraw politically or militarily from any part of the West Bank; not willing to stop the construction of new settlements or the expansion of existing settlements; not willing to withdraw the Israeli settlers from Sinai, or even leave them there under United Nations or Egyptian protection; not willing to acknowledge that United Nations Resolution 242 applies to West Bank–Gaza area; not willing to grant the Palestinian Arabs real authority, or a voice in the determination of their own future to the extent that they can choose between the alternatives outlined above.[147]

According to Carter, although Begin said this was a negative way to express the Israeli position, he did not deny its accuracy. Indeed, with the exception of the settlements in the Sinai, the Israelis held firm to that position. In reality the differences between Israel and the United States were not great—at least not on the Palestinian issue.

Begin returned to Washington on May 1 to join in the American commemoration of the thirtieth anniversary of the birth of Israel. He was warmly received at the White House for a private meeting, followed by a reception for 1,200 people on the South Lawn. Carter delivered an emotional speech reiterating America's unequivocal support for Israel and offered to set up an American memorial for the victims of the Holocaust. Indeed, the president went out of his way to associate himself with Begin's views, commenting, for instance, on the Middle East peace process: "My belief is that a permanent settlement will be based substantially on the home-rule proposal that Prime Minister Begin has put forward."[148] (Significantly, even Ezer

Weizman, Begin's defense minister, did not think much of the home-rule idea. After meeting with Sadat in March, Weizman wrote that Sadat wanted only a fig leaf that could suggest some kind of autonomy for the Palestinians, but that Begin had reduced the autonomy plan to a caricature of genuine self-rule.[149]) In Carter's words the While House celebration with Begin and Israel's American supporters was "a very positive and heartwarming experience." However, the president's hospitality and warmth had little effect on the stalled peace process, the Israeli occupation of Lebanon, or on the extremely negative and vitriolic outpourings of pro-Israeli Americans against the president. Indeed Carter wrote, "I still had serious problems among American Jews, and a few days later we had to postpone two major Democratic fund-raising banquets in New York and Los Angeles because so many Jewish party members had canceled their reservations to attend."[150]

Notwithstanding the unremittingly hostile attitudes of Israel's American supporters and of the Begin government, or perhaps because of them, the United States made a significant policy shift in Israel's favor. Moshe Dayan notes that on May 1 Washington agreed: (1) to interpret the withdrawal clause in Resolution 242 as meaning Israeli withdrawal only from the centers of Arab population, with redeployment elsewhere in the occupied territories, and (2) to accept the Israeli formula that the Arabs in the occupied territories would participate in the determination of their future within the framework of the discussions to be held among Egypt, Jordan, and Israel.[151] Even considering domestic political factors it is difficult to imagine how American policymakers rationalized such a position from the perspective of U.S. national interests—or even how it was justified in terms of Israel's long-range security. The Likud government was obviously pleased, however, and Dayan commented: "The United States is a superpower, but for the attainment of peace between us and the Arabs, our agreement is required. It was up to us to ensure that neither our armed forces nor our settlements would be removed from the West Bank, and that the territory would not come under foreign rule."[152] (Note that Israel considers Palestinians foreigners in their own homeland while Jews from all over the world have the "right" to immigrate to this same land.)

(The point that both Israel and the United States seem to miss is that given Israel's absolute economic dependence on the United States, Washington *has* leverage with which to pressure Israel but never exercises it. On this matter the pro-Israeli forces best serve Israel's interests and contravene American interests. Because of the powerful impact that these groups are able to exert on the electoral process, neither the Congress nor the Executive (especially Democratic presidents) has been willing to use American economic and military aid as a means of influencing Israeli behavior. As Seth P. Tillman, a prominent analyst of the U.S.–Israeli relationship, notes: "It is this and this alone that gives Israel the means to withstand all verbal pressures and reproaches and to continue to impose solutions contrary to the desires and interests of the United States."[153])

Little progress on the peace process occurred from May through July—in fact, there had been no official talks between Israelis and Egyptians since January 1978, when Kamel was recalled from Israel.[154] In an attempt to break the deadlock, an Egyptian–Israeli–U.S. conference was convened by the Americans at Leeds Castle in England on July 18, 1978. Foreign Ministers Dayan and Kamel headed the Israeli and Egyptian delegations, while Vance led the Americans. (In Vienna in early July, prior to the Leeds meeting, President Sadat had talked with Shimon Peres, the leader of Israel's opposition Labor party, and Defense Minister Weizman. Weizman stated publicly that in his talks with Sadat he had obtained agreement from the Egyptian president that after five years of "autonomy" the West Bank would revert to Jordanian control and Gaza to Egyptian control, while Israel could retain military footholds in both areas commensurate with its security requirements.[155] Sadat also apparently promised Weizman that Egypt would sell oil from the Sinai to Israel and would provide water from the Nile to help irrigate the Negev.[156]) However, at Leeds little progress was made in bridging the gap between Israel and Egypt. Dayan was particularly adamant that he did not regard Israel's control over the West Bank and Gaza as temporary and that the reassertion of Jordanian or Egyptian control would be unacceptable.[157] Quandt notes that Vance left the Leeds Castle conference with a few new ideas to consider and with no reason to be optimistic about the chances of bringing the two sides together.[158]

Shortly after the Leeds meeting, on July 23, Begin responded to Sadat's plea for a "goodwill gesture" from Israel—for example, the return of Mt. Sinai—to get the talks going again, with a blunt retort: "Not even one grain of desert sand. Nobody can get anything for nothing," the prime minister declared.[159]

President Carter expressed deep concern over the stalled peace process: "Sadat has demanded that the Israeli military team leave Egypt. I think he's trying to set the stage for us to get involved more deeply in the Middle East dispute. That's our intention, but we want to approach it carefully." And further: "Sadat is meeting with the radical Arabs to try to repair his fences with them, which is not a good omen. My hope is that he still is depending on us and will accommodate what I propose."[160] Carter followed these two notes regarding his concern about Sadat (both of which contain serious implications for American interests in the Middle East) with the statement: "I was really in a quandary. I knew how vital peace in the Middle East was to the United States, but many Democratic members of Congress and party officials were urging me to back out of the situation and to repair the damage they claimed I had already done to the Democratic party and to United States–Israeli relations. It seemed particularly ironic to be so accused, when I was trying to bolster our relations with Israel and strengthen its security."[161] Indeed, "ironic" does not adequately express the situation.

On July 20, Carter told his advisors that he was considering a summit meeting with Begin and Sadat. Quandt comments that "he [Carter] later told Brzezinski that for political reasons he wanted the summit to have a dramatic impact."[162] Ten days later the president informed his aides that he would hold the summit. Carter then sent long, almost identical letters to the Egyptian president and the Israeli prime minister, hand-carried by Secretary Vance, asking them to come to Camp David, the presidential retreat in the mountains of Maryland. Both leaders accepted, and the announcement of the forth-coming meeting was made on August 8.

September 5-17, 1978: At Camp David

Beginning on September 5, 1978, Prime Minister Begin, President Sadat, President Carter, and their respective aides closeted themselves for thirteen days at Camp David. On September 5 Carter met first with Sadat, then Begin. The Egyptian president presented a set of maximalist demands, then told Carter that while he would accept nothing less than the entire Sinai and that no Israeli settlements could remain nor could Israel retain control of the airfields, on every other issue he was prepared to compromise.[163] In addition, the following day Sadat gave Carter, in writing, a series of concessions he was prepared to make—at appropriate moments—in the negotiations. These included the normalization of relations with Israel, free movement of peoples across borders, trade, the indivisibility of Jerusalem, Palestinian representatives to come only from the West Bank and Gaza, and many others.[164] Sadat openly agreed with Carter that there should be no independent Palestinian state; moreover he offered to negotiate on behalf of the Palestinians if Jordan declined, providing a convenient rationale for excluding Jordanian concerns and removing the need to consider Jordan as a partner in the Middle East peace process.[165] Sadat's statements as well as his written list of concessions reassured the Americans that the Egyptian president's public position on the Palestinian issue was pure rhetoric.

Quite simply, Sadat's objective at Camp David was to regain Egyptian territory under full Egyptian sovereignty and to cement his ties with the United States. His strategy was to attempt to fully coordinate and cooperate with Carter to achieve these ends. Sadat had no interest in the West Bank and Gaza per se, though as a result of prodding by his advisors he attempted unsuccessfully to establish certain principles—territory in exchange for peace (the Resolution 242 formula)—by which other Arab countries could negotiate a fair peace with Israel.[166]

Begin also presented a maximalist position on the first day,[167] the difference being that he stuck with his initial demands and in the end compromised only on the issues of airfields and settlements in the Sinai. The Israeli goal was to conclude a separate Egyptian-Israeli agreement without diluting Israel's claim to Jerusalem or the West Bank and Gaza. In fact, the goal was to solidify Israel's position and "right" to Eretz Israel. The Israeli strategy was to avoid making concessions on the points most important to Sadat, such as settlements in the Sinai, until Sadat agreed to drop any (even procedural) demands concerning the West Bank and Gaza.[168] In addition to their requirements regarding the substantive issues under discussion at the summit, the Israelis also insisted on being shown any American proposal before it was presented to Sadat.[169] They based this demand on one of the secret agreements Kissinger had provided in the Sinai II package (that Israel would always be consulted first on any matter relating to its security). Carter complied, but what began as prior consultation was ultimately transformed into prior approval, further undermining the president's ability to structure American interests into the agreement. The Israelis also demanded at the outset, as they had in regard to the Sinai II negotiations, a separate bilateral agreement with the United States as a precondition for signing any agreement with Egypt.

Carter's objective at Camp David (narrower than that of several of his advisors[170]) was primarily to secure an Egyptian-Israeli accord. According to Quandt, he was prepared to do what was necessary to facilitate such a bilateral agreement with or without any genuine link to the broader Palestinian issue.[171] The president's strategy was to relentlessly pressure Sadat for concessions while seeking to meet Begin's conditions, with the exception of Israeli settlements or airfields in the Sinai.[172]

The three leaders met together on the second day, September 6. The sole agreement to emerge from the meeting was that of the three

Sabbaths observed by the men—Sadat on Friday, Begin on Saturday, and Carter on Sunday—only on Saturday would no work be done. Carter writes, however, that despite this agreement the U.S. team did most of the drafting of the texts on Saturday. The three met again together, twice, on September 7, but did not have another personal encounter until the Camp David accords were ready for signature.

The Israelis did not view Sadat's initial position as a posture for Arab consumption, even though Carter had told them that Sadat was willing to be flexible on every point except Egyptian territory and sovereignty. In Dayan's words: "No member of our delegation held any opinion other than that of Prime Minister Begin that the Egyptian proposal should be rejected outright."[173] (Dayan also notes the Israeli concern over the need to embark on a "public information campaign," so that "when" the talks collapsed it could be readily demonstrated that the Egyptians were to blame because of their "stubborn, impractical and unjustified proposals."[174] Dayan's comment illustrates a widely held Israeli assumption, and not an unreasonable one given American political culture, that in any situation Israel could mobilize congressional support, the media, and public opinion in the United States to back its interpretation of events.)

After the Egyptians abandoned their initial rhetorical position, only two areas of disagreement remained as potential stumbling blocks to an accord: (1) the Jewish settlements and airfields in the Sinai and (2) the manner in which the West Bank–Gaza issue would be framed. The former was the more serious: Sadat was adamant that the settlements in the Sinai had to be removed; Begin that they remain. In addition, Israel wanted to maintain control over the airfields while Egypt would not even consider that option. Conflict over a West Bank–Gaza formula mainly involved semantics. Nevertheless, the parties remained deadlocked on both questions until the very end.

On September 15 Carter pledged $3 billion in American aid to assist in the construction of new airfields in the Negev to compensate the Israelis for giving up the bases in the Sinai.[175] The Israelis accepted the offer and agreed to relinquish control over the Sinai airfields. On the issue of settlements, the Israelis agreed, on September 16, to submit to the Knesset the question: "If agreement is reached on all other Sinai issues, will the settlements be withdrawn?" Thus the entire Knesset, not Begin and his cabinet alone, would decide the matter of Israeli settlements in the Sinai and the future of a peace treaty with Egypt. A proposal for an Egyptian-Israeli treaty was thus drafted.

Concerning a formula for the Palestinians on the West Bank and Gaza, a document was drawn up that in Quandt's words "fuzz[ed] over the issue rather than resolv[ed] it."[176] There was no linkage between the two documents—the accord purporting to deal with the Palestinian question and the Egyptian-Israeli agreement—making it possible for Israel to ignore entirely what provisions were written into the first document while enjoying the benefits of a complete peace with Egypt. In addition, while the Palestinians were granted "full autonomy," the meaning of the concept in practice was not spelled out. Israel did not agree to abolish the military government in the occupied territories, only to "withdraw" it; Israel later claimed this meant only that the military government would be physically removed from the West Bank during an interim period, but that it would continue to exist and to have ultimate control over the "self-governing authority" the Palestinians were to elect. The document contained no statements about the "inadmissibility of territory by war" or the applicability of Resolution 242 "to all fronts of the conflict." The Israeli claim to sovereignty over all of Jerusalem was also unchallenged. Sadat did request a separate exchange of letters, so that he could make Egypt's views on Jerusalem part of the public record;[177] but in effect he acquiesced in the continuation of Israeli rule over the entire city. Finally, Israel agreed to no more than a three-month freeze on settlements in the West Bank and Gaza.[178] The issue of settlements led to much subsequent discord between the United States and Israel.

Carter records the following: "We finally worked out language that was satisfactory: that no new Israeli settlements would be established after the signing of this Framework for Peace, and that the issue of additional settlements would be resolved by the parties to the negotiations."[179] Begin denied that he ever agreed to freeze settlements for a period longer than the three months that were to be used to conclude an Egyptian-Israeli treaty. Carter alleges that in a late night meeting on September 16 Begin agreed to a freeze for the five-year duration of the autonomy negotiations. Whether Begin was duplicitous or Carter merely heard what he wanted to hear cannot now be determined with certainty, although both Vance and Quandt lend support to the president's contention. But, in fact, on September 17, Begin gave Carter a letter stating that a settlement freeze would take place for only the three-month period set up for the Egyptian-Israeli negotiations. Moreover, Carter did not even ask Begin for his signature on an American letter stating the U.S. position that the settlement freeze was for the five-year duration of autonomy.[180] In any case, the day after the Camp David accords were signed, Begin publicly discussed Israel's plans for the establishment of new Jewish settlements in the West Bank and as early as October 26 announced plans to begin "thickening" settlements already in place. Washington did nothing.

The two documents produced from the Camp David summit were signed on September 17, 1978, and were formally entitled: (1) A Framework for Peace in the Middle East, and (2) A Framework for the Conclusion of a Peace Treaty between Israel and Egypt.[181]

The evening before the signing, on September 16, Sadat's two key advisors at Camp David, Mohammed Ibrahim Kamel, the Egyptian minister of foreign affairs, and Nabil el-Araby, the legal director of the foreign ministry, resigned. They claimed that they were unable to bear responsibility for Sadat's surrender to Israel on the issues of a comprehensive peace and the Palestinians. Kamel's resignation must have been particularly distressing to Sadat, who had had to accept the resignation of Kamel's immediate predecessor, Ismail Fahmy, over the original peace initiative.[182] (Kamel's successor was Kamal Hassan Ali.) Other advisors who did not resign, such as Boutros Ghali, Osama el-Baz, and Hassan Tuhamy (who had made the initial contacts with the Israelis in the fall of 1977), nevertheless expressed grave reservations about the agreement Sadat had concluded—as did Egyptian intellectuals, journalists, leftists, Islamic groups, and others.

Reaction to Camp David

Reflecting on the Camp David accords, Tahseen Basheer, a senior Egyptian diplomat, expressed the view that the agreements could have been somewhat better from the Egyptian and Arab point of view if Sadat had been less eager and Carter more persevering, but that they could not have been *much* better because the result fell, as it had to, within the parameters of what American domestic politics would allow.[183] Indeed, the importance of domestic political considerations was illustrated repeatedly during the Camp David process. For example, at one point Kamel pointed out to Carter that if reducing Soviet influence in the Middle East was a primary objective of the United States, then a comprehensive settlement would not only reduce it but also end it. Carter replied that a U.S.-Egyptian–Israeli agreement would better accomplish this end.[184] Since the logic of Kamel's statement is so obvious, one must question whether Carter believed his own words, or if he was simply justifying the limits imposed upon him by the Israelis and their American supporters. Mahmoud Riad, another Egyptian diplomat, expressed the general Arab perception when he wrote that Carter's answer was merely a restatement of the Israeli concept for the establishment of a military alliance among the three countries that would enable Israel to control the whole region.[185] In any case it is apparent from the comments of these Egyptians, in addition to the resignations of his advisors, that President Sadat's support within his own country was far from unanimous.

The Soviet reaction to Camp David was pointedly negative. The Soviets described the agreements as a "new measure adopted against the Arabs and an attempt to obstruct the achievement of a just peace"; they asserted that no durable peace could be established unless the Palestinian people won the right to self-determination. The posture of the Soviet Union was not merely one of pique; it was also a position of political realism, acknowledging that without Syria and the PLO no long-term peace was possible. Indeed, while Carter, bowing to the Israelis, excluded the Soviet Union (as well as Syria and the PLO) from the peace process, he failed to end Moscow's role in the region. In fact, he accomplished just the opposite. Several of the Arab regimes that rejected the terms of the Camp David agreements became more closely linked than before to the Soviet Union, requesting and receiving increased aid and arms, which led to further Soviet influence and heightened Soviet presence in the area. This in turn increased the likelihood of another regional war, including the possibility of a U.S.–Soviet confrontation.

The PLO denounced the agreements,[186] though Quandt reports that while Arafat was skeptical of the accords, he "showed a serious interest in finding out if there might be more to Camp David than met the eye."[187] But the Palestinian people within the occupied territories strenuously rejected the outcome of Camp David. A general strike was declared on September 20, and demonstrations swept through all the villages and towns of the West Bank and Gaza. The elected mayor of Halhoul, Mohammed Milhem, expressed his opposition by declaring that the people of the West Bank wanted self-determination and the leadership of the PLO.[188] The elected mayor of Ramallah, Karim Khalef, denounced the Camp David plan, stating that it "will never be accepted by us"; to do so would be "to accept the occupation forever."[189] Mayor Bassam Shak'a of Nablus said that Palestinians would persevere in the struggle for their national rights and that the PLO would determine the appropriate means by which to secure those rights.[190] (These and other elected West Bank mayors were dismissed by the Begin government in 1982 as part of its effort to implement its "solution" for the occupied territories.) Indeed, West Bank leaders from the mayors to university professors to individuals like pharmacist Izzadine Arayan (who was imprisoned for six months and subjected to solitary confinement and torture for initiating and circulating a petition opposing the Camp David accords)[191] were outspoken and emphatic in their rejection of Camp David. Elias Freij, the pro-Jordanian mayor of Bethlehem (the only mayor of a major West Bank town not elected on a pro-PLO slate in 1976), appeared to be the only leader—and even he had considerable reservations—who saw any potentially positive benefits for the Palestinians from this agreement.[192]

An Arab summit meeting convened in Baghdad on November 1 to consider a response to Camp David. All members of the Arab League except Egypt were invited and attended. The group decided to send a delegation to Cairo to persuade Sadat to revoke the Camp David accords, but while the delegation was en route Sadat announced that he would refuse to see it, so the members returned to Baghdad. The Arab states then voted to suspend Egypt from the League and to transfer its seat out of Cairo. They also agreed that the wealthy Arab regimes would extend financial support over a period of ten years to Syria ($1,850 million), Jordan ($1,250 million), the PLO ($250 million), and Palestinians living in the West Bank and Gaza ($150 million). Aid to Egypt was completely suspended. (Egypt had been receiving some $2 billion from Saudi Arabia.)[193] Significantly, however, while condemning the results of Camp David, all the Arab states—even the so-called radicals—agreed to the adoption of resolutions based on U.N. Resolutions 181 and 242, including establishment of a Palestinian state under the leadership of the PLO and Israeli withdrawal to the pre-1967 boundaries. These resolutions indicated the acquiescence of the Arab regimes in the two-state formula as recommended in the 1947 partition resolution and signified the end of Arab state interest in liberating Palestine. The refusal to accept the Camp David arrangement stemmed from the fact that Sadat traded the two-state solution for Israeli domination over all of Palestine.[194]

September 1978 to March 1979: Israel and Egypt Conclude a Separate Peace

The immediate aftermath of Camp David involved five difficult months of bickering and arguing over what appeared for a while to be insurmountable obstacles before an Egyptian-Israeli peace treaty was signed on March 26, 1979. The final treaty contained no important departures from the Camp David framework, except that the first document, the Framework for Peace, was rendered totally meaningless.

The day after the signing of the Camp David accords, September 18, Prime Minister Begin embarked on a speaking tour in the United States in which he repeatedly declared that "Judea and Samaria" (the West Bank) were an integral part of Eretz Israel, which God had given to the Jews and which Israel would never relinquish under any circumstances. He called Jerusalem the "eternal capital" of Israel and promised that it would remain forever united under Israeli control. Further, Begin said that many more new settlements would be constructed and the present ones expanded. He made a number of other statements about the Palestinians and future relationships with Israel's Arab neighbors that President Carter felt violated the spirit of Camp David. Carter notes that he told American Jewish leaders in a White House meeting on September 19 that Begin was acting in a "completely irresponsible way."[195] According to Carter, "Begin continued to disavow the basic principles of the accords. . . . his public statements were in sharp contrast to those of the American and Egyptian delegations. . . . I talked to him privately . . . and warned that his remarks were making it almost impossible for them [other Arab governments or Palestinian Arabs] to join in any future discussions. . . . and I had a feeling that he really did not want any early talks involving the Palestinians and other Arabs. The next day in New York, Begin continued his disruptive comments."[196] Again, the president did nothing to ensure that Begin lived up to the "spirit of Camp David"—whatever that meant in the aftermath of what was concluded at the summit.

On September 27 the United States received word that the Knesset had approved (by a vote of 84 to 19, with 17 abstentions) Israel's evacuation of Sinai if a peace treaty was signed by Israel and Egypt. This action opened the door for the Egyptian-Israeli treaty. Carter then invited the foreign and defense ministers of Egypt and Israel to Washington to work out the details of the final treaty.

An initial trilateral conference convened on October 12. The main issues before the parties were: (1) the stages and lines of Israeli withdrawal and the timing of the establishment of diplomatic relations at the ambassadorial level; (2) the question of linkage between the two documents produced at Camp David (the Israelis wanted no linkage, insisting instead on a separate peace not tied to the process of autonomy negotiations on the West Bank or the Palestinian question; the Egyptians wanted some linkage); (3) the question of "priority of obligations" (the Israelis demanded that the Egyptian-Israeli treaty should supersede and take precedence over all other treaties Egypt had previously concluded with Arab states; Egypt felt this was unreasonable and resisted acquiescing to the demand).

Carter initially took the position that there should be at least a political link (as distinct from a legal link) between the two treaties, so that Egypt could demonstrate to the Arab world that it had not totally capitulated on the Palestinian issue and concluded a separate peace. On Sadat's instructions, the Egyptian delegation indicated that such a non-binding political link—what they termed "correlation"—would be acceptable. The Egyptians also agreed that full diplomatic relations would be established at the ambassadorial level once the Israelis withdrew to the El Arish–Ras Mohammed line; but they strongly objected to giving the treaty with Israel priority over all other Egyptian treaty commitments. At the outset Carter agreed with the Egyptians on the issue of priority of obligations, but pressure from Israel in the ensuing months caused him to change his mind. The Israelis enlisted help from their American supporters to influence the president, employing a variety of tactics. In one instance Eugene Rostow and two of his Yale colleagues, L. Lipson and M. S. McDougal, wrote a statement using an interpretation of international law to back the Israeli position. After Carter surrendered, he then exerted great pressure on Egypt to accede to the Israeli stance, and in the end Sadat did.

The Israelis pressed the administration on a number of other issues, indicating that if they did not receive satisfactory answers, they would not proceed with the treaty negotiations. One involved oil. Israel wanted a written guarantee that the United States would provide oil if Israel could not buy it from Egypt or elsewhere. Israel also wanted economic aid to finance its withdrawal from Sinai (which by November 1 had grown to $3.37 billion) and was presented by Dayan as a precondition for Israeli approval of an Egyptian-Israeli treaty. In addition, Israel wanted firmer commitments from the United States on freedom of shipping and aircraft through the Gulf of Aqaba and the continued operation of the American early-warning stations in Sinai. It requested a review, restatement, and updating of all previous bilateral agreements between the United States and Israel and insisted on U.S. involvement and responsibility in implementation of the peace treaty with Egypt as well as American responsibility to supply an alternative to the U.N. forces (if these should not be forthcoming) and cooperation in constructing new airfields in the Negev to replace the ones in Sinai.[197] These and other demands were granted in two bilateral memoranda of understanding that Washington provided Israel.

After both sides discussed a draft proposal for a treaty, the Israeli negotiating team returned home for consultation on October 21. At that time the president sent Prime Minister Begin a personal message asking for his cooperation in the negotiations. Begin's response came in a public statement announcing plans to expand the West Bank settlements and to move his office to East Jerusalem,[198] a declaration that was humiliating for Carter and embarrassing for Sadat and that caused friction between Washington and Israel.

Israel and the United States also disagreed over a letter President Carter sent to King Hussein.[199] The king had requested a clarification of the American position on certain matters. The administration considered the letter a means for the president to present an "American" interpretation of the Camp David accords to the Arab world in the hope of averting the negative consensus that appeared to be crystallizing among the Arabs over the outcome of Camp David. Assistant Secretary of State Harold Saunders delivered Carter's letter to Hussein on October 19, then went to Israel to give Prime Minister Begin a copy of it. Begin complained bitterly to Saunders about not having been consulted by Carter concerning the letter prior to his giving it to Hussein, and harshly criticized the president's substantive points, arguing, among other things, that they "constituted a grave threat to Israel."[200] The letter resulted in further discord in U.S.–Israeli relations and in Carter's relations with pro-Israeli Americans, although it did nothing to help Washington win support from the Arab states, since it was apparent to Hussein and others that even if the United States disagreed with Israel, it did not have the will or ability to influence the Jewish state or to pursue its stated principles.

The Israeli negotiating team returned to Washington on October 26, and the talks resumed. This round was particularly frustrating, and Carter noted the following in a diary entry on November 8: "It's obvious that the Israelis want a separate treaty with Egypt: they want to keep the West Bank and Gaza permanently. . . . and they use the settlements and East Jerusalem issues to prevent the involvement of the Jordanians and the Palestinians."[201] The foregoing analysis certainly suggests that Carter was aware of Israel's position (and in essence had acceded to it) many months earlier. However, Quandt writes that Carter was "outraged" at this point, feeling that Israel was "backsliding from the commitments made at Camp David."[202] In any case, it is clear, as Israeli officials had continually indicated, that a separate treaty was the maximum to which Israel would ever agree. A typical comment was that of Defense Minister Weizman, in a pointed declaration to Carter: "If anyone, Arab or American, thought that our evacuation of Sinai was to be taken as a model for the other fronts, he was deluding himself. Neither from the West Bank and Gaza, nor from the Golan Heights would we remove our settlements or fail to maintain a military presence."[203]

On November 21 the Israeli cabinet voted to accept the draft peace treaty. On November 24 the Cairo newspaper *Al Ahram* published a partial text of the proposed treaty, leaving out Article 6, which gave the Egyptian-Israeli treaty priority over Egypt's previous treaties with Arab countries. The next day Washington and Israel published the full text of the draft, causing the Egyptians considerable embarrassment and leading to increased tensions between Egypt and Israel.[204]

Carter set a December 17 deadline for the two states to conclude a final treaty. On December 9 Vance went to the Middle East to attempt to bridge the remaining differences between Egypt and Israel. In the wake of the harsh reaction of the Arabs at the Baghdad Summit, Sadat's advisors attempted to press the Egyptian president to insist on some form of linkage between the two accords signed at Camp David. The Egyptians saw that linkage as revolving around a relationship between the formal exchange of ambassadors between Israel and Egypt and the establishment of a self-governing authority on the West Bank and Gaza. Israel refused to consider the idea of even a target date for the setting up of a self-governing authority and was adamant that there be no linkage between such an authority and the exchange of ambassadors. Carter and his advisors seemed to feel that some connection between the two issues was important in order to broaden the peace process in the Arab world. However, Carter's surrender on so many previous issues did not bode well for American interests to prevail on this one, and in the end they did not. Vance found the Egyptians "cooperative," but in Israel the secretary was met with hostility and complete negativism. After his departure the Israeli government released the following statement: "The Government of Israel rejects the attitude and interpretation of the U.S. government with regard to the Egyptian proposals."[205] December 17 came and went without progress.

In an effort to break what appeared to be a serious stalemate, Secretary Vance arranged a meeting in Brussels on December 23, 1978, between Dayan and the new Egyptian prime minister, Mustapha Khalil. At that meeting Khalil stated that the crux of the problem for Egypt was that it wanted peace with Israel, but not total isolation from the Arab world. He argued that the United States and Israel should be urging Egypt to make alliances with the moderate Arab countries, rather than abandoning them; Egypt could not come to the aid of the moderates against the radicals and Islamic fundamentalists that were sweeping the area if Egypt was completely isolated. Dayan asked Khalil what Egypt would do if Syria attacked Israel in the occupied Golan Heights and claimed it was a defensive war, thus rendering operative Egypt's treaty with Syria. Khalil replied that Egypt would side with Syria verbally, but would take no action whatsoever.[206] This answer was not sufficient for the Israelis, who insisted that a priority of obligations clause, in the language that they specified, be written into any final treaty. On this and the other issues the outcome remained a stalemate.

In mid-January 1979 the Iranian revolution deposed the shah, who was then welcomed in Egypt as a guest of Sadat, a situation that added to Sadat's domestic and regional troubles. In addition, the events in Iran suggested to many officials in Cairo that an alliance with the United States could not be relied on to keep a regime in power and thus there seemed to be even less reason for Sadat to align Egypt so completely with Washington. Moreover, the rise of the Ayatollah Khomeini strengthened Islamic fundamentalism in Egypt and buttressed opposition to Sadat, while the popular reaction throughout the Arab world to the Iranian revolution made it seem especially risky for regimes to be perceived as "pro-Israeli" or "pro-American." Sadat appeared oddly oblivious to these considerations, though his advisors were acutely mindful of them.

In Israel, where there had been many doubts all along concerning the prudence of the treaty, events in Iran raised questions about whether it was wise to withdraw from the Sinai at a time when the Middle East was becoming increasingly unstable. The rage of Muslim fundamentalists against the pro-American position of the shah raised questions in Israel about the stability of Sadat's domestic position and thus the wisdom of a territorial compromise. Many Israelis were also wary of giving up the oil fields in Sinai, since Iran, under the shah, had been a principal supplier of oil to Israel, a role that the new regime was not likely to play. Too, like the Egyptians, the Israelis wondered just how much they could count on the United States as they watched Washington sit helplessly by while one of its major allies in the region was deposed. More to the point was the fact that Israel, for years depicted as an outpost of American power and a strategic asset to American interests in the Middle East, was unable to affect in any way the situation in Iran.

For the Carter administration the fall of the shah made the Israeli-Egyptian treaty, regardless of the concessions required to secure it, more attractive, not less, since administration officials assumed—erroneously—that that part of the Middle East would be stable as a result of its further incorporation in the American sphere. Carter also wanted the treaty to present to the American public as a "political success" to offset the disaster in Iran. The importance of domestic politics in Middle East policymaking was evident in a memorandum Brzezinski sent to the president on January 23 expressing his thoughts about the Arab-Israeli issue. The memorandum is striking for its lack of concern with substance (particularly from the highest official in the National Security Council): "Events may make it difficult for us to pursue such a strategy, but I am firmly convinced for the good of the Democratic Party we must avoid a situation where we continue agitating the most neuralgic problem with the American Jewish community (the West Bank, the Palestinians, the PLO) without a breakthrough to a solution. I do not believe that in the approaching election year we will be able to convince the Israelis that we have significant leverage over them, particularly on those issues. . . . We have little time left."[207]

On January 17, 1979, Alfred Atherton was dispatched to Israel to try to iron out some of the semantic problems in the draft treaty. Atherton conveyed the administration's willingness to accept Israel's position on the priority of obligations issue, but the specific wording of the American position was still not acceptable to Israel. As a further concession to induce Israel to sign a treaty with Egypt, the United States agreed—again—to support in writing Israel's massive retaliatory actions against neighboring countries.[208] In Cairo Atherton found the Egyptians unwilling to accept all of Israel's changes in the draft treaty, although they did agree to give Israel first option to buy, at market price, the oil produced in Egyptian fields and the oil yet to be discovered in the A-Tur oil field in Sinai.[209] The Egyptians proposed a renewal of the talks at the ministerial level.

The ministerial talks convened at Camp David on February 21, with Khalil, Vance, and Dayan participating. Camp David II, which lasted four days, turned out to be, in Dayan's words, "cold, short and sterile." Vance attempted to impress upon his visitors Washington's feelings about the urgency of an Egyptian-Israeli peace in light of the Iranian revolution and the negative spirit that had prevailed at Baghdad.[210] Yet it was these very factors that made Sadat's advisors highly reluctant to conclude a separate peace with Israel: indeed almost all of them warned the Egyptian president against such a "peace." The priority of obligations clause was still a contentious issue, as was the fact that Israel had rescinded its agreement to evacuate El Arish in advance of the original date; Egypt had responded by delaying the exchange of ambassadors. In addition, the Americans were now pressuring Egypt to drop the requirement for linkage between the exchange of ambassadors and the establishment of self-government in the West Bank, a position they had previously supported. Carter was not willing to engage in a confrontation with Israel over the issue; thus Sadat was expected to concede.

Begin came to Washington on March 1, at Carter's invitation. Within three days Carter resolved the disagreement on the wording of the priority of obligations clause by acceding to the Israeli position; Carter conceded as well that there should be no linkage of any kind between the Egyptian-Israeli treaty and negotiations on autonomy for the Palestinians on the West Bank. Dayan described it as a "complete turnabout in the American position."[211] After the Begin-Carter agreement, Vance, in Israel on March 7, gave Dayan the Memorandum of Understanding, which the Israelis had demanded at the outset of the process as a prerequisite for their signing a treaty with Egypt. The alliance that emerged between the United States and Israel as a result of that memorandum represents one of the high points in Israeli diplomacy vis-à-vis the United States.

In this Memorandum of Understanding, the United States agreed that in case of a violation or threat of violation to the Treaty of Peace against Israel, it (1) will take "such remedial measures as it deems appropriate, which may include diplomatic, economic and military measures"; (2) "will provide support it deems appropriate for proper actions taken by Israel in response to such demonstrated violations of the Treaty of Peace"; (3) "will be prepared to consider on an urgent basis, such measures as the strengthening of the United States presence in the area, the providing of emergency supplies to Israel and the exercise of maritime rights in order to put an end to the violations"; (4) "will oppose and, if necessary, vote against any action or resolution in the United Nations, which, in its judgement adversely affects the Treaty of Peace"; (5) "will pledge to be responsive to the military and economic requirements of Israel on a long-term basis"; and (6) "will refuse to supply weapons to parties that could use them against Israel and will not supply or authorize the transfer of such weapons from third parties."[212]

Even with the Memorandum of Understanding, Israel still had reservations about concluding the treaty, as did Egypt. In desperation Carter decided to go to the Middle East in an attempt to persuade both sides to finalize the treaty. Within one hour of Carter's arrival in Cairo, and over the opposition of virtually all his advisors, Sadat agreed to accept the treaty, stating: "He [Carter] and I resolved all the questions which still had not been decided after all these months."[213] Carter's notes of the meeting are significant: "In my private visits with Sadat he emphasized again and again that his main concern was about me, and that he wanted my trip to be a 'smashing success.'... It was imperative to him that the United States and Egypt stand together, no matter what might be the outcome of the negotiations."[214] Sadat appeared to have lost sight of a number of important aspects of Egyptian political reality. His infatuation with the United States is indeed striking.

Carter then traveled to Israel on March 10, where he was greeted with considerable hostility and extensive haggling over semantics. The president made an emotional address to the Knesset on March 12 concerning the need for peace between Israel and Egypt that was received in cold silence. One M.K. decried the treaty as "a crime against our people," while another compared Sadat with Hitler. Still others accused the president of "selling out" Israel.[215] Carter wrote of his feelings at the time: "I was convinced that Begin would do everything possible to block a treaty."[216] Quandt notes that the American delegation in Israel "suspected that his [Begin's] real purpose was to hurt Carter politically by depriving him of a much needed foreign policy victory."[217] Finally on March 13 Begin said that most of his "concerns" had been alleviated and that he would submit the much-amended draft treaty (together with the U.S. memorandum) to the cabinet for debate. The cabinet approved the treaty, and Carter returned to Egypt on March 13 to finalize the agreement with Sadat. The president came home on March 14, but wrote that he was "disgusted" with the American press's negative comments about the agreements being "bought" at a price of $10 to $20 billion and involving a mutual defense treaty with Israel.[218]

A copy of the Memorandum of Understanding between the United States and Israel was finally given to Egypt on March 25, 1979. It immediately caused consternation among Egyptian officials. They believed that by virtue of this document the United States had assumed the role of arbiter in determining whether there was a violation or threat of violation of the bilateral treaty and that the article in the treaty that provided for the settlement of disputes was nullified by this extensive American commitment to Israel.[219] That very day Egypt sent Carter a letter expressing its opposition to the memorandum, declaring that this document would adversely affect the whole process of peace and stability in the area. Mahmoud Riad relates the substance of the letter:

The contents of the memorandum were based on alleged accusations against Egypt and provided for certain measures to be taken against her in the hypothetical case of violation, the determination of which was largely left to Israel; the US was supposed to be a partner in a tripartite effort to achieve peace, not to support the allegations of one side against the other or to assume that Egypt was the side liable to violate its obligations; the Memorandum could be construed as an eventual alliance between the US and Israel against Egypt. It offered the US rights that were neither mentioned nor negotiated with Egypt, and empowered the US to impose punitive measures, which raised doubts about future relations and could affect the situation in the whole region; and it gave the US the right to impose a military presence in the region for reasons agreed between Israel and the US. This was a matter Egypt could not accept; in fact, it cast grave doubts concerning the real intention of the US since it could be accused of collaborating with Israel to create such circumstances as would lead to an American military presence in the area, a matter which would certainly have serious implications, especially on stability in the whole area, and could lead to other alliances to counter this one.[220]

Nevertheless, Sadat and Begin signed the Treaty of Peace between the Republic of Egypt and the State of Israel on March 26, 1979, in Washington. Vance and Dayan signed the Memorandum of Understanding the same day.

The second Baghdad conference convened on March 27, and the Arab leaders agreed to withdraw immediately their ambassadors from Egypt and to sever political and diplomatic relations within a month. The conference reaffirmed the boycott regulations, economic sanctions, and suspension of Egypt's membership in the Arab League, which were decided at the first Baghdad summit.

In May 1979 the fruitless negotiations over West Bank–Gaza autonomy were begun.

On February 26, 1980, Israel and Egypt established official diplomatic relations with an exchange of ambassadors.

In August 1980 Sadat, playing into Israeli hands, suspended the autonomy talks in response to Israel's legislation "reunifying Jerusalem" (formally incorporating the eastern sector of the city into Israel).

In June 1981 Israel bombed and destroyed a nearly completed French-built nuclear reactor at the outskirts of Baghdad.

In July 1981 Israel initiated a two-week long series of bombing raids in southern Lebanon that was capped by the bombardment of a residential sector of West Beirut on July 17, during which 300 civilians were killed.

On October 6, 1981, Sadat was assassinated.

In November 1981 the United States and Israel concluded a formal strategic cooperation agreement, suspended three weeks later, but reinstated in November 1983.

In December 1981 Israel annexed the Golan Heights.

In April 1982 Israel completed its withdrawal from the Sinai.

In June 1982 Israel invaded Lebanon, initiating the fifth major Arab-Israeli war.

Camp David surely had not contributed to stability or peace in the Middle East.

Conclusion

It is instructive to ask what benefits Egypt, Israel, and the United States achieved through the Camp David process and to question why the United States did not press for a comprehensive treaty or attempt to find a resolution to the Palestinian issue.

The singular benefit to Egypt was the return of the entire Sinai (with the exception of Taba), reestablishing Egyptian sovereignty and territorial integrity throughout its country. This is not an inconsiderable achievement, even beside the failure on the Palestinian issue. Moreover, states typically place their own national interests before any group interest, and by 1978 the Arab states had become increasingly individualistic—the growing dilution of pan-Arab nationalism since 1967 was strikingly pronounced. Nevertheless, Sadat's disregard of all Arab concerns, including the Golan, Jordanian interests, East Jerusalem, and the question of Palestine seems somewhat extreme. The intense contempt Sadat displayed for other Arab leaders (as well as his own advisors who disagreed with him) suggests a man entirely too confident of himself: perhaps Sadat's self-image as a great statesman and peacemaker clouded his ability to fashion a sound treaty. The extent of Sadat's desire for an alliance with the United States and the lengths to which he went in "cooperating" with Washington to secure such a partnership also appear unusual as well as unrealistic. It should have been apparent to the Egyptian president that regardless of the nature and extent of the concessions he made, Egypt would never enjoy the "special relationship" with the United States that Israel does. In part, Sadat's aspiration for a partnership with the United States stemmed from his belief that it would bring many advantages to Egypt; however, most of the expected benefits did not materialize. For instance, Sadat thought that by making peace with Israel he could decrease Egypt's defense expenditures and divert that money to needed developmental projects. After the treaty some resources were released from defense purposes, but complex economic and political forces seriously reduced the potential impact of developmental plans. Sadat also believed that if Egypt made peace with Israel, foreign investment would be attracted to Egypt because of its new image of stability. This assumption too proved illusory. In addition, while U.S. aid to Egypt did increase substantially, the Arab boycott cost Egypt important sources of income and assistance, and Egypt ended up less well off economically than before the treaty. Moreover, much of the American aid has been used to purchase American weapons. Egypt regained its territory, but little else.

Egypt lost its traditionally influential role in the Arab world and certainly did not acquire the ability to influence Washington or Israel. Egyptian impotence with regard to Israeli actions during the 1982 war in Lebanon was a stark testament to the hollow meaning of its peace treaty with Israel. Moreover, the humiliating manner with which the American Congress and President Reagan has treated Egypt and its new president, Husni Mubarak, so far surely strikes a dissonant cord in every Egyptian. Undoubtedly, too, such humiliation at the hands of the United States feeds the growing Islamic fundamentalist movement in Egypt—a movement that had been given significant impetus by Sadat's flamboyant embrace of the United States. The degree to which President Sadat was out of touch with his people—evidenced in the negative responses of his closest officials as well as in the streets of Asyut and Cairo—will not likely be recorded favorably in Egyptian history.

Israel, on the other hand, realized many benefits from the Camp David process. It attained its first formal peace treaty with an Arab country—a proclaimed objective of the Jewish state from its inception. What is more, the peace was not concluded with just any Arab state, but with the most politically important and militarily strongest country in the Arab world. This is certainly a considerable achievement. As a result of the treaty Israel neutralized any possible threat from its southern flank and was able to pursue military action against its northern neighbors without fear of rearguard response. Such a strategic advantage in the regional context is of enormous significance. Israel assumed the treaty would lead to considerable commercial and economic benefits as well as intimate personal relations with Egypt. These expectations did not materialize—largely because of Israel's aggressive policies against other Arabs (in the West Bank and Gaza, Iraq, Lebanon, and elsewhere). At home Mubarak needed to counter the disapproval of the treaty and to undercut the appeal and demands of Muslim fundamentalists and other opposition groups; within the Arab world he attempted to reduce Egypt's isolation. However, even the "cold" peace served Israel's most important interests. As a direct result of the treaty Israel forged a virtual military alliance with the United States (formalized and expanded in November 1981), including vastly increased economic and military aid, increased political and diplomatic support, a guaranteed supply of oil, and much more. The intensification of the U.S.-Israeli relationship was a major advantage for Israel. Finally, one of the most salient benefits was the written international agreement (the Framework for Peace in the Middle East)—a 1978 "Balfour Declaration"—that "legitimized" Israel's goal of permanent control over the West Bank and Gaza. Such progress toward the achievement of Eretz Israel was enormously important to Begin and the Likud and to many other Zionists as well. Indeed, some Israelis argued that the only reason Israel agreed to the accord with Egypt was because of the second agreement concerning the West Bank.

The balance sheet for the United States is less easily measured. Those individuals who perceive Israel as a strategic asset to American interests undoubtedly consider the intensified U.S.–Israeli alignment a benefit. This analyst views the closer relationship as having a decidedly negative consequence for the United States. Many Americans also considered the new U.S.–Egyptian partnership a gain. However, a contrary argument suggests that given the strictly bilateral character of the Egyptian-Israeli agreement, its decided unpopularity within Egypt and throughout the Arab world, and the multiple negative consequences that flowed directly from the treaty, the Camp David process did not serve American interests.

It is true that as a result of Camp David the United States extended its influence over Egypt and increased Egypt's dependence on Washington. This situation limits the political and military maneuverability of Cairo, particularly its ability to pursue policies inimical to U.S. interests. The desire to bring Egypt fully within the American sphere, a goal of Washington since the early 1950s, was achieved with the Egyptian-Israeli treaty. But the extended influence did not come without cost. The United States promised to provide Egypt with $1.5 billion in aid annually, and in practice that aid has increased yearly. More important, from the perspective of America's long-term and continuing interests in the region, it is difficult to conclude that the Egyptian-Israeli treaty made a positive contribution. As a result of the treaty Soviet influence in the region received a renewed boost; regional instability escalated significantly, culminating in another major war; and U.S. relations with a number of Arab regimes deteriorated. Indeed, Egypt's isolation in the Arab world was reflected in American isolation—a condition that grew profoundly in the next five years. Moreover, the assassination of Sadat and the ascendancy of President Mubarak brought a shift in Egyptian perspectives on the United States. Particularly as the limits of Egypt's ability to influence Washington on matters of concern to Cairo became apparent, Mubarak grew increasingly less enthusiastic about Cairo's place in the American orbit. By 1984 Egypt was attempting to rebuild its relations with the Soviet Union and was moving to reintegrate itself into the Arab world. There were limits, however, to Egypt's ability to pursue nonalignment; the linkages of economic dependence forged at Camp David were indeed constraining. Many individuals interpreted this as a vindication of U.S. Middle East policy.

Thoughtful observers, however, were likely to reflect on the Iranian revolution and to question Washington's ability to impose its will on the Arab world indefinitely, especially given the increasing unpopularity of pro-American Arab elites in their own countries and the growing anti-American sentiment prevalent throughout the region. The United States has not had a history of astutely choosing "partners" among Arab elites. President Eisenhower, for example, preferred the discredited Nuri Said and the illegitimate monarchy in Iraq, because they were "pro-American," to Gamal Abdul Nasser, a leader who genuinely had the support of his people. Similarly, President Carter preferred the slavishly pro-American Sadat, irrespective of how he and his policies were viewed by his own people, to the Palestinian leaders who constituted the most representative and popular leadership in the Arab world. Significantly both Nasser and the PLO attempted to reach a modus vivendi with Israel. In both cases Israeli and American rejection worked against the best interests of the United States and the Jewish state, but the United States also has a history of pursuing policies that contradict its national interest. In the long run, American interests will only be served through U.S. alignments with regimes that have the support of their people and that represent the interests and aspirations of their people, including a genuinely independent and representative Palestinian regime. Indeed, the unresolved question of Palestine was still the central issue in the Middle East after Camp David, yet American policymakers behaved as if they expected it simply to disappear. The real failure of Camp David was the failure to facilitate a just resolution of this festering issue.

In addition to the cost/benefit analysis of the Camp David process, several other factors bear comment in conclusion. Presidential preeminence still appeared to be the norm in Middle East policymaking during the period 1974-75 through 1979. To some extent this was so; but the high profile of President Carter in bringing the Egyptians and Israelis together tended to obscure the extraordinarily intricate and complex relationship that had developed between domestic pro-Israeli elements and Congress and the ways in which this relationship influenced policy outputs. The reader is reminded of but two prominent examples: the Jackson-Vanik amendment in 1974 with its considerable impact on U.S.-Soviet détente, and the May 1975 letter from seventy-six Senators that undermined the Ford administration's attempts to induce Israeli concessions in the Sinai II negotiations. On the other hand, the focus on the Executive in this chapter serves to illustrate the changed reality of the American political system concerning Middle East issues—the most important aspect being the degree to which pro-Israeli forces had come to influence all institutions within the system compared to earlier periods. Still, it must be stated again that if the policymaking elite were to become convinced that providing Israel unqualified support was not in America's fundamental interest, the strength of the pro-Israeli effort would be seriously diminished. For whatever reason—and the reasons are many and varied, despite the fact that they are based on subjective belief, misperception and misinformation—the elite continues to view Israel as a valuable partner and an asset to the realization of American interests.

Even in the Carter administration, where the strategic asset argument was made far less often than during the two previous administrations, and where the president began with fresh ideas including at least the willingness to address the Palestinian issue, the basic inclinations of officials were pro-Israeli. Jimmy Carter, for example, is a born-again Christian for whom the establishment of Israel was the fulfillment of biblical prophecy. Given such a weltanschauung, could the desire of the Palestinians for a state possibly compete with the interests of Israel? Zbigniew Brzezinski was fundamentally a "cold-warrior." Once the Soviet Union intervened in Afghanistan and Washington began to fear a Red tide sweeping the Middle East, could the interests of Israel fail to have been met in the common struggle against the Soviets? Beliefs and misperceptions thus come together in a variety of ways on the question of Israel. It is also true that public opinion is a factor on Middle East issues, and support for Israel within the American public extends far beyond Jewish constituencies. It is worth recalling how many times President Carter expressed apprehension about "public opinion" in addition to concern about his Jewish constituents. Public opinion in the United States—again for a variety of reasons—is immensely supportive of Israel. Unfortunately, it is equally hostile to Palestinians, and nearly as hostile to Arabs and Muslims in general. As rationally inexplicable as these phenomena are, they nevertheless play a part in the interface between domestic politics and Middle East policy. There simply are not any voices of significance in the United States who care about the fate of the Palestinians, and this constitutes a powerful disincentive for a president who is confronted with a prodigious audience that cares passionately about Israel. In such a situation a dispassionate formulation of policy is lost to the pressure of that which is least harmful politically, familiar, and "plays well" with the public.

What is most needed, perhaps, is for all Americans—policymakers and the public—to become better informed about the Middle East and more sensitive to its complex realities. Heightened sensitivity and more rational policies would go a long way in regaining the respect and friendship of Middle East peoples—the loss of which has profoundly affected American national interests.

CHAPTER SEVEN

THE 1982 WAR IN LEBANON

Introduction

The fifth Arab-Israeli war and Israel's third major offensive war against the Arabs began with an aerial bombardment of Beirut on June 4 and 5, 1982. On June 6 Israeli forces launched a massive land, sea, and air invasion of Lebanon, which resulted in the occupation of one-third of the country up to and including the Beirut-Damascus highway; the destruction of all the Syrian missile batteries in the Bekaa Valley; the elimination of over one-quarter of the Syrian air force; and the destruction of all the political, social, and military organizations of the PLO. The invasion included a siege of the western sector of the city of Beirut, which interrupted supplies of electricity, water, food, and medicine to the civilian population.

The campaign lasted for sixty-seven days, past September 1, when the last of the PLO fighters trapped in Beirut evacuated the city. Though the intense hostilities ceased after that, sporadic fighting continued. On September 15 Israel invaded and occupied all of West Beirut. Phalangist forces allied to Israel massacred Palestinian civilians between September 16 and 18 in the refugee camps of Sabra and Shatila while the area was under Israeli control. Israel pulled back from Beirut on September 28 but maintained its occupation of the other parts of Lebanon that it had secured during the war.

On December 27, 1982, Israel and Lebanon began negotiations, under the auspices of the United States, for an Israeli withdrawal. On May 17, 1983, the two states signed an agreement providing for the withdrawal of most Israeli forces and granting Israel many concessions in trade, political influence, and a normalization of relations. Israel did not withdraw, however, and within less than one year, on March 5, 1984, Beirut cancelled the agreement. Despite the maintenance of its military occupation in Lebanon, Israel's political influence (including that with the Phalange) declined drastically. To its detriment, the United States involved itself on a multiplicity of levels with this Israeli adventure.

The International Context, Regional Linkages, and American Interests and Allies

General Trends

As in all periods since the end of World War II, events in the global arena were intensely interconnected with Middle East politics and crises during 1979-82. The era was marked by the collapse of détente between Moscow and Washington, the intensification of Soviet-American competition, and the reemergence among American policymakers of the perception of the Soviet Union as a world revolutionary state intent on dominating the international system and defeating the United States. The transformation in relations between the United States and the Soviet Union was evidenced in the special role the Middle East played in the strategies of both powers—becoming a flash point for their growing hostility.

The Arabian Gulf was one important area that reflected the increasing discord. After the revolution in Iran and in the wake of the Soviet invasion of Afghanistan, Washington strategists depicted the Soviets, rather than indigenous forces, as the major threat to U.S. interests in the Gulf. The formal expression of this new emphasis was the Carter Doctrine—a statement of America's perception of its strategic concerns in the Gulf region and of its readiness to resort to force to secure those interests.

The tension between Moscow and Washington spilled over into the Arab-Palestinian-Israeli conflict and that enmity in turn exacerbated Soviet-American discord. While Jimmy Carter began his presidency with the understanding that cooperation between the United States and the Soviet Union was essential to oversee a peaceful resolution of the Middle East conflict (reflected in his effort to reconvene the Geneva Conference and in the 1977 Soviet-American joint statement), Israel's opposition to that approach resulted in its demise. Thus the Soviets and Soviet regional allies, such as Syria, were excluded from the peace process, and the Palestinian issue was subordinated to the effort to secure an Egyptian-Israeli peace treaty. However, the aftermath of that treaty saw the Arab-Palestinian-Israeli conflict intensify and the Soviet position strengthen. The separate Egyptian peace with Israel heightened Syrian concerns about a possible Israeli-Syrian war and encouraged the formation of a stronger Soviet-Syrian axis to counter the U.S.–Israeli alliance (to which Egypt appeared affiliated in a junior capacity). On October 8, 1980, Syria and the Soviet Union signed a twenty-year Treaty of Friendship and Co-operation. In 1981, after Israel annexed the Golan Heights, relations between Moscow and Damascus grew even closer.

The Egyptian-Israeli treaty contributed in other ways to the expansion of Soviet influence, regional instability, and difficulties for American interests. The ink was barely dry on the treaty when Israel undertook its most extensive phase of colonization in the West Bank and Gaza, sending an unmistakable signal to the world, particularly to the indigenous people, that the Israeli government intended to retain these areas permanently. Concomitant with the intensive colonization were systematic efforts to dispossess the Palestinians of their land and encourage their emigration.[1] Such policies strengthened active resistance by Palestinians in the West Bank and Gaza, resulting in increased Israeli repression. The harsher measures intensified backing of the PLO as their sole, legitimate representative and increased support for an independent Palestinian state as the only solution to the myriad problems among Palestinians under occupation. The PLO, in turn, looked to the Soviet Union and to the Arab states, including the most conservative ones, for help. Saudi Arabia and the Gulf states provided the PLO with financial support and political advocacy in the international arena, while the Soviet Union provided arms. By denying Palestinians the right to self-determination and by excluding the PLO from the peace process, the Egyptian-Israeli treaty afforded the Soviets an opportunity to demonstrate their support for the Palestinians by sending weapons. Paradoxically, however, the more weapons the PLO secured, the less it used them: Palestinian guerrilla activity diminished to its lowest level during this period. Nevertheless, the arms buildup was destabilizing in and of itself, since Israel used it as a pretext for its preemptive strikes in Lebanon and as justification for the 1982 invasion. Moreover, the Israelis used the Soviet-PLO connection as another rationalization for their refusal to consider a Palestinian state on the West Bank and Gaza: such a state, they argued, would be a base for the Soviets in the Middle East. Yet the longer the Palestinian question remained unresolved, the greater was the likelihood of renewed regional conflict.

In addition, the Egyptian-Israeli treaty resulted in a worsening of relations between the United States and several Arab regimes. Most of the Arab governments held Washington responsible for the treaty, which they condemned for ignoring Syrian and Jordanian concerns; for the implications of the neutralization of Egypt in future Israeli military offensives in the absence of a comprehensive settlement; and for ignoring the interests of the Palestinians, while consigning the West Bank and the Gaza Strip to permanent Israeli occupation. Saudi Arabia, a long-standing pro-American state, was placed in a particularly awkward situation by Washington's position as the architect of Camp David and attempted for a time to distance itself from the United States. However, this was during a period when the Saudis were concerned about Soviet influence in South Yemen and Ethiopia, as well as about the threat from Iran's export of Shi'ia fundamentalism. Eventually, their worries regarding the ability of the regime to withstand the currents of change in the region grew so acute that they drew closer to the United States, even to the extent of military collaboration. Indeed, the threat Riyadh felt from Teheran and the Iraq-Iran war led the Saudi regime to request Washington to dispatch four radar surveillance planes (AWACs) to bolster its air defense system. Acting within the framework of his newly enunciated doctrine—the Saudis claimed fear of possible Iranian air attacks in retaliation for their support of Baghdad (a Soviet ally)—President Carter agreed.

The Reagan administration, which assumed office in 1981, was immediately faced with another Saudi request for arms, specifically equipment to upgrade its F-15's. In the context of concern about instability in the Arabian Gulf, threats to Western access to oil, and increased Soviet influence in the region, the administration announced on March 6, 1981, that the United States was prepared to sell Saudi Arabia all of the equipment that it requested, except for bomb racks.[2] Additionally, in April 1981 the administration announced that it would sell Saudi Arabia five AWACs of its own, delivery to be scheduled for 1985. Pending delivery, the four American-manned AWACs, sent by Carter, would remain.[3] The provision of the F-15 equipment and the AWACs became an important policy objective for the Reagan administration, which recognized the utility of having a positive relationship with a pivotal Arab state of such importance in OPEC, significance in geostrategic location, and fervor against Communism.

Indeed, the AWACs had a fundamentally political rather than military significance. They were intended to provide the Saudis with concrete evidence of America's friendship; to give an incentive for Riyadh to continue its pro-Western economic policies; and to encourage the Saudis to support Secretary of State Alexander Haig's plans to forge a "strategic consensus" against Soviet penetration in the region. The planes in no way altered the military balance between the Arabs and Israel. Ronald Reagan would never have permitted such a shift, since both he and Haig were committed to the absolute military superiority of Israel.[4] Haig, a former top aide to Henry Kissinger, strongly advocated the thesis that Israel was an indispensable strategic asset to the United States in containing the Soviet Union. Such an argument undoubtedly appealed to Reagan, whose major preoccupation was with implementing means to limit Soviet expansionism.

No sooner was the proposed AWACs sale announced, however, than Israel decried it as a "threat to its existence,"[5] and the domestic pro-Israeli lobby mounted a campaign in the media and Congress to prevent the sale. The B'nai B'rith (the Jewish anti-defamation league) sponsored full-page advertisements in major American newspapers, calling for opposition to the arms deal with Saudi Arabia, and labeling it "an oil arrogant, oil greedy nation" that opposed the Camp David accords and "financed PLO terrorism."[6] The pro-Israeli campaign nearly succeeded: a large portion of the media, Congress, and public opinion was persuaded to oppose the sale. The Reagan administration and U.S. corporations doing business with the Saudis also waged a powerful campaign, however; and the Senate declined to disapprove the AWACs by a vote of 52 to 48 on October 28, 1981. (The House of Representatives had voted against the sale, 201 to 111.) This represents one of only two major setbacks the Israeli lobby ever experienced and thereafter how a Senator voted on this issue became the most important factor in the lobby's determination of an individual's "friendship" toward Israel. Those who were labeled "unfriendly" faced serious problems at reelection. Illinois Senator Charles Percy was targeted by the lobby in 1984 because of his vote on the AWACs, despite an otherwise virtually unblemished record of support for Israel's interests; his defeat was related in considerable measure to the lobby's efforts.[7]

Contrary to the public's image of Saudi Arabia, the monarchy has been a consistently moderating force in Middle East regional politics and a staunchly pro-American ally. Riyadh has rarely been a flamboyant player in the political arena, but it has repeatedly demonstrated its commitment to regional and international political and economic stability. Two important areas that reflect this Saudi policy in the period under consideration are its peace initiatives and its petroleum policy.

An Arab-Initiated Peace Plan. In August 1981 Saudi Crown Prince Fahd publicly offered an eight-point comprehensive plan for peace in the Middle East, known thereafter as the Fahd Plan. It called for Israeli withdrawal from the territories occupied since 1967, including East Jerusalem; removal of Israeli settlements from these territories; freedom of worship for all religions in Jerusalem; recognition of the right of Palestinians to return to their homes; establishment of a transitional regime for the West Bank and Gaza under the United Nations; establishment of a Palestinian state with East Jerusalem as its capital; affirmation of "the right of all countries of the region to live in peace"; and a guarantee of the settlement by the United Nations or some of its members.[8] The reference to the right of all states to live in peace clearly implied recognition of Israel. The Fahd Plan, reduced to its essentials, was thus a restatement and an affirmation of the two-state solution embodied in the U.N. resolution that partitioned Palestine in November 1947. The closer the majority of Arabs came to formally accepting the idea, however, the more strenuously Israel rejected it. Indeed, Israeli Prime Minister Menachem Begin denounced the Fahd initiative as a plan "to liquidate Israel in stages," and Foreign Minister Yitzhak Shamir described each of the eight points as "a poisoned dagger thrust into the heart of Israel's existence." Israel immediately announced that it would "counter" the peace plan by planting new settlements on the West Bank.[9]

President Reagan met Crown Prince Fahd during the North-South Conference at Cancun, Mexico, in October 1981 and was reported to have given a sympathetic hearing to the Saudi plan. The president stated publicly that while the United States and Israel did not agree with all of Fahd's points, "it is the first time that the Saudis have recognized Israel as a nation and it is a beginning for negotiations." Secretary of State Haig added, "There are aspects in the eight point proposal . . . by which we are encouraged." Assistant Secretary of State Nicholas Veliotes, in testimony before the European and Middle Eastern Subcommittee of the House Foreign Affairs Committee on October 21, spelled out the official American position. In keeping with long-standing policy, the assistant secretary unequivocally reiterated U.S. opposition to the point regarding a Palestinian state. Veliotes said that the United States accepted without qualification the points regarding freedom of worship for all religions and the right of all states in the region to live in peace. Regarding the right of repatriation or compensation for the Palestinian refugees, Veliotes noted that it was "essentially right out of a United Nations resolution" for which the United States had consistently voted. While indicating basic agreement with the point on Israeli withdrawal from the occupied areas, Veliotes restated the American view that such withdrawal should take place in the context of a negotiated peace, which would not preclude modifications of the pre-1967 boundary lines. Veliotes did not rule out the remaining three points—removal of Israeli settlements, a U.N. trusteeship for the West Bank and Gaza for a transitional period, and a guarantee of any peace agreement by the United Nations—"if the parties concerned agreed on them." These were matters to be settled in negotiation, the assistant secretary stated.[10]

On November 2 King Hussein told American officials in Washington that he supported the Fahd Plan.[11] Yasir Arafat (who reportedly helped draft it) gave the plan initial public support, but later, on November 22, under pressure from groups within and external to the PLO, drew back from it.[12] An Arab summit was convened in Fez, Morocco, on November 25 to debate the plan and strategies for implementing its proposals. The summit conference, however, was preceded by meetings of the foreign ministers of all members of the Arab League; here the plan was dealt a serious blow, resulting in the failure of the Fez Summit. In part the conflicts among the Arab states contributed to the debacle at Fez, as did the opposition of Syria to Fahd's proposals—opposition related more to context than the content of the plan, but as one analyst argues, it was in considerable measure Saudi Arabia's inability to deliver American support for the Fahd Plan that resulted in its demise. At a decisive moment in the foreign ministers' meeting on November 22 Prince Saud al-Faisal was asked: "If the Summit approved the Fahd points, do you believe the United States would accept them, and if so, induce Israel to negotiate on those terms?" The prince gave no reply. To the Arabs, the issue was whether a decision to recognize Israel would produce U.S. backing for an international conference of all the parties to discuss the Fahd Plan; the Saudis could give no assurance of such support from Washington.[13] In addition, the Jordanians reported on King Hussein's talks with President Reagan in Washington and said that the king was shocked at how little the president appeared to understand about Jordan's territorial boundaries before and after Israel's independence and since the 1967 war. Moreover, a statement made by Reagan after Hussein's visit, declaring that he preferred Jerusalem to remain under Israeli control, was not only in conflict with the Fahd Plan, which said East Jerusalem should be the capital of a Palestinian state, but ran counter to previous American policy on Jerusalem and touched a sensitive cord in the Arab world.[14]

The foreign ministers' meeting thus ended with Saudi Arabia counting only seven solid supporters: Bahrain, Morocco, Oman, Qatar, Somalia, the Sudan, and Tunisia; Kuwait, Jordan, and the United Arab Emirates offered qualified backing. Mauritania and Lebanon abstained.[15] No one was more pleased by the demise of the Fahd Plan than Israel. The American government continued to profess to see it as constructive, but Washington's interest in it was constrained by Israeli objections.[16] After Fez, a majority of Arab leaders came increasingly to feel that President Reagan did not have the will or the ability to provide credible support for its American friends in the Arab world—a perception not helpful in furthering American influence in the Middle East.

Subsequent to the Fez meeting the Arab world remained divided and in conflict with itself. The lack of response to Israel's war against the Palestinians in Lebanon and its slow destruction of an Arab capital city during the summer of 1982 was evidence of the total disintegration of the Arab "nation." However, after Israel's aggression in Lebanon, the Arab states unanimously adopted a comprehensive peace proposal, called the Fez Plan, at an Arab summit conference in Fez, Morocco, in September 1982, based on the initial eight-point Fahd Plan. Israel again categorically rejected the peace initiative.

Saudi Petroleum Policy. Oil was a major concern of U.S. policymakers throughout 1979-82, but the Saudis kept their end of the bargain implicit in their relationship with the United States by continuing to pursue a policy of price restraint within OPEC and by adjusting their own production levels to meet the industrial world's requirements. Both policies brought market pressure to bear on high-price producers so as to establish unified OPEC prices and hold down the world market price. The Saudis increased production in the summer of 1979 to alleviate the world oil shortage (resulting from a decline in Iranian production after the revolution) and again in the fall of 1980 (to insulate the international petroleum market from the effects of the Iran-Iraq war). At the OPEC meeting in Geneva in May 1981, a time of oil surplus on the world market, Saudi Arabia, which accounts for 40 percent of OPEC's production, declined to participate in a 10 percent cutback in production; it also held its price at $32 a barrel while other OPEC countries set prices from $36 to $41 a barrel. The Saudis thus adhered firmly and continuously to a policy of linking world oil prices to world inflation, economic growth, and currency fluctuations.[17] This Saudi cooperation minimized a U.S. energy crisis potentially so severe that President Carter had asked the nation to view it as the "moral equivalent of war." Moreover, since the United States and, more important, its Western European and Japanese allies would remain dependent on foreign (including OPEC) oil at least until the end of the century, the strength of the U.S.–Saudi relationship was of vital importance.[18] By the spring of 1982 there was a glut of oil on the world market, prices had dropped significantly, and when the Israeli invasion commenced, many observers felt that the Arabs could not use the oil weapon even if they had wanted. Other analysts argued that Saudi Arabia could have cut production during the war in Lebanon, maintaining that if the Saudis had acted with the Libyans and Iranians, as much as two million barrels per day could have been withheld. Producer interests would not have been damaged, but Washington and its allies would have faced significant problems.[19] Assuming the latter analysis was correct, there was all the more reason for the United States to pursue and maintain a good relationship with Riyadh.

The revolution in Iran was particularly significant in the context of global great power and Middle East regional linkages. In addition, it reverberated in American domestic politics. In November 1979, a group of militant Iranian students seized the American Embassy in Teheran after Carter had allowed the deposed shah to come to the United States for medical treatment. Washington retaliated by freezing all of Iran's financial assets in the United States and officially boycotting Iranian oil. The fifty-two Americans were held hostage for 444 days, until January 20, 1981, and President Carter was accused of permitting America's honor to be sullied—a charge that contributed to his defeat in the 1980 election. More significant, however, was the fact that the revolution not only brought an end to the most important pro-Western regime in the Gulf region but also institutionalized a strain of Islamic fundamentalism that was decidedly hostile to the United States. Washington worried that the new government in Teheran might become friendly with Moscow and was concerned about the export of revolutionary fervor and anti-Americanism. The Iraqi regime of Saddam Hussein was an early target of the expansionist tendencies of Iranian revolutionary zeal, which was a major factor in Baghdad's decision to initiate a war with Iran.

Initially Washington believed that both the defeat of the Ayatollah Khomeini *and* Saddam Hussein would serve its interests; thus, the United States maintained a studied neutrality, calculating that the two rivals would bleed each other to death. Later, in 1984, as the pro-Western Arab regimes of the Gulf, including Saudi Arabia, came to feel increasingly threatened by Iran, the U.S. began cautiously to tilt toward Iraq.[20] (From the outset of the war Israel sold weapons on a continuing basis to Iran.[21]) Significantly, however, in the early months of the Reagan administration Saddam Hussein sent a series of signals to the United States, indicating Iraq's interest in a reorientation away from the Soviet Union and toward the West. This interest was no doubt piqued by Moscow's reluctance to support Iraq's war effort against Iran and its delays in sending arms shipments; but the concern went much deeper and had far-reaching implications for U.S. interests. Secretary of State Haig took note of the possibility of improved Iraqi-American relations in testimony to the Senate Foreign Relations Committee in March 1981, and he sent Deputy Assistant Secretary of State Morris Draper to Iraq in early April.[22] Nothing came of the Draper visit, and the only other indication of American willingness to respond to Baghdad was the Reagan administration's decision in March 1982 to exempt Iraq from some restrictions on American exports. (A group of congressmen, spurred on by pro-Israeli pressure, had attached a special export-licensing requirement to the Export Administration Act passed in 1979. The provision was designed to cut off trade to countries designated as supporters of "international terrorism," i.e., the PLO.)

Negotiations were begun between Iraq and Lockheed for the sale of at least six, and possibly twelve, Super-Hercules aircraft. Israel immediately mobilized the American-Israel Public Affairs Committee (AIPAC), the official pro-Israeli lobby, to oppose the sale. Resolutions were introduced into the House and Senate urging the administration to reinstate Iraq on the "terrorist list," and a bill was drafted to prohibit all U.S. military sales to "any country in the Middle East which has not declared its willingness to adhere to the . . . Camp David accords."[23] As a result, the president refused to license the deal, and the Soviets then reappeared with a supply of arms, only too eager to draw Iraq away from its flirtation with the West.[24] Significantly, Egyptian-Iraqi relations warmed in the context of the war, with Egypt supplying Iraq substantial amounts of military equipment—some $1.5 billion worth in an agreement concluded in April 1982 alone. In return, Iraq eased its boycott against Egypt, upgraded its diplomatic representation in Cairo, and boosted economic ties between the two countries.[25] Why the United States was unable to move forward in this important area remains obscure, although clearly both Israeli opposition and American diplomatic ineptitude played crucial roles. In any event, Washington's unresponsiveness sent the Iraqis back into the arms of the Soviets, whether they wished to be or not.

The Soviet invasion of Afghanistan in 1979, like the Iranian revolution, was a significant event in terms of the linkages between great power relations and the Middle East regional context. The invasion, which was prompted by the loss of power of a pro-Soviet regime in Kabul as a result of popular opposition to its extensive social reform measures,[26] was the final blow to détente and was viewed in Washington as constituting a serious threat to American interests in the Arabian Gulf. Carter responded by embargoing millions of tons of grain to the Soviet Union; by refusing to let Americans participate in the 1980 Olympic games scheduled to be held in Moscow; and by enunciating the Carter Doctrine, committing the United States to protecting the security of Arabian Gulf oil-producing states if they were "externally threatened."[27] The announcement of the doctrine was followed by the establishment of the Rapid Deployment Force to give concrete meaning to the political statement.

By the time Reagan became the president, détente was frozen, and the new administration rapidly rekindled the cold war. Regional problems were again viewed exclusively in the context of great power politics, and the world was divided into the forces of good and the forces of evil, with every regional conflict reduced to a simplistic view of American-Soviet competition. It was a Kissingerian view of the world, except that the perception of the Soviet Union was no longer one of a traditional great power pursuing its interests in the context of power politics; rather, it was a reversion to the earlier perception of George F. Kennan, of the Soviet Union as a world revolutionary state.

The reemphasis on great power rivalry provided a convenient rationale for refusing to deal with the real causes of economic and political upheavals around the globe. It also maintained the position and power of the politically dominant classes that served U.S. interests. In addition, as a result of the administration's belief that order had to be sustained by force, a massive buildup of American strategic and conventional power was immediately undertaken. The concepts of parity, deterrence, and balance that had governed the U.S.–Soviet nuclear relationship since the early 1970s were shelved in favor of an all-out effort to achieve absolute American superiority. In the Middle East the priorities for the Reagan administration were decreasing Soviet influence and safeguarding the West's freedom of access to the area's oil. The Reagan-Haig team expanded the Carter Doctrine and gave great stress to the development of the Rapid Deployment Force. The major thrust of Haig's regional strategy was the attempt to create an anti-Soviet security screen—termed a "strategic consensus"—extending from Pakistan to Egypt and including such disparate nations as Turkey, Saudi Arabia, and Israel. A somewhat oversimplified replay of John Foster Dulles's Middle East policy, this strategy overlooked the intractable Arab-Israeli animosity (which precluded cooperation between states like Israel and Saudi Arabia), ignored the centrality of the Palestinian issue and its attendant implications for renewed conflict, obscured the meaning of the Islamic fundamentalist movement that was spreading throughout the area, and denied the fact that Israeli expansionism and militarism, not Communism, were the real threats to regional stability. The administration's ideological mindset was sufficiently strong, however, that these factors did not deter the pursuit of the policy.

The new strategy included an increased program of military assistance to a number of Middle Eastern countries, including Saudi Arabia, other Gulf states, Egypt, and Jordan. The Reagan team, under the direction of Haig and Secretary of Defense Caspar Weinberger, embarked on a five-year plan to construct or expand a string of military bases across the Middle East in support of American naval, ground, and air forces. The most important facility was to be at Ras Banas, the Egyptian port on the Red Sea; in addition, a former British base on the island of Masira, off the coast of Oman in the Arabian Sea, was to be rebuilt. Smaller projects called for improvements in the airfield at Seeb in Oman, near the entrance to the Strait of Hormuz; in the port of Berbera on the Gulf of Aden, close to the entrance to the Red Sea; and in the port at Mombasa, in Kenya on the Indian Ocean. All of these plans, however, were overshadowed by the administration's policy of promoting a substantially increased margin of military superiority for Israel. With the demise of the shah of Iran, Israel was the strongest military power in the area, and Haig and Reagan considered this power a great potential resource. (Later events suggested, however, that Weinberger was less persuaded of the merits of the strategic asset thesis than the president and the secretary of state.)

Moreover, in keeping with its focus on the Middle East as merely another arena of great power competition and its disregarding of the inherent causes of the Arab-Palestinian-Israeli conflict, the Reagan administration was unconcerned about a settlement of the Palestinian problem. On February 3, 1981, contradicting the four preceding administrations, Reagan stated that Israeli settlements in the occupied territories were "not illegal." Asked if he had any sympathy toward the Palestinians, Reagan responded with a flat "No."[28] One week earlier, on January 28, Secretary of State Haig had announced that "international terrorism" would take the place of "human rights" as the focus of U.S. policy, and almost immediately the State Department published a paper purporting to detail Soviet financial aid and training for the PLO as evidence of Soviet-sponsored terrorism.[29] The administration found that Israeli allegations about a Palestinian state being a base for Soviet expansionism in the Middle East perfectly accorded with its world view; thus, the PLO was dismissed as a Soviet proxy, and the Palestinian issue was given no importance at all. For Reagan and Haig, not only was the Arab-Palestinian-Israeli conflict no more than a reflection of U.S.–Soviet competition, but the PLO was simply a terrorist group doing the bidding of the Soviet Union.

The U.S.–Israeli Relationship

Several political and military indicators reflect the importance that the Reagan administration placed on Israel. One of the most important is the amount of aid that Washington sent to Israel during Reagan's first term. Table 5 details this aid from Camp David until 1983.

The effect of this unconditional economic and military aid, together

TABLE 5. U.S. Assistance to Israel, 1978-83

Year	Total Aid	Economic Loans	Economic Grants	Military Loans	Military Grants	Soviet Jews' Resettlement Funds
1978	1,811.8	266.8	525.0	500.0	500.0	20.0
1979	4,815.1	265.1	525.0	2,700.0	1,300.0	25.0
1980	1,811.0	261.0	525.0	500.0	500.0	25.0
1981	2,189.0	0	764.0	900.0	500.0	25.0
1982	2,219.0	0	806.0	850.0	550.0	13.0
1983[a]	2,198.0	0	785.0	850.0	550.0	13.0
TOTAL	15,043.9	792.9	3,930.0	6,300.0	3,900.0	121.0

SOURCE: *The Link,* Dec. 1982, 3.
NOTE: Data are in millions of dollars and do not include loans through the Import-Export bank.
[a] Under the Continuing Appropriations Act, 1983, which expired on Dec. 17, 1982.

with the strength of the pro-Israeli lobby, led Israel to conclude that it had a carte blanche in its regional activities. One manifestation of that attitude was evidenced in the bombardment of a nuclear reactor in Iraq. On June 7, 1981, Israeli pilots, using jet bombers supplied earlier through the American military assistance program, destroyed the reactor on the outskirts of Baghdad, as French technicians were completing its construction. The Reagan administration reacted mildly. The president advised Congress that Israel "may have" violated the 1952 agreement (in which Israel pledged to use American weapons for defensive purposes only). Hearings in the Senate Foreign Relations Committee lasted for two days, and while several Senators expressed some dismay with the Israeli bombing, no action was taken. The House Foreign Affairs Committee also held brief hearings, but no moves to sanction Israel were made there either. The only indication of possible American displeasure was a temporary suspension, ordered by the president, of a shipment of four F-16's to Israel. Israeli Prime Minister Begin condemned the suspension as unjust and unjustifiable. When asked how the Israeli attack affected American interests in the Middle East, he replied that Israel always took American interests into consideration, but added: "If anybody should think that one sovereign country should consult another sovereign country about a specific military operation, in order to defend its citizens, that would be absurd."[30] The delivery of the F-16's was scheduled for July 17, a day on which Israel heavily bombarded Beirut. That resulted in a delay until August 17, when the aircraft, by then increased to fourteen F-16's and two F-15's, were delivered.[31]

Moreover, in keeping with the promises Carter had made in the Memorandum of Agreement, the United States announced that it would veto any U.N. resolution calling for sanctions against Israel because of its attack on the Iraqi reactor. Thus Iraq's ambassador, Saadum Hamaddi, and the U.S. ambassador, Jeane Kirkpatrick, worked out a resolution that "strongly condemned" Israel and called on it to open its nuclear facilities for International Atomic Energy Agency inspections (as the Iraqi facility had been) and to compensate Baghdad for the damages it sustained;[32] Israel never complied with either request. Late in September 1981 the IAEA voted to expel Israel from the agency unless it opened its nuclear facilities to international inspection. The United States voted against the resolution—the only Western country to do so.[33]

Lebanon was another manifestation of the license Israel took in regional policies. During two weeks beginning on July 10, 1981, Israel mounted a series of air attacks in southern Lebanon, supposedly in reprisal for an arms buildup by the PLO. The PLO responded with rocket attacks on northern Israel, and on July 17 Israel bombarded a residential section in Beirut, killing 300 civilians and seriously wounding 800 more. In all, during the two weeks of fighting, 450 Lebanese and Palestinians and six Israelis died. The American response was again mild. President Reagan commented that "I don't think violence is ever helpful to the peace process,"[34] and he delayed delivery of the F-16's for another month. But the president also dispatched Philip Habib as a special ambassador to arrange a cease-fire. With the help of the Saudis, Habib concluded a truce between Israel and the PLO on July 24, a difficult task given that Israel and the United States refused to talk to the PLO. The agreement was thus between Israel and the United States, and between the United States and Lebanon, which dealt with the PLO through the United Nations. The PLO observed the cease-fire (with one exception) despite repeated Israeli violations, and the Israeli side of the border was quiet for eleven months, until Israel's assault on Lebanon in June 1982.

The U.S.–Israeli relationship reached a new high in the fall of 1981, when Defense Secretary Weinberger and Israeli Minister of Defense Ariel Sharon signed a Memorandum of Strategic Cooperation on November 30.[35] The document detailed proposals for collaboration against threats to the Middle East from the Soviet Union or "Soviet controlled forces." The conclusion of the agreement indicated that the mild consternation with which the administration had greeted Israel's bombardment of Iraq and Lebanon would not detract from continuing American support for the Jewish state. The agreement was also designed to allay Israeli anxiety about the American sale of AWACs to Saudi Arabia; indeed, Hirsh Goodman, an Israeli military analyst, wrote that the accord was intended to "underline to the Arab world that . . . Israel remains the focal point of United States interests in the region."[36]

The Arab world did, indeed, view the agreement as a complete partnership between Washington and Israel. Saudi Arabia, in particular, opposed the formalization of the U.S.–Israeli alliance and was acutely embarrassed by a State Department report claiming that Crown Prince Fahd had raised no objections to the collaboration in a meeting he had had with Haig. The official Saudi news agency stated: "We have pointed out that this military support of Israel exposes the security of the Mideast region to incalculable danger and plunges the region into a terrible armament race."[37] The Syrian response was to seek a firmer alliance with the Soviet Union. Even conservative Kuwait moved to open diplomatic relations with Moscow; its leader, Sheik Jaber al-Ahmed al-Sabah, said he did so specifically as a counterweight to the American-Israeli alliance. Despite the condemnation by both conservative pro-American states and less-moderate Soviet-leaning states, the United States initialed the agreement.

Two weeks after the signing, Israel annexed the Golan Heights. Stunned, Washington announced that the strategic cooperation agreement was "suspended" until further notice, although Sharon later claimed that the agreement had remained secretly in effect.[38] This Israeli action gave further impetus to the Soviet-Syrian relationship and increased the fears and insecurities of the Arab states in general, making the Soviets appear as potentially necessary and welcome friends—even to the most moderate regimes. George Ball summarized the dilemma when he noted that the U.S. relationship with Israel is "an enormous inhibition to our achieving any kind of decent political relations with the countries which count most in the area."[39] Moreover, Israel's explicit negation of Resolution 242 made Washington's continuous demands that the PLO accept the resolution hypocritical at best. The requirement concerning PLO acceptance of this resolution had provided Washington with a convenient rationale for not dealing with the PLO as the legitimate representative of the Palestinian people. That rationale would seem to have been nullified by Israel's action, but Washington maintained its position.

It is important to note that the U.S.–Israeli strategic alliance was intended to extend beyond the Middle East, and Israel's ability and willingness to act as an American proxy in other areas of the globe— Asia, Africa, and particularly Central America—explains in part Washington's willingness to tolerate Israel's activities in the Middle East. After the Sandinista victory in Nicaragua in 1979 and in the context of the increasing turbulence throughout Central America, including the "covert" efforts of the Central Intelligence Agency to overthrow the Nicaraguan regime, Israel assumed an increasingly important role in that region. It supplied weapons and technology, trained security forces, aided the "contras," provided expert advice in population pacification, and so forth.[40] One example of Israeli assistance occurred in 1981, when Reagan was searching for ways to provide more aid to El Salvador than Congress had appropriated. Israel agreed to "lend" the administration $21 million from funds that had been approved for Israel. The money was transferred to El Salvador, and Israel was "repaid" in the next fiscal year.[41]

Perhaps the most controversial aspect of the U.S.–Israeli relationship during this period involves Washington's role in Israel's invasion of Lebanon. Washington presented itself as "completely surprised" by the Israeli action and totally uninvolved in its preparations. The facts, however, are to the contrary. Indeed, Ze'ev Schiff, a military analyst for *Ha'aretz,* reported that "Washington was duly informed" of Israel's plans long before the start of the war.[42]

Ariel Sharon, the architect of the invasion, had assumed that the November 30 strategic cooperation agreement would provide the necessary ideological cover for his moves into Lebanon. But when the memorandum was formally suspended, he needed to obtain a separate promise that Washington would not oppose his operation. In February 1982 Major General Yehoshua Saguy, chief of Israeli military intelligence, met with officials at the Pentagon and with Haig; he brought with him the details of the specific military plans for the Lebanon campaign.[43] Subsequently John Chancellor of NBC leaked this plan, reporting in April that Israel intended to launch a major war in Lebanon with 1,200 tanks. According to Chancellor, one column of troops would push northward to block the Syrian armor in the Bekaa Valley, while another would advance to the Palestinian camps near Tyre and Sidon under aerial and naval cover. Chancellor also reported that an assault against Beirut was inevitable.[44]

This NBC report was only one of several that appeared in the media from January 1982 as an effort to prepare public opinion for the "necessity" and "inevitability" of the Israeli invasion. Israel's ambassador to the United States, Moshe Arens, commented to the press in February that an Israeli invasion of Lebanon was "only a matter of time."[45] Indeed, all of the major print media carried extensive and explicit reports throughout the spring of 1982 on the probability of a major Israeli assault against Lebanon. Haig, too, repeatedly "revealed" to the media that Palestinian forces in southern

Lebanon were receiving Soviet rockets and artillery and termed this a serious development, which "could jeopardize United States' efforts to prevent new fighting in that troubled region."[46]

Two key conversations during May 1982, between Haig and Sharon and between Haig and Arens, led the Israelis to conclude that they had America's consent for the invasion. In a meeting in Washington on May 25, twelve days before the war began, Sharon informed Haig that the invasion was imminent and warned the secretary of state that no country had the right to tell another country how best to protect its citizens. Haig's only comment—which he had offered on previous occasions—was that Israel would need a clear breach of the cease-fire to make the action acceptable in the international community.[47] According to one unnamed high American official, "Haig believed that Israel was doing our work for us in Lebanon" and thus gave Sharon a "green light."[48] Sharon reported Haig's "support" for Israel's initiative to Begin and the Israeli cabinet, and within a few days Haig wrote to the Israelis that the substance of Sharon's remarks to him had been passed on to President Reagan.[49] This was also taken by the Israelis as further encouragement. After the second critical meeting—between Arens and Haig—Arens records that he "discussed in a positive atmosphere Israel's need to seize a security zone in southern Lebanon."[50]

Begin and Sharon found more than diplomatic approval for their plans in Washington. Analysts Joe Stork and Jim Paul revealed data from the Pentagon's Defense Security Assistance Agency demonstrating that in the first quarter of 1982 Israel took delivery of $217,695,000 worth of military equipment from the United States— nearly ten times the value delivered in the same period in 1980 and 40 percent more than in 1981. Deliveries included ten F-15's, fourteen tank recovery vehicles, and nineteen 155mm self-propelled howitzers. Shipments of bombs, including "guided bombs" identical to those used during the siege of Beirut, and ammunition were worth $6 million, compared to $1 million for the same period in 1981.[51] In addition, the Pentagon also deployed U.S. naval forces into the eastern Mediterranean in advance of the outbreak of hostilities, presumably to counter potential Soviet intervention. The carrier USS Ranger sailed from San Diego to the Indian Ocean in May, relieving the USS Kennedy, which sailed through the Suez Canal and took up a position off Lebanon just as the Israelis began their invasion. The carrier USS Eisenhower and its escorts steamed out of Naples on June 1 to take up a position off Crete. A task force of U.S. marines and landing equipment was trained and assembled in the Spanish port of Rota and sailed east on June 6, the day the invasion began.

The helicopter carrier *USS Guam* left Norfolk on May 24 and reached Rota on June 3. Two more American carriers and their escorts joined the armada in late June. This fleet of more than fifty warships included the largest number of carriers ever assembled in the Mediterranean. The Pentagon provided a cover for the buildup with the announcement of a "readiness exercise" to "demonstrate an ability to reinforce carrier battle groups in the Mediterranean, to project power ashore in support of land battles, and to demonstrate that NATO in the southern region has the flexibility to take advantage of major short-notice training opportunities."[52] It seems more likely that Washington was sending a strong signal to the Soviets not to interfere with Israel's military operation.

U.S. support for Israel's actions in Lebanon was further evidenced by Washington's response to the invasion. The United States was virtually the only nation in the world that did not issue a statement criticizing the invasion. Moreover, even after the war widened, in approximately one week, Washington put no real pressure on Israel to bring the hostilities to a quick end. According to Schiff, Israel had the impression that it was being given adequate time to accomplish the wide-ranging objectives of the campaign: "There was a general feeling that Israel and the United States were operating in tandem. Even if Haig and other United States officials were surprised by the Israeli move past the 40 kilometer line, the moderate and indifferent United States reaction to that move revealed an American tolerance for the extended war. It appears that Haig intended to enjoy the fruits of the Israeli move."[53] The lack of American opposition also had an important influence on the internal Israeli political dynamic. In Schiff's damning assessment: "A more resolute American response would have strengthened moderate elements in the cabinet and would have prevented the two-month shelling of Beirut. Israeli cabinet ministers who were against extending the war to Beirut said they could not oppose the plans as long as Washington did not come out against them. 'I cannot show myself to be less of a patriot than the Americans,' one minister said."[54]

Israel and Lebanon

Lebanon is a multi-confessional state in which political power and concomitant economic advantage are distributed on the basis of religion as a result of an unwritten agreement, called the National Pact, concluded among the sects in 1943. With French backing, the Maronite Christian sect garnered the greatest amount of political power, though it may not have been numerically the largest group in 1943 (there have been allegations of fraud concerning the 1932 census on which the proportional distribution was based), and has become progressively smaller as time passed. By 1982 the Maronites constituted no more than 20 percent of the population. Historically, three clans have competed for dominance of Maronite politics—and control of Lebanon—in an internecine struggle no less bloody than the other conflicts that have wracked the country. The Chamouns, the Frangiehs, and the Gemayels have each had their own party and their own militia, frequently resorting to violence against one another in murderous quests for power. Other Christian sects as well as Sunni and Shi'ia Islamic sects and the Druze also have had parties and militias, and all played the deadly game of Lebanese politics. Lebanon has been dominated by the Maronites since its independence, but certain elite sectors of the Muslim and Druze groups were part of the political equation until Israel upset the traditional balance in 1982.[55]

In 1948, as a result of the hostilities in Palestine, approximately 128,000 Palestinian refugees fled to Lebanon where they were given what was to be temporary refuge until they could return to their homes. Israel refused to permit their return, and the Lebanese government (fearing a shift in the balance of power between Christians and Muslims) refused to grant them citizenship or integrate them into Lebanese society. Thus they remained refugees in thirteen camps. By 1982 there were approximately 350,000 Palestinians in Lebanon (reflecting additional refugees from the 1967 war, the flight of PLO members after the 1970 Jordanian crisis, and natural increase).[56]

In 1969 the PLO secured the right to an autonomous presence in Lebanon, in an accord with the Lebanese government known as the Cairo Agreement,[57] though Beirut's acquiescence was testament to the weakness of the central government. After 1970 and its forced dispersion from Jordan, the PLO established most of its institutions in Lebanon and became one more armed party in the Lebanese crucible. It is important to emphasize, however, that the PLO was not primarily a military organization in Lebanon. Far more important than its military apparatus were its various social institutions, including the Palestine Red Crescent Society with eleven major hospitals and sixty clinics; SAMED, with forty-six factories providing employment and producing material necessities for Palestinian refugees; its social welfare agency, which by 1980 ministered to over 40,000 persons; its educational organs that provided kindergarten, adult literacy, and vocational programs; its myriad cultural institutions; its research center; and its various unions.[58]

Israel's involvement with Lebanon dates back to 1948, when the Phalange, the party/militia of the Gemayel clan, asked for Israeli help to organize an insurrection to overthrow the Lebanese government. In 1951, in response to another Phalangist appeal, Israel secretly gave approximately $3,000 to the Phalange election campaign. Moshe Sharett, then foreign minister, commented: "This group [the Phalange] is worthy of serious attention on our part. The taking out of Lebanon from the pan-Arab circle and its affiliation with Israel is extremely heartwarming and opens the door to a far-reaching realignment in the whole structure of the Middle East."[59]

In 1954 David Ben-Gurion, in temporary retirement from the prime ministership, suggested to Prime Minister Sharett that the time was "now" appropriate for Israel to "bring about" a Maronite state in Lebanon:

Perhaps (there is never certainty in politics) now is the time to bring about the creation of a Christian State in our neighborhood. . . . Without our initiative and our vigorous aid this will not be done. It seems to me that this is the central duty, or at least one of the central duties, of our foreign policy. This means that time, energy and means ought to be invested in it and that we must act in all possible ways to bring about a radical change in Lebanon. . . . If money is necessary, no amount of dollars should be spared. . . . We must concentrate all our efforts on this issue. . . . This is an historic opportunity. Missing it will be unpardonable. . . . Everything should be done, in my opinion, rapidly and at full steam.[60]

Moshe Dayan fully supported Ben-Gurion's proposals for Lebanon, adding that the territory south of the Litani would have to be annexed to Israel. Sharett's analysis of Dayan's position is revealing: "According to him [Dayan] the only thing that's necessary is to find an officer, even just a major. We should either win his heart or buy him with money, to make him agree to declare himself the savior of the Maronite population. Then the Israeli army will enter Lebanon, will occupy the necessary territory, and will create a Christian regime which will ally itself with Israel. The territory from the Litani southward will be totally annexed to Israel and everything will be all right."[61] Indeed, as early as 1918 Zionist leaders had openly discussed the necessity of controlling the waters of the Litani: "In order to have resources sufficient to allow it to perform its proper function in solving the Jewish problem, Palestine needed control of the Litani."[62] Thus, Israel's interest in fostering exclusive Maronite dominance in Lebanon, in securing jurisdiction over the Litani River, and in annexing southern Lebanon have long historical precedents. The presence of the PLO was not the factor that first peaked Israel's interest in Lebanon, although it was because of the PLO that Israel first took military action against Lebanon.

Israel initiated military activity in Lebanon in 1968, in the form of massive reprisal raids, e.g., the aerial bombardment of Palestinian refugee camps and Lebanese towns and cities and incursions by land. The most spectacular early Israeli operation against Lebanon came in December 1968, when Israeli commandos destroyed thirteen civilian planes of Lebanon's Middle East Airlines on the ground at Beirut International Airport. The raid was allegedly in reprisal for a Palestinian guerrilla attack on one El Al plane at Athens International Airport a few days earlier. In April 1973 some thirty-five Israeli commandos entered Beirut and assassinated three prominent PLO leaders, killing nine civilian bystanders. After the Palestinian attack on Maalot in May 1974, Israeli air force squadrons attacked a number of Lebanese towns and Palestinian refugee camps, killing fifty civilians and wounding more than 200. From mid-1968 to mid-1974 there were forty-four major Israeli air attacks on Lebanese towns and Palestinian refugee camps: 880 Lebanese and Palestinian civilians were killed, and hundreds more were wounded.[63]

In December 1975, in the midst of the Lebanese civil war, Israel launched a major raid into southern Lebanon while it was covertly arming Phalange units in central Lebanon and overtly supporting other Christian militias in southern Lebanon with heavy artillery and air cover. Simultaneously, it initiated the "good fence" policy along the Israeli-Lebanese border, through which Lebanese Christians of all denominations were encouraged to cross the frontier to take jobs in neighboring Israeli workplaces, to seek medical attention, and to shop.[64] Israeli involvement in the Lebanese civil war on behalf of the Maronites (who dominated the rightist coalition) was succeeded by Syrian troop intervention, at the invitation of Maronite President Suleiman Frangieh, when it appeared that the Lebanese groups opposing the rightists might defeat them. (Syrian troops remained in Lebanon as a peacekeeping force, mandated by a joint resolution of the Arab states after the termination of the hostilities.) The opposition, known as the Lebanese National Movement, was dominated by Muslim and Druze groups and had a leftist social democratic orientation; the PLO was reluctantly drawn into the civil strife and supported the leftist coalition. Shortly after becoming prime minister in May 1977, Menachem Begin openly acknowledged Israel's role in the Lebanese civil war and pledged to create an autonomous defense capacity for the Christians in southern Lebanon through an alliance with Saad Haddad and his right-wing militia.[65]

In September 1977 an American-sponsored cease-fire imposed a temporary calm in southern Lebanon; however, the IDF soon resumed its bombing raids in retaliation for PLO attacks on Nahariya. By early 1978 Israel was once again deeply engaged in southern

Lebanon, using Lebanese villages as staging areas and bases from which to attack Palestinian positions. The PLO, in turn, fired on northern Israeli towns. At the same time the Phalange and other Christian militias turned more and more to Israel for military support and economic aid. The hijacking of an Israeli civilian bus by Palestinian guerrillas on March 11, 1978, became the pretext for a major escalation of Israeli involvement in Lebanon, which took the form of a full-scale invasion called Operation Litani.[66] The invasion commenced on March 14, 1978, and resulted in the creation of the "security belt" in southern Lebanon, with the surrogate Haddad placed in control.

Between 1978 and 1981 PLO rocket and guerrilla activity across Israel's northern border decreased markedly, and PLO terrorist activity as at Munich and Maalot ceased altogether. However, the PLO did acquire a supply of small arms and outdated artillery and mechanized equipment from the Soviets, which they stockpiled in various places. The arms buildup occurred simultaneous with the PLO's rapidly increasing international legitimacy and recognition.

In late March 1981 events again began to push Lebanon toward war. Phalangists in Zahle, with Israeli material, weapons, and support, began to build a road in what Syria saw as an effort to cut through Syrian lines and link up with Haddad's forces in the south. As the road construction gathered momentum, the Phalangists also massed 5,000 fighters in Zahle.[67] On April 2, 1981, the Syrians attacked the Phalangist forces and on April 25 Syrian helicopters attacked Phalangist positions on the Sannin Hills to dislodge them from these strategic heights. Syria may have reasoned that domination of the strategic mountaintops would lead to control of Junieh, the Lebanese port through which Israel delivered arms and supplies to the Phalange. The Israelis had similar thoughts and on April 28 shot down two Syrian helicopters over central Lebanon. Syria then moved several batteries of Soviet SAM 6 missiles into the Bekaa Valley on April 29, in the hope of denying Israel the total air supremacy over Lebanon it had enjoyed for years. The Begin government immediately planned to destroy the missiles, but poor weather on April 30 prevented the operation. The United States pleaded with Israel not to attack the missiles, and Begin reluctantly refrained. Elimination of the SAM 6's, however, remained an important Israeli objective until they were destroyed in the first week of the war in the summer of 1982.

Israel mounted an air attack on southern Lebanon on July 10, 1981, claiming the attack was in reprisal for the PLO arms buildup. The PLO retaliated by firing rockets into several northern Israeli towns, and the result was two weeks of intense Israeli air strikes and commando assaults into southern Lebanon and more PLO rocket and artillery attacks on northern Israel. Habib arranged a cease-fire on July 24. Israel repeatedly violated the truce, however, and Begin formally renounced it on May 9 of the next year. Still, the Israeli side of the border was quiet until the Israelis bombarded Beirut on June 4 and 5, 1982, commencing the final assault on the PLO.

The Israeli rationale for intervention in Lebanon is complex and has evolved over time. Israel had three objectives when it first undertook military raids in Lebanon in 1968. The first was to punish the PLO for guerrilla activities against Israel and to deter future operations. However, since the Israeli air and ground assaults generally resulted in high civilian casualties, they served primarily to heighten the guerrillas' determination to press on with their campaign. The second objective was to punish the Lebanese government for allowing the guerrillas to operate from its territory and to pressure it to prevent future guerrilla operations. But the Lebanese government was weak, and its army was fragmented; thus it could not control the Palestinians. Moreover, Israel's continuous bombardments (together with the activities of the PLO and the internal fragmentation of Lebanese society) added to the strains on Lebanon's thin governmental legitimacy, further compromised the armed forces, increased the polarization of Lebanese politics, and generally contributed to the breakdown of the Lebanese political system, which culminated in the civil war of 1975-76.[68] The third objective was to weaken the support for the PLO that existed among the mainly Shi'ite population of southern Lebanon. The high civilian casualty rate did eventually incline the southern Lebanese people to blame the PLO and the Palestinians for the destruction caused by Israel. Indeed, at the outset of the Israeli invasion in 1982 the invaders were welcomed as liberators by many of the Shi'ites. (That attitude shifted, however, once the nature and duration of the Israeli occupation of southern Lebanon became apparent, to intense animosity and violent resistance).

By the mid-1970s the lack of success Israel had realized with two of its three objectives led the Jewish state to augment its military policies with a program for the manipulation of political and military events from within Lebanon. Israel's expanded strategy involved the installation of a government friendly to it, which would cooperate over matters ranging from expulsion of the PLO to water distribution, economic integration, and political and military cooperation. To this end Israel cultivated a close relationship with Bashir Gemayel, who commanded the largest Christian militia in Lebanon, the Kateb, the forces of the Phalange, hoping to facilitate the election of Gemayel as president. Israel expected its alliance with the Phalange to result in the defeat and dispersion of the Palestinians and the conclusion of a formal Lebanese-Israeli peace. As early as 1977 Gemayel began to receive direct military aid from Israel, which reached over $100 million by 1982. Large numbers of Gemayel's men received training in Israel, and Israel provided the Phalange with sophisticated weapons and political and military advice.[69] In addition, Israel supplied Saad Haddad with arms, money, and advice after installing him as commander of the area of southern Lebanon that it controlled following its 1978 invasion.

Israeli strategy with regard to Lebanon and the PLO became more complex after the Camp David accords were signed in September 1978. Israel now was determined to eliminate the PLO completely. The intensification of the campaign against the PLO was related to the Begin government's decision to absorb the West Bank and Gaza (for which Israel needed a compliant Palestinian population). The PLO was first and foremost the symbol of Palestinian nationalist aspirations. Thus Begin and his advisors believed that if the PLO could be destroyed as an organization, the idea of Palestinian nationalism could be suppressed and eliminated, and those Palestinians living under occupation would have to acquiesce in the extension of Israeli sovereignty over all of historic Palestine. Such acquiescence, it was assumed, would then lead to the emigration of the indigenous population, ensuring continued Jewish exclusivity in the state. The nature of this objective made the elimination of the social and political organizations of the PLO even more important than the destruction of its military capability.

Paradoxically, the effort to crush the PLO came at a time when the PLO had begun to prove itself a carefully disciplined, mature organization that honored international agreements, administered a complex civilian infrastructure in Lebanon,[70] had increased its prestige and popularity in the West Bank and Gaza,[71] had gained increasing international legitimacy and recognition, had compromised its objective of a democratic secular state of Palestine for a Palestinian state in the West Bank and Gaza alongside Israel, and appeared to be prepared to relinquish the military option, at least any offensive capability, in favor of diplomacy and politics. Indeed, the PLO was never a serious military threat to Israel, as numerous Israeli military analysts have amply demonstrated.[72] In fact, the real "threat" to Israel came from the transformation in the strategy and objectives of the PLO. The world could not ask Israel to negotiate with a terrorist PLO bent on the destruction of the Jewish state; it could expect it to negotiate with a responsible PLO. But since Israel was unwilling either to negotiate with the PLO or to consider the establishment of a Palestinian state, it had to eliminate the PLO and its influence with West Bank and Gaza Palestinians.[73] Yehoshua Porath, an Israeli scholar of the Palestinians at the Hebrew University, expresses another aspect of Israeli thinking as regards elimination of the PLO: "The Government's hope is that the stricken PLO, lacking a logistic and territorial base will return to its earlier terrorism; it will carry out bombings throughout the world, hijack airplanes and murder many Israelis. In this way, the PLO will lose part of the political legitimacy that it has gained and will mobilize the large majority of the Israeli nation in hatred and disgust against it, undercutting the danger that events will develop among the Palestinians that they might become a legitimate negotiating partner for future political accommodation."[74]

A further strategic concern, which became increasingly important by the end of the 1970s, involved controlling the waters of the Litani River in order to expand Israel's hydroelectric power and the irrigation of its farm land. To realize the full value of the Litani, Israel needed to control an area of Lebanon (either by occupation or through arrangements with a compliant government) far into the Bekaa Valley and well above the Karaoun Dam. By 1982 the waters of the Litani were useless without control of that dam because much of the river was already used for generating electricity in three major power plants, using water extracted by the dam at Karaoun or in existing irrigation projects in the Bekaa Valley. The residual unused flow, a maximum of 200 million cubic meters in an average year, was too small to profit Israel materially if it controlled only the lower reaches of the river. Thus Israel had to secure control over the entire watershed of the Litani as far north as the Beirut-Damascus road to safeguard its own diversion works.[75]

In summary, Israel's objectives in initiating the war in Lebanon in 1982 were: (1) to crush and destroy the organizational infrastructure of the PLO in order to eliminate Palestinian nationalism and to solidify its control over the West Bank; (2) to increase Israeli influence in Lebanese politics through the election of Bashir Gemayel as president of Lebanon and to impose Phalange dominance throughout the Lebanese polity; (3) to gain definitive control over the Litani River; and (4) to destroy the Syrian missile sites in the Bekaa Valley. (This aim involved military and political calculations. On the one hand, it was thought that taking out the missile batteries in a preemptive strike would so weaken Syria militarily that it could not contemplate a war with Israel for at least ten years.[76] On the other hand, some Israelis believed that such a definitive blow would weaken Syrian President Assad and create enough internal dissension to bring about the fall of his government.)[77]

Once the decision to invade Lebanon was formally taken, sometime in November-December 1981, all that Israeli decision makers needed was a pretext for initiating the campaign.[78] Defense Minister Sharon was mindful of Haig's admonitions that Israel would need a "reason" to undertake its military plans, but the PLO's observance of the July 1981 cease-fire afforded no obvious excuse. Thus Israel undertook an extensive provocation campaign, in January 1982, designed to elicit a response from the PLO to which Israel could then retaliate with its invasion.[79]

The Provocation Campaign in Lebanon

Every aspect of the provocation campaign involved explicit Israeli violations of the 1981 cease-fire. The campaign began with the flight of four Israeli jet fighters over Syrian missile sites in the Bekaa Valley. Then the Israeli forces in "Haddadland" let off 5,000 rounds of machine gun fire and 40,000 rounds of small arms fire during "training exercises" in Yarin and Marouahine. U.N. observers reported that tanks were used in Israeli maneuvers in Lebanon and called the action "intensive, excessive and provocative." On February 8 thirty-two Israeli buses entered Lebanon carrying 600 to 700 well-armed troops; the troops left the same day. On March 6, 300 Israeli military vehicles feigned an attack on Khaim, a village close to routes the PLO believed the Israelis would use in a land assault; again the Israelis pulled out the same day. There were also naval provocations. On January 25 an Israeli warship and several torpedo boats intercepted seven Lebanese fishing boats inside Lebanese territorial waters near Tyre. The warship sank two Lebanese boats. U.N. observers reported several incidents on February 10 and 16—these perpetrated by Israeli and Haddad forces stationed at Bayadah.[80]

The provocations continued throughout the spring. One of the most serious occurred on April 21, 1982, when Israeli planes struck deep inside Lebanon, bombing three alleged Palestinian targets and killing twenty-three persons. The Israelis claimed this was in retaliation for the death of an Israeli soldier killed by a land mine in southern Lebanon.[81] Still, the PLO did not respond. After Prime Minister Begin publicly renounced the cease-fire on May 9, Israel bombarded what it said were PLO headquarters in southern Lebanon, killing eleven and wounding fifty-six, few of whom were connected with the PLO.[82] In response, the following day the PLO fired several rounds into northern Israel, although it pointedly and carefully avoided populated areas. There were no deaths or injuries.

The restraint shown by the PLO during the spring of 1982 can be attributed to three factors: (1) it did not want to diminish the political and diplomatic advantages of being seen as the victim of Israeli actions; (2) it did not want to provide Israel with a pretext for further attacks or a large-scale invasion; and (3) it wanted to continue to appear as a responsible party to the cease-fire agreement.[83]

The Provocation Campaign on the West Bank and Gaza

Israel also carried out a provocation campaign on the West Bank and Gaza, designed either to elicit a response by the PLO (which would give Israel an excuse to initiate its war), or, as was expected, to demonstrate the impotence of the PLO to help the 1.3 million Palestinians living under occupation.[84] Israeli officials assumed that the PLO would be discredited and its influence diminished if it remained passive in the face of continuous and intensifying Israeli repression. The Israelis put as much pressure as possible on Palestinians to deflect their loyalty from the PLO and to make clear that there was no option but acquiescence in the Israeli plans for the occupied areas.

The campaign began in mid-March with the dismissal of seven elected pro-PLO mayors. There followed a spiraling cycle of protests, repression, and rebellion. None of the measures the Israelis used to control the Palestinians were new (all had been instituted by earlier Labor governments), but all were employed with greater intensity. They included: extensive personal and collective harassment; detaining individuals without charge; mass round-ups of people for interrogation; imposition of curfews on whole villages for days and weeks on end; blowing up of homes of relatives of individuals suspected of political activism; deportations; increased censorship of Palestinian newspapers; closing of Palestinian universities for lengthy periods (Bir Zeit, for example, was closed for four months); strict censorship of university curriculums; and promulgation of a list of several thousand prohibited books. Israeli soldiers frequently broke into university dormitories at night and dragged students to military headquarters. In addition, Jewish vigilante groups detained and harassed Palestinians at will. In one six-week period thirteen Palestinian civilians were killed by Israeli soldiers and settlers.[85] Moreover, Israel employed the use of torture against Palestinians—some aspects of which were enunciated in a memorandum written by Lieutenant General Rafael Eitan and communicated to Colonel Yaakov Hartabi, who passed it along to all levels of the military administration on the West Bank.[86]

The PLO refrained from any response to this campaign of repression and harassment against Palestinians on the West Bank and Gaza.

On June 3, however, Israel found its pretext for invasion. On that day an assassination attempt was made on the Israeli ambassador to Great Britain, Shlomo Argov, by an anti-PLO Palestinian group headed by Abu Nidal. The PLO immediately disclaimed any responsibility. Argov's assailants were arrested within twenty-four hours, and on June 6 Prime Minister Margaret Thatcher announced that a "hit list," found on one of the arrested suspects, included the name of the PLO's London representative, thus obviously exculpating the PLO.[87] Nevertheless, this incident was used as the justification for launching the invasion of Lebanon, which Israel called "Peace for Galilee."

Israel initiated the war with the bombing of Beirut on June 4 and 5 and invaded Lebanon on June 6. The exact number of Lebanese and Palestinian casualties is unknown. According to Lebanese police figures (which are based on actual counts in hospitals, clinics, and civil defense centers) between June 4 and August 31, 1982, 19,085 people were killed and 30,302 were wounded—the vast majority of these civilians.[88] The estimates of the number of dead in the September 16-17 massacres in the Palestinian refugee camps of Sabra and Shatila are put at between 700 and 1,500, all civilians.[89] The American Friends Service Committee's Advisory Committee on Human Rights estimates that nearly 200,000 Palestinians were made homeless as a result of the IDF's systematic destruction of the Palestinian refugee camps of Rashidiyeh, Bourj el Shemali, el Buss, Ein el Hilweh and Mieh Mieh.[90]

The War in Lebanon

The American Response to Israel's First Week in Lebanon

The American response during the first week of hostilities was minimal. On June 4, after the first reports of the bombing of Beirut, the State Department issued a statement appealing to all parties to "refrain immediately from any further acts of violence."[91] On June 5, the second day of the bombing of Beirut, Secretary of State Haig, with the president at an economic summit meeting in Versailles, said the bombing was "very serious" and announced that Philip Habib would return to the Middle East and seek to restore the July 1981 cease-fire.[92] President Reagan sent a letter to Prime Minister Begin on June 5 asking that Israel use "restraint" in Lebanon.[93] Begin responded with a letter outlining Israel's intentions: "The Israeli army has been ordered to push the Palestinian forces northward to a distance of 40 kilometers [25 miles] from the Israeli border, to place their artillery beyond the range of Israeli territory." Begin pledged that "Israel would not attack any Syrian forces in Lebanon or Syria unless the Syrians engaged the Israelis," and that the invasion was not "aimed at acquiring any Lebanese territory."[94] The American ambassador to Israel, Samuel W. Lewis, conveyed a separate message to the Israeli government on June 5. It contained word from Saudi Arabia that PLO Chairman Yasir Arafat was willing to reinstate the cease-fire even after the two days of Israeli bombardment of Palestinian sections of Beirut.[95] Israel refused to consider a truce. The U.N. Security Council met in emergency session and passed Resolution 508, calling for a cease-fire to go into effect at 0600 hours local time June 6.

On June 6 President Reagan asked Israel to withdraw from Lebanon and dispatched Habib to Israel with a personal appeal to Begin to stop the fighting. Israel flatly rejected the request. The Security Council passed Resolution 509 on the evening of June 6, calling on Israel to withdraw all its military forces immediately and unconditionally to the internationally recognized boundaries of Lebanon, and reaffirmed its request for an immediate cease-fire. The United States used the threat of its veto to insure that neither a condemnation of Israel nor a call for sanctions was included in either resolution.

On June 7 Haig issued a statement saying that the United States wanted a cease-fire in Lebanon and the immediate withdrawal of Israeli forces in accordance with the two Security Council resolutions, but he added that Israeli troops were engaged in "continued fighting at a fast pace and would require time to achieve their objectives." In replying to a question about Israeli losses in the fighting, Haig said in words of clear identification with Israel, "*We* not only lost an aircraft and a helicopter yesterday, there is a claim a second aircraft has been shot down" (emphasis added). Asked whether Israel's use of American arms would run afoul of legislation prohibiting their use for offensive purposes, the secretary of state replied that this was the kind of question that Habib might explore. Haig also noted that the United States was cutting its embassy personnel to about thirty and warning against travel in Lebanon. Haig further commented: "We would like to see the central government of Lebanon strengthened and the border area made secure. Clearly there is going to have to be more than just a cease-fire. There is going to have to be a readjustment of the internal arrangements in Lebanon. And we would hope that would be in the direction of strengthening of the central government."[96]

Haig told a news conference on June 8 that President Reagan had "deferred judgment" on whether Israel's use of American arms in Lebanon constituted justified self-defense or a form of aggression that would violate American law, adding that the United States would not deny Israel the "right of legitimate self-defense."[97] In addition, he issued a statement saying that an expanded U.N. peacekeeping force, to police more effectively a buffer zone in southern Lebanon, and "some lessening" of Syria's 25,000-man military force in Lebanon should be part of a "comprehensive solution" after a cease-fire.[98] These two conditions outlined by Haig were reportedly identical to what Begin had been calling for in talks with Habib in Israel, although the Israelis stated that they preferred a peacekeeping contingent that included American troops rather than an expanded U.N. force. Several senior American officials commented off-the-record that the president was not eager to have Americans engaged in Lebanon.[99] (The question of U.S. troops in Lebanon became an issue of some discord between Washington and Israel, although in the end Israel prevailed.) An announcement was made later in the day that as a gesture of support for the Lebanese government, President Reagan would seek immediate congressional approval for $25 million in emergency humanitarian aid to ease the suffering of Lebanese civilians caught in the conflict.[100]

After a second meeting between Habib and Begin on June 8, administration officials told reporters that Begin had refused to respond to questions about a cease-fire or a withdrawal. The officials parried the reporters' questions with the statement that Habib was "probing Israeli intentions," since Israeli forces were already well beyond the 40 kilometer line and pushing close to Beirut. The Israelis apparently gave Habib no indication of their full agenda. Moreover, Begin made a public declaration directed at President Assad that day, asking him to refrain from engaging Israeli troops and stating: "We are making every effort to refrain from conflict with the Syrians. Our business in Lebanon is with the terrorists." Begin declared: "I call upon President Assad to instruct the Syrian army not to harm Israeli soldiers, and then they will not be touched. In essence we do not want to harm anyone. We want only one thing: that our settlements in the Galilee not be harmed, that our citizens in the Galilee should not have to spend days and nights in shelters anymore. And if we achieve a line 40 kilometers north of our northern border, then our work is done. All fighting will end."[101] At the moment Begin was uttering those words, the IDF was well beyond the 40 kilometer line, and the next day Israel attacked the Syrians.

Indeed, in contradiction to the prime minister's solemn promise not to involve Syria in its campaign, Israel destroyed all the Syrian missile batteries in the Bekaa Valley on June 9. In response, Haig only commented that the Israeli action suggested that "Israel might be shifting its originally announced objective in Lebanon." On the other hand, Haig said, "Israel might well be adhering to its originally stated plan and might have gone beyond the 25 mile zone and engaged the Syrians for 'tactical' reasons."[102] The first statement was a weak justification for Israel's advance on Beirut and a remarkably mild reaction to an Israeli assault on a Soviet ally that could have had serious ramifications for the United States. The second comment implied that Haig was aware that Israel's officially stated objectives were less than its real intentions. Haig also said that U.S. diplomatic activity was aimed at assembling some sort of a peacekeeping force that could go into Lebanon and take over from the Israelis.[103] It is notable that the secretary of state was interested in institutionalizing Israel's actions in Lebanon and that he did not say that the goal of American diplomacy was an Israeli cease-fire or withdrawal.

The potential for a seriously widened conflict was heightened when an official source in Israel threatened (on June 9) that a major collision between Israel and Syria was likely if the substantial Syrian ground force in the Bekaa Valley did not withdraw; he added that there was no certainty that such a confrontation would be limited in scope.[104] Sharon contributed substance to the statement by declaring that it would not be possible to remove the threats to Israeli settlers in the Galilee from the PLO until all Syrian forces were removed from Lebanon.[105] Israel's public pronouncements, together with its military assaults on Syrian positions, were an obvious indication of broadening objectives. The risk that Israel was taking in provoking a Syrian reaction was extremely dangerous. An all-out war between Syria and Israel would have been a grave threat to the stability of the Middle East and could have portended a confrontation between the United States and the Soviet Union. It would thus have been prudent for Washington to have made a serious effort to restrain the Israelis, particularly as regards their campaign against Syria. No such action was taken. In fact, the United States vetoed as "unbalanced" a U.N. resolution condemning Israel on June 9.

On June 10 President Reagan sent Begin a letter containing a message described by his press secretary as "firm," calling for Israeli forces to withdraw. Israel obviously saw no reason to entertain such a request; indeed, the United States gave it no reason to, since the threat of withholding aid or arms or of imposing any other sanction was never raised (and moreover, Israel believed that Washington had given prior approval to the military campaign). Edwin Meese, the president's counselor, informed reporters that Reagan was not considering any sanctions against Israel or contemplating interrupting the flow of American arms. The administration also stated that it would not join Western Europe's public denunciation of the Israeli invasion.[106] Begin replied through Habib, indicating that Israel would consider a cease-fire but would not withdraw from Lebanon until all Israeli conditions were met. These included: (1) a guarantee that the PLO's forces would not be allowed back into a 40 kilometer zone north of the border; (2) a reduction of the 25,000 Syrian troops; and (3) the creation of a Lebanese government free of Syrian and PLO pressure.[107] These conditions provide further evidence that Israel's goals in Lebanon encompassed more than a security zone north of its border. Washington appeared to be unconcerned by the implications of this situation.

Haig announced on June 10 after a meeting between President Reagan and Saudi Foreign Minister Prince Saud al-Faisal that Saudi Arabia had given no indication of any possible interruption in the flow of oil to the West in spite of Arab "anger" over the invasion. Thus the United States was assured at an early date that it had nothing to fear from the Arab oil-producers for its support of Israel's actions in Lebanon. Haig also announced that Reagan had warned Soviet President Leonid Brezhnev about the dangers of outside powers becoming involved in the war in Lebanon. The message was in response to a protest against the Israeli invasion that the Soviet leader had sent to Reagan two days earlier. Haig described the tone of the messages as "frank," but "not threatening." Other American officials "saw no evidence" that the Soviet Union was preparing to intervene militarily in the conflict in any way. It was also noted with satisfaction in Washington that with the exception of one article in *Tass,* all other articles in the Soviet press had avoided any allusion to the possibility of Soviet action.[108]

The administration apparently made the erroneous conclusion that since it had nothing to fear from the Soviet Union or from an Arab oil embargo, it would reap significant benefits from Israel's aggression—at least that was the position of Haig and his mentor, Henry Kissinger, the individual most responsible for institutionalizing the myth that Israel was a strategic asset to American interests. Kissinger expressed his continuing belief in this idea in an article in the *Washington Post,* "From Lebanon to the West Bank to the Gulf." The former secretary of state claimed that Israel's action in Lebanon:

opens up extraordinary opportunities for a dynamic American diplomacy throughout the Middle East. . . . the results [of Israel's actions] are congruent with the interest of the peace process in the Middle East, of all moderate governments in the area and of the United States. . . . the general position of the administration is wise and statesmanlike. . . . [i.e.,] to reestablish a strong Lebanese central government whose authority runs throughout a genuinely neutral country. . . . Lebanon can be another testing ground for proving that radical Arab regimes and Soviet backing offer no solution to any of the central issues of concern in the area. Lebanon thus offers an opportunity for Egypt to reenter Arab politics. . . . The Lebanese crisis creates an opening for American diplomacy to overcome the impasse in the autonomy talks between Egypt and Israel.[109]

Kissinger also argued that Israel's invasion of Lebanon would solve the fourfold crises facing the governments in the Gulf region, i.e., Shi'ite radicalism, Moslem fundamentalism, Iranian revolutionary agitation, and Soviet imperialism.[110] That Kissinger, Haig, and others who made similar arguments were wrong on every single positive outcome they predicted was obvious within less than a year after the end of the war. Thoughtful observers ought to have challenged such assertions at the outset.

On June 10 Vice-President George Bush met with officials from several Jewish groups, including delegations from the Conference of Presidents of Major American Jewish Organizations and the Union of American Hebrew Congregations. Peter Teely, Bush's secretary, said that the Jewish leaders "just wanted to express to the administration the depth of feeling in the Jewish community in support of Israeli actions in Lebanon." Bush assured the Jewish leaders of America's unequivocal support for Israel.[111]

The power of the pro-Israeli lobby was so strong by this time that it not only enabled Israel to resist pressure from Washington to behave in ways conducive to American interests, but it also gave Israel the ability to pressure the United States into pursuing courses of action that were congruent with Israel's objectives. An early intimation of the latter was evidenced in a thinly veiled warning Israel issued to the United States not to interfere with its actions in the context of rapidly escalating military activity. David Kimche, director general of the Israeli foreign ministry, said in an interview that it was true that the advantages Israel had obtained in past military campaigns had been diminished by diplomatic intervention by the United States. This time, he said, all countries should recognize that the invasion was aimed against "terrorism" and was therefore in everyone's general interest.[112] Thus Kimche also attempted to suggest that Israel's actions were serving American interests by relating the Israeli war effort to the Reagan/Haig foreign policy commitment to eradicate Soviet-sponsored "international terrorism." As noted earlier, the tactic of tying Israel into the cold war anti-Communist consensus in the United States was a major aspect of Israel's strategy of presenting itself as a strategic asset to American interests.

On June 11 Israel and Syria announced a cease-fire agreement in Lebanon, although it did not include the PLO. Washington "welcomed" the truce but viewed it as "extremely fragile." State Department officials seemed to suggest that given Begin's adamancy on not withdrawing Israeli forces from Lebanon until certain conditions were met, the United States was prepared "to make the best" of Israel's military actions by trying to translate them into a long-term political solution for Lebanon. Thus the president decided "not to make an issue" of Israel's refusal to accept the Security Council's demand for immediate withdrawal. Officials at the State Department also indicated that they expected finding a formula to resolve the crisis would require long negotiations involving the United States, Syria, the Lebanese, and other Arab governments acting on behalf of the PLO as well as the Israelis themselves.[113] Washington's willingness to follow Israel's lead was clearly apparent. Indeed, in a statement on June 11, Haig again defended Israel's deep penetration into Lebanon: "Well, the further advances are associated with eliminating further threats and whatever tactical positions they feel they wanted to assume for future negotiations."[114]

On June 12 Israel and the PLO agreed to a cease-fire. When Yitzhak Shamir, the Israeli foreign minister, was asked if the cease-fire came in response to U.S. pressure, he replied: "There are no American pressures and there were no American pressures because the Americans have sufficient experience and they know that they will not achieve anything by pressure."[115] Despite Shamir's denials, some reports claimed that the United States had worked intensively to bring about the truce. In fact, Haig met with Arens in Washington and apparently asked that Israel take the lead in announcing a truce. At the same time Habib met with government officials in Israel and urged them to announce a cease-fire. A State Department spokesman said: "We have been in touch with all parties, urging the imperative of an immediate cease-fire."[116] There is no reason to doubt either that American officials urged Israel to agree to a cease-fire or that the United States applied no pressure.

In any event, the cease-fire was broken on June 13, when Israeli troops moved on Baabda and seized control of the Beirut-Damascus highway, closing the last exit from the city. The Israelis denied that this move, which resulted in the encirclement of Beirut, was a breach of the cease-fire, claiming that they were merely "improving their positions." When the PLO retaliated, Israel argued that the PLO had violated the cease-fire and then began to bombard Beirut with repeated air strikes.

Throughout the war Israel continuously alleged that the PLO had breached cease-fires when Israel had, in fact, instigated the resumption of military activity. There were twelve cease-fires in all. Each of the first eleven was shattered by a bombardment of Beirut. During the tenth cease-fire the Israelis "improved their positions" and took over all of the Metn area, in central Lebanon north of Beirut. Israeli military correspondent Hirsh Goodman reported another curious interpretation of cease-fire violations: "The Defense Minister admitted on television on Friday 25 June, that the IDF did not always return fire at the same spot Israeli forces sustained fire. A rifle bullet loosed off by a Syrian soldier in the Bekaa could unleash a 16-hour bombardment of West Beirut. It is a pity that it took the Defense Minister two weeks to admit that this was the IDF's policy."[117]

On June 13 Shamir declared that "Israel will not retreat from its positions in Lebanon before it is ensured that the terrorist organizations will not return to those places which Israel's Army has reached."[118] This statement implied virtually limitless possibilities in terms of long-range Israeli objectives vis-à-vis Lebanon and Syria. Haig stated that same day on ABC's "This Week" that the United States was no longer interested in an unconditional Israeli pullback in Lebanon—contravening a U.N. resolution the United States had voted for only a few days before. Moreover, his comment aligned Washington with Israel's open-ended objectives and provided further substance to the impression that the United States and Israel were working in tandem in Lebanon.[119]

After the military triumph of the first week, Israel spent the remainder of the summer engaged in three parallel activities: (1) consolidating and solidifying its hold over southern Lebanon while imposing Phalange control throughout all areas, as a prelude to fostering the election of Bashir Gemayel as president; (2) attempting to force the PLO to evacuate Beirut; and (3) inflicting punishing blows to Syrian missiles and the Syrian air force while avoiding a direct engagement with the Syrian army.

Israel Consolidates Its Hold over Southern Lebanon and Facilitates the Election of Gemayel

During the weeks following its invasion, Israel was successful in imposing Phalange control throughout the areas it occupied and in effecting a major economic penetration of southern Lebanon.[120] With the election of Bashir Gemayel as president on August 24, it appeared that Israel's plan for Lebanon was well on its way to implementation. Indeed, the Israeli invasion made possible Gemayel's election by parliament without the traditional consensus of the Muslim and Christian communities.[121]

However, almost immediately after his election, Gemayel began to make overtures to his former domestic enemies, including the Muslim and Druze parties, and attempted to form a central government of national unity. At the same time Gemayel tried to distance himself from Israel and sought to replace it with the United States as his major ally. Begin and Sharon were outraged and summoned Gemayel to a secret meeting on September 1 in Nahariya in northern Israel, where they informed the president-elect exactly what was expected of him. The Israeli leaders expressed their anger and disappointment at Gemayel's failure to provide military assistance during the war. They demanded that immediately on assuming the presidency (in three weeks) he sign a formal peace treaty with Israel providing for the normalization of relations and open borders. They also expressed extreme displeasure at Gemayel's overtures to the Muslim and Druze groups. For his part, Gemayel argued that he needed more time to consolidate his power before establishing direct links with Israel and protested Israel's tactics of expanding the area under Haddad's control and the arming of non-Phalange militia in the south. A Lebanese Christian close to the Phalangist leadership summed up the president-elect's dilemma: "Either we become a permanent satellite of Israel, excluded from the Arab world, or we refuse to sign a peace treaty and join the United States."[122] Gemayel chose the latter course.

Two weeks after the Nahariya meeting, on September 14, Gemayel was assassinated, the victim of a massive explosion at Phalange party headquarters. Some analysts believed that Bashir's Israeli connection was his undoing, either because it had been too close or because it was unraveling.[123] However, under continuing Israeli influence the Lebanese parliament selected Amin Gemayel, Bashir's brother, as president. Israel considered Amin less sympathetic to its interests than Bashir, but the dominance of the Phalange party was maintained through his election. Indeed, soon after the inauguration of Amin the impact of the new Phalange order became apparent. As a result of the Israeli invasion and its imposition of Phalange control, the Lebanese political and social system was subject to serious dislocation. In general, the various Israeli military, economic, and political policies contributed to the increasing fragmentation of Lebanese society and to the weakening of Lebanon's state and social institutions. The most serious damage inflicted on Lebanon was the alteration Israel imposed on the traditional balance of power among the various political/confessional groups.[124] In two years, however, the groups vanquished from the power equation through the Israeli/Phalange alliance—primarily the Shi'ites and Druze—had reasserted themselves in a bloody civil war, and Maronite as well as Phalange influence was at a historic low. That situation was paralleled by the virtual exclusion of Israeli influence from Lebanon.

The Assault on the PLO

Simultaneous with extending Phalange dominance throughout Lebanon, Israel engaged in a massive military campaign during the summer of 1982 to force the PLO out of Beirut. The campaign lasted until August 19 with the PLO evacuation commencing on August 21. The main tactics included: (1) intensive, almost daily, bombing raids; (2) a siege of Beirut lasting nearly ten weeks, during which electricity, water, food, fuel, and medicine were curtailed to the entire western sector; and (3) sophisticated psychological warfare. On July 3 Arafat signed a written statement agreeing that the PLO would leave Beirut. Thus the Israeli policies of siege and bombardment from July 4 until August 19 were aimed at forcing the PLO's departure on Israel's maximalist terms. The effect of the physical devastation ultimately became psychological: the PLO evacuated Beirut not because it was militarily defeated, but because, as a statement issued by the PLO said, "the destruction of Beirut over the heads of half a million Muslims is not a mere possibility but has become a reality."[125]

On July 3 Arafat also publicly endorsed a call made jointly by three internationally known Jewish leaders—Pierre Mendes-France, former French prime minister, Nahum Goldmann, former president of the World Jewish Congress and life-long supporter of Israel, and Philip M. Klutznick, president emeritus of the B'nai B'rith, organizer and former chairman of the Conference of Presidents of Major American Jewish Organizations, president emeritus of the World Jewish Congress, and former U.S. Secretary of Commerce—for mutual recognition between Israel and the PLO. Arafat hailed the statement as "a positive initiative toward a just peace."[126] Washington and Israel ignored the declaration and Arafat's response. The PLO also put forward a plan for its withdrawal from Lebanon, in the context of its signed commitment to leave, containing the following proposals: (1) a firm cease-fire; (2) withdrawal of PLO leaders and all guerrillas with their small arms from Beirut to a destination to be decided by the PLO, the Lebanese government, other Arab states, and the United States; (3) a U.S. guarantee of the safety of the PLO leaders and guerrillas along their exit routes and of the Palestinian civilians remaining behind; (4) restoration of control over West Beirut by the Lebanese army, whose entry into the Muslim side would coincide with the arrival of an international peacekeeping force made up possibly of American and French observers; (5) deployment of a multinational force to separate the two armies and ensure the safety of the Palestinian civilians in the camps; (6) collection of heavy weapons by the Lebanese army; (7) withdrawal of Israeli forces from Beirut; (8) a symbolic military presence of two small PLO battalions under the Lebanese army command in Tripoli and in the Bekaa Valley, to be withdrawn from Lebanon when all other foreign armies withdrew; and (9) a PLO political office with diplomatic immunity in Beirut to supervise informational and social welfare activity and help the Lebanese government administer the affairs of the Palestinian civilians in Lebanon.[127]

Israel rejected the PLO plan, demanding complete, immediate, and unconditional withdrawal. Israel was especially adamant that no token political or military representatives be left behind.[128] When Israel finally agreed, on August 19, to a plan for the PLO departure, the only concession it made was to permit the departing fighters to take one small weapon apiece with them.[129]

In the interim the United States provided the PLO with a written agreement guaranteeing the safe evacuation of the departing fighters and assuring "the safety of all persons in the area." The agreement stated: "The United States government fully recognizes the importance of these assurances . . . and will do its utmost to insure that these assurances are scrupulously observed."[130] This was understood by all the parties to mean a U.S. commitment to protect the safety of the Palestinian civilians in the camps, a serious concern for the PLO leadership, who feared the brutality that the Phalange and Haddad militias could inflict on the civilians. The United States also formally agreed to provide marines to take part in a multilateral peacekeeping force to guarantee the safe departure of the PLO and the security of the Palestinians left behind. Israeli officials, who had lobbied hard for the participation of U.S. troops in such a contingent, were pleased by the prospect of direct American military involvement. They saw this initial commitment as "the possible embryo of an American led multinational force in Lebanon," which would provide the stamp of American legitimacy to their military actions.[131] (When the United States agreed to provide the marines, it also acquiesced in the Israeli demand that American troops not come to Beirut until after the PLO left the city.) The PLO too viewed American participation in a peacekeeping force as a positive development, considering it important not only for its value in preventing a massacre of PLO fighters and Palestinian civilians, but also because PLO officials interpreted it as a kind of recognition of the PLO that they hoped would provide the organization with a political face-saving device.[132] Hani al-Hassan, a ranking advisor to Arafat, commented: "We are fighting for that—to force the United States to recognize us. The PLO would be more flexible if there were direct talks with the United States."[133] In addition, Issam Sartawi, a close advisor to Arafat, stated that the PLO was ready for reciprocal recognition of Israel and added: "It is an unequivocal statement directed to the United States government."[134] Israel responded that it did not need or want PLO recognition and, even if recognition was offered, would not reciprocate. The United States bowed to Israel's position, and the State Department issued a terse comment saying that Sartawi's statement "does not appear to meet the position we have laid out for recognizing the Palestinian group."[135] Thus the political hopes that the PLO had foreseen in the American commitment of the marine contingent proved unfounded, as did its expectation of protection for Palestinian civilians. In fact, the Israeli perception was correct: the presence of U.S. troops was viewed throughout the Arab world as further proof of American backing for Israel's war effort.

One complicating factor in negotiating the PLO exodus was that no Arab country wanted the fighters. In an effort to relieve Beirut of the siege and constant bombardment, the PLO (in accord with a suggestion made by the Saudi and Syrian foreign ministers—an offer the ministers attempted to press on Washington during their visit to the capital in July)[136]—proposed to move its fighters out of Beirut and into northern Lebanon temporarily, until the negotiations were complete.[137] Israel rejected the offer and maintained its pressure. On August 21 the first of 15,600 Palestinians began to leave Beirut. At the same time, the French sent a force of 2,000 men; the Americans sent 800 marines, who did not land until August 25; and the Italians sent 800 troops, who arrived on August 26. The marines were scheduled to remain for thirty days; however, on September 10 they abruptly left Beirut—well ahead of schedule—followed by the Italians and the French.

On September 15, after the assassination of Bashir Gemayel, Israel invaded West Beirut, directly violating the American-sponsored ceasefire. The IDF went into the western sector of the city with tanks and troops, under cover of off-shore gun boats, stating that its objective was to prevent disorder and to disarm the leftist Lebanese militias. The Israelis seized armaments from Lebanese Muslim and nationalist militias and arrested many of the militiamen. The Palestinian refugee camps of Sabra, Shatila, and Burj el Barajneh were encircled. By September 16 Israel controlled nearly all of West Beirut. That evening the IDF sent elite units of the Phalange militia, including the Damour Brigade, and allegedly some militia under the command of Saad Haddad—about 1,400 troops in all—into the Palestinian refugee camps with orders to "purify" them.[138] The Phalangists remained in the camps through September 18, in sight of IDF observation posts, and assisted by illumination from flares fired by Israeli mortars.[139] Phalange commanders were in radio contact with IDF officers, and the militia were supplied with IDF rations.[140] During the time they were in the camps the Phalange forces massacred between 700 and 1,500 women, children, and old men. Hundreds more were severely wounded.[141]

Israel successfully destroyed the PLO infrastructure in Lebanon in 1982, including all its social institutions, but it did not destroy the idea of Palestinian nationalism nor weaken the will of West Bank and Gaza Palestinians to resist Israeli encroachments on their land. While Israel instituted a vigorous settlement program in the war's aftermath, no serious analyst has suggested that the war contributed to a resolution of the Palestinian question. Indeed, this war merely heightened attention to the centrality of the Palestinian issue, most particularly the homeless, stateless condition of this people and the extreme anti-Palestinian sentiment that exists against it in the countries wherein Palestinians have been forced to reside since 1948.

The Limited Campaign against Syria

The major goals of the Israeli campaign against Syria were accomplished during the first week of the war when some ninety Israeli jets attacked and destroyed all nineteen of the SAM missile batteries in the Bekaa Valley on June 9. As of June 10 Israel had made a substantial thrust at the Syrian air force, bringing down sixty-one MIG's and five helicopters. In several tank and artillery battles the Syrians lost control of the western part of the Beirut-Damascus highway, which facilitated the Israeli encirclement of Beirut. Syria and Israel agreed to a cease-fire on June 11.

On June 22 Israeli tanks and fighter planes undertook a major offensive against Syrian and Palestinian positions along the central and eastern reaches of the Beirut-Damascus highway, in the region between Jamhur and Hammana. This successful campaign gave Israel extended control over the Beirut-Damascus highway for some sixteen miles east of Beirut and over portions of Lebanese territory five to ten miles north of the road. A second Israeli-Syrian cease-fire went into effect late in the day on June 22; however, it collapsed on the following day when Israeli tanks, planes, and artillery again hit Syrian positions along the highway. Sporadic fighting continued until a third Syrian-Israeli cease-fire was called on June 25.

This truce held until July 22, when Israel initiated air and land attacks along the entire cease-fire line in eastern Lebanon. The city of Baalbek and several Syrian-controlled villages were bombed. On July 24 IDF jets attacked Syrian positions in the Bekaa Valley, knocking out three new SAM batteries that Damascus had installed. Small arms fire was reported for the next few days in the Bekaa until July 28, when another cease-fire was instituted. There was no further action between Syria and Israel until August 31, when Israel shot down a Syrian MIG-25 on a photographic reconnaissance mission over Beirut.

On September 8 IDF jets attacked and destroyed a Syrian antiaircraft missile battery in Dahr el-Baydar, east of Bhamdoun; on September 9 Israeli planes destroyed four more Syrian missile batteries in Lebanon, also east of Bhamdoun. On September 11 there was some ground fire between IDF troops and the Syrians in the Bekaa, and on September 12 the Israelis destroyed a Syrian SAM antiaircraft site in central Lebanon, near Dahr al-Baydar. On September 13 waves of Israeli planes pounded twelve Syrian targets in eastern Lebanon, striking within three miles of the Syrian border. This was the heaviest sustained bombing (lasting eight hours) of Syrian targets since July 22.

All of this Israeli military activity against Syria was part of a campaign to put military and psychological pressure on Damascus to withdraw completely from Lebanon. That the Syrians did not respond to the repeated Israeli provocations with any offensive action indicates their own perception of military inferiority and their desire to avoid a full-scale war with Israel. However, they also did not withdraw their forces from Lebanon.

The Syrian military was shown to be decisively inferior to the Israeli war machine in the summer of 1982; indeed, Damascus and its Soviet sponsor were resoundingly humiliated. However, within a few months after the war ended, the Soviet Union replaced all of the Syrian equipment with more sophisticated weapons and greater quantities of arms than it had previously provided. Some ninety MIG-21's and twelve SAM-5 missiles—with a range sufficient to hit Tel Aviv and Jerusalem—were sent. Later more SAM-5's arrived as well as several thousand Soviet personnel to train and strengthen the Syrian military. Thus even though Israel was successful in destroying the Syrian missile batteries and in inflicting blow after blow on the the Syrian air force while avoiding a direct engagement with Syria, the Israeli offensive gained nothing in the long run. Instead, it contributed to a significant alteration in the regional balance of power by inducing the Soviet Union to undertake a stronger commitment to arm Syria, rebuilding its military with significantly more sophisticated weapons and fueling the regional arms race. At the same time Syria enjoyed a regional political resurgence, and by the spring of 1984 it was again the dominant power in Lebanon. At that time

Damascus presided over Beirut's cancellation of a U.S.–sponsored Lebanese-Israeli agreement. In the final analysis, Israel was reduced to fighting for physical survival in its area of occupation in southern Lebanon, while an indigenous Lebanese resistance, backed by Syria, caused continuous attrition that Israel was unable to suppress despite its massive military might and traditional bombing raids.

The U.S.–Israeli Relationship during the War
(after the First Week)

With the Israeli campaign in southern Lebanon and the encirclement of Beirut completed, the United States directed itself to fulfilling Israel's demands in order to effect a cease-fire and withdrawal. Philip Habib shuttled endlessly among Tel Aviv, East Beirut, Damascus, Riyadh, and other Arab capitals, attempting to arrange an agreement to end the hostilities. The substance of Habib's mission was to sell Israel's demands, in an American package, to the PLO, through the Syrians, the Saudis, and the Lebanese.

Moscow "warned" Israel on June 14 that the Middle East was close to the Soviet Union's southern borders and that developments in that area "cannot help but affect the interests of the USSR."[142] As with the Soviet warning to the United States the previous week, American diplomats were not particularly disturbed by the statement; it was noted that Moscow delayed making a formal comment on the crisis for more than a week while the Palestinians and Syrians suffered crippling losses. American officials suggested that the Soviets merely issued a strong warning "for the record," when it was already too late for any realistic Soviet action that could affect the outcome of the fighting.[143] This seems to have been a dangerously cavalier attitude toward the Soviet Union, considering Moscow's important geostrategic interests in the Middle East, its formal alliance with Syria, and its informal alliance with the PLO. (On the other hand, the "concern" of the Reagan administration with the "threat" from the Soviet Union may have been merely rhetoric for domestic consumption, issued for the purpose of justifying a massive military buildup, which served primarily to enhance the profit margin of certain elite sectors.)

On June 14 Egypt reaffirmed to the United States the stability of its peace treaty with Israel, declaring that despite Israel's actions in Lebanon and the breakdown in the Palestinian autonomy talks, Cairo would not break relations with Israel or renege on the Camp David agreements. "The peace process is a fact," declared Foreign Minister Kamal Hassan Ali.[144] That reassurance, which came four days after Saudi Arabia indicated that it would not use oil as a weapon against the West, relieved the United States of any necessity to be firm with the Israelis. Indeed many in Washington seemed to believe that American hegemony in the Middle East was virtually complete through the Saudi and Egyptian connections and that it was on the verge of becoming absolute as a result of Israel's military campaign to break the PLO and Syria and deliver Lebanon as another link in the American chain.

On June 15 Begin arrived in the United States for talks with Reagan, other governmental officials, and prominent Jewish leaders. He came with a broad framework of goals for Lebanon, which he expected the American government to help him achieve. Chief among his objectives, according to his aides, was "the creation of a stable, Christian-led government in Beirut that would be willing to sign a peace treaty with Israel."[145] This was a major departure from his previously stated goal of a 40 kilometer security belt to ensure peace for Galilee. Begin was apparently confident of American support, for, as one high Israeli official stated: "We've given the West the gift of Lebanon on a silver platter. We've created a vacuum, and all we ask is for them to step into it."[146] (It is worth noting that when Washington did attempt to exert its influence in Lebanon at the war's end, Israel vigorously and successfully opposed it. What Israel wanted was simply American support for *its* objectives in Lebanon.) There had been some speculation in Washington that Reagan might not meet with Begin; but, on receiving reassurances from Israeli officials that Israel would not enter Beirut, Washington announced that the two leaders would meet on June 21.

Between the time of Begin's arrival in the United States and his meeting with Reagan, a number of points of discord surfaced within the administration concerning the nature and degree of support Washington should be providing Israel. One point of contention was evident between Haig and Habib. Habib advocated that Washington take a "stronger line" with the Israelis, feeling that their military actions in the Beirut area were out of proportion to the military need. Haig argued that the United States should put no restraints on the means Israel chose to fulfill its ends. Reagan accepted Haig's judgment. Another area of discord involved the participation of American troops in a peacekeeping force that might go to Beirut. Israel was pushing hard for U.S. involvement. Defense Secretary Caspar Weinberger (and several other officials) opposed the idea, believing that such a contingent should reflect an extension of the mandate of UNIFIL rather than the introduction of Americans in an independent force. Haig disagreed and again won the president's support for Israel's position.[147]

Another area of contention concerned Israel's "divide-and-rule" policies in areas of Lebanon under its control. Habib believed that there could not be a settlement of any kind without a Lebanese government strong enough to make and implement decisions. Israel, however, was undercutting the authority of the central government more seriously each day, primarily through the forcible substitution of Phalangist forces for Lebanese army troops as well as through the installation of Phalangist troops in Muslim and Druze areas (Israeli tanks also surrounded the presidential palace at Baabda). On this issue, too, Haig insisted that no pressure be brought on Israel. Habib also did not think much of the Israeli approach to cease-fires. He felt the cease-fires should be consolidated and observed and that the Lebanese government be given time to forge a consensus.[148] On this issue the special ambassador prevailed, at least in principle: the administration asked Israel to agree to a strict observance of the cease-fires in Lebanon. Haig made the request through Arens. However, given Haig's unequivocal support for Israel's objectives in Lebanon and his public disagreements with Habib, there was no reason why the Israelis should have taken the request seriously. In fact, Israel proceeded with military action. Intimations of further discord within the administration emerged on June 17, when an unconfirmed report alleged that the Pentagon, led by Weinberger, had made an "unprecedented formal dissent" to Reagan on Haig's policy vis-à-vis Israel.[149] In spite of all this, Haig remained the preeminent decision-maker until June 25. The president consistently accepted Haig's analysis and recommendations and disregarded the advice of others.

Meanwhile, in New York on June 17 Begin told a group of prominent Jewish leaders that the Israeli army would remain in Lebanon as long as the PLO posed a security threat to his country. In a warning to the Reagan administration, the prime minister added: "If anybody tries to use pressure against us, Israel is going to behave as the Czechs should have behaved in 1938, but didn't."[150] When Begin addressed a State of Israel Bonds Campaign luncheon on June 18 (at which $27 million was raised), he received his biggest round of applause when he spoke of his determination to resist "the pressure of America" to withdraw the Israeli army from Lebanon before Israel secured all its conditions.[151] The prime minister's reception was less warm later in the day when he addressed the U.N. General Assembly Special Session on Disarmament. Two-thirds of the delegates either boycotted or walked out of the speech in which Begin said that wars of self-defense, as Israel was fighting in Lebanon, "were the noblest concept of mankind."[152]

On June 20 Weinberger openly broke with the policy of unequivocal support for Israel. He said the United States should investigate possible violations of American law by Israel's use of American arms in Lebanon and advised Reagan to reproach publicly the Israelis for their military actions.[153] Israel and its American supporters stridently charged that the defense secretary was not a friend of Israel. It is true that Weinberger was not the enthusiastic advocate of Israel's invasion that Haig was, but certainly he viewed Israel as a friend and an ally. However, he was not convinced that Israel's policies in Lebanon were going to have any positive benefit on U.S. interests, and he feared that Israeli excesses might harm both American and Israeli interests in the long run. The president rejected Weinberger's advice, and on June 21 when Reagan and Begin met for three hours in the White House, there was no rebuke to the prime minister for any of Israel's activities. When the two leaders met reporters after their meeting, they appeared to be in complete accord on the steps to be taken to resolve the Lebanese conflict.[154] Indeed, Reagan's remarks suggested that he fully endorsed Haig's position that Israel could not be expected to withdraw from Lebanon until all Syrian and Palestinian forces had first withdrawn.[155] In addition, a State Department spokesman told reporters that Resolution 509 was no longer relevant. Such comments clearly implied that the administration was prepared to support a long Israeli occupation of Lebanon.

On June 22 Begin met with Senators and Representatives on Capitol Hill and found that not every congressman endorsed Israel's actions as warmly as the president and his secretary of state. The prime minister was questioned about the use of cluster and phosphorous bombs against civilians, although he denied knowledge of their use.[156] However, despite the expressed concern of some members, Congress made no effort to restrain Israel's actions.

Begin left Washington on June 23 and in the aftermath of his visit the differences among officials in the administration became more apparent. Weinberger openly challenged the Reagan-Haig position of unequivocal support for Israel, and Habib expressed increasing displeasure both with Haig's policies and Israel's actions. On the other hand, Edwin Meese reaffirmed publicly that there would be no recriminations by the administration against Israel because it had "good reasons" for going into Lebanon.[157] On June 25 Haig resigned. It was then unclear whether he did so on his own or under pressure, but Haig was angry over a number of issues. For one, William P. Clark, the president's national security advisor, was dealing directly with certain Arab ambassadors, bypassing Haig. During one meeting with the ambassadors Clark apparently told the Saudis that Washington would prevent an Israeli entry into West Beirut. Haig believed that Clark's word to the Saudis had encouraged the Palestinians to resist, undercutting his policy of securing the unconditional evacuation of the PLO from West Beirut. Haig was also apparently unhappy about the two-track diplomatic effort the administration was pursuing—one controlled by himself through Habib (an increasingly contentious relationship); the other supervised by Weinberger and Bush through the Saudis.[158]

However, whether Haig resigned or was fired is less important than that U.S. policy did not undergo any significant change as a result of his departure. Reagan appointed George P. Shultz to succeed Haig, and despite what seemed like a fresh perspective in Shultz's confirmation hearings, as well as some initial efforts by the new secretary to fashion a U.S. Middle East policy that would serve American interests (primarily expressed in the Reagan Plan and an effort to establish American influence in Lebanon, both of which failed), the American approach to the region remained unaltered. The failures of Shultz's initiatives can be ascribed fundamentally to the unwillingness of either Shultz or Reagan to exert any pressure on Israel to accord its policy with U.S. interests.

Reagan sent Begin a message on July 9, expressing "concern" over the blockade and the continued bombardment of Beirut and noting that such actions were hampering Habib's mission. Reagan suggested vaguely that if Habib's mission failed, other alternatives would have to be sought by the United States. Several journalists asked if that message implied that the United States might decide to negotiate directly with the PLO, but State Department officials denied any change in American policy was being contemplated.[159] The American refusal to have anything to do with the PLO was again emphasized in the context of the search to find a new refuge for the Palestinians departing from Lebanon. On July 19 the Saudi foreign minister, Prince Saud al-Faisal, and the Syrian foreign minister, Abdel Halim Khaddam, came to Washington to attempt to solve the problem of where the PLO would go when it left Beirut. Shultz spoke with the ministers that day, and Reagan met with them on July 20. Prior to the Shultz meeting, Prince Saud told reporters that the United States could resolve the situation in Lebanon by dealing directly with the PLO and focusing on the long-term problem of Palestinian self-determination and a permanent national homeland rather than seeking yet another temporary shelter. The State Department promptly said that "the United States [would] have no direct contacts with the PLO unless the PLO [met] all United States conditions."[160] When the Arab ministers met with Reagan, they outlined a plan for breaking the Israeli siege of West Beirut. The main point of their proposal was that the PLO forces in Beirut be moved temporarily to northern

Lebanon until a place could be arranged for them in other countries.[161] Israel's rejection of the idea brought an immediate American rejection.

In a half-hearted attempt to exert pressure on Israel to desist in its massive bombardments of Beirut, Walter J. Stoessel, acting secretary of state after Haig's resignation, delivered a letter to congressional leaders on July 16, which stated that a "substantial violation by Israel" of the Arms Export Control Act of 1952 "may have occurred in Lebanon." A Reagan spokesman also announced on July 16 that the administration was holding up a shipment of cluster-bomb artillery shells to Israel until it received a formal report from Begin on the use of the American-made cluster bombs in Lebanon. (American intelligence sources had reported conclusively that the highly antipersonnel cluster bombs were being used in South Lebanon and in Beirut. Moreover, Israeli military officers had conceded their use, but contended that efforts were being made to reduce civilian casualties.)[162] In any event Stoessel's letter, which was classified to minimize repercussions from the pro-Israeli lobby, stopped far short of declaring that a violation of the law *had* occurred. If either the administration or Congress had found Israel in violation of the self-defense provisions of the law, a halt in export credits for arms sales to Israel would have been mandatory. The administration certainly did not want this; and despite the expressed concern of a few congressmen, Congress would not have wanted to vote on the issue. Neither the Executive nor the Legislature wished to provoke the Israeli lobby.

Israel formally replied to Reagan on July 17, officially acknowledging that it used the bombs in Lebanon but defending their use, arguing that its actions were consistent with Israeli-American agreements. Israel also stated that it used the bombs only against military targets, but, since most PLO military targets were situated in the midst of civilian areas, some of the weapons had probably unintentionally fallen on populated areas.[163] On July 19 Reagan announced that transfer of a shipment of cluster bombs for Israel had been suspended, pending completion of an interagency study on whether Israel's use of the weapons in Lebanon had violated its agreement with the United States.[164] On July 27 the president announced that the suspension was "indefinite," although the administration still refused to make a "legal" determination about whether Israel had violated American law in using the weapons and said it did not plan to do so.[165] This suspension of one shipment of cluster bombs represented the only sanction the United States applied against Israel during the war.

At about the same time the Israeli lobby began a campaign against Philip Habib, who had worked as a consultant for the Bechtel Corporation, which does business in the Arab world. Habib was not on the payroll of Bechtel while he served the Reagan administration, but pro-Israeli individuals and groups began expressing public "concern" that the company's financial relations with Arab countries would "prejudice" Habib against Israel in the negotiations. Thomas A. Dine, the executive-director of the American-Israel Public Affairs Committee, said he "regretted" that Habib's association with Bechtel had not been fully disclosed earlier, but he was hopeful that Habib would "carefully fulfill all of his responsibilities independent of any commercial concerns."[166] The attempt to portray any American deviation from Israel's interests as a "sell-out" to "Arab money" was one way that the Israeli lobby kept pressure on the administration throughout this crisis (and in general used it as a means of intimidating American officials).[167] Both Shultz and Weinberger were also former Bechtel employees, and Israel's American friends continuously expressed their hostility toward Weinberger and their belief that he was "one hundred per cent anti-Israel." "Suspicions" were raised about Shultz, though he comported himself more to Israel's liking and was thus less vilified than the defense secretary.

On July 28, after a meeting between Habib and Begin, Israel announced that it would "grant him [Habib] only a limited time to achieve his goals. It's not months, not even many weeks. . . . After time runs out there will be no other way. We will have to get them out of there."[168] This statement reflected another form of pressure that Israel exerted on the administration—threatening to invade Beirut if the United States did not fulfill its demands. Rather than reversing the pressure as they should—and could—have done, the administration hastened to issue reassuring statements on the intensity of the American commitment to resolve the crisis.[169] At the United Nations the United States also demonstrated its support for Israel by abstaining on Security Council Resolution 515, adopted on July 29, demanding that Israel lift the blockade of Beirut and permit the passage of supplies to the civilian population. Washington had many levers through which it could have exerted pressure on Israel, but chose to employ none of them, even as Israel escalated its military activity and continued its intransigence in the negotiations.

On August 1, in response to a new and more conciliatory plan for its evacuation put forward by the PLO on July 30, Israel unleashed the most massive, intense bombardment of West Beirut to date, lasting some fourteen hours. Reagan refrained from criticizing Israel but said he would be "firm" in his talks with Foreign Minister Shamir, who arrived in Washington that day. On August 2 Shamir held a long meeting with Reagan in the Oval Office. Administration officials told reporters that prior to his session with Shamir, the president had received a series of "blistering" messages from Habib, saying that he had little or no hope of being able to negotiate the withdrawal of Palestinian forces from Lebanon as long as Israel kept breaking the cease-fires and bombing the city. The officials reported that Habib had made it clear that his position as a negotiator was being undercut and that he wanted the president to use his meeting with the foreign minister to put a stop to further Israeli military action. Other officials told reporters that Israel was responsible for most of the violations of the nine cease-fires arranged by Habib. However, despite the impression these officials attempted to convey of the president's new, firmer attitude toward Israel's actions, when reporters asked what threats or warnings the president or secretary of state had employed in their meetings with the Israeli minister, the answer was simply "none."[170]

An Israeli official who had sat in on the meetings with Shamir and Reagan and who was authorized to speak for the Israeli delegation, told reporters: "Our people didn't come out of the meetings with . . . [the] impression that there was any change in the administration's position. The meetings were friendly. We can say that the president was firm in what he wanted to say, but there were no threats." The official also said that there was agreement on "first things first," meaning, he said, that both sides agreed that the first priority was to get the PLO out of West Beirut and then continue with the wider issues of peace. Shamir himself said later that his meetings with Reagan had been conducted in "a friendly atmosphere." Nevertheless, the foreign minister issued another "warning" to the administration, stating that while there was "no deadline" in the negotiations, they "cannot last forever." Shamir elaborated: "We prefer a diplomatic solution. . . . but we are convinced that the PLO will not leave Beirut or Lebanon unless they will be convinced that they have only one choice before them—to leave by negotiations or by other means."[171]

President Reagan received a letter from Soviet Premier Brezhnev on August 2, asking the president "to use most urgently the possibilities at your disposal" to halt the Israeli bombardment. There were several additional, fairly strong statements in the letter, but diplomats in Washington interpreted the message as fitting the pattern set by Moscow officials from the beginning of the Israeli invasion—to limit Soviet involvement to propaganda, diplomatic maneuvers on behalf of the Syrians and Palestinians, and a modest airlift to resupply arms that Syria had lost.[172]

On August 3 Israel undertook a major offensive, moving deeper into West Beirut. According to Lebanese leaders involved in the negotiations, the Israeli thrust came just as the indirect talks between Habib and PLO were making serious progress.[173]

On August 4 Israel once more furiously bombarded West Beirut and also tightened its blockade of the city. This time the onslaught halted the negotiations. Again, Lebanese sources stated that the talks had been making progress, particularly because the PLO had presented a new eleven-point proposal that abandoned the request for a prior disengagement of forces. Instead the PLO now simply asked that a multinational peacekeeping unit be deployed in West Beirut simultaneous with its evacuation in order to protect the departing fighters and to safeguard the Palestinian civilians who would remain behind.[174] Israel insisted that the multinational force not arrive until *after* the PLO departure. Reagan sent a personal message to Begin on August 4 asking him to observe the cease-fire in Beirut as "a necessary first step toward our goal of restoring the authority of the government of Lebanon."[175] In addition, several administration officials commented publicly that Reagan viewed the Israeli thrust as a "direct threat" to Habib's mission: "We had something close to a settlement yesterday with the PLO and for some unexplained reason the Israelis let go last night just about the same time."[176] The "reason" was that Israel was unprepared to accept a settlement whose terms did not dovetail precisely with its demands. Nevertheless, in an attempt to deflect the growing criticism of the administration from domestic pro-Israeli sources, the president issued a sternly worded statement, voicing his "strong conviction" that the PLO "must not delay further its withdrawal from Beirut."[177] The true state of affairs was again made apparent when administration spokesmen were asked about the possible use of sanctions to force the Israelis to observe the cease-fire; the officials declared that the administration was definitely not contemplating any sanctions—"it serves no useful purpose," one commented.[178]

In a public response to Reagan's August 4 message, Begin stated that Israel would continue the siege of West Beirut and the bombardment as long as it saw fit. "Nobody should preach to us," Begin told 200 members of the United Jewish Appeal who were visiting in Israel. Begin vigorously defended Israel's actions in West Beirut and told the Americans: "Nobody, nobody is going to bring Israel to its knees. The Jews do not kneel but to God." Those present gave him a standing ovation.[179]

On August 5 the United States asked Israel to yield the military gains won in its thrust into West Beirut and to withdraw to the cease-fire lines that existed on August 1. The request was accompanied by what administration officials described as a "sharply worded" personal message to Begin suggesting that American-Israeli relations would be threatened unless Israel stopped what Reagan termed "unnecessary bloodshed" in Lebanon. State Department spokesmen said that in delivering the letter, the U.S. charge d'affaires in Israel, William Brown, also requested that Israeli troops be withdrawn.[180] On the same day, however, Reagan assured a delegation from the Conference of Presidents of Major American Jewish Organizations of America's unequivocal support for Israel and reaffirmed that the administration would never use sanctions against the Jewish state.[181] The United States also demonstrated its support for Israel at the United Nations that day. The Security Council, facing a crisis of credibility after the Israeli cabinet formally rejected the U.N. request to pull back its troops in Beirut and permit U.N. observers to monitor the area, debated possible sanctions against Israel. The United States informed the Security Council that it would veto any such attempt.[182]

August 6 brought a new Israeli blitzkrieg on West Beirut, as Begin declared he saw no progress in the American efforts to obtain the PLO withdrawal. However, shortly before the bombardment began, Lebanese Prime Minister Shafik Wazzan had announced "virtual agreement" among United States, Lebanese, and PLO negotiators on the terms of withdrawal. In an attempt to deflect potential American criticism for Israel's military actions and to increase pressure on the administration, Begin sent a strongly worded letter to Reagan, declaring that U.S. proposals for an Israeli pullback in West Beirut were absolutely unacceptable as was the deployment of multinational forces before the PLO evacuated. The letter had its intended effect: that evening the United States vetoed a Security Council resolution calling for sanctions against Israel for its refusal to comply with previous cease-fire resolutions.[183]

However, on August 7, U.S. officials intimated that there were growing disagreements between Washington and Israel. One announcement stated that the Reagan administration had undertaken a "comprehensive assessment" of U.S. relations in the Middle East and had found "very profound differences" with Israel, including Israeli settlements on the West Bank, the dismissal of elected Palestinian mayors, and Israel's opposition to the sale of American weapons to Jordan and Saudi Arabia.[184] The announcement was tempered by the statement that the United States was seeking "fundamental changes" from Jordan and Saudi Arabia in terms of support for the Camp David agreement, and there was no suggestion of how the United States might pursue its interests in the face of these "profound" differences. Nevertheless, Israel quickly responded to the suggestion of divergence in United States and Israeli objectives in the Middle East. Ambassador Arens warned the United States not to consider sanctions against Israel: "It's difficult to see how it [sanctions] would be applied," he said. "Sanctions are applied to an enemy country. We're not an enemy of the United States. On the other hand, I assure you, it's not going to sway Israel from a course necessary for assuring its security."[185] Israel's relentless pressure (backed by the pressure exerted by its American supporters) was again effective: Shultz and Reagan both publicly reiterated their position that sanctions against Israel would never be applied because they would be "counterproductive."

On August 9 Israel answered a personal letter from Shultz (who had asked the Israelis to consider a new plan for the PLO evacuation that Habib had carefully worked out) with a massive air, sea, and land bombardment of West Beirut. That same day two U.S.–made Israeli air force F-16 jet fighters buzzed two American helicopters off the coast of Lebanon, the most recent of three incidents of Israeli harassment of American forces. According to Pentagon officials about a dozen Americans were endangered in the buzzing incident. The secretary of defense formally protested to the Israeli government.[186] Israeli officials apologized, but this was only the beginning of Israel's harassment of American forces, which reached a peak in January–March 1983.

On August 10 Israel launched new attacks on West Beirut while accepting "in principle" the Habib plan. On August 11 and 12 Israel again pounded West Beirut with eleven hour-long bombing raids. At the same time the IDF advanced into strategic positions in northern Lebanon. The bombardment on August 12 was so intense and widespread that the Lebanese authorities suspended negotiations. Wazzan stated: "I have told Philip Habib that I cannot carry on in these talks while these thousands of tons of explosives are wreaking mass destruction in my city, my capital."[187] Reagan was reported to have expressed "outrage" over the continuous bombings in a telephone call to Begin. Larry Speakes, the deputy White House press secretary, told reporters: "The president expressed his outrage over this latest round of massive military action. He emphasized that Israel's action halted the ambassador's negotiations for a peaceful resolution of the Beirut crisis when they were at the point of success. The result has been more needless destruction and bloodshed."[188] However, a State

Department official later made a point of stating that the president had made no threats to the Israelis in his conversation with Begin.[189]

On the evening of August 12 the Security Council voted to renew its demand that Israel permit U.N. officers to monitor the cease-fire in Beirut. The United States voted for the resolution, but only after softening its language to voicing "serious concern about continued military activities in Beirut," instead of singling out Israeli action for condemnation.[190] At the end of the day Israel agreed to a cease-fire. On August 19 the Israeli cabinet formally accepted the plan worked out by Habib, and Reagan expressed his "extreme gratification" with Israel's decision.[191] On August 21 the PLO evacuation began and continued until September 1, when the last fighters departed the city. The U.S. marines landed on August 25, following a meeting between Sharon and Morris Draper in which the Israeli defense minister granted "permission" for the marines and the Italian contingent to take up positions at that time rather than waiting for the departure of all PLO forces. The war against the PLO was officially over, although Israel continued its attacks on the Syrians and would invade West Beirut on September 15.

Sharon arrived in the United States on August 26, with the stated purposes of "setting the record straight" on the alleged "misinformation" the media had disseminated throughout this war and of "mend[ing] fences" with Washington.[192] Leaders of the American Jewish community (who pledged $550 million at a luncheon on August 28 to help Israel pay for the costs of the war) warmly received him.[193] On August 27 Sharon met with Shultz and Weinberger. Sharon commented after the meetings that there were some "differences of opinion" between the United States and Israel, but that as to "the fundamental friendship and the basic partnership and common interests, as well as Israel's contribution to the free world and the Middle East—on these there is no dispute."[194] While American officials said that differences with Israel existed over the concept of "autonomy" for the Palestinians on the West Bank as envisioned in the Camp David accords, they were otherwise in agreement with Sharon about the commonality of interests between the two states. However, one issue of contention between Washington and Israel—foretelling a major area of dispute between the two states—became apparent during Sharon's visit: the Israeli campaign to promote the idea that "Jordan is Palestine" and therefore the "natural" Palestinian state. American officials made a clear effort to distance themselves from this specious proposal, which implicitly called for the overthrow of the Hashimite monarchy. It was not in the interest of the United States to have King Hussein think that Washington in any way supported a plan to oust him and turn Jordan over to the Palestinians. Nevertheless, the domestic propaganda effort over this issue has enjoyed considerable success in some important sectors of American society.

Another source of discord became apparent when Washington attempted to assert its interests in the war's aftermath. Reagan and his top advisors believed that the confluence of events represented by the defeat of the PLO, the weakening of Syria, and the strength of Israel's military and political position was auspicious for an overall Middle East peace settlement. Thus the administration sought to take advantage of the situation by expanding U.S. influence with the new government in Beirut and through the devising of a solution for the Palestinian question. The paradox became apparent immediately, however. The United States could only further its interests in Lebanon and elsewhere in the Arab world by reining in Israel and setting limits on the Jewish state's expansive designs, particularly in Lebanon and in the West Bank. But when the United States attempted to pursue its own interests, both Lebanon and the Palestinian question became issues of serious contention between Washington and Israel. In the end, Israel's interests prevailed, and American interests were again thwarted.

The administration had begun to assert some influence in Lebanon even before the end of the war. Several officials had made overtures to Bashir Gemayel, encouraging him to rely on U.S. support rather than aligning himself exclusively with Israel. The United States was concerned that a Lebanese-Israeli peace treaty on Israel's terms would destabilize Lebanon's domestic politics and the region as a whole.[195] Thus Washington advised Gemayel not to sign such a peace treaty—at least not immediately—as it had earlier encouraged him not to provide the aggressive military support Israel had expected during the war itself.[196] (Washington had feared that such action would render Gemayel unable to unify Lebanon and function as the president of all Lebanese.) Israel was already outraged that Gemayel had not contributed the military support it had requested during the siege of Beirut. Moreover, for Israel a peace treaty with Lebanon on its terms was crucial, since such a treaty would afford an important justification for the casualties, both military and diplomatic, of the invasion. Thus on September 6 Israel increased the pressure on Gemayel for a formal accord. Sharon publicly stated that if a government came into being in Lebanon and refused to sign a peace treaty with Israel, Israel would establish a "special status" for a sector of southern Lebanon up to 40 or 50 kilometers north of the border.[197] Sharon did not define "special status," but it was assumed to mean Israeli control either through a pro-Israeli militia (like Saad Haddad's) or permanent Israeli occupation. The American concern over the implications of Israel's demands was apparent in testimony Shultz gave before the House Foreign Affairs Committee on September 9. Shultz stated that the United States would support a peace treaty between Israel and Lebanon only if it was freely entered into by the Lebanese government and not dictated by Israeli military pressure: "A peace treaty that is signed at the point of a gun is not, in the end, a long lasting peace treaty."[198] Israel was enraged, but in the final analysis Shultz brokered just such a treaty.

While Israel was angry over the U.S. position on a Lebanese-Israeli accord and Washington's independent overtures toward Gemayel, it became even more outraged by American attempts to foster a settlement of the Arab-Israeli conflict and resolve the Palestinian question. Significantly, though Reagan had come to office viewing the Palestinian issue as nothing other than Soviet-sponsored international terrorism, the war apparently made the president aware that this was a larger issue that required resolution. Thus Reagan and Shultz devised a plan that they believed would settle the Palestinian problem while furthering the American interests of regional stability, improving relations with the Arab states, and decreasing opportunities for Soviet expansion. They also firmly believed that such an approach was the best guarantee for Israel's long-term security.

President Reagan sent Prime Minister Begin a letter on August 31, outlining several proposals for a comprehensive Arab-Israeli peace. Reagan asked for a freeze on Jewish settlements in the occupied West Bank and Gaza Strip and suggested that these territories ultimately be linked in a confederation with Jordan. The president specifically asked that Israel not annex the occupied areas. The proposals were placed in the context of a comprehensive plan for the next phase of negotiations under the Camp David formula. Reagan also reiterated his opposition to an independent Palestinian state or a negotiating role for the PLO. But since the major objective of the Israeli campaign had been to ensure final and permanent Israeli sovereignty over the West Bank, the Israeli government considered the president's proposals preposterous and rejected them out of hand. Shamir issued a statement claiming that Reagan's suggestions contradicted the Camp David accords, and Begin canceled a vacation to convene an emergency session of the cabinet in order to devise a strategy for defeating the American plan. Several members of Begin's party demanded that the prime minister create many new settlements immediately; other members passed the contents of the letter to Israel Radio, hoping to rouse the public to derail the initiative.[199] To counter Israeli opposition, Reagan decided to appear on television to explain the proposals to the American public.

President Reagan's televised speech on September 1 was billed as a "fresh start" and a "new initiative" for peace in the Middle East, although the Reagan Plan, as it came to be known, was merely a new expression of ideas and attitudes that had long been U.S. policy, at least in principle. In principle the United States had consistently opposed Israeli annexation of the West Bank and Israeli settlements in the occupied areas (though Reagan had reversed the second principle during his election campaign). In addition, Washington had always viewed Jordan as a desirable partner in a Middle East settlement.[200] Thus in keeping with the traditionally stated maxims of American policy, Reagan called for autonomy for the Palestinians living in the West Bank and Gaza under some form of Jordanian supervision, a freeze on Israeli settlements, and the maintenance of an undivided Jerusalem (implicitly acquiescing in continued Israeli dominance of the city). The president reaffirmed America's "ironclad" support for Israel, reiterated U.S. commitment to the Camp David formula, and ruled out an independent Palestinian state or any role for the PLO in negotiations leading to Palestinian "autonomy."[201]

Washington's inability to produce any innovative ideas is striking; moreover, the Reagan Plan was seriously flawed in that it denied Palestinians the right to self-determination. As such, in the long run the plan could only have led to further regional instability. America's shortsightedness was exceeded, however, by Israel's complete blindness. The Israeli government reacted to the president's speech with statements full of rancor and took immediate moves to torpedo the plan. Begin called the Reagan Plan "suicidal" for Israel and a "betrayal of the Camp David agreements." The Israeli cabinet voted unanimously to reject the plan and to "continue a vigorous program of establishing Jewish settlements on the West Bank in order to consolidate Israel's hold on the area." It announced that forty-two new Israeli settlements would be established in the West Bank within the next five years, with 100,000 new Jewish settlers. The cabinet also reaffirmed its right to sovereignty over the territories after the five-year transition period envisioned at Camp David.[202] Weinberger, who was in Israel, told Begin that he hoped Israel would not dismiss the president's proposals out of hand, but Begin replied that Israel would refuse to participate in any negotiations on the basis of the plan. As to the settlement policy, Begin declared: "Such settlement is a Jewish inalienable right and an integral part of our national security. Therefore, there shall be no settlement freeze."[203] It is true that the Reagan Plan contradicted the most cherished desire of the Begin government—the extension of Israeli sovereignty over the West Bank. It also negated the major reason Israel had undertaken the war in Lebanon. Israeli opposition to the plan was therefore inevitable. But the United States possessed the leverage to induce Israeli agreement if the administration had elected to use it. Reagan and Shultz were explicit from the outset, however, that no pressure would be brought to bear on Israel to encourage its cooperation, thus ensuring the failure of the initiative.

Despite its flaws regarding Palestinian self-determination, the PLO, and Jerusalem, the Reagan initiative was well received in many sectors. Within the United States the president's plan was widely perceived as a serious initiative for peace in the Middle East. For example, Anthony Lewis, a *New York Times* columnist, warmly praised the plan. The Arab world responded with caution, but generally viewed the proposals with optimism. The seriousness with which the Reagan Plan was considered by the Arabs was demonstrated at the Arab summit conference in Fez later in September; in a long series of negotiations between King Hussein and Arafat; and by the attention the plan was given at the meeting of the Palestine National Council in February 1983. King Hussein withheld immediate formal comment on the plan, but made it clear through authorized sources that Jordan's reaction was "favorable." An official Palestinian source said Reagan's statement was "constructive." However, both Jordanian and Palestinian officials expressed skepticism about the administration's "determination," i.e., its will and ability to implement the proposals.[204]

Indeed, even American officials expressed reservations on that score. A senior State Department official commented: "Administration after administration has said the same things in public and in private," but "there were always worries about the 'Jewish vote' and worries that an overall approach would not work with the Israelis, that the Israelis had to be dealt with more gingerly." The official pointed out how the one venture in this direction, the Rogers Plan, had backfired politically and diplomatically and speculated that since the Israelis had rejected Reagan's proposals out of hand, the Arabs would be wary of endorsing them, and all would come to naught.[205] This was, in fact, the outcome.

Administration officials made no attempt to use the enormous leverage the United States possesses vis-à-vis Israel—the amounts and terms of American aid—to influence Israeli behavior or to secure Israeli compliance with the Reagan Plan. Instead, Washington increased the amount of aid that was to go to Israel in the coming year. On October 14, 1982, Israel formally requested $3.2 billion for the 1984 fiscal year, approximately $1 billion more than it was receiving in the 1983 fiscal year.[206] The administration submitted a request to Congress for aid to Israel of $2.5 billion, including $1.7 billion in military credits, of which $500 million would not have to be repaid, and $800 million in economic grants (also non-repayable). Congress then allocated Israel even more money than had been requested by the Executive. The credits that did not have to be repaid were increased to $850 million and $125 million was added to the $800 million in economic assistance.[207] The increased aid more than covered the cost of the new settlement program, estimated at roughly $200 million of the $2.6 billion aid package.[208] It is striking that both the administration and Congress chose, in effect, to "reward" Israel (with more aid at better terms) for its aggression in Lebanon and its absolute rejection of the Reagan Plan. It seems obvious that whatever perceived advantages Israel might offer as a strategic asset could not possibly account for these actions; indeed, such behavior cannot be explained apart from the profound and inextricable ways in which the pro-Israeli lobby is related to the domestic political process.

After the enunciation of the Reagan Plan other areas of strain developed in the U.S.–Israeli relationship. One concerned the Israeli refusal to share military intelligence from the war in Lebanon with the United States.[209] The Reagan administration considered this a direct affront, especially because American military officials attach great importance to Israel's sharing intelligence gathered through the battlefield testing of American military equipment and information learned about Soviet weapons. Indeed, such weapons testing and data collection are the most concrete and important services that Israel provides the United States. In this case the Pentagon was particularly interested in seeing what Israel had learned from its combat with the Syrians, who were using new Soviet weapons systems. Sharon claimed that Israel was unwilling to share the intelligence because of the delay in the U.S. shipment of F-16 aircraft in 1981 (after Israel's bombardment of Iraq and Beirut); because of the suspension of the 1981 Memoranda of Understanding (after Israel annexed the Golan); and because of the suspension of the shipment of cluster bombs during the war in Lebanon.[210] More to the point, the Israeli position was intended to demonstrate to Washington the leverage Israel had and was prepared to use against the United States as a means of pressuring the administration to drop a policy Israel did not agree with—in this case the Reagan initiative.

Israel's efforts to sabotage the Reagan Plan produced strains in its relations with Washington, but the Israelis lost no time in launching their offensive. On September 5 Israel allocated $18.5 million to build three new settlements on the occupied West Bank "immediately" and announced approval to build seven others. Nine of the ten settlements were to be built in the hills around Hebron, a fiercely nationalistic Palestinian city. In addition, $37 million was allocated to transfer high technology factories from Israel proper into the West Bank.[211] On the same day Begin warned Reagan in a letter that the American proposals for the West Bank would lead to a Palestinian state and "a Soviet base in the heart of the Middle East." This, Begin contended, "would endanger our very existence." He rebuked the president: "A friend does not weaken his friend, an ally does not put his ally in jeopardy."[212] In a radio interview on September 5 Sharon predicted the Reagan Plan would die: "The United States will have no alternative but to drop the proposals because they cannot be implemented and Israel will not even discuss them."[213] Reagan's only reaction was to comment that the U.S. position would remain unchanged.[214]

In Fez, Arab leaders debated the Reagan Plan and then undertook a major peace initiative of their own. On September 9 they announced agreement on a peace plan that declared all nations in the Middle East, including an independent Palestinian state, had a right to a peaceful existence. The plan implicitly recognized Israel in that statement and in leaving to the U.N. Security Council the task of guaranteeing the security of states in the region. The plan called for Israeli withdrawal from the lands it had occupied in 1967, and recognized the PLO as the legitimate representative of the Palestinian people.[215] The Fez Plan was directly derived from the Saudi proposals (the Fahd Plan) of 1981 and was based squarely on U.N. Resolutions 181 and 242. King Hassan of Morocco projected the "normalization of relations and diplomatic ties" between the Arab states and Israel following implementation of the Fez Plan.[216] The plan would have served American interests in the region by terminating the Arab-Israeli conflict and resolving the Palestinian issue, thus decreasing markedly Soviet opportunities for expansion, and virtually assuring regional stability (at least in terms of the Arab-Palestinian-Israeli conflict). Undoubtedly it would also have reduced some of the anti-Americanism that pervades the Islamic fundamentalist movement (and much of the region generally) by addressing several major issues of concern to Islamists, i.e., the question of Palestine and the persistent American hostility to Palestinian interests, the perception of U.S.-Israeli imperialism, and Israeli domination of East Jerusalem. In addition, the Fez Plan would have provided a strong guarantee of Israel's future security. It was, by any measure, a more realistic proposal for Middle East peace and the maximization of long-range American national interests than the Reagan Plan.

The U.S. response was cautious, but Shultz stated that he saw the possibility of a "breakthrough" in the Arab leaders' recognition of Israel's right to exist, even though the Arab proposals were "at considerable variance" with Reagan's plan.[217] The Israeli reaction was completely negative. Shamir declared that the plan constituted "a renewed declaration of war on Israel," that it "has no weight, no value. . . . and contains the same hate, the same war against peace, the same coldness" as previous Arab decisions on Israel. "It is another plan for the liquidation of Israel in one stage or two," said Shamir, denouncing the Fez Plan's call for a Palestinian state as a "threat to Israel's existence."[218]

After Israel's rejection of both the Reagan and the Fez plans, the administration put its hopes for some movement toward a comprehensive peace on King Hussein of Jordan. That was unrealistic, however. To engage in a peace process with Israel, the king needed some evidence that the United States would push Israel on a West Bank negotiation. And this Washington was not prepared to do. It did not even exert pressure on Israel to desist in its vigorous settlement policy, leaving the king without the slightest incentive to act. Moreover, as time went on, Hussein came to feel that if the United States could not achieve an Israeli withdrawal from Lebanon, it certainly could not facilitate negotiations over the West Bank. Nevertheless, Hussein engaged in long and painstaking talks with Arafat about the form and content of a possible joint Jordanian-Palestinian negotiation regarding the West Bank. That those talks failed in the end was not because of pressure from PLO "radicals" or a failure of Jordan to take "bold action," as was alleged in Washington. It was simply the failure of the United States to apply any pressure on Israel to halt its settlements or withdraw from Lebanon. In such a context neither the Palestinians nor the Jordanians believed that they had anything to gain from agreeing to negotiate with Israel, which stated repeatedly (and provided fresh evidence daily through its expanding settlement program) that there was nothing to negotiate about.

The Israeli invasion of West Beirut on September 15 led to further strains between Washington and Israel. The United States asked Israel to withdraw its military forces from the city "immediately," noting that the entry of the troops was a "clear violation" of the American-sponsored agreement negotiated by Habib.[219] Israel rejected the American request, responding that its troops would remain in West Beirut until the Lebanese army was able to ensure security in the city.[220] Washington did little to bring about an Israeli withdrawal; indeed, even though the Israelis themselves never made such a claim, President Reagan stated that they had moved into West Beirut only after coming under attack from Lebanese Muslim forces.[221] Whether from ignorance or a desire to exculpate Israel, the president's statement left Washington again looking as if it were a partner in the new invasion. Israel's occupation of Beirut and the actions of its Lebanese allies in Sabra and Shatila worsened Washington's already badly tarnished image in the Arab world and elsewhere. By violating the American-sponsored cease-fire and creating the conditions for the massacre, Israel put the United States in a position of defaulting on its guarantees to the PLO concerning the safety of Palestinian civilians. But the administration never raised the issue of Israel's culpability, either in the massacres themselves or in causing America to violate an international agreement.

Moreover, the United States continued to support Israel at the United Nations. The Security Council convened on September 16; Resolution 520, passed the next day, condemned the Israeli incursion into Beirut and called for a return to the positions occupied by Israel before September 15. The threat of a U.S. veto again ensured that the resolution contained no call for sanctions against Israel. On September 19, the United States threatened once more to use its veto to ensure that a Security Council resolution (521) condemning the massacres in Sabra and Shatila did not mention Israel.

On September 20 the Lebanese government formally called on President Reagan to return the marines. Israel was eager for their return (because the American presence would be perceived as a legitimizing factor) but was not prepared to withdraw from the strategic positions around Beirut, which Washington stated was the precondition for the marines return. In fact, a number of American officials, including the secretary of defense, were opposed to a reintroduction of the marines under any circumstances, pointing out that their mission was unclear and expressing fear that their presence could drag the United States into a combat situation.[222] Israel eventually pulled back (under duress) to facilitate the return of the marines.

U.S.-Israeli Relations, September 29, 1982–May 17, 1983

The marines returned to Lebanon on September 29, 1982, under the rubric of "peacekeepers," and thereafter the administration undertook an intense diplomatic effort to bring about the evacuation of all foreign forces from Lebanon, including Israel's, and to advance the Reagan Plan. Ultimately the former objective proved so elusive that the latter was given scant attention, and in the end Washington failed to achieve either goal. Significantly, both diverged from Israel's interests, and with the aid of its American friends Israel engineered the American failures. Indeed, the two most striking features of this period were Israel's ability to manipulate the United States and Washington's surrender to policies that contravened vital American interests.

On October 10 Israel renewed its demand for a formal peace treaty with Lebanon as a prerequisite for its withdrawal while discord continued between the United States and Israel over the nature of such a treaty. As the postwar situation in Lebanon increasingly diverged from Israel's expectations, the Jewish state became ever more intent on obtaining a treaty that would provide for the full normalization of relations and unrestrained economic intercourse. U.S. officials understood, however, that those conditions would complicate the precarious position of Amin Gemayel's government domestically and would place Lebanon in an untenable situation vis-à-vis the Arab world. Washington wanted to see Gemayel consolidate his power internally and unify the country; in addition, it did not want Lebanon boycotted as Egypt had been in the wake of Camp David. Thus Washington was not anxious to have Israel impose such an agreement.

There were several specific areas of contention regarding an Israeli treaty with Lebanon. First, U.S. officials believed that a formal treaty should not be forced at the point of a gun, which they believed the Israelis were doing. Second, the United States believed that there was no reason why Israel should not withdraw quickly; the Israelis were determined to stay until they had obtained their political objectives, raising the possibility of an indefinite occupation. Third, the administration opposed a role for Saad Haddad in Lebanon, since this automatically precluded the possibility of the Gemayel government extending its control throughout all of Lebanon; Israel was adamant that Haddad's militia be accorded an independent status. Fourth, the United States wanted to build up the U.N. force (UNIFIL) in southern Lebanon as a guarantor of security; Israel insisted on maintaining an Israeli presence and attempted to persuade the United States to participate with it in security arrangements in southern Lebanon. Washington believed this would constitute a permanent compromise of Lebanon's sovereignty. Finally, the United States objected to Israel's demand that both the Syrian troops and the remaining PLO forces in the Bekaa Valley and in the Tripoli area leave before Israel departed, recognizing that this was unrealistic from the Syrian perspective.[223] However, with the exception of joint U.S.–Israeli participation in a security force in southern Lebanon, Israel prevailed on each of the issues—in an agreement brokered by the U.S.

Despite these serious divergencies, the United States declined to put forward a proposal of its own, preferring to "mediate" between Lebanon and Israel. In addition, the administration acquiesced in the establishment of a special Israeli-American "working group" to "consult" about the Israeli position and to facilitate a "compromise." This represents a clear illustration of the privileged position Israel enjoys in Washington. As such, Lebanon could not have hoped to gain an equal hearing for its position on the issues. Moreover, the existence of such a working group inside the American government was another means that Israel used to exert pressure on the administration.

In mid-October Gemayel came to the United States to seek American support. At the Security Council on October 18 the Lebanese president told the delegates that Israel was the chief obstacle to peace in Lebanon: "The withdrawal of Israeli forces constitutes today the fundamental objective called for by your resolutions. This objective must be achieved."[224] Meeting with President Reagan on October 19, Gemayel asked the United States to expand the size and scope of the international peacekeeping force to bring about an early withdrawal of Israeli, Syrian, and Palestinian troops. He also informed American officials that signing even a security agreement with Israel would cause him "a serious problem" domestically and with other Arab nations.[225] In addition, Gemayel reiterated the specific Lebanese objections to the Israeli proposals and asked Reagan for help. However, the pressures applied by Israel and its domestic supporters led the administration to conclude that the political costs of opposing Israel were too great, thus it declined to support Gemayel or pursue its own interests. Gemayel then turned to Damascus for assistance. In the end it was Syria that emerged as the power behind the Beirut government.

On November 6 Reagan announced that there would be a new, high-level effort to bring about the withdrawal of all foreign forces from Lebanon. It was expected that Philip Habib would be sent back to the region. (He returned on November 17.) Administration officials indicated that this effort would involve a "tactical shift in emphasis," putting more time and energy in bringing about the withdrawal of foreign forces from Lebanon and leaving negotiations about Palestinian autonomy on the "back burner"[226] (though the Palestinian negotiations could hardly have been said to have been on the front burner prior to this time). The United States still did not have a plan of its own to expedite troop withdrawals in Lebanon; and the Israelis added to Washington's dilemma by announcing on November 9 that they would refuse to begin talks with Lebanon on the withdrawal of their forces until the Lebanese government first agreed to discuss political normalization.[227] Habib thus made little progress during his trip—either on procedural or substantive issues.

While Washington was deemphasizing Reagan's September 1 initiative, King Hussein continued to support it. In an interview the king stated that he backed the Reagan Plan, although he wanted the United States to gain concessions from Israel on the settlement issue before he would join peace talks.[228] Almost simultaneously the World Zionist Organization announced plans to double the number of Jewish settlers on the West Bank in 1983 and to bring the total to 1.4 million by 2010.[229] Washington had no comment. Moreover, following the American congressional elections in early November, Begin declared that the results "strengthened his hand on the Mideast."[230] AIPAC reported that the elections returned more consistent supporters of Israel, while the lobby took credit for the defeat of one of Israel's most persistent critics, Illinois Representative Paul Findley.[231]

U.S.–Israeli relations warmed briefly toward the end of November when the two countries signed an agreement for an exchange of intelligence on the Lebanese war, although implementation of the agreement was held up for several months because of clauses Washington considered unacceptable. Israel wanted a stipulation requiring Israel's consent before Washington passed on information to America's NATO allies. The Pentagon also balked at a provision that Israeli experts accompany the captured equipment sent to the United States to observe any tests that were made and to be sure that the American conclusions would be shared with Israel.[232]

In December the pro-Israeli lobby intensified its pressure on the administration. With tensions between Israel and the United States escalating, Israel's American supporters became increasingly vocal in their displeasure over the Reagan administration's lack of full support for Israel's interests. Their successful maneuvers with Congress in November regarding the level and terms of repayment of aid to Israel had been viewed with great satisfaction in Israel, and the Israeli government encouraged the lobby to pressure the administration on both Lebanon and the Reagan Plan. One manifestation of that pressure was evident when the lobby induced 175 congressmen to sign a letter to President Reagan demanding that he deny advanced weapons to Jordan unless Jordan engaged in direct negotiations with Israel. This effort was in part a response to a statement Meese had made on December 15, that the United States would sell arms to Jordan regardless of whether or not it entered the peace process. The offer was meant to serve as an inducement to Jordan to join in negotiations, since Washington could not deliver on the settlement freeze.[233] The administration bowed to the pressure exerted by the lobby and announced on December 16 that it would be "unlikely" to sell Jordan any new jet fighter planes or mobile antiaircraft missiles unless King Hussein participated in direct talks with Israel.[234] While the announcement placated pro-Israeli groups, it further undermined United States credibility with the king (who was negotiating intensely with Arafat on the Reagan Plan) and with other moderate Arab states.

Nevertheless, by late December there were indications from Amman, Damascus, and from high-ranking PLO officials that after two months of talks with King Hussein, Arafat was pursuing a diplomatic strategy aimed at bringing the PLO into a position to take part in Reagan's initiative. The strategy involved an attempt on Arafat's part to establish a relationship with Hussein through which the two could coordinate efforts in a negotiation over the West Bank and Gaza and create a general framework for a linkage between Jordan and any future Palestinian entity. Reliable reports suggested that Arafat was prepared to accept a negotiating team made up of Jordanians and non-PLO Palestinians, although the precise nature of the Palestinian entity and its relationship with Jordan had yet to be agreed upon. Reportedly Arafat wanted the king to find out if Reagan was ready to give some assurances on Israeli withdrawal from the West Bank and Gaza before he committed the PLO to the negotiating process.[235]

King Hussein met President Reagan in Washington on December 21 and told the president that Israel's continuous settlement construction on the West Bank and America's inability or lack of will to prevent it were making his task of persuading the PLO to join the Reagan initiative virtually impossible. The king asked the president to end economic aid to Israel if it persisted in defying the president and built more settlements; a gesture of that nature, he argued, could then be presented to the Arab world as evidence of American sincerity. Reagan told the king that such a thing could never be done.[236] Hussein met Reagan again on December 23, and while there were no substantive differences in the discussions from those of December 21, the president later said that he was "cautiously optimistic" that Jordan would enter negotiations.[237]

On December 27 the first Israeli-Lebanese negotiations began at Khalde, Lebanon; the Israeli site for the alternating talks was to be Kiryat Shmoneh. The talks began in an atmosphere of uncertainty and without even an agreement on the agenda. American officials remained cool toward an immediate accord on normalization, rightly fearing that it would contribute to further internal strife in Lebanon, which could then open opportunities to Syria and the Soviet Union for renewed influence.[238] Israel's response to this U.S. concern was that the Israelis would work to stabilize Gemayel's government by continuing to arm and train the Phalangist militia. Israel had earlier attempted to disarm all the Muslim and leftist militias during its invasion of West Beirut; now Israel was proposing to unite the country not by building up the Lebanese army in which all confessions would have an equal role, but by strengthening one militia and having it impose its will. The United States disagreed with this approach and continued to attempt to develop the Lebanese army.

The Lebanese-Israeli Negotiations: January to May 1983

After the start of formal Lebanese-Israeli negotiations, several rounds of talks occurred, with Lebanon stressing troop withdrawal and Israel focusing on political normalization. The United States remained a mediator: it never put forth a set of proposals that reflected American objectives.

On January 5 President Reagan received Israeli President Yitzhak Navon and strongly reaffirmed the U.S. commitment to Israel's security. Reagan also announced that Habib would be sent back to the Middle East as part of another American initiative to break the Lebanon stalemate.[239] On January 13 Habib met with Begin in Israel and presented him with a letter from President Reagan asking the Israelis to demonstrate some flexibility. The president's request was rebuffed, and Habib made no progress on any of the issues under discussion.

At this point Washington officials seemed to become aware of the fact that there was a link between Israel's stalling in Lebanon and its rejection of the Reagan Plan. It was becoming obvious that King Hussein could not join the Reagan initiative as long as Israel remained in Lebanon: if the United States could not deliver on the withdrawal of Israeli forces from Lebanon, the Arabs could not realistically depend on Washington to bring about any positive Israeli movement on the West Bank. Israel made the fullest use of these factors in its strategy. On the one hand, Israel calculated that if it could keep Washington's attention focused on the Lebanese situation, the United States would be less likely to press it on the Reagan Plan. On the other hand, Israeli officials hoped that the stalemate in Lebanon and the rapid construction of new settlements on the West Bank would kill any Jordanian or Palestinian incentive to respond positively to the Reagan Plan, which would then free Israel from responsibility for the demise of the plan. Yet even as the Israeli strategy became clear to the administration, no consideration was given to the possibility of exerting pressure on Israel to withdraw from Lebanon or to halt the construction of new settlements.

In the meantime several other situations were occurring that considerably complicated the Middle East picture in the coming months. The two most important included (1) increased Soviet military assistance to Syria and (2) Israeli harassment of American marines.

By the first week of the new year Washington realized that the Soviet Union was rebuilding Syria's military, and on a far more sophisticated level than previously. The Soviets constructed two new bases in Syria in which they emplaced twelve SAM-5 missiles in addition to sending Syria ninety aircraft, mostly MIG-21's.[240] The major advantage of the SAM-5 is its range—about 155 miles—which put Israeli airfields and cities within target of the Syrian missiles. U.S. intelligence also reported that Syria would have two additional Soviet-armed divisions by 1984, with self-propelled artillery; most tanks would be T-72's, and there would be more commando battalions.[241] By March 3,000 to 4,000 Soviet personnel were in Syria to train the Syrians and staff the missile sites.[242] The supply of advanced Soviet weapons helped Syria achieve its goal of military parity with Israel. By early 1984, in contrast to Israeli calculations in 1982 of an emasculated Syria unable to contemplate a war with Israel for another ten years, Damascus emerged militarily more powerful than at any time in its modern history, and many in Israel feared that the Syrians might initiate a war to retake the Golan Heights.[243] Moreover, with its heightened military power came a resurgence of Syrian political influence, specifically in Lebanon, but also in the Arab world generally. The reemergence of Syria as a dominant regional power factor was directly linked to U.S. diplomacy, which in its surrender to Israel had increased the amount and intensity of Arab animosity to the United States and increased the attractiveness of what the Soviets had to offer.

Israeli harassment of American marines came to light early in January 1983. By the end of that month there had been at least five confrontations between the IDF and the marines. On January 22 Weinberger stated publicly that he was "very worried" that the recent events could "grow into something much more serious."[244] On February 1 a marine captain with a loaded pistol ordered IDF tanks away from a marine checkpoint in Beirut.[245] These confrontations came to a head in March when the commandant of the marine corps, General Robert H. Barrow, charged in a letter to Weinberger that "the Israeli troops are deliberately threatening the lives of American military personnel."[246] The commandant stated that the IDF had persistently "harassed, endangered and degraded" American marines and soldiers. He asserted that the Israeli forces "persist in creating serious incidents" and contended that the incidents had been "timed, orchestrated, and executed for obtuse Israeli political purposes." He stated that the incidents occurred "in life-threatening situations, replete with verbal degradation of the officers, their uniform and country" and that "incidents of this nature are the rule rather than the exception."[247] Israeli spokesmen disavowed the charges, but Pentagon officials disclosed previously confidential details of incidents in which American officers were fired on, barred at gunpoint from routine patrols, and insulted by Israelis. In a statement released on March 18, Weinberger firmly backed the commandant, saying the issue was of "very real concern" at the Pentagon.[248]

The apparent reason for the IDF's actions was Israel's displeasure at the U.S. refusal to engage in a joint military liaison in Lebanon. The United States had not wanted to appear as a partner in Israel's occupation, but Israel hoped to force the United States into just such a role and applied pressure through the lobby and other venues including the episodes on the ground to accomplish its purpose. Following the Barrow letter, Israel issued instructions on March 18 to its soldiers to avoid any further incidents with the marines, and they did indeed cease.[249] The United States did not accede to the Israeli desire for a joint military liaison in Lebanon, and nothing more was said about the humiliating and dangerous experiences of American military personnel at the hands of Israelis.

On February 23 President Reagan publicly indicated American displeasure with the pace of the Israeli-Lebanese talks and repeated his position that an Arab-Israeli resolution of the Palestinian issue would provide "the greatest security for Israel." He reiterated a statement made earlier that if Israel compromised in Lebanon, the United States would help to "guarantee" the Israeli-Lebanese frontier. The president added the inducement that the United States would be willing to enlarge the multinational force so that it could also patrol in southern Lebanon.[250] Still, no sanctions against Israel were even hinted at. February ended with no progress on the negotiations, and on March 1 Israeli officials flatly rejected a compromise that Habib had painstakingly worked out with the Lebanese.[251]

The administration undertook another initiative in mid-March, but it also failed. This effort involved a series of meetings between Reagan and Shamir on March 14 and 15. After the two days of talks officials said that some new "understandings" had been reached and that Israel and the United States agreed on many "principles"; but no progress had been made on how to implement either the "un-

derstandings" or the "principles."[252] On March 21 Defense Minister
Arens, in a fence-mending gesture, said that Israel was now willing
to share the intelligence gained and the technology and tactics used
in the war in Lebanon with the United States, without the previous
conditions that Israel had demanded, i.e., prior consultation before
sharing information with NATO allies and Israeli teams to supervise
the American analyses and inspection of data.[253] This gesture seemed
to portend an improvement in U.S.–Israeli relations; however, when
Israel again flatly refused on March 24 to accept a new set of compromise proposals brought by Habib, the discord intensified.

By the end of March it was apparent that the Reagan Plan was
likely to collapse entirely. In a March 19 interview King Hussein
emphasized that the United States had failed to create any conditions
whereby the Reagan Plan could serve as even a starting point for
negotiations. "Unfortunately," the king said, "the facts are that we
are way behind schedule on the American side in terms of the goals
set for the beginning of this year: total withdrawal of foreign forces
from Lebanon." In addition, Hussein sharply criticized the American
failure to stop Israel from creating new settlements on the West Bank.
Unless the United States could make headway on these two matters
with Israel, the king stated, "It is obvious that talks on a broader
settlement cannot get started. We are still hoping that the United
States will contribute towards enhancing its credibility by pressing
Israel for concessions."[254] Shortly after the king made these comments,
the Israeli government approved eight new settlements on the West
Bank in areas heavily populated with Palestinians. One of the settlements was intended to become a new Jewish city directly over-
looking the largest city on the West Bank, Nablus. The Israelis were
sending Hussein an unmistakable signal. Aware of the likely negative
decision of the king, Reagan made a gesture on March 31, which he
hoped Hussein would interpret as American firmness with Israel.
The president announced that until Israel withdrew its forces from
Lebanon, he would not permit the transfer to Israel of some seventy-
five F-16 fighter jets.[255] (Just a week before, the United States had
proceeded with the sale of 200 Sidewinder missiles to Israel as a
reward for its willingness to share information gathered during the
Lebanese war.[256]) Since the F-16's were not scheduled to be delivered
until 1985, the president's announcement was a symbolic rather than
a substantive measure against Israel.[257] Nevertheless, Israel was incensed, announcing that President Reagan had made "a regrettable
pronouncement" about the F-16's.[258] On April 13 Moshe Arens, the
new defense minister, declared that because of Reagan's decision to
withhold the F-16's, Israel had decided to "reduce Israeli dependence

on American weapons and to build up the domestic arms industry." Arens went on: "I'm afraid there is no precedent to such a statement in relations between Israel and the United States during 35 years. It has never happened that an American president has said that the supply of aid to which the United States obligated itself is conditioned on concessions on policy. Today Lebanon, tomorrow on another front."[259]

The Arens statement provides a telling commentary on U.S.–Israeli relations: Israel views the vast amounts of American military and economic support provided by the United States as an inherent obligation the United States owes to Israel, without any Israeli responsibility or concern for American interests—and Washington has acquiesced in this situation despite the unprecedented nature of the arrangement in international politics. The explanation for this phenomenon resides in the convergence of two factors: (1) the perception held by certain influential policymakers over the span of fifteen or so years that Israel was a strategic asset to U.S. interests and (2) the power of the pro-Israeli lobby on the domestic scene to reinforce that perception and to maintain the policies derived from it, even after the strategic asset thesis had been repeatedly demonstrated as fallacious.

To soothe the Israeli reaction to the F-16 announcement, the administration declared on April 17 that Israel could buy American-designed components for a new fighter-aircraft (the Lavi) that was to be built in Israel. In other words, Washington would now provide the means for Israel to develop an aircraft industry independent of, and potentially in competition with, the United States. Israel obviously could not develop a "domestic arms industry" and "reduce its dependence on American weapons" unless Washington provided the wherewithal for it to do so. The paradoxes in the situation seem endless. Nevertheless, Israel had been pressing Washington for quite a while on the issue and the timing of the president's statement was intended to take the sting out of the F-16 announcement and to encourage some Israeli flexibility in the Lebanese negotiations.[260] The Israelis were reportedly pleased, but made no concessions in the negotiations.

In a last-ditch effort to bring King Hussein to the negotiating table, the Reagan administration issued a statement on April 8 promising that if the king would come forward, the United States "would seek to bring about a halt in the building of Israeli settlements in the West Bank."[261] Administration officials said that Reagan had given Hussein private assurances in the past that he "would do what he could" to change Israeli settlement policy. The April 8 announcement was the first time the president made his pledge public. The officials added, however, that the administration was not planning to use economic or military sanctions to pressure Israel on the settlement issue. Shultz and Reagan were said to believe in "persuasion rather than coercion."[262]

The king may have put some trust in the president's insubstantial statement, but most Palestinian leaders did not. Despite the fact that King Hussein and Arafat had reached an agreement in their talks, the PLO executive committee, including Arafat's Fatah supporters (as well as the "radicals"), rejected the accord on the basis that it would not achieve even the least of the Palestinian objectives. Thus on April 10 Jordan formally rejected the Reagan initiative. The announcement from Amman said simply that Jordan had failed to reach an agreement with the PLO and would not enter American-sponsored talks on the basis of the plan proposed by President Reagan.[263]

The administration then attempted to shift the onus for the failure of the Reagan Plan to the Palestinians and the PLO. On April 12 President Reagan issued a statement saying: "Unless the Palestinian leadership makes 'a bold and courageous move' to break the Middle East deadlock, the Palestinian people will face continued frustration in meeting their national aspirations."[264] Secretary of State Shultz later called on the Palestinians to reject the PLO and find new leadership that was capable of taking and implementing a decision. There is an old phrase about power, Shultz said, "Either use it or lose it." Reagan and Shultz both urged the Arab regimes to circumvent the PLO, though none did.[265]

The Arab states and most Palestinians held the United States responsible for the failure of the Reagan Plan. In a report from the West Bank, David Shipler, a *New York Times* correspondent, noted that while some Palestinians felt that Israel was primarily responsible for discouraging negotiations by continuing construction of Jewish settlements in the territories, most blamed the United States for failing to force Israel to halt the settlements. For example, Mustafa Natshe, the acting mayor of Hebron, said: "The United States is powerful, but they don't use their power in the right way. Washington could have cut aid to Israel and forced a halt in settlement, in which case there would be more trust in the United States, and I think things would have been changed between King Hussein and the PLO."[266]

The Israelis were pleased at the demise of the Reagan initiative, and they, too, pointed to alleged Arab intransigence as the cause.[267] One is reminded, however, of Israel's immediate, categorical rejection of the plan, its defiant intensification of the settlement program, and of statements like Begin's in the Knesset on September 10, nine days after Reagan made the initiative public: "This plan, in my opinion died at its birth. Today it no longer exists, and certainly in the future, there will be no trace of it." Israel's actions in the subsequent months, and American inaction, made the prime minister's prediction a reality. Moreover, on April 17 in a televised speech Begin reiterated that there would never be a freeze on settlements. Israel, the prime minister said, has an "inalienable right" to hold and settle the territories that it has occupied since the 1967 war.[268]

By mid-April administration officials began to think that having excluded Syria from the Lebanese-Israeli withdrawal talks might not have been wise, especially in view of the fact that the United States had agreed to Israel's demand that Israel would withdraw only if there was a simultaneous Syrian withdrawal. Thus, the administration decided to make a "gesture" to Syria, and the president dropped a hint on April 17 that the United States might include Syria's demand for return of the Israeli-occupied (and annexed in 1981) Golan Heights in the context of an overall settlement. American officials, however, hastened to reassure outraged Israelis and pro-Israeli Americans that this was merely an affirmation of America's long-standing policy to support Resolution 242 and did not portend any new American initiative—a rather striking example of the contradiction between principle and practice in American diplomacy. The bid for Syrian support came in a letter from Reagan to Syrian President Hafez Assad, but it was at least eight months too late and had a strong tenor of insincerity.

On April 27 Shultz left for the Middle East to begin a round of shuttle diplomacy between Lebanon and Israel in another attempt to secure an agreement between these two nations. On May 6, eleven months after Israel invaded Lebanon and following four months of negotiations including twelve days of grueling personal diplomacy, Israel grudgingly assented to a Lebanese-Israeli accord worked out by Shultz and Habib, in which it achieved most of its demands and which significantly favored its interests. The Israeli cabinet voted to accept "in principle" this accord but couched its reply in conditional terms, requiring "clarifications" on several points and a separate agreement with the United States as a prerequisite to its signing.[269] Indeed, Israel again demanded a bilateral pact with Washington, involving more American concessions. The administration provided Israel with a Memorandum of Agreement on May 17, which "recognized" that despite the entente with Lebanon, Israel had the right of "self-defense" to retaliate against attacks by "terrorists" in Lebanon.[270] The memorandum was not made public and was intended primarily to cover all possible contingencies for Israeli military activity in Lebanon. Israel wanted to be sure that it would not encounter criticism from the United States if it undertook measures beyond its borders to "ensure its security." The memorandum also reaffirmed that the United States would not expect Israel to withdraw from Lebanon until Syria and the PLO did.[271] In addition, prior to the signing of the Israeli-Lebanese accord, Israel received a reward for its agreement to participate. After the cabinet decision the administration announced that the embargo on the seventy-five F-16 fighter planes would be lifted.[272] Israel and Lebanon signed the American-mediated agreement on May 17 and subsequently U.S.–Israeli relations warmed appreciably.

The agreement was widely depicted as a major foreign policy success for both the United States and Israel, but it was seriously flawed. By the canons of international law, the treaty was without validity, since it was imposed under the duress of Israeli occupation. More important, the agreement amounted to a permanent compromise of Lebanese sovereignty by giving Israel specific military-security rights in southern Lebanon. It provided for normalization of relations between the two countries to begin six months after the agreement was signed; the start of the negotiations, however, was not contingent on Israeli withdrawal. Indeed, under the agreement Israel was not required to withdraw from Lebanon until after the Syrians and the PLO troops in the Bekaa Valley and Tripoli area had withdrawn, leaving open the possibility that it might "legally" never do so.[273] (Israel did not withdraw until the summer of 1985, and then only because of an intense resistance that was mounted by the indigenous Lebanese against the Israeli occupation. The Syrian and PLO forces remained.) Moreover, in addition to these shortcomings, the exclusion of Syria assured the failure of the accord. (On March 5, 1984, under pressure from Damascus, the Lebanese government abrogated the agreement and shortly thereafter forced Israel to close a political liaison office it had established in East Beirut. The cancellation of the Lebanese-Israeli agreement was a serious setback to Israel's objective of increasing its influence with the Lebanese government. More important, it was a resounding defeat for the United States in the Middle East.)

Subsequent to the announcement of the Israeli-Lebanese joint accord, Syria had notified senior Lebanese officials that it objected to virtually every major clause of the understanding. Syria's state-run radio said: "Any reading of the draft agreement shows that Israel has achieved military and political goals that it failed to achieve through its invasion of Lebanon."[274] Shultz traveled to Damascus to attempt to convince the Syrians to accept the accord, but without success. After meeting with Assad, Shultz acknowledged: "We recognize there is a tremendous amount of work still to be done." Nevertheless Shultz presided over the signing of the agreement and then became bitterly resentful of the Arabs when it collapsed. Ghassan Tueni, a former permanent ambassador of Lebanon to the United Nations who served as general coordinator during the Lebanese-Israeli negotiations, commented perceptively about other weaknesses in the agreement: "The Lebanese-Israeli Agreement has proclaimed the 'end of the state of war' where war did not really exist: between Lebanon and Israel. It has ironically increased the risks of war where war did exist: between Syria and Israel."[275] It should be added that given the internal Lebanese political situation, the agreement would inevitably fuel the conflict between the "victorious" Phalange and the various "vanquished" majority groups that objected to the new Israeli-imposed, U.S.–backed, order in Lebanon.[276]

Within three months after the signing of the entente, Lebanon was plunged into renewed civil war. The Druze and the Shi'ites were determined to reject Phalange dominance and found support in Syria. Eventually the United States was drawn into the civil conflict, when in September 1983 it began to exercise military fire power on behalf of the Gemayel government against the opposition groups. America's direct involvement came in the wake of an Israeli pull-back from its postwar occupation position in the Shouf to a more secure, defensible line along the Awali River. After the United States exercised military force—including bombardment from the largest guns on the navy's warships against the Lebanese groups in opposition to the Gemayel regime, the marine headquarters became the target of a bombing attack on October 23, 1983, in which 264 marines were killed. Within six months, by March 1984, the United States withdrew its "peace-keeping" contingent entirely from Beirut, marking the collapse of American influence in Lebanon and the plummeting of U.S. credibility throughout the Arab world. The demise of American influence was paralleled by the resurgence of Syrian influence, backed by Soviet power. By the time Israel withdrew from Lebanon in 1985, after having created a new surrogate force—the South Lebanese Army—to police southern Lebanon on it's behalf, Israel's policies against the Lebanese had created so many enemies among the local population (the same people who had welcomed Israel as liberators in 1982), as well as fueling the Islamic fundamentalist movement in that country, that many in Israel rightly feared that the border with Lebanon would be more insecure after a pullout than it had been before 1982.

Conclusion

The United States supported Israel more completely during the Israeli invasion of Lebanon in 1982 and in the period preceding the war than at any other time in the history of their relationship. This unequivocal support resulted primarily from the Reagan/Haig belief that U.S interests and Israeli interests were parallel in the Middle East, and that whatever objectives and policies Israel chose to pursue, particularly if they were couched in the guise of containing Soviet expansion and Soviet-inspired terrorism, American interests would be served. This was an enormous misperception, as the Lebanon debacle demonstrated. However, when in the war's aftermath, American policymakers confronted the divergence between U.S. and Israeli objectives and attempted to formulate policies that served American interests, the power of the pro-Israeli lobby thwarted every effort, resulting in the failure of the American policy and the triumph of Israel's interests at the expense of the United States.

The Lebanese situation illustrated in the most profound and dramatic way the extensive divergence of interest between Israel and the United States and also the myriad ways in which Israel contravenes American interests in the Middle East. However, Washington does not appear to have learned from this experience. There has been no Lebanese Syndrome to parallel the Vietnam Syndrome, and the dominant perception in policymaking circles remains that Israel serves American interests in the Middle East. The increasingly close U.S.-Israeli relationship in the three years following the Lebanon catastrophe is testament both to the strength of the dominant misperception and to the power of the pro-Israeli forces to reinforce the perception and to ensure U.S. support for Israel's objectives.

As in the preceding chapter, the nature of the event analyzed herein focused the discussion on the Executive branch. While this perspective is obviously useful for understanding the U.S.-Israeli relationship, it obscures both the prominence of the role played by Congress on Middle Eastern issues by this time and the enormous influence of pro-Israeli forces in Congress. The final chapter should serve to restore this balance and to illustrate the importance of congressional input in the formation of policy and the relationship between the electoral process and the policy formation process.

CHAPTER EIGHT

ISRAEL AS A STRATEGIC ASSET
The Israeli Lobby and Its Efforts

Introduction

This book has demonstrated a number of significant distortions in the common wisdom concerning Israel and the Arab-Palestinian-Israeli conflict and their bearing upon U.S.–Israeli relations. One of the most important concerns the continuous threat to Israel's survival that allegedly existed from 1948. In reality, Israel itself has constituted a serious security threat to the Arab states, repeatedly violating the territorial integrity of its neighbors with military raids (termed "reprisals" and "preemptive" strikes) and full-scale invasions. Except during the 1948 war no Arab state launched a regular attack on the territory of Israel (in 1973 Egypt and Syria fought on and for their national territory seized by Israel in 1967). The incursions on Israeli territory have been carried out by Palestinian guerrillas, sometimes with the approval of an Arab regime, usually without it, and often in spite of attempts by Arab governments to prevent them.

A second misperception concerns the nature or causes of the protracted Arab-Palestinian-Israeli conflict. The root cause of the conflict is not Arab state aggression against Israel; it is the unresolved question of Palestine. Israel exists at the expense of the Palestinians: their homes and land were usurped, and they were transformed into stateless refugees as a result of the creation of the Jewish state. Israel, however, has persisted in denying the existence of a Palestinian people, has refused to consider the establishment of the Palestinian state recommended in the 1947 partition resolution (Resolution 181) that legitimized its own existence, and has refused to engage in any diplomatic or political negotiations with the legitimate representatives of the Palestinians—the PLO. What is more, Israel has succeeded in preventing the United States from acknowledging the Palestinian right to self-determination and from including the PLO in any Middle Eastern diplomacy, at the same time successfully depicting "Palestinian" as a synonym for "terrorist." While rightly deploring all acts of Palestinian terrorism, one should also recall that Zionists themselves used terrorism during their struggle to establish Israel, in one memorable instance at Deir Yassin; and Israeli *state* terrorism— mainly implemented from American-made F-16's—has far exceeded in destructive magnitude and civilian casualties all acts of Palestinian terrorism. It is apparent then that Israel's refusal to recognize the Palestinians as a people or to acknowledge their right to self-determination stems not from the fact that some Palestinians have engaged in acts of terrorism, but rather from the concern that to do so might call into question the legitimacy of Israel's "right" to a Jewish state in Palestine. Moreover, defining Palestinians as terrorists is part of a process of dehumanization that makes the denial of Palestinian human rights more palatable to those who persist in the abrogation of those rights.

Although undeniably the Palestinians and the Arab states did not welcome the creation of Israel, they have come to accept the reality of its existence and have demonstrated their willingness to live in peace with it on the basis of the 1947 partition resolution and the 1967 borders. (Egypt's willingness to conclude a peace with Israel that negated Resolution 181 was quickly shown to be a serious error.) It seems clear that if Israel wanted to live in peace and security in the Middle East community, it could do so. However, after eighteen years of a military occupation over the 1.3 million inhabitants of the West Bank and Gaza, including an intensive settlement and colonization program, the annexation of Jerusalem and the Golan, the continuous denial of basic Palestinian human rights, and ongoing attacks on Arab states, one can only conclude that Israel—today the fourth most powerful military in the world and possessed of a significant nuclear capability—does not want peace in any meaningful sense. There seems no way such a situation can accord with American interests or objectives in the Middle East. How can an Israel, committed to policies that a priori assure the perpetuation of regional instability, be considered a strategic asset to American interests?

Nevertheless, in spite of this fundamental contradiction, the American government has provided the Jewish state with extraordinary support. The magnitude of U.S. support for Israel—militarily, politically, economically, and diplomatically—goes beyond any traditional relationship between states in the international system. The partnership cannot be explained in the context of classic great power/ proxy relationships in which the great power provides the surrogate with complete economic and political support, while the surrogate acts to promote the interests and further the influence of the great power. In the U.S.–Israeli relationship the United States has provided

absolute support, but Israel has repeatedly engaged in actions that
have contravened American interests—often significantly harming
them. At the same time the relationship in and of itself has inhibited
the United States from maximizing its most important interests, i.e.,
the containment of Soviet influence and the assurance of Western
access to Middle Eastern raw materials, markets, and investment
opportunities.

Nor can the relationship between Israel and the United States be
considered an "alliance" as that concept is generally understood in
international politics—for example, in the way the United States
and Great Britain are allies. George Ball summarizes succinctly the
contradictions in the alleged U.S.–Israeli alliance. The modern meaning of an alliance, Ball notes, is "a coalition of nations with substantial
common objectives, at least with regard to a specific geographic area,
that consult closely and seek, in concert, to advance and protect their
mutual security interests."[1] However, Israel

has never been prepared to deal with the United States in the manner and
spirit expected of an ally. It does not share with us, as its primary objective,
the establishment of enduring peace in the area, except on its own expansionist terms. It does not—and is not willing to—consult with us or seek
to concert a common policy. It persistently deceives the United States as
to its intended moves, often to the detriment of United States plans and
interests. It ignores the restrictions placed upon the use of United States
military assistance. It consistently demands an expanding subsidy, while
unabashedly using part of the funds to finance policies and practices we
deplore. The central flaw in our relations with Israel . . . [is that] . . . not
only has Israel, from the beginning, refused to work with us on a common
strategy, but Israeli leaders have repeatedly taken the United States by
surprise, launching military adventures that have stultified our diplomacy
and upset our plans and interests. . . . Since then [1956] Israel has con-
temptuously flouted the United Nations, counting on the United States to
use its veto in the Security Council to save it from censure and economic
sanctions.[2]

Ball further stresses Israel's frequent violation of its contractual commitments to the United States through its flaunting of the restrictions
placed on the use of U.S. weapons.[3]

It is often argued that the U.S.–Israeli relationship is based on the
common democratic political cultures of the two countries. Yet while
the United States is a genuinely secular democracy with explicit
constitutional guarantees of equality before the law and a tradition
of equality of opportunity for all people in the context of a pluralist
political culture, Israel is a self-consciously Jewish state in which
Jewish religious law tends increasingly to determine the social laws
of the land. Moreover, while its political institutions are democratic,
Israel is, as Seth P. Tillman has observed, "a sectarian democracy

made possible by the forcible expulsion and continuing subjugation of the native Palestinian population, for all but a small minority of whom—those living as Israeli citizens—Israeli democracy is a bitter irony."[4] However, even Arabs who have Israeli citizenship are not only seriously discriminated against but are also denied full protection under the law.[5] The president of the American-Israeli Civil Liberties Coalition, Philippa Strum, commented on the situation in *Reform Judaism:*

> Israeli Arabs . . . are not permitted to serve in the armed forces . . . which not only precludes their sharing an otherwise universal citizenship experience, but also disqualifies them for such armed service–linked government benefits as government-backed mortgages, government-backed scholarships, and the regular welfare payments all families receive per child. . . . Numerous statistics indicate that Arab municipalities receive far less government funds than do Jewish municipalities for roads, schools, water supply, sewage, etc. Most land in Israel is owned by the Jewish National Fund, which rents it on long-term leases; it will not rent land to Arabs. Most Arab land within Israel proper has been confiscated by the state.[6]

Moreover, Israel has no constitution and no bill of rights; there are no domestic civil courts; there is state censorship over the electronic media; and no newspapers or magazines may be published without a government license.

What then, one must ask, is the basis of the relationship?

The United States has realized two advantages from its close association with Israel: the collaboration between the Israeli intelligence service (the Mossad) and the Central Intelligence Agency, and Israel's battlefield testing of American weapons. The cooperation between the intelligence services has been extensive—throughout Europe, Africa, Asia, and Central and South America as well as the Middle East. Moreover, its frequent military engagements have enabled Israel to test the effectiveness of American arms, including cluster and phosphorus bombs, electronic radar jamming devices, and most other highly sophisticated American weaponry. But beyond these two useful services, it is difficult to see what benefits the United States has derived from its sponsorship of, and partnership with, Israel.[7]

A brief summation of Israel's national interests and foreign policy objectives highlights the contradictions between Israeli and American interests. Israel's major foreign policy objectives have included:

(1) Ratification or legitimization of the territorial status quo at any given time (although Israel has always refused to delimit its own borders) plus expansion of the territory allotted in the 1947 partition resolution to an undefined territorial space that would provide "national security." Indeed, Israel's definition of national security has

frequently been expressed in terms of territory. Israel began expanding in 1948 and grew more committed to such expansion as time went on, until its objectives openly included the extension of Israeli sovereignty over Jerusalem, the West Bank, and Gaza (that is, the totality of historic Palestine) as well as the Golan Heights. In addition, Israel has attempted to extend its control over southern Lebanon and occupied major parts of Egypt for twelve years. Such expansionist policies have kept the Middle East in a constant state of instability and turmoil and helped to afford Moscow countless opportunities to broaden its influence.

(2) The seeking of foreign aid in the most extensive quantities possible, both from private sources (Jews living in the diaspora) and public sources (governments), so that Israel could simultaneously encourage the immigration and facilitate the absorption of Jews from around the world, attain a position of unchallenged military superiority in the region, and pursue economic development (including the attainment of a comfortable enough life for its citizens that Jewish emigration would be discouraged). Between 1949 and 1984 the United States provided Israel with $28.1 billion in military and economic aid, of which over half ($14.6 billion) was given in outright grants.[8] Mohamed El Khawas and Samir Abed Rabbo illustrate the magnitude of the combined public and private aid from the United States:

Official United States aid, however, is by no means the sole source of American assistance received by Israel. Contributions from individuals, private institutions and the sale of Israeli government bonds account for more than $1 billion a year, totaling more than $14 billion between 1948 and 1984. Other forms of aid to Israel, though not as well publicized . . . include: direct American investment in Israeli economic activities (United States investments constitute approximately 55 percent of total foreign investments in Israel), the extension of credit facilities by the United States Import-Export Bank (which exceeded $1.1 billion between 1949 and 1983), the exemption of Israeli products from United States import duties (thus saving Israel the duty on more than $1 billion worth of products annually), free access to highly advanced technical know-how, used primarily to manufacture military hardware that eventually competes with American products in foreign markets, and finally the transfer of billions of dollars, initially deposited in United States branches of Israeli banks.

Keeping both official and unofficial aid in mind then, total assistance received by Israel from United States sources is estimated by some experts to lie between $9 and $10 billion annually. In per capita terms, direct American aid to Israel exceeds $1,000 per person and amounts to more than $10 million per day, much of which is paid for by the United States taxpayer and funneled away from needed social programs for the American poor and unemployed. Direct and indirect annual aid is actually more than $2,000 per person, greater than the average per capita income in the Arab world.[9]

El Khawas and Rabbo thus show that American citizens have sacrificed so that Israeli citizens could enjoy a good life at the same time that the Israeli government pursued policies that contravened America's interests. In the spring of 1984, with Israel's inflation rate over 400 percent, and with Israelis enjoying the highest standard of living they had ever experienced, the U.S. Congress, which had already slashed social programs for all Americans, voted Israel the largest amount of economic and military aid ever provided—and all in outright grants.

(3) Preservation of the ethnic purity of the Jewish state. This has involved both preventing the return of Palestinian Arab refugees and encouraging the emigration of those Arabs living in areas of "Eretz Israel," particularly the West Bank, which Israel wanted to incorporate into the state. Israel's refusal to facilitate the repatriation of the Palestinians or to provide compensation for their properties, as mandated by U.N. Resolution 194 (before 1967) and the nature of its military occupation and settlement and colonization policies (since 1967) have been major sources of conflict in the region.

(4) The encouragement of Jewish immigration. This is a distinct and critical policy objective. However, this policy, in the context of Israel's policy toward the Palestinians, has also been a prominent cause of regional enmity.

(5) The pursuit of national security through aggressive militarism expressed in the policies of "preemptive" and "retaliatory" raids as well as full-scale wars. Force has been considered the best overall means to attain desired territorial and political objectives. However, like its expansionism, Israel's militarism has engendered insecurity among the Arabs and impelled them to make common cause with Moscow. Moreover, this policy has been the most important factor in perpetuating regional instability.

The contradictions between Israeli and U.S. interests are apparent. Nevertheless, American policy toward Israel has been predicated at least since 1967 (and to some extent as early as 1960) on the assumption that Israel serves American interests in the Middle East by acting as an extension of American power. Several factors have contributed to the growth and institutionalization of this perception—fallacious though it is: (1) unwise and inept diplomacy on Washington's part (its inability to devise constructive policies toward the Arab states; its alignment with regional elites lacking popular bases of support, such as the monarchy and Nuri Said in Iraq; its refusal to accept and accommodate itself to Arab nationalism; and its complete failure in dealing with Gamal Abdul Nasser), which resulted in Washington's alienation from the most influential and viable forces and groups in the Arab world; (2) the promotion of the idea of Israel as a strategic asset in elite circles by individuals with access to power, such as Walter and Eugene Rostow and Henry Kissinger; (3) faulty analysis of political reality by important decision-makers, for instance, Lyndon Johnson's misjudgments in 1967; and (4) the enormous efforts of pro-Israeli groups. While the success of the domestic pro-Israeli campaign has been directly related to the *convergence* of its interests with elite perceptions, an analysis of the organizational infrastructure of this "lobby" and the various means it has used to achieve its ends is instructive in and of itself. Thus, the final chapter examines the role of the pro-Israeli lobby in the formation of American Middle East policy.

Political Culture and Popular Perceptions

The role of the pro-Israeli lobby has been alluded to throughout this book—for example, its efforts at forming alliances with crucial sectors in American society such as the labor movement; its success in influencing public opinion; and its ability to tie Israel into the American preoccupation with Communism. (Indeed, as Stephen D. Isaacs noted in *Jews and American Politics:* "Jewish activists on the Hill used the anti-Communist tool broadly for maintaining support for Israel," and "Jewish power has succeeded of late because of Americans' fear of the Soviet Union."[10])

The existence of an intensely emotionally committed and active group of pro-Israeli individuals in the United States has given Israel a tremendous advantage in the effort to win the hearts and minds of Americans. Their effort has been assisted by the reservoir of American guilt and obligation that has existed in the wake of the Holocaust and the concomitant lack of understanding Americans have had for Arabs, due partly to the ineffectiveness of Arab efforts at communicating their perspective, but also to traditional American ignorance of and hostility toward the Arab world, Islam, and the Orient in general. Indeed, Americans have tended to see Israel as a culturally similar "Western" state surrounded by a sea of feudal, "foreign," barbarians. However, as with the perceptions about Israel's democracy, the beliefs about Israeli-American cultural similarity evidence considerable dissemblance from reality. One important reason for the maintenance of this image has been the continued Ashkenazi (i.e., European) dominance in virtually all elite sectors of Israeli society over the majority Oriental/Sephardim Jewish ethnic element.[11]

Moreover, the pro-Israeli sympathy of Americans and the favorable images of Israel that abound in this country are not entirely innate: they have been carefully cultivated by pro-Israeli groups in a myriad of ways. One of the most successful tactics—perhaps *the* most successful—has been the constant invocation of the Holocaust and the specter of anti-Semitism whenever criticism of Israel or organized Jewish activity arises. Pro-Israeli groups have also been able to exercise a critical role in determining the parameters—"the outer limits of respectable debate"—on issues related to Israel, Palestine, and the Arab-Palestinian-Israeli conflict. The efforts of pro-Israeli groups in defining "responsible discourse" have been particularly apparent in the media (films, television, radio, newspapers, and popular literature), which have consistently accorded Israel favorable treatment while keeping major issues concerning the Jewish state out of the realm of public discussion. With some notable exceptions (such as the television coverage by some reporters of the Israeli invasion of Lebanon), the media have essentially functioned to transmit and buttress official policies on U.S.–Israeli relations, to reinforce commonly held American stereotypes of the Arab world, to idealize Israel and exempt it from criticism, and to suppress (usually through self-censorship) information and debate on critical issues, such as levels of aid to Israel and the origins of the Palestinian question. It is most likely that if the "informed public" (that segment of the population—about 20 percent—of interested, concerned citizens who keep abreast of foreign affairs) was presented with minimal facts in a relevant context, it would assuredly question Washington's policies regarding Israel and the Arab world. The activities of pro-Israeli groups are not the sole reason for the pro-Israeli orientation of the media and public opinion,[12] but their efforts cannot be minimized. Several of the activities of such groups in this somewhat amorphous area are illustrative.

For example, the American-Israel Public Affairs Committee (AIPAC) has become increasingly concerned about the efforts of Arabs, especially Palestinians, to communicate directly to the American public, particularly in the universities, and it has undertaken an intensive campaign to ensure that the Israeli prism for perceiving the Middle East continues to predominate in American universities. Since 1980 AIPAC has run a Political Leadership Development Program for pro-Israeli student activists. This has involved (as of June 1983) 350 campus workshops in fifty states and some 5,500 students. Those attending the workshops are made familiar with pro-Israeli and anti-Arab arguments and are taught how to organize on campus to counter pro-Palestinian activities. Special attention is given to influencing campus media. An AIPAC guide on "Making More Ef-

fective Use of the Student Newspaper" notes that this valuable resource has not been properly exploited and offers advice on how to
maximize its effectiveness. Pro-Israeli activists are encouraged to join
the staff of newspapers, if possible, or to find a sympathizer who will.
AIPAC also concentrates on monitoring "anti-Israeli" speakers on
university and college campuses. Tapes and notes are collected, and
files are compiled. AIPAC can thus send summaries of a speaker's
standard points and arguments, a description of his/her question and
answer style, and a list of potentially damaging quotations from
earlier talks to activists in advance. AIPAC also draws up questions
that can be asked and helps plan strategies suited to each campus.[13]

Professor Noam Chomsky of the Massachusetts Institute of Technology has discussed the contents of a file that the B'nai B'rith (the
Jewish anti-defamation league) keeps on him (which he received from
an unnamed source):

It's just like an FBI file—150 pages of material, clips from newspapers
and inter-office memos saying I was going to show up at this or that place,
surveillance of talks I have given, characterization of what was said in the
talks (often falsified . . .). All this material goes into a central source. Then
when I give a talk somewhere, my file will be given to the appropriate
local group, who will be able to dig through it, and come up with statements
that I allegedly made at some time during the last 15 years to be publicized
in unsigned pamphlets. The file is also sent to people with whom I have
public debates so that they can extract fabricated defamatory material from
it. This is done, incidentally, under a tax-free grant to a religious and
educational organization.[14]

AIPAC also suggests means of countering "pro-Palestinian" speakers on campus including packing the meeting with pro-Israelis, arranging a meeting to coincide with the talk, holding a pro-Israeli
meeting immediately beforehand, and using the event to leaflet and
advertise a forthcoming pro-Israeli event. It also tries to build up
political strength on campus that can be used to block pro-Palestinian
activities. This may involve getting friends of Israel into the student
union or academic senate, if these bodies control the booking of
rooms. Otherwise, AIPAC advises that disruptive protests can be
organized, which will discourage the college administration from
arranging future pro-Palestinian speakers.[15]

In addition, AIPAC publishes "guides" or "enemies lists" to advise
its supporters of who is and who is not a "friend of Israel." One
written by Jonathan S. Kessler and Jeff Schwaber, *The AIPAC College
Guide: Exposing the Anti-Israel Campaign on Campus* (Washington,
D.C.: AIPAC Papers on United States–Israeli Relations, 1984; 196
pp.), focuses on individual colleges and universities. Another, a 154-
page publication, *The Campaign to Discredit Israel,* describes in

minute detail twenty-one organizations and thirty-eight individuals that AIPAC has labeled "enemies" of Israel. Those singled out include prominent professors, former diplomats and congressmen, and educational and charitable organizations. A companion to the latter AIPAC publication is a 118-page book, *Pro-Arab Propaganda in America: Vehicles and Voices,* published by the Anti-Defamation League of B'nai B'rith, which similarly details forty-eight organizations and thirty-four individuals. In November 1984 the Middle East Studies Association (MESA), the largest and most prestigious organization in the United States of scholars, academics and professionals concerned with the Middle East, passed a unanimous resolution at its annual meeting, condemning this blacklisting campaign and calling on AIPAC and the B'nai B'rith to "disavow and refrain from" soliciting "unbalanced information on students, faculty, and other parties on American university campuses."[16]

The primary accusation leveled against the groups and individuals listed in the B'nai B'rith and AIPAC books is that they are "pro-Palestinian" or "pro-PLO." Pro-Israeli groups have succeeded in associating the words "Palestinian" and "PLO" with terrorism in the minds of Americans; then with techniques reminiscent of the McCarthy era, they smear their opposition with the label "pro-PLO." Moreover, individuals who do take public positions in support of the PLO often find themselves blacklisted or professionally damaged. For example, pro-Israeli advocates in Boston were able to bring about the cancellation of a contract the Boston Symphony Orchestra had signed with the Academy Award–winning actress Vanessa Redgrave (a vocal supporter of the PLO) to narrate five performances of Igor Stravinsky's *Oedipus Rex* in April 1982.[17]

Redgrave lost $31,000 in the cancellation and was unable to find work for eighteen months thereafter—unemployment that she alleges was related to a blacklisting campaign. A Boston court did not uphold this charge, but Redgrave is appealing the decision. At the time the symphony cancelled her contract, it claimed to fear that violence would erupt at performances because of threats by the Jewish Defense League. In testimony during Redgrave's suit against the orchestra, however, it became apparent that the contract had been cancelled because an orchestra trustee inferred that Jewish financial backing for the symphony would cease if Redgrave were allowed to perform. In a sworn statement trustee Irving Rabb said, "I thought this would be a devastating thing from the point of view of fund raising." Rabb also claimed that he had never heard of specific threats against the symphony and was never told of threats by the JDL.[18]

The pressure that pro-Israeli groups can exert on the media is usually subtle, but can become overt. For instance, in the aftermath of the 1982 war in Lebanon a new group calling itself Americans for a Safe Israel (AFSI) brought an extraordinary amount of pressure to bear on NBC over its coverage of the war. In June 1983 AFSI produced an hour-long documentary, directed by Peter E. Goldman, entitled "NBC in Lebanon: A Study of Media Misrepresentation." Subsequently, the group published a monograph by Edward Alexander, *NBC's War in Lebanon: The Distorting Mirror* (New York: AFSI, 1983) and then filed suit twice, in 1983 and in 1984, with the Federal Communications Commission in an attempt to deny license renewal to WNBC-TV, the NBC station in New York. In addition, it filed petitions with the FCC to deny license renewals to other NBC affiliates in New England, New York, and New Jersey. NBC says that it stands by its coverage of the war in every respect, and both the *Columbia Journalism Review* and the *Washington Journalism Review* support the network. Yet it seems doubtful that this kind of pressure does not have some effect, however subconscious, in influencing media coverage of Israel.

A February 1982 ABC-TV report, "Under the Israeli Thumb," describing Israeli policies in the occupied territories, led to a campaign by pro-Israeli organizations and individuals attempting to "prove" that the documentary was the product of intimidation by the PLO against journalists in Beirut.[19] The major protagonist in the crusade was Ze'ev Chafets, a former head of the Israeli press office in Jerusalem under the Likud government who, according to Robert I. Friedman, "fed his views to *New Republic* publisher Martin Peretz, who dutifully published them in editorials and news stories."[20] In addition, the *New York Times* published an interview with Chafets by its Jerusalem bureau chief, David Shipler, in which the former Israeli official repeated his allegations. The *Times* edited some parts of the interview, and Chafets, outraged by the cuts, "complained loudly in letters and phone calls to editors in the United States until a chastened *Times* reported the incident."[21] Subsequently, Chafets published a book with William Morrow, *Double Vision: How the Press Distorts America's View of the Middle East,* in which he argues that the American press has been unfair to Israel while serving as little more than a public relations agency for the PLO.[22]

Another pro-Israeli organization that was formed after 1982 to monitor the media is the Committee for Accuracy in Middle East Reporting (CAMERA). In November 1983 the National Association of Arab-Americans (NAAA) attempted to undertake a media campaign opposing the levels of aid to Israel and the effort by Congressman Clarence Long to win congressional approval for Israel to spend

U.S. grant dollars to develop a fighter plane (the Lavi) of its own. All fifteen radio stations in Baltimore refused to run the NAAA commercials, although four stations in Washington did. Those four stations were subject to intense pressure from CAMERA and other pro-Israeli groups to stop the commercials. Station WTOP-AM ran the advertisement for two weeks, then refused to run an updated version; it subsequently gave CAMERA free air time to respond to NAAA's message. In December 1984 NAAA again attempted to mount a radio campaign, this time in New York, questioning the increasing amount of aid the United States gives to Israel as social services to Americans are cut. Anticipating retaliation from listeners and advertisers, twenty out of twenty-one stations refused to air the commercial. Mario Mazza of WNCN-NY stated: "I think it would have been programmatic and public relations suicide."[23] The one station that did run it, WMCA-NY, received hundreds of angry calls and letters and lost significant amounts of money as advertising was cancelled.[24]

The entertainment industry has traditionally contributed to the general American sympathy for Israel through popular films and television docudramas such as *Exodus, The Chosen, Golda,* and *Entebbe,* among others. No film was ever made reflecting the Palestinian perspective until Costa Gavras's *Hanna K.* in 1983. Gavras, well known for films such as *Z* and *Missing,* attempted to depict the Palestinian-Israeli conflict in human terms. Hanna Kaufmann, a child of Holocaust survivors and an American-Jewish immigrant to Israel, was a court-appointed lawyer assigned to defend a Palestinian, Salim Bakri, accused of terrorism and infiltration; Bakri claimed that he was trying to regain possession of his family house. Hanna saved him from a jail sentence, but he was deported to Jordan. Salim eventually returned, was jailed for illegal immigration, and again asked for her services. As Hanna investigated his story, she discovered that his family house was now a tourist attraction in Kfar Rimon, a settlement built and lived in by Russian Jews. Salim's village of Kufr Rumaneh had disappeared except for a few stones and trees. The state's attorneys offered Hanna a deal: if she dropped proceedings, they would arrange for Salim to become a South African citizen, and he could then return to Israel and try to get his property back. Hanna was confronted with the fact that one legacy of the Holocaust was the dispossession of the Palestinians while her colleagues attempted to persuade her of the merits of the arrangement for Salim with the argument that Israel must be "defended" even if Palestinians are denied their rights.[25] The film contained a number of aesthetic problems and Hanna's personal life at times overshadowed and muddled the political aspects of the story. Nevertheless, as Edward Said, Parr Professor of English Literature at Columbia University, commented: "As a political as well as a cinematic intervention, then *Hanna K.* is a statement of great and I believe, lasting significance."[26] Unlike previous Costa Gavras films, *Hanna K.* did not turn on emotions and attempted to present the complexity of a multifaceted situation without Gavras's usual heavy hand.

Pro-Israeli groups were extremely concerned about *Hanna K.* and its potential for depicting the Palestinian issue in a sympathetic light. An internal memorandum was circulated by the B'nai B'rith advising members that if the film played in their cities, there were certain comments that could be made in the local press. Attached to the memorandum were two sets of prepared criticisms, written by Shimon Samuels and Abba Cohen from the French headquarters of the B'nai B'rith, outlining the arguments supporters of Israel should make against the film.

Hanna K. opened in several American cities and played for a short time to virtually universally negative reviews (where it was reviewed at all), then was abruptly pulled from circulation by the American distributors of the film. One Chicago distributor commented off-the-record that while it could not be proven that the film was pulled because of political pressure, distributors "understood" that the film was unacceptable to supporters of Israel, who have many friends and are themselves important in the entertainment industry. Michelle Ray-Gavras, the director's wife, commented: "In the United States, a Universal tour that was to have encompassed New York, Boston, Washington, Chicago, and San Francisco was dropped at the last moment and a two-week run in New York substituted. Similar notices were received. Costa Gavras gave scores of interviews to journalists and critics and began to notice a common thread. 'They would come in and say that while they didn't have political objections, a friend or relative had seen the film and thought it was anti-Israeli. After a while we took side bets as to whether the writer we were about to see would have a cousin, sister, neighbor, etc., who'd spotted an anti-Israeli angle!' "[27] Costa Gavras personally advertised the film in the *New York Times* at a cost of $50,000 after Universal refused to. Universal even forbade the director the use of advertisements that had been prepared for the film.[28]

It is not uncommon for views that run counter to the conventional wisdom to be suppressed. The experience of two authors is illustrative. James Ennes, the officer-of-the-deck on the bridge of the *USS Liberty* in June 1967, wrote a book detailing the results of his twelve-year investigation into the Israeli attack on his ship. *Assault on the Liberty* was published by Random House in 1980, received excellent reviews from both military and civilian critics, and then was targeted by pro-Israeli groups who wanted to suppress it. AIPAC and the B'nai B'rith coordinated the nationwide campaign. Ennes himself has said:

> Would-be buyers from New York, Baltimore, and San Francisco wrote to tell me that when, as a last resort, they phoned my publisher to place orders, they were told falsely that Random House had never published such a book, or had suspended publication to avoid a lawsuit. When Random House traced a large order at my request, they discovered that all orders from a major Los Angeles wholesaler had simply "vanished." Ostensibly, all orders for *Assault on the Liberty* had been "lost." In Washington, D.C., the manager of a popular bookstore told me that my book had been unavailable for months following several important reviews . . . even though Random House had an abundance of books on hand at the time. At Walden Books . . . *Assault on the Liberty* was dropped prematurely from stock despite steady demand. At the naval base in San Diego, a large supply of books was returned to the publisher after the base chaplain filed a complaint.[29]

The campaign against the book was not limited to the distribution process; it was directed as well against any media airing of information contained in the book. Thus a producer of ABC's "Good Morning America" invited Ennes to an interview on March 10, 1980, but subsequently cancelled the program after discussing it with the Israeli Embassy. ABC's "Nightline" interviewed four *Liberty* crewmen and prepared a thirty-minute report on the attack, then shelved the program "temporarily" for higher priority news. Later the producers reported that the fully edited studio tape and more than fifteen reels of supporting raw film had disappeared from the "Nightline" film library. The program was never aired, and ABC refuses to comment on the incident.[30]

Roberta Strauss Feuerlicht's book was also the object of an attempt to suppress its distribution. Mark A. Bruzonsky, a former Washington associate of the World Jewish Congress, reported on "the conspiracy to kill" *The Fate of the Jews: A People Torn between Israeli Power and Jewish Ethics* (New York: Times Books, 1983), a book about "the 'true' meaning of Judaism and the predicament of the Jews true to their ethical heritage who face the contradictions of contemporary Zionism." He offered this evidence:

(1) The publisher did not run a single advertisement or arrange any important media appearances for the author.

(2) Feuerlicht received private information that the new editor of Times Books, Jonathan Siegel, had ordered that nothing be done to promote the book. Feuerlicht stated in April 1984 that Times Books

was planning to take the book out of print after the initial run of 7,000.

(3) No major newspaper other than the *Los Angeles Times* reviewed the book—"Not even the one with the motto 'All the News That's Fit to Print,' which is affiliated with the publisher and which has a large Jewish readership."

(4) Pro-Israeli groups and publications attempted to "kill *Fate* through a combination of slander and neglect." For instance, Leonard Fein, editor of *Moment* magazine, dismissed the book as "preposterous . . . easily the worst I've looked at in years." In contrast the book received very favorable comments by the *New York Times* chief correspondent in Jerusalem, David Shipler, and by *Publishers Weekly*.[31]

At the same time, political culture in the United States is deeply affected by commercial films and television movies such as *Little Drummer Girl, Delta Force,* and *Under Siege,* among others in which Arabs are portrayed in an extremely negative, one-dimensional (i.e., terrorist) fashion; and by best-selling books such as Leon Uris's *The Haj,* a historically inaccurate and deeply racist portrayal of the Palestinians, and Joan Peters's *From Time Immemorial: The Origins of the Arab-Israeli Conflict over Palestine,* which critic Norman G. Finkelstein has called one of the "most spectacular frauds ever published on the Arab-Israeli conflict," adding, "In a field littered with crass propaganda, forgeries and fakes, this is no mean distinction. But Peters' book has thoroughly earned it." Finkelstein, a doctoral candidate at Princeton University, detailed the fraudulent statistics and deceptive arguments that Peters used in an attempt to "prove" that historically there were no Palestinian people.[32] Yehoshua Porath, an Israeli historian of Palestinian Arabs who teaches at the Hebrew University, called the book "a sheer forgery."[33] Others who have severely criticized the book and have documented its enormous falsehoods include Sir Ian Gilmour, a Conservative member of the British Parliament, Albert Hourani, a historian of the Middle East at Oxford University, Edward Said, Noam Chomsky, and Alexander Cockburn, who writes for the *Nation*.[34] Nevertheless, pro-Israeli reviewers, such as Walter Reich in the *Atlantic,* Martin Peretz in the *New Republic,* and Daniel Pipes in *Commentary,* the journal of the American Jewish Committee, praised the book highly. Holocaust scholar Lucy Dawidowicz congratulated Peters for having "brought into the light the historical truth about the Mideast."[35] Other pro-Israeli individuals who have endorsed the book include Saul Bellow, Elie Wiesel, and Arthur Goldberg.[36] *From Time Immemorial* has been reprinted eight times as of this writing (in addition to a paperback edition) and is being widely distributed throughout the United States, despite the numerous painstaking documentations of its massive distortions. Likewise, protests from the Arab-American community to the publisher of *The Haj* and to major book distributors concerning its racist nature proved unavailing.

Such multifaceted efforts by pro-Israeli individuals and groups are obviously significant in the larger picture of American support for Israel and the development and perpetuation of the mistaken, misleading, and inaccurate ideas that have become "common wisdom" with regard to the Arab-Palestinian-Israeli conflict and the U.S.–Israeli relationship. But pro-Israeli organizations in the United States have also made an enormous impact in recent years through the domestic political process.

Thus to analyze further the reasons for the institutionalization and continuation of the perception of Israel as a strategic asset and the policies derived from the idea, it is necessary to examine in detail how pro-Israeli groups affect the electoral process as well as to describe the relationship between the electoral process and the formation of policy. To facilitate this analysis, it is instructive to look at the Reagan administration's Middle East policies in the context of the 1984 presidential election. During that election season the problems of American policy in the Middle East were particularly apparent. In the face of escalating tensions in the Arabian Gulf, the disintegration of Lebanon, the resurgence of Syrian power and the concomitant expansion of Soviet influence, the rise in incidents of terrorism— particularly against American individuals and property—and the spread of militant Islamic fundamentalism threatening the internal stability of several Arab regimes, the United States was never in a weaker position to influence events, protect its vital interests, or assist its longtime allies such as Saudi Arabia. Moreover, the contradictions between Israeli and American interests were never more apparent, nor was the relationship between policy formation and the impact of the Israeli lobby on the electoral process ever more starkly outlined.

The 1984 Election: Policies and Electoral Considerations

As the material in Chapter 7 illustrates, from its inception the record of the Reagan administration in the Middle East was one of failure.[37] Both major assumptions on which its policies were based— that the multifaceted and complex issues in the region could be reduced to a simplistic, dichotomous view of American-Soviet competition and Soviet causality, and that Israel was the key strategic asset to contain the Soviets and bring the region securely under the American umbrella—were erroneous. These fallacious assumptions led to one policy blunder after another.

Characteristic was the early and stillborn attempt of Reagan's first secretary of state, Alexander Haig, to forge a strategic consensus between Israel and pivotal Arab states—an attempt that disregarded the regional animosities inherent in the Arab-Palestinian-Israeli conflict and the domestic implications of such an alliance for the Arab regimes. Moreover, the Reagan administration's acquiescence, by virtue of the absence of meaningful sanctions, in every one of Israel's highly aggressive and inflammatory policies, including the bombing of the nearly completed French-built nuclear reactor in Baghdad, the bombing of Beirut (1981), the formal annexation of Jerusalem and the Golan Heights, the intensive settlement policy on the West Bank, and finally the massive war in Lebanon, resulted in American credibility in the Arab world plummeting to unprecedented depths.

In addition, the mistaken premises led Haig to give Israel a "green light" for its invasion of Lebanon—certainly one of the major mistakes of the United States in the Middle East in the post–World War II era. The failure of the Reagan administration to follow through on the peace initiative enunciated by the president on September 1, 1982 (the Reagan Plan) must be counted as another policy blunder. The reintroduction (following the massacres in Sabra and Shatila), conduct, and manner of withdrawal of the U.S. marines in Lebanon was yet another serious error. Israel pressed hard for the return of the marines after the slaughter in the refugee camps, although many in Washington, including Secretary of Defense Caspar Weinberger, opposed their reintroduction. President Reagan, however, was persuaded to support Israel on this issue and the marines were returned—on what was called a "peacekeeping" mission, though its purpose was obscure at best. Eventually the peacekeepers became partisans in an increasingly bitter civil war, and Congress began to discuss the situation in terms of the War Powers Act.

Convinced that he could shore up the Israeli-imposed Phalange regime of the Gemayel clan, in September 1983 the president authorized the use of American firepower against the domestic rivals of the Phalange. The president then enlisted the assistance of AIPAC to ensure that Congress did not force a discussion of the marines' role in Lebanon. The success of AIPAC's efforts was reflected in congressional acquiescence to keeping the marines in Lebanon for an additional eighteen months before requiring consideration of the matter under the War Powers Act. Pleased with the results of AIPAC's lobbying, the president personally phoned Thomas A. Dine, its executive director, and thanked him for his organization's help: "I certainly appreciate it. I know you mobilized the grass-roots organizations to generate support." Dine replied: "We fought very hard because we thought the United States was being tested. We thought you as president and commander-in-chief were being tested by the Syrians and we felt very strongly that American resolve was appropriate here."[38] Shortly thereafter the marine headquarters was bombed in a guerrilla attack, and 264 Americans were killed. On February 7, 1984, President Reagan ordered the withdrawal of the marines in a move so precipitous that American credibility in the Arab world plummeted even lower. Arab leaders had disapproved of the United States taking sides in the war, but were stunned when Washington abandoned the side it had pledged to uphold. More significant was the fact that the withdrawal of the marines was evidence of the marked decline of U.S. influence in Lebanon at a time when the Syrian position was renewed and strengthened.

Another major policy failure was the American-brokered Israeli-Lebanese accord. The United States oversaw the ratification of Israel's objectives while negating its own interests, only to have the Lebanese government, under the influence of Syria, cancel the agreement.

Subsequent to Washington's debacle in Lebanon, the United States suffered another major setback in its Middle East relations. As the 1984 electoral season swung into high gear, the administration, bowing to pressure AIPAC had effectively exerted in Congress, withdrew a proposal (made on March 21, 1984) to sell 1,200 defensive, shoulder-held Stinger missiles to Saudi Arabia and 1,600 to Jordan.

After it had become apparent that Israel would use its power in Congress to defeat the sale, the administration attempted to strike a bargain with AIPAC. Intensive negotiations were carried out between Lawrence Eagleburger, a high State Department official, and Thomas Dine. The administration sought to exchange dropping the Stinger sale in return for AIPAC's agreeing to use its influence to kill a pending bill that would require moving the American Embassy in Israel from Tel Aviv to Jerusalem. The administration lost on both counts.[39] Indeed, when the president decided to cancel the Stinger sale, AIPAC was informed twelve hours before Richard Murphy, the assistant secretary of state for Near Eastern Affairs.[40]

One of the most important functions of the Israeli lobby is preventing the sale of American weapons to Arab countries.[41] The power of the lobby is so great in such matters that a week before the president cancelled the Stinger missile sale, he went before the United Jewish Appeal to seek domestic pro-Israeli support for the weapons policy.[42] He did not get it. But King Hussein viewed the president's appearance before the United Jewish Appeal as an example of Reagan acting as a supplicant to the Israeli lobby to seek aid for Jordan, a situation that he deeply resented. The king gave an interview to Judith Miller of the *New York Times* in which he bitterly criticized American policy. He said that the United States had tilted so far toward Israel that it could no longer be an honest broker. The United States was "succumbing to Israeli dictates," he said, and there was "no way" for Arabs "to sit and talk with Israel as long as things are as they are."[43] Washington then used Hussein's remarks as a pretext—and justification—for the cancellation of the missile sale.

Despite its success in preventing the sale of Stingers to Jordan and Saudi Arabia, AIPAC declined to decrease the pressure it was applying in Congress concerning the American Embassy. Senator Daniel Patrick Moynihan (D., New York) had introduced the bill that would require the U.S. Embassy in Israel be moved from Tel Aviv to Jerusalem. Moynihan argued that the legislation was needed as a sign of American support for Israel. It was also an obvious attempt for the Democratic party to curry favor with Jewish voters in an election year (though Moynihan himself did not come up for reelection until 1986). At its 1984 Annual Policy Conference, AIPAC had set as one of its five goals for the year the "transfer of the American Embassy to Jerusalem, Israel's capital."[44] (The other four objectives included conversion of all U.S. aid to Israel to a grant basis while maintaining existing levels; opposition to U.S. sales of sophisticated weapons to Arab countries that do not negotiate directly and make peace with Israel; development of a meaningful framework for strategic cooperation between the United States and Israel; and establishment of a U.S.–Israeli free trade zone.[45]) Moynihan's initiative thus supported a major goal of the lobby and raised an issue on which Senators and Representatives could demonstrate their loyalty to Israel. Indeed, it is instructive to observe (as discussed below) how Democrats and Republicans competed to fulfill all the objectives set by AIPAC.

By April 1 the Jerusalem bill had thirty-eight co-sponsors in the Senate and 215 in the House, and it appeared that the votes needed for passage were assured, despite the trepidations of many in Congress about the wisdom of the proposed action. But especially in an election year Congress would not want to vote against an issue of such significance to pro-Israeli groups.

This was an issue, however, that deeply touched the emotions of many groups besides pro-Israeli activists. Representatives of Arab and non-Arab Muslim countries alike strongly warned the Reagan administration of the grave consequences that could be expected to American property and lives in those countries if Washington moved its embassy to Jerusalem. Indeed, the international pressure became so intense that the president indicated he would veto the bill if Congress passed it. Nevertheless, impervious to the exigencies of the national interest, Democratic presidential contenders Gary Hart and Walter Mondale argued vociferously, particularly during the New York primary, over who had been for the embassy move longest and most consistently. At one point, speaking before the Conference of Presidents of Major American Jewish Organizations, Hart apologized for a letter sent to the Zionist Organization of America by his Senate office that suggested the embassy be moved to Jerusalem as part of an overall effort to negotiate a Middle East peace treaty. Hart told the Presidents Conference that if elected president he would move the embassy without preconditions. As for the letter, he said: "I apologize for that ambiguity. It is unfortunate. I assume responsibility for it. But the letter does not reflect my position today or my position a year ago, or for that matter six weeks ago."[46]

Congress held hearings on the bill throughout the summer, although there was considerable discussion about rewriting the legislation to reflect a "sense of the Congress," rather than requiring the move. Such a change would permit individuals to vote yes without provoking a constitutional crisis over which branch has responsibility for the formation of foreign policy; it would also obviate the necessity for a presidential veto—something the president and all the Republicans wished to avoid—while assuaging pro-Israeli voters. Thus, in September, proponents of the Jerusalem bill, acknowledging its shaky constitutional basis and faced with an uncompromising White House, dropped the bill and switched to a "Jerusalem Resolution." The nonbinding resolution expressed the sense of Congress that the U.S. Embassy in Israel "should be moved to Jerusalem at the earliest possible date." Just before the close of the 98th Congress in October 1984, after seven hearings and testimony from more than two dozen witnesses, the two House subcommittees charged with the legislation passed the resolution by a voice vote. Opponents of the legislation felt a measure of success for having stalled long enough so that there was insufficient time for consideration by the entire committee and the full House. Proponents were pleased to have completed the first legislative hurdle with congressional support intact and were looking forward to the start of the 99th Congress, when the matter would again become a "live issue."[47]

The embassy debate spawned a related political movement, which its organizers no doubt felt was opportune for pushing during an election season. On April 4, 1984, the American Jewish Congress, meeting in Israel, accused the diplomatically independent U.S. Con-

sulate in Jerusalem of developing political ties with West Bank Palestinians sympathetic to the PLO, at the expense of relations with
Israel and in ways that were inimical to the interests of Israel. The
organization's statement was issued after its members had been briefed
by the Israeli government. The American Jewish Congress subsequently brought pressure on Congress, and on May 17 forty-six
members of the House of Representatives sent Reagan a letter urging
him to "change the status of the United States Consulate in Jerusalem
by placing it directly under the jurisdiction and supervision of the
United States Embassy."[48] This new movement reflected the resentment Israel feels toward the independent contacts the consulate has
with Palestinians on the West Bank and its desire to see this channel
of information severed, forcing American officials to rely exclusively
on Israel for information regarding the occupied territories. An Israeli
success in this area would mean increased Israeli control over American policymaking. It would also send a signal about American Middle East policy as clear as if the embassy were physically moved from
Tel Aviv to Jerusalem. At the time of this writing the status of the
consulate remains unaltered, but pressure for a change is mounting.

Further evidence of election year concern for pro-Israeli sensibilities was apparent in mid-May when Yasir Arafat, PLO chairman,
addressed the congress of the Pan-Hellenic Socialist Movement,
Greece's ruling party. Arafat called for direct negotiations between
Israel and the PLO within the framework of a U.N.–sponsored Middle
East peace conference.[49] This statement, which should have been
welcomed as a breakthrough in the Palestinian-Israeli impasse, elicited no response from the Reagan administration. It may be assumed
that in an election year the president did not wish to risk antagonizing
pro-Israeli constituencies by acknowledging the PLO's initiative, although it is apparent that Washington, in deference to Israel, has
never been willing to recognize overtures made by the PLO.

Electoral considerations were also apparent in Washington's reactions to events in the Arabian Gulf. The four-year-old war between
Iran and Iraq began to take ominous new directions in the spring
of 1984 as both states initiated attacks on the oil tankers of third
countries. Iran hit Saudi Arabian and Kuwaiti ships, and Teheran
increased the stridency of its threats to close the Straits of Hormuz
if Iraq continued its assaults on the Iranian oil facility at Kharg
Island. The major American concern (which was felt even more
strongly by Western European countries and Japan) involved the fear
that the Arabian Gulf oil market might be disrupted, creating short-
term shortages for Japan and Western Europe and eventual oil price

hikes that could affect the entire world economy. America was also concerned that the conservative, pro-Western Gulf states might fall victim to domestic fundamentalist insurgencies or destabilization by Iran and its militant supporters.

On May 22, despite the humiliation the Saudi government suffered in March when Israel forced the administration to deny its first request, King Fahd urgently pleaded with the United States to sell Saudi Arabia 1,200 Stinger missiles so that it could defend itself against further Iranian air attacks. The Saudis, who by this time were spending approximately $4 billion annually on American technology and technical support,[50] believed that in view of the extent to which they had tied their economy to American interests and had worked in OPEC to maintain an oil policy favorable to Western economic concerns, the United States, as a matter of principle, was bound to sell them the equipment they needed. They, like the Jordanians, intensely resented the veto that Israel was able to exercise over such sales, for instance, the American ban on the sale of bomb racks for the F-15's they already have. (That ban was part of an agreement to which the Carter administration submitted in 1978 to gain congressional approval for the sale of the planes.)

From the administration's perspective the sale of the Stingers to Saudi Arabia was an easy way to demonstrate its support for the Saudis in the Gulf crisis without having to make a commitment to undertake military action itself—something the president did not want in an election year and the Saudis did not want at all. For the Saudi government, already concerned about domestic opposition and insurrection, American troops or facilities on its territory would entail a significant risk. "Give us the weapons," Saudi officials argued, "and we will defend ourselves."[51] It is a telling commentary on the position of the United States in the Arab world that considering the close and intricate relationship between Washington and Riyadh, the Saudi regime must fear for its continued existence if it were to align itself with Washington openly. However, the Saudi government was also feeling disillusioned with and humiliated by the United States. The Saudi foreign minister stated that while his nation and the U.S. Congress "may share the goal of protecting the Gulf, the way the Congress actually goes about doing it is unacceptable."[52]

It seems certain that Israel and its supporters in Washington did not seriously regard the Stinger as a threat to Israel since Israel had been supplied the means to neutralize the missiles' guidance system.[53] Nevertheless, the Israeli government immediately objected to the sale and mobilized AIPAC to block congressional approval of it. The apparent motivation was related to Israel's desire to disrupt and destroy the U.S.–Saudi relationship (much as it had wanted and attempted to ruin U.S.–Egyptian relations in the 1950s). In this instance Israel hoped that through its ability to pressure Congress to oppose selling the Stingers to Saudi Arabia, it could alienate the Saudis from the United States and increase their reluctance in the future to seek arms from Washington.[54] Indeed, the desire to humiliate Saudi Arabia and weaken its links with the United States motivated other activities of the pro-Israeli lobby in the spring of 1984, including the leaking of a secret agreement between Washington and Riyadh for the lease of four Stinger missiles for protection of the Saudi royal yacht and the leaking of administration contingency plans for a U.S. military intervention force moving into the Dhahran air field with 100 to 150 combat aircraft, supporting tankers, and some 50,000 troops.[55]

In an attempt to stave off the anticipated Israeli opposition, when the Reagan administration announced, on May 23, that it intended to revive plans to sell Saudi Arabia the Stinger missiles, it simultaneously announced that it was "postponing" plans for an elite Jordanian mobile force intended to assist in the Western defense of the Gulf. The president and his advisors hoped that by abandoning the Jordanian project, Israel could be persuaded not to block congressional approval for the missile sale to Saudi Arabia.[56] (The administration had been quietly but unsuccessfully trying for years to gain congressional support—in the face of Israeli opposition and pressure on Congress—for the Jordanian program, known as the Joint Logistics Planning Program. Plans for this originally highly classified administration-backed project were first leaked over Israeli radio. In November 1983, under pressure from the Israeli lobby, congressional budgetary committees eliminated from the 1984 military spending bill funds for the project. Defense appropriation committees were again about to consider funds for the program when the president withdrew the request.[57]) The administration's public abandonment of the program added fuel to King Hussein's frustration with Washington and to America's generally tarnished image in the Arab world, but it did not deter the Israelis from utilizing their power in Congress to block the sale of the Stingers to Saudi Arabia.

Faced with certain defeat in Congress, and himself under intense pressure from Israel and its domestic supporters, the president elected to circumvent Congress and sell the missiles to the Saudis on an emergency basis under the provisions of a national security waiver in the military sales law, but he tailored the sale to minimize as much as possible the damage with Israel. For example, despite the Saudi request for 1,200 missiles, Washington provided only 400. Additionally, the administration asked AIPAC what its reaction would be to the sale of bomb racks to the Saudis and immediately dropped any further consideration of that Saudi request when the reply was that the American official must be "crazy" to even ask.[58] Moreover, Undersecretary of State Michael Armacost personally informed Meir Rosenne, the Israeli ambassador, of the president's decision.[59] Nevertheless, Israel and its American friends were incensed over the sale of the 400 Stingers, and the administration deferred to Israel when the issue of Stingers for Kuwait came up.

Indeed, it was solely the desire to placate Israel and its domestic supporters that accounted for the administration's refusal to sell Kuwait, which is even more vulnerable than Saudi Arabia in the Gulf crisis, Stinger missiles.[60] Even with the specific disclaimer by the Kuwaiti government that the missiles would not be used against Israel, but only for defensive purposes in the Gulf, the request was refused and Washington announced that further weapons orders from the Gulf should go to Western Europe.[61] Washington subsequently expressed surprise and outrage when Kuwait concluded an accord with Moscow for $325 million worth of Soviet anti-air and other military defense material; the accord reportedly included the dispatch of Soviet military experts and training personnel to Kuwait.[62]

American and Israeli interests were certainly incompatible in the Gulf crisis, as was further evidenced in the spring of 1984 in the context of intensifying hostilities. When Saudi Arabia came under direct attack from Iran, the United States began to tilt, albeit ever so slightly, toward Iraq, fearing the consequences of an Iranian victory on the stability of Saudi Arabia and other Gulf states. Iraq sought financial aid from the United States for the construction of an oil pipeline that would enable Baghdad to export another 2 million barrels a day across Saudi Arabia and Jordan. The pipeline would make up for losses inflicted by Syria, whose wartime alliance with Iran prevented Iraqi oil from reaching the Mediterranean through a pipeline crossing Syrian territory. The United States favored the project; indeed, according to one knowledgeable State Department official: "The real benefit [of the pipeline] would be that it would change the expectations on vulnerability of oil. A significant amount of oil would be moved without travelling through the Gulf."[63] Israel, however, opposed the project, but suggested linking the planned Iraqi-Jordanian pipeline to the Israeli oil terminal at Ashkelon in return for a pledge not to attack the pipeline if it was built.[64] The implicit threat was indicative of Israel's policy toward U.S.–Iraqi relations: Israel took issue with and attempted to thwart all administration efforts to improve relations with Baghdad.[65]

Another example of the incompatibility of interests was revealed by James E. Akins, former U.S. ambassador to Saudi Arabia, who reported that Israel was significantly stepping up its military assistance to Iran.[66] Akins stated that the American-operated AWACs radar planes based in Riyadh had tracked Israeli planes flying north over Lebanon and Syria and then south to Turkey, where they lost them. But Iraqi radar had picked up aircraft moving from there to Iran. Akins assumed the "daily flights" were carrying spare parts and other military supplies and maintained that the Israelis were "lying" when they "categorically den[ied]" that they were regularly supplying Iran.[67] There was no doubt that during the war Israel had been secretly providing arms to Iran. At issue in the spring of 1984, however, were not only the growing divergence of United States and Israeli objectives in the Gulf and Israel's ability to constrain the conduct of American foreign policy, but also the concern about a wider war with potential great power involvement. It had been the hope of Western diplomats that an Iranian shortage of spare parts for its U.S.-made jets could help preclude a full-scale "tanker war" in the Gulf, but with Israel supplying spare parts, and possibly selling other more sophisticated weapons, the chances of averting a major war, which could well have involved the United States, were significantly decreased.

With this overview of events during the Reagan administration as a background, let us now turn to an examination of how the pro-Israeli groups influence policy within the United States.

The Pro-Israeli Lobby

The fundamental orientation of pro-Israeli organizations was succinctly expressed by a spokesman for the Conference of Presidents of Major American Jewish Organizations: "It is our policy to support any democratically-elected government of Israel, and we feel that what is good for Israel is good for the United States."[68] That position was reiterated by Hyman Bookbinder, chairman of the American Jewish Committee: "We bend over backward to help people understand that help for Israel is also in America's strategic interests."[69] That organized pro-Israeli groups have been able to translate their premise into American policy, to have kept the perception of Israel as a strategic asset dominant in American political culture, and to have obtained American support—economic, financial, diplomatic, political, and military—for every one of Israel's policy objectives is, to a great extent, a reflection of their ability to influence the domestic political process.

The term "Israeli lobby" loosely refers to the approximately thirty-eight major Jewish groups that concern themselves with Israel and with influencing U.S. Middle East policy to serve the interests of the Jewish state. (Since the 1982 war in Lebanon there has been a proliferation of new groups, in addition to the thirty-eight, such as AFSI, CAMERA, and others.) Only one of these organizations is registered as a lobby—the American-Israel Public Affairs Committee (AIPAC). It is of interest to note that AIPAC is registered as a domestic, not a foreign, lobby, having been exempted from the Foreign Agents Registration Act. (During the Fulbright hearings of 1963, enough evidence from documents subpoenaed from files of several of the pro-Israeli organizations was found to justify its inclusion in a category described in the title of the published hearings as "Non-Diplomatic Representatives of Foreign Principals"; however, AIPAC's domestic status was maintained.) The issue of "foreign" versus "domestic" lobby is not without importance: pro-Israeli groups are always quick to label supporters of Arab causes as "foreign agents." For example, Thomas Dine, in a speech written for the National Association of Jewish Legislators, said that Arab influence in the United States is directed and financed from "outside." "They," said Dine, "are a foreign lobby... their support is not rooted in American soil."[70] Israel, however, is a foreign nation, and those who actively work for its interests could also be considered agents of a foreign government.

Leaders of the other major Jewish organizations sit on AIPAC's executive committee and this assures that AIPAC's reports on congressional action and its calls for grass-roots pressure go far beyond its own membership, which in 1984 was approximately 44,000.[71] AIPAC is closely associated with the weekly newsletter, *Near East Report,* which all its members receive as part of their $35 annual dues and which it distributes without cost to members of Congress, news media, key government officials, and others influential in the policymaking process.[72]

Most of the organizations represented on AIPAC's board also belong to the New York–based Conference of Presidents of Major American Jewish Organizations. The Presidents Conference is a coordinating body for debate and action on matters relating to Israel and other concerns of American Jewry. Its main functions are to serve as an interpreter of Israel's views and wishes to the American government and to thrash out disagreements among members in private, so others cannot capitalize on them. One of the Israeli lobby's strongest features is the united front it presents to the public, never deviating from the Israeli government line. Traditionally the Presidents Conference has concerned itself primarily with influencing the

Executive branch, while AIPAC has focused on Congress, though these distinctions have become somewhat blurred over time.

Unlike AIPAC, most of the groups belonging to the Presidents Conference live on tax deductible donations and cannot legally devote a major portion of their resources to direct lobbying. They can, however, disseminate information about particular Representatives and Senators and congressional legislation and alert Jews to undertake pressure campaigns. Moreover, several member organizations of the Presidents Conference, such as the American Jewish Committee, the American Jewish Congress, the B'nai B'rith, and the Union of American Hebrew Congregations, have their own Washington representatives who "informally" press Israel's desires on members of Congress and the administration. For example, in 1981 the only issue on which the American Jewish Committee urged a mass mailing to members of Congress was Reagan's proposed AWACs sale to Saudi Arabia.[73] In addition, officials in the Israeli Embassy maintain intimate and continuing ties with members of Congress and with high-ranking staff in the Executive branch.[74]

Important, too, in building support for Israel is a network of Zionist groups, originally organized to work for creation of the state of Israel and now active in supporting it. These include, among others, the Zionist Organization of America, the Zionist Labor Alliance, and Hadassah, the Women's Zionist Organization of America. These groups promote a variety of projects including trips to Israel for politicians and academicians. Indeed, in virtually every metropolis and state throughout the country, pro-Israeli groups facilitate tours to Israel for local civic, religious, and political leaders; state politicians; and Senators, Representatives, and their key aides.

In addition to these various organizations, Israel's interests are advanced by congressional aides with intense pro-Israeli sympathies, who coordinate their efforts with AIPAC.[75] These individuals are not lobbyists as such, but they have considerable influence on the congressmen for whom they work. Morris J. Amitay, former executive director of AIPAC and previously an aide to former Senator Abraham A. Ribicoff (D., Connecticut), explained the contribution of congressional staff members when he was still a Senate aide: "There are now a lot of guys at the working level up here who happen to be Jewish, who are willing to make a little bit extra effort and to look at certain issues in terms of their Jewishness, and this is what has made this thing go very effectively in the last couple of years. These are all guys who are in a position to make the decisions in these areas for these Senators."[76] Besides relying on their own direct efforts, Amitay explained, pro-Israeli congressional aides call, when necessary, for "out-

side help," which means the application of direct pressure on legislators from influential Jewish constituents and pro-Israeli organizations
such as AIPAC.[77] In addition, every president has had a special White
House consultant on relations with the Jewish community, who provides a unique channel of direct access for pro-Israeli groups to the
president.

The individuals and organizations comprising the pro-Israeli lobby
have a myriad of techniques and methods with which to achieve
their objectives. One important method is the careful monitoring of
congressional committees that deal with issues of concern to Israel.
Former Congressman Paul Findley (R., Illinois) relates an example
of the sophistication of the lobby in monitoring committees:

> There was an occasion on which I hadn't even drafted an amendment. I
> hadn't even spoken to anyone else about it except whispering to somebody
> else on the committee with me that I thought I'd offer an amendment to
> cut maybe $50 million out of the aid bill to Israel which is just a tiny
> portion of what was pending. Within half an hour I was visited by two
> other members of the committee who were in the room during that period.
> Clearly they'd had calls from their home districts of concern about what
> this Findley was up to—what amendment he was going to offer. It shows
> the efficiency of the network. Obviously the word was passed very swiftly
> and got out to the districts, then calls came back. That was very impressive.
> Chances are there was an AIPAC representative in the room. They normally
> are present during all deliberations of the committee. They cover the Hill.
> They have four or five people full time that deal with Congress. They don't
> have to cover every committee hearing, just the ones where they need to
> be present.[78]

Another technique important to the pro-Israeli effort is the ability
to exert direct pressure on congressmen from the grass roots. Indeed,
AIPAC possesses a computerized listing of supporters of Israel in
every state and congressional district. A member of Congress who
is undecided or likely to vote against a matter of importance to Israel
can routinely expect to receive letters and telegrams, not merely from
a scattering of leading citizens in his own constituency, but possibly
from past and potential campaign contributors from across the country.[79] AIPAC also has a type of power of attorney from many supporters listed in its computerized files. When a pending matter is
urgent, a Representative or Senator may see telegrams from his
constituents, billed to their home telephone numbers, even before
some of the constituents know the telegrams or mailgrams have been
sent.[80]

More important than the specific lobbying techniques that pro-

Israeli groups employ is their power to deliver money and votes in elections in quantities far greater than the numerical size of these groups would suggest.

Presidential Campaigns

In presidential contests pro-Israeli groups exercise their power through financial contributions, high voter turnout in the primaries, and their demographic distribution in the context of the Electoral College system. One month before the 1984 November election Morris J. Amitay wrote: "In any close presidential election, the Jewish vote, which is concentrated in states with large blocs of electoral votes, becomes crucial, and this November should be no exception."[81]

The approximately six million American Jews, constituting 2.7 percent of the population, are well known for their extremely high turnout at the polls. For example, in the Democratic primary in New York in April 1984, 30 percent of the voters were Jewish and Jews made up 41 percent of Mondale's total vote, accounting for the decisiveness of his victory.[82] The effect of such a concentration of voting strength drives candidates to positions of total support for the wishes of the Jewish community. Note again Hart and Mondale competing to demonstrate which was more committed to moving the American Embassy to Jerusalem. In addition, the nature of the Electoral College, in which a few thousand votes can determine the outcome of a presidential election in a given state by awarding all of a state's electoral votes to one candidate, biases the election results in favor of heavily populated states such as New York, New Jersey, California, and Florida. The winner-take-all system gives these states disproportionate weight. The heavy concentration of Jews in these populous states combined with their high turnout at the polls contributes to their power.

The Democrats were particularly concerned about the Jewish vote in the 1984 presidential election for several reasons. In 1980 the Democratic candidate, President Jimmy Carter, did not receive a majority of the Jewish vote. Carter received 44 percent of the vote, Reagan received 39 percent, and Representative John B. Anderson received 17 percent.[83] Moreover, according to AIPAC's Dine, no Democrat since 1916 has been elected president without winning at least 70 percent of the Jewish vote.[84] In the spring of 1984 Nathan Perlmutter, national director of the Anti-Defamation League of the B'nai B'rith, as well as other prominent leaders of the Jewish community, publicly labeled Democratic primary contender the Reverend Jesse Jackson an anti-Semite and demanded that the Democratic party repudiate him, warning that it could forfeit the support of Jews in November. "There could be a repeat of 1980. . . . Jews will watch their interest closely and we will respond accordingly."[85]

(The labeling of individuals who disagree with the lobby's positions as "anti-Semitic" is a common practice among Israel's advocates. For example, when Senator Charles Mathias [R., Maryland] voted in favor of the AWACs sale to Saudi Arabia, a Jewish newspaper in New York commented: "Mr. Mathias values the importance of oil over the well-being of Jews and the State of Israel. The Jewish people cannot be fooled by such a person, no matter what he said, because his act proved who he was."[86] Former Congressman Paul "Pete" McCloskey [R., California] also has had the charge of anti-Semitism leveled at him: "When I ran for reelection in 1980, I was asked a question about peace in the Middle East, and I said if we were going to have peace in the Middle East we members of Congress were going to have to stand up to our Jewish constituents and respectfully disagree with them on Israel. Well, the next day the Anti-Defamation League of the B'nai B'rith accused me of fomenting anti-Semitism, saying that my remarks were patently anti-Semitic."[87] Indeed, it may be that the weapon of greatest power possessed by the pro-Israeli lobby is its accusation of anti-Semitism. George Ball comments: "They've got one great thing going for them. Most people are terribly concerned not to be accused of being anti-Semitic, and the lobby so often equates criticism of Israel with anti-Semitism. They keep pounding away at that theme, and people are deterred from speaking out."[88] In Ball's view, many Americans feel a "sense of guilt" over the Holocaust, and the result of their guilt is that the fear of being called anti-Semitic is "much more effective in silencing candidates and public officials than threats about campaign money or votes.")[89]

Jackson commented to reporters that he thought the demands of the Jewish leaders for the Democratic party to repudiate him were unfair, and he asked rhetorically what would be said if black leaders demanded that the Democratic party repudiate the Jewish leaders who had slandered him and threatened to withhold their votes and money unless the party complied. Jackson was charged with being anti-Semitic for raising such a question.

Despite the threats made by Jewish leaders in the spring of 1984 to abandon the Democratic party, there was reason to question whether the Jewish vote would go to the Democrats even without the Jackson factor. By this time the general conservatism on both domestic and foreign issues of the Jewish community made it more likely that "voting its interests" would mean voting Republican.[90] On the other hand, as the campaign progressed, Reagan's positions on prayer in the schools and religion in general presented serious and well-founded concerns to Jews. The Democratic leadership did take the threats seriously, however, and considerable attention was focused on this matter. In fact, the question of the Jewish vote and the Jackson issue was extremely prominent throughout the entire campaign. From the outset of his candidacy pro-Israeli groups were intensely disturbed about Jackson's challenge to the dominant perceptions regarding Israel and the Middle East—Jackson was the first major politician in twenty years to state forthrightly that the United States, while not abandoning its special relationship with Israel, must have constructive, positive relationships with all the states in the region. Jackson demonstrated the logic of his argument and the absurdity of American policy by traveling to Syria and talking with the Damascus government in a successful effort to secure the release of an American airman being held prisoner. Moreover, Jackson argued that there can be no peace in the Middle East without a just resolution of the Palestinian question, including the realization of the Palestinian right to self-determination and U.S. willingness to negotiate with the PLO as the legitimate representative of the Palestinian people.

Such "heresy" was intolerable to pro-Israeli groups, who made every effort to discredit Jackson. For example, the Jewish Defense League undertook an aggressive campaign against him. The formal campaign began on November 11, 1983, with an advertisement in the *New York Times* featuring a photograph of Jackson embracing Arafat. Above the photograph, in boldface type, were two questions: "Do you believe that any Jew should support this man? Should any decent American?" The advertisement branded Jackson a threat to Jews, Israel, and America and asked for contributions to help halt his campaign for the presidency. It declared: "We will expose Jesse Jackson for the danger he really is. Ruin, Jesse, Ruin."

Fern Rosenblatt, national director of the Jewish Defense League and associate director of Jews Against Jackson, defended the advertisement: "Jesse Jackson has to be stopped. To recognize the PLO and to negotiate with them . . . is outrageous. To be so openly anti-Semitic is not grounds for being president of the United States."[91] (Actually, the Jewish Defense League's effort against Jackson had been in operation for some time: at nearly every campaign stop Jackson's speeches were being interrupted by militants from the League.) One week after the advertisement's appearance, the Jewish Defense League reported receiving 1,500 letters and $5,000 in contributions and announced the formation of ten additional Jews Against Jackson chapters across the country.[92]

Subsequently, a morally slack and politically foolish reference by Jackson to Jews as "Hymies" and New York as "Hymie-town" (in addition to Jackson's refusal to repudiate Black Muslim leader Louis Farrakhan, though he repeatedly disassociated himself from statements made by Farrakhan) gave Jackson's opponents additional ammunition. Any mistake would have served them equally well. As *The Nation* editorialized: "Their campaign to devalue Jackson's candidacy is aimed at the movement he leads and the threat it presents. Jackson . . . makes demands about class, race, privilege and power that are unique in modern major party politics. It is hardly surprising that those who feel the threat will take the first opportunity to disarm it."[93] Indeed, Jackson's public apology before a synagogue for the Hymie remark made no difference to those (including far more than the fringe members of the Jewish Defense League) who persisted in their efforts to malign him.

The demand by establishment Jewish leaders for Jackson's repudiation was juxtaposed with a new political reality, also created by the Jackson candidacy: the 3.5 million black voters his campaign mobilized in the primaries,[94] a block with potentially greater voting power than the Jewish community. If the Democrats could not win without Jewish voters, they also could not win without the newly enfranchised black voters. Democratic party officials thus found themselves in a quandary, and Jackson received all of the blame for the divisions in the party. In the end, in his speech at the Democratic National Convention, Jackson apologized again for any pain he had created for the Jewish people, specifically acknowledging their right to return to their ancestral homeland and not mentioning the Palestinians. The Democratic party made no changes in its Middle East policy; and under intense pressure from the Jewish community the party defeated Jackson's minority platform plank on affirmative action (Jewish leaders had been adamant that the Democrats not agree to Jackson's demands on behalf of quotas for blacks).

For those who were concerned about the nature of American foreign policy in the Middle East there was hope that the questions the Jackson candidacy had raised would have a positive impact on the political process. Indeed, since both Jackson and former Senator George McGovern (an early Democratic contender who told a synagogue audience that "it is politically risky for any American politician to recognize that the Palestinians have some legitimacy to their claims, or that Israeli political leaders can sometimes be in error"[95]) challenged some of the myths about the Middle East and spoke with honesty about the Palestinian issue, such individuals believed this campaign marked the beginning of a change at the grass roots that could someday reach the halls of Congress. That optimism, however, seems unwarranted.

President Reagan apparently believed that there was political mileage to be gained from exploiting the Democratic concern about the Jewish vote and the Jackson issue. On April 9 Vice-President George Bush, acting on behalf of the president and speaking before AIPAC in Washington, castigated the Democratic presidential contenders for failing to condemn anti-Semitism. Subsequently Larry Speakes, the White House spokesman, confirmed that the Bush statement had been planned by the White House. He said Bush had spoken for the president and other White House officials and that Jackson's "polarizing influence" could help the Republicans next fall.[96] (This was not the first time Reagan attempted to exploit the issue of anti-Semitism. In an effort to win the support of the Jewish community for administration attempts to overthrow the government of Nicaragua, the president accused the Sandinistas of being anti-Semitic. The issue of the alleged anti-Semitism of the Sandinistas became a topic of national concern, although several prominent rabbis and Jewish leaders traveled to Nicaragua to investigate the charges and found them totally without foundation.) Moreover, on October 26 Reagan reminded the congregation of Temple Hillel in Woodmere, Long Island, that while the Republican National Convention in Dallas had approved a platform plank deploring anti-Semitism, the Democrats "couldn't find the moral courage or leadership to pass a similar resolution. Forgive me," the president went on, "but I think they owe you an explanation. What has happened to them? Why, after the issue became so prominent during the primaries, did the Democratic leadership walk away from their convention without a resolution condemning this insidious cancer?" The president also told the Jewish audience that the reason he had sent American troops to Beirut in 1982 was to prevent another Holocaust. He said the Jewish battle cry "never again" should "be impressed on those who question why we went on a peacekeeping mission to Lebanon."[97] Significantly, the Israeli newspaper *Ha'aretz* had editorialized only days earlier: "The loss of several points in the public opinion polls may force the president to court the pro-Israeli bloc in the electorate more seriously."[98]

Money provides the complement to the vote in explaining the impact of pro-Israeli groups on the presidential election process. In his study *Jews and American Politics,* Stephen Isaacs documents that "Jews take enormous pride in their prominence in financing campaigns . . . and give like no other group in society."[99] In late 1983 the *Christian Science Monitor* reported that approximately 50 percent of all Democratic party funds come from the Jewish community.[100] Isaacs elaborates:

The Democrats, meanwhile, have some very wealthy supporters, and, among them, some non-Jews, but the point is that they can't do this fund raising as systematically [as the Republicans] in industry except maybe a couple. Traditionally, textiles was a good industry because it was a combination of the Jews in New York and the Southerners, who were Democrats. Secondly, the entertainment industry, where a lot of Jews made money in movies or are performers. . . . Therefore all that is a prelude to saying that you could typify the Jews as an industry, as a Democratic supportive group that could almost be systematically mined for money.[101]

Moreover, according to Isaacs, Democratic presidential candidates are dependent on Jewish money for success.[102] Isaacs reports the assertion of a prominent non-Jewish national strategist that "you can't hope to go anywhere in national politics if you're a Democrat, without Jewish money."[103] Writing in 1974, Isaacs noted that of reported gifts, the pattern of Jewish predominance in Democratic national campaigns was clear: "In 1968 of the twenty-one persons who loaned $100,000 or more to Hubert Humphrey's campaign, 15 were Jewish, ranging from the $100,000 loans of Edwin L. Weisl and Arnold M. Picker to the $240,000 loans of John Factor and Lew Wasserman. In 1972 . . . Jews were the main source of large gifts to the Democratic campaign."[104]

Changes in campaign finance laws since 1974 have altered the ways in which special interest groups funnel money to favored candidates, thus making it difficult to trace such donations. For example, in a practice known as "bundling," an organization solicits contributions from its membership for a candidate and each individual makes out a check for the maximum allowable legal contribution to the candidate ($1,000 in any one year). The organization collects these "individual" contributions, which may total hundreds of thousands of dollars, and presents them to the candidate, who then knows who his "friends" are. But, insofar as the Federal Election Commission is concerned, the contributions are recorded as individual donations, and it is impossible to demonstrate bundling. There is little doubt that Jewish money played a major role in financing the Mondale campaign in 1984, especially given Mondale's intimate relations with the Jewish community. AIPAC's Dine made a revealing comment about the extent of Mondale's ties to pro-Israeli groups: He "bounces ideas off us on Mideast issues before issuing policy statements. Mondale's well-known and well-liked. He's rooted in our community."[105]

It is apparent that both Jewish money and the Jewish vote are important, if not critical, considerations for the Democratic party. This illuminates several aspects of the 1984 presidential contest, especially the party's concern about the tensions between Jackson and the Jewish community, and it explains the obsequiousness of

Mondale and Hart to the interests of pro-Israeli groups. Moreover, the extremes to which Democratic candidates extend themselves to receive the beneficence of the traditionally Democratic pro-Israeli groups then drives Republican candidates to be even more pro-Israel. It is an endless spiral of competition.

Indeed, Reagan competed ardently for the support of pro-Israeli groups, and this consideration figured prominently in the administration's formation of Middle East policy during the election season, including the cancellation of the plans for the elite Jordanian strike force, the minimal number of Stingers that were supplied to Saudi Arabia, the refusal to supply the Saudis with the requested bomb racks for their F-15's, the refusal to sell Kuwait Stinger missiles, and the reluctance to provide financial assistance to Iraq for the construction of an oil pipeline.

The most important pro-Israeli initiative undertaken by Reagan was the Strategic Co-operation Agreement the president revived (from the suspended 1981 accord) in November 1983. That agreement formalized the U.S.–Israeli relationship in a grand gesture that made the relationship the centerpiece of American policy in the Middle East. The reinstatement of the agreement—especially its timing— was intended in part as a political move, a substantive preemption to anything the Democrats could promise during the campaign. The agreement included the formation of a joint political-military group and joint military exercises, the stockpiling in Israel of American equipment, an increase in military and economic aid and an increase in the amount that would be given in grants, negotiations to establish a free trade arrangement, a special exemption for Israel from foreign military sales laws, permission for Israel to resume buying cluster bombs and to buy cluster bomb fuses enabling it to produce its own bombs, and allegedly discussion of a proposal that Israel become a conduit for American aid to "anti-Communist forces" in Central America and elsewhere through a fund the administration would establish independent of the government budget to finance projects suggested by Israeli experts.[106]

Both Israel and its American supporters were pleased by the president's initiative; however, when it came to implementing strategic cooperation the divergencies between Israeli and American interests were again apparent. For the Reagan administration the main purpose of such military affiliation was to counter "increased Soviet involvement in the Middle East," and the intention was to concentrate on anti-Soviet military contingencies in the region. For Israel, the objective was to assure American support for its traditional interest in fighting land and air wars against the Arabs. Israel viewed the paramount "threat" to the area to be from "radical" Arab governments and PLO "terrorists" and specifically argued that Syria constituted the major threat to peace in the Middle East. Partly because the United States did not perceive the situation in those terms and partly because it did not wish to further alienate friendly Arab regimes, the administration insisted that the focus be on the anti-Soviet character of the alignment. Israeli military commanders were reported to be "alarmed" by this.[107] Israel wanted to assure U.S. backing and assistance for its regional military adventures but was not willing to involve itself in Washington's anti-Soviet crusade. Thus the Israeli military opposed the accord as a diversion from dealing with "traditional Arab threats," while Israeli political leaders opposed it as causing unnecessary problems with the Soviet Union on matters such as Jewish immigration.[108]

Ironically, despite the fact that for years Israeli leaders and the domestic pro-Israeli lobby had argued that Israel was a strategic asset to the American objective of containing Soviet expansionism and that there was a need for a formal Israeli-American strategic cooperation agreement because of the growing Soviet threat in the region, when a U.S. administration finally consented, it turned out that Israel was not interested in joint planning for a direct Soviet attack but was only concerned about the Russian "stalking horses" in the Middle East, i.e., Syria, the PLO, and Iraq. The Israelis, however, reluctantly went along with the American direction so as to ensure the realization of their long-sought accord with Washington, assuming, not unrealistically, that their interests would prevail in the long run.[109] Indeed, it is far more likely that the United States will be dragged into a war in the Middle East in support of some Israeli adventure that prompts Soviet support for one of its friends than that Israel will come to the aid of the United States in a confrontation with the Soviet Union as a result of unilateral Soviet action.

In spite of these contradictions, the exigencies of election season competition impelled the president, against the advice of Secretary of Defense Weinberger (certainly not "soft" on Communism) and with opposition from the air force and the army, to reinstate the agreement and proceed with its implementation. Indeed only the navy seemed to see some advantages in the arrangement—perhaps because the Sixth Fleet would be the primary beneficiary, since Israel could be used for repairs, prepositioning of stocks, shore leave, and combined operations against the Soviet Mediterranean fleet.[110]

On the other hand, reports from Central America in late 1983 and 1984 suggested that Israel and the United States were working together to implement the policies of the Reagan administration in that troubled region.[111] For Israel, the sale of weapons, the dispatching of advisors, and the transfer of technology to the Central American regimes that Reagan was attempting to shore up were ways to intertwine and cement the U.S.–Israeli relationship. Israel seemed to reason that if it could be helpful to the United States in Central America (while at the same time improving its own economy and increasing its international support vis-à-vis the governments it assisted), the United States would be less likely to oppose its Middle East objectives. Indeed, while the thesis of Israel dominating the Middle East in the interests of American power has been demonstrated to be without basis, it is apparent that in other areas such as Central America, Sri Lanka, Zaire, and elsewhere Israel can and often does act to further American objectives. Yet in these regions too, Israel has interests of its own that are often in conflict with American interests (e.g., the sale of weapons and technology): contrary to another currently fashionable argument, the Third World proxy thesis does not always hold up.

But Israel did provide considerable assistance to the United States in Central America during the Reagan administration; moreover, in the particular constellation of political forces that existed in Washington in the spring of 1984, Israel and its American friends were able to help the president with a reluctant Congress by tying Israeli interests to Central American issues, then pressuring Congress for votes favorable to both. For example, the foreign aid bill passed by the House of Representatives in June contained provisions of aid to Central American countries, particularly El Salvador, that were initially opposed by some Representatives. However, since the bill was a package that also contained $2.5 billion for Israel, even those who had most strongly opposed it voted for it. "I displayed my usual cowardice," one House member was reported to have said, deprecating his vote for legislation he had fought strongly against. Why did he vote contrary to his convictions? "Because lobbyists from AIPAC had reminded [him] that for friends of Israel, the vote on the foreign aid bill was crucial."[112]

Negotiations with Israel over the free trade arrangement proposed in the strategic cooperation agreement proceeded rapidly in the spring and summer of 1984, since the administration hoped to sign the deal before the November elections. A number of American industries and agricultural producers strenuously objected to the proposed pact, believing such an arrangement would damage their economic interests. In addition to competing against tariff-free imported goods, it would be difficult for the U.S. market to beat the significantly lower prices of Israeli goods produced by government-subsidized industries (which frequently employ cheap Arab labor). Among the protesting groups were Florida citrus growers, California growers of olives and tomatoes, textile manufacturers and footwear industry associations, jewelry industries, Roses, Inc., the American Farm Bureau, and, surprisingly, the usually pro-Israel AFL-CIO.[113] Despite the domestic opposition, however, the imperatives of the election season made it certain that Congress would not act to block the proposed free trade area, and indeed the administration had an impressive success to present to pro-Israeli constituencies. The legislation giving the administration the go-ahead to negotiate a free trade area with Israel passed the Senate on September 20 as part of an omnibus trade and tariffs bill, which was approved by a vote of 96 to 0. The free trade agreement with Israel—the first of its kind to be negotiated between the United States and any other nation—would, in its purest form, drop all tariff barriers and allow duty-free shipment of each country's products to the other. On October 3 the House passed its own separate Free Trade Area Bill (H.R. 5377) by a vote of 416 to 6. In the House-Senate conference the two bodies reconciled the differing bills and cleared the way for the administration to conclude an accord with Israel.[114]

Another election season decision by the Reagan administration favorable to Israeli interests, but detrimental to American business, was an agreement to buy sophisticated reconnaissance aircraft for the U.S. navy and marine corps from Israel. The Pentagon had budgeted approximately $106 million for 1984 alone for the purchase of the aircraft, known as remote pilotless vehicles (RPVs) which were to be produced by Tadiran Industries. The American corporation that lost the sale was Development Sciences, Inc., of California. Israel had been attempting for years to increase its military sales to the United States and pro-Israeli groups were very pleased by the president's decision.[115]

President Reagan undertook other measures during the 1984 election season, both on matters of substance and form, in an attempt to compete with the Democrats for the Jewish vote. In one instance he upgraded the position of White House consultant on relations with the Jewish community to that of senior special assistant. Marshall Breger, a former University of Texas law professor, held the post at the time. By upgrading the position, the president afforded Breger, and by extension pro-Israeli groups concerned with the content of policy, expanded access to senior administration officials shaping Middle East policy.[116]

Congressional Campaigns

It is in Congress where the grip of the pro-Israeli groups is strongest and where the relationship between the electoral process and the policymaking process is most evident. That relationship is starkly outlined in the phenomenon of Political Action Committees (PACs), organizations through which interest groups fund congressional campaigns.

The importance of PACs resides in the narrow focus of their interests and their ability to channel huge sums of money to candidates who are then not likely to pursue policies that will incur the displeasure of the special interests the PACs represent. Representative James Leach has observed: "Washington has just become a special interest enclave, a city of special interests very different from the rest of society."[117] Moreover, according to M. Margaret Conway, a prominent scholar of the electoral process, despite federal election laws, "There is no limit on the total amount a PAC may spend on behalf of a candidate as long as the PAC does not coordinate its activities in any way with the candidate, his or her representatives, or the campaign committee." She has also demonstrated that federal campaign finance laws give a distinct advantage to multicandidate PACs, those contributing to five or more candidates for federal office.[118]

The interest of pro-Israeli PACs is especially narrowly defined, reflecting the objectives of the Israeli government. Melvin M. Swig, founder of the San Franciscans for Good Government PAC, succinctly commented that the sole purpose of his PAC was to "support candidates whose views are favorable to the State of Israel."[119] Similarly, Robert Golder, president of the Delaware Valley PAC, stated: "This PAC is a group of American Jewish people working for a stronger American position on Israel."[120] Pro-Israeli PACs enjoy the advantages of multicandidate PACs, since they make financial contributions to contenders for the Senate and the House; Democrats and Republicans (although Democratic candidates typically receive the greater share of Jewish PAC money); northerners, southerners, easterners, and westerners; liberals and conservatives—only the individual's fidelity to the objectives and interests of Israel is considered. The identities of the majority of the pro-Israeli PACs are obscured by titles such as the Committee for 18, Arizona Politically Interested Citizens, and the Joint Action Committee for Political Affairs. Mark Siegel, a Carter White House aide, a former political director of the Democratic National Committee, and in 1984 the director of the National Bipartisan Political Action Committee (a pro-Israeli PAC), said that committee names were chosen because of a concern in the

Jewish community that "there are those in the political process who would use the percentage of Jewish money (in a given race) as a negative."[121] (Although AIPAC is not a political action committee and does not sponsor a PAC, a sizeable number of AIPAC's directors, officers, and executive committee and national members are officers of the various pro-Israel PACs around the country.)

In the 1981-82 congressional election season, pro-Israeli PAC contributions, channeled through thirty-three separate PACs, amounted to $1,873,623, representing the largest amount of PAC contributions in the country. The money was divided among 268 individuals. Some, such as Senators Daniel Moynihan (D., New York) who received $11,000, Howard Metzenbaum (D., Ohio) who received $35,175, and Robert Byrd (D., West Virginia) who received $55,000, were not even up for reelection.[122]

The funds dispersed by pro-Israeli PACs are carefully targeted. For example, in 1982 pro-Israeli groups contributed $355,550 to help elect or defeat members of the House Foreign Affairs Committee and the House Appropriations Committee's Foreign Operations Subcommittee, panels that subsequently added more than $125 million to the Reagan administration's request for aid to Israel.[123] Dante Fascell (D., Florida), the chairman of the House Foreign Affairs Committee, received $40,750 from twenty-two pro-Israeli PACs. After Reagan bypassed Congress and sold Saudi Arabia Stinger missiles, Fascell, a strident critic of the sale, called for congressional hearings to determine whether a sufficient emergency existed to warrant the president's provision of 400 missiles to the Saudis.[124] Representative Clarence Long (D., Maryland), chairman of the House Foreign Operations Subcommittee, received $29,250 in the 1981-82 election season from eighteen pro-Israeli PACs[125] and then sponsored the bill that allowed Israel to use $550 million in military credits in fiscal year 1984 to finance the construction of a new fighter plane, the Lavi. A number of American defense industries (e.g., Northrop Corporation) whose planes will be in competition with the Lavi and that receive no government subsidies for construction of their planes vigorously protested. Weinberger, too, argued that it was inappropriate for military credits to be used in this manner.[126] However, under Long's direction Congress approved the Lavi proposal. In 1983 Long received $49,850 from pro-Israeli PACs, which was 74 percent of all the money he received from PACs that year.[127] In total during in the 1983-84 election cycle, Long received $169,300 from fifty-one different pro-Israeli PACs,[128] although ironically he was defeated in the November 1984 election.

By November 1984 the thirty-three pro-Israeli PACs from the 1981-

82 election season had grown to sixty-six and had given $3,426,279 to candidates for the Senate and House, almost double the contributions of the 1981-82 election cycle.[129] According to Federal Election Commission reports, pro-Israeli PACs raised $5,819,455 during the 1983-84 election season and disbursed $6,368,178 during the same period. (The difference between receipts and disbursements reflects the cash balance carried forward from the 1982 election cycle; pro-Israeli PACs began the 1986 cycle with $371,675 in cash-on-hand.)[130] Pro-Israeli PAC money was targeted again on the campaigns of Senate Foreign Relations Committee members and the House Foreign Affairs and Appropriations Committee members. In the Senate, some of the largest sums of money went toward the defeat of Senator Charles Percy (R., Illinois), chairman of the Foreign Relations Committee. Sixty-two pro-Israeli PACs gave $283,850 to his successful opponent, Paul Simon.[131] In addition, twenty pro-Israeli PACs contributed $48,150 to Republican Congressman Tom Corcoran's unsuccessful primary campaign against Percy: only ten other Senate campaigns received more Israeli PAC money than Corcoran.[132] The second largest amount of money—$244,400 from fifty-seven pro-Israeli PACs— went to the unsuccessful campaign of James Hunt, who challenged Jesse Helms (R., North Carolina), next in line to become chairman of the Foreign Relations Committee (although after the election he chose to take another committee chairmanship).[133] Other key people received huge sums of money as well. For example, Senator Rudolph Boschwitz (R., Minnesota), an avid supporter of Israel who chairs the Near Eastern and South Asian Affairs Subcommittee of the Foreign Relations Committee, received $117,950 in his successful re-election bid.[134] Senator Carl Levin (D., Michigan), intensely pro-Israel and an important member of the Armed Services Committee, received $168,163 from pro-Israeli PACs.[135] Tables 6 and 7 list the ranking recipients of pro-Israeli PAC contributions in the 1983-84 election cycle.

An interesting aside that complements these figures is Common Cause's disclosure that the United Jewish Appeal paid more money in lecturing fees to Senators in 1983 than any other group in the United States.[136] For instance, Senator Christopher Dodd (D., Connecticut), a member of the Foreign Relations Committee and an ardent supporter of Israel, received $32,000 from the United Jewish Appeal and another $14,000 from other Jewish groups in 1983 for speaking engagements.[137]

To appreciate the relationship between pro-Israeli PACs and the extent of pro-Israeli influence in Congress, one need only examine the behavior of Senators and Representatives on the issue of aid to

TABLE 6. The Top Recipients of Pro-Israeli PAC Contributions
in Senate Races during the 1983-84 Election Season

Candidate	Party/State	Outcome of Election	Amount	Number of PACs
Paul Simon	D., Illinois	Won	$283,850	62
James Hunt	D., North Carolina	Lost	$224,400	57
Carl Levin	D., Michigan	Won	$168,163	47
Rudolph Boschwitz	R., Minnesota	Won	$117,950	45
Tom Harkin	D., Iowa	Won	$106,830	35
Norman D'Amours	D., New Hampshire	Lost	$ 86,200	34
Albert Gore	D., Tennessee	Won	$ 71,050	29
William Winter	D., Mississippi	Lost	$ 70,990	28
Max Baucus	D., Montana	Won	$ 50,800	22

SOURCE: *Focus* 8, no. 5 (May 1, 1985), 3.

Israel. An associate editor of the *Washington Post* reported a revealing incident:

Earlier, the House and the Senate engaged in a bit of a contest over who would give more to the Israelis this year. The Reagan Administration requested $850 million in economic (as opposed to military) aid for the next year. The Senate Foreign Relations Committee—whose chairman and ranking Democrat are both up for reelection this November—quickly upped the ante to $1.2 billion, an increase of nearly 50 per cent. This worried members of the House Foreign Affairs Committee, according to one senior member: "we can't let them be more generous to Israel, than we are," he quoted colleagues as saying. In the end, the House Committee proposed $1.1 billion, but it will come out of the conference at $1.2 billion, a knowledgeable member predicted.[138]

The editor noted that "episodes like these get no serious coverage in the news media," but in Washington "reporters and politicians share a cynical understanding that Israel and its American friends constitute probably the single most effective lobbying force in the country. Ask a Senator or Congressman on one of the committees involved," he added, "if anyone this year seriously questioned whether the huge amount of American aid to Israel was a good idea, and you are more likely to get a laugh than an answer."[139]

The House Foreign Aid bill, approved in May 1984, gave Israel $2.5 billion for fiscal year 1985: $1.4 billion in military aid and $1.1 billion in economic aid ($439 million more than the administration had requested). The bill also contained three sections specifically relating to the conduct of U. S. policy in the Middle East that were tailored to meet Israel's interests: (1) Section 122 required presidential certification that "Jordan is publicly committed to the recognition of Israel and to prompt entry into direct peace negotiations with

TABLE 7. The Top Fifteen Recipients of Pro-Israeli PAC Contributions in House Races during the 1983-84 Election Season

Candidate	Party/State	Outcome of Election	Committee	Amount	Number PACs
Clarence Long	D., Maryland	Lost	A.	$169,300	51
Larry Smith	D., Florida	Won	F.A.	$ 45,630	41
Ben Erdreich	D., Alabama	Won	—	$ 39,400	30
Mark Siljander	R., Michigan	Won	F.A.	$ 29,850	28
Robert Torricelli	D.,New Jersey	Won	F.A.	$ 29,000	23
Les AuCoin	D., Oregon	Won	A.	$ 27,850	19
Dante Fascell	D., Florida	Won	F.A.	$ 25,250	23
Richard Durbin	D., Illinois	Won	A.	$ 24,981	21
Edward Feighan	D., Ohio	Won	F.A.	$ 24,200	21
Charles Wilson	D., Texas	Won	A.	$ 23,100	18
Peter Kostmayer	D., Pennsylvania	Won	F.A.	$ 22,950	20
Sam Gejdenson	D., Connecticut	Won	F.A.	$ 21,200	13
Harry Reid	D., Nevada	Won	F.A.	$ 21,150	22
Ronald Wyden	D., Oregon	Won	A.	$ 20,000	13
Lee Hamilton	D., Indiana	Won	F.A.	$ 19,350	20

SOURCE: *Focus,* 8, no. 5 (May 1, 1985), 3.

NOTE: A. = Appropriations; F.A. = Foreign Affairs. Note that of these fifteen, nine served on the Foreign Affairs Committee, and four served on the Appropriations Committee in the 98th Congress; Durbin joined the Appropriations Committee in the 99th Congress.

Israel" before certain specified weapons could be sold to Jordan. (2) Section 909 codified and went beyond Kissinger's September 1975 promise to Israel that the United States would not recognize or negotiate with the PLO. "No officer or employee of the United States government and no agent or other individual acting on behalf of the United States government shall negotiate with the P.L.O., or any representatives thereof, and the United States shall not recognize the P.L.O. unless and until the P.L.O. recognizes Israel's right to exist, accepts S.C. Resolutions 242 and 338, and renounces the use of terrorism." (3) Section 911 expressed congressional concern about the difficult Egyptian-Israeli relationship but stated only that Egypt should live up to the relationship.[140]

The Senate Foreign Relations Committee passed a foreign aid bill that increased the amount of aid proposed by the House and provided that all monies to Israel should be outright grants.[141]

In the end the foreign aid program was funded under a continuing resolution, which Congress approved after its scheduled adjournment. As a money saving measure, the House had voted on September 25, 273 to 134, to cut foreign aid spending by 2 percent, except for funds to Israel and Egypt. As a result of the Camp David agreements U.S.

aid to Egypt is pegged on a percentage basis to funds going to Israel. The final foreign aid bill provided Israel with $2.6 billion entirely on a grant basis, with no loans to be repaid. In addition, other features of the bill provided that:

(1) The $1.2 billion in economic aid would be provided to Israel as a cash transfer during the first quarter of fiscal year 1985, that is, before January 1;

(2) Israel could use up to $400 million of its military aid on the development of the Lavi fighter aircraft;

(3) Israel would be able to bid on U.S. Agency for International Development projects; and

(4) Approval of a "sense of the Congress" resolution that all future annual appropriations of economic aid to Israel be at least as much as Israel's annual debt repayment to the United States.[142]

(With regard to the third item in the above list, it is worth noting that A.I.D. had already chosen Israel to build a $10 million settlement project along the Nicaraguan–Costa Rican border as part of a U.S. plan to squeeze Nicaragua from Honduras in the North and Costa Rica in the South.[143])

Another provision stated that an additional $2 million "shall be made available only for cooperative projects among the United States, Israel, and developing countries." This is the essence of a bill introduced earlier in 1984 by Representative Howard Berman (D., California) that aimed at further integrating Israel with U.S. global objectives in the Third World. According to a spokesman in his office, Berman planned to reintroduce his bill in the 99th Congress, and with this precedent hoped to add about $20 million in the next fiscal year for these U.S.–Israeli–Third World "development projects."[144]

What impels Congress to lavish such huge gifts of money on Israel — often far in excess of what an administration requests — to provide such favorable repayment terms (in fiscal year 1985, no repayment at all), and to acquiesce in Israel's every policy demand?

For some congressmen it is their own passionate emotional ties to the Jewish state; for others it is the continuing misperception of Israel as a strategic asset to American interests in the Middle East. For still others, such as former Senator James Abourezk, the answer is the "political terrorism and intimidation" of the Israeli lobby. According to Abourezk, "If a member of Congress refuses to go along with a request, the Israeli lobby threatens him with political defeat."[145] Said another veteran congressional observer, "Congressmen are afraid that the lobby will turn off the contributions and voters if they do not 'toe the line.' "[146]

In 1982 pro-Israeli groups were successful in their concerted effort to defeat a long-time member of the House of Representatives and its Committee on Foreign Affairs who was also an outspoken critic of Israel. Thirty-one pro-Israeli PACs contributed $103,325 to Richard Durbin[147] in his bid to unseat Representative Paul Findley (R., Illinois). The *Wall Street Journal* detailed the sophisticated, nationwide campaign organized against Findley:

Some people went to great effort to defeat Mr. Findley. Robert Asher of Highland Park, Ill., was the treasurer of Citizens Concerned for the National Interest . . . which raised money from the Jewish community in the fashionable North Shore suburbs of Chicago and contributed $5,000 to Mr. Durbin. Mr. Asher also headed the National Committee to Elect Dick Durbin, which solicited individual donations from Jewish leaders across the country with a letter saying: 'This year we have the best chance we will ever have to remove this dangerous enemy of Israel from Congress.' Barbara Anne Weinberg, a Beverly Hills housewife, helped form the Citizens Organized Political Action Committee, a Los Angeles based PAC, . . . that gave $5,000 to Mr. Durbin. According to election-commission records, Mrs. Weinberg and her husband, Lawrence Weinberg, gave $20,000 to the PAC in 1981-1982 and gave an additional $2,000 to Mr. Durbin.[148]

Findley himself suggested the importance of the role of the pro-Israeli groups:

Without the Jewish money, my opponent could not have mounted the attack that tore me to pieces. . . . Without the money to buy that very expensive time [television] and prepare those very expensive ads [newspaper] the attack could not possibly have been so great. An incumbent has enormous resources and can usually overcome a lot of odds. And I almost did. The margin was so close that any of a number of factors could have tipped the scale. But the main factor was that my opponent had a lot of money with which to attack me and that money came mainly from Jewish sources. And had that not been available I would have won. I don't have any doubt.

Further:

My colleagues knew that I went through a real struggle in 1980 and even if I had won last November [1982], my colleagues were aware of the national scope of my challenge and this awareness has a chilling effect. Even if I'd won they would have said "I don't want to go through that. At least I won't take any chances."[149]

Findley also stated that the consistent support for Israel's demands in Congress does not arise out of ideological commitment to Israel's objectives, but rather out of "fear" of the kind of "sticks" the lobby can wield in the electoral process: "They have been able to convince members of Congress that Jewish support is vitally important and that they [the congressmen] would be in trouble if they didn't have it. I think that's the key, by making examples of the few, they can influence the many."[150] The significance of the pro-Israeli activity in the Findley-Durbin race was noted by another congressman:

"There is no question that the Findley-Durbin race was intimidating," says Democratic Representative Mervyn Dymally of California, who often grumbles during subcommittee sessions that aid to Israel is too high, especially after Israel's military adventures in Lebanon. Whenever Rep. Dymally grumbles, he says, he receives a prompt visitation from the American-Israel Public Affairs Committee or one of the Jewish PAC's, usually accompanied by someone from his district. During one recent session, he explained that while he sometimes complains, in the end he always votes for more aid to Israel. "Not once, I told them, have I ever strayed from the cause. And they said, 'Well you abstained once.' That's how good they are."[151]

One of the main individuals targeted for defeat in the 1983-84 election season was Senator Charles Percy, chairman of the Foreign Relations Committee. Percy's concern about the effect of being targeted was evidenced in his eagerness, in the debate over aid to Israel, to increase the amount of aid over what the administration requested as well as in his push to have all the aid given in the form of nonrepayable grants. AIPAC claimed that Percy's defeat was the result of organized pro-Israeli efforts, as it had claimed credit for Findley's defeat in 1982. Explaining why Percy had been targeted, Robert Golder, president of Delaware Valley PAC commented: "Senator Percy is a very powerful Senator. . . . he is a moderate and people listen when he talks, and he has not always been for Israel. He has not been 100 per cent pro-Israel. We would be much happier with Paul Simon, who is 100 per cent pro-Israel."[152] According to Percy's press secretary, Kathy Lydon, the only time Percy voted contrary to Israel's interests was on the sale of AWACs to Saudi Arabia in 1981.[153]

The spiraling costs of campaigning give PACs in general extraordinary and, many argue, dangerous influence. Common Cause, the citizens' lobby, waged a campaign during the 1983-84 election season in support of legislation to curb what it termed "the dangerous and scandalous role played by affluent special interest groups in Congressional elections."[154] Former Congressman William Brodhead, who favored such legislation, remarked: "They're [the PACs] trying to buy votes. There's no other purpose of it. . . . Democracy can't survive in this country if people are going to be buying and selling votes in the lobbies of the United States."[155] The bill to reduce the influence of PACs did not pass in the 98th Congress, which was to be expected, since incumbents, the primary recipients of PAC money, were naturally reluctant to limit their most important financial resources. Nor is it likely that such legislation would pass in the future. Moreover, a decision on April 30, 1984, by the U.S. Supreme Court, in which it refused to rule on the legality of campaign spending limits before the November 6 elections, freed PACs to spend in the 1984 election as never before. It was estimated after the decision that PACs would spend approximately $20 million during 1984, and it was to be assumed that the combined contributions of pro-Israeli PACs would once again top the list of special interests.

It is important to note, however, that despite the phenomenal success of the pro-Israeli lobby on the domestic scene, its interests and efforts are not representative of all Jews in the United States, possibly not even of a majority of Jews. According to one professional on the AIPAC staff: "I would say that at most 2 million Jews are interested politically or in a charity sense. The other 4 million are not. Of the 2 million most will not be involved beyond giving money."[156] Moreover, according to one estimate, all those who provide the political actions for all organizations in United States Jewry probably do not exceed 250,000.[157] It is also interesting to note that five of the thirty-eight "Arab propagandists" listed in *Campaign to Discredit Israel* and six of the thirty-four listed in *Pro-Arab Propaganda in America* are Jewish.

Conclusion

The discussion in this chapter leads to the conclusion that the power of the Israeli lobby over the formation and execution of U.S. Middle East policy has become a virtual stranglehold. It no longer matters whether elected officials subscribe to the perception of Israel as a strategic asset to American interests or not. What matters is that the Israeli lobby is able to maintain the dominance of that perception as virtually unquestionable political truth and to assure that regardless of how severely American interests in the Middle East are compromised by Israel's policies, the U.S. government will continue to provide Israel with complete support. The lobby's effectiveness in impacting on the electoral process and its ability to shape public opinion and affect political culture are major factors in fostering this perception.

That such a situation is a formula for disaster seems self-evident. While the Arab world in 1985 is weak, divided, disorganized, and incapable of challenging Israel's regional hegemony, it is folly to assume that this situation will remain unchanged. History is a succession of the rise and fall of nations: those most susceptible to decline are ones that impose their domination on peoples other than their own. The 160 million Arabs will not forever accept the dictates of three million Israelis, even under the shadow of the United States.

The fall of the shah of Iran at the hands of his own people should give pause to all thoughtful observers, as should the resilience of the spirit and idea of Palestinian nationalism even after the massive destruction Israel inflicted on every Palestinian organization and institution in 1982. It is inconceivable that Syria will accept perpetual Israeli occupation of the Golan; or the Lebanese, Israeli domination of southern Lebanon; or Saudi Arabia and other Muslim countries, Israeli rule over all of Jerusalem. The present Israeli/U.S.-enforced acceptance will assuredly not withstand the test of time. On another level, the Israeli possession of nuclear weapons will inevitably stimulate the development of a nuclear capability among the Arabs, and despite Israel's precedent-setting attack on the Baghdad reactor, some state will succeed. Ultimately instability will give way to renewed war, with the very real potential of nuclear escalation and superpower involvement. Washington's partnership with Israel may thus be the undoing of the United States.

It is also apparent that there will be no peace or stability in the Middle East without a just resolution of the Palestinian question. While Israel is committed to maintaining an exclusive Jewish state *and* the extension of Israeli sovereignty over all of historic Palestine, foreclosing any possibility for a solution to this issue, the Palestinians—repressed and brutalized in every country in which they have been forced to reside since 1948—are more determined than ever to secure a state of their own in which they can protect themselves. In the conflict between the Palestinian quest for survival and the Israeli commitment to deny it resides the core of Middle Eastern instability and the potential for a cataclysm that may not only engulf the Near East but could in this nuclear age swallow the rest of the world. If the Israelis and their American supporters are too shortsighted to grasp this fundamental fact, surely other Americans must have the vision to understand it.

The single hope in this most disheartening situation is for the American people to take an interest in the foreign policy of their government, to attempt to understand the complex reality of the Middle East, including the perceptions and aspirations of the Arab people in general, and the Palestinians in particular, and to regain control of their government so that its policies serve the interests of its citizens—not merely the interests of a dominant elite. It is worth recalling that the opposition of large numbers of Americans to the war in Vietnam and their organization against the Southeast Asian intervention—a policy long supported by an elite consensus—was a major factor contributing to policy change. Must 55,000 American lives—or more—be lost in the Middle East before we rethink our perceptions and policies?

NOTES

PREFACE

1. Michael Parenti, *Power and the Powerless* (New York: St. Martin's Press, 1978), 41-49.

2. For a discussion of the suppression of a book (Roberta Strauss Feuerlicht's *The Fate of the Jews: A People Torn between Israeli Power and Jewish Ethics* [New York: Times Books, 1983], see Cheryl A. Rubenberg, "Pro-Israeli Influence on the Media and United States Middle East Policy," *Mideast Monitor* 2, no. 2 (Mar. 1985), 2. Also see Chapter 8 herein.

3. Nadav Safran, *Israel: The Embattled Ally* (Cambridge, Mass.: The Belknap Press of Harvard University Press, 1978).

4. See Cheryl A. Rubenberg, "Conflict and Contradiction in the Relations between the Arab States and the Palestine National Movement," in *Palestine: Continuing Dispossession,* ed. Glenn E. Perry (Belmont, Mass.: Association of Arab-American University Graduates, Inc. 1986), 121-45.

CHAPTER ONE

1. David Halberstam, *The Best and the Brightest* (New York: Random House, 1969).

2. See, for example, John C. Campbell, "The Security Factor in United States Middle East Policy," *American-Arab Affairs* 5 (Summer 1983), 1. Campbell limits his discussion to the balance of global power and access to the region's oil.

3. See, for example, Bernard Reich's *The United States and Israel: Influence in the Special Relationship* (New York: Praeger, 1984), especially 88, 89, 92, 94, 136, and 138. In general rather than making the argument directly himself, Reich uses the positions of various government officials who subscribe to the thesis to present it, but clearly he adheres to the idea.

4. Seth P. Tillman, *The United States in the Middle East: Interests and Obstacles* (Bloomington: Indiana University Press, 1982), 52 and passim, makes a similar argument, though stated less directly.

5. See, for example, George W. Ball, "What Is an Ally?" *American-Arab Affairs* 6 (Fall 1983), 12, who writes specifically about the impediment the U.S.–Israeli relationship has been to Washington's efforts to increase the stability of pro-American Arab governments.

6. Some books that bring the reality of Israel's policies into sharper perspective include: Livia Rokach's *Israel's Sacred Terrorism: A Study Based on Moshe Sharett's Personal Diary and Other Documents* (Belmont, Mass.: Association of Arab-American University Graduates, Inc. 1980); Amnon Kapeliouk's *Israel: la fin des mythes* (Paris: Albin Michel, 1975); Avri el-Ad's *Decline of Honor* (Chicago: Regnery, 1976); Yoram Peri's *Between Battles and Ballots: Israeli Military in Politics* (Cambridge: Cambridge University Press, 1983); David Hirst's *The Gun and the Olive Branch:*

The Roots of Violence in the Middle East (London: Futura Macdonald, 1983; orig. publ. Farber & Farber, 1977); Simha Flapan's *Zionism and the Palestinians* (New York: Barnes and Noble, 1979); Dov Yermiya's *My War Diary: Lebanon, June 5-July 1, 1982* (Boston: South End Press, 1983); Noam Chomsky's *The Fateful Triangle: The United States, Israel and the Palestinians* (Boston: South End Press, 1983) All of these writers except Hirst and Chomsky are Israelis, and Chomsky is Jewish.

7. Statistics from B. Michael, *Ha'aretz*, July 16, 1982, citing official statistics, quoted in Chomsky, *Fateful Triangle*, 74.

8. Quotation from Goldmann in Tillman, *United States in the Middle East*, 53.

9. Eric Rouleau, *Le Monde*, Feb. 19, 1970, quoted in Chomsky, *Fateful Triangle*, 64. Actually Nasser sought accommodation as early as 1955. See p. 60 herein, and also *New York Times*, Nov. 28, 1982, and Elmore Jackson, *Middle East Mission* (New York: W. W. Norton, 1983).

10. *London Sunday Times*, June 15, 1969, quoted in Chomsky, *Fateful Triangle*, 51.

11. Amos Elon, *Ha'aretz*, Nov. 13, 1981, quoted in ibid., 64.

12. Edward Witten, *Ha'aretz*, Jan. 6, 1983, quoted in ibid., 65.

13. For a detailed analysis of Israel's response to the Jordanian proposal see ibid., 65. In addition, see the discussion of the Jordanian proposal that King Hussein formally transmitted to President Nixon and Henry Kissinger in early 1973 as discussed by Henry Kissinger, *Years of Upheaval* (Boston: Little, Brown, 1982), 216-22. Also see the discussion in the text of Chapter 5 herein.

14. For an analysis of the Security Council resolution and Israel's response, see Noam Chomsky, *Towards a New Cold War: Essays on the Current Crisis and How We Got There* (New York: Pantheon Books, 1982), 267, 300, 461; also Chomsky, *Fateful Triangle*, 67.

15. Bernard Gwertzman, *New York Times*, Aug. 21, 1977, quoted in Chomsky, *Fateful Triangle*, 68.

16. *New York Times*, Mar. 21, 1977, quoted in ibid., 68. Also see pp. 193-96 herein.

17. See the analysis and detail in Chomsky, *Fateful Triangle*, 69. See also pp. 194, 196, 201-2 herein.

18. Richard H. Curtiss, *A Changing Image: American Perceptions of the Arab-Israeli Dispute* (Washington, D.C.: American Educational Trust, 1982), 131-33. See Chapter 8 herein for further discussion of American commercial losses due to the U.S.-Israeli relationship.

19. For a good analysis of the consequences of U.S. "support" for Israel, see George W. Ball, *Error and Betrayal in Lebanon: An Analysis of Israel's Invasion of Lebanon and the Implications for United States-Israeli Relations* (Washington, D.C.: Foundation for Middle East Peace, 1984), passim.

20. See, for example, Peter Grose's *Israel in the Mind of America* (New York: Schocken Books, 1984), and Regina Sharif's *Non-Jewish Zionism: Its Roots in Western History* (London: Zed Press, 1983).

21. Campbell, "Security Factor," 7-8.

22. Seth P. Tillman, "United States Middle East Policy: Theory and Practice," *American-Arab Affairs* 4 (Spring 1983), 9-10 (emphasis in original).

23. Stephen Green, *Taking Sides: America's Secret Relations with a Militant Israel* (New York: William Morrow, 1984), 72; also see 16-75.

24. Marxist analysts would argue that insofar as the elite in American politics is fundamentally dominated by corporate interests and that American foreign policy is essentially a search for global hegemony to maximize U.S. commercial concerns, Israel serves as a surrogate in the grand global scheme. See Ibrahim I. Ibrahim, "The American-Israeli Alliance: *Raison d'etat* Revisited," *Journal of Palestine Studies* 15, no. 3 (Spring 1986), 17-29. I think the weight of evidence in this book indicates that Israel has not fulfilled the surrogate role in the Middle East, although clearly Israel has done so in other parts of the globe. See, for example, Cheryl A. Rubenberg, "Israel and Guatemala: A Case Study in Israeli Foreign Policy," *MERIP Reports* (May-June 1986). That the majority of Arab governments have remained so pro-American and that U.S. interests have not suffered more severely than they have must be accounted for *in spite of,* not *because* of Israel. Additional factors, from an Arab perspective, are weak leadership in the aftermath of Nasser's death and a dependent position in the structural relations of the international economic system, even with the oil resource. See Cheryl A. Rubenberg, "Conflict and Contradiction in the Relations between the Arab States and the Palestine National Movement," in *Palestine: Continuing Dispossession,* ed. Glenn E. Perry (Belmont, Mass.: Association of Arab-American University Graduates, Inc., 1986). Of course, from the American perspective the situation is fortuitous and is a further reason why U.S. policy has remained so wedded to Israel. Seth Tillman and George Ball have argued that pro-Israeli individuals and groups acquired sufficient power, either directly or indirectly, to mold elite perceptions consonant with Israel's interests. Pro-Israeli individuals would argue, much like Marxists, that America's interests are served by its faithful and "only" regional ally, Israel. Some even argue that U.S. and Israeli interests are identical.

25. Chomsky, *Fateful Triangle,* passim. This is the underlying thesis of the book.

26. Ball, "What Is an Ally?" 11-12.

27. For a discussion of the Israeli lobby, see Cheryl A. Rubenberg, "The Middle East Lobbies," *The Link* 17, no. 1 (Jan.-Mar. 1984); Rubenberg, "The Conduct of United States Foreign Policy in the Middle East in the 1983-84 Presidential Election Season," *American-Arab Affairs* 9 (Summer 1984). The most comprehensive and best account of the Israeli lobby on the American scene is Paul Findley's *They Dare to Speak Out: People and Institutions Confront Israel's Lobby* (Westport, Conn.: Lawrence Hill, 1985).

28. Tillman, *United States in the Middle East,* 54.

29. For a discussion of this phenomenon see Cheryl A. Rubenberg, "Pro-Israeli Influence on the Media and United States Middle East Policy," *Mideast Monitor* 2, no. 2 (Mar. 1985). Also see: Edmund Ghareeb, ed., *Split Vision: The Portrayal of Arabs in the American Media* (Washington: American-Arab Affairs Council, 1983); Janice J. Terry, "The Arab-Israeli Conflict in Popular Literature," *American-Arab Affairs* 2 (Fall 1982), 97-104, and *Mistaken Identity: Arab Stereotypes in Popular Writing* (Washington, D.C.: American-Arab Affairs Council, 1985); Jack G. Shaheen, *The T.V. Arab* (Bowling Green, Ohio: Bowling Green State University, 1985), and "Media Coverage of the Middle East: Perception and Foreign Policy," *Annals of the American Academy of Political and Social Science* 482 (Nov. 1985); and Michael C. Hudson and Ronald A. Wolfe, eds., *The American*

Media and the Arabs (Washington, D.C.: Center for Contemporary Arab Studies, Georgetown University, 1980).

30. See, for example, Hassan Haddad and Donald Wagner, *All in the Name of the Bible: Selected Essays on Israel, South Africa, and American Christian Fundamentalism*, PHRC Special Report #5 (Chicago: Palestine Human Rights Campaign, 1985); Bashir Nijim, ed., *American Church Politics and the Middle East* (Belmont, Mass.: Association of Arab-American University Graduates, Inc., 1982); Dewey Beegle, *Prophecy and Prediction* (Ann Arbor: Prior Pettingill, 1979).

31. Earl Raab and Seymour Martin Lipset, *The Political Future of American Jews* (New York: American Jewish Congress, 1985), passim.

32. Ball "What Is an Ally?" 12.

33. Fred J. Khouri, "The Challenge to United States Security and Middle East Policy," *American-Arab Affairs* 5 (Summer 1983), 19, makes this argument very cogently.

34. Ibid., 12, 19.

35. Ibid., 13.

36. Seymour M. Hersh, *The Price of Power: Kissinger in the Nixon White House* (New York: Summit Books, 1983), 225.

37. Khouri, "Challenge," 13.

38. The European consensus on a Palestinian state has been made explicit in numerous official statements, e.g., the June 1980 "Venice Declaration." The United States ignores these statements; in addition, it has openly opposed the Euro-Arab dialogue and European overtures to the PLO. Henry Kissinger once confided in a private document that one basic element in his post-1973 diplomatic strategy was "to ensure that the Europeans and Japanese did not get involved in the diplomacy" concerning the Middle East. Cited in Chomsky, *Fateful Triangle*, 20. Chomsky states that the source is a memorandum obtained under the Freedom of Information Act.

39. Henry Kissinger, *Washington Post*, June 16, 1982. For a quotation from his article see pp. 285-86 herein.

40. See Chapter 8 herein for a full discussion of these issues.

41. See, for example, Maxime Rodinson, *Israel: A Colonial Settler State* (New York: Monad Press, 1973); Philippa Strum, "Israel's Democratic Dilemma," *Reform Judaism*, Publication of the Union of American Hebrew Congregations, 14, no. 2 (Winter 1985-86), 13; Ian Lustick, *Arabs in the Jewish State: Israel's Control of a National Minority* (Austin: University of Texas Press, 1980); Uri Davis, "Israel's Zionist Society: Consequences for Internal Opposition and the Necessity for External Intervention," in EAFORD and AJAZ, eds., *Judaism or Zionism: What Difference for the Middle East?* (London: Zed Books, 1986), 176-205; Elia T. Zureik, *The Palestinians in Israel: A Study in Internal Colonialism* (London: Routledge & Kegan Paul, 1979).

CHAPTER TWO

1. This brief historical overview borrows heavily from the analysis provided by Fred J. Khouri in *The Arab-Israeli Dilemma*, 2d ed. (Syracuse, N.Y.: Syracuse University Press, 1976), 1-3.

2. See Roberta Strauss Feuerlicht, *The Fate of the Jews: A People Torn between Israeli Power and Jewish Ethics* (New York: Times Books, 1983), 1-67, for a brief but excellent, if somewhat revisionist, history of the Jewish

people from the time of the First Temple through the diaspora until 1948. For a more standard history, see Abram Leon Sachar, *A History of the Jews* (New York: Alfred A. Knopf, 1968).

3. For a discussion of the historical connection of the Palestinians to Palestine, see Henry Cattan, "The Question of Jerusalem," *Israel and the Question of Palestine*, special issue, *Arab Studies Quarterly* 7, nos. 2 and 3 (Spring/Summer 1985), 132-33. For a comment on Palestinian identity, see Maxime Rodinson, *Israel and the Arabs*, 2d ed. (New York: Penguin Books, 1982 [orig. publ. 1968]), 216. For the meaning of Jerusalem to Muslims, see Ishaq Musa Husaini, "Jerusalem in Islamic Perspective," in *Jerusalem: Key to Peace in the Middle East*, ed. O. Kelly Ingram (Durham, N.C.: Triangle Friends of the Middle East, 1978), 39-46.

4. For an excellent history of Arab nationalism, see George Antonius, *The Arab Awakening* (New York: G. P. Putnam & Son, 1946).

5. The Hussein-McMahon Correspondence was an exchange of letters between Sir Henry McMahon, the British high commissioner for Egypt, and Sharif Hussein of Mecca (and the Hejaz) between July 14 and Dec. 13, 1915. For a text of these letters, see ibid., 413-27.

6. The Balfour Declaration was a letter dated Nov. 2, 1917, from Lord Arthur James Balfour, the British foreign secretary, to Lord Rothschild. The letter stated, in part, "His Majesty's Government views with favor the establishment in Palestine of a National Home for the Jewish people. . . . it being clearly understood that nothing shall be done which may prejudice the civil and religious rights of existing non-Jewish communities in Palestine." For the full text, see John Norton Moore, ed., *The Arab-Israeli Conflict III: Documents*, American Society of International Law (Princeton, N.J.: Princeton University Press, 1974), 31-32.

7. For a text of the Sykes-Picot Agreement, see ibid., 24-28.

8. For a good standard history of political Zionism, see Ben Halpern, *The Idea of the Jewish State*, 2d ed.(Cambridge, Mass.: Harvard University Press, 1969). For an important critique of Zionism, see EAFORD and AJAZ, eds., *Judaism or Zionism: What Difference for the Middle East?* (London: Zed Press, 1986), especially Norton Mezvinsky, "Humanitarian Dissent in Zionism: Martin Buber and Juda Magnes," 98-119, and Rabbi Elmer Berger, "The Unauthenticity of 'Jewish People' Zionism," 133-47. Mezvinsky and Berger are Jews. Two other important books on Zionism are: Shlomo Avineri, *The Making of Modern Zionism: The Intellectual Origins of the Jewish State* (New York: Basic Books, 1981), and Bernard Avishai, *The Tragedy of Zionism: Revolution and Democracy in the Land of Israel* (New York: Farrar, Strauss and Giroux, 1985). Avineri and Avishai are Israeli.

9. For a text of the Biltmore Program, see Moore, ed., *Documents*, 230-32.

10. The Jewish Agency was an umbrella organization, formed in 1929, that originally subsumed all Jewish groups, Zionist and non-Zionist, political and military, dedicated to the building of a Jewish homeland in Palestine. Eventually it became solely an instrument of Zionist aims.

11. Janet Abu-Lughod, "The Demographic Transformation of Palestine," in Ibrahim Abu-Lughod, ed., *The Transformation of Palestine: Essays on the Origin and Development of the Arab-Israeli Conflict* (Evanston, Ill.: Northwestern University Press, 1971), 140.

12. *Israeli Yearbook*, 1950/51, Jerusalem, 81, cited in ibid., 140.

13. *Census of Palestine*, Jerusalem, 1922, cited in ibid., 142.
14. *Census of Palestine*, Jerusalem, 1931, cited in ibid., 144.
15. Ibid., 150.
16. *General Monthly Bulletin* 12, (Dec. 1947), 686 (Table I), cited in ibid., 155. It has become fashionable to attempt to "prove" that the demographic character of Palestine was other than these statistics suggest. A much heralded new polemic of this genre is Joan Peters's *From Time Immemorial: The Origins of the Arab-Jewish Conflict over Palestine* (New York: Harper and Row, 1984). Princeton University graduate student and critic Norman G. Finkelstein, who painstakingly documented the book's fraudulent statistics and deceptive arguments, has called the book one of the "most spectacular frauds ever published on the Arab-Israeli conflict." *In These Times*, Sept. 5-11, 1984, 12-14. See also pp. 343-44 herein.
17. John Ruedy, "Dynamics of Land Alienation," in I. Abu-Lughod, ed., *Transformation of Palestine*, 124.
18. Ibid., 134-35.
19. Khouri, *Arab-Israeli Dilemma*, 53-54.
20. See Khouri's analysis in ibid., 38-42.
21. See, for example, the analysis by Peter Grose, *Israel in the Mind of America* (New York: Schocken Books, 1984).
22. "Congressional Resolution Favoring the Establishment in Palestine of a National Home for the Jewish People, Sept. 21, 1922," in Moore, ed., *Documents*, 107-8.
23. J. C. Hurewitz, *The Struggle for Palestine* (New York: Schocken Books, 1976 [copyright 1950]), 213.
24. *Congressional Record*, 78th Cong., 2d Sess. vol. 90, part 1, Jan. 10, 1944–Feb. 8, 1944 (Washington, D.C.: Government Printing Office, 1944), 815.
25. Hurewitz, *Struggle for Palestine*, 213-14.
26. Correspondence cited in Robert J. Donovan, *Conflict and Crisis: The Presidency of Harry S. Truman, 1945-1948* (New York: W. W. Norton, 1977), 321, 455.
27. See J. C. Hurewitz, ed., *Diplomacy in the Near and Middle East: A Documentary Record, 1914-1956*, 2 (Princeton, N.J.: Princeton University Press, 1956), 66-74. For excerpts from the King-Crane Commission report, see Moore, ed., *Documents*, 50-63. In addition, for an excellent analysis and contextual article, see M. Thomas Davis, "The King-Crane Commission and the American Abandonment of Self-Determination," *American-Arab Affairs* 9 (Summer 1984), 55-66.
28. "Excerpts from the Report of the United Nations Special Committee on Palestine, Sept. 3, 1947," in Moore, ed., *Documents*, 259-312.
29. Ben-Gurion's statement in quotation with supporting analysis is cited by Ilan Halevi in "Zionism Today," *Israel and the Question of Palestine*, special issue, *Arab Studies Quarterly* 7, nos. 2 and 3 (Spring/Summer 1985), 8. More important, Ben-Gurion's official biographer has recently demonstrated the Israeli leader's belief in military struggle as the only means to secure a Jewish state in Palestine as well as his conviction that a state in part of Palestine was insufficient to fulfill Zionism's aspirations. See Shabtai Teveth, *Ben-Gurion and the Palestinian Arabs: From Peace to War* (New York: Oxford University Press, 1985), passim, but especially pp. 187-88.
30. For a text of the Truman Doctrine, see Ralph H. Magnus, ed., *Documents on the Middle East* (Washington, D.C.: American Enterprise

Institute, 1969), 63-69. For a reasonably balanced discussion of the development of the cold war, see Daniel Yergin, *Shattered Peace: The Origins of the Cold War and the National Security State* (Boston: Houghton Mifflin, 1977), passim. For a critique of the conventional wisdom on the origins of the cold war, see William Appleman Williams, *The Tragedy of American Diplomacy*, rev. ed. (New York: World, 1962).

31. In the debate over the partition of Palestine, the Soviets supported partition and the establishment of the state of Israel, followed through with sales of arms and aircraft in 1948, and voted for Israel's admission to the United Nations in 1949. But as the United States emerged as an ally of Israel, the Soviets swung to support for the Arab position. Significant Soviet influence in the Arab world, however, did not develop until 1955 and the "Czech Arms Deal" with Egypt. Nevertheless, given the growing intensity of the cold war in the 1947-48 period and the very real interests of the United States in the Arab world, it is not surprising that most officials in the State and War departments, including the Joint Chiefs of Staff, opposed American support for the creation of Israel.

32. William Eddy, *F.D.R. Meets Ibn Saud* (New York: American Friends of the Middle East, 1954), 36-37. In general for a discussion of Truman, the Department of State, and the question of Palestine, see Evan M. Wilson, *Decision on Palestine: How the United States Came to Recognize Israel* (Stanford, Calif.: Hoover Institution Press, 1979).

33. Harry S. Truman, *1946-1952, Years of Trial and Hope: Memoirs*, 2 (New York: New American Library [paperback], 1956), 185.

34. Ibid., 185.

35. John Snetsinger, *Truman, the Jewish Vote and the Creation of Israel* (Stanford, Calif.: Hoover Institution Press, 1974), 42. Snetsinger's book provides an excellent discussion of the intricacies of domestic politics and American policy vis-à-vis Palestine and the creation of Israel.

36. *New York Times*, Oct. 5, 1946, cited in ibid., 42.

37. *New York Times*, Nov. 1, 1946, 17, cited in ibid., 44. Also see Walter Millis, ed. (with the collaboration of E. S. Duffield), *The Forrestal Diaries* (New York: Viking Press, 1951), 218.

38. Grose, *Israel in the Mind of America*, 230-31, 272-73, 277, 293, 298. Also see Donovan, *Conflict and Crisis*, 317, 373-76, 386, 428.

39. See Donovan, *Conflict and Crisis*, 324. Also see George F. Kennan, *Memoirs: 1925-1950* (Boston: Little Brown, 1967), 380.

40. See "Report by the Policy Planning Staff on the Position of the United States with Respect to Palestine," Jan. 19, 1948, in *Foreign Relations of the United States, 1948, vol. 5, The Near East, South Asia, and Africa* (in two parts), Part 2, "Israel" (Washington, D.C.: Government Printing Office, 1976), 546-54; "United States Position with Regard to the Question of Palestine," memorandum prepared in the Department of State, *Foreign Relations of the United States, 1947, vol. 5, The Near East, South Asia and Africa*, "Palestine" (Washington, D.C.: Government Printing Office, 1975), 1166-70.

41. For the report of the Anglo-American Committee of Inquiry (published Apr. 20, 1946), see Moore, ed., *Documents*, 243-53.

42. The importance attributed to Middle Eastern oil, even at this early juncture, can be seen in the following sources: Halford L. Hoskins, *Middle East Oil in United States Foreign Policy*, The Library of Congress Legislative Reference Service (New York: Viking Press, 1951); Raymond F. Mikesell

and Hollis B. Chenery, *Arabian Oil: American Stakes in the Middle East* (Chapel Hill: University of North Carolina Press, 1949).

43. See Millis, ed., *Forrestal Diaries,* 323.

44. Truman, *Memoirs,* 186-87.

45. See Thomas J. Hamilton, "Partition of Palestine," *Foreign Policy Reports* (Feb. 15, 1948), 286-95.

46. David Horowitz, *State in the Making* (New York: Alfred A. Knopf, 1953), 301. Also see Donovan, *Conflict and Crisis,* 328-31, who documents in detail the last-minute U.S. lobbying for support of partition. Donovan also takes the position that Truman *ordered* the pressure at the end. Sumner Welles makes the same argument in his *We Need Not Fail* (Boston: Houghton Mifflin, 1948), 63. Also see Alan R. Taylor, *Prelude to Israel: An Analysis of Zionist Diplomacy, 1897-1947* (New York: Philosophical Library, 1959), 103-4.

47. Horowitz, *State in the Making,* 255, 301.

48. Hamilton, "Partition of Palestine," 295. For important documentation to support this view, see also *Foreign Relations of the U.S., 1947,* 1248, 1290, 1291, 1305-9.

49. "Memorandum, Henderson to Marshall, November 10, 1947," ibid., 1249.

50. *Israel: Political and Diplomatic Documents, December 1947–May 1948,* Israel State Archives, Central Zionist Archives (Jerusalem: Israel Government Printer at Akva Press, 1979), 40, 102-4, 112, 113, passim.

51. U.S. Department of State, *Press Release,* no. 949, Dec. 5, 1947.

52. Quoted in Ernest Stock, *Israel on the Road to Sinai: 1949-1956* (Ithaca, N.Y.: Cornell University Press, 1967), 39. Stock's source: Y. Riftin, no. 5 *Israeli Parliamentary Proceedings* (Divrei ha-Knesset), 1572, (May 31, 1950).

53. See Dan Kurzman, *Genesis 1948: The First Arab-Israeli War* (New York: World, 1970), 107-8.

54. "Moshe Shertok: Aide-memoir for F. D. Roosevelt, Jr.," Dec. 24, 1947, *Israel Documents, December 1947–May 1948,* 103.

55. "Report by the Policy Planning Staff on Position of the United States with Respect to Palestine," Washington, Jan. 19, 1948, in *Foreign Relations of the U.S., 1948,* 550-51. In the same volume see also: 556-66, 569-71, 573-81, 587-89, 616-25.

56. See Donovan, *Conflict and Crisis,* 371. The source for Truman's commitment: *Public Papers of the Presidents of the United States: Harry S. Truman, 1948* (Washington, D.C.: Government Printing Office), 229.

57. Truman, *Memoirs,* 188.

58. See, for example, "Report by the Policy Planning Staff on Position of the United States with Respect to Palestine," Jan. 19, 1948, in *Foreign Relations of the U.S., 1948,* 546-54; "The Partition of Palestine and United States Security," memorandum by Samuel K. C. Kooper of the Office of Near Eastern Affairs, Jan. 27, 1948, ibid., 563-66; "Memorandum by the Director of the Policy Planning Staff (Lovett)," Jan. 29, 1948, ibid., 573-81; "The Problem of Palestine," memorandum by the Planning Staff, Feb. 11, 1948, ibid., 619-26.

59. Even before the Czech crisis Truman had expressed his concern over having American troops tied down in Palestine; he referred to these strategic liabilities in a cabinet meeting on Dec. 1, 1947. See Millis, ed., *Forrestal*

Diaries, 346. Also see Snetsinger, *Truman, the Jewish Vote and Israel,* 85-86.

60. See the accounts in Grose, *Israel in the Mind of America,* 272-73, and Donovan, *Conflict and Crisis,* 374-75.

61. See Truman, *Memoirs,* 190; *Foreign Relations of the U.S., 1948,* 637, 745, 746, 749-50; Donovan, *Conflict and Crisis,* 375-79; Ian J. Bickerton, "President Truman's Recognition of Israel," *American Jewish Historical Quarterly* 58 (Dec. 1968), 213, 215-16, 173-240 passim; and "Statement by Secretary of State George Marshall," Mar. 25, 1948, *Foreign Relations of the U.S., 1948,* 759-60.

62. "Moshe Shertok to George Marshall," Apr. 29, 1948, *Israel Documents, December 1947–May, 1948,* 695-96.

63. *New York Times,* May 14, 1948, cited in Snetsinger, *Truman, the Jewish Vote and Israel,* 90.

64. Trygve Lie, *In the Cause of Peace* (New York: Macmillan, 1954), 170.

65. *Foreign Relations of the U.S., 1948,* 974. Also see Snetsinger's analysis in *Truman, the Jewish Vote and Israel,* 94-114.

66. Walter Eytan, *The First Ten Years: A Diplomatic History of Israel* (London: Weidenfeld and Nicolson, 1958), 8.

67. See *Foreign Relations of the U.S. 1948,* 974-76.

68. Snetsinger, *Truman, the Jewish Vote and Israel,* 103, 179, whose source was "The Politics of 1948," Clifford to Truman, Nov. 19, 1947 (Clark M. Clifford Papers, Truman Library, Independence, Mo.).

69. *Foreign Relations of the U.S., 1948,* 974.

70. Snetsinger, *Truman, the Jewish Vote and Israel,* 105, whose source was Truman Papers, Truman Library, Independence, Mo., OF 204-Misc.

71. Truman, *Memoirs,* 193.

72. Chaim Weizmann, *Trial and Error: The Autobiography of Chaim Weizmann* (New York: Harper and Brothers, 1949), 480-81.

73. *Foreign Relations of the U.S., 1948,* 1313. Also see 1300-1301, 1346, 1391.

74. White House Press Release, Jan. 19, 1949.

75. "Memorandum by the Acting Secretary of State (Lovett) to President Truman," May 26, 1948, *Foreign Relations of the U.S., 1948,* 1051-53. Also see 1058-60.

76. See James G. McDonald, *My Mission in Israel* (New York: Simon and Schuster, 1951).

77. *New York Times,* June 23, 1948.

78. *Foreign Relations of the U. S., 1948,* 1131-32, 1140.

79. Snetsinger, *Truman, the Jewish Vote and Israel,* 118, whose source was Truman Papers, OF 204-D.

80. *New York Times,* July 15, 1948, 8.

81. See Stephen D. Issacs, *Jews and American Politics* (Garden City, N.Y.: Doubleday, 1974), passim.

82. *Foreign Relations of the U.S., 1948,* 1027, 1060-61, 1217.

83. *Public Opinion Quarterly* 12 (Fall 1948), 550.

84. *Foreign Relations of the U.S., 1948,* 1152-54.

85. See David Ben-Gurion, *Israel, a Personal History* (New York: Funk and Wagnalls, Sabra Books, 1971), 198-210, 231, 269-71.

86. *Department of State Bulletin,* Oct. 3, 1948, 436.

87. Truman, *Memoirs,* 195.

88. *Foreign Relations of the U.S., 1948*, 1437-38.

89. Ibid.

90. Ibid., 1512-14 ("Statement by the President").

91. Marian Woolfson, "Tricks the Memory Plays on Palestine," *Manchester Guardian Weekly* (England), Apr. 6, 1986.

92. Khouri, *Arab-Israeli Dilemma*, 74-77. Also see Stephen Green, *Taking Sides: America's Secret Relations with a Militant Israel* (New York: William Morrow, 1984), 16-75, for an excellent discussion of Israel's quantitative and qualitative superiority in the 1948 war.

93. *Foreign Relations of the U.S., 1948*, 1215.

94. Lie, *In the Cause of Peace*, 188.

95. *Foreign Relations of the U.S., 1948*, 1337-39.

96. J. Abu-Lughod, "Demographic Transformation of Palestine," 161.

97. Khouri, *Arab-Israeli Dilemma*, 53-54. His figures are taken from U.N. sources. Also see J. Abu-Lughod, "Demographic Transformation of Palestine," 156-61, whose figures are slightly higher and probably more accurate since they are based on her meticulous demographic analysis.

98. Benny Morris, "The Causes and Character of the Arab Exodus from Palestine: The Israeli Defense Forces Intelligence Branch Analysis of June 1948," *Middle Eastern Studies* (London) (Jan. 1986). Morris, an Israeli, published another article, "Operation Dani and the Palestinian Exodus from Lydda and Ramleh in 1948," *The Middle East Journal* (Winter 1986), in which he extends the research and analysis further. He will publish a complete volume on the subject with Cambridge University Press in 1987; see excerpts and analysis in *Al Fajr,* Jerusalem Palestinian Weekly (English) (May 16, 1986), 8-9. Also, in the same issue are excerpts—on the same subject—from an interview with the Israeli analyst, Simha Flapan, that appeared in the *Canadian Jewish News* (Oct. 1985). He makes the same points about Israel's concerted effort—through military means—to rid Palestine of its indigenous people. Flapan has written a book entitled *The Birth of Israel—Myths and Realities,* which will be published late in 1986 (no publisher specified in article). The work of both these Israelis should have a profound impact on the "common wisdom" and conventional historiography concerning Israel's role in driving the Palestinians out of Palestine in 1947-48.

99. See Khouri, *Arab-Israeli Dilemma*, 123-24, for a discussion of the massacre. For an account of another deliberate massacre of unarmed and helpless Palestinians by Zionist soldiers in the village of Biram, see Elias Chacour, *Blood Brothers* (Grand Rapids, Mich.: Chosen Books of the Zondervan Corp., 1984), 36-53. Father Chacour, a Melkite priest born in Palestine, presently lives in Ibillin, Galilee, Israel.

100. Menachem Begin, *The Revolt,* rev. ed. (New York: Nash Publishing, 1977), 216-22.

101. Begin, *The Revolt* (London: W. H. Allen, 1951), quoted in I. F. Stone, "The Other Zionism," in *Underground to Palestine: And Reflections Thirty Years Later* (New York: Pantheon Books, 1978), 258-59. See also Alan Taylor, "The Two Faces of Zionism," in *Judaism or Zionism,* 69-75.

102. Seth P. Tillman, *The United States in the Middle East: Interests and Obstacles* (Bloomington: Indiana University Press, 1982), 190.

103. Snetsinger, *Truman, the Jewish Vote and Israel*, 126-32.

104. Khouri, *Arab-Israeli Dilemma*, 102-22, 123-81.

105. *Foreign Relations of the U.S., 1948*, 1337-39.

106. Ibid., 1704.
107. Ibid., 1546.
108. Ben-Gurion, *Israel*, 151.
109. *Foreign Relations of the U.S., 1948*, 1526-27, 1544-45.
110. For the texts of the armistice agreements, see Moore, ed., *Documents*, 380-414. For a discussion of the international legal meaning of armistices, see Gerhard Von Glahn, *Law among Nations: An Introduction to Public International Law*, 3d ed. (New York: Macmillan, 1976), 574. An armistice is an agreement or contract between belligerents. "Its primary and traditional purpose is to bring about a temporary suspension of active hostilities" (ibid.). Also note, "Normally, armistices envisage a future resumption of hostilities, because they represent merely a suspension of the latter" (ibid.). An armistice is not a peace treaty.
111. Indeed, it has been alleged that Amir Abdullah of Transjordan (the son of Sharif Hussein, who was placed on a British-created throne) and King Farouk of Egypt (a British-sponsored monarch in a country dominated by British influence) undertook specific efforts to ensure that the Palestinian state did not materialize. See, for example, Samir Amin, *The Arab Nation: Nationalism and Class Struggles* (London: Zed Press, 1978), 49; Michael C. Hudson, "The Arab States' Policies towards Israel," in I. Abu-Lughod, ed., *Transformation of Palestine*, 317; Dan Schueftan, "The Palestinians, the Arab States, and the Arab Commitment to the 'Cause of Palestine' as Factors in the Palestinian Dimension of the Arab-Israeli Conflict," in Gabriel Ben Dor, ed., *The Palestinians and the Middle East Conflict* (Ramat Gan, Israel: Turtledove Publishers, 1979), 129-34, and passim. Nevertheless, this does not excuse Washington from its responsibility to see that Resolution 181 was implemented in its totality, especially considering the important role the United States played in securing its initial passage.

CHAPTER THREE

1. For an analysis of U.S. strategic thinking during this period, see John Spanier, *American Foreign Policy since World War II*, 6th ed. (New York: Praeger Publishers, 1973), 115.
2. Dwight D. Eisenhower, *The White House Years: Waging Peace, 1956-61* (Garden City, N.Y.: Doubleday, 1965), 27.
3. Herman Finer, *Dulles Over Suez: The Theory and Practice of His Diplomacy* (Chicago: Quadrangle Books, 1964), 18; for an analysis of the Baghdad Pact, see John C. Campbell, *Defense of the Middle East: Problems of American Policy*, rev. ed. (New York: Harper and Bros., 1960), 54-57.
4. Yair Evron, *The Middle East: Nations, Superpowers and Wars* (New York: Praeger Publishers, 1973), 132-33.
5. Ibid., 132-34. Also see Campbell, *Defense of the Middle East*, 49-62.
6. Seymour M. Hersh, *The Price of Power: Kissinger in the Nixon White House* (New York: Summit Books, 1983), 215.
7. For an analysis of the importance of oil during this period, see Benjamin Shwadran, *The Middle East: Oil and the Great Powers*, 2d ed. (New York: Praeger Publishers, 1959).
8. Campbell, *Defense of the Middle East*, 100-102. Also see Winthrop W. Aldrich, "The Suez Crisis: A Footnote to History," *Foreign Affairs* 45 (Apr. 1967), 541-52.
9. Moshe Dayan, *Diary of the Sinai Campaign* (Jerusalem: Steimatzky's

Agency, 1964; English trans. by Weidenfeld and Nicholson, London, 1966), 3, 1-58, 209-10.

10. See the analysis in Ernest Stock, *Israel on the Road to Sinai 1949-1956, with a Sequel on the Six Day War, 1967* (Ithaca, N.Y.: Cornell University Press, 1967), 62-70.

11. Kennett Love, *Suez: The Twice-Fought War* (New York: McGraw-Hill, 1969), 55-60. Also see Wilbur Crane Eveland, *Ropes of Sand: America's Failure in Middle East* (New York: W. W. Norton, 1980), 73-77, and Stephen Green, *Taking Sides: America's Secret Relations with a Militant Israel* (New York: William Morrow, 1984), 83-87.

12. Eveland, *Ropes of Sand*, 73-77; Love, *Suez*, 55-60; Green, *Taking Sides*, 83-87.

13. Love, *Suez*, 58. Also see David Ben-Gurion, "Israel's Security and her International Position before and after the Sinai Campaign," *Israel Government Yearbook, 5720, 1959/60*, 17.

14. Quoted in Love, *Suez*, 5-20, in the context of a full discussion of the Gaza raid.

15. Ibid., 96-98.

16. Ibid., 476. For an analysis of the Kafr Qasem massacre, which the Palestinians remember as vividly as Deir Yassin, see David Hirst, *The Gun and the Olive Branch: The Roots of Violence in the Middle East* (London: Futura Macdonald, 1978, orig. publ. Farber and Farber, 1977), 185-87. Hirst analyzes Israel's military policies that resulted in the massacre and the "pro forma" trial for and "non-sentences" of those individuals responsible. There is a slight difference in the figures of slain Palestinians between Love (who cites 49) and Hirst (47). Love says seven women were killed; Hirst, fourteen women.

17. See General Assembly Resolution 194 (III), Dec. 11, 1948, in John Norton Moore, ed. *The Arab-Israeli Conflict, III, Documents,* American Society of International Law (Princeton, N.J.: Princeton University Press, 1974), 373-76.

18. For excellent material on the condition of the Palestinian Arabs living within Israel, see Sabri Jiryis, *The Arabs in Israel* (New York: Monthly Review Press, 1976); Elia T. Zureik, *The Palestinians in Israel: A Study in Internal Colonialism* (London: Routledge and Kegan Paul, 1979); Ian Lustick, *Arabs in the Jewish State: Israel's Control of a National Minority* (Austin: University of Texas Press, 1980); Uri Davis, "Israel's Zionist Society: Consequences for Internal Oppression and the Necessity for External Intervention," in EAFORD and AJAZ, eds., *Judaism or Zionism: What Difference for the Middle East?* (London: Zed Books, 1986), 176-205.

19. For an analysis of the Arab boycott of Israel, see Earl Berger, *The Covenant and the Sword: Arab-Israeli Relations 1948-56* (London: Routledge and Kegan Paul, 1965), 144-53.

20. Nadav Safran, *Israel: The Embattled Ally* (Cambridge, Mass.: The Belknap Press of Harvard University Press, 1978), 351, who comments specifically on Israel's efforts to sabotage the prospects of Egypt's joining a Middle Eastern alliance sponsored by the West.

21. See Green, *Taking Sides*, 107-14, for a comprehensive account of the Lavon affair.

22. Fred J. Khouri, *The Arab-Israeli Dilemma*, 2d ed. (Syracuse, N.Y.: Syracuse University Press, 1976), 205, who notes Israel's practice of seizing Arab ships.

23. Safran, *Embattled Ally*, 351.

24. *New York Times*, Nov. 28, 1982. See also Elmore Jackson, *Middle East Mission* (New York: W. W. Norton, 1983).

25. Ibid., Oct. 6, 1955.

26. Mahmoud Riad, *The Struggle for Peace in the Middle East* (New York: Quartet Books, 1981), 7.

27. See "The President's Proposal on the Middle East," *Hearings before the Committee on Foreign Relations and the Committee on Armed Services*, U.S. Senate, 85th Cong., Jan. 14 to Feb. 11, 1957 (Washington, D.C.: Govt. Printing Office), 791. That the United States did offer arms to Egypt was confirmed to me in an interview with a former high State Department official who stated that he had drafted the American proposal. Also see Sir Anthony Eden, *Full Circle: The Memoirs of Anthony Eden* (Boston: Houghton-Mifflin, 1960), 281, and Finer, *Dulles Over Suez*, 26-27.

28. See, for example, Campbell, *Defense of the Middle East*, 72-73.

29. See, for example, Trevor N. Dupuy, *Elusive Victory: The Arab-Israeli Wars, 1947-1974* (New York: Harper & Row, 1978), 131.

30. "Statement on Foreign Affairs by Israeli Premier and Foreign Minister Moshe Sharett, Oct. 18, 1955," quoted in J. C. Hurewitz, ed., *Diplomacy in the Near and Middle East: A Documentary Record, 1914-1956* (Princeton, N.J.: Princeton University Press, 1956), 405-12, specifically, 409.

31. Eisenhower, *Waging Peace*, 25. Also see *Department of State Bulletin* 34 (Feb. 20, 1956), 285-86.

32. See Shimon Peres, *David's Sling* (London: Weidenfeld and Nicholson, 1979), 41.

33. For dollar amounts of American aid to Israel, see Allan C. Kellum, "U.S.-Israeli Relations: A Reassessment," *The Link* 15 (Dec. 1982), 3 (Source: Library of Congress Congressional Research Service).

34. Dayan, *Diary*, 11-12.

35. "Report on the Near & Middle East by Secretary of State John Foster Dulles," June 1, 1953, *Department of State Bulletin* 28 (June 15, 1953), 331-35.

36. Ibid., 341-42.

37. Ibid., 342, 339, and passim. See also Geoffrey Aronson, *From Sideshow to Center Stage: United States Policy toward Egypt, 1946-1956* (Boulder: Lynne Rienner Publishers, 1986).

38. In the Knesset a Mapam spokesman called Dulles "Hitler's helper to power," and a Herut member said Dulles's speech showed America's policy was in fact anti-Israel. See Stock, *Israel on the Road to Sinai*, 59, and passim; also see, Finer, *Dulles Over Suez*, 15, 24; and Nadav Safran, *The United States and Israel* (Cambridge, Mass.: Harvard University Press, 1963), 232.

39. *Divrei ha-Knesset (Israel Parliamentary Proceedings)* 14, 1581ff. (June 15 and 16, 1953), cited in Stock, *Israel on the Road to Sinai*, 59, n. 7, 249.

40. Stock, *Israel on the Road to Sinai*, 60-61.

41. *Department of State Bulletin* 29 (Aug. 10, 1953), 177-78.

42. The most important resolutions on the status of Jerusalem in this period were Resolution 181 (II) Nov. 29, 1947; Resolution 194 (III), Dec. 11, 1948; Resolution 303 (IV), Dec. 9, 1949, in Moore, ed. *Documents*, 313, 373, 457, respectively.

43. See Berger, *Covenant and the Sword,* 116-23; Stock, *Israel on the Road to Sinai,* 62-63.

44. See *Department of State Bulletin* 29 (Nov. 2, 1953), 589-90. Also see ibid., 29 (Nov. 16, 1953), 674-75, and Green, *Taking Sides,* 76-93.

45. *Department of State Bulletin* 29 (Oct. 1953), 552.

46. Ibid., 30 (May 10, 1954), 713.

47. Ibid., 30 (Apr. 26, 1954), 628-33; 30 (May 10, 1954), 708-11.

48. *Divrei ha-Knesset (Israel Parliamentary Proceedings)* 16 (May 12, 1954), 1596, cited in Stock, *Israel on the Road to Sinai,* 65-66, n. 27, 250.

49. Safran, *United States and Israel,* 233-34.

50. *Department of State Bulletin* 31 (Sept. 5, 1955), 378-80.

51. Ibid.

52. See the analysis in *Israel Digest,* Oct. 26, 1955, special supplement.

53. Safran, *United States and Israel,* 278. In a report published by the Office of Planning and Budgeting, Bureau for Program and Policy Coordination, Agency for International Development, entitled *U.S. Overseas Loans and Grants and Assistance from International Organizations: Obligations and Loan Authorizations July 1, 1945–September 30, 1981,* aid to the Arab countries and to Israel is given for eight periods. Except for two periods, 1946-48 and 1953-61 when the Arab states received more aid than Israel, Israel received more aid than all the Arab states combined. For the entire period 1946-81 the Arab states received $13,695.6 (million) compared to $20,639.8 (million) for Israel. The population of Israel ranged from 3 to 4 million while the population of the Arab states from 120 to 160 million.

Aid to the Arab States and Israel
(in millions of dollars)

	1946-48	1949-52	1953-61[a]	1962-77	1978	1979	1980	1981
Arab states[b]	17.8	9.8	935.1	5,238.8	1,321.5	2,975.4	1,387.7	1,809.5
Israel	c	86.5	508.0	9,513.4	1,791.8	4,790.1	1,786.0	2,164.0

[a] The three major recipients of the $935.1 were: $302.3 to Egypt, of which $214.6 was in the Food for Peace program; $71.1 to Iraq, of which $49.4 was military aid given to bolster Iraq's role in the Baghdad Pact until 1958; and $296.8 to Jordan, to shore up the monarchy against domestic opposition.

[b] Arab states include: Bahrain, Egypt, Iraq, Jordan, Kuwait, Lebanon, Oman, Saudi Arabia, Syria, People's Democratic Republic of Yemen, and Yemen Arab Republic.

[c] Israel did not become a state until May 1948.

54. Love, *Suez,* 504; Eden, *Full Circle,* 523; Hugh Thomas, *Suez* (New York: Harper and Row, 1967), 112-15, 124.

55. For a discussion of the military campaign, see Edgar O'Ballance, *The Sinai Campaign, 1956* (London: Faber and Faber, 1959); R. Henriques, *A Hundred Hours to Suez* (New York: Viking, 1957); C. F. Beaufre, *The Suez Expedition, 1956* (London: Faber and Faber, 1969); and Dayan, *Diary,* passim.

56. Eisenhower, *Waging Peace,* 69. Eisenhower records only the first cable, although Dayan, *Diary,* 71, quotes both.

57. See John Robinson Beal, *John Foster Dulles: A Biography* (New York: Harper and Brothers, 1957), 272-73.

58. Dayan, *Diary,* 73-74.

59. Security Council, *Official Records,* 748th Meeting, Oct. 30, 1956, 1, 2.

60. Ibid.

61. Document quoted in Finer, *Dulles Over Suez,* 377.

62. *Department of State Bulletin* 30 (Mar. 11, 1956), 387. Also see Dean Acheson, "Foreign Policy and Presidential Moralism," *The Reporter* 16 (May 2, 1957), 10-14.

63. Eisenhower and Dulles are not generally remembered for their fidelity to principles of international law. For example, this administration engineered the coup in Guatemala in 1954, overthrowing the second freely elected president of that country (Jacobo Arbenz), thus aborting the country's struggle to establish a democratic political system and effect social and economic reform and consigning the country to one of the worst fates of any country in Latin America. Between 1954 and 1984 some 100,000 civilians were murdered in Guatemala by the army and government-sponsored death squads in a "counterinsurgency" campaign first "advised" by the United States and later (1977-84) by Israel. See Michael McClintock, *The American Connection II: State Terror and Popular Resistance in Guatemala* (London: Zed Press, 1986), and Cheryl A. Rubenberg, "Israel and Guatemala: A Case Study in Israeli Foreign Policy," *MERIP Reports* 140 (May-June 1986).

64. For analyses of American interests in the Middle East, see John C. Campbell, "American Efforts for Peace in the Middle East," in *The Elusive Peace in the Middle East,* ed. Malcolm H. Kerr (Albany: State University of New York Press, 1975), 272-73. Also see Campbell, *Defense of the Middle East,* 95-110; Eisenhower, *Waging Peace,* 74-93.

65. "Radio and Television Address by Pres. Eisenhower–Oct. 31, 1956," in Department of State, *United States Policy in the Middle East September 1956–June 1957, Documents,* Department of State Publication 6505, Near and Middle East Series 25 (Washington, D.C.: Government Printing Office, 1957), 148-51.

66. *United States Policy in the Middle East,* 151-57.

67. Ibid., 157-58.

68. Ibid., 158-60.

69. Ibid., 158.

70. Ibid., 160.

71. Ibid., 169-70, 183-86.

72. Ibid., 199-204.

73. Ibid., 199.

74. Ibid., 199-204.

75. T. Robertson, *Crisis: The Inside Story of the Suez Conspiracy* (New York: Atheneum Publishers, 1965), 277-78.

76. Abba Eban, "The Political Struggle in the United Nations and the United States resulting from the Sinai Campaign, Oct. 1956–Mar. 1957," mimeograph on file in the Israeli Embassy, Washington, D.C.

77. Eisenhower, *Waging Peace,* 83.

78. Finer, *Dulles Over Suez,* 392.

79. David Ben-Gurion, *Israel, a Personal History* (New York: Funk and Wagnalls, Sabra Books, 1971), 509.

80. There is a one sentence reference in Walter Eytan, *The First Ten Years: A Diplomatic History of Israel* (London: Weidenfeld and Nicholson, 1958), 140, that indicates sanctions actually were employed.

81. *U.S. Policy in the Middle East,* 211-12.

82. Ibid., 213.

83. Ibid., 212.

84. Abba Eban, *My Country: The Story of Modern Israel* (New York: Random House, 1972), 147.

85. Ibid., 148; and Ben-Gurion, *Israel,* 522.

86. Ben-Gurion, "Address to the Nation on Kol Yisrael, 8 Nov. 1956," printed in Michael Brecher, *Decisions in Israel's Foreign Policy* (London: Oxford University Press, 1974), 289.

87. *U.S. Policy in the Middle East,* 238-39.

88. Brecher, *Decisions in Israel's Foreign Policy,* 292-93.

89. Ben-Gurion, *Israel,* 523.

90. Ibid., 524.

91. Ibid., 523.

92. Eisenhower, *Waging Peace,* 183.

93. Ibid., 178-79.

94. Finer, *Dulles Over Suez,* 468-69, 478, and Campbell, *Defense of the Middle East,* 126-27.

95. Ralph H. Magnus, ed., *Documents on the Middle East* (Washington, D.C.: American Enterprise Institute, 1969), 86-93. For analysis of the doctrine, see Campbell, *Defense of the Middle East,* 124-26.

96. Riad, *Struggle for Peace in the Middle East,* 11.

97. *U.S. Policy in the Middle East,* 253-54.

98. Ibid., 272-76.

99. Ibid., 276-77.

100. Ibid., 277.

101. Ben-Gurion, *Israel,* 525.

102. *U.S. Policy in the Middle East,* 278-79.

103. Ben-Gurion, *Israel,* 525-26.

104. *U.S. Policy in the Middle East,* 290-92.

105. Abba Eban, "Sinai and Suez—A Retrospect," *Midstream* 4 (Winter 1958), 5-14, specifically 7.

106. Ben-Gurion, *Israel,* 527.

107. Brecher, *Decisions in Israel's Foreign Policy,* 297.

108. Eisenhower, *Waging Peace,* 185.

109. *U.S. Policy in the Middle East,* 292-93.

110. Ibid., 293.

111. Brecher, *Decisions in Israel's Foreign Policy,* 297.

112. Ben-Gurion, *Israel,* 527.

113. Brecher, *Decisions in Israel's Foreign Policy,* 297.

114. Sherman Adams, *First Hand Report: The Story of the Eisenhower Administration* (New York: Harper, 1961), 281.

115. For a text of the address, see *U.S. Policy in the Middle East,* 301-7. Also see Eisenhower, *Waging Peace,* 187.

116. *U.S. Policy in the Middle East,* 308-16.

117. Ben-Gurion, *Israel,* 529.

118. Ibid.

119. Finer, *Dulles Over Suez,* 486.

120. Ben-Gurion, *Israel,* 530.

121. Ibid., 530-31.

122. Ibid., 531.

123. The session is discussed in Brecher, *Decisions in Israel's Foreign Policy,* 299.

124. *U.S. Policy in the Middle East,* 328-32.
125. Ibid.
126. Ibid., 322-27.
127. Finer, *Dulles Over Suez,* 488-89.
128. Ben-Gurion, *Israel,* 532.
129. *U.S. Policy in the Middle East,* 332-34.
130. Ben-Gurion, *Israel,* 534.
131. Ibid., 534, 532-33.
132. Ibid., 535.
133. Eban, *My Country,* 150.

CHAPTER FOUR

1. Malcolm Kerr, *The Arab Cold War: Gamal 'Abd al-Nasir and His Rivals, 1950-1969,* 3d ed. (New York: Oxford University Press, 1971), passim.
2. See, for example, Livia Rokach, *Israel's Sacred Terrorism: A Study based on Moshe Sharett's Personal Diary and Other Documents* (Belmont, Mass.: Association of Arab-American University Graduates, 1980).
3. Michael Brecher, *Decisions in Israel's Foreign Policy* (London: Oxford University Press, 1974), 322. See also Brecher, *The Foreign Policy System of Israel: Setting, Images, Process* (New Haven, Conn.: Yale University Press, 1972), 44.
4. Brecher, *Foreign Policy System,* 45.
5. Ibid.
6. See Richard P. Stebbins, ed., *Documents on American Foreign Relations, 1963* (New York: Harper and Row, 1964), 268.
7. See John C. Campbell, "American Efforts for Peace in the Middle East," in *The Elusive Peace in the Middle East,* ed. Malcolm H. Kerr (Albany: State University of New York Press, 1975), 280-81. Also see John S. Badeau, *The American Approach to the Arab World* (New York: Harper and Row, 1968), and Badeau, "U.S.A. and U.A.R.: A Crisis in Confidence," *Foreign Affairs* 43 (Jan. 1965), 281-96.
8. Campbell, "American Efforts for Peace," 280-81.
9. Mahmoud Riad, *The Struggle for Peace in the Middle East* (New York: Quartet Books, 1981), 15-16.
10. Abba Eban, *An Autobiography* (New York: Random House, 1977), 355.
11. Shimon Peres, *David's Sling* (London: Weidenfeld and Nicholson, 1970), 103.
12. See the analysis by William B. Quandt in his *Decade of Decision: American Policy toward the Arab-Israeli Conflict, 1967-1976* (Berkeley: University of California Press, 1977), 10-11.
13. Donald Neff, *Warriors for Jerusalem: The Six Days That Changed the Middle East* (New York: Linden Press/Simon and Schuster, 1984), 80-81, 83-84, 110-11, 113, 143, 156-59, 164, 169-70, 172-73, 191, 211-12, 235-36, 259-60, 307.
14. Joseph E. Johnson, "Arab vs. Israeli: A Persistent Challenge," address given before the American Assembly, Arden House, Harriman, N.Y., Oct. 24, 1963, in Fred J. Khouri, *The Arab-Israeli Dilemma,* 2d ed. (Syracuse, N.Y.: Syracuse University Press, 1976), 146.

15. Lyndon B. Johnson, *The Vantage Point: Perspectives of the Presidency, 1963-1969* (New York: Holt, Rinehart and Winston, 1971), 288.

16. Eugene V. Rostow, "The Middle Eastern Crisis in the Perspective of World Politics," *International Affairs* 47, no. 2 (Apr. 1971), 275, 281.

17. Quandt, *Decade of Decision,* 12-13.

18. Cheryl A. Rubenberg, *The Palestine Liberation Organization: Its Institutional Infrastructure* (Belmont, Mass.: The Institute for Arab Studies, 1983), 1-7. Also see Helena Cobbana, *The Palestine Liberation Organization: People, Power and Politics* (New York: Cambridge University Press, 1984); John W. Amos II, *Palestinian Resistance: Organization of a Nationalist Movement* (New York: Pergamon Press, 1980); William B. Quandt, Fouad Jaber, and Ann Mosely, *The Politics of Palestinian Nationalism* (Berkeley: University of California Press, 1973).

19. Cheryl A. Rubenberg, "Conflict and Contradiction in the Relations between the Arab States and the Palestine National Movement," *Palestine: Continuing Dispossession,* ed. Glenn E. Perry (Belmont, Mass.: Association of Arab-American University Graduates, 1986), 121-45. See also Aaron David Miller, *The PLO and the Politics of Survival* (New York: Praeger, 1983).

20. For a comprehensive biography of Yasir Arafat, see Alan Hart, *Arafat, Terrorist or Peacemaker* (London: Sidgwick and Jackson, 1985).

21. See, for example, the analysis in Khouri, *Arab-Israeli Dilemma,* 229-41.

22. See the analysis by Yair Evron in *The Middle East: Nations, Superpowers and Wars* (New York: Praeger Publishers, 1973), 57-58ff.

23. Ibid., 47-77.

24. Karl von Horn, *Soldiering for Peace* (London: Cassell, 1966), 78, also 69, 79, 123-24. On Israeli provocations in the demilitarized zone, also see "Report by Colonel de Ridder, Acting Chief of Staff," *United Nations Document S/2084,* Apr. 10, 1951; and E. L. M. Burns, *Between Arab and Israeli* (London: Harrap, 1962), 113-14; E. H. Hutchison, *Violent Truce* (New York: Devin-Adair, 1956), 110. Also see Khouri, *Arab-Israeli Dilemma,* 191-97, for a discussion of Israeli-Syrian problems, especially Israel's efforts to monopolize fishing in Lake Tiberias.

25. Charles W. Yost, "The Arab-Israeli War: How It Began," *Foreign Affairs* 46 (Jan. 1968), 305.

26. Khouri, *Arab-Israeli Dilemma,* 234-37.

27. Ibid., 234-36. Also see Riad, *Struggle for Peace in the Middle East,* 17.

28. John Norton Moore, ed., *The Arab-Israeli Conflict III, Documents,* American Society of International Law (Princeton, N.J.: Princeton University Press, 1974), 712-13.

29. *United Nations Document S/7845,* Apr. 9, 1967, cited in David Hirst, *The Gun and the Olive Branch: The Roots of Violence in the Middle East* (London: Futura Macdonald, 1983; orig. publ. by Farber and Farber, 1977), 213.

30. Brecher, *Decisions in Israel's Foreign Policy,* 331-37.

31. Quotation from Y. Rabin, "Shisha Yamin Ve'od Hamesh Shanim" (Six Days and Five More Years), *Ma'ariv,* June 2, 1972, cited in ibid., 334. For an extremely important discussion by a prominent Israeli (a former member of the Stern) on the misuse and manipulation of Holocaust sentiments for political purposes, see Boaz Evron, "The Holocaust: Learning

the Wrong Lessons," *Journal of Palestine Studies* 10, no. 3 (Spring 1981), 16-26.

32. *Ma'ariv*, Mar. 24, 1972, cited in Hirst, *Gun and the Olive Branch*, 210-11.

33. *Le Monde*, Feb. 29, 1968, cited in ibid., 211.

34. For a partial discussion of Israeli policy at this time, see Abba Eban, *My Country: The Story of Modern Israel* (New York: Random House, 1972), 199, and Yost, "Arab-Israeli War," 308-11.

35. See Godfrey Jansen, "New Light on the 1967 War," *Daily Star* (Beirut), Nov. 15, 22, 26, 1973, quoted in Hirst, *Gun and the Olive Branch*, 216.

36. Ibid.

37. Nadav Safran, *Israel: The Embattled Ally* (Cambridge, Mass.: The Belknap Press of Harvard University Press, 1978), 406.

38. *New York Times*, May 13, 1967, cited in Khouri, *Arab-Israeli Dilemma*, 244.

39. See, for example, the analysis by Quandt, *Decade of Decision*, 38-39.

40. Eban, *Autobiography*, 321; Brecher, *Decisions in Israel's Foreign Policy*, 362-63; Michael Bar-Zohar, *Embassies in Crisis: Diplomats and Demagogues behind the Six Day War* (Englewood Cliffs, N.J.: Prentice Hall, 1970), 20.

41. Michael Brecher, *Decisions in Crisis: Israel 1967 and 1973* (Berkeley: University of California Press, 1980), 47, states that "the first Israeli assessment was that Nasser was putting on a show."

42. Eban, *Autobiography*, 321.

43. Ibid., 319.

44. *New York Times*, Aug. 21, 1982.

45. See, for example, Eban, *Autobiography*, 327-28.

46. Quandt, *Decade of Decision*, 41.

47. For one account, see Bar-Zohar, *Embassies in Crisis*, 56.

48. Johnson, *Vantage Point*, 290.

49. Ibid.

50. Ibid., 291.

51. Ibid., 292.

52. Eban, *Autobiography*, 327-28.

53. Quoted from the Egyptian press in Hisham Sharabi, "Prelude to War: The Crisis of May-June 1967," in *The Arab-Israeli Confrontation of June 1967: An Arab Perspective*, ed. Ibrahim Abu-Lughod (Evanston, Ill.: Northwestern University Press, 1970), 53; also see Khouri, *Arab-Israeli Dilemma*, 247, and the analysis by Hirst, *Gun and the Olive Branch*, 206-18, which demonstrates with clarity and incisiveness that Nasser never intended to go to war.

54. Riad, *Struggle for Peace in the Middle East*, 19-20.

55. Ibid., 20.

56. Bar-Zohar, *Embassies in Crisis*, 44-45.

57. Ibid., 56.

58. Johnson, *Vantage Point*, 291.

59. Eban, *Autobiography*, 329. Also see Bar-Zohar, *Embassies in Crisis*, 68-69; Brecher, *Decisions in Israel's Foreign Policy*, 375.

60. Johnson, *Vantage Point*, 291.

61. On the ship movements, see Randolph S. Churchill and Winston S.

Churchill, *The Six Day War* (Boston: Houghton Mifflin, 1967), 43; also Quandt, *Decade of Decision*, 43.

62. See, for example, the analysis in Stephen Green, *Taking Sides: America's Secret Relations with a Militant Israel* (New York: William Morrow, 1984), 199. Also see Ibrahim I. Ibrahim, "The American-Israeli Alliance: *Raison d'etat* Revisited," *Journal of Palestine Studies* 15, no. 3 (Spring 1986), 17-29.

63. See, for example, Quandt, *Decade of Decision*, 60, 39-71 passim.

64. See the analysis in ibid., 56.

65. Eban, *Autobiography*, 334. Also see Brecher, *Decisions in Israel's Foreign Policy*, 378; and Quandt, *Decade of Decision*, 43.

66. Brecher, *Decisions in Israel's Foreign Policy*, 381. He cites Israeli Foreign Ministry sources.

67. Riad, *Struggle for Peace in the Middle East*, 19-21.

68. Green, *Taking Sides*, 201.

69. Ibid.

70. Johnson, *Vantage Point*, 291.

71. Bar-Zohar, *Embassies in Crisis*, 85.

72. Eban, *Autobiography*, 334-35.

73. Ibid., 348-49. Also see Brecher, *Decisions in Israel's Foreign Policy*, 385-86; Moshe Dayan, *Story of My Life: An Autobiography* (New York: William Morrow, 1976), 329.

74. Eban, *Autobiography*, 350.

75. Brecher, *Decisions in Israel's Foreign Policy*, 387. He cites Israeli Foreign Ministry sources.

76. Bar-Zohar, *Embassies in Crisis*, 114-15; he cites interviews with several top officials in Washington as his source. Quandt, *Decade of Decision*, 49, reports the same conclusion.

77. Quandt, *Decade of Decision*, 49.

78. Johnson, *Vantage Point*, 293. Indeed Johnson had received a report on May 26 prepared by the Central Intelligence Agency, the National Security Council, and the State Department confirming that there were no risks for Israel in a war with the Arabs, that it would win such a war in less than a week, and that it would involve heavy Israeli air strikes accompanied by armored penetrations of Arab territory. Also see Green, *Taking Sides*, 199-200.

79. Brecher, *Decisions in Israel's Foreign Policy*, 326.

80. Eban, *Autobiography*, 366.

81. Riad, *Struggle for Peace in the Middle East*, 21.

82. Cited in Khouri, *Arab-Israeli Dilemma*, 247.

83. Bar-Zohar, *Embassies in Crisis*, 167-69. (He confirms the statements made by Riad in his meeting with Yost, as noted earlier in the text.)

84. Interview with former senior State Department official, Washington, Nov. 1976.

85. U.S. Senate, Committee of Foreign Relations, *A Select Chronology and Background Documents Relating to the Middle East*, 1st rev. ed. (Washington, D.C.: Government Printing Office, 1969), 220-22.

86. Bar-Zohar, *Embassies in Crisis*, 159-60.

87. Ibid., 160. Also see Quandt, *Decade of Decision*, 56.

88. Quandt, *Decade of Decision*, 58.

89. Ibid.

90. Brecher, *Decisions in Israel's Foreign Policy*, 420.

91. Eban, *Autobiography,* 394.
92. Ibid., 385.
93. Brecher, *Decisions in Israel's Foreign Policy,* 421; also Dayan, *Story,* 339.
94. Dayan, *Story,* 341-43. Also see Green, *Taking Sides,* 200-201.
95. Eban, *Autobiography,* 404.
96. Ibid., 405.
97. See the open letter that the celebrated Israeli columnist Ephraim Kishon addressed to King Hussein in the *Jerusalem Post,* June 16, 1967.
98. See the analysis in Green, *Taking Sides,* 212-42, on Israeli territorial ambitions. Also see Neff, *Warriors for Jerusalem,* 186, 325.
99. Eban, *Autobiography,* 411.
100. Ibid.
101. Johnson, *Vantage Point,* 301.
102. See Neff, *Warriors for Jerusalem,* 201-86, for a full discussion of the June War.
103. Johnson, *Vantage Point,* 297.
104. Green, *Taking Sides,* 204-11. According to Green, "The principle source for this story claims to have been a participant in the operation described. The author has verified the story circumstantially, that is, by checking Air Force unit histories, commander's names, technical details, and so forth. Furthermore, certain of the details provided by the source would have been very difficult to learn other than by participation in such a mission in Israel. Nevertheless, efforts to confirm this story either through contacts with other individuals who might have participated in such an operation, or through senior officials in the Pentagon, White House, and State Department, have not met with success. During the course of these efforts at verification (July-Sept., 1983) Air Force Intelligence has contacted several former members of the 17th Tactical Reconnaissance Squadron, reminding them of their obligations to maintain silence on any previous intelligence missions in which they may have been involved."
105. Ibid., 210.
106. Riad, *Struggle for Peace in the Middle East,* 25-26.
107. Ibid., 25.
108. Johnson, *Vantage Point,* 301-3.
109. James Bamford, *The Puzzle Palace: A Report on America's Most Secret Agency* (Boston: Houghton Mifflin, 1982), 227-28. Also see James M. Ennes, Jr., *Assault on the Liberty* (New York: Random House, 1979), passim. (Ennes was a lieutenant and the officer on the deck of the *Liberty* at the time it was attacked by Israel.) Also see Green, *Taking Sides,* 212-42; Neff, *Warriors for Jerusalem,* 246-63; "Interview: The USS Liberty Wouldn't Sink; the Survivors Won't go Away," with James M. Ennes and George Golden (also a lieutenant and the only Jewish officer on board), *Israeli Foreign Affairs* 1, no. 5 (Apr. 1985), 4-5. Ennes and Golden were replying to questions raised in an article written by Ze'ev Schiff and Hirsh Goodman, two Israeli military correspondents, that appeared in the *Atlantic Monthly* (Sept. 1984).
110. See Roberta Strauss Feuerlicht, *The Fate of the Jews: A People Torn between Israeli Power and Jewish Ethics* (New York: Times Books, 1983), 161-63, and Melvin I. Urofsky, *American Zionism from Heryl to Holocaust* (New York: Anchor Books, 1976).

CHAPTER FIVE

1. See the analysis by David Hirst, *The Gun and the Olive Branch: The Roots of Violence in the Middle East* (London: Futura Macdonald, 1983; orig. publ. Farber and Farber, 1977), 218-24.

2. Amnon Kapeliouk, *Israel: la fin des mythes* (Paris: Albin Michel, 1975), 28, also 183-222.

3. See Larry L. Fabian, "The Red Light," *Foreign Policy* 50 (Spring 1983), 60.

4. See, for example, the analysis by Daniel Dishon, "Inter-Arab Relations," and Varda Ben Zvi, "The Federation of Arab Republics," both in *From June to October: The Middle East between 1967 and 1973,* ed. Itamar Rabinovitch and Haim Shaked (New Brunswick, N.J.: Transaction Books, 1978), 157-70 and 171-88, respectively.

5. Fouad Ajami, *The Arab Predicament: Arab Political Thought and Practice since 1967* (Cambridge: Cambridge University Press, 1981), makes this argument.

6. See the analysis by Shimon Shamir, "Nasser and Sadat 1967-1973, Approaches to the Crisis," and Itamar Rabinovitch, "Continuity and Change in the Ba'ath Regime in Syria, 1967-1973," in *From June to October,* ed. Rabinovitch and Shaked, 189-218 and 219-30, respectively.

7. See Uriel Dann, "The Jordanian Entity in Changing Circumstances, 1967-1973," and Gabriel Ben Dor, "The Institutionalization of Palestinian Nationalism," *From June to October,* ed. Rabinovitch and Shaked, 231-44 and 245-68, respectively.

8. George M. Haddad, "Arab Peace Efforts and the Solution of the Arab-Israeli Problem," in *The Elusive Peace in the Middle East,* ed. Malcolm H. Kerr (Albany: State University of New York Press, 1975), 206-7.

9. See Mahmoud Riad, *The Struggle for Peace in the Middle East* (New York: Quartet Books, 1981), 76-102. Jordan, of course, did not receive weapons from Moscow, being a loyal client state of Washington.

10. Fred J. Khouri, *The Arab-Israeli Dilemma* (Syracuse, N.Y.: Syracuse University Press, 1968), 313. Also see Riad, *Struggle for Peace in the Middle East,* 71-80, for an analysis of the meaning of the Khartoum conference in terms of Arab willingness to seek a comprehensive settlement with Israel rather than the separate bilateral agreements that Israel and the United States wanted.

11. Haddad, "Arab Peace Efforts," 207.

12. Khouri, *Arab-Israeli Dilemma,* 316.

13. Eric Rouleau, *Le Monde,* Feb. 19, 1970, quoted in Noam Chomsky, *The Fateful Triangle: The United States, Israel and the Palestinians* (Boston: South End Press, 1983), 64.

14. See the analysis in Khouri, *Arab-Israeli Dilemma,* 366. Also see Amos Elon, *Ha'aretz,* Nov. 13, 1981, quoted in Chomsky, *Fateful Triangle,* 64.

15. Edward Witten, *Ha'aretz,* Jan. 6, 1983, quoted in Chomsky, *Fateful Triangle,* 65.

16. For a detailed analysis of Israel's response to the Jordanian proposal see ibid.

17. Haddad, "Arab Peace Efforts," 208-9.

18. Mohammed Heikal, *The Road to Ramadan* (New York: Ballantine Books, 1975), 57-58.

19. Ibid., 48.

20. Edgar O'Ballance, *The Electronic War in the Middle East, 1968-1970* (Hamden, Conn.: Shoe String Press, 1974), 12.

21. For an excellent account of the "Black September" battle, see the analysis by Abu Iyad with Eric Rouleau in *My Home, My Land: A Narrative of the Palestinian Struggle* (New York: Times Books, 1981).

22. For a further analysis of "Black September," see William B. Quandt, Fuad Jabber, and Ann Mosely Lesch, *The Politics of Palestinian Nationalism* (Berkeley: University of California Press, 1973), 193-94. For a text of the Cairo Agreement, signed Nov. 3, 1969, see Walid Khalidi, *Conflict and Violence in Lebanon: Confrontation in the Middle East,* Center for International Affairs (Cambridge, Mass.: Harvard University Press, 1979), 185-87.

23. Michael C. Hudson, "The Palestinian Factor in the Lebanese Civil War," *Middle East Journal* 32, no. 3 (Summer 1976), 267.

24. Ibid.

25. Riad, *Struggle for Peace in the Middle East,* 231. Also see Ismail Fahmy, *Negotiating for Peace in the Middle East* (Baltimore: Johns Hopkins University Press, 1983), 5-9, who gives a similar assessment.

26. Seymour M. Hersh, *The Price of Power: Kissinger in the Nixon White House* (New York: Summit Books, 1983), 216.

27. William B. Quandt, *Decade of Decision: American Policy toward the Arab-Israeli Conflict, 1967-1976* (Berkeley: University of California Press, 1977), 79-80.

28. Fred J. Khouri, "The Challenge to United States Security and Middle East Policy," *American-Arab Affairs* 5 (Summer 1983), 13.

29. *The Middle East* (London), Mar. 1983, 18.

30. Lyndon B. Johnson, "Principles for Peace in the Middle East," *Department of State Bulletin,* July 10, 1967, 31-34.

31. Ibid.

32. See Shlomo Slonim, *United States–Israel Relations, 1967-1973: A Study in the Convergence and Divergence of Interests,* Jerusalem Papers on Peace Problems #8 (Jerusalem: Leonard Davis Institute of International Relations, Hebrew University of Jerusalem, 1974).

33. John Norton Moore, ed. *The Arab-Israeli Conflict III, Documents,* American Society of International Law (Princeton, N.J.: Princeton University Press, 1974), 1034-35.

34. Nadav Safran, *Israel: The Embattled Ally* (Cambridge, Mass.: The Belknap Press of Harvard University Press, 1978), 442. Safran calls Israel's acceptance "a significant policy departure."

35. See Abba Eban, *My Country: The Story of Modern Israel* (New York: Random House, 1972), 254-57. Also see Arthur J. Goldberg, "Withdrawal Needn't Be Total: An Interpretation of Resolution 242," *Washington Star,* Dec. 9, 1973, B-3. (Goldberg was the U.S. ambassador to the United Nations at the time the resolution was written.)

36. See *London Sunday Times,* July 5, 1970. Also see Lord Caradon, "Resolution 242, Camp David and the Future," *American-Arab Affairs* 1 (Summer 1982), 1-2; "The Intent of Resolution 242: A Discussion with Lord Hugh Caradon," *Israel and the Question of Palestine,* special issue, *Arab Studies Quarterly* 7, nos. 2 and 3 (Spring/Summer 1985), 167-74; Hugh Caradon, "Middle East Peace: A Proposal for the United Nations," ibid., 175-80.

37. Riad, *Struggle for Peace in the Middle East,* 68-69.

38. See Elias Sam'o and Cyrus Elahi, "Resolution 242 and Beyond," *Arab World* 17 (Aug./Sept. 1971), 29-36.

39. Bernard Reich, *Quest for Peace: United States–Israeli Relations and the Arab-Israeli Conflict* (New Brunswick, N.J.: Transaction Books, 1977), 136.

40. For an analysis of the historic relationship between Jews and the Democratic party, see Stephen D. Isaacs, *Jews and American Politics* (Garden City, N.Y.: Doubleday, 1974.)

41. President Richard Nixon, news conference on Jan. 27, 1969, *Department of State Bulletin*, Feb. 18, 1969, 142-43.

42. Rowland Evans, Jr., and Robert D. Novak, *Nixon in the White House: The Frustration of Power* (New York: Random House, 1971), 87-88.

43. Hersh, *Price of Power*, 216.

44. Ibid., 219-22, 224.

45. Riad, *Struggle for Peace in the Middle East*, 100-101.

46. Ibid., 100-102.

47. Hersh, *Price of Power*, 217.

48. Ibid., 219.

49. *A Lasting Peace in the Middle East: An American View*, an Address by Secretary of State William P. Rogers, Department of State Publication 8507, Near and Middle East Series 79, Released January 1970, Office of Media Services, Bureau of Public Affairs (Washington, D.C.: Government Printing Office, 1970).

50. Ibid.

51. Ibid.

52. Ibid.

53. Riad, *Struggle for Peace in the Middle East*, 110-11.

54. Abba Eban, *An Autobiography* (New York: Random House, 1977), 464.

55. Hersh, *Price of Power*, 220.

56. Riad, *Struggle for Peace in the Middle East*, 127.

57. *Davar*, Aug. 2, 1970.

58. "Cease-fire Standstill Agreement Between Israel and the United Arab Republic, effective August 7, 1970," Moore, ed., *Documents*, 1064-65.

59. Riad, *Struggle for Peace in the Middle East*, 148-49, 150-51.

60. Ibid., 151.

61. Information provided by a State Department official in an off-the-record interview in Washington, 1976.

62. Hersh, *Price of Power*, 234-36.

63. Ibid., 236-37.

64. Ibid., 237.

65. Richard Nixon, *RN: The Memoirs of Richard Nixon* (New York: Grosset and Dunlap, 1978), 483.

66. Hersh, *Price of Power*, 244-45.

67. Ibid., 240-41.

68. Ibid., 242.

69. Ibid., 244-46.

70. Ibid., 248-49.

71. Safran, *Embattled Ally*, 456, 458, 460.

72. Edward R. Sheehan, *The Arabs, Israelis, and Kissinger: A Secret*

History of American Diplomacy in the Middle East (New York: Reader's Digest Press, Thomas Y. Crowell, 1976), 23.

73. Henry Kissinger, *Years of Upheaval* (Boston: Little, Brown, 1982), 206-7.

74. Ibid., 207.

75. Sheehan, *Arabs, Israelis, and Kissinger,* 25.

76. Riad, *Struggle for Peace in the Middle East,* 237.

77. Quoted in Sheehan, *Arabs, Israelis, and Kissinger,* 26.

78. Kissinger, *Years of Upheaval,* 219, 217-18.

79. Ibid., 219-20.

80. Quandt, *Decade of Decision,* 156.

81. *Washington Post,* Apr. 19, 1973. Later, in December 1973 when Yamani appeared on "Meet the Press," he was asked whether King Faisal had ever warned the United States that Saudi Arabia and other Arab countries might feel compelled to stop oil shipments because of the Arab-Israeli dispute. Yamani replied: "Very much so! I was here in April, and I delivered that message to United States government officials. I explained that our policy is based on full cooperation with the United States of America, that we would like to produce as much as you need. All we want you to do, is to have an evenhanded policy, to implement the 242 Resolution of the Security Council. I told the United States officials this, and we kept saying this, so what happened is not a surprise at all." Quotation printed in Reich, *Quest for Peace,* 237.

82. *Ma'ariv,* July 13, 1973, quoted in Eban, *Autobiography,* 488-89.

83. Chaim Herzog, *The War of Atonement: October 1973* (Boston: Little, Brown, 1975), 278.

84. See Golda Meir, *My Life* (New York: G. P. Putnam's Sons, 1975), 426-27, and Moshe Dayan, *Story of My Life: An Autobiography* (New York: William Morrow, 1976), 461. Meir and Dayan prefer to stress the first reason (i.e., not wanting to risk U.S. support) in their official memoirs. Nixon, Kissinger, and others are clear, however, about Israel's confidence of victory and evaluation of the Arab threat as not serious. See Nixon, *Memoirs,* 921, and Kissinger, *Years of Upheaval,* 488-89 (quoting a report from Israeli Ambassador Dinitz).

85. See Quandt, *Decade of Decision,* 171. He states that Nixon and Kissinger made policy with "occasional inputs" from Defense Secretary James Schlesinger. However a careful reading of the historical record, as well as my own interviews with State Department officials intimately involved in this crisis, suggests that Kissinger acted virtually entirely on his own. Nixon's impairment from the Watergate crisis is certainly clear.

86. See, for example, Leon Jaworski, *The Right and the Power: The Prosecution of Watergate* (Houston: Gulf Publishing Co., 1976), passim.

87. Kissinger, *Years of Upheaval,* 467.

88. Ibid.

89. Ibid., 471.

90. Ibid.

91. Ibid., 476.

92. Ibid., 485.

93. Ibid., 478.

94. Ibid., 480, 485-86.

95. Ibid., 496.

96. Ibid., 501-2.

97. *Aviation Week and Space Technology* 99, no. 24 (Dec. 10, 1973), 16-19.

98. Noyes related this to the Egyptian Foreign Minister Ismail Fahmy; see Fahmy, *Negotiating for Peace in the Middle East*, 32.

99. Sheehan, *Arabs, Israelis, and Kissinger*, 69-70. Also see U.S. Congress, Senate, "Report No. 93-620: Foreign Assistance and Related Programs Appropriations Bill, 1974, Dec. 13, 1973," *Senate Reports*, 93rd Congress, 1st Session, vol. 9 (Miscellaneous Reports on Public Bills) (Washington, D.C.: Government Printing Office, 1973), 121-23.

100. Quandt, *Decade of Decision*, 188. Also see Marvin C. Feurwerger, "The Emergency Security Assistance Act of 1973 and American–Israeli Relations," *Midstream* 20, no. 7 (Aug.-Sept. 1974), 20-38, for a discussion of the significance of the emergency aid.

101. Both interviews were confidential and off-the-record.

102. Quandt, *Decade of Decision*, 184.

103. See Fahmy, *Negotiating for Peace in the Middle East*, 30-31, and Trevor N. Dupuy, *Elusive Victory: the Arab-Israeli Wars, 1947-1974* (New York: Harper and Row, 1978), 501-2, 566-72.

104. Safran, *Embattled Ally*, 482-83.

105. Sheehan, *Arabs, Israelis, and Kissinger*, 34; Matti Golan, *The Secret Conversations of Henry Kissinger: Step by Step Diplomacy in the Middle East* (New York: Quadrangle/Times Books, 1976), 51; and especially Marvin Kalb and Bernard Kalb, *Kissinger* (Boston: Little, Brown, 1974), 464.

106. John F. Roehm, Jr., "Congressional Participation in United States–Middle East Policy, October 1973-1976: Congressional Activism vs. Policy Coherence," in *Congress, the Presidency and American Foreign Policy*, ed. John Spanier and Joseph Nogee (New York: Pergamon Press, 1981), 24-27. On the Israeli lobby generally, see Cheryl A. Rubenberg, "The Middle East Lobbies," *The Link* 17, no. 1 (Jan.-Mar. 1984); also see Robert H. Trice, *Interest Groups and the Foreign Policy Process: United States Policy in the Middle East*, Sage Professional Paper in International Studies, vol. 4, no. 02-047 (Beverly Hills: Sage Publications, 1976).

107. Kissinger, *Years of Upheaval*, 478. Also see Roehm, "Congressional Participation," 31.

108. See the analysis in Edward R. F. Sheehan, "How Kissinger Did It: Step-by-Step in the Middle East," *Foreign Policy* 27 (Spring 1976), 3-71.

109. *Department of State Bulletin*, Oct. 29, 1973, 537.

110. Sheehan, *Arabs, Israelis, and Kissinger*, 34.

111. The Insight Team of the London Sunday Times, *The Yom Kippur War* (Garden City, N.Y.: Doubleday, 1974), 284.

112. Herzog, *War of Atonement*, 284.

113. Golan, *Secret Conversations of Kissinger*, 63.

114. Kissinger, *Years of Upheaval*, 502.

115. Quandt, *Decade of Decision*, 180-83.

116. Kissinger, *Years of Upheaval*, 509.

117. Ibid., 510.

118. Ibid., 504.

119. Golan, *Secret Conversations of Kissinger*, 70-73.

120. Kissinger, *Years of Upheaval*, 550-51.

121. Eban, *Autobiography*, 527-28. Meir, *My Life*, 437-38.

122. Meir, *My Life*, 437-38.

123. Golan, *Secret Conversations of Kissinger*, 77.

124. Ibid., 77-79. Also see Kissinger, *Years of Upheaval*, 559.
125. Kissinger, *Years of Upheaval*, 569.
126. The Insight Team, *Yom Kippur War*, 394, provides some information on the Israeli advance, though the details were provided to me in an off-the-record interview with a senior State Department spokesman.
127. Herzog, *War of Atonement*, 250.
128. Kissinger, *Years of Upheaval*, 571.
129. Ibid., 573.
130. Ibid.
131. Ibid., 579.
132. Ibid., 583.
133. Ibid., 575-91.
134. Ibid., 602 (emphasis in original).
135. Ibid., 605.
136. Ibid., 607.
137. Ibid., 610.
138. *New York Times*, Jan. 26, 1975.
139. Kissinger, *Years of Upheaval*, 611.
140. In response to a question on Feb. 3, 1976, in *Department of State Bulletin*, Feb. 23, 1976, 214.
141. See, for example, the analysis by Quandt, *Decade of Decision*, 202.
142. Quoted in Sheehan, *Arabs, Israelis, and Kissinger*, 201 (emphasis in original).
143. Ibid., 202.
144. Roehm, "Congressional Participation," 31-32.
145. This analysis is derived from Quandt, *Decade of Decision*, 210.
146. Ibid.
147. Roehm, "Congressional Participation," 38-39. Also see Thomas A. Franck and Edward Weisban, *Foreign Policy by Congress* (New York: Oxford University Press, 1979), 103.
148. Kissinger, *Years of Upheaval*, 503, relates the message from Arafat.
149. For a text of the agreement, see Moore, ed., *Documents*, 1149-50.
150. On the decision concerning the lifting of the embargo at the Algiers summit, see Fahmy, *Negotiating for Peace in the Middle East*, 85. For an analysis of the meaning of the Algiers summit, see Riad, *Struggle for Peace in the Middle East*, 264-65.
151. The Insight Team, *Yom Kippur War*, 483-84 illustrates the "logic" that was used to convince the Israelis to forego their concern about the U.N.—i.e., its de facto impotence.
152. Riad, *Struggle for Peace in the Middle East*, 271.
153. Kissinger, *Years of Upheaval*, 790-91.
154. Ibid., 797-98.
155. Ibid., 802.
156. Ibid., 811.
157. See, for example, Golan, *Secret Conversations of Kissinger*, 144-78.
158. For text of the Sinai I Accord see *Search for Peace in the Middle East: Documents and Statements, 1967-1979*, Report prepared for the Subcommittee on Europe and the Middle East of the Committee on Foreign Affairs, U.S. House of Representatives (Washington, D.C.: Government Printing Office, 1979), 1.
159. The memorandum of understanding is described in general terms in the *New York Times*, Jan. 22, 1974.

160. *Washington Post,* Jan. 23, 1974.

161. *The Guardian* (London), Jan. 17, 1974. Also see Alain Gresh, *The PLO: The Struggle Within: Towards an Independent Palestinian State* (London: Zed Books, 1985), 129-210.

162. Gresh, *Struggle Within,* 156-65.

163. Kissinger, *Years of Upheaval,* 846-48.

164. Ibid., 946.

165. Ibid., 948-49.

166. Ibid., 950-51. Also see the account by Fahmy, *Negotiating for Peace in the Middle East,* 90-92. For an analysis of Saudi capitulation to American interests, see Abbas Alnasrawi, "The Rise and Fall of Arab Oil Power," *Arab Studies Quarterly* 6, nos. 1 and 2 (Winter/Spring 1984), 1-12; and Atif A. Kubursi, "The Arab Thrust into the International Arena: Pitfalls and Implications of Strategic Behavior," ibid., 39-69.

167. Kissinger, *Years of Upheaval,* 958.

168. Dayan, *My Life,* 574, 550-51.

169. Hudson, "Palestinian Factor in the Lebanese Civil War," 257.

170. Quoted in Reich, *Quest for Peace,* 293.

171. See Moore, ed., *Documents,* 1193-96.

172. See, for example, Dayan, *My Life,* 578.

CHAPTER SIX

1. For an analysis of the Arab perception of the October War as a victory, see Ismail Fahmy, *Negotiating for Peace in the Middle East* (Baltimore: Johns Hopkins University Press, 1983), 33-34.

2. Fouad Ajami, *The Arab Predicament: Arab Political Thought and Practice since 1967* (Cambridge: Cambridge University Press, 1981), 123.

3. Ibid., passim.

4. Ibid., 10.

5. Ibid., 100-108. Also see Adeed Dawisha, "Comprehensive Peace in the Middle East and the Comprehension of Arab Politics," *Middle East Journal* 37, no. 1 (Winter 1983), and Bahgat Korany and Ali E. Hillal Dessouki, eds., *The Foreign Policies of the Arab States* (Boulder: Westview Press, 1984).

6. Ajami, *Arab Predicament,* 101.

7. Ibid., 101-2.

8. For further reading on Syria see Robert W. Olson, *The Ba'ath and Syria, 1947-82: The Evolution of Ideology, Party and State* (Princeton, N.J.: The Kingston Press, Inc., 1983).

9. Lewis W. Snider, "Inter-Arab Relations," in *Lebanon in Crisis: Participants and Issues,* eds. P. Edward Haley and Lewis W. Snider (Syracuse, N.Y.: Syracuse University Press, 1979), 184. Also see R. D. McLaurin, Mohammed Mughisuddin, and Abraham R. Wagner, *Foreign Policy Making in the Middle East* (New York: Praeger Publishers, 1977), 222-80.

10. For a discussion of this conflict see: Jasim M. Abdulghani, *Iraq and Iran* (Baltimore: The Johns Hopkins University Press, 1984); M.S. El-Azhary, *The Iran-Iraq War: Historical, Economic and Political Analysis* (New York: St. Martins Press, 1984); and Tareq Y. Ismael, *Iraq and Iran: Roots of Conflict* (Syracuse: Syracuse University Press, 1983).

11. Seth P. Tillman, *The United States in the Middle East: Interests and Obstacles* (Bloomington: Indiana University Press, 1982), 109. For a good

general analysis of Saudi Arabia see Christine Moss Helms, *The Cohesion of Saudi Arabia* (Baltimore: The Johns Hopkins University Press, 1981). For more of a sense of the contradictions in that country (and other Gulf states) see Robert W. Stookey, *The Arabian Peninsula: Zone of Ferment* (Stanford: Hoover Institute Press, 1984). For a discussion of the program and measures of the Arab states that emerged from the two Baghdad conferences, especially as they relate to Egypt, see Thomas W. Lippmann, "Economic Boycott of Egypt Imposed by Arab Countries," *Washington Post*, Apr. 1, 1979, and Marvin Howe, "Arabs Agree to Cut All Cairo Ties in Retaliation for Pact with Israel," *New York Times*, Apr. 1, 1979.

12. For a good discussion of Jordan's real position on the West Bank and the Palestinian issue see Naseer Aruri, "The PLO and the Jordanian Option," *MERIP Reports* (Apr. 1984).

13. For a discussion of the reasons for the Islamic upsurge in the Middle East see Ajami, *Arab Predicament*, 137-200. Also see James P. Piscatori, ed., *Islam in the Political Process* (Cambridge: Cambridge University Press, 1983).

14. See Alain Gresh, *The PLO: The Struggle Within: Towards an Independent Palestinian State* (London: Zed Books, 1985), 205-7; Helena Cobban, *The Palestine Liberation Organization: People, Power and Politics* (London: Cambridge University Press, 1984), 84-85; and Sameer Y. Abraham, "The Development and Transformation of the Palestine National Movement," in Naseer H. Aruri, ed., *Occupation: Israel Over Palestine* (Belmont, Mass.: Association of Arab-American University Graduates, 1983), 411-13, who gives important background to the thirteenth PNC meeting from the twelfth meeting in 1974.

15. Cobban, *Palestine Liberation Organization*, 179-80.

16. *Time*, May 24, 1982.

17. See Saleh A. Al-Mani and Salah Al-Shaikhly, eds., *The Euro-Arab Dialogue: A Study in Associative Diplomacy* (N.Y.: St. Martins Press, 1983).

18. See Bradley Graham, "European Summit Urges PLO Role in Middle East Talks," *Washington Post*, June 14, 1981.

19. For a discussion of the conflict between Arab state and Palestinian interests see Cheryl A. Rubenberg, "Conflict and Contradiction in the Relations between the Arab States and the Palestine National Movement," in *Palestine: Continuing Dispossession*, ed., Glenn E. Perry (Belmont, Mass.: Association of Arab-American University Graduates, 1986), 121-45. For a further discussion of the Arab state–PLO relations see Cobban, *Palestine Liberation Organization*, 195-214.

20. On the conditions of Palestinians in Lebanon, see Cheryl A. Rubenberg, "Palestinians in Lebanon: A Question of Human and Civil Rights," *Arab Studies Quarterly* 6, no. 3 (Summer 1984), 194-221. Also see: Hani A. Faris, "Lebanon and the Palestinians: Brotherhood or Fratricide," *Arab Studies Quarterly* 3, no. 4 (Fall 1981) and Elaine Hagopian and Samih Farsoun, eds., *South Lebanon* (Detroit, Mich.: Association of Arab-American University Graduates, August 1978), Special Report no. 2.

21. See the analysis in Tillman, *United States in the Middle East*, 212-13, 117.

22. See, for example, the analysis by Halim Barakat, "The Social Context," in *Lebanon in Crisis*, ed. Haley and Snider, 3-5, (3-20 passim). Also on Lebanon see Walid Khalidi, *Conflict and Violence in Lebanon: Con-*

frontation in the Middle East (Cambridge, Mass.: Center for International Affairs, Harvard University Press, 1979).

23. Barakat, "The Social Context," 19.

24. The causes of the Iran-Iraqi war were far more complex than here suggested. See, for example, "Strange War in the Gulf," *MERIP Reports,* nos. 125/126 (July-Sept. 1984) and "Iraq: The War in the Gulf," ibid., no. 97 (June 1981). Also see sources in note 10 above.

25. See, for example, "President Carter's News Conference of Jan. 30, 1978," *New York Times,* Jan. 31, 1978.

26. *London Sunday Times,* June 15, 1969, cited in Noam Chomsky, *The Fateful Triangle: The United States, Israel and the Palestinians* (Boston: South End Press, 1983), 51.

27. Quoted by Amnon Kapeliouk in *Le Monde Diplomatique,* Aug. 1982, from *Ma'ariv,* Dec. 5, 1975, cited in ibid., 70.

28. *Davar,* Nov. 11, 1982; interview in *Trialogue,* journal of the Trilateral Commission (Winter 1983), cited in Chomsky, *Fateful Triangle,* 112.

29. Jacobo Timmerman, *Prisoner without a Name, Cell without a Number* (New York: Alfred A. Knopf, 1981). Also see Dan Margalit, "Israel Silences Jewish Critic of Argentina," *Kol Ha'ir* (a *Ha'aretz* supplement), Nov. 20, 1981, translated by SUNI News Service (What Israelis Are Saying About Themselves and Their Government), London, Dec. 8, 1981. Also see *Haolam Hazeh,* Dec. 22, 1982, which carried an interview with Timmerman, who states: "I saw with my own eyes how Argentine jailers tortured Jews in person while the Israeli government requested the Jewish community there to remain silent." Also see Eliezer Strauch, "Jews Tortured in Argentina," *Yediot Aharonot,* Jan. 22, 1985, translated by Israel Shahak (Shahak Papers), Collection: "State of Israel and Diaspora Jews: The Case of Argentina," Jerusalem, no date, but circa Feb. 1985. Also see Mario Weinstein, "The Jews of Argentina Who Disappeared and Israel's Responsibility," *Davar,* Feb. 13, 1985, translated by Israel Shahak (Shahak Papers), ibid. Also see the analysis, details, and extensive sources on Israel and Argentina in Noam Chomsky, *Towards A New Cold War: Essays on the Current Crisis and How We Got There* (New York: Pantheon Books, 1982), 291-92. Also see Philip Taubman, "Israel Said to Ship Arms to Argentina," *New York Times,* May 27, 1982; "Israeli Arms Sales Pick Up: Washington May Be Able to Test Argentine Intentions," *Latin America Weekly Report,* Jan. 13, 1984, 5.

30. Tillman, *United States in the Middle East,* 241.

31. "U.S.-U.S.S.R. Joint Communique, October 1, 1977," *The Search for Peace in the Middle East: Documents and Statements, 1967-1979,* Report prepared for the Subcommittee on Europe and the Middle East of the Committee on Foreign Affairs, U.S. House of Representatives (Washington, D.C.: Government Printing Office, 1979), 159-160.

32. William B. Quandt, *Camp David: Peacemaking and Politics* (Washington: The Brookings Institute, 1986), 120.

33. For the Palestinian perspective on Geneva see the analysis in Abraham, "Development and Transformation of the PLO," 411, and Cobban, *Palestine Liberation Organization,* 90-91. For the Arab state perspective on Geneva see Fahmy, *Negotiating for Peace in the Middle East,* 188-251.

34. Quandt, *Camp David,* xi-xiii, discusses his direct involvement in the issues under consideration in this chapter.

35. Ibid., 124-25.

36. Ibid.

37. See the analysis in Mohammed K. Shadid, *The United States and the Palestinians* (N.Y.: St. Martins Press, 1981), 135-36.

38. Ajami, *Arab Predicament,* 129, and Abbas Alnasrawi, ed., "The Impact of Money: Dynamics of Power and Dependency in the Arab World," special issue, *Arab Studies Quarterly* 6, nos. 1 and 2 (Winter/Spring 1984), passim. Also see Alnasrawi, *OPEC in a Changing World Economy* (Baltimore: Johns Hopkins University Press, 1984).

39. For a comprehensive, though unfortunately sensationalistic portrait of this phenomena, see Robin Wright, *Sacred Rage: The Wrath of Militant Islam* (New York: Simon and Schuster, 1985).

40. *Weekly Compilation of Presidential Documents,* Aug. 26, 1974, 1044.

41. Bernard Reich, *Quest for Peace: United States-Israeli Relations and the Arab-Israeli Conflict* (New Brunswick, N.J.: Transaction Books, 1977), 304.

42. Quoted in *Brief,* no. 96, 16-31, Dec. 1974, 1, reprinted in ibid., 334.

43. Embassy of Israel, Washington, D.C., "Policy Background, Current Prospects for an Israeli-Arab Settlement," Feb. 12, 1975, 3, quoted in ibid.

44. See the ten points presented to President Ford by Yigal Allon outlining Israel's demands in Matti Golan, *The Secret Conversations of Henry Kissinger: Step-by-Step Diplomacy in the Middle East* (New York: Quadrangle/Times Books, 1976), 229-30.

45. *Washington Post,* Feb. 17, 1975.

46. Ibid., May 22, 1975.

47. For an analysis of the impact of the congressional letter see John F. Roehm, Jr., "Congressional Participation in United States-Middle East Policy, October 1973-1976: Congressional Activism vs. Policy Coherence," in *Congress, the Presidency and American Foreign Policy,* eds. John Spanier and Joseph Nogee (New York: Pergamon Press, 1981), 35-36.

48. *New York Times,* May 30, 1975, cited in ibid., 35, 43n.

49. Quoted in ibid., 35, cited from Russell Warren House and Sarah Hays Trott, *The Power Peddlers: How Lobbyists Mold American Foreign Policy* (Garden City, N.Y.: Doubleday, 1977), 546.

50. Roehm, "Congressional Participation," 36, cited from Marvin C. Feuerwerger, *Congress and Israel: Foreign Aid Decision-Making in the House of Representatives, 1969-1976* (Westport, Conn.: Greenwood Press, 1979), 170-71.

51. George Ball, "How to Save Israel in Spite of Herself," *Foreign Affairs* 55 (Apr. 1977), 471.

52. See "Second Sinai Disengagement Agreement, Egypt and Israel, September 1, 1975" (plus annexes), in *Search for Peace,* 3-5.

53. For the detailed agreements on all of the above points, see (1) "Memorandum of Agreement between the Governments of Israel and United States," (2) "Memorandum of Agreement between the Governments of Israel and the United States on the Geneva Peace Conference," and (3) "Assurances from the United States to Israel," in ibid., 6-17.

54. Ibid.

55. On the Carter administration's position on the Palestinians see analysis by Shadid, *United States and Palestinians,* 133ff.

56. Quandt, *Camp David,* 58-60.

57. *Weekly Compilation of Presidential Documents,* Mar. 21, 1977, 361.

58. Ibid., May 16, 1977, 706.

59. See, for example, the analysis by Tillman, *United States in the Middle East,* 220-21. Also see Quandt, *Camp David,* passim, who spells out throughout the book the various formulas—"home rule," "autonomy," "trusteeship," and others—that the United States was prepared to consider for the Palestinians, none of them involving self-determination or an independent state of their own.

60. *Department of State News Release,* Vice-President Walter Mondale's address before the World Affairs Council of North California, "A Framework for Middle East Peace," June 17, 1977.

61. William E. Farrell, "United States Move on Mideast Rejected by Israel, Welcomed by Arabs," *New York Times,* Oct. 3, 1977, cited in Tillman, *United States in the Middle East,* 233.

62. William E. Farrell, "Fear They May be a Pawn in Carter's Global Game," *New York Times,* Oct. 4, 1977, cited in ibid., 233.

63. "Mideast Peace Initiative Provokes Criticism in United States," *New York Times,* Oct. 3, 1977, cited in ibid., 234.

64. "Carter's Stance on Palestinians Turns Off Jewish Contributors," *Washington Post,* Oct. 6, 1977, cited in ibid. Quandt, *Camp David,* passim, carries the theme of the importance of the domestic political factor in the formation of U.S. Middle East policy throughout his book although he is very scanty on specifics. He does provide one important source for material on the relationship: Peter Bass, "The Anti-Politics of Presidential Leadership: Jimmy Carter and American Jews," Senior thesis presented to the faculty of the Woodrow Wilson School of International Affairs, Princeton University, Apr. 12, 1985.

65. Quandt, *Camp David,* 126-31.

66. *New York Times,* Oct. 5, 1977.

67. See Sidney Zion and Uri Dan, "Untold Story of the Mideast Talks," *New York Times Magazine,* Jan. 21, 1979, 46ff., and Bernard Gwertzman, "United States Reports Accord with Israel Raises Hopes of Peace Talks," *New York Times,* Oct. 6, 1977. For an analysis of the Dayan-Carter meeting, see Tillman, *United States in the Middle East,* 235-36; Shadid, *United States and Palestinians,* 137; Quandt, *Camp David,* 126-31.

68. Mahmoud Riad, *The Struggle for Peace in the Middle East* (New York: Quartet Books, 1981), 305. Also see Quandt, *Camp David,* 132.

69. Thomas R. Stauffer, *United States Aid to Israel: The Vital Link,* Middle East Problem Paper no. 24 (Washington, D.C.: Middle East Institute, 1983), 2-3 and passim.

70. Moshe Dayan, *Breakthrough: A Personal Account of the Egypt-Israel Peace Negotiations* (New York: Alfred A. Knopf, 1981), 42-54.

71. Ibid., 45.

72. Ibid., 47-50.

73. Ibid., 50-52.

74. Ibid., 46. See Quandt, *Camp David,* 108-110, for a discussion of the Dayan-Tuhamy meeting. Quandt also notes that Dayan held secret talks with King Hussein on August 22 in London, though they did not result in an opening for further negotiations.

75. Quandt, *Camp David,* 111, 113.

76. Ibid., 159.

77. Dayan, *Breakthrough,* 61.

78. Quandt, *Camp David,* 110-14. Also see Jimmy Carter, *Keeping Faith: Memoirs of a President* (New York: Bantam Books, 1982), 304, on Dayan's promise regarding the settlements.

79. Carter, *Keeping Faith,* 292.

80. Dayan, *Breakthrough,* 60-61.

81. Quandt, *Camp David,* 161-62.

82. Fahmy, *Negotiating for Peace in the Middle East,* 198.

83. Quandt, *Camp David,* 115.

84. Address to the Knesset, Nov. 20, 1977, *New York Times,* Nov. 21, 1977.

85. Anwar el-Sadat, *In Search of Identity: An Autobiography* (New York: Harper and Row, 1978), 312.

86. For an analysis see Quandt, *Camp David,* 124-25. He cites Martin Indyk, *To the Ends of the Earth: Sadat's Jerusalem Initiative* (Cambridge, Mass.: Harvard University, Center for Middle Eastern Studies, 1984), 41-43, for further support of this thesis.

87. Quandt, *Camp David,* 124-25, 132-34.

88. Ibid., 150.

89. Dayan, *Breakthrough,* 98.

90. Ibid. Also see Quandt, *Camp David,* 152-55, for more details of the December trip by this American delegation.

91. Quandt, *Camp David,* 155, notes that Begin's idea of autonomy was derived from Vladimir Jabotinsky's writings.

92. On the institutionalized discrimination against Arab citizens of Israel on land tenure (and other matters) see Philippa Strum, "Israel's Democratic Dilemma," *Reform Judaism,* Publication of the Union of American Hebrew Congregations, 14, no. 2 (Winter 1985-86), 13. Also see notes 5 and 6, Chapter 8 herein.

93. "Text of Begin's Plan for West Bank and Gaza Strip," *New York Times,* Dec. 29, 1977.

94. Carter, *Keeping Faith,* 299-300.

95. Quandt, *Camp David,* 157.

96. Tillman, *United States in the Middle East,* 24, whose source was the Office of the White House Press Secretary, "Transcript of an Interview with the President by Barbara Walters, Robert McNeil, Tom Brokaw and Bob Schieffer," Dec. 28, 1977, 5-6.

97. Shadid, *United States and Palestinians,* 138-39, whose source was also the presidential interview cited in n. 96.

98. Quandt, *Camp David,* 171-72. Also see the account by Cyrus Vance, *Hard Choices* (New York: Simon and Schuster, 1983), excerpts reprinted in *American-Arab Affairs* 5 (Summer 1983), 164.

99. Tillman, *United States in the Middle East,* 2-3, whose source was an interview with Sadat in *October Magazine,* Jan. 14, 1978, English translation in *F.B.I.S.,* daily report, Middle East and North Africa, Jan. 16, 1978, D4.

100. "Text of Statements by Sadat and Carter Following Meeting in Aswan," *New York Times,* Jan. 5, 1978.

101. Ibid.

102. "Begin Sees Benefit in Aswan Remarks," ibid.

103. "Remarks by Begin at the Dinner for Participants in Jerusalem Talks," ibid., Jan. 19, 1978.

104. Quandt, *Camp David,* 165, notes that Kamel was opposed to breaking off the talks. He cites a work by Kamel (in Arabic): Muhammad Ibrahim

Kamil, *The Lost Peace in the Camp David Accords* (Jidda: Saudi Research and Marketing Co., 1984), 96-122.

105. William E. Farrell, "Cabinet Acts Quickly," *New York Times,* Jan. 19, 1978.

106. *Newsweek,* Feb. 6, 1978, 42.

107. Quandt, *Camp David,* 166.

108. *Newsweek,* Feb. 13, 1978, 37.

109. Quandt, *Camp David,* 174.

110. Ibid., 167, 174.

111. *Newsweek,* Feb. 13, 1978, 37. Also see Vance, *Hard Choices* (excerpts), 164-65.

112. Quandt, *Camp David,* 176.

113. Ibid., 176, 178.

114. Ibid., 176.

115. Ibid.

116. Ibid., 176-79.

117. Ibid., 179.

118. Ibid., 96-205 illustrates the weakness of Sadat's commitment.

119. Ibid., 204.

120. Ibid.

121. Dayan, *Breakthrough,* 116, 117.

122. *Newsweek,* Feb. 13, 1978, 37.

123. Ibid. Also see Dayan, *Breakthrough,* 117.

124. *Newsweek,* Feb. 20, 1978, 35.

125. Ibid., 36.

126. Dayan, *Breakthrough,* 119.

127. Quandt, *Camp David,* 180.

128. Ibid., 180-81.

129. Ibid., 181.

130. *Newsweek,* Feb. 20, 1978, 36-38.

131. Ibid., Feb. 27, 1978, 32.

132. Quandt, *Camp David,* 191.

133. Ibid., 204.

134. *Newsweek,* Mar. 20, 1978, 25.

135. See Haley and Snider, eds., *Lebanon in Crisis,* 93-98 and note 23 above.

136. *Economist,* Mar. 25, 1978, 62. The *Economist's* figures on dead civilians are lower than given in the text (i.e., 500-600). The higher figure was taken from Haley and Snider, eds., *Lebanon in Crisis,* 101.

137. *Economist,* Mar. 18, 1978, 26.

138. Ibid., Mar. 25, 1978, 60.

139. "U.N. Security Council Resolution 425, March 19, 1978," in *Search for Peace,* 342.

140. *Economist,* June 17, 1978, 67.

141. Jimmy Carter, "Interview," *Penthouse* (Apr. 1983), 170.

142. "Vance's Letter to Congress on Israeli Use of United States Arms," *New York Times,* Apr. 6, 1978.

The illegality of Israel's use of American-supplied weapons for other than strictly defensive purposes resides in two documents. The first: Section 3(c) (2) of the Arms Export Control Act. The use of American weapons for other than defensive purposes is strictly prohibited, and the

President is required to report to Congress promptly any possible violation of that law. See: 'The Use of United States Supplied Military Equipment in Lebanon,' *Hearings,* before the Committee on Foreign Affairs and its Subcommittee on International Security and Scientific Affairs, House of Representatives, July 15 and August 4, 1982, Washington USGPO [Appendix 2—Relevant parts of the Arms Control Export Act], 61-68.

The second: 'Israel, Mutual Defense Assistance Agreement,' effected by exchange of notes signed at Tel Aviv July 1 and 23, 1952; entered into force July 23, 1952: Letters exchanged by the American Ambassador, Monnett B. Davis, and the Israeli Acting Minister for Foreign Affairs, Moshe Sharett. The American statement required that under the terms of the Mutual Defense Assistance Act of 1949, any American assistance furnished to Israel 'must be used solely to maintain its internal security, its legitimate self-defense, or to permit it to participate in the defense of the area of which it is a part, or in United Nations collective security measures, *and that it will not undertake any act of aggression against any other state'* (emphasis added).

The Israelis responded: 'The Government of Israel accepts the undertaking and assurances outlined in that note and concurs with the proposal that this note, together with your note dated July 1, 1952, constitute an agreement covering all transactions for the supply of military assistance under Section 408 (e) of the Mutual Defense Assistance Act of 1949.'

Documents provided by the office of Michael H. Van Dusen, Subcommittee Staff Director of the Subcommittee on Europe and the Middle East (Lee H. Hamilton, Chairman), of the Committee on Foreign Affairs, House of Representatives.

For an excellent discussion of this issue, see William Espinosa and Les Janka, *Defense or Aggression? United States Arms Export Control Laws and the Israeli Invasion of Lebanon* (Washington, D.C.: American Educational Trust, 1983).

143. Vance, *Hard Choices* (excerpts), 168-69. Also see Bernard Gwertzman, "United States Says Israelis in Lebanon Used Cluster Bombs, Breaking Pledge," *New York Times,* Apr. 8, 1978.

144. See his own account: Paul Findley, *They Dare to Speak Out: People and Institutions Confront Israel's Lobby* (Westport, Conn.: Lawrence Hill, 1985), 21-23, 321-22, and passim. Also see the discussion in Chapter 8 herein.

145. See Moshe Dayan's account of the Begin-Carter meetings in *Breakthrough,* 122-29. Also see Vance's account in *Hard Choices* (excerpts), 169-70, and Quandt's in *Camp David,* 184-86.

146. Carter, *Keeping Faith,* 311.

147. Ibid., 311-12.

148. Bernard Gwertzman, "Begin Arrives in the United States and will See Carter about Mideast Issues," *New York Times,* May 1, 1978, quoted in Quandt, *Camp David,* 190.

149. Ezer Weizman, *The Battle for Peace,* (New York: Bantam Books, 1981), 292-301, quoted in Quandt, *Camp David,* 188-89.

150. Carter, *Keeping Faith,* 313.

151. Dayan, *Breakthrough,* 129.

152. Ibid.

153. Seth P. Tillman, "United States Middle East Policy: Theory and Practice," *American-Arab Affairs* 4 (Spring 1983), 9-10.

154. Quandt, *Camp David*, 190-98, discusses a variety of activities aimed at moving the peace process along during this period, including a secret planning group, a trip by Vice-President Walter Mondale to the Middle East, and more.

155. *Economist*, July 15, 1978, 59; ibid., July 22, 1978, 51.

156. Weizman, *Battle for Peace*, 313-24, quoted in Quandt, *Camp David*, 198.

157. *Economist*, July 22, 1978, 51.

158. Quandt, *Camp David*, 201. For a somewhat different analysis see Hermann Frederick Eilts, "Improve the Framework," *Foreign Policy* 41 (Winter 1980-81), 3-20.

159. *Economist*, July 29, 1978, 51.

160. Carter, *Keeping Faith*, 315.

161. Ibid., 315-16.

162. Quandt, *Camp David*, 201, citing Zbigniew Brzezinski, *Power and Principle: Memoirs of the National Security Advisor, 1977-1981* (New York: Farrar, Strauss, Giroux, 1983), 250-51.

163. Carter, *Keeping Faith*, 328-29. See also Dayan, *Breakthrough*, 161-62, for Egyptian demands.

164. Quandt, *Camp David*, 220-23.

165. Dayan, *Breakthrough*, 163.

166. Quandt, *Camp David*, 209-15.

167. Carter, *Keeping Faith*, 332-38.

168. Quandt, *Camp David*, 225-26, 256.

169. Carter, *Keeping Faith*, 333. See also Quandt, *Camp David*, 220.

170. Quandt and Vance in particular disagreed. See: Quandt, *Camp David*, 206-19, 257-58.

171. Ibid., 207, 252.

172. Ibid., 219ff. Quandt notes that this is a reversal of a strategy apparently worked out by Sadat and Carter at their February 1978 meeting during which they agreed on a coordinated Egyptian-American strategy to bring pressure to bear on Israel through confrontationist tactics in order to achieve some progress on the Palestinian issue. See Quandt, *Camp David*, 168-81. But for the reasons discussed earlier in the text, Carter rapidly abandoned his ideas on a comprehensive peace and focused instead on a bilateral Egyptian-Israeli agreement. He never seriously pressured Israel for concessions on the Palestinian question.

173. Dayan, *Breakthrough*, 162.

174. Ibid.

175. Quandt, *Camp David*, 241.

176. Ibid., 244.

177. Carter, *Keeping Faith*, 396-97. Also see Dayan, *Breakthrough*, 171-80.

178. Quandt, *Camp David*, 256.

179. Carter, *Keeping Faith*, 397.

180. For the various conflicting accounts of the settlement dispute see: Quandt, *Camp David*, 247-54, 263-64; Vance, *Hard Choices* (excerpts), 170-73; Dayan, *Breakthrough*, 184-86, 229; Eilts, "Improve the Framework," 8.

181. See "Camp David Framework for Peace, September 17, 1978," and ancillary letters in *Search for Peace*, 18-29.

182. See Fahmy, *Negotiating for Peace in the Middle East*, 252-84.

183. Tillman, *United States in the Middle East*, 26, who cites an interview he had with Basheer in Cairo, Oct. 14, 1978.

184. Riad, *Struggle for Peace in the Middle East*, 323.

185. Ibid.

186. "Arafat Denounces Agreements as 'Dirty Deal' at Summit," *Washington Post*, Sept. 20, 1978.

187. Quandt, *Camp David*, 265.

188. Quoted in Tillman, *United States in the Middle East*, 203, from an interview with Milhem in Halhoul, Nov. 2, 1978.

189. Quoted in ibid., from an interview with Karim Khalaf in Ramallah, Nov. 4, 1978.

190. Quoted in ibid., from an interview with Shak'a in Nablus, Nov. 4, 1978.

191. Interview with Arayan El Bireh, July 1983, by this writer.

192. Tillman, *United States in the Middle East*, 202-5.

193. Quandt, *Camp David*, 271.

194. Riad, *Struggle for Peace in the Middle East*, 329-34. Also see Tillman, *United States in the Middle East*, 201-10 and 106-18 for an analysis of Arab reaction to Camp David.

195. Carter, *Keeping Faith*, 405.

196. Ibid., 405-6.

197. Dayan, *Breakthrough*, 208, 218, 234; also see 356-58 for the texts of the two memorandums (e.g. on the supply of oil and the broader one).

198. Carter, *Keeping Faith*, 408. Also see Quandt, *Camp David*, 277.

199. Dayan, *Breakthrough*, 202.

200. Quandt, *Camp David*, 275.

201. Carter, *Keeping Faith*, 409.

202. Quandt, *Camp David*, 279.

203. Dayan, *Breakthrough*, 228.

204. *Economist*, Dec. 2, 1978, 66. For discussion and detail about the priority of obligations issue, see Quandt, *Camp David*, 259-99.

205. Quandt, *Camp David*, 289.

206. Dayan, *Breakthrough*, 254. Also see Quandt, *Camp David*, 292-93.

207. Quandt, *Camp David*, 295. What is in the text is the totality of what Quandt prints of Brzezinski's memo. He cites merely: Memorandum from Brzezinski to Carter, January 23, 1979—no place or source.

208. Dayan, *Breakthrough*, 257.

209. *Economist*, Jan. 10, 1979, 75.

210. See the account by Dayan, *Breakthrough*, 259.

211. Ibid., 268. Also see Quandt, *Camp David*, 298-302.

212. *Search for Peace*, 55-57.

213. Carter, *Keeping Faith*, 417.

214. Ibid., 418.

215. Jonathan Kandell, "Israelis Listen Silently to Carter," *New York Times*, Mar. 13, 1979.

216. Carter, *Keeping Faith*, 421.

217. Quandt, *Camp David*, 306.

218. Carter, *Keeping Faith,* 426.
219. Riad, *Struggle for Peace in the Middle East,* 336.
220. Ibid., 336-37.

CHAPTER SEVEN

1. For an analysis of Israel's West Bank policy, see Merle Thorpe, Jr., *Prescription for Conflict: Israel's West Bank Settlement Policy* (Washington, D.C.: Foundation for Middle East Peace, 1984). See also notes 85 and 86 below.
2. *New York Times,* Mar. 7, 1981.
3. Ibid., Apr. 16, 1981.
4. For a good analysis of the Reagan administration and Israel, see Naseer Aruri, "The United States and Israel: That Very Special Relationship," in Naseer Aruri, Fouad Moughrabi, and Joe Stork, *Reagan and the Middle East* (Belmont, Mass.: Association of Arab-American University Graduates, 1983), 8-9.
5. *Washington Post,* Apr. 23, 1981.
6. *New York Times,* May 29, 1981.
7. See Paul Findley, *They Dare to Speak Out: People and Institutions Confront Israel's Lobby* (Westport, Conn.: Lawrence Hill, 1985), 18-19, 109-13. It is significant to note that in the spring of 1986 pro-Israeli groups were mobilizing to prevent delivery of the AWACs approved for sale in 1981. A report by Frederick Kempe, "Congress Goes after Saudi AWACs Deal, Imperiling Reagan's Mideast Diplomacy," *Wall Street Journal,* Feb. 13, 1986, noted: "Bolstered by their success in blocking President Reagan's $1.9 billion arms sale to Jordan, some congressmen and pro-Israeli lobbyists are drawing a bead on an even greater prize. Sen. Alan Cranston (D., Calif.) has requested hearings that would set back White House Middle East politics yet again by delaying or stopping this summer's delivery of five AWACs radar planes to Saudi Arabia. . . . The leading pro-Israeli lobby group, the American Israel Public Affairs Committee, or Aipac, asserts the Saudis haven't fulfilled the political terms of the sale. . . . 'Given the track record on Jordan, you have to take the threat seriously,' says a senior administration official who fears a growing loss of U.S. credibility. 'Congress is raising serious questions in the minds of moderate Arab leaders whether the U.S. will stay the course and whether it can follow policies independent of Israel.'" Also see Steven Roberts, "Blending a Chorus of No's to the Saudis on Arms," *New York Times,* May 19, 1986.
8. *New York Times,* Aug. 9, 1981.
9. The quotations are cited in George Rentz, "The Fahd Plan," *Middle East Insight* 2, no. 2 (Jan./Feb. 1982), 21-24.
10. Quotations and analysis are taken from ibid., 22-23.
11. Ibid., 23.
12. See the analysis in Alain Gresh's *The PLO: The Struggle Within: Towards an Independent Palestinian State* (London: Zed Books, 1985), 223-25.
13. See the analysis by Claudia Wright, "The Debacle at Fez," *In These Times,* Dec. 1, 1981, 27.
14. Ibid.
15. Ibid.

16. See, for example, Ned Temko, "Israel Hits Back against Western 'Tilt' to Saudis," *Christian Science Monitor*, Nov. 10, 1981.

17. Seth P. Tillman, *The United States in the Middle East: Interests and Obstacles* (Bloomington: Indiana University Press, 1982), 80.

18. Ibid., 78.

19. See, for example, Claudia Wright, "The Turn of the Screw—The Lebanon War and American Policy," *Journal of Palestine Studies* 11-12 (Summer/Fall 1982), 18-21.

20. See Claudia Wright, "A Tilt Towards Baghdad?" *Middle East* (June 1982), 8. Also see Bernard Gwertzman, "Haig Says United States Seeks Consensus Strategy in Mideast Region: Improved Iraq Ties Possible," *New York Times*, Mar. 20, 1981.

21. Noam Chomsky cites a BBC program in February 1982 during which Jacob Nimrodi, head of the Israeli intelligence agency, Mossad, declared that he believed the West should attempt to stage a military coup against the Khomeini regime. On the same program David Kimche stressed that Israel wants the Iranian army to be strong so that an army takeover would be feasible in Iran. The moderator of the program, Philip Tibenham, commented that "to encourage just such a takeover the Israelis embarked on a series of totally secret deals to supply arms to the Iranian military." Noam Chomsky, *The Fateful Triangle: The United States, Israel and the Palestinians* (Boston: South End Press, 1983), 458-59. Also see William Safire's column in the *New York Times*, May 31, 1982, and the *Christian Science Monitor*, May 30, 1984.

22. See Robert O. Freedman, "Moscow and the Gulf in 1981," *Middle East Insight* 2, no. 2 (Jan.-Feb. 1982), 17.

23. Wright, "A Tilt Towards Baghdad," 7-8.

24. For an excellent account of Washington's loss in not responding to Iraq's initiative, see Adeed I. Dawisha, "Iraq: The West's Opportunity," *Foreign Policy* 41 (Winter 1981-82), 134-53.

25. *Christian Science Monitor*, Apr. 14, 1982.

26. See *A Compassionate Peace: A Future for the Middle East*, a Report Prepared for the American Friends Service Committee (New York: Hill and Wang, 1982), 151-61, for a good analysis of the Afghanistan situation.

27. "Transcript of President's State of the Union Address to Joint Session of Congress," *New York Times*, Jan. 24, 1980.

28. *Mideast Observer*, Feb. 15, 1981.

29. See Joe Stork, "Israel as a Strategic Asset," in Aruri, Moughrabi, and Stork, *Reagan and the Middle East*, 26.

30. *New York Times*, July 14, 1981.

31. For a good analysis of the American non-reaction to the Israeli bombing, see Ghassan Bishara, "The Political Repercussions of the Israeli Raid on the Iraqi Nuclear Reactor," *Journal of Palestine Studies* 11 (Spring 1982), 58-76. Senator Alan Cranston, D., California, a presidential hopeful and a staunch pro-Zionist, wrote an article for the *New York Times*, June 10, 1981, defending Israel's action. For another highly condemnatory critique of Israel's action see Eliot Marshall, "Fallout from the Raid on Iraq," *Science* 213 (July 3, 1981), 116, 125.

32. U.N. Security Council Resolution 487, June 19, 1981.

33. Bishara, "Political Repercussions," 70. On Israel's nuclear capability, see a special issue of the Israeli journal *New Outlook*, "The Dangers of Nuclear Proliferation and Confrontation" (May 1982).

34. *New York Times*, July 19, 1981.

35. *Washington Post*, Dec. 1, 1981.

36. *Jerusalem Post Weekly*, Sept. 20-26, 1981, quoted in Stork, "Israel as a Strategic Asset," 36.

37. John Kifner, "New United States–Israeli Steps May Isolate Arab Allies," *New York Times*, Sept. 16, 1981.

38. See Dan Goodgame, "Latin America Provides Market for Israeli Arms," *Miami Herald*, Dec. 13, 1982, on Sharon's claims regarding the agreement secretly remaining in effect.

39. Ball made these remarks while appearing with Richard Allen on "Meet the Press," Sept. 30, 1980, and they are quoted in Stork, "Israel as a Strategic Asset," 20. Also see George Ball, "How to Save Israel in Spite of Herself," *Foreign Affairs* 55 (Apr. 1977), and Larry L. Fabian, "The Red Light," *Foreign Policy* 50 (Spring 1983), 53-72.

40. See, for example, Cheryl A. Rubenberg, "Israel and Guatemala: A Case Study in Israel's Foreign Policy," *MERIP Reports* 140 (May-June 1986), especially the extensive footnotes providing references to Israel's proxy relationship with the United States in the Third World. Also see Esther Howard, "Israel: The Sorcerer's Apprentice," *MERIP Reports* 112 (Feb. 1983), 16-25; Josh Karliner, "Israel: United States Proxy in Latin America," *Latinamerica Press* 15, no. 29 (Aug. 4, 1983); Clarence Lusane, "Washington's Proxy: Israeli Arms in Central America," *Covert Action* 20 (Winter 1984), 34-37.

41. *Davar* (Hebrew) Jan. 3, 1982.

42. Ze'ev Schiff, "The Green Light," *Foreign Policy* 50 (Spring 1983), 78, and 73-85 passim.

43. Ibid., 79.

44. Ibid., 79-80. Also see Sheila Ryan, "Israel's Invasion of Lebanon: Background to the Crisis," *Journal of Palestine Studies* 11/12 (Summer/Fall 1982), 32.

45. *Washington Post*, Feb. 26, 1982.

46. See, for example, ibid., Feb. 6, 1982.

47. Schiff, "Green Light," 80-81.

48. See James McCartney, "Officials Say Haig Let Israel Think United States Condoned Invasion of Lebanon," *Philadelphia Inquirer*, Jan. 23, 1983.

49. Schiff, "Green Light," 81.

50. Ibid., 82.

51. Joe Stork and Jim Paul, "The War in Lebanon," *MERIP Reports* 108-9 (Sept.-Oct. 1982), 6. Their source was Claudia Wright, Pacific News Service Dispatch, Aug. 19, 1982.

52. Ibid. The source here was Claudia Wright, *In These Times*, Sept. 8-14, 1982.

53. Schiff, "Green Light," 83.

54. Ibid. For fuller details see Ze'ev Schiff and Ehud Ya'ari, *Israel's Lebanon War* (New York: Simon and Schuster, 1984), passim.

55. For a good history of the complex social and political history of Lebanon, see David C. Gordon, *The Republic of Lebanon: Nation in Jeopardy* (Boulder, Colo.: Westview Press, 1983), passim. Also see Jonathan C. Randal, *Going All the Way: Christian Warlords, Israeli Adventurers and the War in Lebanon* (New York: Viking Press, 1983), passim. Schiff and

Ya'ari, *Israel's Lebanon War,* also give a good picture of Lebanese inter-necine strife, especially among the various Maronite clans/militias.

56. See Cheryl A. Rubenberg, "Palestinians in Lebanon: A Question of Human and Civil Rights," *Arab Studies Quarterly* 6, no. 3 (Summer 1984), 194-221.

57. For a text of the Cairo Agreement, see Walid Khalidi, *Conflict and Violence in Lebanon: Confrontation in the Middle East,* Center for International Affairs (Cambridge, Mass.: Harvard University Press, 1979), 185-87.

58. See Cheryl A. Rubenberg, *The Palestine Liberation Organization: Its Institutional Infrastructure* (Belmont, Mass.: Institute of Arab Studies, 1983), passim.

59. David Shipler, " '48 Israeli Tie to Phalangist Revealed," *New York Times,* July 3, 1983; his source was official Foreign Ministry documents, recently uncovered by Benny Morris, an Israeli researcher.

60. Livia Rokach, *Israel's Sacred Terrorism: A Study Based on Moshe Sharett's Personal Diaries and Other Documents,* 2d ed. (Belmont, Mass.: Association of Arab-American University Graduates, 1980), 24-25.

61. Ibid., 29.

62. Ben Halpern, *The Idea of the Jewish State,* 2d ed. (Cambridge, Mass.: Harvard University Press, 1969), 296.

63. Michael C. Hudson, "The Palestinian Factor in the Lebanese Civil War," *Middle East Journal* 32, no. 3 (Summer 1976), 267.

64. Lewis W. Snider et al., "Israel," in *Lebanon in Crisis: Participants and Issues,* ed. P. Edward Haley and Lewis W. Snider (Syracuse, N.Y.: Syracuse University Press, 1979), 93-94.

65. Ibid., 95-96.

66. Ibid., 98. Also see the discussion of the 1978 Israeli invasion of Lebanon in Chapter 6 herein.

67. *New York Times,* Apr. 12, 1981.

68. Hudson, "Palestinian Factor," 261-78.

69. *Miami Herald,* Aug. 25, 1982, reported on the amount of aid Israel had provided to the Phalange between 1977 and 1982.

70. Rubenberg, *Palestine Liberation Organization,* passim.

71. A poll conducted for *Time* magazine by an Israeli firm, with the help of Israeli sociologists and published in *Time,* May 24, 1982, shows that 86 percent of all respondents, randomly selected, wanted an independent Palestinian state, headed solely by the PLO.

72. See Michael Jansen, *The Battle of Beirut: Why Israel Invaded Lebanon* (London: Zed Press, 1982), 24, citing Ze'ev Schiff and other Israeli analysts.

73. The fallacy of Israeli assumptions was clearly demonstrated in the comments made by the mayor of Bethlehem, Elias Freij, and the deposed mayor of Gaza, Rashad Shawa, on NBC's "Meet the Press," Aug. 29, 1982 (reprint from Kelly Press, vol. 82), after the military defeat of the PLO in Lebanon. Freij, considered the most moderate West Bank leader, was asked. "Now that the PLO has been totally defeated, do you feel free to cooperate with the Israelis?" He answered: "The PLO is the official representative and spokesman of all Palestinian Arabs wherever they live in the world." Freij further dismissed the Israeli-sponsored "village-leagues" as collaborators and quislings. Moreover, he stated that Sharon's declaration that Israel will not allow a Palestinian state on the West Bank is "absolutely

rejected by Palestinians." He claimed that the Palestinian people are entitled to a home, to self-determination, and a "state of our own." Shawa likewise stated that the PLO is the only legitimate representative of the Palestinian people, and when asked about the distinction that the Israelis make between the Palestinians and the PLO, he stated: "Since the PLO represents the Palestinians, we are all part and parcel of the PLO." Clearly the military defeat of the PLO had the opposite results on the West Bank from what the Israelis desired.

74. *Ha'aretz*, June 25, 1982.

75. *Christian Science Monitor*, Feb. 8, 1982. Also see Thomas Stauffer's analysis of Israel's water needs in ibid., Jan. 20, 1982. For an analysis of Israel's water policies, see Uri Davis, Antonia E. L. Maks, and John Richardson, "Israel's Water Policies," *Journal of Palestine Studies* (Winter 1980), 3-31.

76. Yohanan Ramati, chairman of the Laam (in the Likud) Foreign Relations Committee, "The Political and Strategic Consequences of the Lebanese War," public lecture, Dec. 2, 1982, Florida International University, Bay Vista Campus, Miami.

77. This was known as the "Yariv Plan," but was never made public. It was discussed with the author in a private interview with an Israeli official.

78. Schiff and Ya'ari, *Israel's Lebanon War*, argue that all the decisions related to the Lebanon War were made by Defense Minister Ariel Sharon alone, possibly with the agreement of Prime Minister Begin, but also possibly without his knowledge. The cabinet, Schiff and Ya'ari argue, was completely in the dark about the war and never knew of what was going to happen until after it happened. This argument, though well presented and seemingly well documented, stretches one's imagination.

79. See, for example, *Christian Science Monitor*, Mar. 18, 1982, which discusses this campaign extensively.

80. Ibid.

81. Ibid., Apr. 26, 1982.

82. *Facts on File Yearbook, 1982,* 414 (June 11, 1982).

83. *Christian Science Monitor*, Apr. 26, 1982, offers a similar analysis.

84. Ibid., Apr. 8, 1982, discusses some of the details of the campaign on the West Bank. For a more complete analysis, see the sources cited in notes 85 and 86 below.

85. For details of these kinds of policies, see *Christian Science Monitor*, Jan. 6, Mar. 11, Mar. 31, Apr. 2, Apr. 7, 1982; *New York Times*, May 2, June 30, July 6, July 9, July 11, 1982. For a detailed discussion of the human rights situation on the West Bank and Gaza, see Cheryl A. Rubenberg, "Israeli Violations of Palestinian Human and Civil Rights in the West Bank and Gaza," *International Journal of Islamic and Arabic Studies* 2, no. 1 (1985), 43-68. Also see *The Bitter Year: Arabs under Israeli Occupation in 1982* (Washington: American-Arab Anti-Discrimination Committee, 1983), and "The Situation on the West Bank," *Hearings before the Subcommittee on Europe and the Middle East of the Committee on Foreign Affairs*, House of Representatives, 97th Cong. 2d sess., May 26, 1982 (Washington, D.C.: Government Printing Office, 1983). Also see Raja Shehadeh, *Occupier's Law: Israel and the West Bank* (Washington, D.C.: Institute for Palestine Studies, 1985).

86. For an analysis of the policy enunciated by Eytan, see *New York*

Times, Jan. 21, 1983, and *Miami Herald,* Jan. 22, 1983. For additional specific documentation of Israeli practices of torture, see Law in the Service of Man, *Torture and Intimidation in the West Bank: The Case of Al-Fara'a Prison* (Ramallah, West Bank: Law in the Service of Man, an affiliate of the International Commission of Jurists, 1984); *Sunday Times* (London), June 19, 1977; Alexandra U. Johnson, "Israeli Torture of Palestinian Political Prisoners in Jerusalem and the West Bank: Three State Department Reports," *Palestine Human Rights Bulletin* 17 (Apr. 1979); *Students behind Bars: A Report on the Prison Experiences of the Fourteen Students Detained Following a Rally at Birzeit University on July 27, 1983* (Birzeit, West Bank: Birzeit University Office of Public Relations, 1985).

87. *New York Times,* June 7, 1982.

88. Figures reported in *Christian Science Monitor,* Dec. 21, 1982.

89. Jean Genet, "Four Hours in Shatila," *Journal of Palestine Studies* 12, no. 3 (Spring 1983), 3-22.

90. See Advisory Committee on Human Rights in Lebanon, *Lebanon: Toward Legal Order and Respect for Human Rights* (Philadelphia: American Friends Service Committee, Aug. 10, 1983).

91. *New York Times,* June 5, 1982.

92. Ibid., June 6, 1982.

93. Ibid.

94. Ibid.

95. Ibid.

96. Ibid., June 8, 1982.

97. Ibid., June 9, 1982.

98. Ibid.

99. Ibid.

100. Ibid.

101. Ibid.

102. Ibid., June 10, 1982.

103. Ibid.

104. Ibid.

105. Ibid.

106. Ibid., June 11, 1982.

107. Ibid.

108. Ibid.

109. *Washington Post,* June 16, 1982.

110. Ibid.

111. *New York Times,* June 11, 1982.

112. Ibid.

113. Ibid., June 12, 1982.

114. See Bernard Gwertzman's analysis in ibid., June 12, 1982.

115. Ibid., June 13, 1982.

116. See Bernard Gwertzman's analysis in ibid.

117. Hirsh Goodman, *Jerusalem Post,* June 28, 1982, reported in Jansen, *Battle of Beirut,* 10.

118. *New York Times,* June 14, 1982.

119. Ibid.

120. See, for example, the analyses of Israeli policies related to Israeli efforts to extend Phalange control throughout Lebanon in: *Washington Post,* July 2, 1982; *Jerusalem Post,* July 16, 1982; *Los Angeles Times,* July 19, 1982; Jansen, *Battle of Beirut,* 114; James F. Clarity, "Lebanese Say Israel

Is Paralyzing Government in Occupied Territories," *New York Times,* Nov. 2, 1982; and the retrospective analysis in the *Miami Herald,* Jan. 23, 1983.

121. See, for example, the analysis by David Lamb, "Lebanese Leader's Links to Israel a Key Question," *Los Angeles Times,* Sept. 6, 1982.

122. *Wall Street Journal,* Oct. 11, 1982. Concerning Haddad, Israel was convinced of the necessity for "its man" to control southern Lebanon independent of the Lebanese army and to be included in the formation of any new government. According to the *Washington Post* (July 2, 1982), Begin specifically stated that "I think he [Haddad] should take part in the central government. He must be a member of the government." He also averred, "We will not leave Major Haddad in the lurch."

123. See the analysis by Lamb in the *Los Angeles Times,* Sept. 6, 1982.

124. For an excellent analysis of the meaning of the alteration of the traditional power equation, see Thomas L. Friedman, "Christians Won Vast New Power in Lebanon War," *New York Times,* Nov. 2, 1982.

125. Jansen, *Battle of Beirut,* 45; the quotation is from the PLO newspaper *Filistin al-Thawra,* Aug. 8, 1982.

126. *New York Times,* July 4, 1982.

127. For details of the plan, see ibid., July 7, 1982; *Miami Herald,* July 5, 1982.

128. *New York Times,* July 8, 1982.

129. Ibid., Aug. 21, 1982.

130. See Milton Viorst, "America's Broken Pledge to the PLO," *Washington Post,* Dec. 19, 1982.

131. *New York Times,* July 7, 1982.

132. Ibid., July 8, 1982.

133. Ibid., July 14, 1982.

134. Ibid., July 15, 1982.

135. Ibid.

136. For an analysis of Saudi and Syrian efforts in Washington, see ibid., July 22, 1982, and *Christian Science Monitor,* July 22, 1982.

137. For the initial PLO proposal, see *New York Times,* July 17, 1982.

138. See the detailed report in ibid., Sept. 20, 1982. Also see the *Economist,* Sept. 25, 1982.

139. *New York Times,* Sept. 20, 1982.

140. Ibid.

141. For a description of the horror of this massacre, see Genet, "Four Hours in Shatila," 3-22. Also see Amnon Kapeliouk, *Sabra and Shatila: Inquiry into a Massacre* (Belmont, Mass.: Association of Arab-American University Graduates, 1984).

142. *New York Times,* June 15, 1982.

143. Ibid.

144. Ibid.

145. Ibid., June 16, 1982. The Israeli prime minister's statement concerning his commitment to a Christian-led government in Lebanon may have, on the one hand, indicated a striking ignorance about the religious, political, historical, and social realities of Lebanon. On the other hand, perhaps it betrayed the thinking of a Zionist leader who believed in domination of the majority by a minority, who harbored a deep "anti-Arab" racism (Christians were not perceived to be "Arab" in the same sense as Muslims were considered Arab) and who distained the basic tenets of democratic principles.

146. Ibid.
147. For an analysis of the differing perspectives within the administration on these issues, see ibid., June 17, 1982.
148. See the analysis in ibid., June 18, 1982.
149. See "Chronology" (June 17, 1982), *Journal of Palestine Studies* 11/12 (Summer/Fall 1982), 146.
150. *New York Times,* June 18, 1982.
151. Ibid., June 19, 1982.
152. Ibid.
153. Ibid., June 21, 1982.
154. See the analysis by Bernard Gwertzman, ibid., June 24, 1982.
155. Ibid., June 22, 1982.
156. Ibid., June 23, 1982.
157. Ibid., June 24, 1982.
158. See the analysis in ibid., June 26 and June 27, 1982. Also see Juliana S. Peck, *The Reagan Administration and the Palestinian Question: The First Thousand Days* (Washington, D.C.: Institute for Palestine Studies, 1984), 57-58.
159. See the analysis in the *New York Times,* July 13, 1982.
160. Ibid., July 20, 1982.
161. Ibid., July 21, 1982.
162. Ibid., July 17, 1982.
163. Ibid., July 19, 1982.
164. Ibid., July 20, 1982.
165. Ibid., July 28, 1982. Also see Kevin Danaher, "Israel's Use of Cluster Bombs in Lebanon," *Journal of Palestine Studies* 11/12 (Summer/Fall 1982), 48-57.
166. *New York Times,* July 27, 1982.
167. For examples of the use of this device, as well as others, including allegations of "anti-Semitism," as ways and means to intimidate Americans (government officials and others) to prevent their deviation from the "line" of the Israeli government, see Findley, *They Dare to Speak Out,* passim. Also see Chapter 8 herein.
168. *New York Times,* July 29, 1982.
169. Ibid., July 30, 1982.
170. Ibid., Aug. 3, 1982.
171. Ibid.
172. Ibid.
173. Ibid., Aug. 4, 1982.
174. Ibid., Aug. 5, 1982.
175. Ibid.
176. Ibid.
177. Ibid.
178. Ibid.
179. Ibid.
180. Ibid., Aug. 6, 1982.
181. Ibid.
182. Ibid.
183. Ibid., Aug. 7, 1982; *Washington Post,* Aug. 7, 1982.
184. *New York Times,* Aug. 8, 1982.
185. Ibid.
186. *Miami Herald,* Aug. 10, 1982.

187. *New York Times,* Aug. 13, 1982.

188. Ibid.

189. Ibid.

190. Ibid., Aug. 13, 1982.

191. Ibid., Aug. 20, 1982.

192. Ibid., Aug. 27, 1982.

193. Ibid., Aug. 29, 1982.

194. Ibid., Aug. 28, 1982.

195. See, for example, the analysis by Rowland Evans and Robert Novak, "Bashir Gemayel's Last Bequest," *Washington Post,* Oct. 6, 1982. Also see David Lamb, "United States Asked to Help Lebanon Rebuild Its Army," *Los Angeles Times,* Sept. 8, 1982.

196. See, for example, the analysis by David Ignatius, "United States Risk in Lebanon Seen Escalating," *Wall Street Journal,* Oct. 11, 1982.

197. See *Jerusalem Post,* Sept. 7, 1982, and *New York Times,* Sept. 8, 1982.

198. *New York Times,* Sept. 10, 1982.

199. Ibid., Sept. 2, 1982.

200. Ibid.

201. Ibid.

202. *Miami Herald,* Sept. 3, 1982; *New York Times,* Sept. 3, 1982.

203. *New York Times,* Sept. 3, 1982.

204. Ibid.

205. Ibid.

206. Ibid., Oct. 15, 1982.

207. Ibid., Dec. 2, 1982.

208. *Facts on File Yearbook, 1984,* 156-57 (Mar. 2, 1984), cited in George W. Ball, *Error and Betrayal in Lebanon: An Analysis of Israel's Invasion of Lebanon and the Implication for U.S.-Israeli Relations* (Washington D.C.: Foundation for Middle East Peace, 1984), 54.

209. *New York Times,* Sept. 3, 1982.

210. Ibid., Sept. 5, 1982.

211. Ibid., Sept. 6, 1982.

212. Ibid.

213. Ibid.

214. Ibid.

215. For a text of the plan, see "Documents," *Journal of Palestine Studies* 12 (Winter 1983), 202-3.

216. *New York Times,* Sept. 11, 1982.

217. Ibid.

218. *Miami Herald,* Sept. 11, 1982; *New York Times,* Sept. 11, 1982.

219. *New York Times,* Sept. 17, 1982.

220. Ibid.

221. Ibid., Sept. 18, 1982.

222. Ibid., Sept. 22, 1982. Also see *Middle East Policy Survey,* Oct. 8, 1982.

223. See *New York Times,* Oct. 11, 1982; *Christian Science Monitor,* Oct. 15, 1982; *New York Times,* Oct. 16, 1982. Israel did not even want the United States to be a party to the negotiations. See, for example, *Middle East Policy Survey,* Nov. 19, 1982.

224. *New York Times,* Oct. 19, 1982.

225. Ibid., Oct. 20, 1982.

226. Ibid., Nov. 7, 1982.
227. Ibid., Nov. 10, 1982.
228. Ibid.
229. See "Chronology," *Journal of Palestine Studies* 12 (Winter 1983), 132.
230. *Miami Herald,* Nov. 11, 1982.
231. Ibid. Also see Cheryl A. Rubenberg, "The Middle East Lobbies," *The Link* 17, no. 1 (Jan./Mar. 1984).
232. *New York Times,* Dec. 14, 1982.
233. Ibid., Dec. 16, 1982.
234. *Miami Herald,* Dec. 17, 1982.
235. Thomas L. Friedman, "Arafat's Strategy: The Jordanian Connection," *New York Times,* Dec. 20, 1982. Also see Cheryl A. Rubenberg, "The PLO's Response to the Reagan Initiative: The PNC at Algiers, February 1983," *American-Arab Affairs* 4 (Spring 1983), 53-69.
236. *New York Times,* Dec. 22, 1982.
237. Ibid., Dec. 24, 1982.
238. Ibid., Dec. 28, 1982.
239. Ibid., Jan. 6, 1983.
240. Ibid., Jan. 11, 1983.
241. "Chronology," *Journal of Palestine Studies* 12 (Spring 1983), 151.
242. *Miami Herald,* Mar. 15, 1983.
243. See, for example, the analysis by David K. Shipler, "The Limits of Israeli Power," *New York Times,* Feb. 26, 1984.
244. *Christian Science Monitor,* Jan. 24, 1983. For background material see *New York Times,* Jan. 11, 1983. Also see *Christian Science Monitor,* Jan. 26, 1983, and *New York Times,* Jan. 26, 1983.
245. *Miami Herald,* Feb. 3, 1983; also see *Christian Science Monitor,* Feb. 4, 1983, and *New York Times,* Feb. 7, 1983.
246. *Miami Herald,* Mar. 17, 1983.
247. *New York Times,* Mar. 18, 1983.
248. Ibid. Also see *Miami Herald,* Mar. 18, 1983.
249. *New York Times,* Mar. 19, 1983.
250. Ibid., Feb. 24, 1983.
251. Ibid., Mar. 2, 1983.
252. *Miami Herald,* Mar. 15, 1983; *New York Times,* Mar. 16, 1983. Also see *Middle East Policy Survey,* Mar. 11, 1983, and Thomas L. Friedman, "Trade Issue Stalls Talks on Lebanon," *New York Times,* Mar. 13, 1983.
253. *Miami Herald,* Mar. 22, 1983; *New York Times,* Mar. 22, 1983.
254. *Miami Herald,* Mar. 20, 1983. Also see *Christian Science Monitor,* Mar. 24, 1983. For excellent analyses of the thinking and politics behind Hussein's decision not to enter the talks, see Karen Elliot House, "King Hussein's Decision," *Miami Herald,* Apr. 17, 1983, reprinted from the *Wall Street Journal;* and Thomas L. Friedman, "Hussein Believes Search for Peace Is at a Dead End," *New York Times,* Apr. 12, 1983.
255. *New York Times,* Apr. 1, 1983.
256. Ibid.
257. *Miami Herald,* Apr. 1, 1983.
258. *New York Times,* Apr. 2, 1983.
259. Ibid., Apr. 14, 1983. Also see *Middle East Policy Survey,* Apr. 8, 1983.

260. *New York Times,* Apr. 18, 1983. Also see *Middle East Policy Survey,* Apr. 22, 1983.
261. *New York Times,* Apr. 9, 1983.
262. Ibid.
263. Ibid., Apr. 11, 1983
264. Ibid., Apr. 13, 1983.
265. Ibid. Also see *Christian Science Monitor,* May 2, 1983.
266. David K. Shipler, "Most West Bank Arabs Blaming United States for Impasse," *New York Times,* Apr. 14, 1983.
267. Ibid., Apr. 17, 1983.
268. *Miami Herald,* Apr. 18, 1983; also see *Wall Street Journal,* Apr. 18, 1983.
269. *New York Times,* May 7, 1983.
270. Ibid., May 18, 1983.
271. Ibid.
272. Ibid., May 7, 1983.
273. For a text of the agreement, see ibid., May 17, 1983. Also see Thomas L. Friedman, "Pullout Pact: Ink on Paper," ibid., May 18, 1983.
274. Ibid., May 3, 1983.
275. Ghassan Tueni, "After the Lebanese-Israeli Agreement," *Middle East Insight* 3, no. 1 (1983), 2-3.
276. See the analysis by Robin Wright, "A Political Split Widens between Muslims and Christians in Lebanon," *Christian Science Monitor,* June 17, 1983.

CHAPTER EIGHT

1. George W. Ball, "What Is an Ally?" *American-Arab Affairs* 6 (Fall 1983), 9.
2. Ibid., 9-10.
3. Ibid., 11.
4. Seth P. Tillman, "United States Middle East Policy: Theory and Practice," ibid., 4 (Spring 1983), 7.
5. See, for example, Sabri Jiryis, *The Arabs in Israel* (N.Y.: Monthly Review Press, 1976); Ian Lustick, *Arabs in the Jewish State: Israel's Control of a National Minority* (Austin: University of Texas Press, 1980); Elie T. Zureik, *The Palestinians in Israel: A Study in Internal Colonialism* (London: Routledge & Kegan Paul, 1979); Uri Davis, "Israel's Zionist Security: Consequences for Internal Oppression and the Necessity for External Intervention," in EAFORD and AJAZ, eds., *Judaism or Zionism: What Difference for the Middle East?* (London: Zed Press, 1986), 176-205.
6. Philippa Strum, "Israel's Democratic Dilemma," *Reform Judaism,* Publication of the Union of American Hebrew Congregations 14, no. 2 (Winter 1985-86), 13. Also see Israel Shahak, "Collection No. 3: Apartheid" (translations from the Israeli Press—Shahak Papers available as of February 1986 to the general public from DAT Press, New York) 2, no. 1 (Feb. 15, 1986). Articles on Israeli apartheid from *Ha'aretz* (4) and *Kol, Ha'ir* (1).
7. There is also dispute as to how cooperative Israel has been in intelligence sharing. See, for example, Harry J. Shaw, "Strategic Dissensus," *Foreign Policy* 61 (Winter 1985-86), 125-41. Shaw challenges more than just this issue—he makes a strong argument against the entire strategic asset thesis. However, Israel has assisted the United States in some of its

objectives in areas outside of the Middle East. See, for example, Cheryl A. Rubenberg, "Israel and Guatemala: A Case Study in Israeli Foreign Policy." *MERIP Reports* (May-June 1986), and the sources cited in note 111 below.

8. Mohamed El Khawas and Samir Abed Rabbo, *American Aid to Israel: Nature and Impact* (Brattleboro, Vt.: Amana Books, 1984), from a review of the book by Mohamed Rabie in *American-Arab Affairs* 8 (Spring 1984), 136.

9. Ibid., 136-37.

10. Stephen D. Isaacs, *Jews and American Politics* (Garden City, N.Y.: Doubleday, 1974), 258-60. For an analysis of the campaign regarding Soviet Jewry, see ibid., 259-60, 262, 264.

11. For analyses of the Ashkenazi-Oriental ethnic and cultural conflict in Israel, see Cheryl A. Rubenberg, "Ethnicity, Elitism, and the State of Israel," in *The Primordial Challenge: Ethnicity in the Contemporary World,* ed. John Stack (Westport, Conn.: Greenwood Press, 1986), and Sammy Smooha, *Israel: Pluralism and Conflict* (Berkeley: University of California Press, 1978).

12. On issues associated with the cold war, journalism typically follows the lead of official Washington. Since Israel is portrayed as a strategic asset to American interests in the global crusade against Communism, it has largely escaped critical scrutiny. See, for example, William A. Dorman and Mansour Farhang, "The U.S. Press and Lebanon," *SAIS Review* 3, no. 1 (1983), 65-81. Journalists' tendency to rely on "official sources" for information contributes to the propagation of government policy. In addition, opinion columns—where "op-ed" writers, using the same official sources, create the illusion of public support for the set of "facts" the journalists are reporting elsewhere—also sustain the conventional wisdom. See Claudia Wright, "The Pressures on the U.S. Media," *Middle East International* (Dec. 23, 1983), 15-16; Claudia Wright, "U.S. Coverage of the Middle East," *Mideast Monitor* 2, no. 1 (Jan. 1985). Also see "The Media Go to War: From Vietnam to Central America," *NACLA Report on the Americas* 17, no. 4 (July/Aug., 1983). In addition, newspapers and television talk shows are inclined to accept "letters to the editor" and "guests," respectively, that represent well-established organizations. At the same time there is a pervasive disinclination toward investigative journalism in diplomacy and foreign affairs and a general hostility to "foreign" ideas in American political culture—all of which help to maintain the official pro-Israeli government line. Wright, in "Pressures on U.S. Media" and "Coverage of the Middle East," discusses these points. Finally, the media are major corporations, sharing interests and perceptions with other elite groups and seeing things the way official sectors see them. In this context cognitive dissonance acts as a powerful shield preventing deviations from the conventional wisdom, even in the face of overwhelming evidence to the contrary. See the analysis by Noam Chomsky in "Interview with Noam Chomsky," *American-Arab Affairs* 10 (Fall 1984), 23ff. Also see Cheryl A. Rubenberg, "Pro-Israeli Influence on the Media and U.S. Middle East Policy," *Mideast Monitor* 2, no. 2 (Mar. 1985), which discusses and summarizes these ideas.

13. "Secret Strategy of the Israeli Lobby," *The Middle East* (Dec. 1983), 28-30. For an analysis of the efforts of pro-Israeli groups on college and university campuses, see Naseer H. Aruri, "The Middle East on the U.S. Campus," *The Link* 18, no. 2, (May/June 1985). Also see "Challenges to Academic Freedom" and "Tucson: Case Study in Intimidation," in Paul

Findley, *They Dare to Speak Out: People and Institutions Confront Israel's Lobby* (Westport, Conn.: Lawrence Hill, 1985) 180-211, and 212-37, respectively.

14. Chomsky, "Interview," 22.

15. "Secret Strategy," 29. For briefing materials given to participants at the 1985 annual seminar for college students held in College Park, Md., July 20-21, 1985, see "AIPAC National Political Leadership Training Seminar Briefing Materials," reprinted in *Journal of Palestine Studies* 15, no. 1 (Autumn 1985) 114-17.

16. See Colin Campbell, "Middle East Scholars Upset by a List," *New York Times,* Jan. 30, 1985.

17. See William Poole, "Redgrave breaks down during testimony," "Actress testifies in symphony lawsuit," "The actress—new testimony," "Redgrave testifies about performance cancellation," *UPI,* Oct. 26, 1984; William Poole, "Redgrave testifies in symphony lawsuit," *UPI,* Oct. 25, 1984; William Poole, "Ozawa says he was unaware of Redgrave's politics," *UPI,* Oct. 24, 1984.

18. See the articles by Poole cited in n. 17. Also see Carol Rosenberg, "Ozawa says he was unfamiliar with Redgrave," "BSO manager says reaction to Redgrave 'not what we expected,' " *UPI,* Oct. 24, 1984; Carol Rosenberg, "Redgrave wants Rabb in courtroom," "The Oscar-winning manager says he feared damage to Redgrave's career," *UPI,* Oct. 23, 1984; Also Carol Rosenberg, no title, *UPI,* Oct. 22, 1984.

19. See Robert I. Friedman, "Book Reviews," *Middle East International,* Jan. 25, 1985.

20. Ibid.

21. Ibid.

22. Ibid.

23. "Israeli Influence in the United States," CBS Morning News, Dec. 27, 1984, transcript of the program.

24. Ibid.

25. See Edward Said's review of *Hanna K., The Village Voice,* Oct. 11, 1983, 45.

26. Ibid.

27. See Hanna Assadi's interview with Michelle Ray-Gavras and her lengthy article in *Al Fajr,* Feb. 8, 1984.

28. Ibid.

29. See James Ennes, Jr., "Assault on *Assault on the Liberty,"* *Middle East International,* Oct. 14, 1983, 13-14.

30. Ibid. Also see Findley, *They Dare to Speak Out,* 165-79.

31. Mark A. Bruzonsky, "Book Review," *Washington Report on Middle East Affairs,* Apr. 2, 1984, 7.

32. See Norman G. Finkelstein, "A Spectacular Fraud: From Time Immemorial," *In These Times,* Sept. 5-11, 1984, 12-14.

33. See the article by Colin Campbell, "Book on Palestine Creates Dispute," *New York Times,* Nov. 28, 1985.

34. To read several of the negative reviews of Peters's *From Time Immemorial,* see Yehoshua Porath, "Mrs. Peters' Palestine," *New York Review of Books* 32, nos. 21 and 22 (Jan. 16, 1986), 36-39; Albert Hourani, *Observer* (London), Mar. 5, 1985; Ian and David Gilmour, "Pseudo-Travellers," *Journal of Palestine Studies* 14, no. 4 (Summer 1985), 129-41 (reprinted

from *London Review of Books,* Feb. 7, 1985); Edward W. Said, "Conspiracy of Praise," *The Nation,* Oct. 19, 1985, 381-86.

35. Finkelstein, "A Spectacular Fraud," 12-14. For important works analyzing the negative portrayal of Arabs in the American media and the policy implications of this, see: Edmund Ghareeb, ed., *Split Vision: The Portrayal of the Arabs in the American Media* (Washington, D.C.: American-Arab Affairs Council, 1983); Janice J. Terry, "The Arab-Israeli Conflict in Popular Literature," *American-Arab Affairs* 2 (Fall 1982), 97-104, and *Mistaken Identity: Arab Stereotypes on Popular Writing* (Washington, D.C.: American-Arab Affairs Council, 1985); Jack G. Shaheen, *The T.V. Arab* (Bowling Green, Ohio: Bowling Green State University, 1985), and "Media Coverage of the Middle East: Perception and Foreign Policy," *Annals of the American Academy of Political and Social Science* 482 (Nov. 1985); and Michael C. Hudson and Ronald A. Wolfe, eds., *The American Media and the Arabs* (Washington, D.C.: Center for Contemporary Arab Studies, Georgetown University, 1980).

36. Campbell, "Book on Palestine."

37. For a good analysis of the ultimate results of Reagan administration policies in the Middle East, see Ned Temko, "Moscow Reaps Windfall Profits in the Middle East," *Christian Science Monitor,* July 16, 1984.

38. *Miami Herald,* Oct. 29, 1983, citing a report by Wolf Blitzer in the *Jerusalem Post.*

39. See Bernard Gwertzman, "Path to Mideast Failure Blazed with Mistakes," *New York Times,* Mar. 25, 1984.

40. Bernard Gwertzman, "Scrapping of Jordanian and Saudi Arms Sales: United States Policy Adrift," ibid., Mar. 22, 1984.

41. For a good analysis, see *Mideast Observer* 7, no. 11 (June 1, 1984).

42. Gwertzman, "Scrapping Arms Sales, Policy Adrift."

43. *New York Times,* Mar. 15, 1984.

44. *Mideast Observer* 7, no. 11 (June 1, 1984), 2.

45. Ibid.

46. *Miami Herald,* Mar. 23, 1984.

47. See Allan Kellum, "Update on Congress," *Washington Report on Middle East Affairs* 3, no. 8 (Oct. 15, 1984).

48. *Mideast Observer* 7, no. 11 (June 1, 1984), 3.

49. James M. Dorsey, "Arafat Calls for Israeli-PLO Talks," *UPI Wire Service,* May 11, 1984. Significantly neither the *New York Times* nor the *Washington Post* carried the story when it occurred, though several months later the *Post* made an offhand reference to it. There were a few stories in smaller papers, such as the *Philadelphia Inquirer,* but they downplayed its significance and failed to place it in relevant context. See Chomsky, "Interview," 23-24.

50. "Reagan to Revive Offer of Missiles to Saudi Arabia," *New York Times,* May 24, 1984.

51. See Bernard Gwertzman, "As Tension Rises in the Gulf, Role for United States Becomes Issue," *New York Times,* May 24, 1984.

52. T. Elaine Carey, "Saudis Spurn United States Offers for Military Aid," *Christian Science Monitor,* May 23, 1984. See note 7, Chapter 7 herein, regarding the efforts of the pro-Israeli lobby in the spring of 1986 to prevent the delivery to Saudi Arabia of the AWACs that were purchased in 1981.

53. Claudia Wright, "Reasons for Keeping Out," *Middle East International,* June 1, 1984, 5.

54. Ibid., 3, for a similar analysis.

55. Ibid.

56. "United States Ends Bid to Form Jordanian Strike Force," *Miami Herald,* May 24, 1984. Also see "Reagan to Revive Offer of Missiles to Saudi Arabia," *New York Times,* May 24, 1984.

57. Ibid.

58. Bernard Gwertzman, "Aids Say Reagan Is Forced to Limit Missiles to Saudis," *New York Times,* May 26, 1984.

59. Jim Anderson, "President Reagan–White House Comment on Stinger Sale," *UPI,* May 25, 1984.

60. For an analysis of Kuwait's vulnerability, see Judith Miller, "Kuwait's Starting to Feel Impact of Shipping War," *New York Times,* May 29, 1984.

61. Judith Miller, "Sidelines Are Hard to Find in the Gulf," ibid., June 3, 1984. Also see Jim Anderson, "No Stingers for Kuwait," *UPI,* June 5, 1984, and Bernard Gwertzman, "United States Tells Kuwait It Can't Have Missiles," *New York Times,* June 20, 1984.

62. Temko, "Moscow Windfall."

63. Charlotte Saikowski, "United States Quietly Boosts Proposed Iraqi Oil Pipeline to the Red Sea," *Christian Science Monitor,* June 14, 1984. Also see Ned Temko, "Hard-Pressed Iraq Seeking Better Ties with Old Foe—the United States," *Christian Science Monitor,"* July 11, 1984.

64. *Middle East International,* June 1, 1984, 5.

65. See Claudia Wright, "A Tilt Towards Baghdad?" *The Middle East* (June 1982), 7-8.

66. *Christian Science Monitor,* May 30. 1984.

67. Ibid.

68. Quotation reported by Richard H. Curtiss, *A Changing Image: American Perceptions of the Arab-Israeli Dispute* (Washington, D.C.: American Educational Trust, 1982), 117.

69. Ben Bradlee, "Israel's Lobby," *Boston Globe Magazine,* Apr. 29, 1984.

70. "Arab, Israel Backers Lobby for Aid, Influence," *The Middle East,* 5th ed. (Washington, D.C.: Congressional Quarterly, 1981), 68.

71. Cheryl A. Rubenberg, "The Middle East Lobbies," *The Link* 17, no. 1 (Jan./Mar. 1984), 3.

72. "Israel Lobby: A Potent, Effective Force on United States Policy," *The Middle East: United States Policy, Israel, Oil and the Arabs,* 4th ed. (Washington, D.C.: Congressional Quarterly, 1979), 89.

73. *The Middle East,* 5th ed. 64-65. Also see Seth P. Tillman, *The United States in the Middle East: Interests and Obstacles* (Bloomington: Indiana University Press, 1982), 118-22. The Israeli lobby used all of its muscle in this battle and, while it lost, made the vote of congressmen on this sale the litmus test for future support, working hard in subsequent elections to defeat those members who voted for the sale.

74. Tillman, *United States in the Middle East,* 65-66.

75. Ibid.

76. Ibid., also see Isaacs, *Jews and American Politics,* 255-56.

77. Tillman, *United States in the Middle East,* 66; Isaacs, *Jews and American Politics,* 256.

78. Interview with former Congressman Paul Findley, Washington, D.C., Sept. 22, 1983.

79. Curtiss, *Changing Image,* 118.

80. Ibid. Also see Findley, *They Dare to Speak Out,* 1-164.

81. Morris J. Amitay, "Just How Friendly Is President Reagan to Israel?" *Jewish Floridian of South County,* Oct. 19, 1984, 7.

82. Ben Bradlee, "Competing for the Jewish Vote," *Boston Globe Magazine,* Apr. 29, 1984.

83. Ari L. Goldman, "Head of Jewish Group Says Jackson Is an Anti-Semite," *New York Times,* June 1, 1984.

84. Bradlee, "Competing for the Jewish Vote."

85. Goldman, "Group Says Jackson Is an Anti-Semite."

86. Charles McC. Mathias, Jr., "Ethnic Groups and Foreign Policy," *Foreign Affairs* 59 (Summer 1981), 995.

87. Grace Halsell, "Interview with Pete McCloskey," *Arab News,* June 15, 1983.

88. Quotation in Findley, *They Dare to Speak Out,* 127.

89. Ibid. For a discussion of the use and misuse of anti-Semitism and a historical analysis that puts the issue of anti-Semitism in an important new light, see the book by French Jewish scholar Maxime Rodinson, *Cult, Ghetto, and State: The Persistence of the Jewish Question* (London: Zed Press, 1983), 172-91 and passim. For an analysis of the use and misuse of the Holocaust, see article by the Israeli writer Boaz Evron, "The Holocaust: Learning the Wrong Lessons," *Journal of Palestine Studies* 10, no. 3 (Spring 1981), 16-26. Also see Sigbert Axelson, "Israel and Anti-Semitism: A Critical View," in *Israel and the Question of Palestine,* special issue *Arab Studies Quarterly* 7, nos. 2 and 3 (Spring/Summer 1985), 11-14.

90. For an analysis of the growing conservatism of the Jewish community in the United States on social, political, and economic issues, see Roberta Strauss Feuerlicht, *The Fate of the Jews: A People Torn between Israeli Power and Jewish Ethics* (New York: Times Books, 1983), passim.

91. *Miami Herald,* Nov. 20, 1983.

92. Ibid.

93. "The Jackson Brothers," editorial, *The Nation,* Mar. 10, 1984, 275-76. Regarding the controversy over Louis Farrakhan, it is worth noting that while the media and Jewish leaders were relentless in their crucifixion of Jackson for his refusal to repudiate the Black Muslim leader, the double standard in American politics was clearly evident in the fact that no one demanded that Ronald Reagan repudiate his California campaign director, John Rousselot, a well-known leader of the John Birch Society. See the letter by Prof. Gerald Horne of Sarah Lawrence College in "Letters to the Editor," *In These Times,* May 9-15, 1984, 10. Nor, as Horne pointed out, were Walter Mondale's role in the anti-Communist purges of the early 1950s, in his capacity as executive secretary of Students for Democratic Action, or his role as architect of the "shafting" of the Mississippi Freedom Democratic party in 1964, or his past use of the ethnic slur "Japs" ever mentioned during the campaign.

94. *Christian Science Monitor,* July 5, 1984.

95. Remarks by George McGovern at Temple Beth Am in Framingham, Mass., as reported by the *UPI Wire Service,* Feb. 8, 1984.

96. John Herbers, "Anti-Semitism Issue Worries Party," *New York Times,* Apr. 11, 1984.

97. Steven R. Weisman, "Reagan Says Foes Fear to Attack Anti-Semitism," ibid., Oct. 27, 1984.

98. Statement reprinted in "Views of the World's Press," *Miami Herald,*
Oct. 29, 1984.

99. Isaacs, *Jews and American Politics,* 116, 119.

100. *Christian Science Monitor,* Nov. 30, 1983.

101. Isaacs, *Jews and American Politics,* 126.

102. Ibid., 120-39.

103. Ibid., 121.

104. Ibid., 121-22.

105. Bradlee, "Competing for the Jewish Vote."

106. The final point is discussed in the *New York Times,* Apr. 22, 1984,
from a report in *Ha'aretz,* although Israel denies any such role.

107. Leslie Gelb, "United States–Israeli Talks Said to Aim at Soviets,"
New York Times, July 20, 1984.

108. Ibid.

109. Ibid.

110. Ibid. For an analysis of the contradictions in "strategic cooperation,"
see Shaw, "Strategic Dissensus."

111. See, for example, Cynthia Arnson, "Israel and Central America,"
New Outlook (Mar./Apr., 1984), 19-22; Esther Howard, "Israel: The Sorcerer's Apprentice," *MERIP Reports* (Feb. 1983), 16-25; George Black,
"Israeli Connection: Not Just Guns for Guatemala," *NACLA Report on the
Americas* 17, no. 3 (May/June 1983), 43-45; Clarence Lusane, "Washington's Proxy: Israeli Arms in Central America," *Covert Action* 20 (Winter
1984), 34-37; Rubenberg, "Israel and Guatemala."

112. Robert G. Kaiser, "Is Dependency on United States Aid Doing
Israel Any Good?" *Miami Herald* (Viewpoint), June 3, 1984.

113. See *Mideast Observer,* Mar. 15, 1984; *Miami Herald* (Business Mon-
day), June 4, 1984, 62; *Voice* 2, nos. 3-4 (Mar./Apr. 1984), 14-15.

114. See Kellum, "Update on Congress," 6. For the complete document,
see "Agreement on the Establishment of a Free Trade Area between the
Government of the United States of America and the Government of
Israel," reprinted in *Journal of Palestine Studies* 15, no. 2 (Winter 1986),
119-31.

115. Richard C. Gross, "Navy Bought Israeli Drones in 'Tremendous
Hurry,'" *UPI,* May 24, 1984. Also see Richard Halboran, "United States
Buys Israeli Pilotless Planes," *New York Times,* May 24, 1984.

116. Bradlee, "Competing for the Jewish Vote."

117. *Miami Herald,* Jan. 18, 1984.

118. M. Margaret Conway, "PACS, the New Politics and Congressional
Campaigns," in *Interest Group Politics,* ed. Allan J. Cigler and Burdett A.
Loomis (Washington, D.C.: Congressional Quarterly Press, 1983), 127. The
currently accepted limits governing PACs are $1,000 per election to a can-
didate for federal office, $20,000 per year to national political party com-
mittees, and $5,000 to another political committee. No individual or or-
ganization may contribute more than $25,000 directly to candidates for
federal election in any one year. A multicandidate committee may contribute as much money as it is able to raise, but still is restricted to giving
no more than $5,000 directly per candidate in each election. However, as
the text states, there are ways around all of these regulations.

119. *Focus* 7, no. 2 (Mar. 1984), 3.

120. Edward Roeder, "Sunshine and Pro-Israel PACs," *Washington Report on Middle East Affairs* 3, no. 8 (Oct. 15, 1984), 3.

121. John J. Fialka, "Jewish Groups Increase Campaign Donations," *Wall Street Journal,* Aug. 3, 1983.
122. *Mideast Observer* 6, no. 19 (Nov. 1, 1983).
123. Fialka, "Jewish Groups Increase Campaign Donations."
124. See William E. Gibson, "Stinger Missile Sale Critics May Force Policy Change," *Sun-Sentinel* (Fort Lauderdale, Fla.), June 5, 1984.
125. *Mideast Observer* 6, no. 19 (Nov. 1, 1983), 3; and Fialka, "Jewish Groups Increase Campaign Donations." The figures given by Fialka and *Mideast Observer* differ slightly in the dollar amount donated to some candidates. The discrepancy may reside in the fact that *Mideast Observer* was able to identify thirty-three pro-Israel PACs, while Fialka identified only thirty. The figures used here are taken from the *Mideast Observer,* and other material is taken from Fialka.
126. *New York Times,* Nov. 11, 1983.
127. *Focus* 7, no. 2 (Mar. 1984), 4.
128. Ibid., 8, no. 5 (May 1, 1985), 3.
129. Ibid., 2.
130. Ibid.
131. Ibid., 3.
132. Ibid.
133. Ibid.
134. Ibid.
135. Ibid.
136. Paula Schwed, *UPI,* May 24, 1984.
137. Ibid.
138. Kaiser, "Is Dependency on U.S. Aid Doing Israel Any Good?"
139. Ibid.
140. *Mideast Observer* 7, no. 8 (Apr. 15, 1984), 3. Also see ibid., 7, no. 5 (Mar. 1, 1984).
141. Ibid., 7, no. 8 (Apr. 15, 1984), 3. Also see ibid., 7, no. 5 (Mar. 1, 1984).
142. Kellum, "Update on Congress," 5-6.
143. See, for example, Lusane, "Israeli Arms in Central America," 37, and "Israeli Militarization of Costa Rica," *Counterspy* (Sept./Nov. 1983), 13.
144. Kellum, "Update on Congress," 6.
145. Quotation from Abourezk, in *The Middle East* (July 1983), 19.
146. Curtiss, *A Changing Image,* 118.
147. *Mideast Observer* 6, no. 19 (Nov. 1, 1983), 3.
148. Fialka, "Jewish Groups Increase Campaign Donations."
149. Interview with former Congressman Findley, Sept. 22, 1983.
150. Ibid.
151. Fialka, "Jewish Groups Increase Campaign Donations."
152. Roeder, "Sunshine and Pro-Israel PACs," 4.
153. Ibid. Also see Andrew H. Malcolm, "Senator Percy's Camp Takes Little for Granted," *New York Times,* Mar. 19, 1984, and Findley, *They Dare to Speak Out,* 109-13.
154. *Miami Herald,* Jan. 18, 1984.
155. Ibid.
156. Quoted in Findley, *They Dare to Speak Out,* 26.
157. Ibid.

INDEX

Abdullah, king of Jordan, 54
Abourezk, James, 372
Abu Rudeis oil field: control of, 209; Egypt's desire for return of, 206
Afghanistan: Soviet-inspired coup in, 201, 202; Soviet invasion of, 255, 263
AFL-CIO: support for Israel, 78, 86, 212, 366. *See also* Meany, George
AIPAC. *See* American-Israel Public Affairs Committee
Ajami, Fouad, 190
Akins, James E., 353
Alawites, 191
Alexander, Edward, 339
al-Fatah. *See* Fatah al-
al-Hani, Hassan, 291
al-Malik, Abd, 24
al-Numairi, Colonel Ja'far, 133
al-Sabah, Sheik Jaber, al-Ahmed, 268
al-Said, Nuri, 16, 54, 85, 251, 334
al-Walid, Caliph, 24
Algeria, 56
Algiers Summit (1973), 178, 179, 184
Ali, Kamal Hassan, 236, 295
Allon, Yigal, 206, 211
American Farm Bureau, 366
American Embassy: efforts to move to Jerusalem, 19, 96, 347-49, 357
American Friends Service Committee's Advisory Committee on Human Rights, 281
American-Israeli Civil Liberties Coalition, 332
American-Israel Public Affairs Committee (AIPAC): and anti-Semitism, 361; campaign efforts of, 362, 368, 374, 375; concern over Arab efforts to communicate with American public, 336-38; lobbying efforts of, 165, 345-46, 350-52, 365; media pressure of, 165, 342; pressure tactics of, 207, 317-18, 356; registration as lobby, 354. *See also* Pro-Israeli lobby
American Jewish Committee, 343, 353, 355
American Jewish Congress, 348-49, 355

American Jews: support Israel, 126, 375. *See also* Pro-Israeli lobby
American national interests: and the June 1867 War, 12, 88-98, 109, 123-26; and the Sinai-Suez Crisis (1955), 52-56; as contravened by Israeli relationship, 330-31; benefits of Israeli relationship to, 332; definition of, 1, 2, 10-11; effect of Camp David, 199, 213, 250-53. *See also* Strategic asset theory
American Schools and Hospital Abroad, 143
Americans for a Safe Israel (AFSI), 339, 354
American University at Beirut, 36
American University at Cairo, 36, 92
Amitay, Morris J., 355, 357
Anderson, John B., 357
Anderson, Robert B., 108, 117
Anglo-American Committee of Inquiry, 33, 41-42
Anglo-Egyptian treaty of 1954, 55
Anti-Defamation League of the B'nai B'rith. *See* B'nai B'rith
Anti-Semite label, 361; as tactic of pro-Israeli lobby, 13, 357-58; in campaign against Jesse Jackson, 19
Aqaba, Gulf of, 82, 83: and the June 1967 War, 110, 112-14; as international waterway, 75, 79; closing of, to Israeli shipping, 112
Arab cold war, 89, 90, 100-101
Arab guerrilla organizations. *See* individual names of groups
Arab League: exclusion of Egypt from Baghdad 1979 summit, 238
Arab nationalism, 25, 54, 93, 100
Arab socialism, 93
Arab states: acceptance of Israel as state, 4, 50, 85; Arab cold war, 89, 90, 100-101; boycott of Israel, 58, 85; political state of, in 1975-76, 190-91; position of Egypt in, 54-55, 60, 85-86, 90, 248-49; post-1973 war, 190-97; relations with U.S., 3, 6-7, 9, 213
Arab Summit conferences: Algiers

NOTE ON THE AUTHOR

Cheryl A. Rubenberg is associate professor of international relations in the department of political science at Florida International University, North Miami. She received her Ph.D. from the School of Advanced International Studies at the University of Miami. She has traveled widely and lived and conducted research throughout the Middle East, including Lebanon, Jordan, Egypt, Israel, the West Bank, and the Gaza Strip. She has published numerous articles on Palestinian human rights, the Palestine Liberation Organization, American policy in the Middle East, and various aspects of the Israeli lobby in the U.S. domestic system.